THEATRE
WORLD

by
JOHN WILLIS

1969-1970 SEASON

Volume 26

CROWN PUBLISHERS, INC.
419 Park Avenue South
New York, N.Y.

TO

HAZEL WILLIS TROTTER

who sublimated theatrical ambitions to utilize her many talents in more important roles: a loving wife to an exemplary husband, a dedicated mother to a beautiful family, and an optimistic crusader for a better world.

ZOE CALDWELL
in "Colette"

Martha Swope Ph

CONTENTS

EDITOR: JOHN WILLIS
Assistant Editor: Stanley Reeves
Staff Photographers: Bert Andrews, Friedman-Abeles, Louis Mélançon,
Van Williams, Zodiac

REVIEWING THE 1969-70 SEASON

The state of the theatre in New York was grim. Attendance was decreasing. Increasing were production and ticket costs, vulgarity without humor, nudity without artistry and obscenity without shock value. On-stage nudity, homosexuality, and vulgarity reached the point of absurdity. Broadway's first all-nude play was quickly dumped with other rubbish. Except for individual performances, impressive sets, and excellent revivals, there was little during 1969-70 in New York's theatres that was not mediocre, depressing, and unrewarding.

Only 26 new plays and 12 new musicals opened on Broadway. Eight survived the season. The total of 62 productions was 5 less than 1968-69. In comparison with the record 264 of 1927-28, it gave little cause for optimism. To holdovers from past seasons (2 plays, 5 musicals) were added two comedies "The Last of the Red Hot Lovers" with James Coco earning stardom and "Butterflies Are Free" with memorable performances by Eileen Heckart, Keir Dullea, and Blythe Danner; the drama "Child's Play"; award-winning musicals "Company" (NY Drama Critics Circle citation), and "Applause" (Tony winner). In her musical debut, Katharine Hepburn scored a personal triumph and made "Coco" a financial success. Neither Tony and Drama Critics Circle awards, nor beautiful ensemble playing by Frank Grimes and company, made "Borstal Boy" a hit. Ethel Merman became a perfect Mrs. Levi in "Hello, Dolly!" that was approaching the musical record held by "My Fair Lady."

Other productions worth noting were "Indians" with Stacy Keach in another commendable characterization, "The Chinese and Dr. Fish" with delightful performances by Alice Drummond and Joseph Bova, and the musical "Purlie." "Buck White" marked the theatrical debut of heavyweight champion Cassius Clay. Shirley Booth returned to Broadway in the musical "Look to the Lilies" with Al Freeman, Jr. another asset. The talents of Maximilian Schell, Dennis King, and its designers did not save the opulent, much-heralded import "A Patriot for Me"; nor could the skillful acting of Anne Jackson and George Grizzard save "Inquest," the much-publicized dramatization of the Rosenberg case. A beautiful production and performances by Robert Weede, Joan Diener, Helen Gallagher, and Steve Arlen were almost the only virtues of "Cry for Us All," the musicalization of the critically acclaimed drama "Hogan's Goat." Beloved Molly Picon and Sam Levene tried valiantly to sustain the unsuccessful comedy "Paris Is Out!" Other performers worthy of praise were Maureen Stapleton, Paul Lipson, Penny Fuller, Linda Lavin, Bonnie Franklin, Brian Bedford, Bernadette Peters, Keene Curtis, Dilys Watling, Lewis J. Stadlen, David Rounds, Melissa Hart, Sam Waterston, and Susan Browning.

It would have been a disastrous year without the abundance of good revivals. Included in the 22 were "Private Lives," "Front Page," "Our Town" with Stage Manager Henry Fonda introducing its impressive cast, "Harvey" with Helen Hayes and James Stewart, "The Boy Friend" with the multi-talented Sandy Duncan. ANTA Theatre provided a showcase for regional companies. Among them was American Shakespeare Festival's controversial production with Len Cariou a laudable "Henry V." San Francisco's American Conservatory Theatre presented praiseworthy revivals of "A Flea in Her Ear," and "Tiny Alice" with Paul Shenar's bravura performance. Lincoln Center's distinctive revivals were "Oklahoma!" with Bruce Yarnell, the Repertory Theater's "The Time of Your Life," "Camino Real" with Jessica Tandy and Al Pacino, and "In the Matter of J. Robert Oppenheimer" — its first success to tour. City Center hosted Le Comedie Francaise, Grand Kabuki, and Marcel Marceau. Another guest, not as well received, was "Rabelais," Jean-Louis Barrault's "total theatre" piece.

Antoinette Perry Awards (Tonys) for best performances in plays went to Tammy Grimes for "Private Lives," Blythe Danner (Supporting Actress) for "Butterflies Are Free," Fritz Weaver and Ken Howard (Supporting Actor) for "Child's Play." Winners in musicals were Lauren Bacall for "Applause," Cleavon Little and Melba Moore (Supporting Actress) for "Purlie," and Rene Auberjonois (Supporting Actor) for "Coco."

Although disappointing in quality, Off-Broadway produced more than ever, and had its surfeit of nude bodies cluttering the stages. Of the 54 new plays, only 4 survived with the 3 plays and 3 musicals from other seasons. "The Effect of Gamma Rays on the Man-in-the-moon Marigolds" with touching performances by Sada Thompson, Pamela Payton-Wright, and Judith Lowry, was the first Off-Broadway play to receive a Drama Critics Circle citation for best American play. Another Off-Broadway first was the Pulitzer Prize to Charles Gordone's "No Place to Be Somebody," a holdover from 1968-69 that made a brief Broadway visit with excellent performances by Ron O'Neal and Nathan George. The Negro Ensemble Company, American Place Theatre, and NY Shakespeare Festival productions; unlike previous seasons, were relatively unimpressive. The Polish Laboratory Theatre aroused excitement with 3 productions in limited exposure.

Zoe Caldwell as "Colette" gave one of the most brilliant performances of any season, anywhere. Katharine Houghton in "A Scent of Flowers" was a rewarding experience, as was Christopher Walken in "Lemon Sky." Other Off-Broadway performers and new plays worth listing were Ron Leibman in "Transfers," Catherine Burns in "Dear Janet Rosenberg...," Fred Stewart and Laurence Luckinbill in "Memory Bank," Kristoffer Tabori in "How Much, How Much?," Jacqueline Brookes in "The Persians," the entire cast of "A Whistle in the Dark," Rue McClanahan and Teresa Wright in "Who's Happy Now?," "Little Boxes," "The White House Murder Case," and "What the Butler Saw."

Musicals fared no better off Broadway than on. The season was initiated with the nude revue "Oh, Calcutta!," that ran through the year. Musical productions and performers deserving mention were Alice Playten and Gilbert Price in "Promenade," Fredricka Weber in "The Last Sweet Days of Isaac," Donny Burks in "Billy Noname," Boni Enten in "Salvation," and the entire cast of "The Me Nobody Knows."

Revivals off Broadway also were among the best entertainment: "Summertree," "Room Service," "Dark of the Moon," "Slow Dance on the Killing Ground," "Awake and Sing" with exceptional performances by everyone, and especially Joan Lorring and Robert Salvio. Additional praiseworthy performers were Colleen Dewhurst, Martin Sheen, Page Johnson, April Shawhan, Ida Kaminska, Terry Kiser, Patricia Roe, Jeremiah Sullivan, Claudia McNeil, Kevin O'Connor, Jan Farrand, Billy Dee Williams, and George Voskovec.

The most encouraging theatre news this year was recorded by Variety's Hobe Morrison: "The road" scored its best season in history. Its gross almost equalled Broadway's. Hopefully, with its increased activity, and that in regional theatres, "The Fabulous Invalid" will survive, acquire new audiences, and regain its revered position among the arts.

Katharine Hepburn

James Stewart

BROADWAY CALENDAR

June 1, 1969 through May 31, 1970

Coco

Lauren Bacall

Ethel Merman

Fritz Weaver

ANTA THEATRE

Opened Saturday, June 14, 1969.*
Bernard M. Weber presents:

A TEASPOON EVERY FOUR HOURS

By Jackie Mason and Mike Mortman; Director, Jeremy Stevens; Scenery, Robert Randolph; Costumes, Winn Morton; Incidental Music, Joseph Raposo; Lighting, John Jay Moore.

CAST

Nat Weiss	Jackie Mason
Mike	Lee Wallace
Trixie	Lee Meredith
David Weiss	Roger Morgan
Bruce Weiss	Barry Pearl
Sylvia Rubin	Marilyn Cooper
Lou Abrams	Bernie West
Patty	Vera Moore
Virginia	Billie Allen

UNDERSTUDIES: Trixie, Sylvia, Pamela Duncan; Bruce, Bruce Adler; David, Jason Howard; Mike, Lou, Michael Vale; Patty, Virginia, Doris Berry.

A Comedy in two acts and nine scenes. The action takes place at the present time in Nat's apartment, the park, and Collins' apartment.

General Manager: Norman Maibaum
Company Manager: Michael Goldreyer
Press: Seymour Krawitz, Ellen Levene, Fred Weterick
Stage Managers: Mortimer Halpern, Leonard Auerbach

*Closed Saturday, June 14, 1969. (1 performance and 97 previews)

Roger Morgan, Jackie Mason, Barry Pearl, Marilyn Cooper
Top Right: Jackie Mason, Billie Allen

Friedman-Abeles Phot

LUNT-FONTANNE THEATRE

Opened Thursday, October 2, 1969.*
Leon H. Gildin presents:

THE NEW MUSIC HALL OF ISRAEL

Staged and Choreographed by Jonathan Karmon; Costumes, Lydia Pinkus Ganay; Executed by Bertha Kwartz; Additional Dialogue, Al Fogel; Assistant Director, Gavri Levi; Musical Direction, Rafi Paz.

CAST

Germaine Onikowski (Mistress of Ceremonies), Leah Dorly Trio, Yoel Dan, Geula Gill, Almoznino, Elisheva and Michael, Boas, Pnina Pery, The Karmon Dancers.

PROGRAM

ACT I: Popular Songs of Israel, Springtime in Israel, Elisheva and Michael, Dance of the Fisherman, Pnina Pery and her Exylaphone, The Legend of Timna, Almonznino, Leah Dorly Trio, A Hassidik Marriage

ACT II: Magic of the Negev, Popular Music of Israel, Rhythms and Dances of the Desert, Lest We Forget, Geula Gill, Mosaic, Israel Joy of Life.

General Manager: Bill Levine
Press: David Lipsky, Lisa Lipsky, Saul Richfield

Leah Dorly Trio
Right Center: Karmon Dancers

*Closed Nov. 29, 1969 to tour after a limited engagement of 77 performances and 3 previews.

**Paul Shenar (also above), DeAnn
Mears Top: Ray Reinhardt, Harry
Frazier in "Tiny Alice"**

ANTA THEATRE

Opened Monday, September 29, 1969.*
The American National Theatre and Academy
(Alfred deLiagre, Jr., Executive Producer;
Jean Dalrymple, Executive Director) presents
the American Conservatory Theatre in re-
pertory in:

TINY ALICE

By Edward Albee; Director, William Ball; Associate Director, Robert Bonaventura; Settings, Stuart Wurtzel; Lighting, John McLain; Men's Costumes, Walter Watson; Miss Mear's Wardrobe,
Ann Roth; Masks, Bruce Harrow.

CAST

Cardinal ....Harry Frazier
Lawyer ....Ray Reinhardt
Brother Julian ....Paul Shenar
Butler ....Philip Kerr
Miss Alice..DeAnn Mears
Monks.................Martin Berman, Robert Simpson

A Drama in three acts and seven scenes. The
action takes place at the present time in the Cardinal's garden, the library of a mansion, a sitting
room.

Original production opened Dec. 29, 1964 and
ran for 167 performances with Irene Worth and
John Gielgud.

Opened Friday, October 3, 1969.*

A FLEA IN HER EAR

By Georges Feydeau; Translated by Barnett
Shaw; Director, Gower Champion; Associate Direc-
tor, Eugene Barcone; Scenery, Stuart Wurtzel;
Costumes, Lewis Brown; Lighting, John McLain.

CAST

Camille Chandel ....Michael O'Sullivan
Antoinette ....Deborah Sussel
Etienne.......................................Barry MacGregor
Finache..Harry Frazier
Serrita..Ann Weldon
Yvonne Chandel ....Carol Teitel
Victor-Emmanuel Chandel...........Rogert Gerringer
Romain Tournel ....Philip Kerr
Don Carlos ....Herman Poppe
At the hotel:
Ferraillon ....Ray Reinhardt
Eugenie ....Izetta Smith
Olivia ....Ruth Kobart
Baptistin ....Robert Lanchester
Rugby ....George Ede
Poche..Robert Gerringer

A Comedy in three acts. The action takes place
in Chandel's home, and in the hotel.

Opened Thursday, October 9, 1969.*

THREE SISTERS

By Anton Chekhov; Director, William Ball;
Associate Director, Eugene Barcone; Scenery,
Paul Staheli; Costumes, Ann Roth; Lighting,
John McLain; Choreography, Ed Mock; Assistant
to Mr. Ball, Kenneth Julian.

CAST

Olga Sergeyevna Prozorov ....Angela Paton
Marya Sergeyevna Prozorov (Masha)............
                              Michael Learned
Irina Sergeyevna Prozorov ....Kitty Winn
Andrey Sergeyevich Prozorov.................Jay Doyle
Fyodor Ilyich Kulygin ....Harry Frazier
Natalya Ivanovna (Natasha)....Carol Mayo Jenkins
Anfisa ....Ruth Kobart
Baron Nikolai Lvovich Tusenbach........Paul Shenar
Ivan Romanich Chebutykin ....William Paterson
Vassily Vassilyevich Solyony ....Robert Lanchester
Lt-Col. Alexander
  Ignatyevich Vershinin.........................Ken Ruta
Alexey Petrovich Fedotik ....Philip Kerr
Vladimir Karlovich Rode...................James Milton
Ferapont.................Michael O'Sullivan, George Ede
SERVANTS: Martin Berman, Mary Markson,
Ed Mock, Frank Ottiwell, Kenneth Julian, Herman
Poppe, Robert Simpson, Izetta Smith, Deborah
Sussel

A Drama in two acts and four scenes. The action
takes place on the Prozorov Estate in Provincial
Russia.

Company Manager: Spofford J. Beadle
Press: Howard Atlee, David Roggensack,
Stanley F. Kaminsky, Irene Gandy, Dennis Powers
Stage Managers: Mark Rodgers, Alan Donovan
*Closed Oct. 25, 1969 after 32 performances in
repertory.

Hank Kranzler Photos

**Angela Paton, William Paterson,
Michael Learned, Kitty Winn Above:
Kitty Winn, Paul Shenar in "Three Sisters"**

**Harry Frazier, Robert Gerringer
Above: Ray Reinhardt, Patricia Falkenhain
in "A Flea in Her Ear"**

IMPERIAL THEATRE

Opened Sunday, October 5, 1969.*
David Merrick Arts Foundation presents:

A PATRIOT FOR ME

By John Osborne; Director, Peter Glenville;
Scenery, Oliver Smith; Costumes, Freddy Wittop;
Lighting, Thomas Skelton; Music, Laurence Rosenthal; Associate Producer, Samuel Liff; Staff Associates, Sylvia Schwartz, John Bonanni; Duel
Staged by Rod Colbin; Assistant to Director, Ronn
Forella; Hairdresser, Vincent Prestia.

CAST

Alfred Redl	Maximilian Schell
August Siczynski	Richard Jordan
Steinbauer	Tom V. V. Tammi
Ludwig Max von Kupfer	Jered Barclay
Kupfer's Seconds	
	Tom Lee Jones, Brian Sturdivant
Lt. Col. Ludwig von Mohl	Staats Cotsworth
Adjutant	John Kramer
Maximilian von Taussig	Robert Stattel
Albrecht	John Horn
Waiter at Anna's	Bryan Young
Officers	Peter Bartlett, Warren Burton,
	Noel Craig, Carl Jessop, Tom Lee Jones,
	Brian Sturdivant
Hilde	Mariclare Costello
Whores	Hedy Sontag, Marilyn Joseph,
	Inge von Reith, Billi Vitali
Anna	Madlyn Cates
Stanitsin	James Dukas
Col. Mischa Oblensky	Keene Curtis
Gen. Conrad von Hotzendorf	Stefan Schnabel
Countess Sophia Delyanoff	Salome Jens
Judge Advocate Jaroslav Kunz	Ed Zimmermann
Flunkeys . Michael Goodwin, Christopher Pennock
Hofburg Guests	Peter Bartlett, Alan Brasington,
	Warren Burton, Madlyn Cates, Luis Lopez-Ceperg,
	Peter Colly, Noel Craig, Carl Jessop,
	Tom Lee Jones, Marilyn Joseph, John Kramer,
	Hedy Sontag, Eugene Stuckmann,
	Brian Sturdivant, Billi Vitali, Inge Von Reith,
	Bryan Young
Young Man in Cafe	Warren Burton
Passersby	Eugene Stuckmann, Marilyn Joseph
Paul	Christopher Pennock
Privates	Tom Lee Jones, John Kramer,
	Brian Sturdivant
Ferdy	Alan Brasington
Salome	Peter Colly
Baron von Epp	Dennis King
Lt. Stefan Kovacs	Michael Goodwin
Tsarina	Bryan Young
Lady of Fashion	Warren Burton
Marie Antoinette	Carl Jessop
Orthodox Priest	Tom Lee Jones
Little Boy	John Kramer
Little Girl	Christopher Pennock
Equestrienne	Eugene Stuckmann
Balkan Chief	Brian Sturdivant
Shepherdesses	Noel Craig, Luis Lopez-Cepero,
	Peter Bartlett
Boy	Tom Lee Jones
2nd Lt. Victor Jerzabek	Noel Craig
Hotel Head Waiter	Eugene Stuckmann
Hotel Waiter	Luis Lopez-Cepero
Musicians	
	Frederic Hand, James Carter, Eric Lewis,
	Ruben Rivera

UNDERSTUDIES: Redl, Ed Zimmermann; von
Epp, von Hotzendorf, von Mohl, Oblensky, Eugene
Stuckmann; Countess, Hilde, Hedy Sontag; Kunz,
von Kupfer, John Kramer; von Taussig, Siczynski,
Christopher Pennock; Stanitsin, Young Man, Adjutant, Brian Sturdivant; Albrecht, Salome, Luis
Lopez-Cepero; Ferdy, Boy, Marie Antoinette,
Peter Bartlett; Kovacs, Paul, Tom Lee Jones;
Steinbauer, Waiter, Carl Jessop; Tsarina, Shepherdesses, John Handy; Jerzabek, Warren Burton;
Head Waiter. James Dukas.

A Drama in two acts and 20 scenes. The action takes place in Lemberg, Warsaw, Prague,
Dresden, Vienna, between 1890 and 1913.

General Manager: Jack Schlissel
Company Manager: Richard Highley
Press: Harvey B. Sabinson, Lee Solters,
David Powers, Edie Kean
Stage Managers: Alan Hall, Geoffrey Johnson,
John Handy

*Closed Nov. 15, 1969. (49 performances)

Martha Swope Photos

Michael Goodwin, Maximilian Schell,
Tom Tammi, Bryan Young, Dennis
King, Alan Brasington, John Horn

Top Left: Keene Curtis, James Dukas, Maximilian
Schell, Below: Staats Cotsworth, Ed Zimmermann,
Stefan Schnabel, Salome Jens, Maximilian Schell

BROOKS ATKINSON THEATRE

Opened Monday, October 13, 1969.*
Lyn Austin, Oliver Smith, Joel Schenker, Roger L. Stevens present:

INDIANS

By Arthur Kopit; Director, Gene Frankel; Setting, Oliver Smith; Lighting, Thomas Skelton; Costumes, Marjorie Slaiman; Music, Richard Peaslee; Choreography, Julie Arenal; Associate Producer, Steven Sinn, Production Assistant, Binti Hoskins.

CAST

Buffalo Bill	Stacy Keach
Sitting Bull	Manu Tupou
Senator Logan	Tom Aldredge
Senator Dawes	Richard McKenzie
Senator Morgan	Jon Richards
Trial Soldiers	Bob Hamilton, Richard Nieves
John Grass	Sam Waterston
Spotted Tail	James J. Sloyan
Grand Duke Alexis	Raul Julia
Interpreter	Yusef Bulos
Ned Buntline	Charles Durning
Geronimo	Ed Rombola
Master Valet	Darryl Croxton
First Lady	Dortha Duckworth
Ol' Time President	Peter MacLean
Wild Bill Hickok	Barton Heyman
Teskanjavila	Dimitra Arliss
Uncas	Raul Julia
White House Orchestra	Tony Posk, Peter Rosenfelt
Valets	Joseph Ragno, Richard Novello, Brian Donohue
Chief Joseph	George Mitchell
Annie Oakley	Pamela Grey
Jesse James	Ronny Cox
Billy the Kid	Ed Rombola
Poncho	Raul Julia
Bartender	Brian Donohue
Cowboys	Richard Nieves, Richard Miller, Clint Allmon, Bob Hamilton
Colonel Forsyth	Peter MacLean
Lieutenant	Richard Novello
Reporters	Ronny Cox, Brian Donohue, Darryl Croxton
Crazy Horse	Dino Laudicina
He-Who-Hears-Thunder	Robert McLean
Red Cloud	Andy Torres
Little Hawk	Jay Fletcher
Kiokuk	Princeton Dean
Satanta	Ed Henkel
Old Taza	Michael Ebbin
Black Hawk	Kevin Conway
Tecumseh	Pascual Vaquer
Yellow Cloud	Wesley Fata
Kicking Bear	Gary Weber
Touch-the-Clouds	Peter DeMaio
Howling Wolf	Ted Goodridge
White Antelope	Tom Fletcher
Low Dog	Philip Arsenault
Naiche	Juan Antonio
Indian Drummers	Leon Oxman, Allan Silverman

UNDERSTUDIES: Buffalo Bill, Peter MacLean; Sitting Bull, Dino Laudicina; Dawes, Joseph, Clint Allmon; Morgan, Reporters, Richard Miller; Logan, President, Forsyth, Kevin Conway; Grass, Hickok, James J. Sloyan; Alexis, Uncas, Poncho, Yusef Bulos; Buntline, Richard McKenzie; Geronimo, Billy the Kid, Princeton Dean; First Lady, Teskanjavila, Pamela Grey; Spotted Tail, Interpreter, Usher, Joseph Ragno; Jesse James, Lt., Richard Nieves.

Presented without intermission. The action takes place between 1846 and 1890.

General Manager: Oscar Olesen
Company Manager: James Walsh
Press: Harvey B. Sabinson, Lee Solters, Sandy Manley, Edie Kean
Stage Managers: Kathleen A. Sullivan, Fritz Holt Moose Peting

*Closed Jan. 3, 1970. (96 performances and 16 previews)

Martha Swope Photos

Sam Waterston, Manu Tupou, Stacy Keach, Jon Richards, Tom Aldredge, Richard McKenzie

Top Left: Manu Tupou, Stacy Keach
Below: Charles Durning, Barton Heyman, Stacy Keach

ROYALE THEATRE

Opened Wednesday, October 15, 1969.*
David Merrick Arts Foundation presents:

THE PENNY WARS

By Elliott Baker; Director, Barbara Harris; Setting, William Ritman; Costumes, Jane Greenwood; Lighting, Martin Aronstein; Associate Producer, Samuel Liff; Staff Associates, Sylvia Schwartz, John Bonanni, Elizabeth Kaye, Linda Bate.

CAST

Ross Bishop	Jeffrey Hamilton
Tyler Bishop	Kristoffer Tabori
Howie Clevenger	Jon Korkes
Mrs. Swerdlov	Rita Karin
Carrie Bishop	Kim Hunter
Frank Bishop	Dolph Sweet
Contestant	Jack Valente
Stage Manager	Ben Kapen
Bert	Brooks Morton
Mrs. Mintz	Lois Holmes
Mrs. Pitkin	Martha Galphin
Rowena Keyhoe	Judy Nugent
Mr. Pitkin	John Anania
Dr. Wolf Axelrod	George Voskovec
Reverend Sickles	John Gerstad
Blacky Roche	Lou Tiano
Dalesandro	Joe Alfasa
Horowitz	Brooks Morton
Witowski	James Doolan
Richie Davis	Mel Winkler
Clarence	Robert Delbert
Margaret O	Catherine Bacon
Lois	Kathryn Bauman
Inez Jackson	Avis McCarther

UNDERSTUDIES: Wolf, John Anania; Carrie, Mrs. Mintz, Martha Galphin; Tyler, Howie, James Woods; Frank, Dalesandro, Horowitz, Witowski, Ben Kapen; Mrs. Swerdlov, Lois Holmes; Ross, Richie, Robert Delbert; Inez, Joyce Wilford; Bert, James Doolan; Contestant, Kathryn Bauman.

A play in three acts. The action takes place in a large industrial city in upstate New York in 1939.

General Manager: Jack Schlissel
Company Manager: Hugh McGauley
Press: Lee Solters, Harvey B. Sabinson, Harry Nigro
Stage Managers: Jeff Chambers, James Doolan, Robert Delbert, Judy Nugent

*Closed Oct. 18, 1969. (5 performances and 1 preview)

Martha Swope Photos

Top Left: Kim Hunter, George Voskovec

Kristoffer Tabori, Kim Hunter, George Voskovec Top: Kathryn Baumann, Catherine Bacon, Tabori, Jon Korkes

LYCEUM THEATRE

Opened Thursday, October 16, 1969.*
Ken Gaston, Leonard Goldberg, Budd Filippo, in association with Henry Stern present:

THREE MEN ON A HORSE

By John Cecil Holm and George Abbott; Director, George Abbott; Settings, Boyd Dumrose; Costumes, A. Christina Giannini; Lighting, Fred Allison; Hairstyles and Makeup, Joey Patton; Production Assistants, Ron Roberts, Ed DeVecchio.

CAST

Audrey Towbridge	Rosemary Prinz † 1
The Tailor	D. Brian Wallach
Erwin Trowbridge	Jack Gilford
Clarence Dobbins	Leon Janney
Delivery Boy	Don Simms
Harry	Wally Engelhardt
Charlie	Hal Linden
Frankie	Al Nesor
Patsy	Sam Levene
Mabel	Dorothy Loudon /2
Dora Lee	Butterfly McQueen
Gloria	Gloria Bleezarde
Al	John Svar
Hotel Maid	Dorothy Chace
Mr. Carver	Paul Ford

UNDERSTUDIES: Carver, Gordon B. Clarke; Patsy, Harry Charlie, Don Simms; Erwin, Clarence, John Svar; Mabel, Gloria Bleezarde; Gloria, Audrey, Dora, Dorothy Chace; Frankie, Tailor, Photographer, D. Brian Wallach.

A Comedy in three acts and six scenes. The action takes place in the middle 1930's in the living room of the Trowbridge house in Ozone Heights, N. J., and in the Lavillere Hotel in New York City.

General Manager: Helen Richards
Company Manager: Barry Hoffman
Press: David Lipsky, Lisa Lipsky
Stage Managers: Wade Miller, Bernard J. Kant

Closed Jan. 10, 1970. (100 performances and 4 previews). Original production opened Jan. 30, 1935 and played 835 performances with Sam Levene, Shirley Booth, Teddy Hart, and Garson Kanin.
† Succeeded by: 1. Mary K. Wells, 2. Gloria Bleezarde.

Bert Andrews Photos

Sam Levene, Dorothy Loudon, Jack Gilford

Top: Jack Gilford, Hal Linden, Dorothy Loudon, Sam Levene, Al Nesor, Butterfly McQueen

ETHEL BARRYMORE THEATRE

Opened Saturday, October 18, 1969.*
Jay H. Fuchs, Jerry Schlossberg with Albert Zuckerman in association with Rolan Mattson present:

THE FRONT PAGE

By Ben Hecht and Charles MacArthur; Director, Harold J. Kennedy; Designed and Lighted by Will Steven Armstrong; Costumes, Sara Brook; Associate Producers, Barry Diamond and Fred Menowitz; Assistant to the Producers, Tom Underwood.

CAST

Wilson, American	Will Gregory † 1
Endicott, Post	Robert Milli † 2
Murphy, Journal	James Flavin
McCue, City Press	Ed Riley
Schwartz, News	Bob Larkin
Kruger, Journal of Commerce	Conrad Janis
Bensinger, Tribune	Harold J. Kennedy
Woodenshoes Eichorn	Walter Flanagan
Diamond Louis	Val Avery
Hildy Johnson, Herald Examiner	Bert Convy
Jenny	Dody Goodman † 3
Mollie Malloy	Peggy Cass † 4
Sheriff Hartman	Charles White
Peggy Grant	Kendall March
Mrs. Grant	Helen Hayes † 5
The Mayor	John McGiver † 6
Mr. Pincus	Bernie West
Earl Williams	Patrick Desmond
Walter Burns	Robert Ryan † 7
Carl, a deputy	Bruce Blaine
Tony	Joseph George
A Policeman	Robert Riesel
Another Policeman	Jack Collard

A Play in three acts. The action takes place in the Press Room of the Criminal Courts Building in Chicago in 1928.

General Managers: Leonard A. Mulhern, George Thorn
Press: Howard Atlee, David Roggensack, Stanley F. Kaminsky, Irene Gandy
Stage Managers: Elissa Lane, Bruce Blaine

* Closed Feb. 28, 1970. (159 performances)

† Succeeded by: 1. Victor Arnold, 2. Will Gregory, 3. Butterfly McQueen, 4. Jan Sterling, 5. Molly Picon, Maureen O'Sullivan, 6. Jules Munshin, Paul Ford, 7. James Flavin, Robert Alda

Original production opened Aug. 14, 1928 and ran for 276 performances with Lee Tracy, Dorothy Stickney, Osgood Perkins, and Walter Baldwin.

Bert Convy
Above: Peggy Cass

Robert Ryan, Dody Goodman, Top Left: Helen Hayes, Robert Ryan

16

BOOTH THEATRE

Opened Tuesday, October 21, 1969.*
Arthur Whitelaw, Max J. Brown, Byron Goldman present:

BUTTERFLIES ARE FREE

By Leonard Gershe; Director, Milton Katselas; Set, Richard Seger; Costumes, Robert Mackintosh; Lighting, Jules Fisher; Associate Producer, Ruth Bailey; Hair Stylist, Joe Tubens; Title Song, Steve Schwartz.

CAST

Don Baker	Keir Dullea
Jill Tanner	Blythe Danner
Mrs. Baker	Eileen Heckart
Ralph Austin	Michael Glaser

A Comedy in 2 acts and 3 scenes. The action takes place at the present time in Don Baker's apartment on East 11th Street in New York City.

General Manager: Marvin A. Krauss
Company Manager: David Wyler
Press: Max Eisen, Cheryl Sue Dolby, Marian Graham
Stage Managers: Elizabeth Caldwell, Preston Fischer

*   Still playing May 31, 1970.

Blythe Danner won "Tony" Award for Best Supporting Actress.

Keir Dullea, Eileen Heckart, Blythe Danner Above: Blythe Danner, Keir Dullea

Blythe Danner Top Left: Keir Dullea, Eileen Heckart

17

WINTER GARDEN

Opened Thursday, October 23, 1969.*
Jack L. Warner in association with Don Saxon presents:

JIMMY

Book, Melville Shavelson; Based on novel "Beau James" by Gene Fowler, and Screenplay by Jack Rose and Melville Shavelson; Music and Lyrics, Bill and Patti Jacob; Scenic Production, Oliver Smith; Director, Joseph Anthony; Associate Producer, Harry Mayer; Costumes, W. Robert Lavine; Lighting, Peggy Clark; Projections, Charles E. Hoefler; Musical Direction and Vocal Arrangements, Milton Rosenstock; Musical Arrangements, Jack Andrews; Dance Arrangements, John Berkman; Musical Numbers Staged by Peter Gennaro; Assistant Choreographer, Bill Guske; Hair Styling, Jim Sullivan; Original Cast Album by RCA Victor.

CAST

Jimmy Walker	Frank Gorshin
Bonnie	Cindi Bulak
Jim Hines	Jack Collins
Al Smith	William Griffis †
Allie Walker	Julie Wilson
Francis Xavier Aloysius O'Toole	Edward Becker
Lawrence Horatio Fink	Stanley Simmonds
Antonio Viscelli	Paul Forrest
Stanislaus Kazimir Wojciezkowski	Henry Lawrence
Mrs. Al Smith	Peggy Hewett
Miss Manhattan	Sally Neal
Miss Bronx	Andrea Duda
Miss Brooklyn	Carol Conte
Miss Richmond	Nancy Dalton
Miss Queens	Cindi Bulak
Stage Manager	Gary Gendell
Betty Compton	Anita Gillette
Texas Guinan	Dorothy Claire
Edward Duryea Dowling	Larry Douglas
Warrington Brock	Clifford Fearl
Charley Hand	Evan Thompson
Moe	Del Horstmann
Izzy	Carl Nicholas
Policeman	Herb Fields
Photographers	Andy G. Bew, Tony Stevens
Secretary	Barbara Andres
Reporter	Frank Newell
Tailor	Carl Nicholas
Politicians	Del Horstmann, Ben Laney, Joe McGrath
Girl in fur coat	Carol Conte
Policeman	Ben Laney
Passerby	Sandi McCreadie
Mrs. Compton	Sibyl Bowan
Band Vocalist	Joseph McGrath
Process Server	John D. Anthony
Recorded Impersonations	Dwight Weist

DANCING ENSEMBLE: Cindi Bulak, Carol Conte, Nancy Dalton, Andrea Duda, Saundra McPherson, Sally Neal, Eileen Shannon, Monica Tiller, Pat Trott, Andy G. Bew, Steven Boockvor, Christopher Chadman, David Evans, Gary Gendell, Scott Hunter, Frank Newell, Harold Pierson, Tony Stevens

SINGING ENSEMBLE: Barbara Andres, Gini Eastwood, Barbara Gregory, Peggy Hewett, Mary Louise, Sandi McCreadie, Claire Theiss, Roberta Vatske, John D. Anthony, Edward Becker, Austin Colyer, Herb Fields, Paul Forrest, Del Horstmann, Ben Laney, Henry Lawrence, Joe McGrath, Carl Nicholas

MUSICAL NUMBERS: "Will You Think of Me Tomorrow?," "The Little Woman," "The Darlin' of New York," "Oh, Gee!," "The Walker Walk," "That Old Familiar Ring," "I Only Wanna Laugh," "They Never Proved A Thing," "What's Out There for Me?," "Riverside Drive," "The Squabble Song," "Medley," "One in a Million," "It's a Nice Place to Visit," "The Charmin' Son-of-a-Bitch," "Jimmy," "Our Jimmy," "Life Is a One Way Street," Finale.

A Musical Play of the life and times of Jimmy Walker in 2 acts and 18 scenes. The action takes place between 1925 and 1931.

General Manager: Al Goldin
Company Manager: G. Warren McClane
Press: Marvin Kohn
Stage Managers: William Ross, Michael Sinclair, Jeanna Belkin, Ellen Wittman

* Closed Jan. 3, 1970. (84 performances and 8 previews)
† Succeeded by Stanley Simmonds

Friedman-Abeles Photos

Anita Gillette, Frank Gorshin, Jack Collins, Peggy Hewett, William Griffis Above: Anita Gillette, Julie Wilson Top: Frank Gorshin, Julie Wilson

THE MUSIC BOX

Opened Thursday, October 30, 1969.*
Elliott Martin Productions and Michael Ellis present:

ANGELA

By Sumner Arthur Long; Director, Jack Ragotzy; Scenery and Lighting, Robert Randolph; Costumes, Jane Greenwood; Associate Producer, Samuel Bronstein; Hair Styles, Steve Atha.

CAST

Angela Palmer	Geraldine Page
Alice	Michaele Myers
Jeff Dolan	Tom Ligon
Brian Palmer	Simon Oakland
TV Repairman	Angelo Mango
The Women	Judith Searle

UNDERSTUDIES: Angela, Michaele Myers; Brian, Repairman, Howard Fischer; Alice, Judith Searle.

A Comedy in 2 acts and 6 scenes. The action takes place at the present time in the master bedroom of the Palmer home in Walton, Mass., an affluent suburb of Boston.

General Manager: Al Goldin
Company Manager: Helen Richards
Press: Mary Bryant, David Rothenberg, Meg Gordean
Stage Managers: Harry Young, Howard Fischer

* Closed Nov. 1, 1969. (4 performances and 4 previews)

Friedman-Abeles Photos

Top: Geraldine Page

Simon Oakland
Above: Michaele Myers

ANTA THEATRE

Opened Monday, November 10, 1969.*
The American National Theatre and Academy (Alfred deLiagre, Jr., Executive Producer; Jean Dalrymple, Executive Director) presents the American Shakespeare Festival's production of:

HENRY V

By William Shakespeare; Director, Michael Kahn; Choreo-Movement, Moni Yakim; Scenery, Karl Eigsti; Costumes, Jeanne Button; Lighting, Thomas Skelton; Sound Environment, Alvin Lucier; Executive Producer, Joseph Verner Reed; Managing Producer, Berenice Weiler; Production Assistant, Bill Stuebing; Junk Sculpture, Ralph Funicello, Robert Yodice.

CAST

Chorus	Michael Parish, Robert Foxworth, Fredric Glenn, Riggs O'Hara
Canterbury	Joseph Maher
Ely	Wyman Pendleton
Voice of Falstaff	Tony van Bridge
Henry V	Len Cariou
Exeter	G. Wood
Westmoreland	Carl Strano
Bedford	Ellis Richardson
Clarence	Bolen High
Gloucester	John LaGioia
Montjoy	Tom Klunis
Nym	Herbert Foster
Bardolph	Roger Omar Serbagi
Pistol	Philip Bruns
Mistress Quickly	Mary Doyle
The Boy, Davy	Kristoffer Tabori
Scroop	Martin Broomfield
Cambridge	Robert Scogin
Grey	Mervyn Haines, Jr.
Charles VI	Wyman Pendleton
Dauphin	Danny Davis
Constable	Jack Ryland
Translators	Madge Grant, Michael Parish
Fluellen	Joseph Maher
Governor of Harfleur	Robert Jackson
Katherine	Roberta Maxwell
Alice	Patricia Elliott
Orleans	Martin Broomfield
Bourbon	Robert Scogin
Gower	Barry Corbin
Erpingham	Herbert Foster
Bates	Michael Parish
Williams	Tony Thomas
York	Anthony Passantino
M. LeFer	Mervyn Haines, Jr.
Isabel	June Prud'homme
Burgundy	Robert Jackson

ENSEMBLE: Gerald Cooper, Gary Copeland, Frank Cossa, Jesse Davis, Michael Diamond, Celeste Grant, Bolen High, James Laurence, Davidson Lloyd, Evan Nichols, Gil Payette, Gary Poe, Tim Riley, Ben Simon, Archibald Walker

Presented in two parts.

Manager: Berenice Weiler
Press: Reginald Denenholz, Anne Woll, Toni Thomas
Stage Managers: R. Derek Swire, Gina Shield

* Closed Nov. 22, 1969 after a limited engagement of 16 performances.

Martha Swope Photos

Roberta Maxwell, Patricia Elliott
Above: Len Cariou

Len Cariou (C)

ANTA THEATRE

Opened Thursday, November 27, 1969.*
The American National Theatre and Academy
(Alfred deLiagre, Jr., Executive Producer;
Jean Dalrymple, Executive Director) presents
the Plumstead Playhouse (Martha Scott,
Alfred de Liagre, Jr., Directors) production of:

OUR TOWN

By Thornton Wilder; Director, Donald Driver;
Scenery, Edward Burbridge; Costumes, David
Toser; Lighting, Jennifer Tipton; Hairstyles,
Randy Coronato.

CAST

Stage Manager	Henry Fonda
Dr. Gibbs	Ed Begley
Joe Crowell	Bryant Fraser
Howie Newsome	Thomas Coley
Mrs. Gibbs	Mildred Natwick
Mrs. Webb	Irene Tedrow
George Gibbs	Harvey Evans
Rebecca Gibbs	Denise Nickerson
Wally Webb	Stephen Gustafson
Emily Webb	Elizabeth Hartman
Professor Willard	John Fiedler
Mr. Webb	John Randolph
Woman in the balcony	Enid Kent
Man in the auditorium	Martin Shakar
Lady in the box	Enid Kent
Simon Stimson	John Beal
Mrs. Soames	Margaret Hamilton
Constable Warren	Milo Boulton
Si Crowell	Bryant Fraser
Baseball players	John Tormey, John Ventantonio, Martin Shakar, Lee Danielson, Steve Alpert
Sam Craig	Martin Shakar
Joe Stoddard	William Robertson
Farmer McCarthy	Delos V. Smith, Jr.
People of the town	Leah M. Edlin, Terry Ross, Ruth Wright, Stellar Bennett, Diane Deering, Helen Ross, Lee Sanders, Edward Stevlingson

The entire action of the play takes place in
Grover's Corners, New Hampshire.

General Manager: C. Edwin Knill
Company Manager: Helen Richards
Press: John Springer, Louise Weiner,
Howard Haines
Stage Managers: Nicholas Russiyan,
Martin Shakar

* Closed Dec. 27, 1969 after a limited engagement
of 36 performances and 3 previews.

Original production opened Feb. 4, 1938 with
Frank Craven, John Craven, Martha Scott.

Ray Fisher Photos

Ed Begley, Mildred Natwick
Above: Henry Fonda

Elizabeth Hartman, Harvey Evans, Henry Fonda
Top Left: Fonda, Margaret Hamilton, Mildred
Natwick, John Beal

GEORGE ABBOTT THEATRE

Opened Tuesday, December 2, 1969.*
Zev Bufman in association with High John Productions presents:

BUCK WHITE

Music and Lyrics, Oscar Brown, Jr.; Book adapted by Oscar Brown, Jr. from play by Joseph Dolan Tuotti; Staged by Oscar Brown, Jr. and Jean Pace; Musical Arrangements, Mike Terry, Merl Saunders; Orchestrations, Mike Terry; Musical Direction, Merl Saunders; Scenery, Edward Burbridge; Lighting, Martin Aronstein; Costumes, Jean Pace; Production Assistant, Judi McAllister; Original Cast Album by Buddah Records.

CAST

Hunter	Herschell Burton
Honey Man	David Moody
Weasel	Ted Ross
Rubber Band	Charles Weldon
Jive	Ron Rich
Buck White	Muhammad Ali
	(a/k/a Cassius Clay)
Whitey	Eugene Smith
Black Man	Don Sutherland

UNDERSTUDIES: Honey Man, Jive, Don Sutherland; Weasel, Van Kirksey; Rubber Band, Arnold Williams; Whitey, Paul F. Canavan

MUSICAL NUMBERS: "Honey Man Song," "Money, Money, Money," "Nobody Does My Thing," "Step Across That Line," "H.N.I.C.," "Beautiful Allelujah Days," "Tap the Plate," "Big Time Buck White Chant," "Better Far," "We Came in Chains," "Black Balloons," "Look at Them," "Mighty Whitey," "Get Down."

A Musical in 2 acts. The entire action takes place in the meeting hall of the Beautiful Allelujah Days organization.

General Manager: Robert Kamlot
Company Manager: Irving Cone
Press: Robert Ganshaw, John Prescott
Stage Managers: Martin Gold, Van Kirksey

* Closed Dec. 6, 1969. (7 performances and 16 previews)

Bob Green Photos

Ron Rich, Cassius Clay Top: Ted Ross, Charles Weldon, Clay, Rich, David Moody, Eugene Smith

BILLY ROSE THEATRE

Opened Thursday, December 4, 1969.*
(Moved April 27, 1970 to Broadhurst Theatre)
David Merrick presents the APA production of:

PRIVATE LIVES

By Noel Coward; Director, Stephen Porter; Settings and Lighting, James Tilton; Costumes, Joe Eula; Miss Grimes' Costumes, Barbara Matera; Associate Producer, Samuel Liff; Artistic Director, Ellis Rabb; Producing Manager, Charles Kondek; Staff Associates, Sylvia Schwartz, John Bonanni, Linda Bate, Elizabeth Kaye; Hairstylist, Marie Ardron-Finley.

CAST

Sibyl Chase ....Suzanne Grossmann
Elyot Chase ....Brian Bedford
Victor Prynne ....David Glover
Amanda Prynne..............................Tammy Grimes
Louise ....J. J. Lewis

A Comedy in 3 acts. The action takes place on the terrace of a hotel in France in summer, and in Amanda's flat in Paris.

General Manager: Jack Schlissel
Company Manager: David Lawlor
Press: Harvey B. Sabinson, Lee Solters, Ted Goldsmith, Sandra Manley, Edie Kean
Stage Managers: Lo Hardin, Bob Beard

* Closed May 30, 1970. (204 performances)
Original production opened Jan. 27, 1931 and ran for 256 performances with Noel Coward, Gertrude Lawrence, Laurence Olivier, Jill Esmond.
Tammy Grimes received "Tony" Award for Best Actress.

Carl Samrock Photos

Tammy Grimes, Brian Bedford Top:
Suzanne Grossmann, Bedford, Grimes, David Glover 23

ROYALE THEATRE

Opened Thursday, December 11, 1969.*
Helen Bonfils and Morton Gottlieb by arrangement with Olympia Productions present:

THE MUNDY SCHEME

By Brian Friel; Director, Donal Donnelly; Scenery and Lighting, William Ritman; Costumes, Noel Taylor; Production Assistant, Dorothy Araujo.

CAST

Roger Nash	Patrick Bedford
Sally	Risa McCrary
F. X. Ryan	Godfrey Quigley
Neil Boyle	Leo Leyden
Mrs. Ryan	Dorothy Stickney
Mick Moloney	Jack Cassidy
Dan Mahon	Horace McMahon
Charles Hogan	Neil Fitzgerald
Pat Toye	Ann Sweeny
Sean Grady	Liam Gannon
Tony Hanlan	William Rooney
Owen	Sean Dillon

UNDERSTUDIES: F. X., Mick, Laurence Hugo; Mrs. Ryan, Sally, Pat, Sylvia O'Brien

A Comedy in 3 acts and 4 scenes. The action takes place in the home of the Prime Minister, F. X. Ryan, at the present time.

General Manager: Richard Seader
Press: Dorothy Ross, Ruth Cage
Stage Managers: Warren Crane, William Rooney

* Closed Dec. 13, 1969. (4 performances and 13 previews.

Bert Andrews Photos

Patrick Bedford, Risa McCrary, Godfrey Quigley, Dorothy Stickney
Top Left: Neil Fitzgerald, Jack Cassidy, Horace McMahon, Leo Leyden, Godfrey Quigley

LUNT-FONTANNE THEATRE

Opened Sunday, December 14, 1969.*
Charles K. Peck, Jr., and Canyon Productions, Inc. Present:

LA STRADA

Book, Charles K. Peck, Jr.; Music and Lyrics, Lionel Bart; Based on film by Federico Fellini; Director, Alan Schneider; Dances and Musical Numbers staged by Alvin Ailey; Sets, Ming Cho Lee; Costumes, Nancy Potts; Lighting, Martin Aronstein; Musical Direction, Hal Hastings; Orchestrations Eddie Sauter; Dance Music Arrangements, Peter Howard; Hair Stylist, Steve Atha.

CAST

The Old Man	John Coe
Gelsomina	Bernadette Peters
Mother	Anne Hegira
Elsa	Lisa Belleran
Eva	Mary Ann Robbins
Sophia	Susan Goeppinger
Zampano	Stephen Pearlman
Castra	Lucille Patton
Acrobats	Paul Charles, Harry Endicott
Mario, the Fool	Larry Kert
Mama Lambrini	Peggy Cooper
Alberti	John Coe
Sister Claudia	Susan Goeppinger

COMPANY: Loretta Abbott, Glen Brooks, Henry Brunjes, Connie Burnett, Robert Carle, Paul Charles, Barbara Christopher, Peggy Cooper, Betsy Dickerson, Harry Endicott, Anna Maria Fanizzi, Jack Fletcher, Nino Galanti, Susan Goeppinger, Rodney Griffin, Mickey Gunnersen, Kenneth Kreel, Don Lopez, Joyce Maret, Stan Page, Odette Panaccione, Mary Ann Robbins, Steven Ross, Larry Small, Eileen Taylor.

UNDERSTUDIES: Gelsomina, Lyn Lipton; Mario, Henry Brunjes; Mother, Castra, Peggy Cooper

MUSICAL NUMBERS: "Seagull, Starfish, Pebble," "The Great Zampano," "What's Going on Inside?," "Belonging," "Wedding Dance," "I Don't Like You," "Encounters," "There's A Circus in Town," "You're Musical," "Only More!," "What a Man," "Everything Needs Something," "Sooner or Later," "The End of the Road."

A Musical in 2 acts and 14 scenes. The action takes place in and around the cities and villages of Southern Italy in the early 1950's.

General Managers: Joseph Harris, Ira Bernstein
Company Manager: Sam Pagliaro
Press: Frank Goodman, Barbara Schwei
Stage Managers: Terence Little, William Callan, Stan Page, Lola Shumlin

* Closed Dec. 14, 1969. (1 performance and 12 previews).

Bernadette Peters, Stephen Pearlman
Top: Bernadette Peters, Larry Kert
(R) Bernadette Peters

25

MARK HELLINGER THEATRE

Opened Thursday, December 18, 1969.*
Frederick Brisson presents:

COCO

Book and Lyrics, Alan Jay Lerner; Music, Andre Previn; Director, Michael Benthall; Musical Numbers and Fashion Sequences Staged by Michael Bennett; Sets and Costumes, Cecil Beaton; Orchestrations, Hershy Kay; Lighting, Thomas Skelton; Dance Music Continuity, Harold Wheeler; Music Direction, Robert Emmett Dolan; Associate Producer, Fred Hebert; Production Supervisor, Stone Widney; Hair Styles, Joe Tubens; Film Sequences, Milton Olshin, Fred Lemoine; Produced by Frederick Brisson for Brisson Productions, Inc., and Montfort Productions; Associate Choreographer, Bob Avian.

CAST

Coco	Katharine Hepburn
Louis Greff	George Rose
Pignol	Jeanne Arnold
Helene	Maggie Task
Sebastian Baye	Rene Auberjonois
Armand	Al DeSio
Albert	Jack Beaber
Docaton	Eve March
Georges	David Holliday
Loublaye	Gene Varrone
Varne	Shirley Potter
Marie	Margot Travers
Jeanine	Rita O'Connor
Claire	Graciela Daniele
Juliette	Lynn Winn
Madelaine	Carolyn Kirsch
Lucille	Diane Phillips
Colette	Rosemarie Heyer
Simone	Charlene Ryan
Solange	Suzanne Rogers
Noelle	Gale Dixon
Dr. Petitjean	Richard Woods
Claude	David Thomas
Dwight Berkwit	Will B. Able
Eugene Bernstone	Robert Fitch
Ronny Ginsborn	Chad Block
Phil Rosenberry	Dan Siretta
Lapidus	Gene Sarrone
Nadine	Leslie Dnaiel
Grand Duke Alexandrovitch	Bob Avian
Voice	Jack Dabdoub
Charles, Duke of Glenallen	Michael Allinson
Julian Lesage	Paul Dumont
Papa	Jon Cypher

MODELS, SEAMSTRESSES, CUSTOMERS, FITTERS: Vicki Allen, Karin Baker, Kathy Bartosh, Kathie Dalton, Alice Glenn, Maureen Hopkins, Linda Jorgens, Tresha Kelly, Nancy Killmer, Jan Metternich, Marilyn Miles, Joann Ogawa, Jean Preece, Ann Reinking, Skiles Ricketts, Marianne Selbert, Pamela Serpe, Bonnie Walker, Oscar Antony, Roy Barry, William James, Richard Marr, Don Percassi, Gerald Teijelo.

MUSICAL NUMBERS: "But That's the Way You Are," "The World Belongs to the Young," "Let's Go Home," "Mademoiselle Cliche de Paris," "On the Corner of the Rue Cambon," "The Money Rings out like Freedom," "A Brand New Dress," "A Woman Is How She Loves," "Gabrielle," "Coco," "The Preparation," "Fiasco," "When Your Lover Says Goodbye," "Ohrbach's Bloomingdale's, Best & Saks," "Always Mademoiselle."

STANDBY for Coco, Joan Copeland.

A Musical in 2 acts and 9 scenes. The action takes place in the Maison Chanel, Rue Cambon, Paris — either in the Salon, the apartment above, or the memory. It begins in the late fall of 1953 and ends in the late spring of 1954.

General Manager: Ben Rosenberg
Company Manager: Ralph Roseman
Press: Lee Solters, Harvey B. Sabinson, Leo Stern, Edie Kean
Stage Managers: Jerry Adler, Edward Preston, Robert L. Borod

* Still playing May 31, 1970. Rene Auberjonois received a "Tony" Award for Best Supporting Actor in a Musical, Cecil Beaton for Best Costume Designer.

Friedman-Abeles Photos

Top Right: Katharine Hepburn (c)
Below: Rene Auberjonois, Charlene Ryan

Jeanne Arnold, George Rose, Katharine Hepburn, Gale Dixon, Jack Beaber Above: Chad Block, Dan Siretta, Hepburn, Robert Fitch, Will B. Able

KATHARINE HEPBURN
in "Coco"

THE MUSIC BOX

Opened Monday, December 22, 1969.*
Shepherd Productions presents:

LOVE IS A TIME OF DAY

By John Patrick; Director, Bernard Thomas;
Sets, Lighting, Costumes, Lloyd Burlingame;
"Mongrel" played by Charley I.

CAST

April MacGregor.............................Sandy Duncan
Skipper Allen ....Tom Ligon

UNDERSTUDIES: Wendy Lesniak, Paul Thorne

A Comedy in 2 acts and 6 scenes. The action
takes place at the present time in a student apartment in a state university town.

General Manager: William Craver
Press: Merle Debuskey, Faith Geer,
M.J. Boyer
Stage Managers: Chuck Stockton, Paul Thorne

* Closed Dec. 27, 1969. (8 performances and 16
  previews)

Friedman-Abeles Photos

**Sandy Duncan, also above
with Tom Ligon**

28

James Coco, Marcia Rodd
Above: Doris Roberts, Coco
Right: Linda Lavin, Coco

EUGENE O'NEILL THEATRE

Opened Sunday, December 28, 1969.*
Saint-Subber presents:

LAST OF THE
RED HOT LOVERS

By Neil Simon; Director, Robert Moore; Scenic
Production, Oliver Smith; Costumes, Donald
Brooks; Lighting, Peggy Clark; Hair Styles, Joe
Tubens, Michael Chianese.

CAST

Barney Cashman ....James Coco
Elaine Navazio ....Linda Lavin
Bobbi Michele ....Marcia Rodd
Jeanette Fisher.......................................Doris Roberts

STANDBYS: Barney, Tom Lacy; Elaine, Doris
Belack; Bobbi, Elizabeth Farley; Jeanette, Stella
Longo

A Comedy in 3 acts. The action takes place at
the present time in an apartment in the East 30's
in New York City.

General Manager: C. Edwin Knill
Company Manager: James Turner
Press: Harvey B. Saginson, Lee Solters,
Harry Nigro
Stage Managers: Tom Porter, George Rondo

* Still playing May 31, 1970.

Friedman-Abeles Photos

29

Opened Tuesday, December 30, 1969.*
The American National Theatre and Academy
(Alfred de Liagre, Jr., Executive Producer;
Jean Dalrymple, Executive Director) presents
the New York Shakespeare Festival Public
Theater (Joseph Papp, Producer; Gerald
Freedman, Artistic Director; Bernard Gersten,
Associate Producer) production of:

NO PLACE TO BE SOMEBODY

By Charles Gordone; Director, Ted Cornell; Set
and Lighting, Michael Davidson; Scenery Supervision, David Mitchell; Lighting Supervision, Martin
Aronstein; Costumes, Theoni V. Aldredge; Production Assistant, Judy Rasmuson.

CAST

Gabe Gabriel	Ron O'Neal
Shanty Mulligan	Ronnie Thompson
Johnny Williams	Nathan George
Dee Jacobson	Susan G. Pearson
Evie Ames	Lynda Westcott
Cora Beaseley	Marge Eliot
Melvin Smeltz	Henry Baker
Machine Dog	Christopher St. John
Mary Lou Bolton	Laurie Crews
Ellen	Margaret Pine
Sweets Crane	Walter Jones
Mike Maffucci	Nick Lewis
Louie	Michael Landrum
Judge Bolton	Ed VanNuys
Sgt. Cappaletti	Charles Seals
Harry	Malcolm Hurd

UNDERSTUDIES: Gabe, Melvin, Nick Smith;
Johnny, Charles Gordone; Evie, Cora, Mary Alice;
Sweets, W. Benson Terry; Shanty, Judge, Cappaletti, Michael Landrum; Dee, Mary Lou, Margaret Pine; Mike, Charles Seals.

A Drama in two acts. The action takes place in
the past 15 years in Johnny's Bar in the West Village, New York City.

Manager: David Black
Press: Merle Debuskey, Faith Geer
Stage Managers: Adam G. Perl, Malcolm Hurd
* Closed Jan. 10, 1970 after a limited engagement
of 16 performances; re-opened Off Broadway
Tues., Jan. 20, 1970 at the Promenade Theatre,
and still playing May 31, 1970. Winner of the
1970 Pulitzer Prize.

Friedman-Abeles Photos

**Nathan George, Laurie Crews Top Right: Ron O'Neal,
George, Nick Lewis, Walter Jones**

**Ron O'Neal, Nathan George
Above: George, Marge Eliot**

Opened Monday, January 12, 1970.*
The American National Theatre and Academy
(Alfred de Liagre, Jr., Executive Producer;
Jean Dalrymple, Executive Director) presents
Eugene O'Neill Memorial Theatre Center's:

THE NATIONAL THEATRE
OF THE DEAF

Managing Director, David Hays; Technical Director, Robert Steinberg; Administrative Assistant, Patricia Flynn.

SGANARELLE

By Moliere; Translation by Albert Bermel; Director, Jack Sydow; Adapted by Eric Malzkuhn, Robert Panara; Setting and Costumes, Fred Voelpel; Lighting, John Gleason.

CAST

Street Cleaners	Jacqueline Awad, Lou Fant, William Rhys
Lisette, Celie's chaperone	Dorothy Miles
Celie, daughter of Gorgibus	Fredericka Norman
Gorgibus	Patrick Graybill
Sganarell	Bernard Bragg
Martine	Mary Beth Miller
Servants	Linda Bove, Phyllis Frelich
Grosrene, Lelie's valet	Edmund Waterstreet
Lelie	Richard Kendall
Dorante	John Basinger
Villebrequin	Peter Wechsberg

Intermission

SONGS FROM MILK WOOD

From "Under Milk Wood" by Dylan Thomas; Adapted by Bernard Bragg with Dorothy Miles; Director J. Ranelli; Music, John Basinger; Setting, David Hays; Costumes, Fred Voelpel; Lighting, John Gleason.

Second Voice	Jacqueline Awad
Mr. Pugh, Sinbad Sailors	John Basinger
Mae Rose Cottage, Mrs. Cherry Owen	Linda Bove
First Voice	Bernard Bragg
Captain Cat	Lou Fant
Polly Garter	Phyllis Frelich
Mog Edwards, Rev. Jenkins	Patrick Graybill
Willy Nilly, Mr. Ogmore	Richard Kendall
Myfannwy Price, Mrs. Pugh	Dorothy Miles
Bessie Bighead, Mrs. Pritchard	Mary Beth Miller
Rosie Probert, Mrs. Dai Bread	Fredericka Norman
Second Voice	William Rhys
Mr. Waldo, Cherry Owen	Edmund Waterstreet
Nogood Boyo, Mr. Pritchard	Peter Wechsberg

General Managers: George Thorn,
Leonard A. Mulhern
Company Manager: Michael Goldreyer
Press: Reginald Denenholz, Anne Woll
Stage Managers: Ken Swiger, Rilla Bergman

* Closed Jan. 17, 1970 after a limited engagement of 8 performances, to begin national tour.

**Edmund Waterstreet (C) Top Right:
Linda Bove, Bernard Bragg in
"Songs from Milk Wood"**

**Richard Kendall, Bernard Bragg
Above: Fredericka Norman, Dorothy
Niles in "Sganarelle"**

31

BROOKS ATKINSON THEATRE

Opened Monday, January 19, 1970.*
David Black in association with Donald J. Trump presents:

PARIS IS OUT!

By Richard Seff; Director, Paul Aaron; Scenery, Douglas W. Schmidt; Costumes, Florence Klotz; Lighting, Martin Aronstein; Production Manager, Charles Gray.

CAST

Hattie Fields	Dorothy Sands
Hortense Brand	Molly Picon
Daniel Brand	Sam Levene
Roger Brand	Terry Kiser
Arlene Kander	Zina Jasper
Andrew Grael	Gary Tigerman
Charlotte Grael	Gwyda DonHowe
Hellevi Gessnehr	Laryssa Lauret

UNDERSTUDIES: Hortense, Beatrice Pons; Daniel, Jack Somack; Hattie, Beatrice Pons; Charlotte, Arlene, Hellevi, Jane Singer; Roger, John Towey; Andrew, Garth Dolderer

A Comedy in 2 acts and 4 scenes. The action takes place at the present time in New York City.

General Manager: Jose Vega
Company Manager: R. Tyler Gatchell, Jr.
Press: Betty Lee Hunt, Henry Luhrman, Ruth D. Smuckler, Harriet Trachtenberg
Stage Managers: Bert Woods, Garth Dolderer

* Closed Sunday matinee Apr. 19, 1970. (96 performances and 16 previews)

Zodiac Photos

Sam Levene, Molly Picon Above: Levene, Picon, Dorothy Sands Top: Zena Jasper, Terry Kiser, Levene, Picon

Terry Kiser, Zena Jasper, Molly Picon Above: Picon, Levene, Kiser

ANTA THEATRE

Opened Wednesday, January 21, 1970.*
The American National Theatre and Academy (Alfred de Liagre, Jr., Executive Producer; Jean Dalrymple, Executive Director) presents The Playwrights Unit (Richard Barr, Edward Albee, Charles Woodward) production of:

WATERCOLOR
&
CRISS-CROSSING

By Philip Magdalany; Director, Chuck Gnys; Settings and Costumes, Peter Harvey; Lighting, Richard Nelson; Sound Tapes, David Walker; Production Assistant, Jack Custer; Production Associate, Richard Lipsett; Production Manager, Lynne Prather; Announcer's Voice, Jennifer Harmon.

CAST
"Criss-Crossing"

Adolph	Lee Goodman
Augustus	Robert Reiser
Arnold	Patrick Baldauff
Barbara	Judith Granite
Constance	Cathryn Damon
Catherine	Patricia O'Connell
Carlotta	Mary Louise Wilson

The action takes place at the present time in a city somewhere in the United States.

"Watercolor"

Andrew	Donald Warfield
Benjamin	Peter Lazer
Diane	Jacqueline Brookes
Edith	Kate Wilkinson
Gloria	Jennifer Salt

The action takes place at the present time on a beach somewhere in the United States.

General Managers: Michael Goldreyer, Michael Kasdan
Press: Betty Lee Hunt, Henry Luhrman, Harriet Trachtenberg
Stage Managers: Robert Moss, Gregory Mayrer

* Closed Jan. 24, 1970. (7 performances)

Ted Yaple Photos

Jacqueline Brookes Top: Patrick Baldauff, Judith Granite, Lee Goodman, Cathryn Damon, Robert Reiser, Patricia O'Connell

JOHN GOLDEN THEATRE

Opened Wednesday, January 28, 1970.*
Michael Byron and Mel Weiser present:

BRIGHTOWER

By Dore Schary; Director, Mel Weiser; Sets,
Tom Munn; Costumes, Noel Taylor; Lighting,
John Gleason; General Assistant, David Kolatch;
Hairstylist, Kenneth; Produced by B/W Produc-
tions; Production Consultant, Sally Goldwater.

CAST

Jess	Will Hussung
Sara Brightower	Geraldine Brooks
Daniel Brightower	Robert Lansing
Clay Benson	Arien Dean Snyder
Lori Granger	Martha Galphin
Nick Hagen	Paul McGrath
Bill Canfield	Richard Buck

UNDERSTUDIES: Sara, Lori, Michaele Myers;
Jess, Daniel, George L. Smith; Clay, Bill, Andy
M. Rasbury.

A Drama in 4 scenes with one intermission. The
action takes place in the home of Daniel Brightower
in Vermont in the present and the past.

General Manager: Richard Seader
Press: Bill Doll & Co., Midori Lederer,
Virginia Holden
Stage Managers: Harry Young, Andy M. Rasbury

* Closed Wed., Jan. 28, 1970. (1 performance and
2 previews)

Martha Swope Photos

Robert Lansing, Martha Galphin
Top Right: Will Hussung, Robert Lansing, Geraldine Brooks

HELEN HAYES THEATRE

Opened Saturday, January 31, 1970.*
Roger L. Stevens, Robert Whitehead, Robert W. Dowling present:

SHEEP ON THE RUNWAY

By Art Buchwald; Director, Gene Saks; Settings, Peter Larkin; Costumes, Jane Greenwood; Lighting, Jules Fisher; Production Assistant, Doris Blum; Production Consultant, Frodo Productions, Ltd.; Speeches recorded by Jeremiah Morris.

CAST

Ambassador Raymond Wilkins	David Burns
Martha Wilkins	Elizabeth Wilson
Sam	Jeremiah Morris
Holly	Margaret Ladd
Joseph Mayflower	Martin Gabel
Fred Slayton	Will Mackenzie
Prince Gow	Richard Castellano
General Fitzhugh	Barnard Hughes
Edward Snelling	Remak Ramsay
Colonel Num	Neil Flanagan
Guards	Kurt Garfield, Henry Proach

UNDERSTUDIES: Joseph, Jeremiah Morris; Wilkins, Fitzhugh, Howard Fischer; Gow, Jeremiah Morris, William Becker; Martha, Helen Stenborg; Slayton, Snelling, Russell Horton; Holly, Eda Zahl; Num, William Becker; Sam, Henry Proach.

A Comedy in 2 acts and 4 scenes. The action takes place at the present time in the living room of the United States Embassy in the Kingdom of Nonomura, a remote monarchy in the Himalayas.

General Manager: Oscar E. Olesen
Company Manager: David Hedges
Press: Seymour Krawitz, Fred Weterick
Stage Managers: Frederic de Wilde,
Howard Fischer, William Becker

* Closed May 2, 1970. (97 performances and 16 previews). Moved to Washington, D.C. and closed there May 23, 1970.   Leo Friedman Photos

Margaret Ladd, Elizabeth Wilson, David Burns, Richard Castellano, Will Mackenzie, Martin Gabel
Top Right: Remak Ramsey, David Burns, Barnard Hughes

Charles Aznavour

THE MUSIC BOX

Opened Wednesday, February 4, 19⁷
Norman Twain in association with A
I. Fill presents:

CHARLES AZNAVOUR

Musical Director and Pianist, Henri Byrs
duction Supervisor, Leon Sanossian; Unless
wise noted, Mr. Aznavour is composer and
cist for all songs in the show.

PROGRAM

PART ONE: "Le Tamos," "I Will Give To
"Happy Anniversary," "We'll Drift Away,
Toreador," "Sunday's Not My Day," "Apa
Luz," "Isabelle," "I Will Warm Your Heart
My Daughter," "Et Pourtant," "The W
Youth," "Yesterday When I Was Young,"
menez-Moi," "It Will Be My Day."

PART TWO: "All Those Pretty Girls," "
Avoir Aimer," "My Hand Needs Your I
"You've Let Yourself Go," "Desormais," "
"Reste," "Venice Dressed in Blue," "La Bo
"August Days in Paree," "Les Comediens,"
I in My Chair," "You've Got to Learn," "Les
Moments."

A one-man show with 11 musicians.

General Manager: Sherman Gross
Press: Frank Goodman, Les Schecter

* Closed Feb. 22, 1970. (23 performance
1 preview)

ANTA THEATRE

Opened Wednesday, February 4, 1970.*
The American National Theatre and Academy
(Alfred de Liagre, Jr., Executive Producer;
Jean Dalrymple, Executive Director) presents
the La Mama Experimental Theatre Club
production of:

GLORIA AND ESPERANZA

Written and Directed by Julie Bovasso; Associate
Director and Choreographer, Raymond Bussey;
Assistant Choreographer, William Pierce; Setting,
Daffi; Lighting, Keith Michael; Settings and Cos-
tumes Supervised by Peter Harvey; Costumes,
Ella Luxembourg and the Birdie Sisters; Lighting
Supervisor, Richard Nelson.

CAST

ACT I: A Basement Apartment
Julius Esperanza, a poet ....Kevin O'Connor
Gloria B. Gilbert, his girlfriend ....Julie Bovasso
Professor Poe ....Herve Villechaize
Solange, an 8 foot chicken...............................Daffi
Agitators ....Alex Beall, Reigh Hagen,
 Wes Williams, Alan Wynroth
Guru Children ....Maria D'Elia, Sara Dolley,
 Daffi, John Bacher, Deirdre Simone, Dennis Sokal,
 Ella Luxembourg, Laverne Jamison, Jane Sanford
Soldiers ....William Pierce, Louis Ramos,
 Peter Bartlett, Carl Wilson
Fred the Mailman...............................Ted Henning
Terry Wong Fu, oriental landlord........Dan Durning
The Emergency Room:
Psychiatrist.............................Leonard Hicks
Dr. Brown, another psychiatrist........Maury Cooper
Attendants ....Louis Ramos, Alan Wynroth
Gladiators ....John Bacher, William Pierce,
 Peter Bartlett, Carl Wilson
ACT II: In the Madhouse: Saints and Martyrs
Jack Sinistre, Black Prince....................Alex Beall
Steissbart, his Demon ....Herve Villechaize
St. Teresa............................Reigh Hagen
St. Augustine..............................Ted Henning
St. Ambrose...............................Maury Cooper
St. Anthony, really Lt. Col. Moore..........
 Leonard Hicks
St. John, a shell-shocked soldier ....John Bacher
St. Dominic, a mongoloid...................Dennis Sokal
St. Boniface, an hysteric ....Wes Williams
St. Agnes, a spastic ....Sara Dolley
St. Felicite, a gatatonic ....Deirdre Simone
Mary and Martha..........
 Maria D'Elia, Ella Luxembourg
St. Bernard, a schizophrenic ....Daffi
Back in the Basement:
Eric von Schtutt, internal revenue man ....
 Tom Rosica
Marsha, Gloria's friend ....Jane Sanford
The Alvin and His Mother TV Show:
Alvin, a cocker spaniel ....Ted Henning
Alvin's mother...................................Dennis Sokal
Basketball Ballet Girls ....Sara Dolley,
 Laverne Jamison, Myra Lee, Deirdre Simone,
 Jane Sanford
Oriental Guerrilla Dancers ....John Bacher,
 William Pierce, Peter Bartlett
The Revelations Revue:
Horsewomen Showgirls of the Apocalypse..........
 John Bacher, Maria D'Elia, Sara Dolley,
 Jane Sanford
Star Angels ....Laverne Jamison, Myra Lee,
 Ella Luxembourg, Deirdre Simone
Sword Angels ....Reigh Hagen, Wes Williams,
 Carl Wilson, Alan Wynroth
Trumpet Angels........Peter Bartlett, William Pierce
Woman clothed in the sun ....Dennis Sokal
Alpha and Omega ....Louis Ramos
Dragon...............................Ted Henning

Business Administrator: Jules Weiss
Press: Howard Atlee, David Roggensack,
 Stanley F. Kaminsky, Irene Gandy
Stage Managers: Glen Nielsen, Wes Jensby

* Closed Feb. 14, 1970. (15 performances)

Bert Andrews Photos

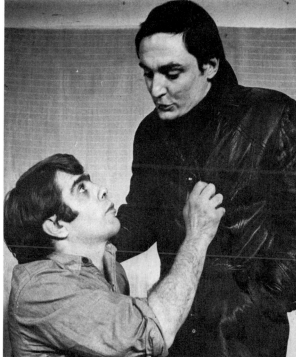

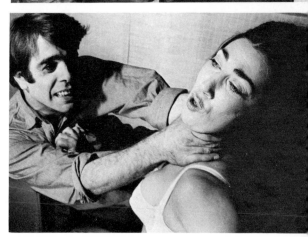

**Top Right: William Pierce, Louis Ramos, Carl Wilson,
Reigh Hagen, Peter Bartlett, Alan Wynroth**

**Kevin O'Connor, Julie Bovasso
Above: O'Connor, Alex Beall**

37

Robert Shaw, Rita Moreno Above: Bob Gorman,
David Sabin, Zale Kessler, Ted Thurston

GEORGE ABBOTT THEATRE

Opened Saturday, February 14, 1970.*
Joseph Cates and Jerry Schlossberg present:

GANTRY

Book, Peter Bellwood; Adapted from novel "Elmer Gantry" by Sinclair Lewis; Music, Stanley Lebowsky; Lyrics, Fred Tobias; Directed and Staged by Onna White; Scenery, Robin Wagner; Costumes, Ann Roth; Lighting, Jules Fisher; Orchestrations, Jim Tyler; Musical Direction, Arthur Rubinstein; Dance Arrangements, Dorothea Freitag; Associate to Director, Martin Allen; Assistant Choreographer, Patrick Cummings; Production Manager, Ben Janney; Associate Producer, Fred Menowitz; Hair Styles, Ernest Adler; Production Supervised by Robert Weiner; Original Cast Album, RCA Records; Vocal Arrangements, Stanley Lebowsky.

CAST

Bill Morgan	Tom Batten
Sister Doretha	Dorothea Freitag
Adelberta Shoup	Gloria Hodes
Sharon Falconer	Rita Moreno
Elmer Gantry	Robert Shaw
Jim Lefferts	Wayne Tippit
George F. Babbitt	Ted Thurston
Rev. Garrison	Kenneth Bridges
Trosper	Bob Gorman
Gunch	David Sabin
Prout	Zale Kessler
Rev. Toomis	David Hooks
Architect	Robert Donahue
Photographer	James N. Maher
Deaf Man	J. Michael Bloom
His Wife	Beth Fowler

TOWNSPEOPLE, ETC: Chuck Beard, J. Michael Bloom, Kenneth Bridges, Patrick Cummings, Robert Donahue, Sandy Ellen, Carol Estey, Beth Fowler, Gloria Hodes, Keith Kaldenberg, Clyde Laurents, Robert Lenn, James N. Maher, Kathleen Robey, Dixie Stewart, Diane Tarleton, Maralyn Thoma, Terry Violino, Mimi Wallace

UNDERSTUDIES: Sharon, Beth Fowler; Lefferts, Kenneth Bridges; Babbitt, David Sabin; Morgan, Toomis, Robert Donahue; Gunch, Trosper, Keith Kaldenberg; Prout, J. Michael Bloom; Adelberta, Diane Tarleton; Garrison, Robert F. Donahue; Deaf man, Robert Lenn; His wife, Dixie Stewart.

MUSICAL NUMBERS: "Wave a Hand," "Gantry Gets the Call," "He Was There," "Play Ball with the Lord," "Katie Jonas," "Thanks, Sweet Jesus!," "Someone I've Already Found," "He's Never Too Busy," "We're Sharin' Sharon," "We Can All Give Love," "Foresight," "These Four Walls," "Show Him the Way," "The Promise of What I Could Be," "Gantry's Reaction."

A Musical in 2 acts and 14 scenes.

General Managers: Robert Weiner, Nelle Nugent
Press: David Powers
Stage Managers: Ben Janney, William Letters, Mary Porter Hall

* Closed Feb. 14, 1970. (1 performance and 32 previews)

Martha Swope Photos

Rita Moreno (C)
Top Left: Rita Moreno (L),
Robert Shaw (R)

ROYALE THEATRE

Opened Tuesday, February 17, 1970.*
David Merrick presents:

CHILD'S PLAY

By Robert Marasco; Director, Joseph Hardy; Scenery and Lighting, Jo Mielziner; Costumes, Sara Brook; Sound, Gary Harris; Associate Producer, Samuel Liff; Associate Designer, John H. Doepp; Staff Associates, Sylvia Schwartz, John Bonanni, Linda Bate, Elizabeth Kay, Robert Pearlstein; Assistant to the Director, Ben Gerard.

CAST

Faculty:
Paul Reese	Ken Howard
Father Penny	David Rounds
Father Griffin	Peter MacLean
Jerome Malley	Fritz Weaver
Joseph Dobbs	Pat Hingle
Father Mozian	Michael McGuire

Students:
Carre	Bryant Fraser
Medley	Christopher Deane
Banks	Robbie Reed
Jennings	Mark Hall
O'Donnell	Frank Fiore
Shea	Patrick Shea
Wilson	Ron Martin
McArdle	Lloyd Kramer
Travis	John Handy

UNDERSTUDIES: Dobbs, Joseph Hill; Malley, Michael McGuire; Reese, Patrick Shea; Shea, Ron Martin

A Drama presented without intermission. The action takes place at the present time in mid-winter in St. Charles' School.

General Manager: Jack Schlissel
Company Manager: Hugh McGauley
Press: Harvey B. Sabinson, Lee Solters,
Sandra Manley
Stage Managers: Mitchell Erickson, John Handy,
Joseph Hill

* Still playing May 31, 1970.
Fritz Weaver received "Tony" Award for Best Actor, Ken Howard for Best Supporting Actor, Joseph Hardy for Best Director, and Jo Mielziner for Best Lighting and Best Scenic Design.

Martha Swope Photos

Howard, Fritz Weaver Above: David Rounds, (C) Top: hael McGuire, Fritz Weaver, Ken Howard holding Robbie Reed, Pat Hingle, Peter MacLean, David Rounds

LYCEUM THEATRE

Opened Thursday, February 19, 1970.*
Harold D. Cohen presents:

NORMAN, IS THAT YOU?

By Ron Clark, Sam Bobrick; Director, George
Abbott; Scenery, William and Jean Eckart; Costumes, Florence Klotz; Lighting, Fred Allison;
Assistant to Producer, Michael Davenport; Hair
Styles, Rusty Buonaccorso; Produced by arrangement with Augustus Productions.

CAST

Norman Chambers	Martin Huston
Garson Hobart	Walter Willison
Ben Chambers	Lou Jacobi
Mary	Dorothy Emmerson
Beatrice Chambers	Maureen Stapleton

UNDERSTUDIES: Beatrice, Mary, Janice Mars;
Norman, Garson, Sean Simpson.

A Comedy in 2 acts and 5 scenes. The action
takes place at the present time in a New York City
apartment.

General Manager: Richard Horner
Company Manager: Al Jones
Press: Lee Solters, Harvey B. Sabinson,
Jay Russell, Edie Kean
Stage Managers: Bernard Pollock, Peter Simpson

* Closed Feb. 28, 1970 after 12 performances and
20 previews.

Zodiac Photos

**Dorothy Emmerson, Lou Jacobi, Martin Huston
Top: Walter Willison, Maureen Stapleton, Lou Jacobi**

ANTA THEATRE

Opened Tuesday, February 24, 1970.*
The American National Theatre and Academy
(Alfred de Liagre, Jr., Executive Producer;
Jean Dalrymple, Executive Director) presents
the Phoenix Theatre (T. Edward Hambleton,
Managing Director) production of:

HARVEY

By Mary Chase; Director, Stephen Porter; Scenery and Lighting, James Tilton; Costumes, Nancy Potts; Hair Styles, Steve Atha; Assistant to Managing Director, Daniel Freudenberger; Staff Assistants, Dina Alkalay, Connie Berry; Production Assistant, Maribeth Gilbert; Portrait, Don Lamb; Production Assistants, Arthur N. Burleigh, Kathy Kelly.

CAST

Myrtle Mae Simmons	Marian Hailey
Veta Louise Simmons	Helen Hayes
Elwood P. Dowd	James Stewart
Ethel Chauvinet	Dorothy Blackburn
Ruth Kelly	Mariclare Costello
Duane Wilson	Jesse White
Lyman Sanderson	Joe Ponazecki
William Chumley	Henderson Forsythe
Betty Chumley	Peggy Pope
Judge Gaffney	John C. Becher
E. J. Lofgren	Dort Clark

A Comedy in 3 acts and 5 scenes. The action takes place at the present time in a city in the Far West in the library of the old Dowd family mansion and the reception room of Chumley's Rest Home.

General Manager: Marilyn S. Miller
Press: Sol Jacobson, Lewis Harmon
Stage Managers: Bruce Hoover, Don Lamb

* Closed May 2, 1970 after 80 performances and 8 previews. Original production opened Nov. 1, 1944 and ran for 1775 performances. Original cast included Josephine Hull, Frank Fay, and Jesse White.

Van Williams Photos

Henderson Forsythe, Jesse White, Marian Hailey, John C. Becher Above: Peggy Pope, Joe Ponazecki, Forsythe, Mariclare Costello

James Stewart, Helen Hayes, also top left with Jesse White

WINTER GARDEN

Opened Thursday, February 26, 1970.*
Fred Coe in Association with Joseph P. Harris
and Ira Bernstein presents:

GEORGY

Book, Tom Mankiewicz; Based on novel by
Margaret Forster, and screenplay by Miss Forster
and Peter Nichols; Lyrics, Carole Bayer; Music,
George Fischoff; Director, Peter Hunt; Choreo-
graphy, Howard Jeffrey; Settings and Lighting,
Jo Mielziner; Costumes, Patricia Zipprodt; Musi-
cal Direction and Vocal Arrangements, Elliot
Lawrence; Orchestrations, Eddie Sauter; Dance
Music Arranged by Marvin Laird; Hairstyles,
Ernest Adler; Production Manager, Porter Van
Zandt; Original Cast Album on Bell Records;
Assistants to the Producers, Ann Levack, Nancy
Simmons; Associate Designer, John H. Doepp;
Production Assistant, Regina Lynn; Audio De-
sign, Robert Liftin.

CAST

Georgy	Dilys Watling
James Leamington	Stephen Elliott
Ted	Louis Beachner
Meredith	Melissa Hart
Peg	Helena Carroll
Jos	John Castle
Peter	Richard Quarry
Health Officer	Cynthia Latham

SINGERS: Susan Goeppinger, Del Horstmann,
Don Jay, Geoff Leon, Regina Lynn
CHILDREN: Kelley Boa, Mona Daleo, Jackie Paris,
Donna Sands, Jill Streisant, Dewey Golkin, Jeffrey
Golkin, Anthony Marciona, Roger Morgan, Johnny
Welch
PARTY GUESTS, ETC.: Kathryn Doby, Sherry
Durham, Patricia Garland, Margot Head, Mary
Jane Houdina, Jane Karel, Barbara Monte-Britton,
Michon Peacock, Mary Zahn, Rick Atwell, Pi
Douglass, Arthur Faria, Charlie Goeddertz, Neil
Jones, Sal Pernice, Richard Quarry, Allan Sobek,
Tony Stevens.
UNDERSTUDIES: Georgy, Carol Prandis; Mere-
dith, Barbara Monte-Britton; James, Ted, John
O'Leary; Peg, Health Officer, Myra Carter; Peter
Allan Sobek.
MUSICAL NUMBERS: "Howjadoo," "Make It
Happen Now," "Ol' Pease Puddin;" "Just for the
Ride," "So What?," "Georgy," "A Baby," "That's
How It Is," "There's a Comin' Together," "Some-
thing Special," "Half of Me," "Gettin' Back to
Me," "Sweet Memory," "Life's a Holiday," Finale.

A Musical in 2 acts and 16 scenes.
General Managers: Joseph H. Harris, Ira Bernstein
Company Manager: Sam Pagliaro
Press: Karl Bernstein, Dan Langan
Stage Managers: Philip Mandelker, James Haire,
Lynn Montgomery
* Closed Feb. 28, 1970 after 4 performances and
7 previews.

**Stephen Elliott, Dilys Watling
Top Right: John Castle, Dilys Watling**

Leo Friedman Photos

ETHEL BARRYMORE THEATRE

Opened Tuesday, March 10, 1970.*
Gilbert Cates presents:

THE CHINESE AND DR. FISH

By Murray Schisgal; Director, Arthur Storch;
Settings, William Pitkin; Costumes, Sara Brook;
Lighting, Martin Aronstein; Production Assistant,
Janice Bogard; Hair Styles, Stanley Williams.

CAST

"Dr. Fish"

Charlotte Mendelsohn......................Charlotte Rae
Mrs. Fish ....Paula Trueman
Dr. Fish ....Marvin Lichterman
Marty Mendelsohn ....Vincent Gardenia

A Comedy in one act. The action takes place
at the present time at Dr. Fish's.

"The Chinese"

Mr. Lee..Joseph Bova
Mrs. Lee ....Alice Drummond
Chester Lee ....William Devane
Gladys Hoffman ....Louise Lasser
Pu Ping Chow................Marcia Jean Kurtz

A Comedy in one act. The action takes place
at the present time at the Lees'.

UNDERSTUDIES: Mrs. Lee, Charlotte, Mrs.
Fish, Vera Lockwood; Mr. Lee, Marty, William
Callan; Gladys, Marcia Jean Kurtz; Pu Ping,
Louise Lasser.

General Manager: Robert Kamlot
Company Manager: Peter Neufeld
Press: Harvey B. Sabinson, Lee Solters,
Marilynn LeVine
Stage Managers: Martin Gold, William Callan
* Closed Apr. 21, 1970. (15 performances)

Carl Samrock Photos

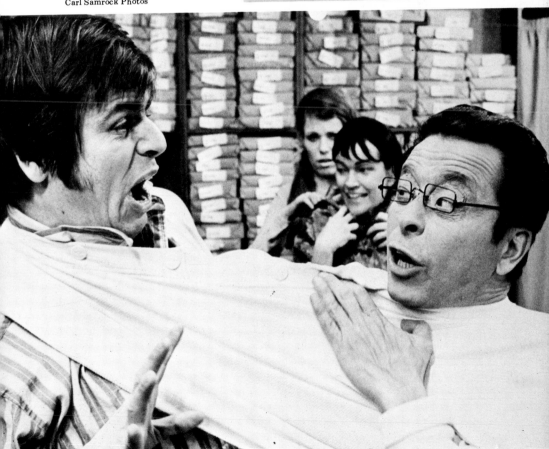

William Devane, Louise Lasser, Alice Drummond, Joseph Bova in "The Chinese"
Top Right: Charlotte Rae in "Dr. Fish"

43

BROADWAY THEATRE

Opened Sunday, March 15, 1970.*
Philip Rose presents:

PURLIE

Book, Ossie Davis, Philip Rose, Peter Udell;
Based on play "Purlie Victorious" by Ossie Davis;
Music, Gary Geld; Lyrics, Peter Udell; Director,
Philip Rose; Choreography, Louis Johnson; Scen-
ery, Ben Edwards; Lighting, Thomas Skelton;
Costumes, Ann Roth; Hair Styles, Ernest Adler;
Orchestrations and Choral Arrangements, Garry
Sherman, Luther Henderson; Musical Supervisor,
Garry Sherman; Musical Conductor, Joyce Brown;
Dance Music Arranged by Luther Henderson,
Original Cast Album by AMPEX.

CAST

Purlie	Cleavon Little
Church Soloist	Linda Hopkins
Lutiebelle	Melba Moore
Missy	Novella Nelson
Gitlow	Sherman Hemsley
Charlie	C. David Colson
Idella	Helen Martin
Ol' Cap'n	John Heffernan

DANCERS: Loretta Abbott, Hope Clark, Judy
Gibson, Lavinia Hamilton, Arlene Rowlant, Ella
Thompson, Myrna White, Morris Donaldson,
George Faison, Al Perryman, Harold Pierson,
William Taylor, Larry Vickers.

SINGERS: Carolyn Byrd, Barbara Christopher,
Denise Elliott, Synthia Jackson, Mildred Lane,
Alyce Webb, Mildred Pratcher, Peter Colly, Milt
Grayson, Tony Middleton, Ray Pollard

UNDERSTUDIES: Purlie, Robert Jackson; Lutie-
belle, Synthia Jackson; Soloist, Alyce Webb; Git-
low, Ted Ross; Ol' Cap'n, Charlie, Curt Williams;
Idella, Alyce Webb; Swing Dancer, Ted Goodridge

MUSICAL NUMBERS: "Walk Him up the Stairs,"
"New Fangled Preacher Man," "Skinnin' a Cat,"
"Purlie," "The Harder They Fall," "Charlie's Songs,"
"Big Fish, Little Fish," "I Got Love," "Great White
Father," "Down Home," "First Thing Monday Morn-
in'," "He Can Do It," "The World Is Comin' to a
Start," Finale.

A Musical in 2 acts and 6 scenes, with prologue
and epilogue. The action takes place in South
Georgia not too long ago.

General Manager: Helen Stern Richards
Press: Merle Debuskey, Faith Geer
Stage Managers: Leonard Auerbach,
Mortimer Halpern, Charles Briggs

* Still playing May 31, 1970.
Cleavon Little received "Tony" Award for Best
Musical Actor, and Melba Moore for Best Sup-
porting Actress in a Musical.

Zodiac Photos

Top Right: Cleavon Little, Melba Moore

Cleavon Little, Melba Moore, John Heffernan, Sherman Hemsley Above: Moore, Novella Nelson, Little

BELASCO THEATRE

Opened Monday, March 16, 1970.*
Barnett Wolfe Plaxen presents:

GRIN AND BARE IT!
and
POSTCARDS

Director, Ronny Graham; Designed by David Mitchell; Costumes, Dominic Poleo; Lighting, Martin Aronstein; Associate Producers, Judith Robin, Sandra Yanowitz; Production Associate, Alan Coffield.

CAST

"Postcards"
by James Prideaux

Margaret .... Kate Wilkinson
Leonard .... Ray Stewart

"Grin and Bare It!"
by Tom Cushing;
Adapted by Ken McGuire

Diana Smith .... Joleen Fodor
Derek Leet .... David Christmas
Agamemnon Smith .... James Burge
Katinka .... Blanche Dee
Mitzi Braun .... Jeanne paslé-green
Heinrich Braun .... Tom Fuccello
Prof. Persius Smith .... William LeMassena
Mrs. Smith .... Barbara Lester
Aunt Minna .... Avril Gentles
Understudy: Philip Larson

A Comedy in one act. The action takes place in the summer of 1929 in the Smiths' home outside of Los Angeles.

Manager: G. Warren McClane
Press: Mary Bryant, Meg Gordean,
David Rothenberg
Stage Managers: D. W. Koehler, Charles Kindl

* Closed Mar. 28, 1970 after 16 performances and 21 previews.

Leo Friedman Photos

**Joleen Fodor, William LeMassena, David Christmas
Top: Blanche Dee, Christmas, James Burge
Left: Kate Wilkinson** 45

JOHN GOLDEN THEATRE

Opened Sunday, March 22, 1970.*
Seymour Vall, Louis S. Goldman in association with Rick Mandell, Bjorn I. Swanstrom present:

BLOOD RED ROSES

Book and Lyrics, John Lewin; Music, Michael Valenti; Director, Alan Schneider; Musical Numbers Staged by Larry Fuller; Scenery, Ed Wittstein; Costumes, Deidre Cartier; Lighting, Tharon Musser; Musical Direction, Milton Setzer; Orchestrations, Julian Stein, Abba Bogin; Assistant Director, Joan Thorne; Assistants to Producers, Maggie Vall, Janet Burton; Production Assistant, Wendy Chernis.

CAST

Grenadier Guards ....William Tost, Bill Gibbens
Fitzroy Somerset, Lord Raglan,
   Commander-in-Chief ....Sydney Walker
Prince Albert ....Ronald Drake
Queen Victoria ....Jeanie Carson
Pvt. William Cockcroft ....Jess Richards
Pvt. John Smalls ....Philip Bruns
Alice Crabbe, a bawd ....Jeanie Carson
W. H. Russell, London Times ....Jay Gregory
Russian Soldier ....Charles Abbott
Cornet Edwin May ....Lowell Harris
Florence Nightingale ....Jeanie Carson

UNDERSTUDIES: Lowell Harris—Russell, Charles Abbott—Smalls, Jay Gregory—Prince Albert, William Tost—Cornet May and Russian Soldier, Bill Gibbens—Lord Raglan, Cockcroft; Frances Sternhagen for Miss Carson.

MUSICAL NUMBERS: Overture, "The Cream of English Youth," "A Garden in the Sun," "Song of How Mucked Up Things Are," "Song of Greater Britain," "Black Dog Rum," "In the Country Where I Come From," "The English Rose," "Soldiers Prayer," "Blood Red Roses," "The Fourth Light Dragoons," "Song of the Fair Dissenter Lass," Finale.

A Play with Songs in 2 acts and 9 scenes. The action takes place in England and the Crimean Peninsula during the Crimean War of 1854-55

General Manager: Diana Shumlin
Company Manager: Paul Groll
Press: Abby Hirsch, Ellen Rosenberg
Stage Managers: Richard Thayer, Louis Pulvino

* Closed Mar. 22, 1970 after 1 performance and 9 previews.

Ted Yaple Photos

Sydney Walker, Jeanie Carson, Ronald Drake
Top Left: Philip Bruns, Jeanie Carson

Daniel Fortus, Lewis J. Stadlen, Shelley Winters, Irwin Pearl, Alvin Kupperman

IMPERIAL THEATRE

Opened Thursday, March 26, 1970.*
Arthur Whitelaw, Max J. Brown, Byron Goldman present:

MINNIE'S BOYS

Book, Arthur Marx, Robert Fisher; Music, Larry Grossman; Lyrics, Hal Hackady; Director, Stanley Prager; Musical Numbers Staged by Marc Breaux; Production Consultant, Groucho Marx; Settings, Peter Wexler; Costumes, Donald Brooks; Lighting, Jules Fisher; Musical Direction and Vocal Arrangements, John Berkman; Orchestrations, Ralph Burns; Dance Arrangements and Incidental Music, Marvin Hamlisch, Peter Howard; Music Publisher, Tommy Valando; Hairstylist, Joe Tubens; Associate Producer, Peter N. Grad; Staff Associates, Carol Young, Rosemary Borello; Production Assistant, Susan Bell; Assistant Choreographer, Dennis Cole; Original Cast Album by RCA Records.

CAST

Julie Marx (Groucho)	Lewis J. Stadlen
Leonard Marx (Chico)	Irwin Pearl
Adolph Marx (Harpo)	Daniel Fortus
Herbie Marx (Zeppo)	Alvin Kupperman
Milton Marx (Gummo)	Gary Raucher
Mrs. Flanagan	Jean Bruno
Mrs. Krupnik	Jacqueline Britt
Minnie Marx	Shelley Winters
Sam (Frenchie) Marx	Arny Freeman
Hochmeister	Merwin Goldsmith
Al Shean	Mort Marshall
Cop	Doug Spingler
Sidebark	Ronn Hansen
Acrobats	Evelyn Taylor, David Vaughan, George Bunt
Cindy	Marjory Edson
Maxie	Richard B. Shull
Telegraph Boy	Stephen Reinhardt
Robwell	Casper Roos
Harpist	Jean Bruno
Theatre Manager	Gene Ross
E. F. Albee	Roland Winters
Mrs. McNish	Julie Kurnitz
Murdoch	Jacqueline Britt
Sandow the Creat	Richard B. Shull
Miss Taj Mahal	Lynne Gannaway
Miss White House	Marjory Edson
Miss Eiffel Tower	Vicki Frederick

ENSEMBLE: Jacqueline Britt, Jean Bruno, Bjarne Buchtrup, George Bunt, Dennis Cole, Deede Darnell, Joan B. Duffin, Marjory Edson, Vicki Frederick, Marcelo Gamboa, Lynne Gannaway, Ronn Hansen, Elaine Manzel, Stephen Reinhardt, Casper Roos, Gene Ross, Carole Schweid, William W. Sean, Doug Spingler, Evelyn Taylor, David Vaughan, Toodie Witmer, Mary Zahn.

UNDERSTUDIES: Minnie, Thelma Lee; Sam, Al, Merwin Goldsmith; Mrs. McNish, Jacqueline Britt; Groucho, Chico, Gary Raucher; Zeppo, Stephen Reinhardt; Harpo, George Bunt; Gummo, William Sean; Maxie, Albee, Casper Roos; Hochmeister, Sidebark, Robwell, Ci Herzog

MUSICAL NUMBERS: "Five Growing Boys," "Rich Is," "More Precious Far," "Four Nightingales," "Underneath It All," "Mama, A Rainbow," "You Didn't Have to Do It For Me," "If You Wind Me Up," "Where Was I When They Passed Out Luck?," "The Smell of Christmas," "You Remind Me of You," "Minnie's Boys," "Be Happy," "The Act," Finale.

A Musical in 2 acts and 12 scenes.

General Manager: Marvin A. Krauss
Press: Max Eisen, Warren Pincus, Bob Satuloff
Stage Managers: Frank Hamilton, John Andrews, Ci Herzog, Doug Spingler

* Closed May 30, 1970 after 80 performances and 64 previews.

Top Left: Arny Freeman, Shelley Winters

LUNT-FONTANNE THEATRE

Opened Sunday, March 29, 1970.*
Edgar Lansbury, Max J. Brown, Richard
Lewine and Ralph Nelson present:

LOOK TO THE LILIES

Book, Lyrics, Sammy Cahn; Based on "Lilies of the Field" by William E. Barrett; Music, Jule Styne; Scenery and Lighting, Jo Mielziner; Costumes, Carrie F. Robbins; Director, Joshua Logan; Musical Direction, Milton Rosenstock; Vocal Arrangements and Direction, Buster Davis; Orchestrations, Larry Wilcox; Dance Arrangements, John Morris; Production Associate, Joseph Beruh; Hairstylist, Ronald DeMann; Audio Design, Robert I. Liftin; Production Assistant, David Loveless; Associate Designer, John H. Doepp; Original Cast Album by Warner Brothers Records.

CAST

Homer Smith	Al Freeman, Jr.
Sister Gertrude	Maggie Task
Sister Elizabeth	Virginia Craig
Sister Agnes	Linda Andrews
Mother Maria	Shirley Booth
Sister Albertine	Taina Elg
Lady Guitarist	Anita Sheer
Juanita	Patti Karr
Rosita	Carmen Alvarez
Juan Archuleta	Titos Vandis
Bartender	Marc Allen III
Policemen	Joe Benjamin, Richard Graham
Courtroom Guards	Paul Eichel, Michael Davis
Judge	Joe Benjamin
District Attorney	Don Prieur
Defense Attorney	Ben Laney
Monsignor O'Hara	Richard Graham
Poker Players	Michael Davis, Paul Eichel, Don Prieur
Children	Lisa Bellaran, Lori Bellaran, Ray Bellaran

SINGERS: Marian Haraldson, Sherri Huff, Suzanne Horn, Maggie Worth, Marc Allen III, Michael Davis, Paul Eichel, Tony Falco, Ben Laney, Don Prieur

DANCERS: Carol Conte, Maria DiDia, Tina Faye, Ravah Malmuth, Glenn Brooks, Harry Endicott, Gary Gendell, Steven Ross

UNDERSTUDIES: Homer, Clifton Davis; Maria, Maggie Task; Juan, Ted Beniades; Albertine, Shirley Potter; Rosita, Carol Conte; Juanita, Tina Faye; Gertrude, Elizabeth, Agnes, Marian Haraldson; Judge, Policemen, Paul Eichel; Monsignor, Policemen, Michael Davis

MUSICAL NUMBERS: "Gott Is Gut," "First Class Number One Bum," "Himmlisher Vater," "Follow the Lamb," "Meet My Seester," "Don't Talk about God," "When I Was Young," "On That Day of Days," "You're a Rock," "I Am What I Am," "I'd Sure Like to Give It a Shot," "I Admire You Very Much, Mr. Schmidt," "Look to the Lilies," "Some Kind of Man," "Homer's Pitch," "Casamagordo, New Mexico," "One Little Brick at a Time," "I, Yes Me, That's Who," "Prayer"

A Musical in 2 acts and 16 scenes.

General Manager: Joseph Beruh
Company Manager: Jewel Howard
Press: Max Eisen, Warren Pincus, Bob Satuloff
Stage Managers: Wade Miller, Gigi Cascio, Bail Bell

* Closed Sun., Apr. 19, 1970 after 25 performances and 31 previews.

Top Right: Maggie Task, Virginia Craig, Al Freeman, Linda Andrews, Taina Elg, Shirley Booth

Carmen Alvarez, Patti Karr, Al Freeman, Shirley Booth Above: Freeman, Booth

LYCEUM THEATRE

Opened Tuesday, March 31, 1970.*
Michael McAloney and Burton C. Kaiser in association with The Abbey Theatre of Dublin present:

BORSTAL BOY

By Frank McMahon; Adapted from Brendan Behan's autobiography of the same name; Directed and Designed by Tomas MacAnna; Scenic Supervision and Lighting, Neil Peter Jambolis; Costume Supervision, Robert Fletcher; Associate Producer, Joyce Sloane; Assistant to the Producers, Roslyn Dickens.

CAST

Brendan Behan	Niall Toibin
Young Behan	Frank Grimes
Sheila	Patricia McAneny
Mrs. Gildea	Mairin D. O'Sullivan,†
I.R.A. Men	Brenday Fay, Liam Gannon, Don Billett, Michael Cahill
Liverpool landlady	Phyllis Craig
Inspector	John MacKay
Detective Vereker	Dean Santoro
Sergeant	Joseph Warren
Charlie Millwall	Bruce Heighley
First Warder, Mr. Whitbread	Francis Bethencourt
Second Warder, Mr. Holmes	Arthur Roberts

Prisoners at Walton:

Hartigan	Norman Allen
Smith	Don Billett
Callan	Liam Gannon
James	Drout Miller
Dale	James Woods
Tubby	Kenneth McMillan
Brownie	Terry Lomax
Prison Chaplain	Stephen Scott
Library Warder	Brendan Fay
Prison Governor	John MacKay
Voice of the Judge	Brendan Fay
Welsh Warder	Arthur Roberts
Governor of Borstal	Stephen Scott
Minister	Kenneth McMillan
Warder O'Shea	Joseph Warren
Italian Priest	Don Perkins
Cook	Kenneth McMillan
Warder's Wife	Amy Burk
Emmigration Official	Brendan Fay

Borstal Boys:

Harty	Norman Allen
Joe	Drout Miller
Ken Jones	George Connolly
Chewlips	Michael Cahill
Jock	Don Billett
Tom Meadows	James Woods
Rivers	Liam Gannon
Cragg	Dean Santoro
Shaggy	Terry Lomax

CROWD, OFFICIALS, ETC.: Tom Signorelli, Richard Yesso, Marilyn Crawley, Richard Yanko, Roslyn Dickens, Peter Hock.

UNDERSTUDIES: Behan, Cook, Brendan Fay; Young Behan, George Connolly; Millwall, Norman Allen; Warder, Governor, Official, John MacKay; Warder, Chaplain, Kenneth McMillan; Tubby, Governor, Don Perkins; Inspector, Sgt., Stephen Scott; Callan, James Woods; Dale, Judge, Dean Santoro; IRA Men, Drout Miller; James, Brownie, Shaggy, Harty, Tom Signorelli; Warder, Verecker, Rivers, Warder, Richard Yanko; Chewlips, Tom, Cragg, Richard Yesso; Joe, Ken, Jock, Priest, Peter Hock; Mrs. Gildea, Landlady, Marilyn Crawley; Sheila, Amy Burk; Warder's Wife, Roslyn Dickens.

A Drama in 2 acts. The many scenes start in Liverpool in the summer of 1939 when the Irish Republican Army was engaged in its bombing campaign to free Northern Ireland; then to Dublin, back to Liverpool, Hollesley Bay, aboard a ship for Ireland, and on the Dublin quayside.

General Manager: Richard Horner
Company Manager: Al Jones
Press: Lee Solters, Harvey B. Sabinson, Jay Russell, Stanley F. Kaminsky, Edie Kean
Stage Managers: Bernard Pollock, William G. Johnson
* Still playing May 31, 1970. Winner of "Tony" Award for Best Play
† Succeeded by Helena Carroll

Top Right: Niall Toibin, Frank Grimes

Patricia McAneny, Frank Grimes, Mairin D. O'Sullivan, Niall Toibin
Above: Frank Grimes

49

**Bonnie Franklin Above: Brandon Maggart,
Ann Williams, Lauren Bacall**

PALACE THEATRE

Opened Monday, March 30, 1970.*
Joseph Kipness and Lawrence Kasha in association with Nederlander Productions and George M. Steinbrenner, III, present:

APPLAUSE

Book, Betty Comden, Adolph Green; Based on film "All About Eve" and the original story by Mary Orr; Music, Charles Strouse; Lyrics, Lee Adams; Director and Choreographer, Ron Field; Scenery, Robert Randolph; Costumes, Ray Aghayan; Lighting, Tharon Musser; Musical Direction and Vocal Arrangements, Donald Pippin; Orchestrations, Philip J. Lang; Dance and Incidental Music Arranged by Mel Marvin; Production Associate, Phyllis Dukore; Directorial Assistant, Otto Pirchner; Choreographic Assistant, Tom Rolla; Hairstylist, Joe Tubens; Original Cast Album by ABC Records.

CAST

Tony Announcer	John Anania
Tony Host	Alan King
Margo Channing	Lauren Bacall
Eve Harrington	Penny Fuller
Howard Benedict	Robert Mandan
Bert	Tom Urich
Buzz Richards	Brandon Maggart
Bill Sampson	Len Cariou
Duane Fox	Lee Roy Reams
Karen Richards	Ann Williams
Bartender	Jerry Wyatt
Peter	John Anania
Bob	Howard Kahl
Piano Player	Orrin Reiley
Stan Harding	Ray Becker
Danny	Bill Allsbrook
Bonnie	Bonnie Franklin
Carol	Carol Petri
Joey	Mike Misita
Musicians	Gene Kelton, Nat Horne, David Anderson
TV Director	Orrin Reiley
Autograph Seeker	Carol Petri

SINGERS: Laurie Franks, Ernestine Jackson, Sheilah Rae, Jeannette Seibert, Henrietta Valor, Howard Kahl, Orrin Reiley, Jerry Wyatt.

DANCERS: Renee Baughman, Joan Bell, Debi Carpenter, Patti D'Beck, Marily D'Honau, Marybeth Kurdock, Carol Petri, Bill Allsbrook, David Anderson, John Cashman, Jon Daenen, Nikolas Dante, Gene Foote, Gene Kelton, Nat Horne, Mike Misita, Ed Nolfi, Sammy Williams

UNDERSTUDIES: Eve, Sheilah Rae; Bill, Tom Urich; Howard, John Anania; Buzz, Ray Becker; Karen, Laurie Franks; Duane, Gene Foote; Bonnie, Carol Petri; Bert, Stan, Jerry Wyatt.

MUSICAL NUMBERS: "Backstage Babble," "Think How It's Gonna Be," "But Alive," "The Best Night of My Life," "Who's That Girl?," "Applause," "Hurry Back," "Fasten Your Seat Belts," "Welcome to the Theater," "Inner Thoughts," "Good Friends," "She's No Longer a Gypsy," "One of a Kind," "One Hallowe'en," "Something Greater," Finale.

A Musical in 2 acts and 16 scenes. The entire action takes place at the present time in and around New York City.

General Manager: Philip Adler
Company Manager: S. M. Handelsman
Press: Bill Doll & Co., Dick Williams, Midori Lederer, Virginia Holden, Susan Schulman
Stage Managers: Terence Little, Donald Christy, Lanier Davis, Howard Kahl

* Still playing May 31, 1970. Winner of "Tony" Award for Best Musical, Best Director, Best Choreographer, and for Miss Bacall, Best Actress in a Musical.

**Top Left: Lauren Bacall, Len Cariou
Below: Penny Fuller, Lauren Bacall**

LAUREN BACALL
in "Applause"

LONGACRE THEATRE

Opened Monday, April 6, 1970.*
Virginia Snow, John Carter, Cash Baxter present:

CANDIDA

By George Bernard Shaw; Director, Lawrence Carra; Costumes, Miles White; Sets, John Braden; Lighting, John Gleason.

CAST

Proserpine Garnett....................Cavada Humphrey
Rev. James Morell............................Wesley Addy
Rev. Alexander Mill ....Paxton Whitehead
Mr. Burgess......................................Keith Mackey
Candida...Celeste Holm
Eugene Marchbanks ....Robert Browning

UNDERSTUDIES: Candida, Proserpine, Paddy Croft; Morell, Paxton Whitehead; Marchbanks, Mill, William McLuckey

A Comedy in 3 acts. The entire action takes place in St. Dominic's Parsonage, Victoria Park, London, in October 1905.

General Manager: Sherman Gross
Press: Frank Goodman, Les Schecter
Stage Managers: Mary Porter Hall,
William McLuckey

* Closed Apr. 11, 1970 after 8 performances and 5 previews.

Original production opened Dec. 9, 1903 with Arnold Daly, Dorothy Donnelly, Dodson Mitchell and ran for 133 performances. Last revival Apr. 22, 1952 with Olivia de Havilland, Terrance Kilburn, Ron Randell for 32 performances.

Cavada Humphrey, Paxton Whitehead
Above: Wesley Addy, Robert Browning

Top: Wesley Addy, Celeste Holm

BROADHURST THEATRE

Opened Wednesday, April 8, 1970.*

Mitch Leigh in association with C. Gerald Goldsmith presents:

CRY FOR US ALL

Book, William Alfred, Albert Marre; Based on play "Hogan's Goat" by William Alfred; Music, Mitch Leigh; Lyrics, William Alfred, Phyllis Robinson; Book and Musical Staging, Albert Marre; Choreography, Todd Bolender; Setting and Lighting, Howard Bay; Costumes, Robert Fletcher; Musical Direction, Herbert Grossman; Music Supervision, Sam Pottle; Orchestrations, Carlyle Hall; Production Coordinator, Dwight Frye; Assistant Choreographer, John Mandia; Production Assistant, Jack Davidson; Hairstylist, Dorman Allison; Original Cast Album on Project 3 Records.

CAST

Street-rats:

Miggsy	Scott Jacoby
Flylegs	Darel Glaser
Cabbage	Todd Jones
Matt Stanton, Leader of Brooklyn's 6th Ward, and owner of Court Cafe	Steve Arlen
Kathleen Stanton	Joan Diener
Edward Quinn, Mayor of Brooklyn	Robert Weede
Petey Boyle	Tommy Rall
Bessie Legg	Helen Gallagher
Maria Haggerty	Dolores Wilson
John "Black Jack" Haggerty	Paul Ukena
James "Palsy" Murphy, Brooklyn Boss	Edwin Steffe
Father Stanislaus Coyne	William Griffis
Senator Thomas Walsh	Jay Stuart
Mortyeen O'Brien, Fire Commissioner	Charles Rule
Peter Mulligan	John Ferrante
Father Maloney	Elliott Savage
Cruelty Man	Taylor Reed
Mrs. Teresa Tuohy	Fran Stevens
Fiona Quigley	Elaine Cancilla
Jack O'Banion	Jack Trussel
Mrs. Mortyeen O'Brien	Dora Rinehart
Aloysius "Wishy" Doyle	Bill Dance
Mutton Egan	Ronnie Douglas

UNDERSTUDIES: Kathleen, Willi Burke; Petey, Coyne, Haggerty, Maloney, Ted Forlow; Matt, Jay Stuart; Quinn, Edwin Steffe; Bessie, Elaine Cancilla; Maria, Fran Stevens; Murphy, O'Brien, Taylor Reed; Miggsy, Flylegs, Cabbage, Ronnie Douglas; Walsh, Mulligan, Jack Trussel; Cruelty Man, Wishy Doyle, Jim Stevenson.

MUSICAL NUMBERS: "See No Evil," "The End of My Race," "How Are Ya Since?," "The Mayor's Chair," "The Cruelty Man," "The Verandah Waltz," "Home Free All," "The Broken Heart of The Wages of Sin," "The Confessional," "Who to Love if not a Stranger?," "Cry for Us All," "Swing Your Bag," "Call in to Her," "That Slavery Is Love," "I Lost It," "Aggie, Oh Aggie," "The Leg of the Duck," "This Cornucopian Land."

A Musical presented without intermission. The action takes place in Brooklyn during a five-day period around the first of May in 1890.

General Manager: Edward H. Davis
Company Manager: J. Ross Stewart
Press: Harvey B. Sabinson, Lee Solters, Ted Goldsmith, Sandra Manley
Stage Managers: James S. Gelb, Bob Burland, Jim Stevenson, Bill Dance

* Closed Apr. 15, 1970 after 8 performances and 18 previews.

Zodiac Photos

Top Right: Helen Gallagher, Steve Arlen, Elaine Cancilla

Helen Gallagher, Tommy Rall, Robert Weede

AMBASSADOR THEATRE
Opened Tuesday, April 14, 1970.*
John Yorke, Don Saxon, Michael Hellerman
present:

THE BOY FRIEND

Book, Music and Lyrics by Sandy Wilson; Director, Gus Schirmer; Dances and Musical Numbers Staged by Buddy Schwab; Settings and Costumes, Andrew and Margaret Brownfoot; Lighting, Tharon Musser; Costume Supervision, Stanley Simmons; Hairstylist, D. Rusty Bonaccorso; Musical Director, Jerry Goldberg; Associate Producer, Robert Saxon; Production Assistant, Ronald Snyder; Orchestrations, Ted Royal, Charles L. Cooke; Original Cast Album on Decca Records.

CAST

Hortense	Barbara Andres
Nancy	Lesley Secombe
Maisie	Sandy Duncan
Fay	Mary Zahn
Dulcie	Simon McQueen
Polly	Judy Carne
Marcel	Marcelo Gamboa
Alphonse	Ken Mitchell
Pierre	Arthur Faria
Madame Dubonnet	Jeanne Beauvais
Bobby Van Husen	Harvey Evans
Percival Browne	Leon Shaw
Tony	Ronald Young
Phillipe	Tony Stevens
Monica	Carol Culver
Lord Brockhurst	David Vaughan
Lady Brockhurst	Marie Paxton
Gendarme	Jeff Richards
Waiter	Tony Stevens
Pepe	Marcelo Gamboa
Lolita	Mary Zahn

UNDERSTUDIES: Polly, Carol Culver; Tony, Jeff Richards; Percival, Paul Tracey; Madame, Barbara Andres; Bobby, Arthur Faria; Brockhurst, Paul Tracey; Dulcie, Lesley Secombe; Lady Brockhurst, Hortense, Fay, Lolita, Eleonore Treiber; Nancy, Maisie, Mimi B. Wallace; Marcel, Pepe, Arthur Faria; Marcel, Pierre, Alphonse, Tony Stevens.

MUSICAL NUMBERS: "Perfect Young Ladies," "The Boy Friend," "Won't You Charleston with Me?," "Fancy Forgetting," "I Could Be Happy with You," "Sur La Plage," "A Room in Bloomsbury," "It's Nicer in Nice," "You Don't Want to Play with Me Blues," "Safety in Numbers," "The Riviera," "It's Never Too Late to Fall in Love," "Carnival Tango," "Poor Little Pierrette," Finale.

A Musical Comedy of the 1920's in 3 acts. The action takes place in the drawing-room of the Villa Caprice, Mme. Dubonnet's finishing school on the outskirts of Nice, on the beach, and at the Cafe Pataplon.

Production Supervisor: Tharon Musser
Press: Saul Richman, Sy Sandler,
Peggy Mitchell
Stage Managers: Phil Friedman, Larry Ziegler,
Eleonore Treiber

* Closed July 18, 1970 after 119 performances and 3 previews. Original production opened Sept. 30, 1954 and ran for 483 performances with Julie Andrews and Bob Scheerer.

Barry Kramer Photos

Jeanne Beauvais, Leon Shaw Top Right: Harvey Evans, Sandy Duncan

Simon McQueen, Lesley Secombe, Leon Shaw, Carol Culver, Mary Zahn Above: Ronald Young, Judy Carne

**Konrad Matthaei, Cathryn Damon,
Marian Mercer (Foreground)**

ETHEL BARRYMORE THEATRE

Opened Saturday, April 18, 1970.*
Ken Gaston and Leonard Goldberg with
David G. Meyers present:

A PLACE FOR POLLY

By Lonnie Coleman; Director, Ronny Graham;
Setting and Lighting, Clarke Dunham; Costumes,
Frank Thompson; Associate Producer, Henry
Stern; Incidental Music, William Fisher; Coordinator for Producers, Joel Dein; Production Assistant, Brian Richmond; Hairstylist, D. Rusty
Bonaccorso.

CAST

Tony	Alan Manson
Joyce	Evelyn Russell
Polly	Marian Mercer
George	William Mooney
Otis	Konrad Matthaei
Angela	Cathryn Damon
Mr. Bigelow	Daniel Keyes
Mrs. Bigelow	Dortha Duckworth
Dan Da Vinci	Robert Moberly

A Comedy in 2 acts and 4 scenes. The action
takes place at the present time in an apartment in
Greenwich Village.

General Manager: Helen Richards
Company Manager: Jesse Long
Press: David Lipsky, Lisa Lipsky
Stage Managers: D.W. Koehler, Didi Francis

* Closed Apr. 18, 1970 after 1 performance and
9 previews.

Ted Yaple Photos

**Dortha Duckworth, Alan Manson Top: William
Mooney, Cathryn Damon, Evelyn Russell**

JOHN GOLDEN THEATRE

Opened Wednesday, April 22, 1970.*
Edward Padula, a division of Eddie Bracken
Ventures, Inc., presents:

PARK

Book and Lyrics, Paul Cherry; Music, Lance
Mulcahy; Director, John Stix; Lighting, Martin
Aronstein; Arrangements and Musical Direction,
Oscar Kosarin; Scenery and Costumes, Peter
Harvey; Musical Staging, Lee Theodore; Assistant
to Producer, Bill Harris; Technical Supervisor,
Mitch Miller.

CAST

Young Man .... Don Scardino
Young Woman .... Joan Hackett
Man .... David Brooks
Woman .... Julie Wilson

PARK BAND: Oscar Kosarin, Richard Cooper,
Bernie Karl, Rick Loewus, Bruce Scott, Gregory
Squires

MUSICAL NUMBERS: "All the Little Things in
the World Are Waiting," "Hello Is the Way Things
Begin," "Bein' a Kid," "Elizabeth," "He Talks to
Me," "Tomorrow Will Be the Same," "One Man,"
"Park," "I Want It Just to Happen," "I Can See,"
"Compromise," "Jamie," "I'd Marry You Again."

A Musical in two acts. The action takes place at
the present time in Spring in a park.

General Manager: Helen Richards
Company Manager: Peter Neufeld
Press: Marc Olden
Stage Managers: Henry Garrard, Robert Tucker
* Closed Apr. 25, 1970 after 5 performances and
5 previews.

Zodiac Photos

**Joan Hackett, Don Scardino,
also top with David Brooks**

Julie Wilson

THE MUSIC BOX

Opened Thursday, April 23, 1970.*
Lee Guber, Shelly Gross present:

INQUEST

By Donald Freed; Based on "Invitation to an Inquest" by Walter and Miriam Schneir; Director, Alan Schneider; Associate Producer, Bernard King; Settings, Karl Eigsti; Costumes, Sara Brook; Lighting and Projection Consultant, Jules Fisher; Projections, Ken Isaacs; Sound, Gary Harris; Production Manager, Mark Wright; Assistant Director, Rhoda Grauer; Production Assistants, Rod McGovern, Dorothy Fields; Hairstylist, Ray Iagnocco.

CAST

Ethel Rosenberg	Anne Jackson
Julius Rosenberg	George Grizzard
Emanuel Bloch	James Whitmore
Clerk	Allen Garfield
Bailiff	Abe Vigoda
Irving Sapol	Mason Adams
Roy Cohn	Mike Bursten
Judge Kaufman	Michael Lipton
Reporters	Charles Kindl, David Clarke
David Greenglass	Jack Hollander
FBI Agents	Ed Bordo, Abe Vigoda, David Clarke
Tessie Greenglass	Sylvie Straus
Matron	Sylvia Gassell
Harry Gold	Phil Leeds
Rabbi	Allen Garfield
Ruth Greenglass	Hildy Brooks

UNDERSTUDIES: Bloch, David Clarke; David Greenglass, Harry Gold, Allen Garfield; Saypol, Abe Vigoda; Kaufman, Julius, Ed Bordo; Ethel, Ruth, Tessie, Sylvia Gassell, Cohn, Charles Kindl

A Drama presented without intermission. The action takes place in The Courtroom, The World, The Past.

General Manager: Irving Cone
Press: Mike Merrick, Nancy Love, Marcia Bell
Stage Managers: Bill Callan, Charles Kindl

* Closed May 16, 1970 after 28 performances and 8 previews.

Barry Kramer Photos

James Whitmore (top), Anne Jackson, George Grizzard
(also above)

Charles Braswell, Elaine Stritch

ALVIN THEATRE

Opened Sunday, April 26, 1970.*
Harold Prince in association with Ruth Mitchell presents:

COMPANY

Music and Lyrics, Stephen Sondheim; Book, George Furth; Director, Harold Prince; Sets and Projections, Boris Aronson; Costumes, D.D. Ryan; Lighting, Robert Ornbo; Musical Direction, Harold Hastings; Orchestrations, Jonathan Tunick; Dance Music Arrangements, Wally Harper; Music Publisher, Tommy Valando; Musical Numbers Staged by Michael Bennett; Production Supervisor, Ruth Mitchell; Associate Choreographer, Bob Avian; Hairstylists, Roberto Vega, Mr. Vincent; Original Cast Album by Columbia Records.

CAST

Robert	Dean Jones †
Sarah	Barbara Barrie
Harry	Charles Kimbrough
Susan	Merle Louise
Peter	John Cunningham
Jenny	Teri Ralston
David	George Coe
Amy	Beth Howland
Paul	Steve Elmore
Joanne	Elaine Stritch
Larry	Charles Braswell
Marta	Pamela Myers
Kathy	Donna McKechnie
April	Susan Browning
Vocal Minority	Cathy Corkill, Carol Gelfand, Marilyn Saunders, Dona D. Vaughn

UNDERSTUDIES: Robert, Larry Kert; Joanne, Jessica James; Peter, Paul, David, James O'Sullivan; Larry, Harry, Bob Roman; Kathy, April, Virginia Sandifur; Susan, Jenny, Marta, Alice Cannon; Amy, Sarah, Audre Johnston.

MUSICAL NUMBERS: "Company," "The Little Things You Do Together," "Sorry-Grateful," "You Could Drive a Person Crazy," "Have I Got A Girl for You," "Someone Is Waiting," "Another Hundred People," "Getting Married Today," "Side by Side By Side," "What Would We Do Without You," "Poor Baby," "Tick Tock," "Barcelona," "The Ladies Who Lunch," "Being Alive."

A Musical Comedy in two acts. The action takes place at the present time in New York City.

General Manager: Carl Fisher
Press: Mary Bryant, Meg Gordean
Stage Managers: James Bronson, Fritz Holt, George Martin

* Still playing May 31, 1970.
† Succeeded by Larry Kert.

Zodiac and Martha Swope Photos

Top Right: George Coe, Teri Ralston, Dean Jones Below: Dean Jones, Susan Browning

Pamela Myers, Susan Browning, Donna McKechnie Above: Barbara Barrie, Dean Jones, Charles Kimbrough

ANTA THEATRE

Opened Wednesday, May 6, 1970.*
The American National Theatre and Academy
(Alfred de Liagre, Jr., Executive Producer;
Jean Dalrymple, Executive Director) presents
the John Fernald Company of the Meadow
Brook Theatre at Oakland University in
Rochester, Michigan (John Fernald, Artistic
Director; Donald R. Britton, Managing
Director) in their production of:

THE CHERRY ORCHARD

By Anton Chekhov; Translated by J. P. Davis;
Director, John Fernald; Scenery, Richard Davis;
Costumes, Ross B. Young; Lighting, Pat Simmons;
Technical Director, Lyalls Phillips; Production
Assistant, Phil Baker.

CAST

Dunyasha	Rhonda Rose
Yermolai Alexeyevich Lopahin	Toby Tompkins
Semyen Pantalyeevich Yepihodof	K. C. Wilson
Feerce	Richard Curnock
Lyoubof Andreyevna Ranyevskaya	Jenny Laird
Varya	Bonnie Hurren
Anya	Andrea Stonorov
Leonid Nadreyevich Gayef	Marshall Borden
Charlotta Ivanovna	Janet McIntire
Boris Borisovich Simeonof-Pischic	William Needles
Yahsa	Michael Tolaydo
Peter Sergeyevich Trofimof	Jeremy Rowe
Tramp	Pat Freni
Station-Master	James Sutorius
Post Office Official	Pat Freni
Guests and Domestics	David Richmond

UNDERSTUDIES: Dunyasha, Varya, Andrea
Stonorov; Yermolai, Tramp, Michael Tolaydo;
Semyen, Leonid, Station Master, David Richmond;
Feerce, Boris, K. C. Wilson; Lyoubof, Janet McIntire;
Anya, Rhonda Rose; Yasha, Pat Freni; Peter,
James Sutorius.

A Drama in 4 acts. The action takes place on
Madame Ranyevskaya's estate in Russia bout the
year 1900.

Company Manager: Michael Goldreyer
Press: Howard Atlee, David Roggensack,
Irene Gandy, Frank Bollinger
Stage Managers: Leon Leake, Bruce L. Blakemore,
John Page Blakemore, Ralph Valatka, Jr.

* Closed May 9, 1970 after 5 performances and
1 preview.

Left: Marshall Borden, Jenny Laird
Above: Bonnie Hurren, Jenny Laird,
Andrea Stonorov

Marshall Borden, Richard Curnock, Jenny Laird, Bonnie Hurren, Toby
Tompkins, Andrea Stonorov, William Needles

HELEN HAYES THEATRE

Opened Thursday, May 21, 1970.*
Edgar Lansbury and J. I. Rodale in association with Nan Pearlman present:

THE ENGAGEMENT BABY

By Stanley Shapiro; Director, Gene Frankel; Scenery, Robin Wagner; Costumes, Ann Roth; Lighting, Jules Fisher; Music, Charles Gross; Production Associate, Joseph Beruh; Sound, Gigi Cascio.

CAST

Roger Porter	Clifton Davis
Walter Whitney	Barry Nelson
Victor Bard	Tom Aldredge
Vivian Whitney	Constance Towers
Constanzia	Antonia Rey
Mary Ann	Holly Peters
Nelson Longhurst	Henderson Forsythe
Receptionist	Marie Puma
Dr. Brien	Angus Cairns
Rev. Henning	James Karen
Neusom	Norman Matlock
Miss Stone	Candy Azzara
Wino in alley	Gigi Cascio
Other man in alley	Lenard Norris
Job Dispenser	James Karen
Voice from Cave	Angus Cairns

UNDERSTUDIES: Walter, Victor, James Karen; Roger, Neusom, Lenard Norris; Nelson, Henning, Angus Cairns; Vivian, Miss Stone, Mary Ann, Constanzia, Marie Puma.

A Comedy in two acts. The action takes place at the present time in New York City.

General Manager: Joseph Beruh
Company Manager: Al J. Isaac
Press: Max Eisen, Warren Pincus
Stage Managers: William Dodds, Gigi Cascio

* Closed May 23, 1970 after 4 performances and 8 previews.

Constance Towers, Barry Nelson, also Top Right with Holly Peters, Clifton Davis

ANTA THEATRE

Opened Tuesday, May 26, 1970.*
The American National Theatre and Academy
(Alfred de Liagre, Jr., Executive Producer;
Jean Dalrymple, Executive Director) presents
the Trinity Square Repertory Company's
production of:

WILSON
IN THE PROMISE LAND

By Roland Van Zandt; Director, Adrina Hall;
Settings, Eugene Lee; Costumes, John Lehmeyer;
Original Music Composed by Richard Cumming;
Technical Director, Steve Crowley; Technical Co-
ordinator, Brigido Cavazos.

CAST

Woodrow Wilson	William Cain
Edith Bolling Wilson	Marguerite H. Lenert
Rev. Dr. Joseph Wilson	Donald Somers
Dr. Cary T. Grayson	William Kamkoehler
George Washington	Martin Molson
Thomas Jefferson	David C. Jones
Andrew Jackson	Dan Plucinski
Abraham Lincoln	James Gallery
Theodore Roosevelt	George Martin
Franklin D. Roosevelt	Ronald Frazier

The Hippies:

The Youth	Richard Kavanaugh
Hippie 1, (The Scribe)	Robert J. Colonna
Hippie 2, (Gen. Sherman)	David Kennett
Hippie 3, (Woman singer)	Barbara Meek
Hippie 4, (Young Wilson at 16)	James Eichelberger
Hippie 5, (Facts)	Ed Hall
Hippie 6, (Musician)	Robert Black
Hippie 7, (Man with gun)	Richard Steele
Hippie 8, (Wilson at 6)	Ann Sachs
Hippie 9, (Klu Kluxer)	William Damkoehler
Hippie 10, (Nurse)	Marguerite H. Lenert

A Drama in two acts. The action begins and ends
in the White House during the last two years of
Wilson's administration (1919-1920). The Hippies
provoke the action of the play.

General Manager: James E. Walsh
Press: Betty Lee Hunt, Henry Luhrman,
Harriett Trachtenberg
Stage Managers: Franklin Keysar,
Robert Applegarth

* Closed May 30, 1970, after 7 performances and
1 preview.

Images Photos

**Ann Sachs, James Eichelberger, William Gain Top:
David C. Jones, Ronald Frazier, James Callery, Cain, Martin
Molson, Dan Plucinski, George Martin**

ST. JAMES THEATRE

Opened Thursday, January 16, 1964.*
David Merrick presents:

HELLO, DOLLY!

Book, Michael Stewart; Based on "The Match-maker" by Thornton Wilder; Music and Lyrics, Jerry Herman; Director, Gower Champion; Re-Staged by Lucia Victor; Dance Assistant, Jack Craig; Settings, Oliver Smith; Costumes, Freddy Wittop; Lighting, Jean Rosenthal; Dance and Incidental Music Arrangements, Peter Howard; Orchestrations, Philip J. Lang; Musical Direction, Saul Schechtman; A David Merrick and Champion-Five Inc. Production; Staff Associates, Sylvia Schwartz, Lynn Middleton, Linda Patton; Original Cast Album by RCA Victor.

CAST

Mrs. Dolly Gallagher Levi	Pearl Bailey† 1
Ernestina	Mable King † 2
Ambrose Kemper	Roger Lawson
Horse	Dianne Conway, Leu Camacho
Horace Vandergelder	Cab Calloway
Ermengarde	Edloe
Cornelius Hackl	Jack Crowder
Barnaby Tucker	Winston DeWitt Hemsley
Irene Molloy	Emily Yancy † 3
Minnie Fay	Sherri "Peaches" Brewer
Mrs. Rose	Marki Bey
Rudolph	Jimmy Justice
Judge	Walter P. Brown
Court Clerk	James Kennon-Wilson

TOWNSPEOPLE: Marki Bey, Leu Camacho, Joetta Cherry, Dianne Conway, Merle Derby, Demarest Grey, Lavinia Hamilton, Patti Harris, Ernestine Jackson, Waltye Johnson, Laverne Ligon, Gail Nelson, Joni Palmer, Jozella Reed, Freda Vanterpool, Clifford Allen, Guy Allen, Bryant Baker, Walter P. Brown, Donald Coleman, Peter Colly, Eugene Edwards, Sargent Faulkner, Larry Ferrell, Julius Fields, Ray Gilbert, Pi Douglass, Reginald Jackson, Don Jay, Bob Johnson, James Kennon-Wilson, Kenneth Scott, E. B. Smith, Luke Stover, Melvin Taylor.

UNDERSTUDIES: Dolly, Thelma Carpenter; Vandergelder, Walter P. Brown; Irene, Ernestine Jackson; Cornelius, Eugene Edwards; Minnie Fay, Marki Bey, Leu Camacho; Barnaby, Larry Ferrell; Ermengarde, Merle Derby; Ernestina, Laverne Ligon; Ambrose, Donald Coleman; Judge, E. B. Smith; Rudolph, Guy Allen.

MUSICAL NUMBERS: "I Put My Hand In," "It Takes A Woman," "Put On Your Sunday Clothes," "Ribbons Down My Back," "Motherhood," "Dancing," "Before The Parade Passes By," "Elegance," "Waiters' Gallop," "Hello, Dolly!," "It Only Takes A Moment," "So Long Dearie," Finale.

A Musical Comedy in 2 acts and 15 scenes. The action takes place in the past in Yonkers and New York City.

General Manager: Jack Schlissel
Press: Lee Solters, Harvey B. Sabinson, Shirley Herz
Stage Managers: Jack Timmers, Bob Bernard, E. B. Smith

The Bailey-Calloway company (succeeded by Phyllis Diller Co.) closed to tour on Dec. 20, 1969. The tour was canceled May 17, 1970 because of Miss Bailey's illness. For original production starring Carol Channing, see THEATRE WORLD, Vol. 20.

† Succeeded by: 1. Thelma Carpenter at matinees. 2. Alyce Webb, 3. Ernestine Jackson.

Friedman-Abeles Photos

Top Right: Winston DeWitt Hemsley, Jack Crowder, Cab Calloway

Cab Calloway, Pearl Bailey (also above)

ST. JAMES THEATRE

Opened Friday, December 26, 1969.*
David Merrick presents:

HELLO, DOLLY!

Book, Michael Stewart; Based on play "The Matchmaker" by Thornton Wilder; Music and Lyrics, Jerry Herman; Re-staged by Lucia Victor after original direction and choreography by Gower Champion; Dance Assistant, Jack Craig; Settings, Oliver Smith; Costumes, Freddy Wittop; Lighting, Jean Rosenthal; Dance and Incidental Music Arrangements, Peter Howard; Musical Direction, Saul Schechtman; Orchestrations, Philip J. Lang; A David Merrick and Champion-Five Production; Staff Associates, Sylvia Schwartz, Elizabeth Kaye, John Bonanni; Coiffures, Hector Garcia; Original Cast Album by RCA Victor.

CAST

Mrs. Dolly Gallagher Levi	Phyllis Diller† 1
Ernestina	Marcia Lewis
Ambrose Kemper	Ronald Young† 2
Horse	Patty Pappathatos, Ellen Elias
Horace Vandergelder	Richard Deacon† 3
Ermengarde	Andrea Bell† 4
Cornelius Hackl	Bill Mullikin† 5
Barnaby Tucker	Danny Lockin
Irene Molloy	June Helmers
Minnie Fay	Georgia Engel
Mrs. Rose	Joyce Dahl
Rudolph	James Beard
Judge	George Blackwell
Court Clerk	Dick Crowley

TOWNSPEOPLE, WAITERS, ETC.: Beverly Baker, Maggie Benson, Monica Carter, Joyce Dahl, Ellen Elias, Gwen Hillier, Lee Hooper, Irma Kingsley, Janice Painchaud, Patty Pappathatos, Jacqueline Payne, Pat Trott, Elise Warner, Paul Berne, George Blackwell, Ted Bloecher, Wayne Boyd, Jack Craig, Ron Crofoot, Dick Crowley, Richard Dodd, Mark East, David Evans, Ed Goldsmid, Jerry Gotham, Joseph Helms, Jim Hovis, Robert L. Hultman, J. David Kirby, Sean Nolan, Alex Orfaly.

UNDERSTUDIES: Dolly, Bibi Osterwald, Vandergelder, George Blackwell; Cornelius, Sean Nolan; Irene, Joyce Dahl; Barnaby, Ed Goldsmid; Minnie, Patricia Cope; Ermengarde, Patty Pappathatos; Ambrose, Ted Bloecher; Ernestina, Elise Warner; Rudolph, Judge, Robert L. Hultman.

MUSICAL NUMBERS: "I Put My Hand In," "It Takes a Woman," "Put on Your Sunday Clothes," "Ribbons Down My Back," "Motherhood," "Dancing," "Before the Parade Passes By," "Elegance," "Waiters' Gallop," "Hello, Dolly!," "It Only Takes a Moment," "So Long, Dearie," Finale.

Two songs were added for Miss Merman: "World, Take Me Back," "Love, Look in My Window."

A Musical Comedy in 2 acts and 15 scenes. The action takes place in the past in Yonkers and New York City.

General Manager: Jack Schlissel
Press: Lee Solters, Harvey B. Sabinson, Leo Stern, Edie Kean
Stage Managers: Jack Timmers, Bob Bernard, Robert L. Hultman

* Still playing May 31, 1970; for original production starring Carol Channing, see THEATRE WORLD, Vol. 20.
† Succeeded by: 1. Ethel Merman (Mar. 28, 1970), 2. David Gary, 3. Jack Goode, 4. Patricia Cope, 5. Russell Nype

Friedman-Abeles Photos

Top Right: Bill Mullikin, Phyllis Diller, June Helmers Below: Ethel Merman, Russell Nype, Danny Lockin, Georgia Engel, June Helmers

Ethel Merman, and above with Jack Goode

ANTA WASHINGTON SQUARE
THEATRE

Opened Monday, November 22, 1965.*
(Moved to Martin Beck, March 19, 1968)
Albert W. Selden and Hal James present:

MAN OF LA MANCHA

Book, Dale Wasserman; Music, Mitch Leigh;
Lyrics, Joe Darion; Book and Musical Staging,
Albert Marre; Choreography, Jack Cole; Settings
and Lighting, Howard Bay; Costumes, Howard
Bay, Patton Campbell; Musical Direction, R. Ben-
nett Benetsky; Dance Arrangements, Neil War-
ner; Musical Arrangements, Music Makers; Hair-
stylist, Charles LoPresto; Technical Adviser,
John Higgins; Production Assistant, Dwight
Frye; Original Cast Album by Kapp Records.

CAST

Don Quixote (Cervantes)	Bob Wright †1
(matinees, David Holliday †2)	
Sancho	Joey Faye †3
Aldonza	Gaylea Byrne
(matinees, Barbara Williams †4)	
Innkeeper	Ray Middleton
Padre	Robert Rounseville
Dr. Carrasco	David Holliday †5
(matinees, Renato Cibelli)	
Antonia	Dianne Barton
The Barber	Leo Bloom
Pedro, Head Muleteer	Shev Rodgers †6
Anselmo	Wilson Robey
Housekeeper	Eleanore Knapp
Jose	Will Carter †7
Juan	John Aristides
Paco	Bill Stanton
Tenorio	Carlos Macri †8
Maria	Rita Metzger
Dancing Horses	Bill Stanton, Will Carter †7
Horses	Leo Bloom, Carmine Caridi
Fermina	Marcia Gilford †9
Captain of the Inquisition	Renato Cibelli
(matinees, Ray Dash)	
Guitarist	Stephen Sahlein
Guards	Ray Dash, Jonathan Fox †10, Toby Tompkins †11, John Fields †12

UNDERSTUDIES: Don Quixote, Jack Dabdoub,
Renato Cibelli; Sancho, Eddie Roll, Wilson Robey;
Aldonza, Emily Yancey, Violet Santangelo; Inn-
keeper, Jack Dabdoub, Renato Cibelli, Paul Mi-
chael; Padre, Ralph Farnworth, Wilson Robey;
Carrasco, Renato Cibelli, Alfred Leberfeld; Bar-
ber, Eddie Roll, Alfred Leberfeld; Antonia, Fer-
mina, Patricia Lens; Pedro, David Wilder, Renato
Cibelli; Maria, Violet Santangelo; Housekeeper,
Rita Metzger; Captain, Ray Dash; Swing Dancer,
John Gorrin.

MUSICAL NUMBERS: "Man of LaMancha,"
"It's All the Same," "Dulcinea," "I'm Only Thinking of Him," "I Really Like Him," "What Does
He Want of Me," "Little Bird," "Barber's Song,"
"Golden Helmet of Mambrino," "To Each His Dulcinea," "The Quest," "The Combat," "The Dubb-
ing," "The Abduction," "Moorish Dance," "Aldonza," "Knight of the Mirrors," "A Little Gos-
sip," "The Psalm."

A Musical Play suggested by the life and works
of Miguel de Cervantes y Saavedra, and performed
without intermission. All the characters are im-
prisoned in a dungeon in Seville at the end of
the 16th century. The entire action takes place
there, and in various other places in the imagina-
tion of Cervantes.

General Manager: Walter Fried
Company Manager: Gino Giglio
Press: Merle Debuskey, Faith Geer
Stage Managers: Marnel Sumner, Michael Turque,
Alfred Leberfeld, Renato Cibelli

* Still playing May 31, 1970. For original production with Richard Kiley, see THEATRE
WORLD Vol. 22.

† Succeeded by: 1. David Atkinson, Claudio Brook,
Keith Michell, Somegoro Ichikawa, Charles
West, 2. Jack Dabdoub, 3. Tony Martinez, Titos
Vandis, 4. Marilyn Child, Emily Yancey, 5. Tim-
othy Jerome, 6. Carmine Caridi, 7. Bert Michaels,
8. Don Bonnell, Robert Rayow, 9. Marcia O'-
Brien, Violet Santangelo, 10. James Leverett,
11. Robert Einenkel, David Wilder, 12. Angelo

Friedman-Abeles & Zodiac Photos

Gaylea Byrne, Somegoro Ichikawa
Above: Ichikawa, Leo Bloom

Top Left: Keith Michell, Timothy Jerome

PLYMOUTH THEATRE

Opened Wednesday, February 14, 1968.*
Saint-Subber presents:

PLAZA SUITE

By Neil Simon; Director, Mike Nichols; Scenic
Production, Oliver Smith; Costumes, Patricia
Zipprodt; Lighting, Jean Rosenthal; Hairstylist,
Ernest Adler; Produced by Nancy Enterprises.

CAST

"Visitor from Mamaroneck"
Bellhop..............................Robert Gerlach
Karen Nash ....Maureen Stapleton † 1
Sam Nash ....Dan Dailey † 2
Waiter ....Jose Ocasio
Jean McCormick ....Lynda Myles
"Visitor from Hollywood"
Waiter ....Jose Ocasio
Jesse Kiplinger.....................Dan Dailey † 2
Muriel Tate ....Maureen Stapleton † 1
"Visitor from Forest Hills"
Norma Hubley ....Maureen Stapleton † 1
Roy Hubley ....Dan Dailey † 2
Borden Eisler ....Robert Gerlach
Mimsey Hubley......................Lynda Myles

UNDERSTUDIES: Shirley Cox, Larry Weber,
Judith Barcroft, Gary Barton

These three one-act plays take place at the present time in a suite of the Plaza Hotel in New
York City.

General Manager: C. Edwin Knill
Company Manager: James Turner
Press: Harvey B. Sabinson, Lee Solters,
Harry Nigro, Cheryl Sue Dolby
Stage Managers: Wisner Washam, Gary Barton

* Still playing May 31, 1970. For original pro-
  duction see THEATRE WORLD, Vol. 24.
† Succeeded by: 1. Elizabeth Wilson (for 1 week),
  Peggy Cass (who was succeeded for 2 weeks by
  Maureen Stapleton), 2. Don Porter.

Martha Swope Photos

Don Porter, Peggy Cass
Top Right: Maureen Stapleton

Jonathan Kramer, Robin McNamara,
Larry Marshall, John Aman, Oatis Stephens

BILTMORE THEATRE

Opened Monday, April 19, 1968.*
Michael Butler presents:

HAIR

Book and Lyrics, Gerome Ragni, James Rado; Music, Galt MacDermot; Executive Producer, Bertrand Castelli; Director, Tom O'Horgan; Assistant Director, Dan Sullivan; Dance Director, Julie Arenal; Musical Director, Galt MacDermot; Costumes, Nancy Potts; Scenery, Robin Wagner; Lighting, Jules Fisher; Hairstylist, Wig City; Original Cast Album by RCA Victor Records.

CAST

Claude	Erik Robinson † 1
Berger	Oatis Stephens
Woof	Bert Sommer † 2
Hud	Donny Burks † 3
Sheila	Heather MacRae † 4
Jeanie	Sally Eaton
Dionne	Melba Moore † 5
Crissy	Shelley Plimpton † 6
Mother	Sally Eaton, Jonathan Kramer, Obie Bray
Father	Rick Granat, Debbie Offner, Larry Marshall
Principal	Rick Granat, Debbie Offner, Larry Marshall
Tourist Couple	Jonathan Kramer, Clifford Lipson † 7
Waitress	Natalie Mosco † 8
Young Recruit	Charles O. Lynch † 9
General Grant	Charles O. Lynch † 1 0
Abraham Lincoln	Lorrie Davis
Sergeant	Donny Burks † 1 1
Parents	Linda Compton † 8, Clifford Lipson † 1 0

THE TRIBE: John Aman, Obie Bray, Hazel Bryant, Jim Carrozo, Lorrie Davis, Denise Delapenha, Robin Eaton, Leata Galloway, Steve Gamet, Rick Granat, Jessica Harper, Joan Johnson, Fluffer Hirsch, Jonathan Kramer, Emmaretta Marks, Holly Near, Debbie Offner, Angie Ortega, George Tipton, Singer Williams, Lillian Wong.

UNDERSTUDIES: Berger, Jim Carrozo, John Aman; Sheila, Denise Delapenha; Claude, Robin Eaton; Woof, Fluffer Hirsch; Jeanie, Lorrie Davis; Crissy, Debbie Offner; Dionne, Denise Delapenha; Alternate Hud, Obie Bray.

MUSICAL NUMBERS: "Aquarius," "Donna," "Hashish," "Sodomy," "Colored Spade," "Manchester," "Ain't Got No," "Dead End," "I Believe in Love," "Air," "Initials," "I Got Life," "Going Down," "Hair," "My Conviction," "Easy to Be Hard," "Don't Put It Down," "Frank Mills," "Be-In," "Where Do I Go," "Electric Blues," "Black Boys," "White Boys," "Walking in Space," "Abie Baby," "Three-Five-Zero-Zero," "What a Piece of Work Is Man," "Good Morning Starshine," "The Bed," "The Flesh Failures," "Let the Sun Shine In."

The American Tribal-Love Rock Musical in 2 acts.

Company Manager: William Orton
Press: Gifford/Wallace, Tom Trenkle, Michael Gifford, Dyanne Hochman
Stage Managers: Robert D. Currie, Ronald Schaeffer, Robert Goldberg

* Still playing May 31, 1970. For original production see THEATRE WORLD, Vol. 24.
† Succeeded by: 1. Allan Nicholls, 2. Robin McNamara, 3. Larry Marshall, 4. Melba Moore, Victoria Medlin, 5. Joan Johnson, 6. Lillian Wong, 7. John Aman, 8. Debbie Offner, 9. Jonathan Kramer, 10. Rick Granat, 11. Obie Bray

Martha Swope Photos

Top Left: "Aquarius"
Left Center: (front) Fluffer Hirsch, Oatis Stephens, Robin McNamara, (rear) Lorrie Davis, Robin Eaton, Sally Eaton, Allan Nicholls, Larry Marshall, Rick Granat, Debbie Offner

SAM S. SHUBERT THEATRE

Opened Sunday, December 1, 1968.*
David Merrick presents:

PROMISES, PROMISES

Book, Neil Simon; Based on Screenplay "The Apartment" by Bill Wilder and I.A.L. Diamond; Music, Burt Bacharach; Lyrics, Hal David; Director, Robert Moore; Musical Numbers Staged by Michael Bennett; Settings, Robin Wagner; Costumes, Donald Brooks; Lighting, Martin Aronstein; Musical Direction and Dance Arrangements, Harold Wheeler; Orchestrations, Jonathan Tunick; Associate Producer, Samuel Liff; Assistant Choreographer, Bob Avian; Hairstylist, Joe Tubens; Musical Director, Arthur Azenzer; Staff Associates, Sylvia Schwartz, John Bonanni, Linda Bate, Elizabeth Kaye; Original Cast Album on United Artists Records.

CAST

Chuck Baxter	Jerry Orbach
J. D. Sheldrake	Edward Winter
Fran Kubelik	Jill O'Hara
Bartender Eddie	Dick Sabol
Mr. Dobitch	Paul Reed
Sylvia Gilholley	Adrienne Angel
Mr. Kirkeby	Norman Shelly †1
Mr. Eichelberger	Vince O'Brien †2
Vivien Della Hoya	Donna McKechnie †3
Dr. Dreyfuss	A. Larry Haines †4
Jesse Vanderhof	Dick O'Neill
Dentist's Nurse	Rita O'Connor †5
Company Nurse	Carole Bishop
Company Doctor	Gerry O'Hara †6
Peggy Olson	Millie Slavin
Lum Ding Hostess	Baayork Lee †7
Waiter	Scott Pearson †8
Madison Square Garden Attendant	Michael Vita †9
Dining Room Hostess	Betsy Haug
Miss Polansky	Margo Sappington †10
Miss Wong	Baayork Lee †7
Bartender Eugene	Michael Vita †9
Marge MacDougall	Marian Mercer †11

Clancy's Lounge Patrons..........Carole Bishop,
Rita O'Connor, Julane Stites, Rod Barry,
Gene Cooper, Bob Fitch, Neil Jones,
Scott Pearson, Michael Shawn, Carolyn Kirsch,
Melissa Stoneburn, Pam Blair, Sandra West,
Dick Korthaze, Fred Benjamin, Joe Nelson,
Ralph Nelson

Clancy's Employees.............Graciela Daniele †12,
Betty Haug, Margo Sappington †13

Helen Sheldrake	Kay Oslin
Karl Kubelik	Dick Sabol
New Young Executive	Rod Barry †14

Interns and Dates.................Barbara Alston,
Graciela Daniele †12, Gerry O'Hara †15,
Michael Shawn †6

Orchestra Voices..............Kelly Britt †16,
Margot Hanson †17, Bettye McCormick,
Ilona Simon

UNDERSTUDIES: Fran, Patti Davis; Dobitch, Dick O'Neill; Vanderhof, Henry Sutton; Eichelberger, Ronn Carroll; Kirkeby, Dick Korthaze; Marge, Peggy, Kay Oslin; Vivien, Betsy Haug; Karl, Frank Pietri; Sylvia, Carol Hanzel; Swing Dancers, Debra Lyman, Don Lopez

MUSICAL NUMBERS: "Half as Big as Life," "Upstairs," "You'll Think of Someone," "Our Little Secret," "She Likes Basketball," "Knowing When to Leave," "Where Can You Take a Girl?," "Wanting Things," "Turkey Lurkey Time," "A Fact Can Be a Beautiful Thing," "Whoever You Are," "A Pretty Young Girl Like You," "I'll Never Fall in Love Again," "Promises, Promises."

A Musical in 2 acts and 14 scenes. The action takes place at the present time in New York.

General Manager: Jack Schlissel
Company Manager: Vince McKnight
Press: Harvey B. Sabinson, Lee Solters, Marilynn LeVine, Edie Kean
Stage Managers: Charles Blackwell, Robert St. Clair, May Muth

* Still playing May 31, 1970. For original production, see THEATRE WORLD, Vol. 25.
† Succeeded by: 1. Ronn Carroll, 2. Henry Sutton, 3. Baayork Lee, 4. Norman Shelly, 5. Carolyn Kirsch, Sandra West, 6. Joe Nelson, 7. Barbara Monte-Britton, 8. Gene Cooper, 9. Frank Pietri, 10. Julane Stites, Barbara Alston, 11. Pam Zarit, 12. Carol Hanzel, 13. Eileen Casey, 14. Frank Newell, 15. Ronn Forella, 16. Patti Davis, 17. Marylou Sirinek

Ed Winter, Jill O'Hara Above:
Jerry Orbach (C) Top: Orbach, O'Hara

Friedman-Abeles & Zodiac Photos

Opened Tuesday, September 22, 1964.*
(Moved Feb. 27, 1967 to Majestic)
Harold Prince presents:

FIDDLER ON THE ROOF

Book, Joseph Stein; Based on Sholom Aleichem's stories; Music, Jerry Bock; Lyrics, Sheldon Harnick; Director-Choreographer, Jerome Robbins; Settings, Boris Aronson; Costumes, Patricia Zipprodt; Lighting, Jean Rosenthal; Orchestrations, Don Walker; Musical Direction, Vocal Arrangements, Milton Greene; Dance Music Arrangements, Betty Walber; Hairstylist, D. Rusty Bonaccorso; Original Cast Album by RCA Victor Records.

CAST

Tevye, the dairyman	Jerry Jarrett † 1
Golde, his wife	Rae Allen † 2
His daughters:	
Tzeitel	Bette Midler † 3
Hodel	Adrienne Barbeau
Chava	Tanya Everett † 4
Shprintze	Peggy Longo † 5
Bielke	Leslie Silvia
Yente, the matchmaker	Florence Stanley
Motel, the tailor	David Garfield † 6
Perchik, the student	Richard Morse
Mordcha, the innkeeper	Zvee Scooler
Lazar Wolf, the butcher	Boris Aplon
Rabbi	Gluck Sandor † 7
Mendel, his son	Larry Ross † 1 9
Avram, the bookseller	Reuben Schafer † 8
Nachum, the beggar	David Masters † 9
Grandma Tzeitel	Jan Myers † 10
Fruma-Sarah	Marta Heflin † 1 1
Constable	Joseph Sullivan
Fyedka	Don Atkinson † 12
Shandel, Motel's mother	Laura Stuart † 13
The Fiddler	Ken LeRoy

VILLAGERS: Bagel Man, Dan Tylor; Streetsweeper, Marc Scott; Fishmonger, Lorenzo Bianco; Seltzer Man, Ben Gillespie; Surcha, Sarah Felcher † 1 4 ; Woodsman, Tony Gardell; Potseller, Victor Pieran; Grocer, Ross Gifford; Baker, Dan Jasinsky; Knifeseller, Allan Gruet; Fredel, Harriet Slaughter † 1 5 ; Bluma, Jan Myers † 1 0 ; Berille, Christine Jacobs; Mirala, Charlet Oberley; Sima, Carolyn Mignini † 1 6 ; Rivka, Ann Tell; The Cobbler, Del Franklin; Anya, Phyllis Wallach; Hatmaker, Allan Byrns; Vladimir, Frank Coppola † 1 7 ; Sasha, Samuel Ratcliffe † 1 8

UNDERSTUDIES: Tevye, Jerry Jarrett; Golde, Yente, Elaine Kussack; Tzeitel, Gretchen Evans; Hodel, Christine Jacobs; Chava, Jill Harmon; Sprintze, Bielke, Phyllis Wallach; Perchik, Allan Gruet; Motel, Larry Ross; Fyedka, Don Lawrence; Rabbi, Reuben Schafer; Nachum, Dan Tylor; Constable, Ross Gifford; Mendel, Dan Jasinsky; Lazar, Jerry Jarrett; Avram, Reuben Schafer; Grandma, Phyllis Wallach; Fruma-Sarah, Gretchen Evans; Shandel, Charlet Oberley; Fiddler, Marc Scott; Mordcha, Tony Gardell.

MUSICAL NUMBERS: "Tradition," "Matchmaker," "If I Were a Rich Man," "Sabbath Prayer," "To Life," "Miracles," "The Tailor," "Sunrise, Sunset," "Bottle Dance," "Wedding Dance," "Now I Have Everything," "Do You Love Me?," "I Just Heard," "Far From the Home I Love," "Anatevka," Epilogue.

A Musical in 2 acts. The action takes place in Anatevka, a village in Russia, in 1905 on the eve of the revolutionary period.

General Manager: Carl Fisher
Press: Sol Jacobson, Lewis Harmon
Stage Managers: Ruth Mitchell, Ed Aldridge,
Jay Jacobson, David Wolf

* Still playing May 31, 1970. For original cast with Zero Mostel see THEATRE WORLD, Vol. 21.
†Succeeded by: 1. Paul Lipson, 2. Peg Murray, 3. Rosalind Harris, Judith Smiley, 4. Peggy Longo, 5. Faye Menken, 6. Peter Marklin, 7. Sol Frieder, 8. Jerry Jarrett, 9. Reuben Schafer, 10. Anna Perez, 11. Harriet Slaughter, 12. John-Michael Savaige, 13. Elaine Kussack, 14. Maralyn Nell, 15. Gretchen Evans, 16. Jill Harmon, 17. Ronn Steiman, 18. Don Lawrence, 19. James McDonald.

Zodiac Photos

Top Right: Leslie Silva, Faye Menken, Peg Murray, Paul Lipson, Ken LeRoy

Paul Lipson, Peg Murray Above: Adrienne Barbeau, Judith Smiley, Peggy Longo

FORTY-SIXTH STREET THEATRE

Opened Sunday, March 16, 1969.*
Stuart Ostrow presents:

1776

Book, Peter Stone; Based on conception by Sherman Edwards; Music and Lyrics, Sherman Edwards; Scenery and Lighting, Jo Mielziner; Costumes, Patricia Zipprodt; Musical Direction, Peter Howard; Orchestrations, Eddie Sauter; Director, Peter Hunt; Musical Numbers Staged by Onna White; Associate to Miss White, Martin Allen; Dance Music Arrangements, Peter Howard; Vocal Arrangements, Elise Bretton; Hairstylist, Ernest Adler; Assistant to Producer, Judy Korman; Assistant to Director, Margi Suisman; Assistant Designer, F. Mitchell Dana; Original Cast Album by Columbia Records.

CAST

John Hancock, President of the Continental Congress	David Ford †1
Dr. Josiah Bartlett, New Hampshire	Paul-David Richards
John Adams, Massachusetts	William Daniels
Stephen Hopkins, Rhode Island	Roy Poole
Roger Sherman, Connecticut	David Vosburgh
Lewis Morris, New York	Ronald Kross
Robert Livingston, New York	Henry LeClair
Rev. Jonathan Witherspoon, New Jersey	Edmund Lyndeck †2
Benjamin Franklin, Pa.	Howard DaSilva
John Dickinson, Pa.	Paul Hecht
James Wilson, Pa	Emory Bass
Caesar Rodney, Delaware	Robert Gaus
Col. Thomas McKean, Dela.	Bruce MacKay
George Read, Dela.	Duane Bodin
Samuel Chase, Maryland	Philip Polito
Richard Henry Lee, Va.	Ronald Holgate
Thomas Jefferson, Va.	David Cryer †3
Joseph Hewes, N.C.	Charles Rule †4
Edward Rutledge, S.C.	John Fink †5
Dr. Lyman Hall, Georgia	Jonathan Moore †6
Charles Thomson, Secretary	Ralston Hill
Andrew McNair, Custodian	William Duell
A Leather Apron	B. J. Slater
Courier	Scott Jarvis
Abigail Adams	Virginia Vestoff †7
Martha Jefferson	Betty Buckley †8

UNDERSTUDIES: Adams, John Cullum; Franklin, Dickinson, Bruce MacKay; Rutledge, Paul-David Richards; McKean, Hancock, William Stenson; Jefferson, Hopkins, Thomas, Hall, Edmund Lyndeck; Courier, B. J. Slater; Abigail, Martha, Jamie Thomas; Lee, Hal Norman; Rodney, David Vosburgh; Wilson, Ronald Kross; McNair, Duane Bodin; General Understudies, Hal Norman, Arthur Anderson; Franklin, Rex Everhart.

MUSICAL NUMBERS: "Sit Down, John," "Piddle, Twiddle and Resolve," "Till Then," "The Lees of Virginia," "But, Mr. Adams," "Yours, Yours, Yours," "He Plays the Violin," "Cool, Cool, Considerate Man," "Momma Look Sharp," "The Egg," "Molasses to Rum," "Is Anybody There?"

A Musical Play in 7 scenes presented without intermission. The action takes place in May, June, and July of 1776 in a single setting representing the Chamber and Anteroom of the Continental Congress, in Philadelphia, and certain reaches of John Adams' mind.

General Managers: Joseph Harris, Ira Bernstein
Press: Harvey B. Sabinson, Lee Solters, Cheryl Sue Dolby, Sandra Manley
Stage Managers: Peter Stern, Lee Murray, Herman Magidson
* Still playing May 31, 1969. Winner of "Tony" and NY Drama Critics Circle Awards for 1969.
† Succeeded by: 1. Charles Cioffi, 2. Arthur Anderson, 3. Peter Lombard, 4. William Stenson, 5. Jon Cypher, John Cullum, 6. Edmund Lyndeck, 7. Ellen Hanley for 2 months, 8. Mary Bracken Phillips.

Top Right: Henry LeClair, Howard DaSilva, David Vosburgh

Peter Lombard, Mary Bracken Phillips, Howard DaSilva, William Daniels Above: Daniels, Virginia Vestoff

Peter Galman, June Allyson

MOROSCO THEATRE

Opened Thursday, December 26, 1968.*
David Merrick presents:

FORTY CARATS

By Jay Allen; Adapted from play by Barillet and Gredy; Director, Abe Burrows; Scenery, Will Steven Armstrong; Costumes, William McHone; Lighting, Martin Aronstein; Associate Producer, Samuel Liff; Hairstylist, Ernest Adler; Produced in association with Beresfor Productions, Ltd.; Staff Associates, Sylvia Schwartz, Ellen Reiss, John Bonanni.

CAST

Ann Stanley	Julie Harris[†1]
Peter Latham	Marco St. John[†2]
Mrs. Adams	Iva Withers
Mrs. Margolin	Polly Rowles[†3]
Billy Boylan	Murray Hamilton[†4]
Eddy Edwards	Franklin Cover
Maud Hayes	Glenda Farrell[†5]
Trina Stanley	Gretchen Corbett[†6]
Mrs. Latham	Nancy Marchand
Mr. Latham	John Cecil Holm
Pat	Michael Nouri

UNDERSTUDIES: Ann, Iva Withers; Maud, Eleanor Phelps; Billy, Alan Manson; Peter, Michael Nouri; Trina, Susan King

A Comedy in 2 acts. The action takes place at the present time in the apartment and office of Ann Stanley in New York, after a prologue somewhere in the Greek islands.

General Manager: Jack Schlissel
Company Manager: Richard Highley
Press: Harvey B. Sabinson, Lee Solters, Harry Nigro, Sandra Manley, Edie Kean
Stage Managers: James Burrows, Jeff Chambers, Michael Nouri, Susan King

* Still playing May 31, 1970. For original production, see THEATRE WORLD, Vol. 25.

† Succeeded by: 1. June Allyson, Zsa Zsa Gabor, 2. Michael Nouri, Peter Galman, 3. Sudie Bond 4. Tom Poston, 5. Violet Dunn, Eleanor Phelps, Lilia Skala, 6. Judy Rolin

Martha Swope Photos

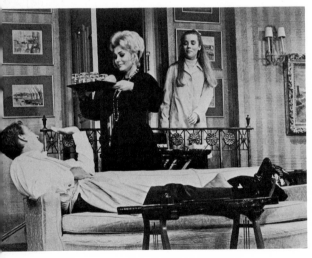

Tom Poston, Zsa Zsa Gabor, Judi Rolin

Tom Poston, June Allyson, Iva Withers

BROADWAY PRODUCTIONS FROM OTHER SEASONS THAT CLOSED DURING THIS SEASON

Title	Opened	Closed	Performances
Mame	May 24, 1966	Jan. 3, 1970	1508
Cabaret	Nov. 20, 1966	Sept. 6, 1969	1166
The Great White Hope	Oct. 3, 1968	Jan. 31, 1970	546
Play It Again, Sam	Feb. 12, 1969	Mar. 14, 1970	453
Hadrian VII	Jan. 8, 1969	Nov. 15, 1969	359
Zorba	Nov. 17, 1968	Aug. 9, 1969	305

NEW YORK CITY CENTER SEASON

CITY CENTER OF MUSIC & DRAMA

Opened Wednesday, September 10, 1969.*
Pacific World Artists Inc. in association with
City Center of Music and Drama, Inc. presents:

THE GRAND KABUKI
in

"Chushingura" (The Treasury of Loyal Retainers)
Lord Hangan ....Baiko
Moronao, Governor of Kamakura ....Shoroku
Tadayoshi, Brother of Shogun ....Kuroemon
Lord Wakasanosuke ....Tatsunosuke
Lady Kaoyo, Hangan's wife ....Kikunosuke
Ishido, Shogun's envoy ....Kuroemon
Yakushiji, Shogun's envoy ....Roen
Goemon ....Kikuzo
Rikiya, Yuranosuke's son ....Minosuke
Yuranosuke, Hangan's chief retainer ....Shoroku
Narrators.................................Takemoto O-Gidayu,
　　　　　　　　　　　　　　Tokatake Wasadayu

with

"Kagami-Jishi" (The Mirror Lion Dance)
Shogun's Retainer ....Karoku
Steward ....Rokuya
Elderly Lady-in-waiting ....Kikuzo
Yayoi, later the lion spirit ....Baiko
Butterfly Dancers ....Kikunosuke, Kirujuro
Stage Attendants....................Umesuke, Umeji

This program was performed through Sept. 16,
1969.*

Opened Wednesday, September 17, 1969.*
"Kumagai Jinya" (General Kumagai's Battle Camp)
Farmers, later Soldiers ....Yaenosuke,
　　　　　　　　　　　　　Umesuke, Umejuro
Lady Fuji-No-Kata ....Kikuzo
Gunji, aide-de-camp to Kumagai ....Ginnosuke
Sagami, wife of Kumagai ....Kikunosuke
General Kumagai ....Shoroku
Kumagai's Stage Attendant ....Senroku
Lord Yoshitsune,
　　Kumagai's Commander ....Tatsunosuke
Offstage Voice ....Matsuji
Kajiwara, a spy against Kumagai.................Karoku
Midaroku, in reality Yahei ....Kuroemon
Retainers of Yoshitsune ....Kikujuro,
　　　　　　　Rokuya, Umejuro, Matsutaro
Narrators ....Takemoto O-Gidayu,
　　　　　　　　　　　　Toyotake Wasadayu
Samisen Players ....Toyozawa Enjaku,
　　　　　　　　　　　　Toyozawa Isaburo

with

"Momiji-Gari" (The Maple-Leaf Viewing Picnic)
Taira Koremochi, young warrior............Kuroemon
Ugenta, his attendant...................................Roen
Sagenta, another attendant ....Tatsunosuke
Ladies' Maids ....Kikunosuke, Kikujuro,
　　　　　　　　　　　Takinojo, Senroku,
　　　　　　　　　　　Umeo, Otome
Lady-in-Waiting ....Kikuzo
Princess Sarashina, and The Demon of
　　Mount Togakushi ....Baiko
God of the Mountain ....Minosuke

Company Manager: Alfred Fischer
Press: Bill Doll & Co.
Stage Manager: Ronald Bates

* Closed Sept. 21, 1969 after a limited engagement
of 18 performances and began national tour.

Top Right: Baiko in "Kagami-Jishi"

**"Momiji-Gari" Above:
Baiko in "Kagami-Jishi"**

71

Opened Tuesday, February 3, 1970.*
S. Hurok by arrangement with the French
Government presents a Moliere Festival by:

COMEDIE FRANCAISE

Maurice Escande, Administrateur General;
Roger Hoff, Directeur General; Olivier Bernard,
Musical Director; Norbert Scmucki, Choreograph-
er; Simultaneous English Translation by Helen
Gillespie Atlas and Edward Greer.

LA TROUPE DU ROI

A Homage to Moliere produced by Paul-Emile
Deiber; Text, Moliere, La Grange and Boileau;
Musical Accompaniment taken from Jean-Baptiste
Lully and Marc Antoine Charpentier; Scenes from
"Les Precieuses Ridicules," "Monsieur de Pour-
ceaugnac," "L'Ecole des Femmes," "Le Bourgeois
Gentilhomme," "Tartuffe," "Les Fourberies de
Scapin," and "L'Avare."

CAST

Le Grange	Georges Descrieres
Moliere	Jean Piat
Brecourt	Simon Eine
Du Croisy	Marcel Tristani
Mlle. du Parc	Genevieve Casile
Mlle. Bejart	Berengere Dautun
Mlle. de Brie	Catherine Hiegel
Mlle. du Croisy	Denise Gence
Mlle. Herve	Francoise Seigner
Mascarille	Jean-Paul Roussillon
Cathos	Catherine Samie
Magdelon	Denise Gence
Arnolphe	Jacques Eyser
Agnes	Catherine Hiegel
Lysidas	Simon Eine
Boleau	Jacques Toja
Tartuffe	Robert Hirsch
Dorine	Francoise Seigner
Elmire	Claude Winter
Harpagon	Georges Chamarat
Eraste	Jean Piat
M. de Pourceaugnac	Jacques Charon
Dancing Teacher	Jacques Buron
M. Jourdain	Jacques Charon
Scapin	Jean-Paul Roussillon
Geronte	Jean-Louis Jemma
Toinette	Catherine Samie
Argan	Jean Piat
Beralde	Marcel Tristani

Intermission

Jean Piat, Robert Hirsch in "Amphitryon"

AMPHITRYON

By Moliere; Director, Jean Meyer; Decor and
Costumes, Suzanne Lalique.

CAST

Sosie	Robert Hirsch
Mercure	Jean Piat
Argatiphontidas	Jacques Eyser
Amphitryon	Georges Descrieres
Jupiter	Jacques Toja
Naucrates	Simon Eine
Posicles	Marcel Tristani
Polidas	Jacques Buron
Cleanthis	Denise Gence
Alcmene	Genevieve Casile
Goddess of the Night	Berengere Dautun

Presented for 6 performances.

Opened Friday, February 6, 1970.

DOM JUAN

By Moliere; Director, Antoine Bourseiller; Decor
and Costumes, Oskar Gustin.

cast

Sganarelle	Jacques Charon
M. Dimanche	Georges Chamarat
Dom Louis	Jacques Eyser
Dom Juan	Georges Descrieres
Pierrot	Jean-Paul Roussillon
Ragotin, La Ramee	Jacques Toja
Dom Gusman	Jean-Louis Jemma
Dom Alonse	Simon Eine
Statue of the Commandant	Marcel Tristani
Dom Carlos	Jacques Buron
Charlotte	Catherine Samie
Elvire	Genevieve Casile
Servant, The Ghost	Berengere Dautun
Mathurine	Catherine Hiegel

Presented for 5 performances.

Opened Friday, February 13, 1970.

LES FEMMES SAVANTES

By Moliere; Director, Jean Meyer; Decor and
Costumes, Suzanne Lalique.

CAST

Chrysale	Jacques Charon
Vadius	Georges Chamarat
Ariste	Jacques Eyser
Trissotin	Georges Descrieres
Clitandre	Jacques Toja
Notary	Jean-Louis Jemma
Lepine	Jacques Buron
Julien	Marcel Tristani
Belise	Denise Gence
Martine	Catherine Samie
Armande	Genevieve Casile
Philaminte	Francoise Seigner
Henriette	Catherine Hiegel

Presented for 5 performances.

Opened Tuesday, February 17, 1970.

LE MALADE IMAGINAIRE

By Moliere; Director, Jean-Laurent Cochet;
Decor and Costumes, Jacques Marillier; Choreography, Norbert Scmucki.

CAST

Argan	Jacques Charon
Purgon	Georges Chamarat
Diafoirus	Jacques Eyser
Beralde	Jacques Toja
Bonnefoi	Simon Eine
Fleurant	Marcel Tristani
Cleante	Jacques Buron
Thomas Diafoirus	Jean-Luc Moreau
Toinette	Francoise Seigner
Beline	Berengere Dautun
Angelique	Catherine Hiegel

Presented for 8 performances.

Company Manager: Joseph Brownstone
Press: Martin Feinstein, Dale Heapps,
James Murtha
Stage Managers: Henri Salles, Andre Malloux,
Bruce Bassman

* Closed Feb. 22, 1970 after a limited engagement
of 24 performances.

Jacques Charon, Georges Chamarat, Francoise Seigner Above: Bernegere Dautun, Charon, Catherine Hiegel in "Le Malade Imaginaire" Top: Genevieve Casile, Jacques Toja in "Amphitryon"

Georges Descrieres, Jacques Charon Above: Descrieres in "Dom Juan" Top: Francoise Seigner, Jacques Charon, Denise Gence in "Les Femmes Savantes"

Jean-Louis Barrault (front)
Top: Marcel Marceau

NEW YORK CITY CENTER

Opened Tuesday, April 7, 1970.*
Ronald A. Wilford Associates Inc. in association with City Center of Music and Drama Inc. presents:

MARCEL MARCEAU

Administrative Director, Alain Mangel; Presentation of Cards by Don Diego Cristian.

PROGRAM

STYLE PANTOMIMES: The Kite, The Cage, The Man and His Boat, The Magician, Circus Performer, The Hands, The Painter, Revolt of the Automat, Creation of the World, The Circus, Remembrances, The Trial, The Bureaucrats, Walking Against the Wind, The Staircase, The Tight Rope Walker, The Sculptor, The Park, The Public Garden, The Bill Poster, The Mask Maker, Contrasts, Youth, Maturity, Old Age and Death, The Seven Deadly Sins

BIP PANTOMIMES: BIP as a Concert Performer, a Matador, Don Juan, Traveller, Subway Rider, Baby Sitter, Violin Virtuoso, Guest at a Society Party, Lion Tamer, Suicide, Skater, Soldier, David and Goliath, Street Musician, Fireman, Modern and Future Life, and BIP at a Ballroom, Travelling by the Sea, Hunting Butterflies, Looking for a Job.

Production Manager: Tennent McDaniel
Company Manager: Charles K. Jones
Press: Herbert H. Breslin, Richard O'Hara
Stage Manager: Antoine Casanova

* Closed Apr. 26, 1970 after a limited engagement of 24 performances.

Herbert Breslin Photo

NEW YORK CITY CENTER

Opened Tuesday, May 19, 1970.*
City Center of Music and Drama, Inc. (Norman Singer, General Administrator) in association with Melvin Kaplan, Inc. presents La Compagnie Renaud-Barrault in:

RABELAIS

Author and Director, Jean-Louis Barrault; Costumes, Matias; Choreography, Velerie Camille; Music, Michel Polnareff; Orchestrations, Jean Claudric; Technical Director, Hans Sondheimer; Sound Technician, Briouze; Simultaneous Translation and Running Commentary by Faubion Bowers.

CAST

Ladies:
Dancer, Lantern...............................Maddly Bamy
Marguerite of Navarre, Queen of Lanternland
.........Velerie Camille
Lady-in-waiting......................Marie-Helene Daste
Dancer, Lantern, Lady of Abbey
.........Huguette Dathane
Dancer, Lantern ....Sharon O'Connell
Dancer, Lantern..........................E. Pareze-Belda
Dancer Lantern ....Michele Rimbold
Dancer, Lady-in-waiting to Gargamelle
.........Celine Salles
Gargamelle, Hostess of Abbey,
Princess Bacbuc.........Jacqueline Staup

Gentlemen:
Grandgousier, Grimalkin....................Jacques Alric
Friar John of the Funnels.........Georges Audoubert
Humanist, Ponocrates............Jean-Louis Barrault
Pillot, Orator, Beggar ....Victor Beniard
Pantagruel ....Jean-Pierre Bernard
Young Gargantua ....Gerard Boucaron
Dancing Actor ....Richard Caron
Monk, Singer ....Claude Del Vitto
Dancer, Sailor ....Michael Devay
Shepherd Frogier, Carpalim ....Louis Fremont
Dunghill, Xenomanes ....Pierre Gallon
Farmer, Sailor, Triboulet ....Jean-Renaud Garcia
Play-Leader, Picrocole............Jean-Pierre Granval
Touchfaucet, Aeditus ....Hubert De Lapparent
Thubal Holofernes, Putherbeus ....Regis Outin
Early Pear, Ding-dong..........Dominique Santarelli
Friar John, Wrestler ....Frank Valois
Trepelu, Wrestler ....Bernard Vignal
Panurge ....Henri Virlojeux

Presented in two parts with a prologue.

Company Manager: Catherine Parsons
Press: Seymour Krawitz
Stage Manager: Jean-Pierre Mathis

* Closed May 31, 1970 after a limited engagement of 16 performances.

NEW YORK STATE THEATER

Opened Monday, June 23, 1969.*
The Music Theater of Lincoln Center (Richard Rodgers, President and Producing Director) presents:

OKLAHOMA!

Book and Lyrics, Oscar Hammerstein 2nd; Based on play "Green Grow the Lilacs" by Lynn Riggs; Music, Richard Rodgers; Director, John Kennedy; Choreography, Gemze de Lappe; Scenery and Lighting, Paul C. McGuire; Costumes, Miles White; Musical Director, Jay Blackton; Orchestrations, Robert Russel Bennett; Assistant Conductor, Robert Stanley; Hairstylist, John Quaglia.

CAST

Aunt Eller	Margaret Hamilton
Curly	Bruce Yarnell
Laurey	Lee Beery
Ike Skidmore	Sam Kirkham
Slim	Del Horstmann
Joe	Kurt Olson
Will Parker	Lee Roy Reams
Jud Fry	Spiro Malas
Ado Annie Carnes	April Shawhan
Ali Hakim	Ted Beniades
Gertie Cummings	June Helmers
Donna	Donna Monroe
Judith	Judith McCauley
Dixie	Dixie Stewart
Joyce	Joyce Tomanec
Andrew Carnes	William Griffis
Cord Elam	John Gerstad

UNDERSTUDIES: Curly, John Almberg; Laurey, Judith McCauley; Aunt Eller, Maggie Task; Ado Annie, June Helmers; Will Parker, Andy G. Bew; Cord, Del Horstmann; Carnes, Sam Kirkham; Skidmore, John Dorrin; Dancing Curly, Henry Boyer; Dancing Laurey, Gilda Mullett; Dancing Jud, Michael Lane; Ali, Jud, Alex Orfaly; Gertie, Maggie Worth.

SINGERS: Bobbi Lange, Judith McCauley, Donna Monroe, Eleanor Rogers, Dixie Stewart, Maggie Task, Joyce Tomanec, Maggie Worth, John Almberg, John D. Anthony, Lester Clark, John Dorrin, Mark East, Del Horstmann, Robert Lenn, Joe McGrath, Kurt Olson, Alex Orfaly, Ken Richards, Tom Trelfa.

DANCERS: Graciela Daniele, Katherine Gallagher, Mary Lynne McRae, Gilda Mullett, Sally Ransone, Audrey Ross, Lana Sloniger, Eileen Taylor, Lee Wilson, Toodie Wittmer, Jenny Workman, Mary Zahn, Paul Berne, Andy G. Bew, Henry Boyer, Bjarne Buchtrup, Michael Ebbin, William Glassman, Michael Lane, Ralph Nelson.

MUSICAL NUMBERS: "Oh, What a Beautiful Mornin'," "The Surrey with the Fringe on Top," "Kansas City," "I Cain't Say No," "Many a New Day," "It's a Scandal! It's an Outrage!," "People Will Say," "Pore Jud," "Lonely Room," "Out of My Dreams," "The Farmer and the Cowman," "All Er Nothin'," "Oklahoma!," Finale.

A Musical in 2 acts and 6 scenes. The action takes place just after the turn of the century in Indian Territory (now Oklahoma).

General Manager: Morris Jacobs
Company Manager: Ronald Bruguiere
Press: Frank Goodman, Ruth Cage
Stage Managers: Sammy Lambert, Phil King, James Stevenson

* Closed Sept. 6, 1969 after 88 performances. Original production opened Mar. 3, 1943 and ran for 2202 performances.

Top Right: Lee Roy Reams
Below: Bruce Yarnell, Lee Beery

Margaret Hamilton, Bruce Yarnell, Lee Beery

VIVIAN BEAUMONT THEATER

Opened Thursday, June 26, 1969.*
The Repertory Theater of Lincoln Center under the direction of Jules Irving (Robert Symonds, Associate Director) presents:

IN THE MATTER OF
J. ROBERT OPPENHEIMER

By Heinar Kipphardt; Freely adapted from the documents; Translation, Ruth Speirs; Director, Gordon Davidson; Setting, Peter Wexler; Lighting, John Gleason; Costumes, Constance Ross; Still Projections, Elinor Bunin, Peter Wexler.

CAST

J. Robert Oppenheimer	Paul Sparer
Gordon Gray	John Beal
Ward V. Evans	Robert Symonds
Thomas A. Morgan	Ben Hammer
Curtis Moffat, Jr.	Philip Bosco
H. Thomas Spalding	Robert Phalen
Aaron Stein	Ralph Bell
Franklin S. Hardiman	Cec Linder
Major Nicholas Radzi	Robert Levine
John Lansdale	Stephen Elliott †
Edward Teller	Herbert Berghof
Hans Bethe	Sandor Szabo
Walker LeRoy Adams	Ronald Weyand
Jacob Lehmann	Ray Fry
Stenographers and Guards	Frank Bayer, Martin Herzer, Patrick Horrigan, Joseph Schroer

UNDERSTUDIES: Ray Fry, Ben Hammer, Robert Levine, Joseph Schroer, Richard Woods

A Drama in 2 acts. The action takes place in Room 2022, Building T3, Atomic Energy Commission Washington, D.C., during the period April 12-May 6, 1954.

Production Manager: Robert D. Currie
Press: Susan Bloch, Linda Gerber, Sedgwick Clark
Stage Managers: Barbara-Mae Phillips, Frank Bayer, Martin Herzer, Patrick Horrigan

* Closed Oct. 12, 1969 after 126 performances. For original NY production, see THEATRE WORLD, Vol. 25. Company began tour Oct. 13, 1969 at the National in Washington, D.C., and closed in San Francisco on Jan. 10, 1970.

† Succeeded by Shepperd Strudwick

Martha Swope Photos

Robert Symonds, John Beal, Ben Hammer, Herbert Berghof
Top Right: Paul Sparer

VIVIAN BEAUMONT THEATER

Opened Thursday, November 6, 1969.*
The Repertory Theater of Lincoln Center
(Jules Irving, Director; Robert Symonds, Associate Director) presents:

THE TIME OF YOUR LIFE

By William Saroyan; Director, John Hirsch; Settings, Douglas W. Schmidt; Costumes, Carrie Fishbein Robbins; Lighting, John Gleason; Production Assistant, Julia Fremon.

CAST

Joe	James Broderick
Arab	Ralph Drischell
Nick	Philip Bosco
Willie	Lenny Baker
Sam	Bill Cunningham
Newsboy	Marc L. Vahanian
	or Scott Jacoby
Drunkard	Jack Fletcher
Tom	Biff McGuire
Kitty Duval	Susan Tyrrell
Dudley	Matthew Cowles
Harry	Leonard Frey †
Wesley	Lorenzo Fuller
Lorene	Marcia Lewis
Blick	Joseph Mascolo
Mary L	Priscilla Pointer
McCarthy	Ralph Bell
Krupp	Gene Troobnick
Kit Carson	Robert Symonds
A Sailor	Ronald Hale
Killer	Helene Winston
Babs	Barbara eda-Young
Elsie	Laura Esterman
A Society Lady	Leta Bonynge
Society Gentleman	Patrick McVey
A Cop	Robert Levine
Another Cop	Robert Keesler

UNDERSTUDIES: Joe, Michael Miller; Kit, Ralph Drischell; Kitty, Mary, Barbara eda-Young; Nick, Joseph Mascolo; Dudley, Druck, Sailor, Arthur Sellers; Harry, Lenny Baker; Willie, Ronald Hale; McCarthy, Arab, Robert Keesler; Krupp, Blick, Robert Levine; Society Man, Jack Fletcher; Society Woman, Helene Winston; Wesley, Bill Cunningham, Lorene, Leta Bonynge.

A Comedy in 2 acts. The action takes place in October of 1939 in Nick's Pacific Street Saloon in San Francisco, and in a hotel room around the corner.

Press: Susan Bloch, Jan Henry James,
Sedgwick Clark
Stage Managers: Barnett Epstein,
Jean-Daniel Noland

* Closed Dec. 20, 1969 after 52 performances and 13 previews.

† Succeeded by Danny Sullivan.

Martha Swope Photos

James Broderick, Philip Bosco, Leonard Frey
Top: (foreground) Susan Tyrrell, Biff McGuire, Broderick

Judd Jones, Robyn Goodman in "Antigone"

Leora Dana, Harold Gould in
"The Increased Difficulty of Concentration"

REPERTORY THEATER-IN-THE-SCHOOLS

Opened Monday, November 17, 1969.*
The Repertory Theater of Lincoln Center
(Jules Irving, Director; Robert Symonds,
Associate Director) presents:

ANTIGONE

By Jean Anouilh; Director, Tim Ward.
CAST
Antigone ....Robyn Goodman
Creon ....Judd Jones
Ismene ....Ceci Perrin
Guard ....Joseph Mydell
Guitarist..................................Arthur Miller

A Drama performed without intermission.

Press: Susan Bloch, Jan Henry James,
Sedgwick Clark
Stage Manager: Eastern Hale

* Closed Apr. 19, 1970 after 123 performances.

FORUM THEATER

Opened Thursday, December 4, 1969.*
The Repertory Theater of Lincoln Center
(Jules Irving, Director; Robert Symonds, As-
sociate Director) presents:

THE INCREASED DIFFICULTY OF CONCENTRATION

By Vaclav Havel; Translation, Vera Blackwell;
Director, Mel Shapiro; Sets and Costumes, David
I. Mitchell; Sound, Pril Smiley Delson; Hairstylist,
James Sullivan.

CAST
Dr. Eduard Huml, social scientist ....Harold Gould
Vlasta Huml, his wife ....Jane Hoffman
Renata, his mistress.................Jacqueline Brookes
Blanka, his secretary ....Alix Elias
Dr. Anna Balcar, social scientist ....Leora Dana
Karel Kriebl, technician.....................Sam Schacht
Emil Machal, surveyor ....Sam Umani
Mr. Beck, supervisor ....George Bartenieff
UNDERSTUDIES: Huml, George Bartenieff;
Kriebl, Machal, Beck, Luis Avalos, Female roles,
Trazana Beverley

A Comedy in 2 acts. The action takes place at the
present time in Dr. Huml's flat.

Press: Susan Bloch, Jan Henry James,
Sedgwick Clark
Stage Managers: Jane Ward, Martin Herzer,
Patrick Horrigan

ALICE TULLY HALL

Opened Friday, December 20, 1969.*
David Dretzin presents The Paper Bag Players in:

"DANDELION" and "GROUP SOUP"

Conceived and Designed by Judith Martin;
Assisted by Irving Burton; Dialogue, Judith Martin, Irving Burton, Donald Ashwander, Betty Osgood; Music, Donald Ashwander; Director, Judith
Martin; Assistant Director, Irving Burton; Administrator, Judith Liss; Stage Manager, Daniel
Rosenfels.

CAST
Judith Martin
Irving Burton
Pilar Garcia
Joseph Medalis

* Closed Jan. 4, 1970 after a limited engagement
of 24 performances.

Martha Swope Photos

**Left Center: Harold Gould, Jacqueline Brookes
Alix Elias in "The Increased Difficulty
of Concentration"**

VIVIAN BEAUMONT THEATER

Opened Thursday, January 8, 1970.*
The Repertory Theater of Lincoln Center
(Jules Irving, Director; Robert Symonds, Associate Director) presents:

CAMINO REAL

By Tennessee Williams; Director, Milton Katselas; Scenery and Costumes, Peter Wexler; Lighting, John Gleason; Music Composed by Bernardo Segall.

CAST

Don Quixote	Patrick McVey
Sancho Panza	Michael Enserro
Gutman	Victor Buono
Abdullah	Jose Perez
Prudence Duvernoy	Leta Bonynge
Jacques Casanova	Jean-Pierre Aumont
Loan Shark	Ralph Drischell
Olympe	Barbara eda-Young
Waiters	Arthur Sellers, Luis Avalos
Survivor	Michael Levin
Rosita	Joan Pringle
Officer	Joseph Mascolo
Guards	Sam Umani, Michael Miller
Lady Mulligan	Priscilla Pointer
La Madrecita	Antonia Rey
Her Son	Jose Barrera
The Dreamer	Roberto Reyes
The Gypsy	Sylvia Syms
Esmeralda, her daughter	Susan Tyrrell
Nursie	Arnold Soboloff
Kilroy	Al Pacino
Street Cleaners	Paul Benjamin, Robert Keesler
Lord Mulligan	Robert Symonds
A. Ratt	Ralph Bell
Baron de Charlus	Philip Bosco
Lobo	Nick Cantrell
Marguerite Gautier	Jessica Tandy
Lord Byron	Clifford David
Pilot	Michael Levin
Navigator	Dan Sullivan
Eva	Barbara eda-Young
Voice of the Bum	Ralph Drischell

STREET PEOPLE: Luis Avalos, Michael Miller, Jean-Daniel Noland, Robert Riggs, Raymond Singer, Barbara Spiegel, Dan Sullivan, Sam Umani

UNDERSTUDIES: Marguerite, Priscilla Pointer; Casanova, Michael Levin; Gutman, Joseph Mascolo; Gypsy, Leta Bonynge; Esmeralda, Rosita, Olympe, Eta, Barbara Spiegel; Byron, Raymond Singer; Baron, Ralph Drischell; Quixote, Mulligan, Michael Miller; Nursie, Michael Enserro; Kilroy, Dan Sullivan.

A Drama in 3 acts with prologue. The action takes place where Camino Real ends and Camino Real begins.

Press: Susan Bloch, Jan Henry James,
Sedgwick Clark
Stage Managers: Tim Ward, Barnett Epstein,
Michael Judson

* Closed Feb. 21, 1970 after 52 performances and 13 previews.

Martha Swope Photos

**Jean-Pierre Aumont, Jessica Tandy,
Victor Buono Above: Aumont, Tandy**

**Philip Bosco, Al Pacino
Top Left: Jessica Tandy (C)**

FORUM THEATER

Opened Thursday, January 29, 1970.*
The Repertory Theater of Lincoln Center
(Jules Irving, Director; Robert Symonds, Associate Director) presents:

THE DISINTEGRATION OF
JAMES CHERRY

By Jeff Wanshel; Director, Glenn Jordan; Setting, Douglas W. Schmidt; Costumes, James Hart Stearns; Lighting, John Gleason; Hairstylist, Jim Sullivan.

CAST

James Cherry	Stephen Strimpell
Elizabeth Cherry	Priscilla Pointer
William Cherry	James Ray
Betsey Cherry	Catherine Burns
Grandmother Cherry	Margaret Linn
Mendacious Porpentine	Robert Symonds
Tunbunny	Jacque Lynn Colton
Charley Johnson	James Cahill
Gus	Raymond Singer
Bill	John Merensky
Dirty Gertie, Ophelia Beans, Nicotine Flightpath	Carolyn Coates
Teacher, Susquehanna B Hominy, Traffic Policeman, Zoo Official, Erasmus Pygmy, Policeman, State Trooper	Jay Garner

UNDERSTUDIES: James, Bill, Raymond Singer; William, Porpentine, Jay Garner, Robert Riggs; Elizabeth, Carolyn Coates, Margaret Linn; Grandmother, Priscilla Pointer; Betsey, Jacque Lynn Colton; Tunbunny, Barbara Spiegel; Charley, Gus, John Merensky.

A Comedy in two acts.

Press: Susan Bloch, Jan Henry James, Sedgwick Clark, Jayne Brindle
Stage Managers: Jane Ward, Michael Judson

* Closed Feb. 21, 1970 after 28 performances and 7 previews.

Martha Swope Photos

Catherine Burns, Stephen Strimpell
Top Right: Jay Garner, Strimpell

Margaret Linn, James Ray, Stephen Strimpell,
Priscilla Pointer, Catherine Burns

Paul Sparer, Roberts Blossom, Joseph Mascolo, Philip Bosco

VIVIAN BEAUMONT THEATER

Opened Thursday, March 12. 1970.*
The Repertory Theater of Lincoln Center (Jules Irving, Director; Robert Symonds, Associate Director) presents:

OPERATION SIDEWINDER

By Sam Shepard; Director, Michael A. Schultz; Sets, Douglas W. Schmidt; Costumes, Willa Kim; Lighting, John Gleason; Music Composed and Performed by The Holy Modal Rounders; Musical Directors, Marvin Sylvor, Jeff Cutler; Hairstylist, Jim Sullivan; Production Assistant, Diane Mitchell: Original Cast Album on United Artists Records; Presented by special arrangement with Alvin Ferleger Associates.

CAST

Dukie	Robert Phalen
Honey	Barbara eda-Young
Mechanic	Michael Miller
Young Man	Andy Robinson
Forest Ranger	Robert Riggs
Billy	Roberts Blossom
Colonel Warner	Joseph Mascolo
Captain	Robert Phalen
Cadet	Gus Fleming
Mickey Free	Don Plumley
1st Cohort to Mickey	Ralph Drischell
2nd Cohort to Mickey	Arthur Sellers
Carhop	Catherine Burns
Blood	Garrett Morris
Blade	Paul Benjamin
Dude	Charles Pegues
General Browser	Paul Sparer
Doctor Vector	Ray Fry
Spider Lady	Michael Levin
Edith	Joan Pringle
Captain Bovine	Philip Bosco
Desert Tactical Troop	Robert Riggs, Robert Phalen, Michael Miller

INDIANS: Jose Barrera, Paul Benjamin, Gregory Borst, Gus Fleming, Robert Keesler, Michael Levin, Clark Luis, Richard Mason, Muriel Miguel, Louis Mofsie, Santos Morales, Garrett Morris, Jean-Daniel Noland

UNDERSTUDIES: Young Man, Arthur Sellers; Honey, Carhop, Barbara Spiegel; Vector, Santos Morales; Mickey, Browser, Ralph Drischell; Bill, Warner, Paul Sparer; Blood, Charles Pegues; Spider, Joan Pringle; Bovine, Michael Miller; Captain, Clark Luis; Dukie, Robert Riggs.

MUSICAL NUMBERS: "Catch Me," "Alien Song," "Euphoria," "Don't Leave Me Dangling in the Dust," "Synergy," "Do It Girl," "Bad Karma," "C.I.A. Man," "Generalonely," "Float Me Down Your Pipeline," "I Disremember Quite Well," "Hathor."

A Play in 2 acts and 12 scenes.

Press: Susan Bloch, Jan Henry James, Sedgwick Clark, Jayne Brindle
Stage Managers: Barbara-Mae Phillips, Patrick Horrigan, Paul Bengston, Michael Judson, Jean-Daniel Noland

* Closed Apr. 25, 1970 after 52 performances and 13 previews.

Barbara eda-Young, Robert Phalen
Above: Catherine Burns

FORUM THEATER

Opened Thursday, April 2, 1970.*
The Repertory Theater of Lincoln Center
(Jules Irving, Director; Robert Symonds,
Associate Director) presents:

"LANDSCAPE" and "SILENCE"

By Harold Pinter; Director, Peter Gill; Settings,
Douglas W. Schmidt; Based on designs by John
Gunter; Costumes, Douglas W. Schmidt; Based on
designs by Deirdre Clancy; Lighting, John Gleason; Hairstylist, Jim Sullivan.

CAST

"Landscape"
Duff ....Robert Symonds
Beth ....Mildred Dunnock

Intermission

"Silence"
Ellen ....Barbara Tarbuck
Rumsey ....Robert Symonds
Bates ....James Patterson

UNDERSTUDIES: Barbara Tarbuck, Robert
Phalen.

General Manager: Alan Mandell
Press: Susan Bloch, Jan Henry James,
Sedgwick Clark, Jayne Brindle
Stage Managers: Tim Ward, Jane Ward

* Closed May 17, 1970 after 53 performances.

Martha Swope Photos

Robert Symonds, Mildred Natwick
Top: Symonds, Barbara Tarbuck, James Patterson

VIVIAN BEAUMONT THEATER

Opened Thursday, May 14, 1970.*
The Repertory Theater of Lincoln Center
(Jules Irving, Director; Robert Symonds,
Associate Director) presents:

BEGGAR ON HORSEBACK

By George S. Kaufman and Marc Connelly;
Director, John Hirsch; Scenery and Costumes,
Michael Annals; Lighting, John Gleason; Music,
Stanley Silverman; Songs, Stanley Silverman and
John Lahr; Musical Direction, Abba Bogin; Move-
ment Sequences, Marvin Gordon; Production
Assistant, Richard Bookman; Hairstylist, Jim
Sullivan; Electronic Music, Pril Smiley Delson
and Stanley Silverman.

CAST

Dr. Albert Rice	Biff McGuire
Cynthia Mason	Susan Watson
Neil McRae	Leonard Frey
Mrs. Cady	Tresa Hughes
Homer Cady	Robert Phalen
Gladys Cady	Cherry Davis
Mr. Cady	Jay Garner
Jerry	Les "Bubba" Gaines
Train Vendor	Art Ostrin
Miss Hey	Barbara Spiegel
Miss You	Beryl Towbin
Flower Girls	Dorothy Frank, Elaine Handel, Michon Peacock
Policemen	Robert Keesler, Raymond Singer
Newsboys	Clark Luis, Arthur Sellers
Second Juror	Robert Weil
Candy Vendor	Luis Avalos
Guide	Ralph Drischell
Novelist	Ray Fry
Poet	Bob Daley
Singer	Bobby Lee

PEOPLE IN NEIL'S DREAM: Jose Barrera,
John Beecher, Roger Braun, Tommy Breslin, Peter
Norman, Charles Pegues, Vickie Thomas

UNDERSTUDIES: Neil, John Beecher; Cynthia,
Barbara Spiegel; Gladys, Beryl Towbin; Cady,
Robert Keesler; Mrs. Cady, Elaine Handel; Homer,
Luis Avalos; Albert, Clark Luis; Miss Hey, Miss
You, Vickie Thomas; Jerry, Bobby Lee.

A Comedy in 2 acts. The action takes place in
1924 in Neil's cold-water flat in Greenwich Village.

General Manager: Alan Mandell
Press: Susan Bloch, Jan Henry James,
Sedgwick Clark, Jayne Brindle
Stage Managers: Tim Ward, Barnett Epstein,
Barbara-Mae Phillips, Paul Bengston,
Patrick Horrigan, Michael Judson

* Closed June 27, 1970 after 54 performances and
13 previews

Martha Swope Photos

**Jay Garner, Barbara Spiegel, Leonard Frey,
Beryl Towbin Top: Frey (kneeling), Biff
McGuire (aloft), Art Ostrin (R)**

**Susan Watson, Leonard Frey
with Butterfly Girls**

83

Opened Tuesday, October 21, 1969.*
Equity Library Theatre presents:

IMPRESSIONS ON LOVE

A program of sketches, prose and poetry readings from Dorothy Parker, William Shakespeare, Tennessee Williams, George Bernard Shaw, Oscar Wilde, Neil Simon.

CAST

Grace Kimmins
Ken Kimmins

* Presented for 3 performances, closing Oct. 23, 1969.

Opened Monday, December 8, 1969.*
Equity Library Theatre presents:

THE CAINE MUTINY COURT-MARTIAL

By Herman Wouk; Director, John Harkins.
CAST

Lt. Stephen Maryk	Victor Argo
Lt. Barney Greenwald	Leonard De Martino
Lt. Comdr. John Challee	Kent Broadhurst
Capt. Blakely	Murray Moston
Lt. Cmdr. Phillip Francis Queeg	Nick Padula
Lt. Thomas Keefer	Patrick Sullivan
Signalman Junius Urban	Harvey Keitel
Lt. JG. Willis Seward Keith	Jim Lyttle
Dr. Forrest Lundeen	Paul Geier
Dr. Bird	David Gallagher

* Presented for 3 performances, closing Dec. 10, 1969.

Opened Monday, February 2, 1970.*
Equity Library Theatre presents:

MARJORIE DAW

A One-Act Musical by Sally Dixon Wiener; Based on story by Thomas Bailey Aldrich; Director, Miriam Fond; Musical Direction, Theo Carus; Costumes, Norvie Bullock; Lighting, Gwen Jo Hamill; Choreography, Osa Danam; Technician, Lee Perry; At the Piano, Bob Waxman.

CAST

Dr. Patrick Dillon	Merrill E. Joels
Edward Delaney	James Donahue
John Flemming	Richard Balin
Watkins	George Cavey
Marjorie Daw	Gail Johnston
Navy Lieutenant	Tom Roberts
Rector	Allin Leslie
Society Swell	Bill Oransky
The First Miss Kingsbury	Susan Lehman
The Second Miss Kingsbury	Heddy Zirin

The action takes place in New York and New Hampshire during the summer of 1872.

Stage Managers: Mark Richter, Robert J. Schiraldi

* Presented for 3 performances, closing Feb. 4, 1970.

FORUM THEATER

Opened Thursday, May 28, 1970.*
The Repertory Theater of Lincoln Center (Jules Irving, Director; Robert Symonds, Associate Director) presents:

AMPHITRYON

By Peter Hacks; Translation, Ralph Manheim; Director, Robert Symonds; Setting, Costumes, Masks, James Hart Stearns; Lighting, John Gleason.

CAST

Jupiter	Philip Bosco
Mercury	James Ray
Sosias	Harold Gould
Amphitryon	James Patterson
Alcmene	Priscilla Pointer
Night	Dan Sullivan

A Comedy in 3 acts.

General Manager: Alan Mandell
Press: Susan Bloch, Jan Henry James, Sedgwick Clark, Jayne Brindle
Stage Managers: Jane Ward, Paul Bengston, Michael Judson

* Closed June 20, 1970 after 30 performances and 7 previews.

Martha Swope Photo

Opened Monday, May 4, 1970.*
Equity Library Theatre presents:

SOME OTHER TIME

Director, Richard Mogavero; Musical Director, Ed Linderman; Designer, Anthony Hancock; Choreographer, Barbara Frank.
CAST

"Les Jardins Publique"
Book, Mark Lamos; Music and Lyrics, Mr. Lamos and Philip Killian

Mademoiselle	Laurie Hutchinson
Bandleader	Paul Keith
Georges	Christopher Barrett
Edouard	Horton Willis
M. Montpelier	Hal Watters
Mme. Montpelier	Charlotte Lane
Colette	Susan Ginsberg
Celine	Jessica Hull
Lady in fur hat	Joan Maniscalco
Gentleman in grey	Anthony Hancock

MUSICAL NUMBERS: "Les Jardins Publique," "Sunday Morning," "Listen to the Band," "So Happy," "How Funny and Old," "You, My Dear," "Strange Frightening Feeling."

A One-Act Musical. The action takes place about 1900 in a park in provincial France.

"And I Bet You Wish You Was Me Now"
Book, Sue Kosoff; Music, Jane Staab; Lyrics, Philip Killian

Harry	Hal Watters
Lily	Suellen Estey
Mrs. Watts	Joan Maniscalco
Mrs. Carson	Jessica Hull
Mrs. Slocum	Penny White

MUSICAL NUMBERS: "Lovely Music," "Ellisville," "Xylophone Man," "Lily," "Hope Chest," "And I Bet You Wish You Was Me Now," Finale.

A One-Act Musical. The action takes place in a small rural town in Mississippi.

* Presented for 2 performances, closing May 5, 1970.

Philip Bosco, Prscilla Pointer in "Amphitryon"

OFF-BROADWAY PRODUCTIONS

FORTUNE THEATRE

Opened Tuesday, June 3, 1969.*
Barry Hoffman presents:

THE WORLD OF
MRS. SOLOMON

CAST

"Another Chance"

Bertha Solomon	Henrietta Jacobson
Mrs. Rossteen	Rashel Novikoff
Ada Kaplan	Helen Blay
Mr. Olansky	Morris Strassberg

The action takes place at the present time in Mrs. Solomon's kitchen.

"The Second Mrs. Aarons"

Rosalie Aarons	Robin Lane
Sam Rosenfeld	Leonard Yorr
Dr. John Gaylord	Martin Shakar

The action takes place at the present time in the Aarons' living room.

Associate Manager: Sol Posnack
Press: Max Gendel
Stage Manager: Clifford Ammon

* Closed June 8, 1969 after 8 performances.

Irene Fertik Photo

Right: Henrietta Jacobson

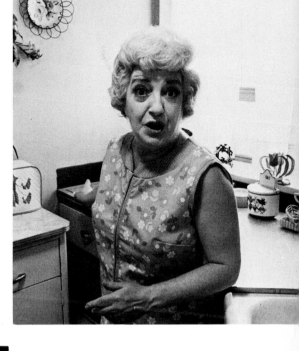

ACTORS PLAYHOUSE

Opened Tuesday, June 10, 1969.*
Harlan P. Kleiman, Jeffrey C. Reiss, Orin Lehman present:

TONIGHT IN LIVING COLOR

By A. R. Gurney, Jr.; Director, Jered Barclay; Scenery, Merrill Sindler; Costumes, Yvonne Bronowicz; Lighting, Andie Wilson Kingwill; Original Music, Orville Stoeber; Production Assistant, Gary Trudeau.

CAST

"The Golden Fleece"

Betty	Rue McClanahan
Bill	Tim O'Connor

"The David Show"

Samuel	Jerome Raphel
David	Anthony Call
Saul	Barney Martin
Jonathan	F. Murray Abraham
Ham	George Patterson
Bathsheba	Holland Taylor

General Manager: Robert S. Fishko
Press: Robert Ganshaw,
John Prescott, Ted Goldsmith
Stage Manager: Sean S. Cunningham

* Closed June 29, 1969 after 23 performances.

Holland Taylor, George Patterson, Anthony Call in "The David Show"

PROMENADE THEATRE

Opened Wednesday, June 4, 1969.*
Edgar Lansbury and Joseph Beruh present:

PROMENADE

Book and Lyrics, Maria Irene Fornes; Music, Al Carmines; Director, Lawrence Kornfeld; Scenery, Rouben Ter-Arutunian; Costumes, Willa Kim; Lighting, Jules Fisher; Orchestrations, Eddie Sauter; Musical Director, Al Carmines; Musical Conductor, Susan Romann; Production Assistant, Dennis Stafford.

CAST

105	Ty McConnell †1
106	Gilbert Price †2
Jailer	Pierre Epstein
Servant	Madeline Kahn †3
Miss I	Margot Albert
Miss O	Carrie Wilson
Miss U	Alice Playten
Mr. R	Marc Allen III
Mr. S	Glenn Kezer
Mr. T	Michael Davis †4
Waiter	Edmund Gaynes
Rosita	Florence Tarlow
Dishwasher	Art Ostrin
Mayor	George S. Irving †5
Mother	Shannon Bolin †6

STANDBYS: Al Settimio, Igors Gavon, Marie Santell.

MUSICAL NUMBERS: "Promenade Theme," "Dig, Dig, Dig," "Unrequited Love," "Isn't That Clear?," "Don't Eat It," "Four," "Chicken Is He," "A Flower," "Rosita Rodriguez," "Apres Vous," "Bliss," "The Moment Has Passed," "Thank You," "The Clothes Make the Man," "The Cigarette Song," "Two Little Angels," "The Passing of Time," "Capricious and Fickle," "Crown Me," "Mr. Phelps," "Madeline," "Spring Beauties," "A Poor Man," "Why Not," "The Finger Song," "Little Fool," "Czardas," "The Laughing Song," "A Mother's Love," "Listen, I Feel," "I Saw a Man," "All Is Well in the City."

A Musical in 2 acts and 7 scenes.

Company Manager: Jewel Howard
Press: Max Eisen, Cheryl Sue Dolby
Stage Manager: Larry Whiteley

* Closed Jan. 18, 1970 after 259 performances.
† Succeeded by: 1. Kenneth Carr, 2. Anthony Falco, 3. Pamela Hall, Marie Santell, Sandra Schaeffer, 4. Gene Varrone, 5. Elliott Savage, Seymour Penzner, 6. Mary Jo Catlett.

Top Left: Florence Tarlow, Carrie Wilson, Margot Albert, Alice Playten

Madeline Kahn, Shannon Bolin, Ty McConnell, Gilbert Price Above: Glenn Kezer, Alice Playten, Michael Davis

Pierre Epstein, George S. Irving, Carrie Wilson

VILLAGE SOUTH THEATRE

Opened Wednesday, June 11, 1969.*
Jacqueline Donnet and Joan Shigekawa in
association with Guthrie productions present:

FIREWORKS

By Jon Swan; Director, Kent Paul; Scenery
and Lighting, Stephen Hendrickson; Costumes,
Michael Arceneaux; Special Sequences, Patricia
Birch; Technical Director, Jim Wallace.

CAST

"The Report"
Ben Bran ....Stephen Joyce
Meg Lehmann ....Monica Moran

"Football"
The Coach ....Stephen Joyce
Claymore ....Haig Chobanian
Norden ....Colgate Salsbury
Geiger....................................John Wardwell
Mrs. Ashland....................................Laurinda Barrett
Gore ....Arnold Wilkerson

"Fireworks for a Hot Fourth"
Waiter ....Arnold Wilkerson
Gloria ....Laurinda Barrett
Growth ....John Wardwell
Anna....................................Kristina Callahan
Belle ....Monica Moran
Old Local ....Stephen Joyce
Sidney ....Colgate Salsbury
Harold ....Haig Chobanian

General Manager: Joe Beruh
Company Manager: Al Isaac
Press: Dorothy Ross, Fred Weterick
Stage Manager: James Greek

* Closed June 14, 1969 after 4 performances.

Martha Swope Photo

Rear: **Laurinda Barrett, Stephen Joyce, John
Wardwell,** Front: **Colgate Salsbury, Arnold
Wilkerson, Haig Chobanian**

PROVINCETOWN PLAYHOUSE

Opened Friday, June 13, 1969.*
Philip Bell in association with Alexander
Maissel presents:

TIME FOR BED—
TAKE ME TO BED

By Charles Love; Director, Paul Weidner; Sets
and Costumes, David Loveless; Lighting, William
Mintzer; Associate Producers, Albert Perry,
Kenneth Panoch; Entr'act Music, Peter Hadreas;
Production Coordinator, Zora Margolis; Produc-
tion Assistant, Ric Cane.

CAST

"Time for Bed"
Fred Abernathy ....Victor Arnold
Mildred Katz ....Alice Spivak

The action takes place at the present time in
an apartment in NY City's West 80's.

"Take Me to Bed"
Sylvia....................................Alice Spivak
Harry ....Victor Arnold

The action takes place at the present time in
a Greenwich Village apartment.

Press: Seymour Krawitz, Ellen Levene
Stage Managers: Robert Stevenson,
Robert Vervoordt

* Closed June 21, 1969 after 11 performances and
6 previews.

Friedman-Abeles Photo

Victor Arnold, Alice Spivak

87

THE BITTER END

Opened Monday, June 16, 1969.*
(Moved July 3, 1969 to Sheridan Square Playhouse)
Allen Swift presents:

WHORES, WARS & TIN PAN ALLEY

An Evening of Kurt Weill's Music; Lyrics, Bertolt Brecht, Marc Blitzstein, George Tabori, Arnold Weinstein, Will Holt, Jacques Deval, Paul Green, Ogden Nash, Alan Jay Lerner, Maxwell Anderson, Ira Gershwin; Accompaniment, Ronald Clairmont; Lighting, Barry Arnold.

CAST

Martha Schlamme
Alvin Epstein

PROGRAM

PART I: "Alabama Song," "Moritat," "Barbara Song," "Havanna," "Instead of Song," "Ballad of Sexual Slavery," "Zuhalterballade," "Seerauber-Jenny," "Kanonensong," "Ballade vom Soldaten Weib," "Essen," "Wie Man Sich Bettet"
PART II: "Le Roi D'Aquitaine," "Medley from Johnny Johnson," "That's Him," "Speak Low," "Susan's Dream," "September Song," "The Saga of Jenny," "Lost in the Stars," "Songs from Happy End," "The Survival Song."

Press: Robert Ganshaw, John Prescott,
Ted Goldsmith
Stage Manager: Michael Roy Denbo

* Closed Aug. 17, 1969 after 72 performances.

MERCURY THEATRE

Opened Sunday, June 29, 1969.*
William W. Rippner in association with Sumac Productions Corp. presents:

PEQUOD

By Roy Richardson; Director, Burt Brinckerhoff; Setting and Lighting, David F. Segal; Costumes, Joseph G. Aulisi; Special Electronic Score and Lyrics, Mildred Kayden; Sound Technician and Production Assistant, Bill Burd.

CAST

Jim	James Seymour
John	John Caffin
Sharon	Sharon Klaif
Merrylen	Merrylen Sacks
Arleen	Arleen Wetzel
Youth	Gary Sandy
Director's Assistant	Dorothy Lyman
Director	John Tillinger
Wife	Bella Jarrett
Pip	Jason Miller
Boomer	Robert Eckles
Dr. Bunger	Don Lochner
Mary	Kelly Wood
Stub	John Mahon
Carpenter	John Randolph Jones
Captain Ahab	Richard Kronold
Starbuck	Jeff David
Queequeg	Lloyd Hollar

A Play presented without intermission. The action takes place at the present time on the stage of the theatre.

General Manager: Norman E. Rothstein
Company Manager: Patricia Carney
Press: Robert Ganshaw, John Prescott,
Ted Goldsmith
Stage Manager: David Semonin

* Closed June 29, 1969 after 1 performance.

JAN HUS THEATRE

Opened Monday June 30, 1969.*
Jan Maher presents:

THE GLORIOUS RULER

By Michael Ackerman; Director, Paul John Austin; Production Design, Lorenzo Nasca; Music and Musical Effects, Rudolph Crosswell; Production Assistants, Amy Oppenheimer, Holly Cavrell; Technical Director, Tom Randol.

CAST

First Woman	Mary Carter
Second Woman	Eileen Mitchell
First Man	John Branon
Second Man	Tom Tarpy
Creon	Don Silber
Oedipus	Jordan Charney
Teiresias	James La Ferla
Jocasta	Mary Hara
Antigone	Valerie Lee
Polinices	P. Raymond Marunas

A Drama in 2 acts. The action takes place beneath the Palace at Thebes.

General Manager: James Walsh
Press: Dorothy Ross
Stage Manager: Tony Giordano

* Closed July 6, 1969 after 8 performances.

Bert Andrews Photo

Jordan Charney, P. Raymond Marunas, Don Silber Top Alvin Epstein, Martha Schlamme Left Center: Richard Kronold, Lloyd Hollar, John Tillinger, Jason Miller, Dorothy Lyman

EDEN THEATRE

Opened Tuesday, June 17, 1969.*
Hillard Elkins in association with Michael White, Gordon Crowe and George Platt presents:

OH! CALCUTTA!

Devised by Kenneth Tynan; Contributors: Samuel Beckett, Jules Feiffer, Dan Greenburg, John Lennon, Jacques Levy, Leonard Melfi, David Newman and Robert Benton, Sam Shepard, Clovis Trouille, Kenneth Tynan, Sherman Yellen; Music and Lyrics: The Open Window, Robert Dennis, Peter Schickele, Stanley Walden; Choreography, Margo Sappington; Conceived and Directed by Jacques Levy; Musical Director, Norman Bergen; Scenery, James Tilton; Costumes, Fred Voelpel; Lighting, David F. Segal; Projection Media Designed by Gardner Compton, Emile Ardolino; Production Supervisor, Michael Thoma; Production Associate, Bill Liberman; Technical Director, Sam Bealieu; Associate Producer, George Platt; Still Photography, Michael Childers; An E.P.I.C Production.

CAST

Raina Barrett	Margo Sappington †6
Mark Dempsey †1	Nancy Tribush
Katie Drew-Wilkinson †2	George Welbes †7
Boni Enten †3	Robert Dennis
Bill Macy †4	Peter Schickele
Alan Rachins	Stanley Walden
Leon Russom †5	The Open Window

PROGRAM

PART I: "Prologue," "Taking off the Robe," "Dick and Jane," "Suite for Five Letters," "Will Answer All Replies," "Paintings of Clovis Trouille," "Jack and Jill," "Delicious Indignities," "Was It Good for You Too?"
PART II: "Much Too Soon," "One on One," "Rock Garden," "Who: Whom," "Four in Hand," "Coming Together, Going Together."

Company Manager: Edmonstone Thompson, Jr.
Press: Samuel J. Friedman
Stage Managers: John Actman, Harry Chittenden, Greg Taylor

* Still playing May 31, 1970.
† Succeeded by: 1. Mel Auston, Martin Speer, 2. Lynn Oliver, 3. Kathrin King, 4. Eddie Phillips, Jr., 5. Mitchel McGuire, 6. Maureen Byrnes, 7. Michael S. Riordan, Michael Cavanaugh

Friedman-Abeles Photos

Top Right: Leon Russom, Boni Enten

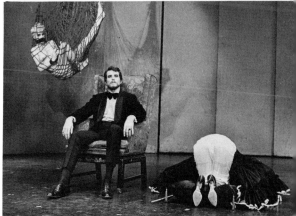

Mark Dempsey, Katie Drew-Wilkinson, George Welbes, Leon Russom, Nancy Tribush, Bill Macy, Raina Barrett, Alan Rachins, Boni Enten, Margo Sappington Right Center: Katie Drew-Wilkinson, Mark Dempsey, Nancy Tribush

JONES BEACH THEATRE

Opened Thursday, July 3, 1969.*
Guy Lombardo presents:

SOUTH PACIFIC

Book, Oscar Hammerstein 2nd; Adapted from James Michener's novel "Tales of the South Pacific"; Music, Richard Rodgers; Lyrics, Oscar Hammerstein 2nd, Joshua Logan; Director, William Hammerstein; Scenery, Fred Voelpel; Costumes, Winn Morton; Lighting, Peggy Clark; Choreography, Jane McLaughlin; Orchestrations, Robert Russell Bennett; Musical Direction, Frederick Dvonch; Entire Production under supervision of Arnold Spector.

CAST

Ngana	June Angela
Jerome	Paul Timothy
Henry	Paul Flores
Phillippe	Robert Monteil
Ensign Nellie Forbush	Nancy Dussault
Emile de Becque	Jerome Hines
Bloody Mary	Martha Larrimore
Bloody Mary's Assistant	Doris Galiber
Stewpot	Brad Sullivan
Luther Billis	Jerry Lester
Professor	James Woods
Lt. Joseph Cable	Nolan Van Way
Capt. George Brackett	Art Barnett
Cmdr. William Harbison	Webb Tilton
Yeoman Herbert Quale	Clark Salonis
Radio Operator Bob McCaffrey	
	David Rummery
Ensign Dinah Murphy	Jamie Thomas
Liat	Sarah Jane Smith
Lt. Buzz Adams	John Felton
Officer	Jess Green

NURSES, NATIVES, ETC.: Karen DeBergh, Marybeth Lahr, Sherry Lambert, Vera Moore, Barbara Perlow, Mary Ann Rydzeski, Marilyn Saunders, Dana Shimizu, Jamie Thomas, Beryl Jo Title, Elise Warner

SAILORS, SEABEES, NATIVES, ETC.: Perer Clark, Bill Collins, Bob Daley, Jack Fletcher, Larry Farrar, John Felton, Paul Flores, Wuitman Fludd III, Nino Galanti, Ted Goodridge, Jess Green, Greg Macosko, Robert Monteil, David Rummery, Clark Salonis, John-Michael Savaige, Keenan Shimizu, Marshall Thomas, Gordon Voorhees

UNDERSTUDIES: Emile, Webb Tilton; Nellie, Jamie Thomas; Luther, Brad Sullivan; Bloody Mary, Doris Galiber; Liat, Sherry Lambert; Stewpot, Buzz, David Rummery; Professor, Marshall Thomas; Ngana, Dana Shimizu; Jerome, Keenan Shimizu; Henry, Robert Monteil

MUSICAL NUMBERS: Overture, "Dites-moi Pourquois," "A Cockeyed Optimist," "Twin Soliloquies," "Some Enchanted Evening," "Bloody Mary Is the Girl I Love," "There Is Nothin' Like a Dame," "Bali Ha'i," "I'm Gonna Wash that Man Right Outa My Hair," "I'm in Love with a Wonderful Guy," "Younger than Springtime," "Happy Talk," "Honey Bun," "You've Got to Be Carefully Taught," "This Nearly Was Mine," Finale.

A Musical in 2 acts. The action takes place on 2 islands in the South Pacific, during WW II.

Company Director: Martin Cohen
Press: Saul Richman
Stage Managers: Mortimer Halpern, Leonard Auerbach, William Krot

* Closed Monday, Sept. 1, 1969. For original production, see THEATRE WORLD, Vol. 5.

Barry Kramer Photos

Jerome Hines, Nancy Dussault

**Top Left: Brad Sullivan, Jerry Lester,
Nancy Dussault, James Woods**

MERCURY THEATRE

Opened Tuesday, July 29, 1969.*
Leticia Jay presents:

THE HOOFERS

Director, Derby Wilson; Conceived and Coordinated by Leticia Jay; Music, Tiny Grimes' Band.

CAST

Chuck Green
Lon Chaney
Jerry Ames
Sandman Sims
Mabel Lee
Tony White

Jimmy Slyde
Rhythm Red
Derby Wilson
Raymund Kaaland
Leticia Jay
Eva Turner

A Musical Entertainment with tap and rhythm dancers.

Boris Bakehy Photo

Right: Sandman Sims

HAMILTON FISH PARK

Opened Sunday, August 3, 1969.*
The Puerto Rican Traveling Theatre and Mayor John V. Lindsay's Urban Action Task Force with the Parks, Recreation and Cultural Affairs Administration (August Heckscher, Administrator) present:

CROSSROADS

By Manuel Mendez Ballester; Translated by Roberto Boss; Producer, Miriam Colon; Director, Robert Rodriguez Suarez; Scenery and Costumes, Anibal Otero; Lighting and Sound, RIC-LO Productions; Costume Coordinator, Barbara N. Cohen; Project Director, Robert Buzzell; Technical Director, Kenneth Daniels; Production Assistant, Inez Perez.

CAST

Cayetano .... Alex Colon
Dona Patricia .... Miriam Goldina
Don Alfonso .... Pat McNamara
Chana .... Maria De Landa
Mario .... Walter Rodriguez
Jack .... Dermot McNamara
Felipe .... Lou Ciulla
Irma .... Maria Soledad Romero
Marta .... Virginia Arrea
Antonio .... Louis Quinones
Lorna .... Bette Craig
Cop 1 .... Alex Colon
Cop 2 .... Irving Brady

A Play in 2 acts. The action takes place in the late 1950's in an apartment in NYC's Spanish Harlem.

Company Manager: Gilberto Zaldivar
Press: Marian Graham
Stage Managers: Lathrop Robbins, Alex Colon

* Closed in Sheep Meadow, Central Park, NYC, on Aug. 31, 1969, after 25 performances. Presented at Town Hall for one performance on Saturday, Nov. 8, 1969.

Bert Andrews Photo

Right Center: Pat McNamara, Walter Rodriguez, Lou Ciulla, Miriam Goldina

BERT WHEELER THEATER

Opened Monday, August 4, 1969.*
The United States of America presents:

BUTTERFLY McQUEEN AND FRIENDS

Pianist, Joe Burns; Costumes, African Market, Inc.; Technician, Joseph Bly.

CAST

Butterfly McQueen
Wanetta Hope
Jonathan Nicoll
Paul Searcy

Delilah Jackson
Jill Jackson
William Hoffler
Mitchell Marco

A "Happening" in 2 acts.

* Closed Sept. 15, 1969 after 7 performances on Mondays only.

Butterfly McQueen

TAMBELLINI'S GATE THEATRE

Opened Wednesday, July 30, 1969.*
(Moved Oct. 7, 1969 to Frances Adler Theatre)
Woodie King Associates in cooperation with
Chelsea Theatre Center presents:

A BLACK QUARTET

Setting, John Jacobson; Costumes, Gloria
Gresham; Lighting, Marshall Williams; Sound,
Helmuth Lesold; Associate Producer, Ed Pitt.

CAST

"Prayer Meeting or the First Militant Minister"
by Ben Caldwell; Director, Irving Vincent
Burgler .... Carl Boissiere †
Minister .... L. Errol Jaye

"The Warning: A Theme for Linda"
By Ronald Milner; Director, Woodie King
Linda .... Vikki Summers
Nora .... Louise Heath
Joan .... Loretta Greene
Paula .... Jo-Ann Robinson
Grandfather .... L. Errol Jaye
Nasty Old Man .... Gerald Anthony
Donald .... Paul Rodger-Reid
Grandmother .... Joan Pryor
Mother .... Minnie Gentry

Intermission

"The Gentleman Caller"
by Ed Bullins; Director, Allie Woods
The Maid .... Minnie Gentry
The Gentleman .... Carl Boissiere †
Madame .... Sylvia Soares
Mr. Mann .... Frank Carey

"Great Goodness of Life (A Coon Show)"
by LeRoi Jones; Director, Irving Vincent
Voice of the White Judge .... Frank Carey
Court Royal .... L. Errol Jaye
Attorney Breck .... Jimmy Hayeson
Young Man .... Sam Singleton
Hood 1 & 3 .... Jimmy Hayeson
Hood 2 & 4 .... Paul Rodger-Reid
Young Woman .... Anna Maria Horsford
Leader .... Carl Boissiere †

General Manager: Jeff Britton
Company Manager: Sam Wright
Press: Bill Cherry
Stage Manager: David Semonin

* Closed Nov. 2, 1969 after 111 performances.
† Succeeded by Dennis Tate

**L. Errol Jaye, Carl Boissiere
Top Right: Arnold Johnson**

PROVINCETOWN PLAYHOUSE

Opened Tuesday August 5, 1969.*
J&S Productions present:

SOURBALL

By Robert Shure; Director, James Kerans; Sets,
Jeery N. Rojo; Lighting, Edmund Seagrave; Cos-
tumes, Deborah Foster; Technical Assistant, Ken
Petrovic; Production Assistants, Gail Julian, Bob
Woods, Wendy Mogel.

CAST

Tom	Richard Niles
Jim	Atherton Knight
Sara	Kate Hawley
Danny	Scott Robinson
Sullivan	Bernie Passeltiner
Mrs. Brick	Enid Rodgers
Nuster	Patrick McVey
Grady	Jeremiah Morris

A Grim Comedy in 2 acts. The action takes place
at the present time in a basement.

General Manager: William E. Hunt
Press: Saul Richman, Stan Brody

* Closed August 5, 1969 after 1 performance.

Barry Kramer Photo

Kate Hawley, Enid Rodgers, Patrick McVey

"Arena Conta Zumbi"

ST. CLEMENT'S CHURCH

Opened Monday, August 18, 1969.*
Theatre of Latin America presents:

ARENA CONTA ZUMBI

By Gianfrancesco Guarnieri and Augusto Boal;
Director, Augusto Boal; Music, Edu Lobo; Musical Direction, Theo de Barros; Performed in Por-
tugese.

CAST

Lima Duarte	Zezinha Duboc
Renato Consorte	Germano Batista
Antonio Pedro	Vera Regina
Rodrigo Santiago	Theo de Barros
Cecilia Thumim	Jose Alves

A Drama in 2 acts telling the story of Zumbi,
the last of the kings who reigned in Palmares, a
black republic in the heart of Brazil from 1605 to
1695.

General Manager: Levy Rossell
Press: Sol Jacobson, Lewis Harmon

* Closed Tuesday, Sept. 16, 1969 after a limited
engagement of 16 performances.

Derly Marques Photo

GRAMERCY ARTS THEATRE

Opened Thursday, August 21, 1969.*
(Moved March 4, 1970 to Pocket Theatre)
Mortimer Levitt and Arthur Cantor present
the Daytop Theatre Company in:

THE CONCEPT

Evolved as a total group effort of Daytop Vil-
age; Director, Jacobina Caro; Scenery and Lighting, Katherine Bird Paquette

CAST

Gerald Gentile	Lance Martin
Ray Grosso	Augie Nigro
Ed Kapelsohn	Louis Pedrosa
Nestor Laracuente	Stephanie Richards

Press: Elizabeth Roberts

* Closed June 28, 1969 after 268 performances.

"The Concept"

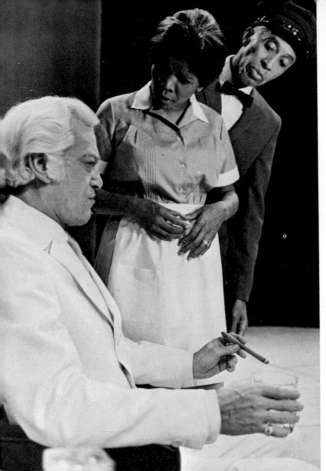

ST. MARKS PLAYHOUSE

Opened Thursday September 4, 1969.*
Hooks Productions, Inc. presents:

THE RECKONING

By Douglas Turner Ward; Director, Michael A. Schultz; Scenery, Edward Burbridge; Lighting, Martin Aronstein; Costumes, Gertha Brock; Special Sound, James Reichert; Associate Producers, Clarence Avant, Al Bell Jr., Sam Engler, presented in co-operation with the Negro Ensemble Company.

CAST

Scar .... Douglas Turner
Baby .... Jeannette DuBois
Off-Stage News Announcer .... Richard Pyatt
Governor .... Lester Rawlins
Son .... Conard Fowkes
Missy .... Louise Stubbs
Josh .... Joseph Attles

A play presented without intermission. The action takes place past, present, or possibly the future (take your pick) in the State Capitol of a deep southern state.

General Manager: Krone-Olim Management, Inc.
Press: Howard Atlee, David Roggensack, Irene Gandy
Stage Manager: Charles Roden

* Closed Nov. 23, 1969 after 94 performances.

Bert Andrews Photos

Conard Fowkes, Lester Rawlins Top: Rawlins, Louise Stubbs, Joseph Attles

Top: Jeannette Dubois, Douglas Turner, Lester Rawlins

ACTORS PLAYHOUSE

Opened Monday, September 8, 1969.*
Darius V. Phillips presents:

SILHOUETTES

By Ted Harris; Director, John Camilla; Scenery and Costumes, Joseph C. Davies; Lighting, Barbara Nollman.

CAST

Annie ....Maude Higgins
Gloria ....Ann Stafford
Chuck ....Fred Forrest
Georgie ....James Racioppi
Randy ....Bill Haislip

A Comedy presented in 2 parts. The action takes place at the present time in a New York East Village Apartment.

General Manager: James Walsh
Press: Howard Atlee, David Roggensack,
Irene Gandy
Stage Manager: Charles J. Golden

* Closed Sept. 16, 1969 after 8 performances.

Bert Andrews Photo

Top Right: Bill Haislip, Maude Higgins, James Racioppi, Ann Stafford, Fred Forrest

VILLAGE SOUTH THEATER

Opened Thursday September 11, 1969.*
Joel M. Reed presents:

THE END OF ALL THINGS NATURAL

By G. Zoffer; Director, Gail Bell; Sets and Lighting, Barry Arnold; Costumes, Mike Masse; Assistant to Producer, Alice Gunther; Production Assistant, Claudia Quest.

CAST

Professor Anton Solviev ....Nicholas Saunders
Yekaterina Lobov ....Joyce Marcella
Pyotr Kurakov ....Alexander Orfaly
Ivan Lobov ....Michael Levin
Vasili Rhizov ....David Ellin
Nadeja Uzhina ....Margaret Brewster
Klementi Radischev...............................Muni Seroff
KGB Agent ....Franc Geraci
Nicolai Simonov ....Rudy Caringi
Prosecutor ....Thomas Kubiak
Judge ....David Ellin
Understudy: Phillip Giambri

A Drama in 2 acts. The action takes place at the present time in the parlor of a Russian country home — a dacha in the village of Vyeshin, several hundred miles from Moscow and a courtroom.

Company Manager: Lawrence Rothman
Press: Max Eisen, Jeanne Gibson Merrick,
Cheryl Sue Dolby,
Stage Manager: Michael J. Frank
Assistant Stage Manager: Phillip Giambri

* Closed September 14, 1969 after 5 performances.

Right Center: Michael Levin, Nicholas Saunders, Joyce Marcella, Muni Seroff, Alexander Orfaly

Richard B. Shull, Jane Hoffman, Jack Fletcher, Dorothy Lyman, Bill Hinnant, Liz Sheridan

THE NEW THEATRE

Opened Tuesday, September 16, 1969.*
Leonard Sillman and Orin Lehman present:

THE AMERICAN HAMBURGER LEAGUE

By Norman Kline; Director, George Luscombe; Settings and Costumes, Nancy Jowsey; Lighting, Paul Sullivan; Incidental Music, Arthur Siegel; Presented by special arrangement with Toronto Workshop Productions.

CAST

Jack Fletcher
Bill Hinnant
Jane Hoffman
Dorothy Lyman
Liz Sheridan
Richard B. Shull
STANDBYS: Jane Buchanan, Henry Calvert,
Phil Piro

PROGRAM

ACT I: "Prologue," "They're Here," "They've Put Up a New Lampost," "I Know What You're Thinking," "Are You Charles Waltz?," "I Have Always Had a Plain Face," "Where's Seth?," "Once a Week I Put My Television Set on the Windowsill," "Nice Shot," "Do You Clean Birthday Suits?," "Yoo-Hoo, Raymond, Breakfast Is Ready," "Mary, I'm a Fool," "I'm a Member in Good Standing of a Reform Congregation," "Charles, This Isn't Easy for Me to Have to Say," "All Those Who Want Their Hamburger Rare, Raise Their Hand."

ACT II: "Are You Waiting for Vito?," "I Have These Pains in My Back," "Who Would Write Something Like That?," "Are You Coming Bowling with Me Tonight, or Not?," "Candlelight Graces a Woman's Face," "Who Is It? The Grocery Boy," "I Have Come to the Conclusion that I Am Unable to Compete in the Normal Labor Market," "Where Did You Come From?," "Closeup of Jack Entering Room," "No-Cal, Norma?"

A Revue in two acts and 25 scenes.

Press: Howard Atlee, David Roggensack,
Irene Gandy
Stage Manager: Bud Coffey

* Closed Sept. 16, 1969 after 1 performance.

Bert Andrews Photos

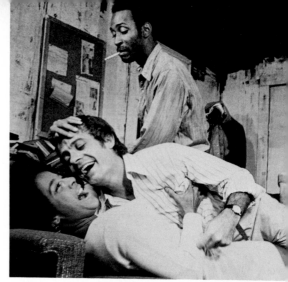

STAGE 73

Opened Monday, September 15, 1969.*
(Moved to New Theatre Oct. 7, 1969)
Harlan P. Kleiman presents:

THE OFAY WATCHER

By Frank Cucci; Director, Jerry Adler; Settings and Lighting, Dahl Delu; Costumes, Yvonne Bronowicz; Associate Producers, Jeffrey C. Reiss, Patrick McNamara; Production Assistant, Martha Larson; A Kleiman—Reiss Production.

CAST

Rufus...Cleavon Little
Bruce Jennings.....................................Terry Kiser
Daisy...Billie Allen

A Drama in 3 acts. The action takes place at the present time in Bruce's apartment in the East Village in New York.

Company Manager: Joanne Malley
Press: Robert Ganshaw, John Prescott
Stage Manager: Martha Knight

* Closed Oct. 19, 1969 after 40 performances.

Bert Andrews Photos

Billie Allen, Terry Kiser, Cleavon Little
(also top right)

IDAN SQUARE PLAYHOUSE

ened Thursday, September 18, 1969.*
rmit Bloomgarden in association with Com-
nwealth United Entertainment and Jona-
an Burrows presents:

ELLO AND GOODBYE

athol Fugard; Director, Barney Simon;
ion Design, William Ritman.

CAST

....Martin Sheen
....Colleen Dewhurst

gi-comedy in 2 acts. The action takes place
he summer of 1965 in Port Elizabeth, South

Company Manager: Al Isaac
Press: Max Eisen, Cheryl Sue Dolby
Stage Manager: Patrick J. Latronica

Oct. 26, 1969 after 45 performances.

Martin Sheen, Colleen Dewhurst

JAN HUS PLAYHOUSE

Opened Wednesday, September 24, 1969.*
David Black presents:

SALVATION

Book, Music, and Lyrics by Peter Link and C. C. Courtney; Director, Paul Aaron; Designed by Joan Larkey; Dance Movement, Kathryn Posin; Music Arrangements, Kirk Nurock; Conductor, Jon Bauman; Played by Nobody Else; Production Supervisor, Charles Gray; Production Assistants, Mary Anne Newfield, Ellen Rapaport; Original Cast Album on Capital Records.

CAST

Ranee	Yolande Bavan
Farley	Peter Link † 1
Monday	C. C. Courtney † 2
Mark	Joe Morton
Boo	Boni Enten
Dierdre	Annie Rachel
Betty Lou	Marta Heflin † 3
LeRoy	Chapman Roberts † 4

MUSICAL NUMBERS: Overture, "Salvation," "In Between," "1001," "Honest Confession Is Good For the Soul," "Ballin'," "Let the Moment Slip By," "Gina," "Stockhausen Potpourri," "If You Let Me Make Love to You, Then Why Can't I Touch You?," "There Ain't No Flies on Jesus," "Deadalus," "Deuteronomy XVII Verse 2," "For Ever," "Footloose Youth and Fancy-Free," "Schwartz," "Let's Get Lost in Now," "Back to Genesis," "Tomorrow Is the First Day of the Rest of My Life."

A Rock Musical in 19 scenes without intermission.

General Manager: Jose Vega
Company Manager: R. Tyler Garchell, Jr.
Press: Gifford/Wallace, Tom Trenkle
Stage Managers: Curt Dempster, Judy Fisher

* Closed Apr. 19, 1970 after 239 performances.
† Succeeded by: 1. Clifford Lipson, 2. Barry Bostwick, Jim Hall, 3. Bette Midler, 4. Northern Calloway.

Kenn Duncan Photos

Yolande Bavan, Boni Enten, Joe Morton
Top: Annie Rachel

Peter Link, Joe Morton

FORTUNE THEATER

Opened Monday, October 6, 1969.*
Linda Otto presents:

CALLING IN CRAZY

By Henry Bloomstein; Director, Robert Greenwald; Settings, Kert Lundell; Lighting, F. Mitchell Dana; Special Sound, James Reichert; Assistant to the Producer, Susan Stoller; Production Assistant, Harry Chittenden.

CAST

Dutch	Rick Lenz
Violet	Jill Clayburgh
Mrs. Ortega	Kay Carney
The Applicant	Ed Preble
Nerissa	Marcia Wallace
A Company Official	Ed Preble
Quester	Ed Preble

A Comedy in 2 acts. The action takes place in 1947 in Dutch's apartment, and the offices of Mrs. Ortega, Nerissa, and Mr. Bradford.

General Managers: George Thorn
Leonard A. Mulhern
Press: Robert Ganshaw, John Prescott
Stage Manager: Mary Porter Hall

* Closed October 19, 1969 after 15 performances.

Left: Jill Clayburgh, Rick Lenz

EASTSIDE PLAYHOUSE

Opened Tuesday, October 14, 1969.*
Bernard Sahlins presents:

FROM THE SECOND CITY

Director, David Lynn; "Flower Song" Lyrics by Sandy Holt; Setting, Steven Holmes; Sound and Lighting, Gary Harris; Composer and Musical Director, Fred Kaz; An Arts and Leisure Corp. Production; Production Assistant, Vincent Cangiano.

CAST

J. J. Barry
Murphy Dunne
Martin Harvey Friedberg
Burt Heyman
Pamela Hoffman
Ira Miller
Carol Robinson

A Satirical Revue devised by the company.

General Manager: William Craver
Press: Merle Debuskey, Faith Geer, M. J. Boyer
Stage Manager: Harvey M. Schaps

* Closed Nov. 9, 1969 after 31 performances.

Friedman-Abeles Photos

Right Center: J. J. Barry, Martin Harvey Friedberg, Murphy Dunne, Pamela Hoffman, Ira Miller, Carol Carol Robinson, Burt Heyman

Carol Robinson, Ira Miller, Pamela Hoffman

99

MERCURY THEATRE

Opened Wednesday, October 8, 1969.*
Josh Productions in association with Moe
Weise present:

A WHISTLE IN THE DARK

By Thomas Murphy; Director, Arvin Brown;
Settings, Kert Lundell; Lighting, Ron Wallace;
Costumes, Vanessa James; Production Assistant,
Maribeth Gilbert.

CAST

Harry Carney	Charles Cioffi
Hugo Carney	Anthony Palmer
Betty Carney	Roberta Maxwell †1
Mush O'Reilly	Dermot McNamara
Iggy Carney	Don Plumley †2
Michael Carney	Michael McGuire
Michael Carney, Sr.	Stephen Elliott †3
Des Carney	Tom Atkins

A Drama in 3 acts. The action takes place at the
present time in the living-room of Michael Carney's
house in Coventry, England.

General Managers: Gugleotti-Black
Company Manager: J. Ross Stewart
Press: Max Eisen, Lenny Traube,
Cheryl Sue Dolby
Stage Manager: James O'Connell

* Closed Jan. 4, 1970 after 100 performances.

† Succeeded by: 1. Barbara Hayes, 2. William
Devane, 3. Richard McKenzie.

**Roberta Maxwell, Michael McGuire Top:
Tom Atkins, Anthony Palmer, Charles Cioffi,
Stephen Elliott**

ROOSEVELT THEATRE

Opened Sunday October 12, 1969.*
The Yiddish Repertory Theater presents:

THE TREES DIE STANDING

By Alejandro Casona; Adapted and Directed
by Ida Kaminska; Production Assistant, Victor
Melman; Scenery, James E. French.

CAST

Helen	Rachela Relis
Priest	David Ellin
Juggler	Jaime Lewin
Marta-Isabel	Ruth Kaminska-Turkow
Mr. Fernando Balboa	Marian Melman
Beggar	Chaim Towber
The Hunter	George Guidall
Director	Karol Latowicz
Genovfa	Helen Blay
Felissa	Sylvia Tylbor
The Grandmother	Ida Kaminska
The Stranger	Jack Rechtzeit

A Drama in 3 acts. The action takes place at
the present time in the office of the Director, and
in the home of Mr. and Mrs. Balboa.

General and Company Manager:
Lawrence Rothman
Press: Max Eisen, Benjamin Rothman,
Cheryl Sue Dolby
Stage Manager: Chaim Towber

* Closed December 14, 1969 after 72 performances.

Ida Kaminska Marian Melman, Ruth Kaminska
Top: Helen Blay, Ida Kaminska

101

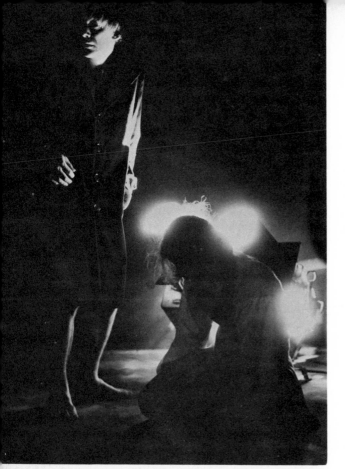

WASHINGTON SQUARE
METHODIST CHURCH

Opened Thursday, October 16, 1969.*
The Brooklyn Academy of Music in association with Ninon Tallon Karlweis and the Committee to Welcome the Polish Lab Theatre presents in repertory:

THE LABORATORY THEATRE OF POLAND
Jerzy Grotowski, Director

THE CONSTANT PRINCE

Scenario and Direction, Jerzy Grotowski; Calderon's Text Adapted by J. Slowacki; Costumes, Waldemar Krygier; Scenery, Jerzy Gurawski; Literary Adviser, Ludwik Flaszen.

CAST

The Constant Prince ....Ryszard Cieslak
King ....Antoni Jaholkowski
Fenixana ....Rene Mirecka
Tarudant ....Zygmunt Molik
Mooley ....Zbigniew Cynkutis
Henri, the prisoner...................Stanislaw Scierski

Opened Tuesday, November 4, 1969.*

ACROPOLIS

Scenario and Direction, Jerzy Grotowski; Based on text by Stanislaw Wyspianski; Scenery, Jerzy Gurawski; Costumes and Properties, Jozef Szajna.

CAST

Jacob-Priam, chief of the dying tribe
.........Zygmunt Molik
Rebecca-Cassandra ....Rena Mirecka
Isaac-Troyan Guardian ....Antoni Jaholkowski
Esau-Hector ....Ryszard Cieslak
Angel-Paris ....Zbigniew Cynkutis
Leah-Helen of Troy.........Stanislaw Scierski
and Andrzej Paluchiewicz

Opened Tuesday, November 18, 1969.*

APOCALYPSIS CUM FIGURIS

Scenario and Direction, Jerzy Grotowski; Assistant Director, Ryszard Cieslak; Literary Adviser, Ludwik Flaszen; Costumes, Waldemar Krygier; Citations from The Bible, Dostoyevsky, T. S. Eliot, Simone Weil.

CAST

Simon Peter...........................Antoni Jaholkowski
Judas.................................Zygmunt Molik
Lazarus.............................Zbigniew Cynkutis
Mary Magdalene ....Elizabeth Albahaca
John...............................Stanislaw Scierski
The Simpleton ....Ryszard Cieslak

* Closed Dec. 15, 1969 after 68 performances.

Bernand and Zaiks Photos

"Acropolis"

Rena Mirecka, Ryszard Cieslak in "The Constant Prince" Top: Cieslak, Elizabeth Albahaca in "Apocalypsis"

BOUWERIE LANE THEATRE

Opened Sunday, October 19, 1969.*
Swen Swenson and Michael Devereaux present:

AND PUPPY DOG TAILS

By David Gaard; Director, Michael Devereaux; Set, Harry Pinkerton; Lighting, James Greek; Production Supervisor, M. Sanford Kaplan; Production Assistants, Dolores Towey, Rita Southworth, David Rolhuff.

CAST

John Hendrix	George Reeder
Tommy Spencer	Edward Dunn
Bud Kelcorn	Ken Kliban
Carey-Lee Dunbar	Horton Willis

A Comedy in 2 acts and 4 scenes. The action takes place at the present time in John and Carey-Lee's apartment on the upper East Side of New York City.

Press: Max Eisen, Cheryl Sue Dolby
Stage Manager: James Greek

* Closed Jan. 11, 1970 after 141 performances. Previews were presented in the Astor Place Theatre from Sept. 17 through Sept. 28, 1969, before moving to Bouwerie Lane.

Ken Kliban, George Reeder Top: Kliban, Edward Dunn, Reeder, Horton Willis

TAMBELLINI'S GATE THEATRE

Opened Sunday, October 19, 1969.*
Bacherway Productions in association with
Jay Fiondella presents:

GO FLY A KITE!
(The Story of an Uncommon Man)

Entire Production Conceived by Fredd Wayne;
Additional Dialogue, Sidney Dorfman; Lighting,
Marshall Spiller; Techincal Director, Steven Holmes

CAST

Fredd Wayne

A One-Man show extracted from the works of
Benjamin Franklin, and presented in two acts.

General Manager: Paul B. Berkowsky
Company Manager: Bob MacDonald
Press: Bill Doll Associates
Stage Manager: Steven Holmes

* Closed Oct. 26, 1969 after 8 performances.

Fredd Wayne as Benjamin Franklin

ASTOR PLACE THEATRE

Opened Sunday, October 26, 1969.*
Henry Fownes, Frank Bessell, Bruce Hoover,
with Leonard Mulhern and George Thorn
present:

CRIMES OF PASSION

By Joe Orton; Director, Michael Kahn; Settings,
William Ritman; Lighting, Richard Nelson; Cos-
tumes, Jane Greenwood; Musical Director, Conrad
Susa.

CAST

"The Ruffian on the Stair"
Joyce ....Sasha Von Scherler
Mike ....Richard A. Dysart
Wilson ....David Birney

"The Erpingham Camp"
Erpingham ....Richard A. Dysart
Chief Redcoat Riley ....John Tillinger
Lou....................................Sasha Von Scherler
Ted ....Tom Tarpey
Eileen ....Lynn Milgrim
Kenny ....David Birney
W. E. Harrison ....James Cahill
Padre ....Tom Lacy
Jessie Mason ....Bette Henritze
Redcoats and Campers....................Zoe Kamitses,
    Josef Warik, Catherine Wright, Mark MacCauley

UNDERSTUDIES: Erpingham, Mike, Tom Lacy;
Jessie, Joyce, Zoe Kamitses; Kenny, Wilson, Josef
Warik; Riley, Tom Tarpey; Eileen, Catherine
Wright; Ted, Harrison, Mark MacCauley.

General Managers: George Thorn,
Leonard A. Mulhern
Company Manager: Frank Hartenstein
Press: Howard Atlee, David Roggensack,
Stanley F. Kaminsky, Irene Gandy
Stage Managers: Stephen Sobel, Josef Warik

* Closed Nov. 2, 1969 after 9 performances.

CASTLE THEATRE

Opened Monday, October 27, 1969.*
Gallery Productions presents:

THE HAUNTED HOST

By Robert Patrick; Director, Eric Concklin;
Scenery, Martin L. H. Reymert; Lighting, David
Adams; Music and Lyrics, Robert Patrick; Music
and Lyrics Arranged and Performed by Jon Bau-
man, Brad Burg; Assistant to the Producers,
Julia Willis.

CAST

Jay, The Host....................................Neil Flanagan
Guest....................................Joseph Pichette

A play in 2 acts. The action takes place in the
living room of Jay's Greenwich Village apartment.

General Manager: Edmonstone Thompson, Jr.
Press: Reginald Denenholz
Stage Manager: Judith Kayser

* Closed November 2, 1969 after 8 performances.

Eeva Photo

Joseph Pichette, Neil Flanagan
Left Center: David Birney, Bette Henritze

MARTINIQUE THEATRE

Opened Monday, October 20, 1969.*
Lawrence Goossen and Susan Richardson
present:

A SCENT OF FLOWERS

By James Saunders; Director, Brian Murray;
Scenery, Ed Wittstein; Lighting, David F. Segal;
Costumes, Diedre Cartier; Producing Associate,
Melinda Hamilton; Production Assistant, Jane
Neufeld; Produced by the J/B Company.

CAST

Zoe..Katharine Houghton
Fred ....Jeremiah Sullivan† 1
Sid...John Colenback† 2
Godfrey...John Glover
Scrivens...Roderick Cook
Grandmother ....Donna Barry
Edgar ....Sydney Walker
Agnes ....Carolyn Coates
David ....James Noble† 3

STANDBYS: Zoe, Agnes, Jo Henderson; Fred,
Sid, Godfrey, Montgomery Davis; Scrivens, Edgar,
David, Nick Savian.

A Drama in 3 acts.

Press: Max Eisen, Cheryl Sue Dolby
Stage Manager: Barbara Tuttle

* Closed Dec. 21, 1969 after 72 performances.
† Succeeded by: 1. Montgomery Davis, 2. George
Backman, 3. Nick Savian

Martha Swope Photos

**Left: Katharine Houghton, John Glover
Top: Katharine Houghton, Carolyn Coates,
James Noble**

**Jeremiah Sullivan, Katharine Houghton,
John Colenback**

Roderick Cook, Katharine Houghton

STAGE 73

Opened Wednesday, October 22, 1969.*
Kenneth Waissman and Maxine Fox present:

FORTUNE AND MEN'S EYES

By John Herbert; Director, Sal Mineo; Setting and Costumes, Alan Kimmel; Lighting, Ken Billington; Special Sounds, Gary Harris.

CAST

Rocky	Bartholomew Miro, Jr.
Mona	Jeremy Stockwell
Queenie	Michael Greer†
Guard	Joe Dorsey
Smitty	Mark Shannon
Catsolino	George Ryland

STANDBYS: Queenie, Jesse Deane; Smitty, Rocky, Mona, Christopher Glason

A Drama in 3 acts. The action takes place at the present time in a boy's prison.

General Manager: Edward H. Davis
Press: Betty Lee Hunt, Henry Luhrman, Harriett Trachtenberg
Stage Managers: Gigi Cascio, George Ryland

* Closed May 10, 1970 after 231 performances. For original NY production, see THEATRE WORLD, Vol. 23.
† Succeeded by Jesse Deane, then Robert Redding.

Kenn Duncan Photos

**Left: Jeremy Stockwell,
Mark Shannon, Joe A. Dorsey**

Bartholomew Miro, Jr., Mark Shannon

Michael Greer

PROVINCETOWN PLAYHOUSE

Opened Tuesday, October 28, 1969.*
JanMar Productions, Ltd. presents:

ROSE

By Emanuel Fried; Director, Charles Olsen;
Scenery and Costumes, Misha Petrow; Lighting,
Michael C. Davidson; Sound, Gary Harris; Pro-
duction Assistant, John Welsh.

CAST

Rose Elmstead	Nadyne Turner
Michael Milovich	Gil Rogers
Ellen Milovich	Judy Jordan
Bertram Tompkins	Raymond Thorne
Mr. Elmstead	David Clarke

UNDERSTUDIES: Mike, Bert, Mr. Elmstead,
Andrew Johns; Rose, Ellen, Annette Hunt.

A Play in 3 acts. The action takes place between
1938 and 1958 in Upstate New York and in New
York City.

General Manager: Lily Turner
Press: Dorothy Ross
Stage Manager: Stephen Jarrett

* Closed Nov. 2, 1969 after 8 performances.

Bert Andrews Photo

David Clarke, Nadyne Turney

**Emilio Rodriguez, Lolina Gutierrez,
Miriam Rodriguez in "La Difunta"**

THEATRE EAST

Opened Friday, October 31, 1969.*
The Greenwich Mews Spanish Theatre,
Frances Drucker, and Gilberto Zaldivar
present:

PROGRAM OF 3 ONE-ACTERS

"La Difunta"

By Miguel De Unamuno; Director, Luz Castanos; Scenery, Manuel Yescas; Costumes, Barbara Naomi Cohen; Lighting, Ray McCutcheon.

CAST

Fernando	Emilio Rodriguez
Ramona	Inez Ivette Perez
	or Miriam Rodriguez
Marcelo	Pablo De La Torre
Dona Engracia	Lolina Gutierrez

"Cruce De Vias"

By Carlos Solorzano; Director, Luz Castanos;
Scenery, Manuel Yescas; Costumes, Barbara
Naomi Cohen; Lighting, Ray McCutcheon.

CAST

El Guardavia	Joe Vega
El Tren	Inez Ivette Perez
	or Miriam Rodriguez
El Hombre	Antonio Canal
	or Tony Diaz
La Mujer	Gay Darlene Bidart
	or Fini Moreno

"Las Pericas"

By Nelson Dorr; Director, Rene Buch; Scenery,
Zita Gomez de Kanelvas; Costumes, Barbara
Naomi Cohen; Lighting, Ray McCutcheon.

CAST

Rosita	Shelly Pearson
Panchita	Miriam Cruz
Felina	Linda Monteiro
Serafina	Milagros Horrego

Press: David Lipsky, Marian Graham,
Enrique Fernandez

* Closed Dec. 21, 1969 after 26 performances on
weekends only.

Bert Andrews Photos

**Miriam Cruz, Shelly Pearson, Linda
Monteiro, Milagros Horrego in "Las Pericas"** 107

ACTORS PLAYHOUSE

Opened Monday, November 3, 1969.*
Len Gochman, Jon Peterson, James Stevenson
present:

THE LOCAL STIGMATIC

By Heathcote Williams; Director, Arthur Storch;
Settings, Milton Duke; Lighting, Molly Friedel;
Costumes, Elaine Yokoyama; Music, Conrad Susa;
Associate Producers, Lionel Stern, C. Michael
Lane; Production Assistant, Donna Sorbello;
"Sketches," Harold Pinter.

CAST

"Sketches"

"Applicant"
Lamb ....Joseph Maher
Interviewer..Sudie Bond

"Interview"
Jakes ....Joseph Maher
Interviewer ....Paul Benedict

"Last to Go"
Counterman ....Joseph Maher
News Seller ....Paul Benedict

"Request Stop"
Woman..Sudie Bond
Men...........................Joseph Maher, Paul Benedict

"That's All"
Woman..Sudie Bond
Man ....Paul Benedict

"That's Your Trouble"
Man ....Paul Benedict
Woman..Sudie Bond

"Trouble in the Works"
Wills ....Paul Benedict
Mr. Fibs ....Joseph Maher

"The Local Stigmatic"

Graham ....Al Pacino
Ray..Michael Hadge
A Man ....Paul Benedict
David ....Joseph Maher

Presented in 6 scenes.

General Managers: Gatchell and Neufeld
Press: Max Eisen, Jeanne Gibson Merrick,
Warren Pincus
Stage Managers: Lawrence Spiegel, Jayme Daniel
* Closed Nov. 9, 1969 after 8 performances.

Kenn Duncan Photos

Al Pacino, Michael Hadge

HUDSON WEST

Opened Wednesday, November 5, 1969.*
Rick Hobard presents:

RONDELAY

Book and Lyrics, Jerry Douglas; Based on "La
Ronde" by Arthur Schnitzler; Music, Hal Jordan;
Sets and Costumes, Raoul Pene Du Bois; Lighting,
Neil Peter Jampolis; Director, William Francisco;
Musical Numbers Staged by Jacques d'Amboise;
Musical Direction and Vocal Arrangements, Karen
Gustafson; Orchestrations, Philip J. Lang; As-
sociate Producers, Martin Hodas, James Jennings;
Production Coordinator, F. Mitchell Dana; Pro-
duction Assistant, Vincent Cangiano; Hairstylist,
Ted Azar.

CAST

The Whore ....Barbara Lang
The Soldier ....Terence Monk
The Parlor Maid ....Carole Demas
The Student......................................Peter York
The Young Wife ....Louise Clay
The Professor...................................Dillon Evans
The Sweet Thing..............................Barbara Minkus
The Poet ....Shawn Elliott
The Diva...Gwyda DonHowe
The Count ....Paxton Whitehead

CHORUS: Andrea Fulton, Betty Lynn, Maureen
Maloney, Susan Schevers, Brown Bradley, John
Kordel, Stephen Lehew, Terrence McKerrs

UNDERSTUDIES: Whore, Andrea Fulton; Maid,
Betty Lynn; Wife, Susan Schevers; Sweet Thing,
Maureen Maloney; Diva, Andrea Fulton; Soldier,
Stephen Lehew; Student, Terrence McKerrs; Pro-
fessor, Brown Bradley; Poet, John Kordel; Count,
Brown Bradley

MUSICAL NUMBERS: "Rondelay," "Lovers of
the Lamplight," "One Hundred Virgins," "Angel
Face," "Tonight You Dance with Me," "Easy,"
"The First Kiss," "Afterward," "She Deserves
Me," "Closer," "Honor," "The Answer," "Failure,"
"Success," "The Days of My Youth," "I've Got
a Surprise for You," "Reidhof's," "Champagne,"
"Dessert," "Masquerade," "When Lovers Fall in
Love," "What You Are," "A Castle in India," "Back
to Nature," "Saint Genesius," "Opera Star," "Not
So Young Love," "Auf Wiedersehen," "Gusto,"
"Happy Ending," "I'll Show You the World To-
night," "Reflections," "Before Breakfast," "Give
and Take."

A Musical in 2 acts and 10 scenes. The action
takes place in Vienna in 1905 and 1906.

General Manager: William Craver
Company Manager: Janet Spencer
Press: Max Eisen, Cheryl Sue Dolby
Stage Managers: Frank Hamilton, R. L. Middleton
* Closed Nov. 14, 1969 after 11 performances.

Barbara Lang

VILLAGE SOUTH THEATRE

Opened Monday November 17, 1969.*
Michael Ellis and Samuel Bronstein present:

WHO'S HAPPY NOW?

By Oliver Hailey; Director, Stanley Prager;
Music, Michael Barr; Lyrics, Dion McGregor;
Scenery, Howard Barker; Costumes, Gertha Brock;
Lighting, Shirley Prendergast; Technical Director,
Calvin Leasure.

CAST

Richard Hallen ....Ken Kercheval
Pop ....Stuart Germain
Mary Hallen.....................................Teresa Wright
Horse Hallen....................................Robert Darnell
Faye Precious ....Rue McClanahan
Understudy: Mary, Faye, Connie Van Ess

A Drama in 3 acts. The action takes place in a
Texas bar between 1941 and 1955.

General Manager: Edward H. Davis
Press: Michael Alpert
Stage Manager: Otis Bigelow

* Closed Dec. 21, 1969 after 24 performances.

Bert Andrews Photos

ht: **Stuart Germain, Robert Darnell, Ken Kercheval**
Below: **Germaine, Darnell, Rue McClanahan,
Teresa Wright**

Franz Matter, Maria Sebaldt in "Philipp Hotz"

BARBIZON-PLAZA THEATRE

Opened Wednesday, November 19, 1969.*
The Gert Von Gontard Foundation under
the auspices of the Swiss Ambassadors to
the United States and Canada present the
ZURICH SCHAUSPIELTRUPPE in:

THE MARRIAGE OF
MR. MISSISSIPPI

By Friedrich Durrenmatt; Director, Robert
Freitag; Settings and Costumes, Theo Schweizer;
Technical Director, Edwin Schaedlich; Masks,
Gertrud Krull.

CAST

Frederic Rene Saint-Claude..............Fred Haltiner
A Maid...Susi Aeberhard
Anastasia ....Marla Becker
Florestan Mississippi ....Robert Freitag
Diego ....George Weiss
Bodo von Uebelohe-Zabernsee...........Franz Matter
Professor Ueberhuber ....Otto Freitag

Opened Wednesday, November 26, 1969.

"PHILIPP HOTZ"
and
"THE FIREBUGS"

By Max Frisch; Directors, Fred Haltiner, Maria
Becker; Settings and Costumes, Theo Schweizer.

CAST

"Philipp Hotz"

Philipp Hotz ....Robert Freitag
Girl ....Susi Aeberhard
Old Porter ....George Weiss
Young Porter ....Guido von Salis
Wilfrid...Franz Matter
Dorli..Maria Sebaldt
Clarissa ....Maria Becker
Customs Agent....................................Otto Freitag

"The Firebugs"

Herr Biedermann...............................Franz Matter
Anna ....Susi Aeberhard
Schmitz..Robert Freitag
Babette ....Maria Sebaldt
Eisenring ....Fred Haltiner
Policeman ....Otto Freitag
Mrs. Knechtling ....Maria Becker
Ph. D ....Guido von Salis

* Closed Nov. 30. 1969.

109

BROOKLYN ACADEMY OF MUSIC

Opened Wednesday, November 19, 1969.*
Chelsea Theater Center (Robert Kalfin, Artistic Director; Michael David, Executive Director) in association with Woodie King presents:

SLAVE SHIP

By LeRoi Jones; Director, Gilbert Moses; Design, Eugene Lee; Choreography, Oliver Jones; Music, Archie Shepp, Gilbert Moses; Production Coordinator, Burl Hash; Sound, Paul Jaeger, Mary Lou Lehman; Additional Music, Leopoldo Fleming, Richard Fells, John Griggs, Bob Ralston, Michael Ridley, Charles Davis; Yoruba Consultant, Mr. Ogundipe; Musical Director, Leopoldo Fleming; Maskes, Hilary Scharrad; Yoruba Music Consultant, Joe Comadore.

CAST

Atowoda, Auctioneer	Frank Adu
Tawa	Gwen D. Anderson
Akoowa, Modern Preacher	Preston Bradley
Iyalosa (Tsia)	Lee Chamberlin
Akano	Bill Duke
Segilola	Jackie Earley
Adufe	Phyllis Espinosa
Olala	Ralph Espinosa
Dademi	Maxine Griffith
Lalu, Plantation Tom	Garrett Morris
Salako, Rev. Turner	Tim Pelt
Sailor	C. Robert Scott
Noliwe	Seret Scott
Imani	Marilyn Thomas
Oyo	Reeta White

A Drama presented without intermission. The action takes place in the hold of a ship.

Press: Saul Richman
Stage Managers: Peter Turner, David Eidenberg, Joan Lebowitz, Laurence Cohen

* Closed Jan. 11, 1970 and re-opened Tuesday, Jan. 13, 1970 at Washington Square Methodist Church. Cast walked out Jan. 23 in protest to physical conditions of theatre, returned on Jan. 27, and was closed Jan. 28, 1970 because of a fire.

Bert Andrews Photo

NEW LINCOLN THEATRE

Opened Tuesday, December 2, 1969.*
Lee Hessel and Sam Fleishman present:

THE WAY IT IS!!!

Conceived and Written by Jerry Clark; Music, Buddy Bregman; Lyrics, Michael Greer, Kelly Montgomery; Directed and Staged by Buddy Bregman; Choreography, Eddie Gasper; Settings, Mike Goldberg; Costumes, Gloria Gresham; Lighting, Joe Pacitti; Vocal Arrangements and Musical Direction, Jack Lee; Orchestrations, Wally Harper.

CAST

Jacqueline Britt
Deborah Bush
Jerry Clark
Gene Foote
Milton Earl Forrest
Ann Hodges
David Lile
Renee Lippin
Veronica Redd

ACT I: "Adam and Eve," "Superman," "Does America Need a Third Party," "Obscene Phone Call," "Goldberg's Gripe," "Smut Mail," "Generation Gap/I See in You," "Orgy," "Sexual Anonymous," "Shakespeare Today," "The Nude-Nik Hora," "Campus Life," "Pornography," "Tune of the Hickory Stick," "Could I Be Kidding Myself," "The Vice President and the Call Girl," " 'Tis the Season," "Times Have Changed," "My Ghost Writer," "The Brand New Fourth Estate."

ACT II: "Local Hookers' Local," "Intermission Interviews," "I Feel So Lost," "Sexicare," "Operations Trade-In," "The Producers," "A Little Something on the Side," "Film Discussion Show," "Praise to the Blessed Builders," "Apollo 69," "Graffiti," "A Nude Encounter," "The Way It Is."

An Adult Musical in 2 acts and 33 scenes.

General Managers: Solomon Posnack, Barry Hoffman
Company Manager: Ethelyn Thrasher
Press: Dorothy Ross, Ruth Cage
Stage Manager: Clifford Annon

* Closed Jan. 20, 1970 after 60 previews only.

"Slave Ship"

PERFORMING GARAGE

Opened Thursday, November 20, 1969.*
The Performance Group presents:

MAKBETH

By Richard Schechner and the Performance Group; Based on play by William Shakespeare; Director, Richard Schechner; Setting, Jerry Rojo; Costumes, Jerry Rojo, Lewis Rampino; Music Composed and Directed by Paul Epstein; Technical Adviser, Ed Madden; Maze Environment, Brooks McNamara.

CAST

Banquo	Remi Barclay
Macduff	Stephen Borst
Dark Power	Jason Bosseau
Duncan	Tom Crawley
Dark Power	Richard Dia
Makbeth	William Finley
Dark Power	Joan MacIntosh
Malcolm	William Shepard +
Lady Makbeth	Ceil Smith

Stage Managers: Vicki Strang, Phil Phelan

† Succeeded by Ernie Schank.

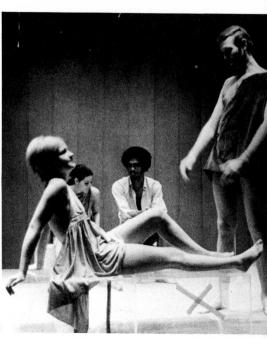

Deborah Bush, Jacqueline Britt, Milton Earl Forrest, David Lisle

Bert Andrews Photo

THE NEW THEATRE

Opened Wednesday, December 3, 1969.*
Leonard S. Field and N. Lawrence Golden
present:

LITTLE BOXES

By John Bowen; Director, Perry Bruskin;
Scenery, Helen Pond, Herbert Senn; Costumes,
Pamela Schofield; Lighting, Molly Friedel; Staff
Assistant, Maureen Anderman.

CAST

"The Coffee Lace"

Lilly	Leona Maricle
Mr. Davis	Jon Beam
Sonny	Tony Tanner
Iris	Beulah Garrick
Rose	Lucie Lancaster
Jimmy	Norman Barrs
Johnny	Frederic Tozare

"Trevor"

Jane Kempton	Jo Henderson
Sarah Lawrence	Jennifer Tilston
Trevor	Tony Tanner
Mrs. Lawrence	Rosalind Ross
Mr. Lawrence	Norman Barrs
Mrs. Kempton	Beulah Garrick
Mr. Kempton	Frederic Tozare
Mr. Hudson	Dillon Evans

UNDERSTUDIES: Richard Flanders, Susan Leek

A Comedy in two parts. The action takes place
at the present time in the top-floor flat of a reno-
vated Victorian House.

General Manager: Ben Rosenberg
Company Manager: Peter Neufeld
Press: Seymour Krawitz, Ruth D. Smuckler
Stage Manager: Janet Beroza

* Closed Dec. 14, 1969 after 15 performances.

Friedman-Abeles Photo

Top Right: Norman Barrs, Tony Tanner, Jo Henderson,
Jennifer Tilston

Peter DeAnda Right Center: Robert Loggia,
Oliver Clark, Tresa Hughes

SHERIDAN SQUARE PLAYHOUSE

Opened Sunday, December 7, 1969.*
Capricorn Co., Kleiman-Reiss Productions,
and Studley-Traub present:

PASSING THROUGH
FROM EXOTIC PLACES

By Ronald Ribman; Director, Eugene Lesser;
Sets, C. Murawski; Lighting, William Mintzer;
Costumes, Joseph Aulisi; Production Assistant,
Martha Larson.

CAST

"The Son Who Hunted Tigers in Jakarta"

Charles Ferris	Vincent Gardenia
Edna	Tresa Hughes
Mr. Sweeney	Robert Loggia

Intermission

"Sunstroke"

Tomqualaturatu	Peter DeAnda
Arthur Goldblatt	Oliver Clark
Mr. Aldous Shawcross	Robert Loggia
Mrs. Shawcross	Tresa Hughes

Intermission

"The Burial of Esposito"

Nick Esposito	Vincent Gardenia
His wife	Tresa Hughes
His brother-in-law	Robert Loggia
His son	Jay Hammer

Company Manager: Jeffrey H. Knox
Press: Robert Ganshaw, John Prescott
Stage Manager: Martha Knight

* Closed Dec. 28, 1969 after 25 performances.

Bert Andrews Photos

**Elayne Barat, Herve Villechaize
in "The Moondreamers"**

Opened Monday, December 8, 1969.*
Peter Moreau, Herschel Waxman, Maury Kanbar present:

THE MOONDREAMERS

Written and Directed by Julie Bovasso; Designed by Bernard X. Bovasso; Lighting, John P. Dodd, Keith Micharl, Lee Fitzgerald; Technical Director, Daffi; Costomes, Randy Barcelo; Musical Director, LaMar Alford.

CAST

Soldiers	Louis Ramos, Alan Wynroth, Alan Harvey
Stockbrokers	Chris Christianson, Carl Wilson, Wes Williams
The Bride, tourist, squaw	Vincenza DiMaggio, Constantine Poutous
Indian, Gold Star Mother	Laura Simms, Ching Yeh, Evan Ritter
Rene Utray	Tom Rosica
Sandra, his wife	Jane Sanford
Mimi, the Dreamboat Girl	Zina Jasper
Doublemint Opera Trio	Lamar Alford, Maria D'Elia, Ella Luxembourg
The Mother	Jean David
The Lawyer	Ted Henning
The Doctor	Leonard Hicks
Zen Buddhist, Geisha	Ching Yeh, Laura Simms
Salvation Army Singer	Reigh Hagen
Mick a copper	Alex Beall
Mack, another copper	Lamar Alford
Chief of Police	Herve Villechaize
Bubu, his companion	Elayne Barat
Apple Boy	Douglas Stone
Two Dancing Swells	John Bacher, Lanny Harrison
Strange Fruit Dancer	Raymond Bussey
The Groom	Fred Muselli
The Father	Alan Harvey
Ira, The Astronaut	Daffi
Man at the end	Louis Ramos
Ziegfeld Nurses, Hula Girls	Maria D'Elia, Roberta Hammer, Diedre Simone
Flappers, Vamps	Janda Lee, Mossa Ossa, Ella Luxembourg
Dancehall Boys	John Bacher, Chris Christian, Reigh Hagen
Sheiks, Space Boys	William Pierce, Carl Wilson, Lawrence Sellars

CHORUS OF CONSTANTLY PRESENT PEOPLE: Elayne Barat, Lanny Harrison, Constantine Poutous, Douglas Stone, Robert Ullman, Steven Verakus, Dennis Sokal.

"A Demonic American Saga with funky music and a truly rotten chorus."

General Manager: Edward H. Davis
Press: Seymour Krawitz, Ruth D. Smuckler
Stage Managers: Wes Jensky, Reigh Hagen

* Closed Dec. 28, 1969 after 24 performances.

Opened Monday, December 15, 1969.*
John Bernard Myers in association with Bob Cato presents:

GERTRUDE STEIN'S FIRST READER

Conceived and Directed by Herbert Machiz; Words and Plays, Gertrude Stein; Music and Musical Adaptation, Ann Sternberg; Set, Kendall Shaw; Lighting, Patrika Brown; Production Assistants, Leonard Stein, Digger St. John, Charles Somers; Hairstylist, Joe Patton.

CAST

Michael Anthony
Joy Garrett
Frank Giordano
Sandra Thornton
Ann Sternberg at the piano

PROGRAM

ACT I: "Sunshine," "Wildflowers," "A Dog," "Writing Lesson," "Johnny and Jimmy," "The Blackberry Vine," "Big Bird," "The Three Sisters Who Are Not Sisters," "Be Very Careful."

ACT II: "New World," "Jenny," "How They Do, Do," "Soldier," "Baby Benjamin," "In a Garden."

General Manager: Malcolm Allen
Press: Betty Lee Hunt, Henry Luhrman, Harriett Trachtenberg
Stage Manager: Douglas Wallace

* Closed Jan. 18, 1970 after 40 performances.

**Joy Garrett, Michael Anthony, Frank Giordano,
Sandra Thornton, Ann Sternberg at piano**

PLAYERS THEATRE

Opened Tuesday, December 9, 1969.•
(Moved to Actors Playhouse April 14, 1970)
Sanford Farber and Eddie White present:

SUMMERTREE

By Ron Cowen; Director, Stephen Glassman;
Settings, Janet Murray; Lighting, David F. Segal;
Production Assistant, Doug Laidlaw.
CAST

Young Man	Lenny Baker
Little Boy	Scott Jacoby†1
Mother	Janet Ward
Father	Hy Anzell†2
Girl	Elizabeth Walker†3
Soldier	Hector Troy

A Play in two acts. The action takes place at the present time.

Press: David Rothenberg, Joe Cali
Stage Manager: Iris Merlis

* Closed May 17, 1970 after 184 performances
† Succeeded by: 1. Michael Bersell, Michael Vahanian, 2. Maurey Cooper, 3. Linda DeCoff

Friedman-Abeles Photos

Left: Lenny Baker, Elizabeth Walker

Hy Anzell, Janet Ward

Scott Jacoby, Janet Ward

CIRCLE IN THE SQUARE

Opened Tuesday December 16, 1969.*
Circle in the Square, Inc. (Theodore Mann,
Artistic Director; Paul Libin, Managing
Director; Gillian Walker, Associate Director)
presents:

SEVEN DAYS OF MOURNING

By Seymour Simckes; Sets, Marsha Louis Eck;
Costumes, Joseph G. Aulisi; Lighting, David F.
Segal; Production Coordinator, Kate Siegel.

CAST

Barish Shimansky	Tony Schwab
Mrs. Charpolsky	Carol Teitel
Varda Shimansky (Ma)	Paula Laurence
Zelo Shimansky (Dad)	Stefan Gierasch
Yanina Leishik	Nancy Franklin
Feivel Leishik	David Margulies
Pildesh Leishik (Alternates)	Timmy Michaels, Jonny Allen
Vossen Gleich	Shimen Ruskin
Blindde	C. D. Creasap
Trupke	Michael Talcott
Shtummer	Michael Thompson
Datya	Camilla Ritchey

UNDERSTUDIES: Barish, Stuart Silver; Mrs.
Charpolsky, Varda, Peggy Elcar; Zelo, Michael
Thompson; Yanina, Camilla Ritchey; Feivel, C. D.
Creasap; Vossen, David Margulies.

A Fable in 2 acts.

Production Manager: Charles Hamilton
Press: Merle Debuskey, Faith Greer
Stage Manager: Owney Ryan

* Closed February 1, 1970 after 55 performances.

Friedman-Abeles Photo

Nancy Franklin, Carol Teitel, David Margulies, Shir
Ruskin, Stefan Gierasch, Paula Laurence, To
Schwab, Timmy Michaels (under table)

ACTOR'S PLAYHOUSE

Opened Wednesday, December 17, 1969.*
Roy Franklyn Presents:

THE BROWNSTONE URGE

By Gladys S. Foster and Allan Rieser; Director,
Tom Hinton; Sets and Costumes, Ken Lewis;
Lighting, Tony Quintavalla.

CAST

Mr. MacCumber	Martin Starkland
Salley Tippet	Donna Wandrey
Randy Tippet	Donn Whyte
David Gresham	Ron Burrus
Skip	Reggie Baff
Inspector	Ci Herzog
Fritz Gribbleman	Frank Torren
Desiree	Jillian Lindig
Cora Trevelyan	Estelle Omens

A Comedy in 3 acts. The action takes place at
the present time in the livingroom of a New York
brownstone.

Press: Sol Jacobson, Lewis Harmon
Stage Manager: Howard Crampton-Smith

* Closed Dec. 21, 1969 after 7 performances.

Lee & Patrick Owens Photo

ROOSEVELT THEATRE

Opened Thursday December 25, 1969.*
The Jewish Repertory Theatre presents:

MIRELE EFROS

By Jacob Gordin; Adapted and Directed by
Ida Kaminska; Costumes, Sylvia Friedlander;
Simultaneous English Translation, Raphael Roth-
stein; Production Assistant, Victor Melman.

CAST

Mirele Efros	Ida Kaminska
Josele, her eldest son	David Ellin
Donie, her younger son	Moisha Rosenfeld
Machle, the maid	Sylvia Tylbor
Reb-Szalman, Mirele's Administrator	Marian Melman
Nuchemtse	Karol Latowicz
Chane Dwore, his wife	Rose Bozyk
Schendele, their daughter	Ruth Kaminska
Shlumele, her son	Mitchell & Neil Rouda
Cantor	Jaime Lewins
Wedding guests	Helen Blay, Rachela Relis, Leonard Whiteman, Leo Weingarten
Oksana	Helena Shmunes

A drama in 4 acts. The action takes place in
Sluck and Grodno in the second half of the 19th
century.

General & Company Manager: Lawrence Rothman
Press: Max Eisen, Benjamin Rothman,
Cheryl Sue Dolby

* Closed January 4, 1970 after 16 performances.

Left Center: Ida Kaminska, Marian Melman

Estele Omens, Donna Wandrey,
Donn Whyte, Ron Burrus

CHERRY LANE THEATRE

Opened Monday December 29, 1969.*
Sarah Beldner and Lois Wahl present:

LOVE YOUR CROOKED NEIGHBOR

By Harold J. Chapler; Director, Sidney Walters;
Sets, Fred Sammut; Lighting, Chuck Vincent;
Costumes, Robert Anderson; Music, John Bran-
cati.

CAST

Faith Detweiler .... Cara Duff-MacCormick
Ralph Nelson .... Don Warfield
Frank .... Robert Weil
Margaret Nelson .... Dale Berg
Tony Nelson .... David Kerman
Understudy: Ralph, Dick Vogell

A Comedy-Drama in 2 acts. The action takes
place at the present time in the west 70's and 80's
in New York City.

General Manager: Joseph Beruh
Company Manager: Gary Gunas
Press: Max Eisen, Warren Pincus, Bob Satuloff
Stage Manager: Will Mott

* Closed January 4, 1970 after 8 performances.

**Top Right: Dale Berg, David Kerman,
Cora Duff-MacCormick**

Mary Jane Mowat, Hugh Thomas   David Ware Photo

SHERIDAN SQUARE PLAYHOUSE

Opened Tuesday, January 6, 1970.*
Joseph Beruh presents:

INSTRUCTIONS FOR THE RUNNING OF TRAINS, ETC. ON THE ERIE RAILWAY TO GO INTO EFFECT JANUARY 1, 1862

Director, Omar Shapli; Musical Coordination,
William Bolcum, Sarah Eigerman; Set, Karl Eigsti; Lighting, Molly Fridel.

CAST
(Section 10)

Trazana Beverley   Noel McCoy
Sarah Eigerman   Mike Morgan
Charles Esposito   Charles Pegues
John Ferraro   Barbara Quinn
Steve Hymes   Vincent Schiavelli

Presented in two parts.

Press: Max Eisen, Bob Satuloff

* Closed Jan. 11, 1970 after 7 performances.

HUNTER COLLEGE PLAYHOUSE

Opened Monday, December 29, 1969.*
Hunter College Concert Bureau presents the
Oxford and Cambridge Sheakespeare Com-
pany in:

TWELFTH NIGHT

By William Shakespeare; Director, Jonathan
Miller; Designer, Hugh Durrant; Lighting, Tony
Corbett; Music, Henry Ward; Assistant Director,
Michael Coveney; Technical Director, Tom Price.

CAST

Orsino .... Mike Wood
Sebastian .... John Madden
Antonio .... Adrian Webster
Sea Captain .... David Wright
Valentine .... Darien Angadi
Curio .... Stephen Wright
Sir Toby Belch .... Jonathan Manes-Moore
Sir Andrew Aguecheek .... Mark Wing Davey
Malvolio .... Hugh Thomas
Fabian .... Alan Strachan
Feste .... Don MacIntyre
Lords .... Charles Metcalfe, Stephen Oliver
Olivia .... Mary Jane Mowat
Viola .... Hilary Henson
Maria .... Barbara Gravenor
Ladies in waiting .... Olivia Harris, Susan Berry

PRIESTS, SAILORS, ETC.: Darien Angadi,
Susan Berry, Olivia Harris, Charles Metcalfe,
Stephen Oliver, David Wright, Stephen Wright,
Nicholas Pickwoad

A Comedy presented in 3 acts. The action takes
place in Illyria.

Press: David Frost
Stage Managers: Chris Nash, Hugh Pile

* Closed Jan. 4, 1970 after a limited engagement
of 9 performances.

Sarah Eigerman, John Ferraro, Michael Moran

Friedman-Abeles Photo

TAMBELLINI'S GATE THEATRE

Opened Sunday, January 11, 1970.*
Davis Weinstock, Michael Pantaleoni, Lewis
E. Lehrman in association with First Circle
Associates Ltd. present:

THE MEMORY BANK

By Martin Duberman; Director, Harold Stone;
Settings and Costumes, Fred Voelpel; Lighting,
Paul Sullivan; Sound, Garry Harris; Production
Assistant, Joan Tannen.

CAST

"The Recorder"
Smyth (interviewer) ....Jeff David
Andrews ....Fred Stewart
"The Electric Map"
Ted ....Laurence Luckinbill
Jim ....Gil Rogers

General Manager: Norman E. Rothstein
Company Manager: Patricia Carney
Press: Howard Atlee, David Roggensack,
Irene Gandy
Stage Manager: Steven Zweigbaum

* Closed Feb. 1, 1970 after 25 performances.

Bert Andrews Photo

**Fred Stewart, Jeff David, Gil Rogers, Laurence
Luckinbill (with earphones) in "Memory Bank"**

MERCER-HANSBERRY THEATRE

Opened Wednesday, January 7, 1970.*
Ruth Kalkstein and Edward Specter Productions by arrangement with Dorian Productions, Louis Negin and The National Arts
Centre of Canada present:

LOVE AND MAPLE SYRUP

Devised and Compiled by Louis Negin; Words
and Music from Canada; Designed by Charles L.
Dunlop; Lighting, Barry Arnold; Production
Assistant, Maxine Zeifman; Hairstylist, Hernan
Girlado; Title Song by Gordon Lightfoot; Asso-
ciate Producers, Art and Burt D'Lugoff.

CAST

Sandra Caron
Gabriel Gascon
Judy Lander
Ann Mortifee
Louis Negin
Margaret Robertson
Bill Schustik

PROGRAM

ACT I: Prologue, "The Gypsy," "Alouette," "Mon
Pays," "Introduction," "Salish Song of Longing,"
"Duet," "The Dimple," "Attempt," "Tonite Will
Be Fine," "Celebration," "Zalinka," "The Last
Time I Saw Her Face," "Des Mots," "Bonne En-
tente," "Emmene-moi," "Queen Victoria," "Motet,"
"Imperial," "Misunderstanding," "A Person Who
Eats Meat," "Springhill Mine Disaster," "Anerca,"
"Making Songs," "The Sculptors," "Eskimo Table-
aux," "Boss Man," "Over the Pacific," "Kivkaq,"
"Etude No. X"

ACT II: "Epilogue," "Happy Stoned Song,"
"Dance, My Little One," "The Sorcerer," "Grand-
mere et Grandpere," "Love and Maple Syrup,"
"Hagar Shipley," "I Had a King," "Bitter Green,"
"Cuckold's Song," "Quand Vous Mourrez de Nos
"Anti-Romantic," "Oh, Canada," "Proverb," "Love
at Robin Lake," "The Poor Little Girls of Ontario,"
"On the Virtues of Being Canadian," "After Dark,"
"Where the Blue Horses," "L'Exile," "Un Canadian
Errant," "Hey, That's No Way to Say Goodbye."

General Manager: Joseph R. Burstin
Company Manager: Archie Thompson
Press: David Lipsky, Marian Graham,
Lisa Lipsky
Stage Manager: D. W. Koehler

* Closed Jan. 18, 1970 after 15 performances.

**Top Left: Louis Negin, Gabriel Gascon, Sandra Caron,
Judy Lander, Margaret Robertson, Bill Schustik,
Ann Mortifee**

ACTORS PLAYHOUSE

Opened Friday January 16, 1970.*
J. Carduner and The Opposites Company
present:

HEDDA GABLER

By Henrik Ibsen; Director, Ted van Griethuysen; Scenery, Linda Wukovich; Costumes, Sandra
LeMonds; Lighting, Robert A. Freedman; Assistant Director, Roy Harris; Technical Director,
Robert A. Freedman.

CAST

Juliana Tesman....................................Cindy Ames
Berthe ....Norma Novak
Jorgan Tesman ....Peter Brett-Hansen
Hedda Tesman, nee Gabler ......Rebecca Thompson
Thea Elvsted ....Anne Fielding
Judge Brack...Aldo Bonura
Ejlert Lovborg ....Dov Newman

A Drama in 4 acts. The action takes place in
the drawing room of the Tesman villa in 1890,
in Christiania, Norway.

Company Manager: Ellen Brody Kimmelman
Press: Howard Atlee, David Roggensack,
Irene Gandy
Stage Managers: David Sage, Roy Harris

† Succeeded by Ted van Griethuysen.
* Closed Mar. 29, 1970 after 81 performances.

VILLAGE SOUTH THEATER

Opened Thursday, January 22, 1970.*
Herman and Diana Shumlin, Robert L. Livingston present:

TRANSFERS

By Conrad Bromberg; Director, Herman Shumlin; Scenery and Costumes, Peter Harvey; Lighting, Roger Morgan; Production Assistant, Wendy C. Henris.

CAST

"Transfers"
Stan ....Ron Leibman
Mack..Garrett Morris
Ralph ....Gilbert Lewis

The action takes place in the vestibule of an abandoned brownstone in Harlem at the present time.

"The Rooming House"
Elie ....Patricia Roe
Bob ....Ron Leibman
Bill ....Don Billett

The Action takes place at the present time in a New London, Conn., rooming house.

INTERMISSION

"Dr. Galley"
Dr. Galley ....Ron Leibman

The action takes place at the present time in a un versity classroom.

UNDERSTUDIES: Stan, Bob, Don Billet; Elie, Barbara Louis; Mack, Ralph, Tony Major.

Company Manager: Lynda Patrie
Press: Seymour Krawitz, Fred Weterick
Stage Manager: Larry Ziegler

* Closed Feb. 22, 1970 after 36 performances.

Bert Andrews Photos

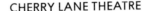

Top Left: Ron Leibman, Patricia Roe Below: Gilbert Lewis, Ron Leibman, Garrett Morris

CHERRY LANE THEATRE

Opened Sunday, January 25, 1970.*
Edward Schreiber in association with Alexander Beck presents:

UNFAIR TO GOLIATH

By Ephraim Kishon; Adaptation and Lyrics, Herbert Appleman; Directors, Ephraim Kishon, Herbert Appleman; Music and Musical Direction, Menachem Zur; Scenery and Lighting, C. Murawski; Costumes, Pamela Scofield; A Project of Thalia Films, Brighton Films, Screencom International.

CAST

Hugh Alexander
Jim Brochu
Jay Devlin
Corinne Kason
Laura May Lewis

Standbys: Fiddle Viracola, Paul Keith

PROGRAM

ACT I: Overture, "The Danger of Peace Is Over," "In the Reign of Chaim," "A Bus Driver," "The Salesman," "What Kind of Baby?," "The Patter of Little Feet," "The Oldtimer," "A Parking Meter Like Me," "The Hardest Currency," "Unfair to Goliath," "Hello," "The Generation Gap," "The Sabra," "Incognito," "The Famous Rabbi," "Back to Back," "2x2 = Schultz"

ACT II: Overture, "In the Desert," "When Moses Spake to Goldstein," "The Rooster and the Hen," "Poloygamy," "Waiting," "Brief Romance," "What Abraham Lincoln Once Said", "High Number Wins," "We're Together," "Sallah and the Social Worker," "The Song of Sallah Shabet," "It's a Country."

A Satirical Revue in 2 acts and 28 scenes.

General Manager: J. Britton
Press: Samuel J. Friedman, Ruth Cage
Stage Manager: Rick Rotante

* Closed March 29, 1970 after 75 performances.

chu, Laura May Lewis   Corinne Kason, Jay Devlin

Leo Friedman Photos

EASTSIDE PLAYHOUSE

Opened Monday, January 26, 1970.*
Haila Stoddard, Mark Wright, Duane Wilder present:

THE LAST SWEET DAYS OF ISAAC

Book and Lyrics, Gretchen Cryer; Music, Nancy Ford; Director, Word Baker; Sets, Ed Wittstein; Costumes, Caley Summers; Lighting, David F. Segal; Musical Direction and Arrangements, Clay Fullum; Production Assistant, Carolyn Richter; Music performed by The Zeitgeist.

CAST

"The Elevator"

Isaac...Austin Pendleton
Ingrid.....................................Fredricka Weber †1

MUSICAL NUMBERS: Overture, "The Last Sweet Days of Isaac," "A Transparent Crystal Moment," "My Most Important Moments Go By," "Love You Came to Me."

INTERMISSION

"I Want to Walk to San Francisco"

Isaac...Austin Pendleton
Alice ....Fredricka Weber †1
Policeman...............................C. David Colson †2

MUSICAL NUMBERS: "I Want to Walk to San Francisco," "Touching Your Hand Is Like Touching Your Mind," "Yes, I Know That I'm Alive,"

The action takes place at the present time.

General Managers: Leonard A. Mulhern, George Thorn
Press: Michael Alpert, Dennis Helfend
Stage Managers: T. L. Boston, Charles Collins

* Still playing May 31, 1970.
† Succeeded by: 1. Alice Playten, 2. John Long

Jack Mitchell Photos

Right: Austin Pendleton, Fredricka Weber

Fredricka Weber, Austin Pendleton

Austin Pendleton, John Long, Louise Heath, Charles Collins, Alice Playten

118

THE NEW THEATRE

Opened Tuesday, January 27, 1970.*
Sunbar Productions presents the High-John
Production of:

JOY

A Musical Come Together with Music and Lyrics by Oscar Brown, Jr.; Lighting Designer, F. Mitchell Dana; Original Cast Album by RCA-Victor Records.

CAST

Oscar Brown, Jr.
Jean Pace
Sivuca
Musicians: Norman Shobey, James Benjamin, Everaldo Ferrerra

General Manager: William Craver
Press: Gifford/Wallace, Tom Trenkle
Stage Managers: Robert Koch, Vincent Cangiano

* Closed July 26, 1970 after 205 performances.

Top Right: Jean Pace, Sivuca, Oscar Brown, Jr.

MERCER-O'CASEY THEATER

Opened Sunday, February 8, 1970.*
Stephanie Sills and Parallel Productions, Ltd. present:

EXCHANGE

Music and Lyrics, Mike Brandt, Michael Knight, Robert J. Lowery; Spoken Material, Eric Levy; Director, Sondra Lee; Musical Direction and Arrangements, Tom Janusz; Settings, Peter Harvey; Costumes, Stanley Simmons; Lighting, William Mintzer; Associate Producers, Kleiman-Reiss Productions.

CAST

Penelope Bodry
Mike Brandt
Igors Gavon
Megan Kay
Michael Knight
Pamela Talus

MUSICAL NUMBERS: ACT I: "All Over My Mind," "If You Listen to My Song," "Anthem," "If I Had the Answers," "Why Don't You Believe Me?," "Wondering," "A Madrigal," "Never Ever Land," "Dancing Through Lifetimes," "The Flower Song," "Carrion Train," "Come on Train," "Train," "L. A. Incident"

ACT II: "Santa Barbara," "Puddles," "Flying Somehow," "Mumble Nothing," "Understand It," "King," "Pied Piper," "Coonskin Cap," "Maybe Tomorrow," "I Can Make It."

A Musical Entertainment in two acts.

Company Manager: Jeffrey H. Knox
Press: Bob Ullman, Ruth Cage
Stage Manager: James Doolan

* Closed Feb. 8, 1970 after one performance.

BROOKLYN ACADEMY OF MUSIC

Opened Wednesday, January 28, 1970.*
Chelsea Theater Center (Robert Kalfin, Artistic Director; Michael David, Executive Director) presents:

THE BRASS BUTTERLY

By William Golding; Director, Allan Leicht; Design, Douglas Higgins; Costumes, Linda Fisher; Musical Director, Robert Barlow; Lighting, Spencer Mosse; Production Supervisor, Burl Hash; Technical Director, David Eidenberg; Sound Tape, Mary Lou Lehman.

CAST

Mamillius	Christopher Leahy
Captain of the Guard	Robert Barry
Postumus	Gastone Rossilli
Emperor	Paxton Whitehead
Usher	Jerrold Ziman
Phanocles	Sam Waterston
Euphrosyne	Arlene Nadel
Sergeant	Mark Rootstein
Attendants	Daniel Gregory, Karen Fredericks, Edward Cannan, Clint Jakeman, Carmichael Wolfschmidt

A Drama in 3 acts. The action takes place in the Emperor's villa on the Isle of Capri.

Stage Managers: Joan Lebowitz, Jane Boland

* Closed Jan. 31, 1970 after a limited engagement of 6 performances. Played 2 additional performances on Feb. 21 and 22, 1970.

Deidi von Schaewen Photo

Left Center: Paxton Whitehead, Sam Waterston

Igors Gavon (C)

**Alan Bergmann, Elizabeth Shepherd,
Michael Pataki**

PROVINCETOWN PLAYHOUSE

Opened Thursday, February 12, 1970.*
Sam Levine presents:

I DREAMT I DWELT IN BLOOMINGDALE'S

Book, Jack Ramer; Music, Ernest McCarty;
Lyrics, Ramer and McCarty; Director, David Dun-
ham Scenery, Ed Wittstein; Clothes by Blooming-
dale's; Lighting and Projection Designs, Jim
Hardy; Musical Staging, Bick Goss; Musical
Arrangements, Ernest McCarty; Performed by
The Wet Clam; Production Assistant, Jane Krensky.

CAST
Window Dresser ....Tom Hull
Father ....Michael Del Medico
Naomi ....Lucy Saroyan
Jessica ....Erika Petersen
Mother ....Liz Ott
Lenny ....Richard Darrow
Ronnie ....Linda Rae Hager
Sue ....Erika Petersen
Bernie ....Michael Del Medico

THE WET CLAM: Richard Malfitano, Dawn Cul-
ton, Joseph Prinzo, Ronald Jackowski, Steve
Gibba

MUSICAL NUMBERS: "Ballad of Dry Dock
Country," "Makin' Believe," "Who Will I Be?,"
"I Dreamt I Dwelt in Bloomingdale's," "We Didn't
Ask to Be Born," "Any Spare Change?." "Brown
Paper Bag," "Naomi," "Smart."

An Absurd Rock Fable in two acts.

General Manager: Roy Franklyn
Press: Sol Jacobson, Lewis Harmon
Stage Manager: Barbara Wood

* Closed Feb. 15, 1970 after 5 performances and
14 previews.

Lee & Patrick Owens Photo

Barry Primus, Linda Selman, Penelope Allen

FORTUNE THEATRE

Opened Monday February 9, 1970.*
Qualis Productions, David Hocker and Chandler Warren present:

THE JUMPING FOOL

By Shirl Hendryx; Director, Allen Savage; Sets,
Bil Mikulewicz; Lighting, Dennis Parichy; Costumes, John David Ridge.

CAST
Maria Benoy ....Elizabeth Shepherd
Susan Calish ....Ann Whiteside
George S. Benoy ....Alan Bergmann
Carl Cartwright ....Jay Gerber
Augie Benoy ....Roger Raiford
Claude Benoy ....Richard Raiford
Suphkin ....Michael Pataki
Harry ....Brendan Hanlon
Psychiatrist ....Grant Sheehan
Ticket Seller ....William Poore

A play in 2 acts. The action takes place at the
present time.

General Manager: Elias Goldin
Press: Nat Dorfman
Stage Managers: Michael D. Moore, Karen Hendel

* Closed Feb. 22, 1970 after 16 performances.

Zodiac Photo

**Liz Otto, Michael Del Medico, Richard Darrow
Lucy Saroyan**

SHERIDAN SQUARE PLAYHOUSE

Opened Wednesday February 25, 1970.*
Phoenix Theatre (A project of Theatre Incor-
porated; T. Edward Hambleton, Managing
Director) presents:

THE CRIMINALS

By Jose Triana; Adapted by Adrian Mitchell;
Director, David Wheeler; Scenery and Lighting,
James Tilton; Costumes, Nancy Potts; Assistant
Manager, Sharon B. Rupert; Staff Assistants,
Dina Alkalay, Connie Barry; Production Assistant,
Arthur N. Burleigh: Producing Director, John
Houseman.

cast
Lalo ....Barry Primus
Beba ....Penelope Allen
Cuca ....Linda Selman

Standbys: Joseph Hindry, Margery Shaw

A Play performed without intermission. The
action takes place in an attic.

General Manager: Marilyn S. Miller
Press: Reginald Denenholz, Anne Woll
Stage Managers: Daniel Freudenberger, E. Reiss

* Closed March 8, 1970 after 15 performances
and 16 previews.

HUDSON WEST THEATRE

Opened Wednesday, February 11, 1970.*
Michael P. Iannucci presents:

THIS WAS BURLESQUE

Entire Production Conceived, Supervised, and Directed by Ann Corio; Based on her recollections; Staged and Choreographed by Richard Barstow; Costumes, Rex Huntington; Miss Corio's Gowns by Raymond Martier; Lighting, Steven Zweigbaum; Musical Conductor, Nick Francis; Technician, Thom Kirby.

CAST

Ann Corio	Pepper Powell
Steve Mills	Count Gregory
Claude Mathis	Tom Dillon
Harry Ryan	Beautiful Marlene
Tami Roche	Harry Conley

THE BURLY CUTIES: Helen Levit, Marilyn Simon, Jinny Jasper, Vickie Daigle, Susan Stewart, Tricia Sandburg, Jennie Chandler, B. J. Hanford

PROGRAM

ACT I: Overture, "The Queen of Burlesque," "Hello Everybody," "Flirtation Scene," "Dance L'Oriental," "Music Teacher," "Pussy Cat Girl," "Minnie Scene," "Special Attraction," "Packing the Trunk," "Minstrel Days," "Pantomime," "Mills and O'Brien," "School Days," "Feature Attraction," Finale.

ACT II: "Powder My Back," "Transformer Scene," "Dance—Then and Now," "White Cargo," "Hall of Fame," "Crazy House," "Memories," Grand Finale

Press: Saul Richman, Peggy Mitchell
Stage Manager: George Sibbald

* Closed May 3, 1970 after 96 performances.

Steve Mills, Ann Corio Top: Burly-Cuties Right: Harry Conley, Marilyn Simon Below: Claude Mathis and Burly-Cuties

Barry Kramer Photos

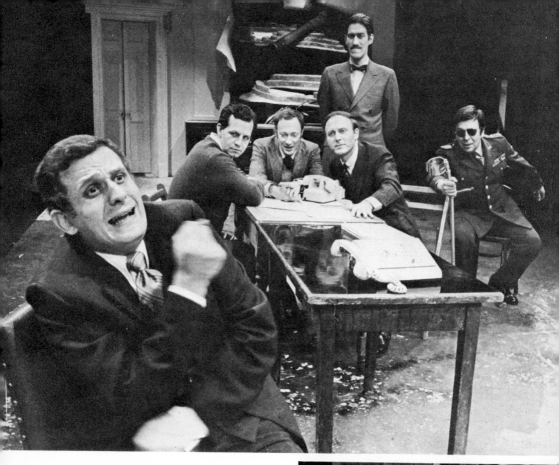

CIRCLE IN THE SQUARE

Opened Wednesday February 18, 1970.*
Theodore Mann, Paul Libin, Harold Leventhal, Orin Lehman present:

THE WHITE HOUSE
MURDER CASE

By Jules Feiffer; Director, Alan Arkin; Sets, Marsha Louis Eck; Lighting, David F. Segal; Costumes, Albert Wolsky; Production Manager, Charles Hamilton; Production Coordinator, Kate Siegel.

CAST

Col. Dawn	Richard Libertini
Lt. Cutler	Edward J. Moore
General Pratt	J. J. Barry
Sweeney	Anthony Holland
Mrs. Hale	Cynthia Harris
Stiles	Paul Benedict
Cole	Paul Dooley
Parson	Andrew Duncan
President Hale	Peter Bonerz
Weems	Bob Balaban

A Comedy in 2 acts. The action takes place several presidential elections hence.

Press: Merle Debuskey, M. J. Boyer, Faith Geer
Stage Manager: Jan Moeral

* Closed May 31, 1970 after 119 performances.

Zodiac Photos

Top: Peter Bonerz, Paul Dooley, Anthony Holland, Paul Benedict, Andrew Duncan, J. J. Barry

Paul Dooley, Andrew Duncan, Peter Bonerz, Paul Benedict, Anthony Holland

TRUCK & WAREHOUSE THEATRE

Opened Monday, March 2, 1970.*
Robert E. Richardson and Joe Davis present:

BILLY NONAME

Book, William Wellington Mackey; Lyrics and Music, Johnny Brandon; Director, Lucia Victor; Sets, Jack Brown; Costumes, Pearl Somner; Lighting, David F. Segal; Musical Direction and Dance Music Arrangements, Sammy Benskin; Orchestrations, Clark McClellan; Vocal Arrangements, Benskin and McClellan; Choreography, Talley Beatty; Associate Producer, William H. Ferguson, Jr.' Production Assistant, Frances Wragg; Hairstylist, Ida Epps; Original Cast Album on Roulette Records.

CAST

Billy Noname	Donny Burks
Louisa, his mother	Andrea Saunders
Li'l Nick	Andy Torres
Big Nick	Charles Moore
Young Billy	Roger Lawson
Young Tiny	Thommie Bush
Rev. Fisher	Eugene Edwards
Dolores	Hattie Winston
Tiny Shannon	Alan Weeks
Mr. Milton	Eugene Edwards
Barbara	Glory Van Scott
Harriet Van Witherspoon	Urylee Leonardos

PEOPLE OF BAY ALLEY, U.S.A.: Thommie Bush, Doris DeMendez, Eugene Edwards, J. L. Harris, Marilyn Johnson, Roger Lawson, Urylee Leonardos, Charles Moore, Joni Palmer, Andrea Saunders, Andy Torres, Glory Van Scott, Alan Weeks, Hattie Winston.

MUSICAL NUMBERS: "King Joe," "Seduction," "Billy Noname," "Boychild," "A Different Drummer," "Look Through the Window," "It's Our Time Now," "Hello, World," "At the End of the Day," "I Want to Live," "Manchild," "Color Me White," "We're Gonna Turn on Freedom," "Mother Earth," "Sit In — Wade In," "Movin'," "The Dream," "Black Boy," "Burn, Baby, Burn," "We Make a Promise," "Get Your Slice of Cake."

A Musical in 2 acts and 15 scenes. The action takes place in Bay Alley, U.S.A., between 1937 and 1970.

General Manager: Lily Turner
Press: Merle Debuskey, Faith Geer
Stage Managers: Smith Lawrence,
Douglas Brenner
* Closed April 12, 1970 after 48 performances.

Martha Swope Photo

Urylee Leonardos (L), Alan Weeks, Glory Van Scott (C), Donny Burks (R)

EDISON THEATRE

Opened Thursday, March 5, 1970.*
Lorin E. Price in association with Barbara Lee Horn presents:

SHOW ME WHERE THE GOOD TIMES ARE

Book, Lee Thuna; Suggested by Moliere's "The Imaginary Invalid"; Music, Kenneth Jacobson; Lyrics, Rhoda Roberts; Director, Morton Da Costa; Choreography, Bob Herget; Sets, Tom John; Costumes, Gloria Gresham; Lighting, Neil Peter Jampolis; Musical Direction and Vocal Arrangements, Karen Gustafson; Orchestrations, Philip J. Lang; Hairstylist, Ronald DeMann; Original Cast Album on RCA Victor Records.

CAST

Aaron	Arnold Soboloff
Rachel	Gloria LeRoy
Annette	Neva Small
Bella	Cathryn Damon
Maurice	John Bennett Perry
Kolinsky	Christopher Hewett
Rothstein	Edward Earle
Dr. Perlman	Mitchell Jason
Thomas Perlman	Michael Berkson
Madame Schwartz	Renee Orin

MEN AND WOMEN OF LOWER EAST SIDE: Austin Colyer, Kevin Daly, Denny Martin Flinn, Lydia Gonzalez, Maria Hero, Peggy Hewett, Sara Louise, Donna Monroe, James E. Rogers, Peter Sansone.

UNDERSTUDIES: Perlman, Rothstein, Austin Colyer; Thomas, Denny Martin Flinn; Annette, Sara Louise; Rachel, Renee Orin.

MUSICAL NUMBERS: "How Do I Feel?," "He's Wonderful," "Look Up," "Show Me Where the Good Times Are," "You're My Happiness," "Cafe Royale Rag," "Staying Alive," "One Big Happy Family," "Follow Your Heart," "Look Who's Throwing a Party," "When Tomorrow Comes," "The Test," "I'm Not Getting Any Younger," "Who'd Believe," Finale.

A Musical in 2 acts. The action takes place in the bedroom of Aaron's house on Henry Street in New York, and various places on the lower East Side in 1913.

General Manager: Paul Vroom
Company Manager: Bill Dean
Press: David Lipsky
Stage Managers: Burry Fredrik,
Schorling Schneider, Kevin Daly
* Closed Mar. 29, 1970 after 29 performances.

Arnold Soboloff, Gloria LeRoy, Neva Small, Michael Berkson, Cathryn Damon

Zodiak Photo

TAMBELLINI'S GATE THEATRE

Opened Monday, March 9, 1970.*
Jonathan Burrows, in association with Ruthe
Feldman presents:

CONTRIBUTIONS

By Ted Shine; Director, Moses Gunn; Sets and
Lighting, Clarke Dunham; Costumes, Judith Hau-
gan; Production Managers, Lindsay Law, Orin
Charm, Michael David; Produced in association
with Ken Gaston Productions.

CAST

"Shoes"

Travis	Donald Griffith
Ronald	Charles Grant
Marshall	Jim Jones
Mr. Mack	Joe Attles
Mr. Wisley	Stanley Greene

The action takes place at the present time in the
employees' locker room of a country club outside
Dallas.

Intermission

"Plantation"

Roscoe	Stanley Greene
Martha	Claudia McNeil
Bishop	Leonard Elliott
Papa Joe Vesquelle	Jay Garner
Mrs. Vesquelle	Yvonne Sherwell

The action takes place at the present time on the
verandah of a plantation mansion outside New
Orleans.

Intermission

"Contribution"

Mrs. Grace Love	Claudia McNeil
Eugene Love	Donald Griffith
Katy Jones	Louise Stubbs

The action takes place in the early 1960s in a
small southern town.

General Manager: Ken Gaston
Press: David Lipsky, Lisa Lipsky
Stage Manager: Lindsay Law

* Closed March 22, 1970 after 16 performances.

Bert Andrews Photo

Louise Stubbs, Donald Griffith, Claudia McNeil

Norma Jean Wood, Peter DeAnda, Jonelle Allen,
Ann Hodapp, Kathleen Miller

124

ELLEN STEWART THEATRE

Opened Wednesday, March 18, 1970.*
William H. Semans and Richard K. Shapiro
in association with Marshall Naify present:

THE HOUSE OF LEATHER

Book, Frederick Gaines; Based on a theme by
Dale F. Menten; Music, Dale F. Menten; Lyrics,
Dale F. Menten, Frederick Gaines; Scenery and
Lighting, David F. Segal; Costumes, Judith Cooper,
James K. Shearon; Musical Director, Dale F. Men-
ten; Director, H. Wesley Balk; Music performed by
Hugo; Original Cast Album on Capitol Records;
Production Assistant, Jimmie Wright.

CAST

Copper	Peter DeAnda
First Woman	Ann Hodapp
Second Woman	Kathleen Miller
First Man	John Kuhner
Second Man	Robert Rovin
Dixie	Kia Coleman
Yankee	Beverly Wideman
Donny Brook	Barry Bostwick
Mrs. Grimm	Norma Jean Wood
Butler Ramsey	John Parriott
Sara Jane	Jonelle Allen
Preacher	Dennis Libby

MUSICAL NUMBERS: "Swanee River Overture,"
"House of Leather Theme," "Sara Jane," "Grad-
uates of Mrs. Grimm's Learning," "Do You Recall
the House of Leather?," "Copper's Creed," "Here I
Am," "Mrs. Grimm," "Time Marches On," "Chil-
dren's Song/Recess with Mrs. Grimm," "Steady
Job," "Imagine You're Alive," "Dixie Prelude/Civil
War," "Armies of the Right," "God Is Black," "I'd
Give to Her the World of Diamonds," "There's Love
in the Country," "Now It's Gone, Gone, Gone,"
"Sherman's March to the Sea," "Death and Reality,"
"Epilogue in Suede."

An Ante-Bellum Rock Musical in 2 acts. The action takes place in Mrs. Grimm's house of prostitu-
tion in New Orleans, and Donny Brook Farm outside the city, before, during, and after the Civil War.

General Manager: Paul B. Berkowsky
Press: Gifford/Wallace, Tom Trenkle
Stage Manager: Paul John Austin

* Closed Mar. 18, 1970 after 1 performance.

FORTUNE THEATRE

Opened Thursday March 19, 1970.*
Stuart Goodman, Peter Skolnik, Bert Steinberg present:

NOBODY HEARS A BROKEN DRUM

By Jason Miller; Director, Peter Skolnik; Settings and Lighting, James F. Gohl; Costumes, Joseph Aulisi; Incidental Music, Tom Ambrosio; Sound, Terry Ross.

CAST

Pat O'Malley	John Coe
Mike Manley	Dan Morgan
Tom Reilly	Anthony Palmer
Matt McGiley	Pat McNamara
Joe Mack, An Idiot	Don O'Hara
Daniel Dyer	Jac Kissel
John O'Hanlin	Richard McKenzie
Paul Shayne, John's son-in-law	T. Atkins
Jamie O'Hanlin, John's son	John P. Ryan
William Evans, a mine foreman	Garry Mitchell
George Griffith, the mine owner	Conrad Bain
Mr. Mangan, his secretary	Martin Shakar
Young soldier	Padraic Conroy
Recruiting Officer	Joe Jamrog
Father Hanley	John Mahon
Mary Shayne, John's daughter	Lisa Richards
Kerrigan, The Shebeen Keeper	Robert Haines
Jenny Malone, a widow	Marilyn Chris
Mr. Flannelly, Northern labor leader	Joe Jamrog
Interpreter	Padraic Conroy

A drama in 2 acts. The action takes place in the Southern Anthracite Region of Pennsylvania in 1862 and 1872.

General Manager: Norman Rothstein
Company Manager: Patricia Carney
Press: Ruth Cage, Bob Ullman
Stage Manager: Howard Crampton-Smith, Joe Jamrog

* Closed March 22, 1970 after 6 performances.

Barry L. Cohen Photo

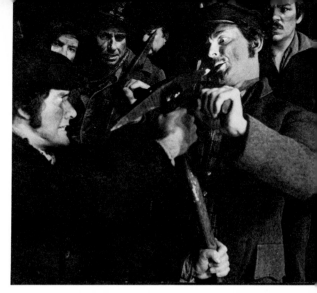

John P. Ryan, Don O'Hara, Anthony Palmer, Richard McKenzie, Garry Mitchell, T. Atkins

McALPIN ROOFTOP THEATRE

Opened Friday, March 20, 1970.*
Marilyn Cantor Baker presents:

LYLE

Book, Chuck Horner; Based on books by Bernard Waber; Music, Janet Gari; Lyrics, Toby Garson; Director, Marvin Gordon; Settings and Lighting, Jack Blackman; Costumes, Winn Morton; Wardrobe, Franklin Simon; Musical Direction and Arrangements, Robert Esty; Production Assistant, Marc Lans.

CAST

Lyle	Steve Harmon †
Hector	Joey Faye
Mr. Grimble	Jack Fletcher
Bob Primm	Stanley Grover
Joan Primm	Ann Vivian
Josh Primm	Steven Paul
Mr. Long	Matthew Tobin
Secretary	Ellyn Harris
Policeman	Dick Bonelle
Guard	Matthew Tobin
European Announcers	Noreen Nichols, Ellyn Harris
Postman, Antonio	Dick Bonelle
Mr. Mamakos	Matthew Tobin
Mr. Carruthers	Dick Bonelle

UNDERSTUDIES: Harmon, Grover, Dick Bonelle; Fay, Fletcher, Matthew Tobin; Vivian, Ellyn Harris

MUSICAL NUMBERS: "Always Leave 'Em Wanting More," "I Can't Believe It's Real," "Generation Gap," "I Belong," "Me, Me, Me," "Alternate Parking," "Try to Make the Best of It," "Loretta," "Look At Me," "Crocodiles Cry," "On the Road," "Lyle's Turn," "Suddenly You're a Stranger," "Everybody Wants to Be Remembered," "Lyle," "Things Were Much Better in the Past," "We Belong."

A Musical Fable in 2 acts and 14 scenes. The action takes place at the present time.

General Manager: Norman Rothstein
Company Manager: Patricia Carney
Press: Bob Ullman, Ruth Cage, Daisy Robards
Stage Manager: Martha Knight

* Closed Mar. 22, 1970 after 4 performances.
† Carleton Carpenter in previews.

Joey Faye, Jack Fletcher (above), Carleton Carpenter

Leo Friedman Photo

VILLAGE SOUTH THEATRE

Opened Friday, March 20, 1970.*
Greenwich Mews Spanish Theatre (Frances Drucker and Gilberto Zaldivar, Producers) presents:

DONA ROSITA, THE SPINSTER

By Federico Garcia Lorca; Director, Rene Buch; Scenery, John Braden; Costumes, Barbara Naomi Cohen; Lighting, Ray McCutcheon; Musical Direction, Juan Viccini; Production Assistant, Andres Nobregas.

CAST

Tio	Esteban Chalbaud
Ama	Lolina Gutierrez
Tia	Fini Moreno
Rosita	Miriam Cruz
Primo	Andres Nobregas
First Manola	Lourdes A. Pedroso
Second Manola	Ana Maria Romagosa
Third Manola	Miriam Rodriguez
Senor X	Emilio Rodriguez
Mother Soltera	Shelly Pearson
First Soltera	Angela Mahnken
Second Soltera	Milagros Horrego
Third Soltera	Magaly Alabau
First Ayola	Mecca
Second Ayola	Candy Rose Cameron or Rosita Cabrera
Don Martin	Tony Diaz
First Obrero	Raul Moncada
Second Obrero	Walter Aguirre
Muchacha	Pablo De La Torre

A Play in 3 acts. The action takes place in Granada between 1885 and 1913.

Press: David Lipsky, Marian Graham, Enrique Fernandez Giraudy

* Closed May 31, 1970 after 33 performances on weekends only.

Bert Andrews Photo

Ana Maria Romagosa, Miriam Cruz, Miriam Rodriguez

SOKOL THEATER

Opened Sunday, March 22, 1970.*
Blanche Yurka presents:

THE MADWOMAN OF CHAILLOT

By Jean Giraudoux; Adaptor, Maurice Valency; Director, Robert Henderson; Decor, Robert Fletcher; Costumes, Charles Tomlinson

CAST

The Prospector	Leonard Sillman
The Sergeant	Roger Oakley
The President	Frederick O'Neal
The Baron	Erik Rhodes
Therese	Hilda Simms
Pauline	Jean Baur
The Waiter	Bryan Young
The Little Man	Joe Young
The Street Singer	Jean Richards
The Flower Girl	Sydney Carroll
The Ragpicker	Manu Tupou
The Deaf-Mute	Vincent Baggetta
Helene	Cynara Reeves
Charles	Hugh Sheppard
Irma	Celia Gregory
The Shoelace Peddler	B.J. DeSimone
The Broker	William Ade
The Street Juggler	James McMahon
Dr. Jardin	Robert Henderson
Countess Aurelia, Madwoman of Chaillot	Blanche Yurka
The Concierge	Kay Strozzi
Pierre	Peter Lucas
The Sewer-man	Staats Cotsworth
Mme. Constance, Madwoman of Passy	Peggy Wood
Mle. Gabrielle, Madwoman of Suplice	Lois Wilson
Mme. Josephine, Madwoman of La Concorde	Jacqueline Susann
The Presidents	Frederick O'Neal, Erik Rhodes, Robert Henderson
The Prospectors	Leonard Sillman, William Ade, B.J. DeSimone
The Ladies	Hilda Simms, Sydney Carroll, Jean Richards
The Voice of Adolphe Bertaut	Erik Rhodes

A Comedy in 2 acts. The action takes place at the present time on the cafe terrace of Chez Francis, Paris, and in the Countess' cellar.

General Managers: Norman Maibaum, Malcolm Allen
Press: Dorothy Ross
Company Manager: Ronald Muchnick
Stage Manager: Leslie Robinson

* Closed March 29, 1970 after 7 performances.

Lois Wilson, Blanche Yurka, Peggy Wood, Jacqueline Susann

Zodiac Photo

BOUWERIE LANE THEATRE

Opened Monday, March 23, 1970.*
George W. Webb presents:

NATURE OF THE CRIME

By Larry Cohen; Director, Lonny Chapman; Settings, William Ritman; Lighting, Paul Sullivan; Costumes, Sara Brook; Sound, Gary Harris; Production Executive, Katina Commings; Production Assistant, Barbara Rosoff; Administrative Assistant, Linda Caputi.

CAST

Daniel Aronoff	Tony Lo Bianco
James Garret	James Antonio
Samuel Ullman	Robert F. Simon
Kirsch	Adam Keefe
Theodore Benjiman	Gerald Gordon
Ruth Aronoff	Barbara Babcock
The Judge	John Benson

A Drama in 3 acts. The action takes place at the present time.

General Manager: Joel Thurm
Press: Howard Atlee, David Roggensack, Irene Gandy
Stage Manager: Charles Hayman

* Closed Apr. 26, 1970 after 41 performances.

Martha Swope Photo

Robert F. Simon, Tony LoBianco

Lillian Hoffman, Harry Van Ore, William Severs, center) Danny Hedaya, Lara Parker, Kenneth Ackles, Ronald Gilbert, Geoffrey Scott

ASTOR PLACE THEATRE

Opened Wednesday, April 1, 1970.*
Albert Poland presents:

"THE UNSEEN HAND" and "FORENSIC AND THE NAVIGATORS"

By Sam Shepard; Director, Jeff Bleckner; Sets, Santo Loquasto; Costumes, Linda Fisher; Lighting, Roger Morgan; Music, Paul Conly with Lothar and the Hand People; Associate Producer, June Stevens; Production Assistant, Jerry Creamer.

CAST

"The Unseen Hand"

Blue Morphan	Beeson Carroll
Willie (The Space Freak)	Lee Kissman
Cisco Morphan	David Selby
The Kid	David Clennon
Sycamore Morphan	Tom Rosica

Intermission

"Forensic and the Navigators"

Forensic	Peter Maloney
Emmett	David Clennon
Oolan	O-lan Johnson-Shepard
1st Exterminator	Tom Rosica
2nd Exterminator	Ron Abbott

The action takes place at the present time during the night in the outskirts of Azusa, California.

General Managers: Gatchell and Neufeld
Press: Robert Ganshaw, John Prescott
Stage Manager: Elissa Lane

* Closed April 19, 1970 after 21 performances and 14 previews.

SHERIDAN SQUARE PLAYHOUSE

Opened Friday, March 27, 1970.*
Mari Saville Presents the Metropolitan Repertory Theatre production of:

LULU
(Earth Spirit)

By Frank Wedekind; Director, Morton Siegel; Scenery and Lighting, David Chapman; Costumes, Deidre Cartier; Composer Scriabin; Translation, Morton Siegel, Mari Saville.

CAST

Dr. Schon	(Harlequin)	Danny Hedaya
Schwarz	(Pedrolino)	Geoffrey Scott
Dr. Goll	(Pantelone)	Ronald Gilbert
Lulu	(Columbine)	Lara Parker
Alvu	(Young Harlequin)	Harry Van Ore
Henriette	(Zanni)	Judith Valentine
Schigolch	(Brighella)	William Severs
Escerny	(Inamorato)	Duane Jones
Geschwitz	(Il Captiano)	Lillian Hoffman
Rodrigo	(Zanni)	Kenneth Ackles
Hugenberg	(Zanni)	Judith Valentine

A Play in 4 acts. The action takes place at the turn of the century. The scene is a Commedia del Arte troupe in their dressing room, improvised in a circus tent, which becomes at varying times an artist's studio, a drawing room, backstage of a theatre, and the salon of a mansion.

Press: Seymore Krawitz, Fred Weterick
Stage Manager: Eastern Hale

* Closed March 29, 1970 after 1 performance.

Bert Andrews Photo

David Selby

Margaret Howell, Chandler Hill Top: Joseph Daly, Margaret Howell, Earl Hindman, Rue McClanahan, Peter DeMaio, Charles Beard, Susan Slavin

MERCER-SHAW ARENA THEATRE

Opened Friday, April 3, 1970.*
Herbert Nitke and Dyot Productions, Inc. present:

DARK OF THE MOON

By Howard Richardson and William Berney; Script Supervision, Howard Richardson; Directed and Designed by Kent Broadhurst; Additional Music, Didi Favreau; Lighting, Molly Friedel; Sound, Gary Harris.

CAST

Barbara Allen	Margaret Howell †
John	Chandler Hill
Dark Witch	Christine Cooper
Fair Witch	Carole Lockwood
Fair Witch Boy	George Wargo
Dark Witch Boy	Bill Hall
Red Witch	Lisa Tracy
Mr. Bergen	Thomas Craft
Uncle Smelicue	Carlo Grasso
Hank Gudger	Charles Beard
Floyd Allen	Patrick Cook
Mrs. Bergen	Jean David
Burt Bergen	Robert Brown
Edna Summey	Susan Slavin
Miss Metcalf	Marcia Wallace
Mrs. Summey	Elizabeth Wilson
Mr. Summey	Robert Baines
Marvin Hudgins	Earl Hindman
Marvin Hudgins	Earl Hindman
Mrs. Allen	Rue McClanahan /2
Mr. Allen	Peter DeMaio
Preacher Haggler	Joseph Daly

A Drama in 2 acts and 9 scenes. The action takes place in the Smokey Mountains.

General Manager: Norman E. Rothstein
Company Manager: Patricia Carney
Press: Sol Jacobson, Lewis Harmon
Stage Managers: Charles Roden, Patrick Cook, Charles Beard

* Closed June 14, 1970 after 86 performances.
† Succeeded by: 1. Claudia Jennings, 2. Shirley Bodtke

Lee and Patrick Owens Photos

BARBIZON-PLAZA THEATRE

Opened Tuesday, April 7, 1970.*
L'Association Francaise D'Action Artistique of the French Foreign Ministry under the patronage of Alliance Francaise de New York by special arrangement with Seff Associates presents LE TRETEAU DE PARIS (Jean De Rigault, Executive Producer) in:

LE GRAND VIZIR
and
LE COSMONAUTE AGRICOLE

By Rene De Obaldia; Director, Jorge Lavelli; Setting, Roland Deville; Technical Director, Louis Fremont.

CAST

"Le Grand Vizir"
Arthur ....Roland Bertin
Ernest ....Gilles Guillot
Hortense ....Maia Simon

"Le Cosmonaute Agricole"
Eulalie ....Josine Comellas
Le Cosmonaute................................Roland Bertin
Zephyrin ....Pierre Baton

Opened Wednesday, April 15, 1970.

LETTRE MORTE
and
ARCHITRUC

By Robert Pinget; Sets and Costumes, Georges Richar; Sound Effects, Jean Jus Forgues; Technical Director, Erik Retsin D'Ambroise.

CAST

"Lettre Morte"
Directed by Michel De Re

M. Levert..................................Olivier Hussenot
Boy..Michel Robbe
Fred.......................................Franics Lax
Lilli......................................Anne-Marie Coffinet

"Architruc"
Directed by Olivier Hussenot

Architruc..................................Michel De Re
Baga.......................................Olivier Hussenot
Le Cuisiner................................Georges Richar

Opened Friday, April 24, 1970.

OH, LES BEAUX JOURS

By Samuel Beckett; Director, Roger Blin.

CAST

Winnie.....................................Madeleine Renaud
Willie.....................................Olivier Hussenot

Opened Tuesday, May 5, 1970.

THREE BY EUGENE IONESCO

Director, Jacques Mauclair; Settings and Costumes, Jacques Noel; Managing Director, Jacques Courtines.

CAST

"La Jeune Fille A Marier"

La Dame ....Claude Genia
Le Monsieur..................................Marc Dudicourt
Le Monsieur-Fille ....Michel Degand

"La Lacune"

L'Academicien ....Jacques
La Femme de L'Academicien ....Claude Genia
L'Ami..Jean-Paul Cisiphe
La Bonne ....Monique Saintey

"Les Chaises"

La Vieille ....Tsilla Chelton
Le Vieux ....Jacques Mauclair
L'Orator ....Jean-Paul Cisiphe

* Closed May 10, 1970.

(No picture available)

GRAMERCY ARTS THEATRE

Opened Sunday, April 5, 1970.*
John Flaxman and Ralph Rosenblum, in association with Richard Pilbrow present:

DEAR JANET ROSENBERG, DEAR MR. KOONING

By Stanley Eveling; Director, Max Stafford-Clark; Lighting, Jules Fisher; Production Assistant, Arlene Caruso.

CAST

"Dear Janet Rosenberg, Dear Mr. Kooning"

Janet Rosenberg ....Catherine Burns
Alec Kooning ....Kevin O'Connor
Standbys: Janet, Penelope Allen;
Alec, Marion Killinger

Intermission

"Jakey Fat Boy"
Alice ....Penelope Allen
Jake ....Kevin O'Connor

General Manager: Edward H. Davis
Press: Mary Bryant, Meg Gordean
Company Manager: Leo K. Cohen
Stage Manager: Lewis Rosen

* Closed May 17, 1970 after 48 performances.

Zodiac Photos

Kevin O'Connor, Penelope Allen
Above: Catherine Burns, Kevin O'Connor

MERCER-O'CASEY THEATRE

Opened Tuesday, April 7, 1970.*
Orin Lehman presents:

THE EFFECT OF GAMMA RAYS ON MAN-IN-THE-MOON MARIGOLDS

By Paul Zindel; Director, Melvin Bernhardt; Music and Sound, James Reichert; Settings, Fred Voelpel; Lighting, Martin Aronstein; Costumes, Sara Brook; Associate Producer, Julie Hughes; Production Assistant, Peggy Cohen.

CAST

Tillie	Pamela Payton-Wright
Beatrice	Sada Thompson
Ruth	Amy Levitt
Nanny	Judith Lowry
Janice Vickery	Swoosie Kurtz

Understudies: Beatrice, Mary Hara; Tillie, Ruth, Swoosie Kurtz.

A Drama in 2 acts. The action takes place at the present time in the home of Beatrice.

* Still playing May 31, 1970.

Bert Andrews Photos

Right: Sada Thompson, Pamela Payton-Wright, Amy Levitt

Judith Lowry, Sada Thompson

Amy Levitt, Judith Lowry, Sada Thompson, Pamela Payton-Wright

MERCURY THEATRE

Opened Thursday, April 9, 1970.*
Ann McIntosh, Honor Moore and Thayer
Burch present:

THE NEST

By Tina Howe; Director, Larry Arrick; Setting,
Robert U. Taylor; Lighting, Roger Morgan; Costumes, Lizbeth Fullemann; Sound, Douglas Simon;
Production Assistant, Susan Odgers.

CAST

Walters	Lois Markle
Lo	Sharon Gans
Aimee	Jill Clayburgh
Stephen	Lane Smith
Virgil	Jack Aaron

A Comdey in 2 acts. The action takes place at
the present time in the apartment of the 3 girls.

General Manager: James Walsh
Company Manager: Louisa Rawle
Press: Alan Eichler, David Powers
Stage Manager: Robert Stevenson

* Closed April 12, 1970 after 6 performances.

Martha Swope Photo

**Top Right: Lane Smith, Jill Clayburgh, Lois
Markle, Sharon Gans, Jack Aaron in "The Nest"
Right: Francesca DeSapio, Sam Waterston**

LINCOLN SQUARE THEATRE

Opened Friday, April 10, 1970.*
Michael Todd, Jr. presents:

AND I MET A MAN

By Lawrence Weinberg; Director, Timmy Everett; Designed by Mischa Petrow; Lighting by
The Joshua Light Show and Thomas Shoesmith.

CAST

Warren	Sam Schacht
Nora	Francesca De Sapio
Aaron	Sam Waterston

A Play in 3 acts. The action takes place at the
present time in the apartments of Warren and Nora,
and Aaron.

Company Manager: Max Gendel
Press: Bill Doll & Company, Inc.,
Midori Lederer, Virginia Holden
Stage Manager: Paul Holland

* Closed April 11, 1970 after 3 performances.

Christopher Cable, Marie Santell, Susan Rush

13th STREET THEATRE

Opened Monday, April 13, 1970.*
Bro Herrod in association with Peter Perry
presents:

THE DRUNKARD

By W. H. S. Smith; Music, Lyrics, Orchestrations, Musical Director, Barry Manilow; Director,
Bro Herrod; Choreography and Musical Staging,
Carveth Wells; Costumes, Carol Luiken; Lighting,
Bill Hall.

CAST

Mary, the widow's daughter	Marie Santell
Mrs. Wilson, the widow	Donna Sanders
Lawyer Cribbs, the villain	Christopher Cable
Edward Middleton, the hero	Clay Johns
William Dowton, his foster brother	Drew Murphy
Agnes, his sister	Joy Garrett
Preacher	Lou Vitacco
Barkeep	Lou Vitacco
Barmaids	Susan Rush, Donna Sanders
Mrs. Carry Nation	Joy Garrett
Julia, from Heaven	Susan Rush
Old Man's Darling	Joy Garrett
Salvation Worker	Donna Sanders

MUSICAL NUMBERS: "Something Good Will
Happen Soon," "Whispering Hope," "Don't Swat
Your Mother, Boys," "Strolling Through the Park,"
"Good Is Good," "Mrs. Mary Middleton," "Have
Another Drink," "The Curse of an Aching Heart,"
"For When You're Dead," "A Cup of Coffee," "Garbage Can Blues," "Shall I Be An Old Man's Darling," "Julia's Song," "I'm Ready to Go," "Do You
Wanna Be Saved?"

A Musical Adaptation of the 19th Century Melodrama in 10 scenes with one intermission.

Production Manager: Diane Kirkpatrick
Press: Reginald Denenholz, Anne Woll
Stage Manager: David Moyer

* Closed May 24, 1970 after 48 performances.

Norman Seeff Photo

Stephen McHattie, Raul Julia, Robert Stattel,
Tom Crawley, Patricia Elliott
Below: Jacqueline Brookes

ST. GEORGE'S CHURCH

Opened Wednesday, April 15, 1970.*
Phoenix Theatre (T. Edward Hambleton,
Managing Director; Gordon Duffey, Artistic
Director) in cooperation with St. George's
Church presents:

THE PERSIANS

By John Lewin; Freely adapted from the "Persae" of Aeschylus; Director, Gordon Duffy; Scenery, Lighting, and Props, Jack Brown; Costumes, Masks, and Props, Nancy Potts; Music, Nasser Rastegar-Nejad; Production Assistant, Sharon Jones.

CAST

Chorus Leader, and Elder................Robert Stattel
Persian Elder ....Tom Crawley
Persian Elder ....Raul Julia
Young Woman of the Chorus...........Patricia Elliott
Atossa, Queen of Persia ....Jacqueline Brookes
Messenger ....J. A. Preston
The Ghost of Darius, formerly King of Persia
..........David Spielberg
Xerxes, King of Persia ....Stephen McHattie

UNDERSTUDIES: Atossa, Young Woman, Carol Emshoff; Xerxes, Darius, Elder, Edwin Owens; Messenger, Chorus Leader, Elder, Robert Lanchester.

A Tragedy presented without intermission. The action takes place in 480 B.C. at Susa, in front of the royal palace, and at the tomb of Darius.

Manager: Sharon Rupert
Press: Sol Jacobson, Lewis Harmon, Dan Langan
Stage Managers: Daniel Freudenberger, E. Reiss

* Closed May 2, 1970 after a limited engagement of 21 performances.

Lee and Patrick Owens Photos

PROVINCETOWN PLAYHOUSE

Opened Monday, April 20, 1970.*
Ashley Feinstein & George Gilbert present

HOW MUCH, HOW MUCH?

By Peter Keveson; Director, Richard Altman; Sets and Lights, William Ritman; Costumes, Whitney Blausen.

CAST

Peggy Monash...........................Nancy Andrews
Carl Monash.................................Hy Anzell
Joycie Monash ....Neva Small
Charley Gordon ....Kristoffer Tabor
Joe Raidy ....Al Neson
Sara ....Donna Pearson
Max ....Maurice Brenner
Paul Gordon ....Hugh Franklin

A Comedy in 2 acts. The action takes place in the Monash apartment, Columbus Ave. and 85th Street.

General Managers: Gatchell & Neufeld
Press: Michael Alpert, Dennis Helfend
Stage Managers: Jane Clegg, David Ross

* Closed May 10, 1970 after 24 performances

Martha Swope Photos

Neva Small, Nancy Andrews, Hy Anzell,
Kristoffer Tabori (also Right Center)

ANDERSON THEATRE

Opened Tuesday, April 28, 1970.*
Carmen Capalbo and Abe Margolies present:

THE RISE AND FALL OF THE CITY OF MAHAGONNY

Book, Bertolt Brecht; Music, Kurt Weill; English Adaptation, Arnold Weinstein; Conceived and Directed by Carmen Capalbo; Musical Director, Samuel Matlovsky; Associate Conductor, Theodore Saidenberg; Setting, Robin Wagner; Costumes, Ruth Morley; Lighting, Thomas Skelton; Color Projections, Larry Rivers; Associate Producer, Charles Rome Smith; Original Cast Album on Atlantic Records.

CAST

Commentator	Evan Thompson
Trinity Moses	Val Pringle
Fatty	Jack De Lon
Leocadia Begbick	Estelle Parsons
Jenny	Barbara Harris
John Hancock Schmidt	Alan Crofoot
Alaska Wolf Joe	Bill Copeland
Billy Bankbook	Don Crabtree
Jimmy Mallory	Frank Porretta
Pianist	Louis St. Louis
Toby Higgins	Richard Miller
Camera Men	Ray Camp, Clint Elliot
Bellhops	Kenneth Frett, James Hobson, Gordon Minard, Tracy Moore

GIRLS AND MEN OF MAHAGONNY: Holly Hamilton, Sayrah Hummel, Anne Kaye, Lani Miller, Jacqueline Penn, Veronica Redd, Lou Rodgers, Adrienne Whitney, Rudy Challenger, Jack Fletcher, Jimmy Justice, Keith Kaldenberg, Richard Miller, Alexander Orfaly

UNDERSTUDIES: Jimmy, Bill Copeland; Trinity, Jimmy Justice; Fatty, Schmidt, Keith Kaldenberg; Leocadia, Lou Rodgers; Jenny, Jacqueline Penn; Joe, Jack Fletcher; Billy, Richard Miller

A Musical in 3 acts and 22 scenes. The action takes place in the City of Mahagonny.

General Manager: James E. Walsh
Press: Seymour Krawitz, Fred Wetrick
Stage Managers: Bob Troy, Nicholas Russiyan, Rudy Challenger

* Closed May 3, 1970 after 8 performances and 69 previews.

Lee Bolton Photo

Estelle Parsons, Frank Porretta, Barbara Harris in "Mahagonny"

THE CUBICULO

Opened Wednesday, April 29, 1970.*
The Cubiculo presents:

TWO NEW PLAYS BY TWO POETS

Settings, Richard Hubbard; Lighting, William Lambert.

CAST

"Frog Frog"

by Mary Feldhaus-Weber; Staged by Clinton Anderson, Deborah Jowitt

with Michael Crosby, Tiffany Hendry, John High, Nancy Zala

"Eleganterooneyrismusissimus"

by Michael Goldman; Directed by Clinton Anderson

with Deborah Jowitt, Philip LeStrange

* Closed May 2, 1970 after limited engagement of 6 performances.

MERCURY THEATRE

Opened Monday, May 11, 1970.*
George Martin in association with K-R Productions presents:

THE MOTHS

Written and Directed by Ralph Arzoomanian; Set, Jason B. Fishbein; Costumes, Whitney Blausen; Lighting, William Mintzer; Production Associate, Jeffrey H. Knox.

CAST

Alexander Zanikyan	Philip Bruns
Anise Zanikyan	Joy Claussen
Sophie	Magda Harout
Father Nikos	Dimo Condos
Auntie	Miriam Lehmann-Haupt
Marco	Michael Vale
Larry	Charles "Chick" Ganimian
Momo	James Howard Laurence

A Play in 2 acts. The action takes place at the present time in Zanikyan's bedroom.

Company Manager: Jeffrey H. Knox
Press: Ruth Cage, Bob Ullman
Stage Manager: James Doolan

* Closed May 11, 1970 after 1 performance.

Ted Yaple Photo

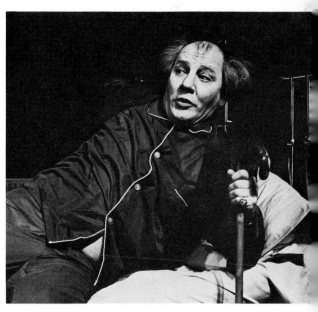

Philip Bruns in "The Moths"

Mc ALPIN ROOFTOP THEATRE

Opened Monday, May 4, 1970.*
Charles Woodward and Michael Kasdan,
by arrangement with Lewenstein-Delfont
Prods. Ltd. and H. M. Tennent Ltd. present:

WHAT THE BUTLER SAW

By Joe Orton; Director, Joseph Hardy; Production Designed by William Ritman; Costumes, Ann Roth; Production Assistant, Jack Custer.

CAST

Dr. Prentice	Laurence Luckinbill
Geraldine Barclay	Diana Davila
Mrs. Prentice	Jan Farrand
Nicholas Beckett	Charles Murphy
Dr. Rance	Lucian Scott
Sargeant Match	Tom Rosqui

UNDERSTUDIES: Nicholas, Match, Allen Williams; Mrs. Prentice, Geraldine, Elaine Hyman.

A Comedy in 2 acts. The action takes place at the present time in the consulting room of an exclusive, private psychiatric clinic in London.

General Manager: Michael Kasdan
Press: Betty Lee Hunt, Henry Luhrman, Ellen Levene, Harriett Trachtenberg
Stage Managers: Murray Gitlin, Allen Williams

* Still playing May 31, 1970.

Martha Swope Photos

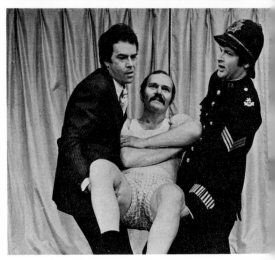

134   Laurence Luckinbill, Diana Davila
Above: Lucian Scott, Jan Farrand

Laurence Luckinbill, Tom Rosqui, Charles
Murphy Above: Diana Davila, Charles Murphy

Zoe Caldwell, Mildred Dunnock

Keene Curtis, Zoe Caldwell, Barry Bostwick
Above: Caldwell, Charles Siebert, Holland
Taylor Top: Caldwell

ELLEN STEWART THEATRE

Opened Wednesday, May 6, 1970.*
Cheryl Crawford in association with Mary W. John presents:

COLETTE

Adapted by Elinor Jones; Based on "Earthly Paradise," the collection of Colette's autobiographical writings by Robert Phelps; Director, Gerald Freedman; Original Music, Harvey Schmidt; Lyrics, Tom Jones; Scenery, David Mitchell; Costumes, Theoni V. Aldredge; Lighting, Roger Morgan; Technical Director, Steven Holmes; Management Associate, Marianne Selbert; Production Assistants, Mark Richter, James Kiernan.

CAST

Colette .... Zoe Caldwell
Sido, her mother .... Mildred Dunnock † 1
Willy, her husband ....Charles Siebert † 2
The Captain (her father), Max (a friend),
 George Wague (her partner), Reporter
 .... Keene Curtis † 3
Daniele (a secretary), Polaire (an actress), Ida
 (a weightlifter), Amalia (an aging actress),
 Marguerite (a close friend), Reporter
 .... Holland Taylor
Leo (Colette's brother), Jacques (Willy's secretary),
 Pierre (Polaire's lover), Jean (a young actor),
 Henri de Jouvenel (Colette's second husband),
 Maurice Goudeket (her third husband)
 .... Barry Bostwick

Composer and Pianist .... Harvey Schmidt

UNDERSTUDIES: Misses Caldwell and Dunnock, Janet Dowd; Mr. Siebert, Mr. Curtis, Bo Brundin; Mr. Bostwick, James Kiernan

A Play in two acts. The action takes place in France between 1873 and 1954.

General Manager: Paul B. Berkowsky
Company Manager: Bob MacDonald
Press: David Powers, Alan Eichler
Stage Manager: Gage Andretta

* Closed Aug. 2, 1970 after 101 performances and 14 previews.
† Succeeded by: 1. Ruth Nelson, 2. Louis Turenne, 3. Tom Aldredge

Martha Swope Photos

135

Ron Leibman Top: Alek Primrose, Tom Brannum, Lucy Saroyan, George Bartenieff, Leibman, Paul B. Price, Jerome Dempsey

EDISON THEATRE

Opened Tuesday, May 12, 1970.*
Jay H. Fuchs & Jerry Schlossberg in association with Jerry Cutler Enterprises & John Murray present:

ROOM SERVICE

By John Murray & Allen Boretz; Director, Harold Stone; Scenery & Lighting, D. Atwood Jenkins; Costumes, Leigh Rand; Associate Manager, Gary Fifield; Production Associate, Ben Bernstein.

CAST

Gordon Miller	Ron Leibman †1
Sasha Smirnoff	Michael Lombard
Joseph Gribble	Paul B. Price
Harry Binion	Frank Savino
Faker Englund	George Bartenieff
Christine Marlowe	Lucy Saroyan
Leo Davis	Tom Brannum †2
Hilda Manney	Barbara Dana
Gregory Wagner	Jerome Dempsey
Simon Jenkins	Darrell Zwerling
Timothy Hogarth	Joel Wolfe
Dr. Glass	Alek Primrose
Bank Messanger	Christopher Guest
House Detectives	Edmund Williams, Smith Lawrence
Senator Blake	Fred Stewart

UNDERSTUDIES: Miller, Frank Savino; Sasha, Wagner, Joel Wolfe; Davis, Christopher Guest; Binion, Jenkins, Bank Messenger, Hogarth, Smith Lawrence; Faker, Dr. Glass, Blake, Gribble, Edmund Williams; Christine, Hilda, Aida Berlyn.

A Comedy in 3 acts. The action takes place in 1937 in Gordon Miller's hotel room near Times Square.

General Managers: George Thorn,
Leonard A. Mulhern
Press: Marvin Kohn
Stage Managers: Steve Zweigbaum,
Smith Lawrence, Aida Berlyn

* Closed July 11, 1970 after 71 performances and 9 previews.
† Succeeded by: 1. Dick Shawn, 2. Stanley Myron Handelman.

UNIVERSITY OF THE STREETS THEATRE

Opened Saturday, May 9, 1970*
The Theatre of the University of the Streets presents:

PEANUT BUTTER AND JELLY

Written and Directed by Harris Freedman; Music, Nancy Day and Harris Freedman; Performed by Nancy Day Freedman; Technical Director, K. C. Craddock; Lighting, Alfred Hart.

CAST

Woman	Katherine Garnett
Man	Michael Moriarty
Second Man	Jared Fey
Second Woman	Judy Joseph
Old Man	Louis Schaefer
Mother	Anne Linden
Arthur	Brian Hall

A Tragicomedy in 2 acts. The action takes place "on a particular morning" in a man's soul.

Stage Manager: Alfred Hart

* Closed May 24, 1970 after a limited engagement of 10 performances on weekends only.

Michael Moriarty, Judy Joseph, Anne Linden, Katherine Garnett, Brian Hall

SHERIDAN SQUARE PLAYHOUSE

Opened Wednesday, May 13, 1970.*
Ruth Kalkstein and Center Stage Associates present:

SLOW DANCE ON THE KILLING GROUND

By William Hanley; Director, John Stix; Sets, Jason Phillips; Costumes, Ritchie Spencer; Lighting, C. Mitch Rogers; Associate Producer, Zvi Kolitz; Technical Director, Dennis Shank; Production Assistant, Lynn Montgomery.

CAST

Glas	George Voskovec
Randall	Billy Dee Williams
Rosie	Madeline Miller

Understudy for Randall, Gilbert Price

A Drama in 3 acts. The action takes place in 1962 in a small store in the warehouse district of Brooklyn.

* Closed June 14, 1970 after 36 performances.

Zodiac Photo

Right Center: George Voskovec, Billy Dee Williams, Madeline Miller

FORTUNE THEATRE

Opened Friday, May 15, 1970.*
Mark Durand, Ken Kaiserman, Debir Productions present:

"THE SHEPHERD OF AVENUE B"
and
"STEAL THE OLD MAN'S BUNDLE"

Director, Peter Galambos; Scenery, Edward Burbridge; Lighting, Dennis Parichy, Associate Producer, Howard Kane; Production Assistants, Gina Horowitz, Parmelee Wells.

CAST

"The Shepherd of Avenue B"
by Lawrence Holofcener

Maria Tucci
Lee Wallace

The action takes place at the present time in a basement apartment on New York's Lower East Side.

Intermission

"Steal the Old Man's Bundle"
by Kenneth Pressman

Roger De Koven
Ted LePlat

The action takes place at the present time in a basement apartment on New York's Upper West Side.

General Manager: Mark Durand
Press: Fred Weterick
Stage Manager: Rick Rotante

* Closed May 17, 1970 after 5 performances.

Roger DeKoven, Ted LePlat

137

Bert Andrews Photo

PLAYHOUSE THEATRE
Opened Sunday, May 17, 1970.*
Haila Stoddard, Mark Wright, Duane Wilder, present the Buffalo Studio Arena production of:

LEMON SKY

By Lanford Wilson; Director, Warren Enters; Set and Costumes, Stephen Hendrickson; Lighting, David Zierk.

CAST

Alan ....Christopher Walken
Douglas ....Charles Durning
Ronnie (His Wife) ....Bonnie Bartlett
Penny ....Kathryn Baumann
Carol ....Lee McCain
Jerry ....Steven Paul
Jack ....Willie Rook

A Drama in 3 acts. The action takes place in the present on the stage of the theater.

General Managers: Leonard A. Mulhern, George Thorn
Press: Michael Alpert, Dennis Helfend
Stage Manager: Louis Pulvino

* Closed May 31, 1970 after 16 performances and 5 previews.

Left: Christopher Walken, Lee McCain, Kathryn Baumann

ORPHEUM THEATRE
Opened Monday, May 18, 1970.*
Jeff Britton in association with Sagittarius Productions presents:

THE ME NOBODY KNOWS

Spoken Text written by children (7-18) attending NYC public schools; Edited by Stephen M. Joseph; Music, Gary William Friedman; Lyrics, Will Holt; Original Idea, Herb Schapiro; Director, Robert H. Livingston; Musical Numbers Staged by Patricia Birch; Scenery and Lighting, Clarke Dunham; Costumes, Patricia Quinn Stuart; Media Design and Photography, Stan Goldberg and Mopsy; Additional Lyrics, Herb Schapiro; Arrangements and Orchestrations, Gary William Friedman; Musical Director, Edward Strauss; Assistant to Producer, Erlinda Zetlin; Production Assistant, Steve Cohen.

CAST

Rhoda ....Melanie Henderson
Lillian ....Laura Michaels
Carlos ....Jose Fernandez
Lillie Mae...Irene Cara
Benjamin ....Douglas Grant
Catherine ....Beverly Ann Bremers
Melba ....Gerri Dean
Donald ....Paul Mace
Lloyd ....Northern Calloway
Clorox ....Carl Thoma
William ....Kevin Lindsay
Nell ....Hattie Winston

MUSICAL NUMBERS: "Dream Babies," "Light Songs," "This World," "Numbers," "What Happens to Life," "Take Hold the Crutch," "Flying Milk and Runaway Plates," "I Love What the Girls Have," "How I Feel," "If I Had a Million Dollars," "Fugue for Four Girls," "Rejoice," "Sounds," "The Tree," "Robert, Alvin, Wendell and Jo Jo," "Jail-Life Walk," "Something Beautiful," "Black," "The Horse," "Let Me Come In," "War Babies."

A Musical Entertainment in 2 acts. The action takes place at the present time in New York City's ghetto.

General Manager: Malcolm Allen
Company Manager: Ronald Muchnick
Press: Samuel J. Friedman, Rod Jacobson, Jane Friedman
Stage Manager: Martha Knight

* Still playing May 31, 1970.

Bert Andrews Photos

Northern Calloway, Paul Mace, Carl Thoma

MARTINIQUE THEATRE

Opened Monday, May 25, 1970.*
Circle-in-the-Square, Theodore Mann, Paul Libin present:

CHICAGO 70

Improvised and Developed by the Toronto Workshop Company; Director, George Luscombe; Designed by Nancy Jowsey; Lighting, John Faulkner; Production Assistant, Barbara Walther; Production Manager, Charles Hamilton; Based on the Conspiracy and Trial Transcripts in Chicago, plus the Prophetic Inspiration of Lewis Carroll's "Alice in Wonderland"; Imperialist Units by Brent Larson.

CAST

Bobby Seale	Calvin Butler
Mark Lane	Jim Lawrence
Arlo Guthrie	Ray Whelan
Mayor Daley	Neil Walsh
Allen Ginsberg	George Meteskey
Abbie Hoffman	Francois Regis Klanfer
Country Joe	Neil Walsh
Linda Morse	Diane Grant
Dee Jay	Murray Blanc

and David Yorston, Jack Beauscholte, Carol Carrington

A "Political Experience" presented in 2 parts. The action takes place in Chicago in 1970.

Company Manager: June Faulkner
Press: Merle Debuskey, Faith Geer
Stage Manager: John Faulkner

* Closed May 14, 1970 after 24 performances.

Zodiac Photo

Jack Beauscholte, Carol Carrington, Francois Regis Klanfer, Calvin Butler, Jim Lawrence, David Yorston

BIJOU THEATRE

Opened Wednesday, May 27, 1970.*
Willard W. Goodman, Catalyst Company, Robert J. Gibson, in association with Jane Cohen Productions present:

AWAKE AND SING

By Clifford Odets; Director, Arthur A. Seidelman; Set, Ethel Green; Lighting, Molly Friedel; Costumes, Pamela Scofield; Associate Producer, Marvin Pletzke; Assistant Production Manager, Rick Alfieri; Production Associate, Terrell Bennett; Production Assistants, Pasquel Vaquez, Robin Schwartz; A Theatre Vanguard Production.

CAST

Ralph Berger	Robert Salvio
Myron Berger	Salem Ludwig
Hennie Berger	Phoebe Dorin
Jacob	Morris Strassberg
Bessie Berger	Joan Lorring
Schlosser	Peter Bosche
Moe Axelrod	Roger Serbagi
Uncle Morty	Bill Macy
Sam Feinschreiber	Irwin Rosen

UNDERSTUDIES: Hennie, Linda Gale; Ralph, Rick Alfieri; Myron, Sam, Peter Bosche; Moe, Morty, Irwin Rosen.

A Drama in 3 acts. The action takes place in 1935 in the Berger's Bronx Apartment.

General Managers: Gatchell and Neufeld
Press: Leslie Coven
Stage Manager: Clint Jakeman

* Closed June 28, 1970 after 41 performances.

Betty Nettis Photo

Salem Ludwig, Joan Lorring, Phoebe Dorin

MERCER-HANSBERRY THEATRE

Opened Thursday, May 28, 1970.*
The People's Company (Studley-Traub Associates, Inc., Melanie Herman) in association with A. & B. D'Lugoff presents:

CANDAULES, COMMISSIONER

By Dan Gerould; Director, Roy Levine; Sets, Lester Polakov; Costumes, Donna Tomas; Lighting, William Mintzer; Music and Sound, James Reichert; Producer, Julien J. Studley; Associate Producer, Melanie Herman.

CAST

Candaules, High Commissioner of Economic Assistance to Lydia	Seth Allen
Gyges, native Lydian bodyguard	Robert Stocking
Nyssia, Candaules' wife	Marilyn Roberts

The action takes place in Sardis, the capitol of Lydia.

General Manager: Melanie Herman
Press: Ruth Cage, Bob Ullman
Stage Manager: Ken Glickfeld

* Closed May 31, 1970 after 5 performances.

Ted Yaple Photo

Marilyn Roberts, Seth Allen

THE NEGRO ENSEMBLE COMPANY
Artistic Director, Douglas Turner Ward   Executive Director, Robert Hooks
Administrative Director, Gerald S. Krone

ST. MARKS PLAYHOUSE

Opened Wednesday, July 2, 1969.*
The Negro Ensemble Company presents:

MAN BETTER MAN

By Errol Hill; Director, Douglas Turner Ward; Music, Coleridge-Taylor Perkinson; Choreography, Percival Borde; Sets, Edward Burbridge; Costumes, Bernard Johnson; Lighting, Buddy Butler; Technical Director, Charles Vincent Dingley.

CAST

Tim Briscoe	David Downing
Portagee Joe	Graham Brown
Swifty	Allie Woods
Inez Briscoe	Rosalind Cash
Hannibal	Tony McKay
Tiny Satin	Samual Blue, Jr.
Crackerjack	Arthur French
Petite Belle Lily	Hattie Winston
Cutaway Rimbeau	Julius W. Harris
Dagger Da Silva	Aston Young
Alice Sugar	Esther Rolle
Coolie	Norman Bush
Peloo	Afolabi Ajayi
Pogo	William Jay
Diable Papa	Damon W. Brazwell
Minee Woopsa	Mari Toussaint
1st Village Woman	Frances Foster
2nd Village Woman	Clarice Taylor

OTHER VILLAGERS: Louise Heath, Marilyn McConnie, Richard Roundtree, Lennal Wainwright, Anita Wilson

MUSICIANS: Herb Bushler, Harold Vick, Montego Joe, Eric Bibb.

MUSICAL NUMBERS: "Procession," "Tiny, the Champion," "I Love Petite Belle," "One Day, One Day, Congotay," "One, Two, Three," "Man Better Man," "Petite Belle Lily," "Thousand, Thousand," "Me Alone," "Girl in the Coffee," "Colie Gone," "War and Rebellion," "Beautiful Heaven," "Briscoe, the Hero."

A Musical in 3 acts and 7 scenes. The action takes place at the turn of the century in a small village on the island of Trinidad, West Indies.
Press: Howard Atlee, David Roggensack, Irene Gandy

* Closed July 20, 1969 after 32 performances.

8/6-CT
Theatre World-Crown-OB-189

Esther Rolle, Aston Young, Hattie Winston, Arthur French in "Man Better Man"

ST. MARKS PLAYHOUSE

Opened Tuesday, January 13, 1970.*
The Negro Ensemble Company presents:

THE HARANGUES

By Joseph A. Walker; Director, Israel Hicks; Music, Dorothy A. Dinroe; Musical Direction, Margaret Harris; Choreography, Percival Borde; Sets, Chuck Vincent; Costumes, Gertha Brock; Lighting, Buddy Butler; Project Coordinator, Edmund Cambridge; Technical Director, Chuck Vincent.

CAST

"Tribal Harangue One"

Ayo	Rosalind Cash
Obataiye	Damon W. Brazwell, Jr.

The action takes place in an African slave dungeon off the coast of West Africa in the 14th or 15th century

"Tribal Harangue Two"

Zoe Walton	Irene Bunde
Cal	Robert Hooks
Jake	David Downing
Walton	Robert G. Murch
Doctor	Willam Jay
Black Men	Julius W. Harris, Douglas Turner

The action is the present in an apartment in Washington, D.C.

"Tribal Harangue Three"

Ayo	Rosaline Cash
Obataiye	Damon Brazwell, Jr.

The action takes place in the future.

Intermission

"Harangue"

Gorilla	Julius W. Harris
Lee	William Jay
Cooper	Elliot Cuker
Billy Boy	Linda Carlson
Asura	Douglas Turner

The action takes place at the present time in a bar on Avenue B in New York's lower East Side.

UNDERSTUDIES: Billy Boy, Irene Bunde; Zoe, Linda Carlson

General Manager: Frederick Garrett
Press: Howard Atlee, David Roggensack, Stanley F. Kaminsky, Irene Gandy
Stage Manager: James S. Lucas, Jr.

* Closed Feb. 15, 1970 after 56 performances.

Elliot Cuker, Douglas Turner, William Jay, Linda Carlson in "The Harangues"

Bert Andrews Photo

ST. MARKS PLAYHOUSE

Opened Tuesday, March 17, 1970.*
The Negro Ensemble Company presents:

"BROTHERHOOD"
and
"DAY OF ABSENCE"

Written and Directed by Douglas Turner Ward;
Sets, Chuck Vincent; Lighting, Ernest Baxter;
Costumes, Gertha Brock; Special Sound, James
Reichert; Production Coordinator, Edmund Cambridge.

CAST
"Brotherhood"

Tom Jason	Tom Rosqui
Ruth Jason	Tiffany Hendry
James Johnson	William Jay
Luann Johnson	Frances Foster

The action takes place at the present time in the
living room of a typical suburban home.

Intermission

"Day of Absence"
(A Reverse Minstrel Show)

Clem	Allie Woods
Luke	Norman Bush
John	David Downing
Mary	Rosalind Cash
First Operator	Esther Rolle
Second Operator	Frances Foster
Third Operator	Anita Wilson
Supervisor	Clarence Taylor
Jackson	William Jay
Mayor	Arthur French
First Man	Bill Duke
Second Man	Allie Woods
Third Man	Norman Bush
Industrialist	Bill Duke
Businessman	Allie Woods
Clubwoman	Clarice Taylor
Courier	David Downing
Announcer	Tom Rosqui
Clan	Norman Bush
Aide	Esther Rolle
Pious	David Downing
Rastus	Bill Duke

The action takes place at the present in an un-
named Southern town.

General Manager: Frederick Garrett
Press: Howard Atlee, David Roggensack,
Irene Gandy
Stage Manager: James S. Lucas, Jr.

* Closed May 3, 1970 after 54 performances.

**Bill Duke, Clarice Taylor, Arthur French,
Allie Woods Above: William Jay, Rosalind Cash
in "Day of Absence"**

ST. MARKS PLAYHOUSE

Opened Tuesday, May 26, 1970.*
The Negro Ensemble Company presents:

AKOKAWE
(Initiation)

Traditional and Modern African Writings Selec-
ted and Directed by Afolabi Ajayi; Sets, Chuck
Vincent; Lighting, Ernest Baxter; Special Dance
Movement, Percival Borde; Project Coordinator,
Edmund Cambridge

CAST

NEGRO ENSEMBLE COMPANY: Norman Bush,
Frances Foster, Esther Rolle, Clarice Taylor, Andre
Womble (Guest Performer)

MBARI-MBAYO PLAYERS: Afolabi Ajayi,
Amandina Lihamba, Paul Makgoba, Ifatumbo
Oyebola, Babafemi Akinlana, Louis Espinosa

PROGRAM

ACT I: Traditional Times: "Opening Call of Drums,"
"Poem of Greetings," "Song of Ojo," "Song of Wis-
dom," "The Storyteller," The First Contact: "The
European," "The Prayer That Got Away," "Song
of War."

ACT II: Poets in Exile: "Invocation," "New York,"
"First Impressions," "Vending Machine," "American Impressions," "New York Skyscrapers," "Telephone Conversation," "Paris in the Snow," Negri-
tude Poets: "Prayer to Masks," "Africa," "Nights
of Sine." "Dawn in the Heart of America," "De-
fiance Against Force," New Songs: "Merinda
Love Song," "Popular Love Song," "Song of Pro-
verbs," Drum Finale.

General Manager: Frederick Garrett
Press: Howard Atlee, David Roggensack,
Irene Gandy
Stage Manager: James S. Lucas, Jr.

* Still playing May 31, 1970.

**Amandina Lihamba, Esther Rolle,
Clarice Taylor
in "Akokawe"**

Bert Andrews Photos

MASTER THEATRE

Opened Thursday, October 16, 1969.*
Equity Library Theatre presents:

LEND AN EAR

Sketches, Lyrics and Music, Charles Gaynor; Director, Sue Lawless; Dances and Musical Numbers Staged by Judith Haskell; Musical Direction, James Kay; Sets and Lighting, John A. Baker III; Costumes, Pamela Scofield.

CAST

Gene Aguirre	Anthony Inneo
Christopher Carroll	Charles Leipart
William J. Coppola	Sara Louise
Donna Curtis	Ted Pugh
Georgia Engel	Maureen Silliman
James Harder	Joan Porter
Douglas Hill	Miriam Welch
Pamela Hunt	Pam Zarit

UNDERSTUDIES: Marsha Meyers, Charles Murphy, Louis Garcia

ACT I: "After Hours," "Give Your Heart a Chance," "Neurotic You and Psychopathic Me," "I'm Not in Love," "Do It Yourself," "Friday Dancing Class," "Ballade," "When Someone You Love Loves You," "The Gladiola Girl," "Join Us in a Cup of Tea," "Where Is the She for Me," "I'll Be True to You," "Doin' the Old Yahoo Step," "A Little Game of Tennis," "In Our Teeny Little Weeny Nest."

ACT II: "Santo Domingo," "I'm on the Lookout," "Three Little Queens of the Silver Screen," "Molly O'Reilly," "All the World's," "Who Hit Me," "Words Without Song," Finale.

Press: Sol Jacobson, Lewis Harmon
Stage Managers: Philip M. Kagan,
Steven Aronson

* Closed Nov. 2, 1969 after a limited engagement of 20 performances.

MASTER THEATRE

Opened Thursday, November 13, 1969.*
Equity Library Theatre presents:

THE LOWER DEPTHS

By Maxim Gorki; Adaptation, Maurice Noel; Director, Robert Moss; Scenery, Chuck Vincent; Lighting, Judith Ann Binus; Costumes, Robert Anderson; Music, Michael Valenti; Technical Director, Ira S. Stoller.

CAST

The Baron	Dan Mason
Kvashnya	Jeanne Kaplan
Bubnov	Louis Galterio
Andrei Mitrich Klesch	John Ventantonio
Nastya	Caroline Faulkner
Anya Klesch	Trudi Mathes
Satin	Al Cohen
The Actor	George Addis
Michail Ivanich Kostilyov	Robert Milton
Vaska Pepel	Pierrino Mascarino
Natasha Karpovna	Susan Kaslow
Luka	Apollo Dukakis
Alyoshka	John Costopoulos
Vasilissa Karpovna Kostilyova	Geraldine Court
Abram Medvyedev	Frank T. Wells
The Tartar	Zito Kirros

A Drama in 2 acts and 4 scenes. The action takes place in the cellar of a flophouse in Russia at the turn of the century.

Press: Sol Jacobson, Lewis Harmon
Stage Managers: John A. Baker III,
Megan Rosenfeld

* Closed Nov. 23, 1969 after a limited engagement of 14 performances.

Right: Geraldine Court, Caroline Faulkner in "The Lower Depths"

MASTER THEATRE

Opened Thursday, December 11, 1969.*
Equity Library Theatre presents:

ROMEO AND JEANNETTE

By Jean Anouilh; Translation, Miriam John; Director, Peter Galambos; Sets, James Singelis; Costumes, Sydney Lee Brooks; Lighting, Edward M. Greenberg.

CAST

Julia	Arlene Nadel
Mother	Lynn Archer
Frederic	Peter Haig
Lucien	Robert Shea
Father	Richard Graham
Jeannette	Marie Puma
Postman	John Copeland

A Drama in 4 acts. The action takes place in a room in the Maurin home, and in a summer house in a small town.

Press: Sol Jacobson, Lewis Harmon
Stage Managers: Charles Hayman,
Gene S. Minkow

* Closed Dec. 21, 1969 after a limited engagement of 14 performances.

Herbert Fogelson Photos

Peter Haig, Richard Graham, Arlene Nadel, Lynn Archer in "Romeo and Jeannette"

MASTER THEATRE

Opened Thursday, January 15, 1970.*
Equity Library Theatre presents:

GETTING MARRIED

By George Bernard Shaw; Director, Clinton Atkinson; Setting, Sandi Marks; Lighting, Atlee Stephan III; Costumes, Betsey Potter.

CAST

Mrs. Bridgenorth	Enid Rodgers
William Collins	John High
General Bridgenorth	Edward Stevlingson
Lesbia Grantham	Deborah Jowitt
Reginald Bridgenorth	Michael Hawkins
Leo Bridgenorth	Tiffany Hendry
Bishop of Chelsea	John M. LeGrand
St. John Hotchkiss	Philip LeStrange
Cecil Sykes	Roger Middleton
Edith Bridgenorth	Kathleen Coyne
Soames	Michael Crosby
The Beadle	Bill Sherwood
Mrs. George	Merle Albertson

A Comedy at the turn of the century. The action takes place in the Norman kitchen in the palace of the bishop of Chelsea.

Press: Sol Jacobson, Lewis Harmon
Stage Managers: Ned Farster, Bill Sherwood

* Closed Jan. 25, 1970 after a limited engagement of 14 performances.

Deborah Jowitt, Tiffany Hendry, Kathleen Coyne, Enid Rogers, Roger Middleton, John M. LeGrand, Philip LeStrange Below: LeStrange, Merle Albertson in "Getting Married"

MASTER THEATRE

Opened Thursday, February 12, 1970.*
Equity Library Theatre presents:

LITTLE MARY SUNSHINE

Book, Music, and Lyrics, Rick Besoyan; Staged by Larry Whiteley; Musical Director, Marjorie J. Brewster; Assistant Choreographer, Joe Conrad; Settings, Clyde Philip Wachsberger; Lighting, Sally Small; Pianists, Marjorie J. Brewster, Mark Needleman.

CAST

Chief Brown Bear	Richard Wyr
Forest Rangers:	
Slim	Bill Littleton
Tex	Randy Beal
Pete	James Hamel
Buster	Tony Rosato
Hank	Bryan Dunlap
Tom	Peter Ligeti
Cpl. Billy Jester	Roger Ochs
Capt. "Big Jim" Warington	Jon Peck
Little Mary Sunshine	Eleanor Rogers
Mme. Ernestine Von Lieberdich	Nancy Zala
Finishing School Ladies:	
Gwendolyn	Marlene Caryl
Mabel	Merry Flershem
Henrietta	Rei Golenor
Cora	Ora McBride
Maude	Susan Schevers
Blanche	Marsha Zamoida
Nancy Twinkle	Fran Brill
Fleet Foot	George Harris II
Yellow Feather	Joel Conrad
General Oscar Fairfax	Tom Sinclair

MUSICAL NUMBERS: "The Forest Ranger," "Little Mary Sunshine," "Look for a Sky of Blue," "You're the Fairest Flower," "In Izzenschnooken on the Lovely Essenzook Zee," "Playing Croquet," "Swinging," "How Do You Do," "Tell a Handsome Stranger," "Once In A Blue Moon," "Colorado Love Call," "Every Little Nothing," "What Has Happened," "Such a Merry Party," "Say Uncle," "Me A Heap Big Injun," "Naughty, Naughty Nancy," "Mata Hari," "Do You Ever Dream of Vienna?," "A Shell Game," "Coo Coo," Finale.

A Musical in 2 acts and 10 scenes. The action takes place in Colorado.

Company Manager: Gene S. Minkow
Press: Sol Jacobson, Lewis Harmon
Stage Managers: Thomas Lynn Greene,
Julia Fremon, Laurence Nadell

* Closed Mar. 1, 1970 after a limited engagement of 22 performances.

Herbert Fogelson Photos

Jon Peck, Eleanor Rogers,
Nancy Zala
in "Little Mary Sunshine"

143

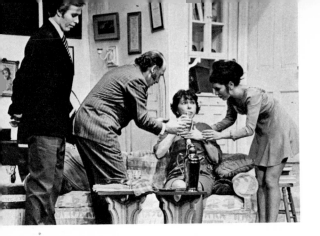

Opened Thursday, March 12, 1970.*
Equity Library Theatre presents:

BAREFOOT IN THE PARK

By Neil Simon; Director, Christian Grey; Setting, Charles L. Gillette; Costumes, Robert Anderson; Lighting, William Marshall; Max Murphy, Art Director; Sound Technician, Constance Gasque; Technical Director, Ira S. Stoller.

CAST

Corie Bratter	Wendy Lesniak
Telephone Repairman	Bill McIntyre
Delivery Man	Lloyd Hubbard
Paul Bratter	Michael Saposnick
Mrs. Banks	Anita Bayless
Victor Velasco	Gonzalo Madurga

A Comedy in 3 acts and 4 scenes. The action takes place at the present time on the top floor of a NYC brownstone.

Press: Lewis Harmon, Sol Jacobson
Stage Managers: Walter Sharp,
Roseanna Richardson, Richard Fink

* Closed Mar. 22, 1970 after a limited engagement of 14 performances.

Top Left: Michael Saposnick, Gonzalo Madurga, Anita Bayless, Wendy Lesniak in "Barefoot in the Park"

MASTER THEATRE

Opened Thursday, April 9, 1970.*
Equity Library Theatre presents:

A HATFUL OF RAIN

By Michael V. Gazzo; Director, Kent Paul; Setting, Bil Mikulewicz; Lighting, Richard Miller; Costumes, Beverly Sherman; Technicians, Duke Sparks, Tom Tyderek.

CAST

Johnny Pope, Sr.	Joe Kottler
Johnny Pope	John Costopoulos
Celia Pope	Crickett Cannon Coan
Mother	Alex Colon
Apples	Roger Lawson
Chuck	Irwin Rosen
Polo Pope	Bruce Weitz
A Man	Ira Stoller
Putski	Elizabeth Harryman

A Drama in 3 acts and 6 scenes. The action takes place in a remodeled apartment on the lower East Side of NYC in 1955.

Press: Sol Jacobson, Lewis Harmon
Stage Managers: Michael Burke,
Wendy Johnson, Dorothy Harris,
Ama Victor

* Closed Apr. 19, 1970 after a limited engagement of 14 performances.

MASTER THEATRE

Opened Thursday, May 14, 1970.*
Equity Library Theatre presents:

ME AND JULIET

Book and Lyrics, Oscar Hammerstein 2nd; Music, Richard Rodgers; Director, Charles Willard; Musical Direction and Arrangements, Thom Janusz; Dances Staged by George Bunt; Sets, Jeffrey B. Moss; Costumes, Jay Liebman; Lighting, Edward Greenberg; Technical Director, Ira S. Stoller; Pianist, John R. Williams.

CAST

Jeanie	Susan Blanchard
Susie	Deborah St. Darr
Sidney	Ted Story
Chris	Bob Shephard
Ruby	David Toll
Bob	Robert Berdeen
Sheila	Jan MacKenzie
Monica	Jane Ann Sargia
Larry	John Johann
Isabel	Bonnie Hinson
Houston	Robert E. Land
Mac	John Swearingen
Kelly	Rita Fitzgerald
Charlie	Way Geis
Lily	Susan Schevers
Jim	Rick Atwell
Joe	Dennis Grimaldi
Jerry	Donald Mark
Michael	J.B. Annegan
Hilda	Rita Fitzgerald
Marcia	Jan MacKenzie
Betty	Patti Mariano

MUSICAL NUMBERS: Prologue, "Very Special Day," "That's the Way It Happens," "We Deserve," "Dream Ballet," "Marriage Type Love," "We Deserve Each Other," "Big Black Giant," "No Other Love," "It's Me," "Intermission Talk," "Night Club Routine," "It Feels Good," "I'm Your Girl," "Keep It Gay," "Family Type Love," Finale.

A Musical in 2 acts with prologue. The action takes place in an off Broadway theatre in which "Me and Juliet," a spoof of 1950 musicals, is currently playing.

Press: Lewis Harmon, Sol Jacobson
Stage Managers: John Weeks, Peter Riegert

* Closed May 24, 1970 after a limited engagement of 14 performances.

Susan Blanchard, John Johann in "Me and Juliet"

Herbert Fogelson Photos

THE BLACKFRIARS' GUILD
Rev. Thomas F. Carey, Moderator
29th Season

BLACKFRIARS' THEATRE

Opened Tuesday, October 14, 1969.*
The Blackfriars' Guild presents:

REUNION OF SORTS

By Mary Drahos; Director, Walter Cool; Settings and Lighting, T. Fabian; Costumes, Alice Merrigal.

CAST

Olga	Hazel G. Wolffs
	or Mary Ann Strossner
Pops Smithson	Robert Kerr
	or Bill Begley
Miss Stuart	Shirley Gusky
	or Kathleen Phillips
Donna	Maureen FitzGerald
	or Erica Weingast
Mrs. Liz Read	Jeanne Fields
	or Amy Yaekerson
Mrs. Ellen Coswell	Mary Jennings Dean
	or Claire Wilbur
Dr. Abbott	Ott Selby
	or Doc Slevin
Jeff Read	Robert Gulliver
	or Joseph P. McCartney
Brad Coswell	David Archer Tardell
	or Raymond Carter

A Comedy-Drama in 3 acts and 6 scenes. The action takes place at the present time in Room 615 of a New York hospital.

Stage Managers: Robert Charles, Richard Dunham
* Closed Nov. 23, 1969 after 41 performances.

Charles Guttilla Photos

Robert Gulliver, Ott Selby, Maureen FitzGerald, Hazel G. Wolffs, Jeanne Fields, Mary Jennings Dean, Shirley Gusky, Robert Kerr, David Arthur Tardell in "Reunion of Sorts"

Leonard Fredrick (seated), David O'Sullivan, Joe Fishback in "Five Star Saint"

BLACKFRIARS' THEATRE

Opened Tuesday, February 10, 1970.*
The Blackfriars' Guild presents:

FIVE STAR SAINT

By Rev. Edward A. Molloy; Director, Walter Cool; Settings and Lighting, T. Fabian; Costumes, Robert Charles; Assistant Director, Ellis Nassour.

CAST

Brother Romito	Kenneth Thompson
	or Michael Bahr
Father De Paula	Dave Hutchison
	or Michael Doran
Father Majone	Joe Fishback
	or Cavan Reilly
Father Villani	David O'Sullivan
	or Richard Scribner
Father Alphonsus	Leonard Frederick
	or Robb McIntire
Father Roberto	Jeff Druce
	or Shelly Kurz
Regent Bernard Tanucci	Herbert DuVal
	or Herbert Jarvis
Joseph Cardinal Castelli	Ott Selby
	or Burt Grosselfinger
Toni	Sterling Roberts
	or Danton LaPenna

A Drama in 3 acts and epilogue. The action takes place in Pagani, Italy, in a modest abode for priests, and in the Bishop's residence in Sant' Agata, near Capua, Italy, between 1755 and 1780.

Stage Managers: Robert Charles, Richard Dunham
* Closed Mar. 22, 1970 after 41 performances.

ROUNDABOUT THEATRE

Opened Sunday, October 12, 1969.*
Roundabout Theatre presents the American Premiere of:

TRUMPETS AND DRUMS

By Bertolt Brecht; Translated by Rose and Martin Kastner; Director, Gene Feist; Music, Erich Bulling; Scene Design, Stuart Wurtzel; Costumes, Patrizia van Brandenstein; Lighting, Gary Long; Choreography, Charon Lee Cohen; Musical Coordinator, David Lipton; Production Assistants, Lisa Bryon, David Cooper, Bob Saturn.

CAST

Captain William Plume	Winston May
Captain Brazen	Sterling Jensen
Sergeant Kite	Bennett Yahya
Mr. Balance	Eric Carlson
Victoria	Elizabeth Owens
Mr. Worthy	Julian Sulmonetti
Mr. Smuggler	Charles Anatra
Simpkins	Marc Devon
Melinda Moorhill	Caroline Thomas
Lucy	Lisa Bryon
Lady Prude	Shirley Peck
Rose	Leslie Ray
Bullock	Vincent Lattuca
Thomas Appletree	Tim Moses
Costar Permain	Steve Clements
William	Lyle J. Lorentz
Maggie	Suzanne Beckman
Sally	Hillary Wyler
Mike	Joe Fishback
Bridewell	Norman Lind
Priscilla	Andrea Joyce
Silvia	Janet Novick
Patience	Cecily Floyd
A Miner	Chris Miller
Miner's Wife	Karen Gawel
A Pimp	Gary Raucher
Kitty	Pamela Bevan
Pickpocket	Mierre
Workless	Bill Roulet
Mrs. Workless	Lucille King
A Big Man	Richard Dahlia

A Play in 11 scenes with one intermission. The action takes place in Shrewsbury, England, in 1776.

Production Manager: Paul Bengston
Press: Michael Fried

* Closed Nov. 22, 1969 after 40 performances.

**Winston May, Elizabeth Owens
in "Trumpets and Drums"**

ROUNDABOUT THEATRE

Opened Sunday, December 21, 1969.*
The Roundabout Theatre presents:

MACBETH

By William Shakespeare; Director, Bill Accles; Scenery, Robert Winkler; Costumes, Mimi Maxmen; Electronic Score, John Kraus, Lighting, James Greek.

CAST

Witches	Lisa Bryon, Joan Kaszas, Andrea Joyce
Duncan	Lyle J. Lorentz
Malcolm	Edwin Lewis
Donalbain	Mierre
Sergeant	Roger Kelly
Macduff	Robert Eder
Lennox	Marc Eliot
Ross	Will Patent
Angus	Marc Devon
Macbeth	Sterling Jensen
Banquo	Jack Axelrod
Lady Macbeth	Elizabeth Owens
Seyton	Bill Roulet
Fleance	Joe Mitchell
Porter	Bill Roulet
Murderers	Will Charles Reilly, John Guerrasio
Lady Macduff	Caroline Thomas
Son to Macduff	Grant Marder
Doctor	Gary Raucher
Siward	Vincent D'Alessio
Young Siward	John Guerrasio
Officers, Soldiers	Richard Bell, David Cooper, William Griesel, Will Charles Reilly

Presented with one intermission.

* Closed Jan. 18, 1970 after 37 performances.

**Sterling Jensen, Elizabeth Owens
in "Macbeth"**

Arthur Alexander Photos

ROUNDABOUT THEATRE

Opened Sunday, February 15, 1970.*
The Roundabout Theatre presents:

OEDIPUS

Adapted by Anthony Sloan; Director, Gene Feist; Assistant Director, Mierre; Lighting, Gary Long; Set, Lorna Hainesworth; Costumes, Helen Frank; Technical Director, Lorna Hainesworth.

CAST

Oedipus, the Ruler	Gordon Heath
Jocasta, his wife	Elizabeth Owens
Antigone, eldest daughter	Charlotte Forbes
Ismene, youngest daughter	Alexis Greene
Polynices, their son	Edwin Lewis
Eteocles, his twin	in exile
Creon, Jocasta's brother	Sterling Jensen
Haemon, his son	Thomas McCann
Nurse	Pamela Bevan
Tiresias	Woodrow Leafer
Girl	Cecily Floyd
Servants	Paul Bennett, John Guerrasio, Michael Groob

A Drama in 2 acts. The action takes place in the early 1930's in the reception hall of a Presidential Palace of a Central American land in the Carribean.

Stage Managers: Linda Paiser, Edward Kramer

* Closed Apr. 12, 1970 after 52 performances.

**Elizabeth Owens, Gordon Heath
in "Oedipus"**

**Gloria Starita, Brian Hartigan
in "The Lady from Maxim's"**

ROUNDABOUT THEATRE

Opened Sunday, May 3, 1970.*
The Roundabout Theatre presents the American Premiere of:

THE LADY FROM MAXIM'S

By Georges Feydeau; Adapted by Gene Feist; Based on translation by Catherine Perebinossoff and Mierre; Director, Gordon Heath; Music and Lyrics, Gordon Heath; Set, Lorna Hainesworth; Costumes, Mimi Maxmen; Lighting, Gary Long; Assistant Director, Paul Bennett; Technical Director, Lorna Hainesworth; Sound, Al Tritt; Choreographer, Rosalind Walker; Musical Director, and Incidental Music, Mathew Greenbaum.

CAST

Dr. Lucien Petipon	Brian Hartigan
Gabrielle	Gloria Starita
Etienne	Edwin Lewis
Dr. Mongicourt	Sterling Jensen
Gen. Petipon	Norman Lind
Clementine	Jennifer Boyd
Lt. Corignon	Charles Anatra
Simone	Yvonne Patterson
The Lady	Marsha Katzakian
Duke of Valmonte	Philip Campanella
Street Cleaner	Robert McCrary
Village Priest	Anthony DeVito
Brother Julian	Tony Zanetta

A Farce in 2 acts. The action takes place at the turn of the century in Paris.

Stage Manager: Elizabeth Owens

* Closed June 14, 1970 after 50 performances.

AMERICAN PLACE THEATRE
Wynn Handman, Director
Michael Tolan, Associate Director Julia Miles, General Manager
Sixth Season

ST. CLEMENT'S CHURCH

Opened Monday, October 27, 1969.*
The American Place Theatre (Wynn Handman,
Director) presents:

MERCY STREET

By Anne Sexton; Director, Charles Maryan;
Scenery and Costumes, Douglas Higgins; Light-
ing, Roger Morgan; Special Sound, James Reichert;
Music Selected and Arranged, McNeil Robinson;
Technical Director, Ted Abramov; Production As-
sistants; Paul Leavin, Patricia White.

CAST

Dr. Alex	Jerome Raphel
Daisy	Marian Seldes
Judith	Virginia Downing
Amelia	M'el Dowd
Arthur	William Prince
Acolytes	Robert Bass, Chris Kalfayan
	Paul Leavin, Fritz Stokes

UNDERSTUDIES: Daisy, Tanny McDonald;
Amelia, Judith, Elizabeth Thurman; Alex, Arthur,
Donald Symington.

A Drama presented without intermission. The time
is now with the exception of time recalled, time
relived, and time to come.

Stage Managers: George Blanchard, Errol Selsby
Press: Howard Atlee, David Roggensack,
Irene Gandy

* Closed Nov. 21, 1969 after 52 performances.

ST. CLEMENT'S CHURCH

Opened Thursday, January 1, 1970.*
The American Place Theatre presents:

FIVE ON THE
BLACK HAND SIDE

By Charlie L. Russell; Director, Barbara Ann
Teer; Scenery, Edward Burbridge; Costumes,
Gertha Brock; Lighting, Shirley Predergast; Spec-
ial Sound, James Reichert; Technical Director,
Rafe Friedman.

CAST

Mr. Brooks	L. Errol Jaye †1
Mrs. Brooks	Clarice Taylor
Gail	Jonelle Allen
Booker T	Matthew Bernard Johnson, Jr.
Gideon	William Adell Stevenson III
Stephanie	Patricia A. Edomy
Sampson	Thabo Quinland R. Gordon
Nia	Nia Anderson
Ruby	Theresa Merritt
Stormy Monday	Judyann Elder
Sweetmeat	Gerry Black
Slim	Ed Bernard
Fun Loving	Tchaka Almoravids
Black Militant	Eugene Reynolds
Evangelist	Marilyn B. Coleman
Rolls Royce	Joseph Attles †2
First Junkie	Demond Wilson
Second Junkie	Eugene Reynolds
Marvin	Lisle Wilson

UNDERSTUDIES: Brooks, Gerry Black; Mrs.
Brooks, Theresa Merritt; Gail, Nia Anderson;
Booker, Lisle Wilson; Gideon, Thabo Quinland
R. Gordon; Ruby, Stormy, Marilyn B. Coleman;
Sweetmeat, Ed Bernard; Marvin, Willie A. Faison,
Jr.

A Comedy in 2 acts. The action takes place at
the present time in Harlem.

Press: Howard Atlee, David Roggensack,
Irene Gandy
Stage Managers: George Blanchard, Errol Selsby

* Closed Jan. 31, 1970 after 55 performances.
† Succeeded by: 1. Maxwell Glanville, 2. Kirk
Kirksey

**Left: Marian Seldes (also below),
William Prince
in "Mercy Street"**

**Nia Anderson, William Adell Stevenson III, Cl
Taylor, L. Errol Jaye, Thabo Q. R. Gordon, Ed Be**

ST. CLEMENT'S CHURCH

Opened Monday, March 9, 1970.*
The American Place Theatre (Wynn Handman, Director) presents:

TWO TIMES ONE

Scenery and Costumes, Kert Lundell; Lighting, Roger Morgan; Special Sound, James Reichert; Production Assistants, Paul Leavin, Parmelee Welles.

CAST

"The Last Straw"
By Charles Dizenzo; Director, Gregory C. Meland.

Dr. Frank ....Edward Kovens
Anthony ....Oliver Clark

The action takes place at the present time in a Manhattan office

Intermission

"Duet for Solo Voice"
By David Scott Milton; Director, Martin Fried

Leonard Pelican ....Herb Edelman
Vassily Chort ....Vassily Chort
The action takes place Now in a 43rd Street Hotel.

Press: Howard Atlee, David Roggensack,
Irene Gandy
Stage Managers: George Blanchard, Errol Selsby
* Closed Apr. 11, 1970 after 35 performances.

**Right: Herb Edelman
Above: Edward Kovens, Oliver Clark
in "Two Times One"**

ST. CLEMENT'S CHURCH

Opened Wednesday, May 20, 1970.*
The American Place Theatre (Wynn Handman, Director) presents:

THE PIG PEN

By Ed Bullins; Director, Dick Williams; Scenery, Douglas Higgins; Costumes, Gertha Brock; Lighting, Ernest Baxter; Music, Gene McDaniels; Production Assistants, Oyamo, Paul Leavin;

CAST

Ray Crawford ....Basil A. Wallace
Len Stover ....Tony Thomas
Sharon Stover...............................Laura Esterman
Margie ....Avis McCarther
Bobo Carroll ....Lou Courtney
John Carroll ....Milton Earl Forrest
Henry Carroll ....Elbert Bernard Pair
Mackman ....Edward Clinton
Ernie Butler...............................Michael Coleman
Carlos.....................................J. Herbert Kerr, Jr.
Pig Pen ....Robert Patterson
Understudies: Judy Mills, Ondine Vaughn

A Play without intermission. The action takes place in a cabin in the hills near Glendale, California, in February of 1965.

Press: Howard Atlee, David Roggensack,
Irene Gandy
Stage Managers: Errol Selsby, George Blanchard
* Closed June 6, 1970 after 35 performances.

Martha Holmes Photos

**Tony Thomas, Laura Esterman, Edward Clinton,
Avis McCarther, Basil A. Wallace in "The Pig Pen"** 149

NEW YORK SHAKESPEARE FESTIVAL PUBLIC THEATER
Joseph Papp, Producer
Gerald Freedman, Artistic Director   Bernard Gersten, Associate Produce

PUBLIC THEATER

Opened Thursday, November 13, 1969.*
The New York Shakespeare Festival (Joseph
Papp, Producer) presents:

STOMP

A "Multimedia Protest Rock Musical" in two
parts, conceived and performed by the 23 members
of The Combine. No other credits available.

* Closed April 19, 1970 after 161 performances.

**Right: "Stomp" Company Below: Hattie Winston,
Janice Lynn Montgomery, Ron Steward, Gerri Dean
in "Sambo"**

PUBLIC THEATER

Opened Sunday, December 21, 1969.*
The New York Shakespeare Festival presents:

SAMBO

Music, Ron Steward, Neal Tate; Words, Ron
Steward; Director, Gerald Freedman; Choreo-
graphy, Tommy Jonsen; Scenery, Ming Cho Lee
Marjorie Kellogg; Costumes, Milo Morrow; Light-
ing, Martin Aronstein; Musical Director, Neal
Tate; Musical Supervision, John Morris.

CAST

Sambo ....Ron Steward
Tigers ....Camille Yarbrough, Rob Barnes
Jenny O'Hara, Robert LaTourneaux, Sid Marshall
Henry Baker
Untogether Cinderella ....Gerri Dean
Miss Sally Muffat.........Janice Lynne Montgomery
Little Boy Blue ....Kenneth Carr
Jack Horney ....George Turner
Bo Peep ....Hattie Winston

UNDERSTUDIES: Sambo, Rob Barnes; Jack
Tiger, Sid Marshall; Cinderella, Bo Peep, Camille
Yarbrough; Boy Blue, Robert LaTourneaux

MUSICAL NUMBERS: "Sing a Song of Sambo,"
"Hey Boy," "I Am a Child," "Young Enough to
Dream," "Mama Always Said," "Baddest Mammy
jammy," "Sambo Was a Bad Boy," "Pretty Flow-
er," "I Could Dig You," "Do You Care Too Much,"
"Be Black," "Let's Go Down," "Astrology," "The
Eternal Virgin," "Boy Blue," "The Piscean," "Ar-
ies," "Untogether Cinderella," "Peace Love and
Good Damn," "Come on Home," "Black Man,"
"Get an Education," "Ask and You Shall Receive,"
"Son of Africa," "I Am a Child."

A Black Opera with White Spots in 2 acts.

Production Manager: Andrew Mihok
Press: Merle Debuskey, Faith Geer
Stage Managers: Adam G. Perl, Andrew J. Traister

* Closed Jan. 11, 1970 after 25 performances

MOD DONNA

Book and Lyrics, Myrna Lamb; Music, Susan
Hulsman Bingham; Director, Joseph Papp; Cos-
tumes, Milo Morrow; Lighting, Martin Aronstein;
Choreography, Ze-eva Cohen; Musical Direction
and Orchestrations, Liza Redfield; Conductor,
Dorothea Freitag.

CAST

Donna ....April Shawhan
Chris ....Sharon Laughlin
Jeff ....Larry Bryggman
Charlie....................................Peter Haig

CHORUS OF WOMEN: Ellen Barber, Jani Brenn,
Katharine Dunfee, June Gable, Deloris Gaskins,
Liz Gorrill, Zora Margolis, Maureen Mooney,
Madge Sinclair

UNDERSTUDIES: Donna, Chris, Mary Jo Walters; Jeff, Charlie, Sam Schacht; Chorus, Nancy
Franklin

MUSICAL NUMBERS: "Trapped,""Earthworms,"
"The Incorporation," "Invitation," "All the Way
Down," "The Deal," "Liberia," "The Morning
After," "Charlie's Plaint," "Creon," "The Worker
and The Shirker," "Food Is Love," "First Act
Crisis," "Astrociggy," "Second Act Beginning,"
"Hollow," "Seduction Second Degree," "Panassoci-
ative," "Earth Dance," "Trinity," "Special Bul-
letin," "Take a Knife," "Second Honeymoon,"
"Jeff's Plaints," "Incantation," "Beautiful Man,"
"Sacrifice," "Now!," "We Are the Whores."

"A Space Age Musical Soap" in two acts.

General Manager: David Black
Press: Merle Debuskey, Faith Geer
Stage Managers: Jane Neufeld, Robert Blacker

* Closed June 7, 1970 after 56 performances.

Friedman-Abeles Photos

**April Shawhan, Sharon Laughlin
in "Mod Donna"**

ANTA MATINEE SERIES
Lucille Lortel, Artistic Director
Fourteenth Season

THEATRE DE LYS

Monday, October 27, and Tuesday matinee October 28, 1969.

A ROUND WITH RING

An "Entertainment" in two parts adapted from the writings of Ring Lardner, and the music of Vincent Youmans, G. Harris White, Jerome Kern, Nora Bayes, Lee Roberts, and Ring Lardner; Coordinator, John Toland; Costumes, Cynthia Barrington; Lighting, Chenault Spence; Stage Manager, Tom Hull.

CAST

Orson Bean	Melinda Dillon
Ann Hodapp	James Pritchett
Bob Lydiard	George Hall

Monday, November 10, 1969, and Tuesday matinee November 11, 1969.

OH, PIONEERS

Written and Directed by Douglas Taylor; Lighting, William Mintzer; Stage Managers, James Doolan, Anne O'Donnell.

CAST

Sue .... Sarah Cunningham
Juliet .... Barbara Baxley
Willie .... Keith Charles
Fred .... Frank Borgman

A Play in 3 acts. The action takes place at the present time in a smallish Mid-Western town.

Monday December 15, 1969 and Tuesday matinee, December 16, 1969.

DREAM OF A BLACKLISTED ACTOR

By Conrad Bromberg; Director, Arthur Sherman; Designer, Parmelee Welles; Lighting, Roger Morgan; Songs, John Duffy; Production Assistant, Jackie Siegel; Sound, Gary Harris.

CAST

Edward Morris .... Rip Torn
Cookie Morris .... Janet Ward
Teresa Morris .... Catherine Burns
Joe Morris .... Kristoffer Tabori
Grace .... Judith Kercheval
Miss Barrow .... Jackie Siegel
Mr. Bennet .... Rick Cane
Mr. Warren .... Alan Garfield
First FBI Man .... Patrick Baldauff
Second FBI Man .... Gerard Hilpert

A Play in 3 acts. The action takes place in the not-too-distant past.

Monday, January 5, and Tuesday matinee, January 6, 1970.

"CRUISING SPEED 600 MPH" and "MRS. SNOW"

Director, Robert Moss; Lighting, Timmy Harris; Stage Manager, Dennis Keith.

CAST

"Cruising Speed 600 MPH"
By Anna Marie Barlow

Rosie .... Janet Ward
Pete .... Donald Gantry

The action takes place at the present time inside an airplane departing from Kennedy Airport, N.Y.

Intermission

"Mrs. Snow"
By Kenneth Pressman

Mrs. Snow .... Patricia O'Connell
Iva .... Janet League
Allen .... Dennis Keith

General Manager: Paul B. Berkowsky
Company Manager: Bob MacDonald
Series Coordinator: Ken Richards
Press: Saul Richman

THE OPEN THEATER
Joseph Chaikin, Director

WASHINGTON SQUARE
METHODIST CHURCH

Opened Tuesday, May 26, 1970*
The Open Theater presents in repertory:

TERMINAL

A collective work created by the Open Theater Ensemble; Co-Directors, Joseph Chaikin, Roberta Sklar; Text, Susan Yankowitz; Costumes, Gwen Fabricant; Lighting, Will Mott; Administrative Director, Marianne De Pury; Production Supervisor, Dale Whitt.

OPEN THEATER ENSEMBLE: James Barbosa, Raymond Barry, Shami Chaikin, Brenda Dixon, Ron Faber, Jayne Haynes, Ralph Lee, Peter Maloney, Mark Samuels, Ellen Schindler, Tina Shepard, Barbara Vann, Lee Worley, Paul Zimet.

Opened Friday, May 29, 1970.*

THE SERPENT

A Play created by the Open Theater Ensemble; Words and Structure by Jean-Claude Van Italie; Director, Joseph Chaikin; Associate Director, Roberta Sklar; Bruitage, Richard Peaslee, Stanley Walden; Associate, Patricia Cooper; Lighting, Will Mott; Production Supervisor, Dale Whitt; Administrative Director, Marianne de Pury.

Opened Saturday, May 30, 1970.*

ENDGAME

By Samuel Beckett; Director, Roberta Sklar; Production Supervisor, Dale Whitt; Costumes, Gwen Fabricant; Scenic Adviser, Bil Michelevich; Lighting, Will Mott; Administrative Director, Marianne De Pury.

CAST

Clov .... Peter Maloney
Hamm .... Joseph Chaikin
Nagg .... James Barbosa
Nell .... Jayne Haynes

Press: Howard Atlee, David Roggensack, Irene Gandy

* Closed June 14, 1970 after a limited engagement of 18 performances in repertory.

James Barbosa in "Endgame"
Above: "Terminal"

SULLIVAN STREET PLAYHOUSE

Opened Tuesday, May 3, 1960.*
Lore Noto presents:

THE FANTASTICKS

Book and Lyrics, Tom Jones; Suggested by Edmond Rostand's play "Les Romantiques"; Music, Harvey Schmidt; Director, Word Baker; Musical Direction and Arrangements, Julian Stein; Designed by Ed Wittstein; Associate Producers, Sheldon Baron, Dorothy Olim, Robert Alan Gold; Original Cast Album by MGM Records.

CAST

The Narrator	Joe Bellomo † 1
The Girl	Anne Kaye † 2
The Boy	Craig Carnelia † 3
The Boy's Father	Donald Babcock † 4
The Girl's Father	John J. Martin
The Actor	Justin Gray † 5
The Man Who Dies	Tom Lacy † 6
The Mute	Ron Prather † 7
At the piano	Bill F. McDaniels
At the harp	Sally Foster

STANDBYS: Narrator, Joe Bellomo; Girl, Carole Demas; Boy, Jimmy Dodge

MUSICAL NUMBERS: "Try to Remember," "Much More," "Metaphor," "Never Say No," "It Depends on What You Know," "Soon It's Gonna Rain," "Rape Ballet," "Happy Ending," "This Plum Is Too Ripe," "I Can See It," "Plant a Radish," "Round and Round," "They Were You."

A Musical in two acts.

General Manager: Bob MacDonald
Company Manager: Jeffrey H. Knox
Press: Harvey Sabinson, David Powers, Sandra Manley
Stage Managers: Geoffrey Brown, Edward Garrabrandt, Robert Crest

* Still playing May 31, 1970. For original NY production, see THEATRE WORLD, Vol.16.
† Succeeded by: 1. Michael Tartel, 2. Carolyn Mignini, 3. Erik Howell, Samuel D. Ratcliffe, Michael Glenn-Smith, 4. Charles Goff, Charles Welch, 5. Ron Prather, 6. Peter Blaixill, Samuel As-said, Bill McIntyre, 7. Les Shenkel

Van Williams Photos

(from top) Charles Welch, John J. Martin, Sa... Ratcliffe, Carolyn Mignini, Michael Tartel, Sa... As-Said, Ron Prather, Les Shenkel

Donald Babcock, Samuel D. Ratcliffe, John J. Martin, Carolyn Mignini

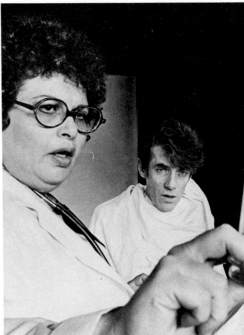

Elaine Shore, William Hickey in "Next"

THEATRE 80 ST. MARKS

Opened Tuesday, March 7, 1967.*
Arthur Whitelaw and Gene Persson present:

YOU'RE A GOOD MAN, CHARLIE BROWN

Book, John Gordon; Based on comic strip "Peanuts" by Charles M. Schulz; Music and Lyrics, Clark Gesner; Director, Joseph Hardy, Sets and Costumes, Alan Kimmel; Lighting, Jules Fisher; Musical Supervision, Arrangements, Additional Material, Joseph Raposo; Associate Producer, Stanley Mann; Production Assistant, Kathleen Huber, Madelyn Buzzard; Original Cast Album by MGM Records.

CAST

Linus	Gene Kidwell
Charlie Brown	Alfred Mazza
Patty	Karen Johnson
Schroeder	Jimmy Dodge
Snoopy	Don Potter
Lucy	Ann Gibbs

UNDERSTUDIES: Charlie, Linus, Schroeder, Carter Cole; Snoopy, Don Kyle; Lucy, Patty, Minnie Gaster

MUSICAL NUMBERS: "You're a Good Man, Charlie Brown," "Schroeder," "Snoopy," "My Blanket and Me," "Kite," "Dr. Lucy," "Book Report," "The Red Baron," "T.E.A.M.," "Glee Club Rehearsal," "Little Known Facts," "Suppertime," "Happiness."

A Musical in 2 acts. The action takes place at the present time during an average day in the life of Charlie Brown.

Company Manager: Larry Goossen
Press: Max Eisen, Jeanne Gibson Merrick, Warren Pincus
Stage Managers: Pat Carney, Barbara Tuttle

* Still playing May 31, 1970. For original production, see THEATRE WORLD, Vol. 23.

ight: (from top) Don Potter, Gene Kidwell, Karen ohnson, Jimmy Dodge, Ann Gibbs, Alfred Mazza

GREENWICH MEWS THEATRE

Opened Monday, February 10, 1969.*
Lyn Austin and Oliver Smith, Seymour Vall in association with Robert J. Gibson and IPC present:

"ADAPTATION" — "NEXT"

Director, Elaine May; Scenery, William Pitkin; Lighting, Michael Davidson; Production Associate, Tessie Hill; Production Assistant, Eda Zahl.

CAST

"Adaptation" by Elaine May

Games Master	Graham Jarvis /1
Players (male)	Paul Dooley /2
Players (female)	Carol Morley /3
R. G. Brown /4	R. G. Brown /4

"Next" by Terrence McNally

Marion Cheever	Dick Van Patten /5
Sgt. Thech	Elaine Shore /6

UNDERSTUDIES: Players (male), Dick Yarmy; Games Master, Marion Cheever, Kenneth Kimmins; Contestant, Phillip R. Allen; Players (female), Sgt. Thech, Grace Kimmins.

General Manager: Steven Sinn
Company Manager: Patricia King
Press: Alan Eichler, David Powers
Stage Managers: Paul Holland, Patricia King

* Still playing May 31, 1970. For original NY production, see THEATRE WORLD, Vol. 25.
† Succeeded by: 1. Frank Freda, Dick Yarmy, Phillip R. Allen, Kenneth Kimmins, 2. Marvin Lichterman, Richard Ramos, 3. Stockard Channing, 4. Mark Gordon, Dick Yarmy, Phillip R. Allen, 5. William Hickey, 6. Patricia Fay.

Leo Friedman Photos

Dick Yarmy, Richard Ramos, Carol Morley, Mark Gordon in "Adaptation"

(front) George Pentecost, Page Johnson, Bill Moor,
Alan Castner, (back) Paul Rudd, Rex Robbins, Robert
Christian, Donald Clement

Curt Dawson, Carleton Carpenter

THEATRE FOUR

Opened Sunday, April 14, 1968.*
Richard Barr and Charles Woodward, Jr
present:

THE BOYS IN THE BAND

By Mart Crowley; Director, Robert Moor
Designed by Peter Harvey; Administrative D
rector, Barry Plaxen; Administrative Assistar
Henry Avery; Production Assistant, Jack Custe
CAST

Michael	David Daniels †
Donald	Leon Russom †
Emory	Matthew Tobin †
Larry	Christopher Bren
Hank	Wayne Tippit †
Bernard	Harold Scott †
Cowboy	Ted LePlat †
Alan	David O'Brien †
Harold	Edward Zang †

UNDERSTUDIES: Donald, Larry, Cowboy, Wi
iam Leet; Bernard, Lisle Wilson; Harold, Emor
John Mintun; Hank, Alan, Jered Mickey

A Comedy-Drama in 2 acts. The action tak
place at the present time in Michael's apartme
in New York.

General Manager: Michael Kasdan
Company Manager: Richard Grayson
Press: David Rothenberg, Joe Cali,
Betty Lee Hunt, Henry Luhrman
Stage Managers: Robert Schear, Richard Foltz

Still playing May 31, 1970. For original NY pr
duction, see THEATRE WORLD, Vol. 24.
† Succeeded by: 1. Carleton Carpenter, Geor
Pentecost, Philip Cusack, 2. Paul Rudd, 3. Je
Admire, Page Johnson, 4. John Devlin, Rex Ro
bins, 5. Robert Christian, 6. Donald Clemer
7. Curt Dawson, Nicholas Pryor, Jered Micke
8. Bill Moor.

VILLAGE GATE

Opened Monday, January 22, 1968.*
3W Productions, Inc. presents:

JACQUES BREL IS ALIVE AND WELL AND LIVING IN PARIS

Production, Conception, English Lyrics, Additional Material, Eric Blau and Mort Shuman; Based on Brel's Lyrics and Commentary; All Dialogue Adapted from works of Jacques Brel; Music, Jacques Brel; Director, Moni Yakim; Music Arranged and Conducted by Wolfgang Knittel; Musical Direction, Mort Shuman; Consultant, Nat Shapiro; Scenery, Henry E. Scott III; Costumes, Ilka Suarez; Vocal Direction, Lillian Strongin; Lighting, James Nisbet Clark; Production Supervised by Eric Blau; Assistant Conductor, Bertha Melnik; Production Assistant, Jerry Lee.

CAST

Elly Stone †	Shawn Elliot
Mort Shuman	Alice Whitefield

MUSICAL NUMBERS: "Marathon," "Alone," "Madeleine," "I Loved," "Mathilde," "Bachelor's Dance," "Timid Frieda," "My Death," "Girls and Dogs," "Jackie," "The Statue," "Desperate Ones," "Sons Of," "Amsterdam," "The Bulls," "Old Folks," "Marieke," "Brussels," "Fannette," "Funeral Tango," "The Middle Class," "You're Not Alone," "Next," "Carousel," "If We Only Have Love."

A Musical Entertainment in two acts.

General Manager: Lily Turner
Press: Ivan Black
Stage Managers: James Nisbet Clark, Philip Price

* Still playing May 31, 1970. For original production, see THEATRE WORLD, Vol. 24.
† / During the season, the following appeared in this production: June Gable, Aileen Fitzpatrick, Chevi Colton, Joe Silver, Jack Blackton, John C. Attle, Sally Cooke, Rita Gardner, Joe Masiell, Teri Ralston, Stan Porter, Norman Atkins, Betty Rhodes, Margery Cohen, J. T. Cromwell.

Margery Cohen   **J. T. Cromwell**   **Chevi Colton**
Above: Joe Masiell

John C. Attle
Above: Rita Gardner

Top Right: Elly Stone, Mort Shuman

OFF-BROADWAY PRODUCTIONS FROM OTHER SEASONS THAT CLOSED DURING THIS SEASON

Title	Opened	Closed	Performances
Your Own Thing	Jan. 13, 1968	Apr. 5, 1970	937
Curley McDimple	Nov. 22, 1967	Jan. 25, 1970	931
Dames at Sea	Dec. 20, 1968	May 10, 1970	575
Little Murders	Jan. 5, 1969	Nov. 30, 1969	400
To Be Young, Gifted and Black	Jan. 2, 1969	Dec. 7, 1969	380
Ceremonies in Dark Old Men	Apr. 28, 1969	Feb. 15, 1970	320
Peace	Jan. 27, 1969	July 13, 1969	192
DeSade Illustrated	May 12, 1969	Aug. 24, 1969	117
Dance of Death	May 25, 1969	July 27, 1969	54

NEW YORK SHAKESPEARE FESTIVAL
Delacorte Theater, Central Park
Joseph Papp, Producer
Gerald Freedman, Artistic Director
July 15 through Aug. 30, 1969

DELACORTE THEATER

Opened Tuesday, July 15, 1969.*
The New York Shakespeare Festival in cooperation with the City of New York presents:

PEER GYNT

By Henrik Ibsen; Directed and Adapted by
Gerald Freedman; Translated by Michael Meyer;
Setting, Ming Cho Lee; Lighting, Martin Aron-
stein; Costumes, Theoni V. Aldredge; Songs and
Music, John Morris; Choreography, Joyce Trisler;
Assistant Director, Amy Saltz; Associate Pro-
ducer, Bernard Gersten, Technical Director,
Michael Wheeler; Production Assistants, Evan
Morris, Stephen Yardley.

CAST

Peer Gynt	Stacy Keach
Aase, his mother	Estelle Parsons
Kari, her friend	Janet Dowd
Aslak, Admiral-at-Sea, Asylum Keeper	
	Michael Baseleon
Solveig's Father, Priest, Button Moulder	
	John Heffernan
Solveig	Judy Collins
Helga, her sister	Lisa Griffin
Solveig's Mother	Paulita Sedgwick
Ingrid, Greenclad Lady, Anitra	
	Olympia Dukakis
Bridegroom Mads-Moen, General-at-Sea, Pen,	
Thin Person	Robert Stattel
Bridegroom's Father, Troll Prime Minister,	
Strange Passenger	Albert Stratton
Ingrid's Father, Troll King, Diplomat-at-Sea	
	James Cahill
Saeter Girls	Marilyn Meyers, Esther Koslow,
	Maria Di Dia
The Boyg, Peer Gynt	Stacy Keach
Troll Brat	Francis Patrelle

VILLAGERS, TROLLS, ETC.: Bruce Cobb, Tom
Crawley, James DeMarse, Kevin Gardiner, Philip
C. Harris, Robert Keesler, Esther Koslow, Marilyn
Meyers, Mary Nall, Michael Rives, Joseph Rose,
Paulita Sedgwick, Patrick Shea, Sam Tsoutsouvas

DANCING ENSEMBLE: Loretta Abbott, Eileen
Barbaris, Rodney Griffin, Edward Henkel, Sharron
Miller, Francis Patrelle, David Radner, Clay Talia-
ferro, Nina Trasoff, Margo Travers

UNDERSTUDIES: Aase, Janet Dowd; Aslak,
Sam Tsoutsouvas; Solveig's Father, Tom Crawley;
Solveig, Esther Koslow; Helga, Nina Trasoff;
Ingrid, Marilyn Meyers; Bridegroom, Philip C.
Harris; Bridegroom's Father, Robert Keesler;
Ingrid's Father, James DeMarse.

A Drama presented in two parts.

Press: Merle Debuskey, Faith Geer
Stage Managers: Michael Chambers,
Dean Compton, Gage Andretta

* Closed Aug. 2, 1969 after 17 performances.

Friedman-Abeles Photos

**Top Right: Estelle Parsons, Stacy Keach, Judy Collins
Below: Stacy Keach, Olympia Dukakis**

Judy Collins, Stacy Keach

DELACORTE THEATER

Opened Tuesday, August 12, 1969.*
The New York Shakespeare Festival in co-operation with the City of New York presents:

TWELFTH NIGHT

By William Shakespeare; Director, Joseph Papp; Setting, Douglas W. Schmidt; Lighting, Martin Aronstein; Costumes, Theoni V. Aldredge; Songs and Music, Galt MacDermot; Swordplay, Albert Quinton; Technical Director, Michael Wheeler; Associate Producer, Bernard Gersten; Assistant Director, Paul Schneider; Production Assistant, Robert Mandel; Hairstylist, Dieter Schade.

CAST

Orsino	Ralph Waite
Curio	Philip C. Harris
Valentine	Stephen Collins
Viola	Barbara Barrie
Sea Captain	Albert Quinton
Sir Toby Belch	Stephen Elliott
Maria	Jennifer Darling
Sir Andrew Aguecheek	Tom Aldredge
Feste	Charles Durning
Olivia	Sasha von Scherler
Malvolio	Robert Ronan
Antonio	Albert Stratton
Sebastian	Peter Simon
First Officer	Sam Tsoutsouvas
Second Officer	Paul McHenry
Priest	Albert Quinton
Servants	Bruce Cobb, Kevin Gardiner
Honor Guard	Thomas Crawley, James De Marse, Patrick Shea
Musicians	Leonard Handler, John McLeod, Stephen Wilensky

UNDERSTUDIES: Viola, Olivia, Elzbieta Chizeska; Maria, Sarah Harris

A Comedy presented in two parts. The action takes place in Illyria.

Press: Merle Debuskey, Faith Geer
Stage Managers: Michael Chambers, Dean Compton

* Closed Aug. 30, 1969 after 17 performances.

MOBILE THEATER

Opened Tuesday, August 5, 1969 in Washington Square Park.*
The New York Shakespeare Festival in co-operation with the City of New York presents:

ELECTRA

By Sophocles; Translated by H. D. F. Kitto; Director, Gerald Freedman; Music, John Morris; Setting, Ming Cho Lee; Lighting, Lawrence Metzler; Costumes, Theoni V. Aldredge; Chorus Direction, Amy Saltz, Gerald Freedman; Chorus Staging and Choreography, Louis Johnson; Assistant Director, Amy Saltz; Tour Director, Charles Haid; Production Assistant, Frances Wragg.

CAST

Paedagogus, attendant of Orestes	Mel Winkler
Orestes, son of Agamemnon and Clytemnestra	Thurman Scott
Electra, daughter of Agamemnon and Clytemnestra	Olivia Cole
Chorus Leader	Robbie McCauley
Chrysothemis, daughter of Agamemnon and Clytemnestra	Joan Harris
Clytemnestra	Josephine Premice
Aegisthus	Clee Burtonya
Pylades, friend of Orestes	Herbert Jefferson, Jr.
Attendants to Clytemnestra	Deatra Lambert, Emma Slaughter

CHORUS OF WOMEN: Laura Cooper, Deloris Gaskins, Aldine King, Ceci Perrin, Leslie Rivers, Lea Scott, Pawnee Sills, Yvonne Stafford, Ella Thompson, Gwynne Tomlan

UNDERSTUDIES: Paedagogus, Clee Burtonya; Orestes, Herbert Jefferson, Jr.; Electra, Clytemnestra, Deloris Gaskins; Chorus Leader, Ceci Perrin; Chrysothemis, Robbie McCauley; Aegisthus, Charles Turner

A Drama presented without intermission. The action takes place before the royal palace.

Press: Merle Debuskey, Faith Geer
Stage Managers: Charles Turner, Philip Parker

* Closed Aug. 30, 1969.

Friedman-Abeles Photos

Sasha Von Scherler, Barbara Barrie Above: Barbara Barrie, Stephen Elliott, Tom Aldredge in "Twelfth Night"

Josephine Premice, Olivia Cole in "Electra"

AMERICAN SHAKESPEARE FESTIVAL
Stratford, Connecticut
Joseph Verner Reed, Executive Producer
June 18 through Sept. 14, 1969

Managing Producer, Berenice Weiler; Artistic Director, Michael Kahn; Production Manager, Lo Hardin; Press, Ben Kornzweig, Reginald Denenholz, Anne Goodrich; Music Director and Conductor, Conrad Susa; Directors, Michael Kahn, Peter Gill, John Dexter; Sets, Karl Eigsti, Ed Wittstein, William Ritman; Costumes, Jane Greenwood, Jeanne Button; Lighting, Thomas Skelton; Sound, Alvin Lucier; Music and Songs, Al Carmines; Choreography, William Burdick; Associate Director, Moni Yakim; Mime, Elizabeth Keen.

COMPANY

Brian Bedford, Len Cariou, Morris Carnovsky, Charles Cioffi, Barry Corbin, Danny Davis, Herb Davis, Mary Doyle, Patricia Elliott, Robert Foxworth, Fredric Glenn, William Glover, James Greene, Mervyn Haines, Jr., William Hickey, Tom Klunis, Joseph Maher, Roberta Maxwell, Michael McGuire, Riggs O'Hara, Edwin Owens, Michael Parish, Wyman Pendleton, June Prud'Homme, Kate Reid, Marian Seldes, Roger Omar Serbagi, Carl Strano, Kristoffer Tabori, Tony Thomas, Toby Tompkins, Maria Tucci, Tony van Bridge, Martin Broomfield, Madge Grant, Anthony Passantino, Ellis Richardson, Frederick Rivera, Robert Scogin, Gerald Cooper, Gary Copeland, Frank Cossa, James Davis, Michael Diamond, Michael Donaghue, Sidney Goldstein, Sylvia Grant, Bolen High, Marc Jacobs, Archie Johnson, Davison Lloyd, James Nichols, Gary Poe, Timothy Riley.

PRODUCTIONS

"Henry V," "Much Ado About Nothing," "Hamlet," "The Three Sisters"

Martha Swope Photos

Len Cariou as Henry V

"Much Ado About Nothing"
Above: The French War Machine
in "Henry V"

William Glover, Roberta Maxwell, Robert Foxworth, Len Cariou in "Much Ado"

Morris Carnovsky, Brian Bedford
in "Hamlet"

Kate Reid, Brian Bedford
in "Hamlet"

Michael McGuire, Marian Seldes, Morris Carnovsky,
Len Cariou, Maria Tucci, Kate Reid in
"The Three Sisters"

SAN DIEGO NATIONAL SHAKESPEARE FESTIVAL
San Diego, California
Craig Noel, Producing Director
June 10 through Sept. 14, 1969
Twentieth Season

Associate Director, William Roesch; Art Director, Peggy Kellner; Business Manager, Adrienne Butler; Press, William B. Eaton; Technical Director, Bernard de Selm; Production Assistant, William Gonzalez; Directors, Richard Easton, Jack O'Brien, Ellis Rabb; Music and Songs, Bob James; Sets and Costumes, Peggy Kellner, Clifford Capone, Nancy Potts; Lighting, Bruce Kelley; Additional Music, Conrad Susa; Sound, Dan Dugan; Stage Managers, Nikos Kafkalis, Michael Vine, Charles Kondek, Domingo Tobar

COMPANY

Leon Charles, Peter Coffield, Richard Easton, Laurence Guittard, Katherin Henryk, Peter Jacob, John McMurtry, Priscilla Morrill, Sada Thompson, Tom Toner, James Tripp, Christopher Walken, James Whittle, Kathleen Bishop, Steve Brown, Diana Durnell, Joseph Kawaja, Albert Lord, Tom McCorry, Arthur Ross, Brendan Smith, Carolyn Wyatt, Eugene Carroll, Tom Corcoran, Daniel Erwine, Richard Geer, Tad Geer, Stephen Hawxhurst, William Lehrke, Michael Sinor

PRODUCTIONS

"Julius Caesar," "A Comedy of Errors," "Macbeth"

**Priscilla Morrill, Richard Easton
in "Julius Caesar"**

**Sada Thompson, Richard Easton
in "Macbeth"**

**Christopher Walken, John McMurty
in "Julius Caesar"**

160

**Laurence Guittard, Richard Easton,
Leon Charles in "Julius Caesar"**

**Tom Toner, Katherine Henry,
in "Julius Caesar"**

Laurence Guittard, John McMurtry,

**Christopher Walken, John McMurtay,
James Whittle in "Comedy of Errors'**

161

OREGON SHAKESPEAREAN FESTIVAL
Ashland, Oregon
Angus L. Bowmer, Producing Director
July 19, through Sept. 7, 1969
29th Season

Directors, Richard D. Risson, Edward S. Brubaker, Hugh C. Evans, Patrick Hines, Carl Ritchie; General Manager, William W. Patton; Press, Robert F. Knoll; Designers, Clayton L. Karkosh, Richard L. Hay, Jean Schultz Davidson, Steven A. Maze; Technical Director, Larry Davidson; Stage Manager, Pat Patton; Choreographer, Shirlee Dodge; Musical Director, W. Bernard Windt

COMPANY

John Arnone, Jim Baker, Hal Bergem, Candace Birk, Ray Birk, Larry Carpenter, Jose Carrillo, Carol Condon, Philip K. Davidson, Tom Donaldson, Charles Edelman, Allen Fearon, Dorothy French, Curtis F. Hanson, John Herzog, Steven James Horton, Christopher Howard, Dana Holm Howard, Robin Hubbard, Terry W. Judd, Roger Kozol, Idalah Luria, Amanda McBroom, Mark Murphey, Tom Oleniac, Shirley Patton, Theodore Pejovich, David Perkovich, Dan Plucinski, Mary Ed Porter, Scott Porter, Myshkin Sletteland, Dennis Smith, Doug Soesbe, J. W. Swearingen, George Taylor, Steven White, Mark York, A. Ryan Allen, Todd Barton, Mark W. Blankfield, Tom Breidenthal, Emily Carpenter, Donna Federico, Jennifer Graham, Robert Ground, Jo Guthrie, Larry Alan Haynes, Carlista Holland, Jon B. Holland, Ghent Howell, Randall S. Moore, Rosa Morin, Carolyn Norton, Debbie Quinn, Michal Dean Scolman, Robert M. Singleton, Joe Tulloch, Gary D. von Stein, Scott Wagoner, Diane Winder

PRODUCTIONS

"The Tempest," "Romeo and Juliet," "Twelfth Night," "King John," "Virtue in Danger"

Carolyn Mason Jones Photos

America's first Elizabethan theatre designed after the Fortune Theatre

Patrick Hines, Dorothy French in "The Tempest"

Roger Kozol, Patrick Hines, Carolyn Norton in "Romeo and Juliet"

**Philip Davidson, Carol Condon
in "King John"**

**Robert Ground in
"Virtue in Danger"**

**Jim Baker, Theodore Pejovich,
Scott Porter in "Twelfth Night"**

**Charles Edelman, Jim Baker
in "The Tempest"**

STRATFORD FESTIVAL OF CANADA
Jean Gascon, Executive Artistic Director
May 26 through Oct. 11, 1969
Seventeenth Season

Associate Artistic Director, John Hirsch; General Manager, William Wylie; Musical Director, Victor di Bello; Administrative Director, Victor Polley; Production Director, John Hayes; Press, Mary Webb, Lillian Bowland; Production Manager, Jack Hutt; Production Coordinator, Grania Mortimer; Directors, Jean Gascon, David Giles, John Hirsch, Marvin Gordon; Designers, James Hart Stearns, Michael Annals, Robert Prevost, Robert Fletcher, Sam Kirkpatrick, Kenneth Mellor; Stage Managers, Keith Green, Thomas Hooker, Patrick McEntee, Christopher Root, Paul Foley, Ron Francis, Ian Gaskell, Elspeth Gaylor, Vincent Berns, Alex Stephenson

COMPANY

William Hutt, Douglas Anderson, Mervyn Blake, Leo Ciceri, Neil Dainard, John Gardiner, George Neilson, Anne Anglin, Mary Hitch, Linda Rice, Jennifer Phipps, Bernard Behrens, Stephen McHattie, Kenneth Pogue, Tedde Moore, Joel Kenyon, Karin Fernald, Joyce Campion, D. M. Hughes, Peter Scupham, John Cutts, Saul Rubinek, Elaine Wood, David Lindsay, Diana Barrington, David Lindsay, Robin Marshall, Kenneth Welsh, Guy Bannerman, Lawrence Benedict, Clyde Burton, Patrick Christopher, Alan Clarey, Ronald East, Stephen Markle, Gary Reineke, Richard Rhude, Jason Robards, Don Sutherland, David Yanovitz, Horace Hinds, Frank Blander, Lanny Levine, James Blendick, Powys Thomas, Kenneth Welsh, Eric Donkin, Jane Casson, Patrick Crean, Gary Reineke, Hume Cronyn, Margaret Braidwood, Amelia Hall, Paul Harding, Edward McPhillips, Paul Harding, Donald Ewer, Louis Guss, P. L. Pfeiffer, Paul Craig, Jack Saunders, Malcolm Armstrong, John Maddison, Joseph Rutten, Tyrus Cheney, Edmund Glover, Leo Phillips, Reginald Rowland, Jr., Peter Sturgess, Thomas Alway, Ian Gaskell, Richard Kelley, Alain Montpetit, Jack Roberts, Wendell Smith, Hans Werner, Joseph Wynn, Donald Davis, Jack Creley, Marilyn Gardner, Alan Crofoot, Irving Harmon, Arnold Soboloff, James Tolkan, Robert Weil, Dinah Christie, Jeri Archer, Stephen Foster, David Drummond, Kevin Kamis, Marc Mantell, Bargaret Rowan, Diane Young

PRODUCTIONS

"Measure for Measure," "Hamlet," "Hadrian VII," "Tartuffe," "The Alchemist," "The Satyricon"

Douglas Spillane Photos

Anne Anglin, Kenneth Welsh in "Hamlet"

Paul Harding, Hume Cronyn in "Hadrian VII"

Kenneth Welsh, Bernard Behrens, William Hutt, Robin Marshall in "Measure for Measure"

**Angela Wood, William Hutt
in "Tartuffe"**

**Jane Casson, William Hutt
in "The Alchemist"**

**Karin Fernald, Neil Dainard
in "Measure for Measure"**

**Marilyn Gardner, Jack Creley
in "The Satyricon"**

"ADAPTATION"-"NEXT"

Directed by Elaine May; "Adaptation" by Elaine May; "Next" by Terrence McNally; Associate Director, Wayne Carson; Scenic Designer, William Pitkin; Lighting, David F. Segal; Technical Director, Geoffrey Richon; Presented by The Theatre Company of Boston in association with Lyn Austin and Oliver Smith, Seymour Vall, Robert J. Gibson, I.P.C. Opened Sept. 17, 1969 in Boston, and closed there on Jan. 18, 1970.

CAST

"Adaptation"
Games Master..Bill Story
Players (male).....................................Don Billett
Players (female).....................Stockard Channing
Contestant....................................Phillip R. Allen
"Next"
Marion Cheever................................William Young
Sgt. Thech......................................Joan Tolentino

General Manager: Steven Sinn
Press: Alan Eichler
Stage Managers: Ronald Schaeffer, Arthur Merrow

Presented by the Los Angeles Music Center at the Mark Taper Forum; Under the supervision of Eda Zahl. Opened October 23, 1969 and closed December 7, 1969.

CAST

"Adaptation"
Games Master..............................Graham Jarvis
Players (male) ....Bob Barend
Players (female).............................Rose Arrick †1
Contestant...Gabriel Dell
"Next"
Marion Cheever ....James Coco †2
Sgt. Thech ....Elaine Shore

General Manager: Steven Sinn
Company Manager: Jerry Arrow
Press: Alan Eichler
Stage Managers: Tom Larson, Wallace Chappell
† Succeeded by: 1. Jeannie Berlin, 2. Dick Van Patten.

Presented by The Happy Medium, Chicago. Opened February 27, 1970 and closed May 31, 1970.

CAST

"Adaptation"
Games Master....................................William Wise
Players (male)..Joe Greco
Players (female).........................Fawne Harriman
Contestant...................................Spencer Milligan
"Next"
Marion Cheever ....Mike Nussbaum
Sgt. Thech ....Karin Woodward

Company Manager: Mary Jane Spencer
Press: Alan Eichler, David Powers
Stage Manager: Ronald Shayne

For original New York production, see THEATRE WORLD, Vol. 25.

Top Right: Phillip R. Allen, Stockard Channing in "Adaptation" (Bradford Herzog Photo) Below: Elaine Shore, Dick Van Patten in "Next"

(Friedman-Abeles Photo)

Bob Barend, Gabriel Dell, Rose Arrick in "Adaptation" (Steven Keull Photo)

Karin Woodward, Mike Nussbaum in "Next"

THE BOYS IN THE BAND

By Mart Crowley; Director, Murray Gitlin; Designed by Peter Harvey; Resident Director, Arthur Meyer; Technical Director, William Freese; Presented by Marshall Naify and Richard Norris in association with Keith Rockwell and Arthur Meyer. Opened Friday, October 31, 1969 in the Committee Theater, and closed there March 7, 1970.

CAST

Michael	Dennis Cooney
Donald	Brian Taggert
Emory	Joseph Palmieri
Larry	Richard Krisher
Hank	Thomas Connolly
Bernard	Guy Edwards
Alan	Richard Roat
Cowboy	Steven Davis
Harold	Gerald Taupier

General Manager: Keith Rockwell
Press: Claire Harrison, Joe Cali,
David Rothenberg
Stage Managers: Madeline Puzo, Patrick Foley

Director, Robert Moore; Lighting, V. C. Fuqua; Administrative Plaxen; Production Assistant, Jack Custer; Presented by Richard Barr and Charles Woodward. Opened Sunday, January 18, 1970 at the Studebaker in Chicago, and closed there Jan. 24, 1970.

CAST

Michael	George Pentecost
Donald	Paul Rudd
Emory	Page Johnson
Larry	Alan Castner
Hank	Rex Robbins
Bernard	Robert Christian
Alan	Jered Mickey
Cowboy	Donald Clement
Harold	Bill Moor

UNDERSTUDIES: Michael, Philip Cusack; Donald, Larry, Cowboy, Scott Pearson; Hank, Alan, Ron Vaad; Bernard, Peter Norman; Emory, George Monk.

General Managers: Michael Goldreyer,
Michael Kasdan
Company Manager: Oscar Abraham
Press: George Deber, David Rothenberg,
Joe Cali
Stage Managers: Robert Schear, Philip Cusack

For original New York production, see THEATRE WORLD, Vol. 24.

Dennis Cooney, Brian Taggert, Guy Edwards, Thomas Connolly, Benny Masters, Gerald Taupier, Richard Krisher, Joe Palmieri, Steven Davis

George Pentecost, Page Johnson, Bill Moor, Paul Rudd, Robert Christian, Donald Clement, Rex Robbins, Alan Castner Right Center: Page Johnson, Donald Clement

BUTTERFLIES ARE FREE

By Leonard Gershe; Director, Milton Katselas; Set, Richard Seger; Costumes, Robert Mackintosh; Lighting, Jules Fisher; Associate Producer, Ruth Bailey; Hairstylist, Joe Tubens; Presented by Arthur Whitelaw, Max J. Brown, Byron Goldman. Opened Wednesday, May 20, 1970 at the Huntington Hartford Theatre, Los Angeles, Calif., and still playing May 31, 1970.

CAST

Don Baker	Wendell Burton
Jill Tanner	Ellen Endicott-Jones
Mrs. Baker	Eve Arden
Ralph Austin	William Tynan

UNDERSTUDIES: Mrs. Baker, Marijane Maricle; Don, Ralph, Lloyd Kramer; Jill, Janice Lynde

A Comedy in 2 acts and 3 scenes. The action takes place at the present time in Don Baker's apartment on East 11th Street in New York.

General Manager: Marvin A. Krauss
Company Manager: Archie Thomson
Press: Max Eisen, Maurice Turet
Stage Managers: Victor Straus, William Tynan, Lloyd Kramer

Martha Swope Photos

Wendell Burton, William Tynan, Ellen Endicott-Jones, Eve Arden
Top Left: Wendell Burton, Eve Arden

CABARET

Book, Joe Masteroff; Based on play "I Am A Camera" by John Van Druten, and stories by Christopher Isherwood; Music, John Kander; Lyrics, Fred Ebb; Director, Harold Prince; Dances and Cabaret Numbers by Ronald Field; Scenic Production, Boris Aronson; Costumes, Patricia Zipprodt; Lighting, Jean Rosenthal; Musical Direction, Gilbert Bowers; Orchestrations, Don Walker; Dance Music Arrangements, David Baker; Original Cast Album by Columbia Records; Presented by Harold Prince in association with Ruth Mitchell. Opened Tuesday, Aug. 19, 1969 in State Fair Music Hall, Dallas, and closed May 23, 1970 in Columbus, Ohio.

CAST

Master of Ceremonies	Jay Fox
Clifford Bradshaw	Franklin Kiser
Ernst Ludwig	Bryan Hull
Custom Officials	Ray LaManna, Laried Montgomery
Fraulein Schneider	Alexandra Damien
Herr Schultz	Woody Romoff
Fraulein Kost	Sally Champlin
Telephone Girl	Joan Weisberg
Kit Kat Band	Judy Gorman, Avalon Lee, Mary Taylor
Maitre d'	John Bartholomew
Max	Ray LaManna
Bartender	Laried Montgomery
Sally Bowles	Tandy Cronyn
Taxi Driver	Jay Bonnell
Two Ladies	Sharon Wylie, Stefani Richards
German Sailors	Richard Cash, Greg Rodgers, T. Schuyler Smith, Fabian Stuart
Frau Wendel	Patricia Hall
Herr Wendel	Jay Bonnell
Herr Erdmann	Fred Cline

Kit Kat Girls:

Lulu	Mickie Bier
Fritzie	Dana Holby
Texas	Diane de Kopf
Frenchie	Lois Etelman
Marlene	Tracy Lee Christopher
Hulda	Carol Perea
Greta	Stefani Richards
Bobby	J. Richard Beneville
Victor	Allan Miller
Greta	Gia DeSilva
Felix	Pat McCann
German Soldier	Joe Stahl

UNDERSTUDIES: Sally, Joan Weisberg; Schultz, Jay Bonnell; Bradshaw, John Bartholomew; Fraulein Schneider, Patricia Hall; M. C., J. Richard Beneville; Ernst, Ray LaManna; Fraulein Kost, Gia DeSilva

MUSICAL NUMBERS: "Willkommen," "So What?," "Don't Tell Mama," "Telephone Song," "Perfectly Marvelous," "Two Ladies," "It Couldn't Please Me More," "Tomorrow Belongs to Me," "Why Should I Wake Up?," "Money Song," "Married," "Meeskite," "If You Could See Her," "What Would You Do," "Cabaret," Finale.

A Musical in 2 acts. The action takes place in Berlin before the start of the Third Reich in 1929-1930.

General Manager: Carl Fisher
Company Manager: James O'Neill
Press: Mary Bryant, Robert W. Jennings, Bernard Simon
Stage Managers: Ruth Mitchell, William Letters, Paul Waigner, Laried Montgomery

For original production see THEATRE WORLD, Vol. 23.

Friedman-Abeles Photos

Top Right: Tandy Cronyn, Jay Fox Below: Woody Romoff, Alexandra Damien, Franklin Kiser

Franklin Kiser, Bryan Hull, Tandy Cronyn

CANTERBURY TALES

Book, Martin Starkie, Nevill Coghill; Based on a translation of Chaucer by Nevill Coghill; Music, Richard Hill, John Hawkins; Lyrics, Nevill Coghill; Director, James Hammerstein; Choreography, Tommy Tune; Musical Direction and Vocal Arrangements, Richard Parrinello; Scenery, Derek Cousins; Re-Designed by C. Murawski; Costumes, Loudon Sainthill; Lighting, Neil Peter Jampolis; Consultant to Producers, Sammy Bayes; Technical Supervisor, John Higgins; Original Cast Album by Capitol Records; Presented by Hal James in association with National Performing Arts. Opened Monday, December 29. 1969 at the Playhouse, Wilmington, Del., closed April 11, 1970 at National in Washington, D.C.

CAST

Chaucer	Martyn Green
Host	Eric Berry
Miller	Patrick Hines
Wife of Bath	Constance Carpenter
Cook	David Steele
Merchant	Richard Neilson
Knight	Reid Shelton
Steward	Ray Walston
Prioress	Luce Ennis
Nun	Mary Jo Catlett
Priest	Llewellyn Thomas
Clerk of Oxford	Terry Eno
Squire	Walter McGinn
Friar	Bill Starr
The Sweetheart	Louisa Flaningam

and Leslie Bromley, Leigh Carole, Ciya Challis, Georgia Sparks, Jane Robertson, Julie Pars, Larry Levy, Chet D'Elia, Raymond Bussey, Marybeth Lahr, Lee Winston.

UNDERSTUDIES: Steward, Reid Shelton; Wife of Bath, Mary Jo Catlett; Chaucer, Richard Neilson; Host, Miller, Merchant, Lloyd Harris; Squire, David Steele; Sweetheart, Julie Pars; Clerk, Raymond Bussey; Nun, Jane Robertson; Prioress, Marybeth Lahr; Friar, Chet D'Elia; Swing Dancer, Leigh Carole.

MUSICAL NUMBERS: "Overture," "Song of Welcome," "Good Night Hymn," "Canterbury Day," "Pilgrim Riding Music," "I Have a Noble Cock," "Darling, Let Me Teach You How To Kiss," "There's the Moon," "It Depends on What You're At," "Love Will Conquer All," "Chanticleer," "Beer Is Best," "Come on and Marry Me, Honey," "Where Are the Girls of Yesterday," "Hymen, Hymen," "If She Has Never Loved Before," "I'll Give My Love a Ring," "I Am All A-Blaze," "What Do Women Want?," "April Song."

A Musical in 2 acts. The action passes between the "Tabard Inn," London, and Canterbury Cathedral in the spring during the latter part of the 14th century.

General Manager: Julian Olney
Company Manager: Edward Fisher
Press: William Tostevin
Stage Managers: Ian Cadenhead,
Christopher Detmer, Chet D'Elia

For original New York production, see THEATRE WORLD, Vol. 25.

Betty Nettis Photos

Top Left: Terry Eno, Louisa Flaningam, Walter McG
Below: Richard Neilson, Terry Eno, Reid She
Mary Jo Catlett, Luce Ennis, Ray Walston, W
McGinn, Constance Carpenter, Patrick Hines, D
Steele, Llewellyn Thomas

Constance Carpenter, Ray Walston
Above: Martyn Green

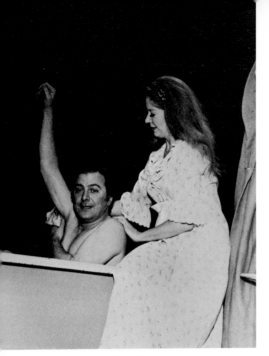

Jack Aranson, Sally Kemp

DYLAN

By Sidney Michaels; Director, Phillip Pruneau; Setting, Stuart Wurtzel; Costumes, Patrizia Von Brandenstein; Lighting, Ward Russell; Production Devised by Jack Aranson; Presented by the San Francisco Theatre Co. in association with the Dublin Theatre Festival. Opened Mar. 11, 1970 in the Denver, Colo., Auditorium Theatre, and closed May 30, 1970 in Philadelphia's Forrest Theatre.

CAST

Dylan Thomas	Jack Aranson
Caitlin Thomas	Mary Rose McMaster
John Malcolm Brinnin	William Whitman
Angus Marius	Oren Curtis
A Clubwoman	Karen Kondan
Meg Stuart	Sally Kemp
Annabelle Graham Pike	Coralie Persse
Robert Mattock	Terry Moore
Bartender	Jay Moreno
Katherine Anne Porter	Eve Porter
Thelma Wonderland	Veleka Gray
Rev. Breathwhate	Richard Spore
Elena Antone	Karen Kondan
Jay Henry Antone	Jim Nolan
Doctor	Terry Moore

REPORTERS, GUESTS, ETC.: Jay Moreno, Richard Spore, Veleka Gray, Eve Porter, Jim Nolan.

A Drama in 2 acts. The entire action of the play takes place in the early 1950's in America and Wales.

Company Manager: James S. Miller
Press: Theresa L. Cone, Dorathi Bock Pierre
Stage Managers: William Browder, Terry Moore

For original NY production, see THEATRE WORLD, Vol. 20.

FORTY CARATS

Adapted by Jay Allen from a play by Pierre Barillet and Jean-Pierre Gredy; Director, Abe Burrows; Scenery, Will Steven Armstrong; Costumes, Sara Brook; Lighting, Martin Aronstein; Associate Producer, Samuel Liff; Presented by David Merrick; Opened Sept. 29, 1969 at the Shubert in Cincinnati, and still playing May 31, 1970.

CAST

Ann Stanley	Barbara Rush
Peter Latham	Stephen Collins
Mrs. Adams	Doris Ingraham
Mrs. Margolin	Imogene Bliss
Billy Boylan	Scott McKay
Eddy Edwards	Gene Blakely
Maud Hayes	Audrey Christie
Trina Stanley	Sylvia Grand
Mrs. Latham	Eileen Letchworth
Mr. Latham	Art Barnett
Pat	William Cox

UNDERSTUDIES: Ann, Eileen Letchworth; Billy, Eddy, Latham, John Dutra; Peter, William Cox; Maud, Mrs. Margolin, Mrs. Adams, Marcie Stringer; Trina, Erin Connor; Mrs. Latham, Doris Ingraham.

A Comedy in 2 acts. The action takes place at the present time in the apartment and office of Ann Stanley in New York City, after a prologue somewhere in the Greek islands.

General Manager: Jack Schlissel
Company Manager: Albert H. Rosen
Press: Harvey B. Sabinson, Lee Solters, Gertrude Bromberg
Stage Managers: Robert Crawley, William Cox, Erin Connor

For original NY production, see THEATRE WORLD, Vol. 25.

Martha Swope Photo

Stephen Collins, Sylvia Grand, Audrey Christie, Barbara Rush, Gene Blakely

FIDDLER ON THE ROOF

Book, Joseph Stein; Based on Sholom Aleichem Stories; Music, Jerry Bock; Lyrics, Sheldon Harnick; Director-Choreographer, Jerome Robbins; Settings, Boris Aronson; Costumes, Patricia Zipprodt; Lighting, Jean Rosenthal; Orchestrations, Don Walker; Musical Director, Joseph Lewis; Dance Music Arranged by Betty Walberg; Vocal Arrangements, Milton Greene; Presented by Harold Prince; Opened Tuesday, April 19, 1966 at the Music Center, Los Angeles, and closed Jan. 17, 1970 at the Shubert in Philadelphia.

CAST

The Fiddler	Mark Stone
Tevye	Paul Lipson
Golde	Mimi Randolph
Tzeitel	Susan Lehman †1
Hodel	Barbara Coggin †2
Chava	Elizabeth Hale
Shprintze	Erica Greene
Bielke	Pamela Greene
Yente	Jennie Ventriss †3
Motel	Peter Marklin
Perchik	Virgil Curry †4
Lazar Wolf	Merwin Goldsmith †5
Mordcha	Fyv Finkel
Rabbi	Baruch Lumet †6
Mendel	James McDonald †7
Avram	Maurice Brenner
Nachum	George Stauch
Russian Dancer	Myron Meljie
Russian Singer	Bob Garrett
Grandma Tzeitel	Edward Androse
Fruma-Sarah	Maralyn Nell
Constable	Michael Burke
Fyedka	James Hobson †8
Shandel	Anne Piacentini

VILLAGERS: Tog Richards, Neil McNelis, Stuart Craig Wood, Peter Hamparian, Judith Brenner, Bob Garrett, Steve Bohm, Ralph Vucci, Verna Pierce, Bill Pugh, Melanie Lerner, Stephanie Satie, Barbara Logan, Martha Cataldo, Emily Byrne, Richard Folmer

A Musical in 2 acts. The action takes place in 1905 in Antevka, a village in Russia, on the eve of the revolutionary period.

General Manager: Carl Fisher
Company Manager: Al Jones
Press: Sol Jacobson, Lewis Harmon, Morris Yuter,
Stage Managers: Ruth Mitchell, Ben Strobach, Jay Jacobson, Christopher Scott

† Succeeded by: 1. Gretchen Evans, 2. Chris Callan, 3. Marise Counsell, 4. Keith Baker, 5. Bob Carroll, 6. Wil Albert, 7. Lewis J. Stadlen, 8. Alan Wilson.

For original NY production, see THEATRE WORLD, Vol. 21.

Friedman-Abeles Photos

Top Right: Paul Lipson, Mimi Randolph

Conn Fleming, Sanford Seeger, Stacy McAdams, Doreen Dunn, Bob Carroll, Elaine Kussack

FIDDLER ON THE ROOF

Book, Joseph Stein; Based on Sholom Aleichem's Stories; Music, Jerry Bock; Lyrics, Sheldon Harnick; Directed and Choreographed by Jerome Robbins; Settings, Boris Aronson; Costumes, Patricia Zipprodt; Lighting, Jean Rosenthal; Vocal Arrangements, Milton Greene; Musical Direction, Harold Glick; Dance Music Arranged by Betty Walberg; Orchestrations, Don Walker; Hairstylist, D. Rusty Bonaccorso; Presented by Harold Prince in association with Theatre Now, Inc. (William Court Cohen, President); Opened Dec. 27, 1969 in Dade County Auditorium, Miami, Fla., and still touring May 31, 1970.

CAST

Tevye	Bob Carroll †1
Golde	Elaine Kussack †2
Their Daughters:	
Tzeitel	Doreen Dunn
Hodel	Mary Ann Chinn
Chava	Alexandra Stoddart
Shprintze	Laurie Scandurra
Bielke	Jacqueline Clark
Yente	Charlotte Jones †3
Motel	Stacy McAdams
Perchik	Sidney Ben-Zali
Lazar Wolf	Joel Wolfe †4
Mordcha	Leon Spelman †5
Rabbi	Sanford Seeger
Mendel	Conn Fleming †6
Avram	Joel Fredrick
Grandma Tzeitel	Fannie Cusanelli
Fruma-Sarah	Jane Stevens †7
Constable	George Emch
Fyedka	Lewis Jacobson
Shadel	Nina Miller
Fiddler	Neal Thompson
Bottle Dancers	Teak Lewis, Vito Durante, Mark Goldman, Gary Dutton

VILLAGERS: Jerry Bell, Fannie Cusanelli, Vito Durante, Gary Dutton, George Emch, John Fennessy, Conn Fleming, Joel Fredrick, Mark Goldman, Jay Grimes, Sharon Hayes, Lewis Jacobson, Teak Lewis, Bess Meisler, Nina Miller, Naomi Robin, Jane Stevens, Neal Thompson, Jeff Warren

UNDERSTUDIES: Tevye, Ronald Coralian; Golde, Nina Miller; Lazar, Rabbi, Joel Fredrick; Hodel, Chava, Frumah, Naomi Robin; Tzeitel, Shereth Friedman; Perchik, Constable, Jeff Warren; Motel, Michael Hardstark; Yente, Grandma, Bess Meisler, John Fennessy; Mordcha, Teak Lewis; Mendel, Neal Thompson; Bielke, Shprintze, Sharon Hayes; Shandel, Fannie Cusanelli; Avram, Vito Durante; Fiddler, Mark Goldman

A Musical in 2 acts. The action takes place in 1905 in Anatevka, a village in Russia, on the eve of the revolutionary period.

General Manager: Carl Fisher
Company Manager: John Scott
Press: Sol Jacobson, Lewis Harmon, Robert W. Jennings, Bernard Simon
Stage Managers: Kenneth Porter, Paul Waigner, Robert Altshuler, Vito Durante, John Fennessy

† Succeeded by: 1. Harry Goz (temporarily), 2. Fritzi Burr, 3. Lila Teigh, 4. Ronald Coralian, 5. Joey Fitter, 6. Michael Hardstark, 7. Shereth Friedman

THE GREAT WHITE HOPE

By Howard Sackler; Director, Milton Katselas; Scenery, Robin Wagner; Costumes, David Toser; Lighting, Jules Fisher; Music Arranged by Charles Gross; Choral Supervision and Arrangement, Howard A. Roberts; Presented by Herman Levin; Opened Monday, Sept. 15, 1969 at the Hanna Theatre in Cleveland, O., and closed Jan. 10, 1970 at the Ahmanson in Los Angeles.

CAST

Jack Jefferson	Brock Peters
Eleanor Bachman	Claudette Nevins
Cap'n Dan	Clifford A. Pellow
Goldie	Marty Greene
District Attorney	Paul Jenkins
Klossowski	Darrell Sandeen
Tick	Tiger Haynes
Fred	George Harris II
Smitty	Martin J. Cassidy
Clara	Gloria Edwards
Mrs. Jefferson	Gertrude Jeannette
Pop Weaver	Donald Marye
Brady	J. O. Dooley
Roller	Steve Zulick
Bettor	J. R. Marks
Tout	John Bentley
Blackface	Vincent Milana
Colonel Cox	William Martel
Deacon	Lance Taylor
Young Negro	Andrew Marshall III
Barker	Frank Wilson
Mr. Donnelly	George Axler
Mrs. Bachman	Ann Driscoll
Mr. Dixon	Tom Noel
Pastor	Ensley
Rudy	Gene Whittington
Mr. Eubanks	Ron Millkie
Mr. Treacher	Joseph Boley
Handler	Steve Zulick
Sir William Griswold	William Major
Mr. Coates	Robert Nadder
Mrs. Kimball	Joi Staton
Mr. Farlow	Sam Nudell
Ragosy	Victor Burgess
African Student	Herbert Jefferson, Jr.
Juggler	Jack Parker
Paco	Ramon Alicea
Government Agent	Jimmy Hayes
The Kid	Darrell Sandeen
Cuban Boy	Andrew Marshall III

and Joseph De Nicola, Peter Rockwell, Bob Molock, Leu Camacho, Dorothi Fox, Birdie M. Hale, Marion L. Matthews, Maxine F. McCrey, Danette M. Small, Jean Taylor, Beau Gillingslea, Juan De Carlos, Billy Reid, Merritt Smith, Gordon Fearing, Earl Hindman, William McIntyre, Craig Thomas, Jack Parker, J. D. Marns, Ellen Tovatt

A Drama in 3 acts and 19 scenes. The action takes place in the years before and during World War I.

General Manager: Philip Adler
Company Manager: Milton M. Pollack
Press: Martin Shwartz, Nate Schenker
Stage Managers: Ben D. Kranz, Patricia Drylie, Steve Zulick

For original NY production, See THEATRE WORLD, Vol. 25.

Friedman-Abeles Photos

Brock Peters, Gertrude Jeannette Top Right: Brock Peters, Claudette Nevins

Marty Greene, Claudette Nevins, Brock Peters Above: Tiger Haynes, Peters, Nevins

HADRIAN VII

By Peter Luke; Director, Jean Gascon; Settings and Costumes, Robert Fletcher; Lighting, Lloyd Burlingame; Presented by Lester Osterman Productions, Bill Freedman, Charles Kasher; Opened Tuesday, Aug. 5, 1969 at the Stratford, Ontario, Canada, Shakespeare Festival, and closed May 30, 1970 at the Fisher in Detroit.

CAST

Frederick William Rolfe ....Hume Cronyn
Mrs. Nancy Crowe ....Margaret Braidwood
Agnes ....Amelia Hall †1
First Bailiff ....Paul Harding
Second Bailiff ....Edward McPhillips
Dr. Talacryn, Bishop of Caerleon.......Paul Harding
Dr. Courtleigh, Cardinal-Archbishop
  of Pimlico ....Edward McPhillips
Jeremiah Sant ....Donald Ewer
Cardinal Ragna....................................Louis Guss
Cardinal Berstein ....P. L. Pfeiffer †2
Father of St. Albans ....Paul Craig
Rector of St. Andrews ....Jack Saunders
George Arthur Rose ....Malcolm Armstrong
Cardinal-Archdeacon ....John Maddison
Paper Chamberlain ....Joseph Rutten
Cardinals...................Tyrus Cheney, J. Leo Gagnon,
          Edmund Glover, Reginald Rowland, Jr.,
                   Peter Sturgess, Malcom Wells
Choral Leader ....Jack Roberts

GUARDS, ACOLYTES, ETC.: Thomas Alway, Ian Gaskell, Richard Kelley, Alain Montpetit, Jack Roberts, Wendell Smith, Hans Werner, Joseph Wynn

UNDERSTUDIES: Rolfe, Paul Craig; Rose, Thomas Alway; Rector, Tyrus Cheney; Chamberlain, Edmund Glover; Regna, John Maddison; Talacryn, Reginal Rowland, Jr.; Father St. Albans, Peter Sturgess; Agnes, Mrs. Crowe, Collette Melville.

A Drama in 2 acts. The action takes place in the early 20th century in London and Rome.

General Manager: Richard Horner
Company Manager: Martin Cohen
Press: Harvey B. Sabinson, Lee Solters,
                     Willard Keefe
Stage Managers: Paul A. Foley, Ron Francis,
                     Ian Gaskell

† Succeeded by: Liza Cole, 2. Reginald Rowland, Jr.

For original NY production, see THEATRE WORLD, Vol. 25.

Paul Harding, Hume Cronyn
Top Right: Edward McPhillips, Cronyn

Margaret Braidwood (L), Hume Cronyn (C),
Donald Ewer (seated)

ROSENCRANTZ AND GUILDENSTERN ARE DEAD

By Tom Stoppard; Director, Jacqueline Britton; Designed by Leo B. Meyer; Costumes, Sara Brook; Music, Marc Wilkinson; Assistant to Producers, Linda D. Ford; Presented by Producing Managers Company (James B. McKenzie, Spofford J. Beadle, Ralph Roseman); Opened Monday, Sept. 8, 1969 in the Mechanic Theatre, Baltimore, Md., subsequently presented in repertory with "Hamlet," and closed Apr. 25, 1970 at Kent State University, Ohio.

CAST

Rosencrantz	John Church
Guildenstern	Clebert Ford
The Player	Robert Burr
Alfred	Ian Wilder
The King	Bruce Clayton-Brown
The Poisoner	Michael Aronson
The Spies	Con Roche, David Rosenbaum
Hamlet	Harvey Solin
Ophelia	Margo Ann Berdeshevsky
Claudius	Edwin Owens
Gertrude	Mary Hara
Polonius	Frederic Warriner
Soldier	Anthony Mainionis
Ambassador	Elliot Levine
Horatio	Michael Holmes

UNDERSTUDIES: Rosencrantz, Bruce Clayton-Brown; Guildenstern, Anthony Mainionis; Player, Michael Aronson; Alfred, David Rosenbaum; Tragedians, Michael Holmes; Ophelia, Gertrude, Rene Savich; Hamlet, Con Roche; Claudius, Polonius, Elliot Levine; Horatio, Anthony Mainionis.

For original NY production see THEATRE WORLD, Vol. 24.

John Church, Mary Hara, Edwin Owens, Clebert Ford Top: (L) Ford, Church, Robert Burr in "Rosencrantz & Guildenstern..."

HAMLET

By William Shakespeare; Director, Peter Levin; Designed by Leo B. Meyer; Costumes, Sara Brook; Original Music and Sound, Don Heckman; Presented by Producing Managers Co.; Opened Monday, Sept. 22, 1969 at the Mechanic Theatre, Baltimore, subsequently presented in repertory with "Rosencrantz and Guildenstern Are Dead," and closed Apr. 25, 1970 at Kent State University, Ohio.

CAST

Ghost	Frederic Warriner
Francisco	Anthony Mainionis
Bernardo	Con Roche
Marcellus	David Rosenbaum
Horatio	Michael Holmes
Hamlet	Robert Burr
Claudius	Edwin Owens
Cornelius	Bruce Clayton-Brown
Voltemand	Ian Wilder
Laertes	Harvey Solin
Polonius	Frederic Warriner
Gertrude	Mary Hara
Ophelia	Margo Ann Berdeshevsky
Reynaldo	Michael Aronson
Rosencrantz	John Church
Guildenstern	Elliot Levine
First Player	Clebert Ford
Prologue	Bruce Clayton-Brown
Player King	Con Roche
Player Queen	Ian Wilder
Fortinbras	Michael Aronson
Captain	David Rosenbaum
Queen's Attendant	Rene Savich
Messenger	Anthony Mainionis
Gravedigger	Elliot Levine
Priest	Bruce Clayton-Brown
Osric	Ian Wilder
Ambassador	Elliot Levine

UNDERSTUDIES: Hamlet, John Church; Claudius, Ghost, Michael Aronson; Gertrude, Ophelia, Rene Savich; Laertes, Players, Priest, David Rosenbaum; Polonius, Elliot Levine; Guildenstern, Horatio, Anthony Mainionis; Rosencrantz, Con Roche; Gravedigger, Osric, Clebert Ford.

Company Manager: Robert Hulter
Press: Lee Solters, Harvey B. Sabinson, Margie Clay, Bernard Simon
Stage Managers: Heinz Hohenwald, Michael Aronson, Rene Savich

Robert Burr, Margo Ann Berdeshevsky in "Hamlet"

HAIR

Book and Lyrics, Gerome Ragni, James Rado; Music, Galt MacDermot; Director, Tom O'Horgan; Executive Producer, Bertrand Castelli; Dance Director, Julie Arenal; Costumes, Nancy Potts; Scenery, Robin Wagner; Lighting, Jules Fisher; Musical Director, Danny Hurd; Sound, Guy Costa; Presented by Michael Butler, Ken Kragen, Tom Smothers, Ken Fritz; Opened at the Aquarius Theatre, Los Angeles, Nov. 22, 1968 and still playing May 31, 1970.

CAST

Claude	Robert Corff, Teddy Neeley
Delores	Delores Hall
Berger	Willie Weatherly, Ben Vereen
Woof	Alan Braunstein
Hud	Ben Vereen, Frankie Karl
Sheila	Gloria Jones
Jeanie	Teda Bracci
Crissy	Kay Cole
Mother	Teda Bracci, Frankie Karl, Joey Richards
Father	Greg Arlin, Kay Cole, Tyron Scott
Principal	Greg Arlin, Frankie Karl, Genie Brown
Tourist Couple	Greg Arlin, Gene Krischer
Supremes	Elaine Hill, Delores Hall, Genie Brown
Young Recruit	Joey Richards
General Grant	Joey Richards
Abraham Lincoln	Delores Hall
Booth	Kay Cole
Coolidge	Lynn Baker
Gable	Genie Brown
Scarlett	Rhonda Oglesby
Butterfly McQueen	Corinne Broskett
Custer	Teda Bracci
Indians	Ben Vereen, Gene Krischer, Elaine Hill, Lee King
Sergeant	Lee King

and Tom Eure, Lee Montgomery, Christine Adams, Lady Helena Walquer, Dobbie Gray, Red Shepard, Gar MacRae, David Hunt, Randy Keys. Joel Christie.

MUSICAL NUMBERS: "Aquarius," "My Donna," "Hashish," "Sodomy," "Colored Spade," "Manchester," "Ain't Got No," "Dead End," "Air," "Initials," "I Got Life," "Going Down," "Hair," "My Conviction," "Easy to Be Hard," "Don't Put It Down," "Frank Mills," "Hare Krishna," "Where Do I Go?," "Electric Blues," "Black Boys," "White Boys," "Walking in Space," "Abie Baby," "3-5-0-0," "What a Piece of Work Is Man," "Good Morning Starshine," "The Bed," "Flesh Failures," "Let the Sunshine In."

The American Tribal Love-Rock Musical in 2 acts.

General Manager: Richard Osorio
Company Manager: James Preston
Press: Dennis F. Shanahan

Theatre World-Crown-215 (Cont.)

Red Shepard, Teddy Neeley

Frankie Karl, Lee King, Ben Vereen

HAIR

Dances Re-staged by Jerry Combs; Musical Director, Steve Gillette; Opened Friday, Aug. 29, 1969 at the Geary Theatre, San Francisco, and still playing May 31, 1970.

CAST

Claude	Eron Tabor
Berger	Bruce Hyde
Woof	Karl Richey
Hud	Philip M. Thomas
Sheila	Lydia Phillips
Jeanie	Marsha Faye
Crissy	Jolie Kanat
Mother	Marsha Faye, Reggie Mack, James Wigfall
Father	Michael B. Brown, Star Donaldson, Soni Moreno
Principal	Arsenio S. Avizado, Gayle Hayden, Danny Lawyer
Tourist Couple	Tom Bullock, Robert Marcum
Supremes	Paulette Ellen Jones, Merria A. Ross, Jeannie Wood
Young Recruit	Michael B. Brown
Maria	Maria-Elena Cordero
Nancy	Nancy Blossom
Roger	Rogert Kent Cruz
General Grant	James Wigfall
Abraham Lincoln	Annie Sampson
Booth	Susan Madley
Coolidge	Elizabeth Caveness
Gable	Paulette Ellen Jones
Scarlett	Gayle Hayden
Butterfly McQueen	Toad Attell
Custer	Marsha Faye
Sergeant	Charles Weldon

and Shezwae Powell, Roscoe S. Blount, Robert G. Castro, Bruce M. Paine, Rhoda Heller

Managing Director: Richard Osorio
Company Manager: Carl Killebrew
Press: Gifford/Wallace, Dennis Powers, Cheryle Elliott
Stage Managers: Jose Sevilla, Fred Kopp, Joel Rudnick

**Michael Meadows, Kenneth Griffin
Above: Valerie Williams**

**Karl Richey, Bruce Hyde, James
Wigfall, Philip M. Thomas**

HAIR

Presented by Michael Butler and Paul Butler; Sound System, Dan Dugan; Artistic Director, Fred Reinglas; Production Assistants, Sharon Scarff, Mike Montell, Lowell Sherman, Joe Falcetti; Opened Monday, Oct. 13, 1969 at the Shubert in Chicago and still playing May 31, 1970.

CAST

Claude	Ken Griffin
Gary	Gary Keyes
Berger	Robert Golden
Woof	Michael Meadows
Hud	James O. McCloden
Sheila	Rosemary Llanes
Jeanie	Arlene Vrhel
Crissy	Helen Pollock
Mother	Arlene Vrhel, Andre DeShields, Blake Anderson
Father	Stan Shaw, Ellen Crawford, Joe Mantegna
Principal	Julienne Ciukowski, Joe Mantegna, Carol Ruth
Tourist Couple	Dennis Cooley, Tom Bowden
Young Recruit	Joe Mantegna
General Grant	Dylan Dunbar
Abraham Lincoln	Valerie Williams
Mother	Kathleen Johnson
Father	Tom Bowden
Sergeant	Chuck McKinney, John Dickson, Joe Mantegna

and Rita Simonini, Eamon O'Neill, Ellen Crawford, Mary Mendum, Charlotte Crossley, Tiny Reed, Ursuline Kairson, Richard Almack, Chuck McKinney, Steven Klatch, Linda Rios, Freida Williams

Managing Director: Richard Osorio
Company Manager: James H. Hulse
Press: Gifford/Wallce, Bill Wilson
Stage Managers: Clint Spencer, Galen McKinley, Kenneth Cox

HAIR

Musical Director, George Taros; Assistant Director, Joe Donovan; Dances Re-staged by Natalie Mosco; Co-Directed by Gerome Ragni and James Rado; Presented by Michael Butler in Association with Glen Warren Productions; Opened 'Sunday, Jan. 11, 1970 at the Royal Alexandra Theatre, Toronto, and still playing May 31, 1970.

CAST

Claude	Doug Barnes
Dionne	Tobi Lark
Berger	Robin White
Woof	Paul Ryan
Hud	Rudy Brown
Sheila	Gale Garnett
Jeanie	Harriet Cohen
Crissy	Rachel Jacobson
Mother	Harriet Cohen, Lee, Freddie Nicolaidis
Father	Brenda Gordon, Colleen Peterson, Frank Moore
Principal	Doug Barnes, Avril Chown, Rachel Jacobson
Tourist Couple	Graham Teear, Frank Moore
General Grant	Michael Kennedy
Abraham Lincoln	Tobi Lark
Granny	Rachel Jacobson
Sergeant	Dorian Clark

and Terence Black, Avril Chown, Jacquie David, Brenda Gordon, Tabby Johnson, Jan Kudelka, Susan Little, Mary Ann McDonald, Jim Peters, Betty Richardson, Wayne St. John, Shelly Sommers, Lynda Squires.

Company Manager: Jerry Livengood
Press: Gifford/Wallace, Fiona Mitchell, Madeleine Page
Stage Managers: Walter Cavalieri, Susanna Dales, Richard Pochinko

Ian R. Samson Photos

Top Left: Doug Barnes, Terence Black, Paul Ryan Below: Michael Kennedy, Robin White, Avril Chown Shelley Sommers, Rachel Jacobson, Tobi Lark Betty Richardson

HAIR

Re-Staged by Joe Donovan; Dances Re-staged by Rhonda Oglesby; Assistant Director, Celttoras; Presented by Michael Butler in association with William D. Owens, G. H. Burke Garrett; Opened Thursday, Apr. 16, 1970 at the Moore Theater in Seattle, Wash., and still playing May 31, 1970.

CAST

Claude	Skip Bowe
Berger	Eric
Woof	Jonathon Johnson
Hud	Tyrone Miles
Shelia	Janis Gotti
Jeanie	Karen Gardner
Crissy	Rooth Dye
Mother	Karen Gardner, Michael Rhone, Tony Lake
Father	Alice Campbell, Janice Dobbs, Bob Bingham
Principal	Raul Arellano, Rose Barbee, Charles Irwin
Tourist Couple	Kevin Mason, Jeffrey Hillock
Supremes	Debbie Walker, Alice Campbell, Michael Rhone
Young Recruit	Todd Tressler
Les	Claude Carlson
General Grant	Don Copeland
Abraham Lincoln	Alice Campbell
Booth	JoAnn Harris
Collidge	Robin Turrill
Gable	Stephanie Janecke
Scarlett	Cathy Chamberlain
Aretha	Debbie Walker
Custer	Karen Gardner
Sergeant	Arthur Dillingham

and Joan Daniels, Burke Wallace, Marcus Mukai, Linda Milburn, Todd Tressler, Barbara Hempleman, Otis Carr, Charles Irwin.

Managing Director: Ken Myers
Company Manager: John Corkill
Press: Gifford/Wallace, Jan Crites
Stage Managers: Brent Peek, Dan Sedgwick, Kent Laundre

Don Copeland, Eric, Burke Wallace

For original NY production, see THEATRE WORLD, Vol. 24.

Mimi Hines, Phil Ford

I DO! I DO!

Book and Lyrics, Tom Jones; Based on play "The Fourposter" by Jan de Hartog; Music, Harvey Schmidt; Director, Lucia Victor; Scenic production, Oliver Smith; Costumes, Freddy Wittop; Musical Direction, Norman Geller; Orchestrations, Philip J. Lang; Associate Producer, Samuel Liff; Presented by David Merrick; Opened Thursday, Sept. 11, 1969 in the Playhouse, Wilmington, Del., and closed Apr. 11, 1970 in the Santa Monica Civic Auditorium.

CAST

He (Michael) ....Phil Ford
She (Agnes) ....Mimi Hines

UNDERSTUDIES: Charlotte Frazier, Mark Alden

MUSICAL NUMBERS: Prologue, "Good Night," "I Love My Wife," "Something Has Happened," "My Cup Runneth Over," "Love Isn't Everything," "Nobody's Perfect," "A Well Known Fact," "Flaming Agnes," "The Honeymoon Is Over," "Where Are The Snows?," "When the Kids Get Married," "The Father of the Bride," "What Is a Woman?," "Someone Needs Me," "Roll Up the Ribbons," "This House".

A Musical in 2 acts with prologue. The action takes place in a bedroom, and covers fifty years of a marriage, beginning just before the turn of the century.

General Manager: Jack Schlissel
Company Managers: Boris Bernardi,
James Mennen
Press: Harvey B. Sabinson, Lee Solters,
Morton Langbord, Bernard Simon
Stage Managers: Robert Vandergriff,
Dorothy Hanning, James Noya

For original NY production, see THEATRE WORLD, Vol. 23.

PLAZA SUITE

By Neil Simon; Staged by Robert V. Straus; Scenic Production, Oliver Smith; Costumes, Patricia Zipprodt; Lighting, Jean Rosenthal; Production Assistant, Donal Rothey; Hairstylist, Pat Stanford; Produced by Nancy Enterprises; Presented by Saint-Subber; Opened June 17, 1969 at the Fisher in Detroit, and closed Feb. 14, 1970 at the Mechanic in Baltimore, Md.

CAST

"Visitor from Mamaroneck"
Bellhop ....Mark Hampton
Karen Nash ....Betty Garrett
Sam Nash ....Forrest Tucker †
Waiter ....Emil Belasco
Jean McCormack ....Paulette Sinclair

"Visitor from Hollywood"
Waiter ....Emil Belasco
Jesse Kiplinger ....Forrest Tucker †
Muriel Tate ....Betty Garrett

"Visitor from Forest Hills"
Norma Hubley ....Betty Garrett
Roy Hubley ....Forrest Tucker †
Borden Eisler ....Mark Hampton
Mimsey Hubley ....Paulette Sinclair

UNDERSTUDIES: Alan North, Kathryn Terwilliger, Ronn Cummins

The action of these 3 one-act plays takes place at the present time in a suite in the Plaza Hotel in New York City.

General Manager: C. Edwin Knill
Company Manager: Morry Efron
Press: Harvey B. Sabinson, Lee Solters,
Robert Reud
Stage Managers: Victor Straus, Ronn Cummins

† Succeeded by Howard Keel, Larry Parks.
For original NY production, see THEATRE WORLD, Vol. 24.

Paulette Sinclair, Howard Keel, Betty Garrett, Mark Hampton Above: Larry Parks, Betty Garrett

MAME

Book, Jerome Lawrence, Robert E. Lee; Based on novel "Auntie Mame" by Patrick Dennis and play by Lawrence and Lee; Music and Lyrics, Jerry Herman; Director, John Bowab; Settings, William and Jean Eckart; Costumes, Robert Mackintosh; Lighting, Tharon Musser; Orchestrations, Philip Lang; Dance Music Arranged by Roger Adams, Musical Direction, William Cox; Dances and Musical Numbers Re-created by Diana Baffa from original by Onna White; Production Coordinator, Lester Tapper; Hairstylist, James Amarel; Presented by Lee Guber and Shelly Gross; Opened at the Bushnell in Hartford, Conn., Sept. 25, 1969 and closed May 13, 1970 at the Fisher in Detroit.

CAST

Patrick Dennis at 10	Darel Glaser † 1
Agnes Gooch	Isabelle Farrell † 2
Vera Charles	Sandy Sprung
Mame Dennis	Sheila Smith † 3
Ralph Devine	Mark Hudson
Bishop	Bill Biskup
M. Lindsay Woolsey	Alan Sanderson
Ito	Arsenio Trinidad
Doorman	Dick Corrigan
Elevator Boy	Jeff King
Dwight Babcock	Sam Kressen
Leading Man	Craig Sandquist
Stage Manager	Jeff King
Madame Branislowski	Hazel Steck
Gregor	Jeff King
Beauregard Jackson	
Pickett Burnside	Brian Moore
Uncle Jeff	Alan Sanderson
Cousin Fan	Janice Winkelman
Sally Cato	Anne Russell
Mother Burnside	Hazel Steck
Patrick Dennis at 19	Peter Shawn
Junior Babcock	Bill Biskup † 4
Mrs. Upson	Hazel Steck
Mr. Upson	Ed Fuller
Gloria Upson	Sandi Smith
Pegeen Ryan	Deborah St. Peter
Peter Dennis	Kenny Knox † 5

MAME'S FRIENDS: Nikki Braniff, Jane Caveny, Bonnie Philips, Deborah St. Peter, Sandi Smith, Jacqueline Solotar, Janice Windelman, Bill Biskup, Jan Bruce, Lonnie Chase, Dick Corrigan, Ray George, Mark Hudson, Joe La Vigna, Robert Lunny, Craig Sandquist, Ella Toon

UNDERSTUDIES: Agnes, Bonnie Philips; Beauregard, Alan Sanderson; Uncle Jeff, Robert Lunny; Branislowski, Mother Burnside, Janice Winkelman; Sally, Gloria, Jane Caveny; Ito, Dick Corrigan; Lindsay, Jeff King; Junior, Mark Hudson; Patrick at 10, Kenny Knox; Mame, Anne Russell

MUSICAL NUMBERS: "St. Bridget," "It's Today," "Open a New Window," "The Man in the Moon," "My Best Girl," "We Need a Little Christmas," "The Fox Hunt," "Mame," "Bosom Buddies," "Gooch's Song," "That's How Young I Feel," "If He Walked into My Life Today," Finale.

A Musical in 2 acts and 15 scenes.

General Manager: Bernard King
Company Manager: Robert Rapport
Press: Jim McCormick, Mae S. Hong
Stage Managers: Neil Phillips.
Michael Frank, Jeff King

† Succeeded by: 1. Stephen Gustafson, 2. Donna Curtis, 3. Patrice Munsel, Anne Russell, 4. Joe LaVigna, 5. Ralph Morrison

For original NY production, see THEATRE WORLD, Vol. 22.

Top Right: Kenny Knox, Sheila Smith Below: Sheila Smith (aloft), Sandy Sprung, Craig Sandquist

Anne Russell, Hazel Steck, Alan Sanderson, Sheila Smith, Brian Moore

THE PRICE

By Arthur Miller; Director, Mr. Miller; Settings and Costumes, Boris Aronson; Production Supervisor, Del Hughes; Production Assistant, Doris Blum; Presented by Robert Whitehead in association with Robert W. Dowling; Opened Sept. 24, 1969 at the Shubert in New Haven, and closed Apr. 25, 1970 at the Studebaker in Chicago.

CAST

Victor Franz	Michael Strong
Esther Franz	Betty Field
Gregory Solomon	Harold Gary
Walter Franz	Shepperd Strudwick

STANDBYS: Victor, Raymond Parker; Esther, Diana Mathews; Walter, Dalton Dearborn; Gregory, Herman O. Arbeit

A Drama presented without intermission. The action takes place on the attic floor of a Manhattan brownstone.

General Manager: Oscar E. Olesen
Company Manager: Abe Cohen
Press: James D. Proctor, John L. Toohey
Stage Managers: Eddie Dimond, Raymond Parker

For original NY production, see THEATRE WORLD, Vol. 24.

Raymond Olivere Photos

Right: Michael Strong, Betty Field, and below with Harold Gary, Shepperd Strudwick

THE PRICE

By Arthur Miller; Director, Joseph Anthony; Scenery and Lighting, Robert T. Williams; Presented by the Producing Managers Co.; Assistant to Producers, Linda D. Ford; Opened Jan. 13, 1970 at Paper Mill Playhouse, Milburn, N.J., and closed Apr. 23, 1970 in Wichita, Kan., Music Hall.

CAST

Victor Franz	Douglass Watson
Esther Franz	Betty Miller
Gregory Solomon	Joseph Buloff
Walter Franz	Carl Bensen

UNDERSTUDIES: Victor, Walter, Bill Lazarus; Gregory, Carle Bensen; Esther, Libby Lester

A Drama in 2 acts. The action takes place at the present time on the attic floor of a Manhattan brownstone house.

Company Manager: Lucille Liberatore
Press: Lee Solters, Harvey B. Sabinson, Seth Shapiro, Bernard Simon
Stage Managers: Charles Durand, Bill Lazarus

For original New York production, see THEATRE WORLD, Vol. 24.

Douglass Watson, Joseph Buloff, Carl Bensen, and above with Betty Miller

1776

Book, Peter Stone; Based on a conception by Sherman Edwards; Music and Lyrics, Sherman Edwards; Scenery and Lighting, Jo Mielziner; Costumes, Patricia Zipprodt; Musical Direction, Jonathan Anderson; Orchestrations, Eddie Sauter; Hairstylist, Ernest Adler; Associate Dance Director, Martin Allen; Director, Peter Hunt; Musical Numbers Staged by Onna White; Original Cast Album by Columbia Records; Presented by Stuart Ostrow; Opened Thursday, Apr. 23, 1970, and still playing May 31, 1970.

CAST

John Hancock	David Ford
Dr. Josiah Bartlett	Lee Winston
John Adams	Patrick Bedford
Stephen Hopkins	Truman Gaige
Roger Sherman	Stanley Simmonds
Lewis Morris	Ray Lonergan
Robert Livingston	Larry Devon
Rev. John Witherspoon	Robert Goss
Benjamin Franklin	Rex Everhart
John Dickinson	George Hearn
James Wilson	Ed Preble
Caesar Rodney	William Boesen
Col. Thomas McKean	Gordon Dilworth
George Read	Michael Shaw
Samuel Chase	Leon Spelman
Richard Henry Lee	Gary Oakes
Thomas Jefferson	Jon Cypher
Joseph Hewes	Walter Charles
Edward Rutledge	Jack Blackton
Dr. Lyman Hall	Richard Mathews
Charles Thomson	Louis Beachner
Andrew McNair	Stuart Germain
Leather Apron	Michael Makman
Courier	Ty McConnell
Abigail Adams	Barbara Lang
Martha Jefferson	Pamela Hall

UNDERSTUDIES: Adams, Richard Mathews; Franklin, Gordon Dilworth; Rutledge, Lee Winston; Hancock, Walter Charles; Jefferson, Lee, Robert Goss; Abigail, Martha, Chris Callan; Rodney, Stanley Simmonds; Bartlett, Larry Devon; McNair, Michael Shaw; Courier, Michael Makman; Wilson, Ray Lonergan; Others, John Dorrin.

MUSICAL NUMBERS: "Sit Down, John," "Piddle, Twiddle and Resolve," "Till Then," "The Mall," "The Lees of Virginia," "But, Mr. Adams," "Yours, Yours, Yours," "He Plays the Violin," "Cool, Cool, Considerate Men," "Momma Look Sharp," "The Egg," "Molasses to Rum," "Is Anybody There?"

A Musical Play without intermission. The action takes place in the Chamber and Anteroom of the Continental Congress in Philadelphia, and certain reaches of John Adams' mind during May, June and July 1776.

General Managers: Joseph Harris, Ira Bernstein
Company Manager: Milton M. Pollack
Press: Lee Solters, Harvey B. Sabinson, Harry Davies
Stage Managers: Ben D. Kranz, Patricia Drylie, Michael Makman

For original NY production, see THEATRE WORLD, Vol. 25.

Martha Swope Photos

Barbara Lang, Jon Cypher, Rex Everhart, Pamela Hall, Patrick Bedford Above: Everhart, Bedford, Gary Oakes

Patrick Bedford, Jack Blackton Top Left: Truman Gaige, Robert Goss, Larry Devon, John Dorrin, David Ford

SPOFFORD!

By Herman Shumlin; Based on novel "Reuben, Reuben" by Peter DeVries; Director, Herman Shumlin; Settings, Donald Oenslager; Custumes, Costumes Associates; Lighting, Tharon Musser; Presented by Diana Shumlin in association with James Nederlander and George M. Steinbrenner III; Opened Sept. 8, 1969 at the Fisher Theatre, Detroit, and closed Mar. 21, 1970 at Clowes Memorial Auditorium, Indianapolis, Ind.

CAST

Spofford	Hans Conried
George	Edmund Williams
Mare	Martha Miller
Mrs. Wilcox	Linda Parrish
Mrs. Punck	Mary Cooper
Mrs. Beauseigneur	Peggy Winslow
Geneva	Kathleen Morrison
Tad	Phillip Schopper
Mrs. Crane	Karen Ford
Pycraft	Fred Miller
Mrs. Springer	Peggy Hagan
Gromler	Grant Gordon
Gowan McGland	Jerome Dempsey
Committeeman	Fred Miller

UNDERSTUDIES: Spofford, Fred Miller; Mare, Karen Ford; Gowan, Edmund Williams; Tad, Gromler, George, James Wilcher; Mrs. Crane, Linda Parrish.

A Comedy in 2 acts. The action takes place at the present time in a town in Connecticut.

General Manager: George MacPherson
Press: Gino Empry, Bernard Simon
Stage Managers: Greg Adams, James Wilcher

For original NY production, see THEATRE WORLD, Vol. 23.

lip Schopper, Hans Conried, Kathleen Morrison
Above: Martha Miller, Morrison, Mary Cooper,
Jerome Dempsey

YOUR OWN THING

Book, Donald Driver; Suggested by Shakespeare's "Twelfth Night"; Music and Lyrics, Hal Hester, Danny Apolinar; Director, Donald Driver; Assistant Director, Rudy Tronto; Associate Producer, Walter Gidaly; Settings, Robert Guerra; Visual Projection Effects, Des Pro Studios; Lighting, Tom Skelton; Costumes, Albert Wolsky; Musical Conductor, David Lewis; Orchestrations, Hayward Morris; Dance Arrangements, Charles Schneider; Technical Direction, Richard Thayer; Original Cast Album by RCA-Victor Records; Presented by Zev Bufman and Dorothy Love; Opened Oct. 2, 1969 at Jorgensen Auditorium, Storrs, Conn., and closed Apr. 18, 1970 in Clowes Memorial Auditorium, Indianapolis, Ind.

CAST

Danny	Walter Willison
John	Gregg Stump
Michael	Ron Tannas
Orson	Roger Rathburn
Olivia	Sandra Harrison
Viola	Jacqueline Mayro
Sebastian	Steve Skiles
Purser	Tony Aylward
Nurse	Lee Billington
Stage Manager	Tony Aylward

UNDERSTUDIES: Orson, Tony Aylward; Sebastian, Gregg Stump; Viola, Sharon Paige; Apocalypse, Hank Schob.

MUSICAL NUMBERS: "No One's Perfect, Dear," "The Flowers," "I'm Me," "Baby, Baby," "Come Away, Death," "I'm on My Way to the Top," "Let It Be," "She Never Told Her Love," "Be Gentle," "What Do I Know?," "The Now Generation," "The Middle Years," "When You're Young and in Love," "Hunca Munca," "Don't Leave Me," "Do Your Own Thing."

A Musical presented without intermission.

General Manager: Claire Teitel
Company Manager: Hilmar Sallee
Press: Bernard Simon
Stage Managers: Roger Franklin, Bob Fahey, Hank Schob

For original NY production, see THEATRE WORLD, Vol. 24.

Jacqueline Mayro, Walter Willison, Steve Skiles, Ron Tannas, Gregg Stump in "Your Own Thing"

YOU'RE A GOOD MAN, CHARLIE BROWN

Book, John Gordon; Based on the comic strip "Peanuts" by Charles M. Schulz; Music and Lyrics, Clark Gesner; Sets and Costumes, Alan Kimmel; Lighting, Jules Fisher; Director, Joseph Hardy; Musical Staging, Patricia Birch; Musical Conductor, Edmund Assaly; Musical Supervision, Arrangements, Additional Material, Joseph Raposo; Original Cast Album on MGM Records; Presented by Arthur Whitelaw and Gene Persson; Opened Monday, Dec. 23, 1968 at Coconut Grove Playhouse, Miami, and still touring May 31, 1970.

CAST

Linus	Joel Kimmel † 1
Charlie Brown	Ken Kube † 2
Patty	Linda Sherwood † 3
Schroeder	Jonathan Hadary † 4
Snoopy	T.D. Johnston † 5
Lucy	Ann Gibbs † 6

UNDERSTUDIES: Alfred Roberge, Janice Lorri, Howard Feuer, Rena Fredrics

MUSICAL NUMBERS: "You're a Good Man, Charlie Brown," "Schroeder," "Snoopy," "My Blanket and Me," "Kite," "Dr. Lucy," "Book Report," "The Red Baron," "T.E.A.M.," "Glee Club Rehearsal," "Little Known Facts," "Suppertime," "Happiness."

A Musical in 2 acts. The action takes place during an average day in the life of Charlie Brown.

General Manager: Marvin A. Krauss
Company Manager: Stanley Brody
Press: Richard Falk, Max Eisen
Stage Managers: John Andrews, Howard Feuer

† Succeeded by: 1. George Connolly, 2. Bob Lydiard, Richard Whelan, 3. Janice Lorri, 4. Trip Plymale; 5. Alfred Roberge; 6. Carol Anne Ziske

For original NY production, see THEATRE WORLD, Vol. 23.

Opened Wednesday, Sept. 17, 1969 at the American Theatre, St. Louis, and closed April 15, 1970 at the Vest Pocket Theatre, Detroit.

CAST

Linus	Derek McGrath
Charlie Brown	Alan Lofft
Patty	Marylu Moyer
Schroeder	Dennis Phillips
Snoopy	Grant Cowan
Lucy	Andrea Martin

UNDERSTUDIES: Lucy, Marylu Moyer; Patty, Robin Charin; Charlie, Snoopy, Linus, Schroeder, Danny Turner

General Manager: Marvin A. Krauss
Company Manager: John Corkill
Press: Max Eisen, Maurice Turet
Stage Managers: Frank Birt, Danny Turner

Andrea Martin, Alan Lofft Top Right: Richard Whelan, Carol Anne Ziske, Alfred Roberge

Andrea Martin, Dennis Phillips, Alan Lofft, Marylu Moyer, Derek McGrath, Grant Cowan Above: Janice Lirri, Trip Plymale

(Failure to meet deadline unfortunately necessitated omission of several companies)

ACTORS THEATRE OF LOUISVILLE
Louisville, Ky.
Jon Jory, Producing Director
Oct. 16, 1969 through Apr. 26, 1970

General Manager, Alexander Speer; Press, Trish Pugh; Associate Artistic Director, Ken Jenkins; Sets and Lighting, Hal Tine; Costumes, Bill Walker; Technical Director, Johnny Walker; Production Manager, David Semonin; Stage Manager, Donna Seigfreid; Properties, Debbie Shoss; Assistant Technical Director, Stephen Lee; Technical Assistant, Kirby Camm; Wardrobe Mistress, Laura Haller; Directors, Jon Jory, Ken Jenkins, Christopher Murney, David Semonin.

COMPANY

Patrick Boxill, David C. Burrow, Clyde Burton, Peggy Cowles, James Cromwell, Leora Dana, MacIntyre Dixon, George Ede, Lee Anne Fahey, Denise Fergusson, Sheila Haney, Jean Inness, Ken Jenkins, Victor Jory, Betty Leighton, Matthew Lewis, Saundra MacDonald, Christopher Murney, Adale O'Brien, Walter Rhodes, Albert Sanders, Devin Scott, Paul Villani, Max Wright

PRODUCTIONS

"Under Milk Wood," "The Killing of Sister George," "Staircase," "Star Spangled Girl," "See How They Run," "Hamlet," "Cat on a Hot Tin Roof," "Tobacco Road," "Beyond the Fringe," "A Thousand Clowns."

Gavin C. Whitatt Photos

**Right: Victor Jory, Leora Dana in "Tobacco Road"
Above: Sheila Haney, Christopher Murney, Lee Anne Fahey, Ken Jenkins, Saundra MacDonald, MacIntyre Dixon, Denise Fergusson, Paul Villani, Adale O'Brien in "Under Milk Wood"**

**MacIntyre Dixon, Patrick Boxill
in "Staircase"**

**Denise Fergusson, Sheila Haney in
"The Killing of Sister George"**

185

ALLEY THEATRE
Houston, Texas
Nina Vance, Producing Director
Oct. 16, 1969 through May 31, 1970

Managing Director, Iris Siff; Business Manager, Bill Pogue; Producing Associate, Herschell Wilkenfeld; Press, Bob Feingold, Claudia Autrey; Company Manager, R. Edward Leonard; Staff Directors, Beth Sanford, William Hardy; Designers, Jerry Williams, Paul Owen; Lighting, Richard D. Cortright, John Hagen; Costumes, Pat Nielson; Stage Managers, Bettye Fitzpatrick, Judy Schoen.

COMPANY

Bill Andes, Jerome Ballew, Jack Bell, James Broderick, Pat Brown, John Carpenter, Kendall Clark, Jeannette Clift, Dale Carter Cooper, Barry Cullison, David Dukes, Lillian Evans, Clarence Felder, Karen Filer, Roy Frady, Margaret Hamilton, William Hardy, I. M. Hobson, Bruce Hall, Dominic Hogan, Irene Hogan, Jerome Kilty, Nancy Evans Leonard, R. Edward Leonard, Loraine Meyer, Daniel Mooney, Donna O'Connor, Kathleen O'Meara Noone, Bill E. Noone, Michael O'Sullivan, Susan Peretz, Dorothy Price, Alexander Reed, Lou Rodgers, Jay Sheffield, Erika Slezak, Robb Webb, Lynn Wood, Norma Jean Wood.

PRODUCTIONS

"The Rose Tattoo," "Everything in the Garden," "Tartuffe," "The Andersonville Trial," "Dear Liar," "Charley's Aunt," "The World of Carl Sandburg," "Blithe Spirit."

Robb Webb Photos

Top Left: Daniel Mooney, Kathleen O'Meara No David Dukes, Erika Slezak, Dominic Hogan in "Char Aunt" Below: I. M. Hobson, Michael O'Sullivan, J nette Clift in "Tartuffe"

Nancy Evans Leonard, Lynn Wood, Jay Sheffield, Pat Brown in "Everything in the Garden"

Irene Hogan, Margaret Hamilton in "Blithe Spirit"

AMERICAN CONSERVATORY THEATRE
San Francisco, California
William Ball, General Director
Apr. 1 through July 25, 1970

Executive Producer, James B. McKenzie; Executive Director, Edward Hastings; Directors, Mark Healy, Louis Criss, Edward Gilbert, Gilbert Moses, Allen Fletcher, William Ball, Jack O'Brien, Ellis Rabb; Press, Dennis Powers, Cheryle Elliott; Sets, Paul Staheli, Milton Duke, Robert Fletcher, Jackson DeGovia; Costumes, Walter Watson, Robert Fletcher, Regina Cate, Alfred Lehman; Lighting, Ward Russell, John McLain, Jules Fisher; Stage Manager, Dorothy Fowler; Technical Manager, Robert Lemon.

COMPANY

Jim Baker, William Bechtel, Martin Berman, Joy Carlin, Michael Cavanaugh, Jeff Chandler, Robert Chapline, Suzanne Collins, Peter Donat, Kathy Donovan, William Douglas, Jay Doyle, Robert Fletcher, Lois Foraker, Herbert Foster, Harry Frazier, David Gilliam, Robert Ground, John Hancock, Kathleen Harper, Carol Mayo Jenkins, Dennis Kennedy, Philip Kerr, Michael Learned, Gilbert Lewis, Fanny Lubritsky, Winifred Mann, James Milton, Ed Mock, Frank Ottiwell, William Patterson, Angela Paton, Rick Poe, Ellis Rabb, Ray Reinhardt, Ken Ruta, John Schuck, Paul Shenar, R. E. Simpson, Deborah Sussel, Tom V. V. Tammi, Ann Weldon, Mark Wheeler, G. Wood, Kitty Winn.

PRODUCTIONS

"Oedipus," "St. Joan," "Six Characters in Search of an Author," "The Rose Tattoo," "Rosencrantz and Guildenstern Are Dead," "The Blood Knot," "Hadrian VII," "The Importance of Being Earnest," "Little Malcolm and His Struggle Against the Eunuchs," "The Tempest," "The Tavern."

Ganslen Studio Photos

Left: Carol Mayo Jenkins, Paul Shenar in "Oedipus Rex" Above: Ken Ruta, Philip Kerr, James Milton in "Rosencrantz and Guildenstern Are Dead" Top: Deborah Sussel, Michael Learned in "The Importance of Being Earnest"

Ann Weldon, Tom V. V. Tammi in "The Rose Tattoo"

Jay Doyle, Peter Donat in "Hadrian VII"

187

ARENA STAGE
Washington, D.C.
Zelda Fichandler, Producing Director
June 17, 1969 through July 5, 1970

Directors, Gilbert Moses, Alfred Ryder; Sets, Leo Kerz, Robin Wagner; Costumes, Marjorie Slaiman, Linda Fisher; Lighting, Leo Kerz, William Eggleston; Production Manager, Hugh Lester; Stage Managers, Florine Pulley, Simon Siegl; Technical Director, Henry R. Garfein, Jerome Rosenberger; Executive Director, Thomas C. Fichandler; Business Manager, JoAnn M. Overholt; Press, Alton Miller, Susanne Roschwalb, Mary Catherine Wilkins.

COMPANY

Fleury Dantonakis, Stan Porter, John C. Attle, Sally Cooke, Elinor Ellsworth, Dominic Chianese, Rick Cluchey, Micil Murphy, Ernie Allen, Randolph Dobbs, Henry Everhart, Martin Turner, Marketa Kimbrell, James Luisi, Anne Meacham, Phyllis Somerville, David Darlow, Morris Engle, Howard Witt, Gloria Maddox, Carol Gustafson, Anne Ives, Martha McIntyre, Eda Reiss Merin, Robert Prosky, Richard Bauer, Grayce Grant, Phyllis Somerville, Helen Martin, Max Wright, John Marriott, William Hansen, Pamela Dunlap, Richard K. Sanders, T. J. Escott, Humphrey Davis, Dorothea Hammond, Dan Ahearn, Peter Cassella, Gene Gross, Kaye McKiernan, Joe Naylor, Gary Young, Margaret Cataldi, Roscoe Born, B. J. Hoos, Arden Staroba, Lynn Milgrim, Paul Carr, Michael Lipton, Yosef Bulos, Liesel Flashenberg, Ned Beatty, Rip Torn, Viveca Lindfors, Mitchell Ryan, Robert Walden, Julie Garfield, Richard Sanders, Chuck Daniel, Robert Guillaume, Norma Donaldson, Marilyn B. Coleman, Jay Fletcher, Marjorie Lynne Feiner, Patronia Johnson, Robert Louis Stephens, St. Clair Christmas.

PRODUCTIONS

"Jacques Brel Is Alive and Well and Living in Paris," "The Cage," "Edith Stein" (World Premiere), "You Can't Take It With You," "The Cherry Orchard," "The Chemmy Circle," "Enchanted Night," "The Police," "Dance of Death," "No Place To Be Somebody."

Roland Freeman, Fletcher Drake Photos

Top Right: Gloria Maddox, Robert Guillaume, Richard Bauer, Norma Donaldson in "No Place to Be Somebody" Below: Pamela Dunlap, Carol Gustafson, Gloria Maddox in "The Cherry Orchard"

Marketa Kimbrell, James Luisi in World Premiere of "Edith Stein"

Viveca Lindfors, Mitchell Ryan, Rip Torn in "Dance of Death"

ASOLO STATE THEATER COMPANY
Sarasota, Florida
Richard G. Fallon, Executive Director
Feb. 19 through Sept. 6, 1970

Managing Director, Howard J. Millman; Artistic Directors, Robert Strane, Eberle Thomas; Designer, Holmes Easley; Guest Directors, Richard D. Meyer, Peter Frisch; Technical Director, Victor Meyrich; Stage Managers, Marian Wallace, William Pitts; Lighting, John Gowans; Sound, Ted Shell; Press, Edith Anson.

COMPANY

Stuart Culpepper, Patrick Egan, David Mallon, Macon McCalman, William Pitts, Barbara Redmond, Sharon Spelman, Robert Strane, Henry Strozier, Eberle Thomas, Isa Thomas, Bradford Wallace, Carol Williard, Joyce Milman.

PRODUCTIONS

"Blithe Spirit," "The Glass Menagerie," "Misalliance," "The Physicists," "Oh Dad, Poor Dad, Mama's Hung You in the Closet and I'm Feelin' So Sad," "Doctor Faustus," "A Flea in Her Ear," "Life with Father," "All's Well That Ends Well," "The Price," "The Tortoise and the Hare."

Von Guttenberg, Hente Photos

...ht: Patrick Egan, Barbara Redmond, William Pitts, ...ron Spelman in "Misalliance" Above: Isa Thomas ...William Pitts (C) in "Oh Dad, Poor Dad..." Below: ...con McCalman, Barbara Redmond, Robert Strane, ...C. David Colson in "The Hostage"

Eberle Thomas, Sharon Spelman
in "The Lark"

Asolo Theatre from up-stage center
Above: "Oh What a Lovely War"

189

BARTER THEATRE
Abingdon, Va.
May 22 through Oct. 12, 1969
37th Season

Founder-Managing Director, Robert Porterfield; Business Manager, Pearl Hayter; Press, Owen Phillips; Directors, Owen Phillips, Jerome Lawrence; Sets, Michael Stauffer, Marvin Roarke, Thomas Rowland; Costumes, Johorne; Lighting, Robert Hammel, Henry Millman, Michael Casteel; Stage Managers, Howard Crampton-Smith, Mark Krause, Owen Phillips, Roy Clary, Walter Williamson; Technical Directors, Lester Zellan, Carol Madeira.

COMPANY

Dorothy Marie, Linde Hayen, Ginger Guffee, Robert Foley, Harold Herman, Stephen Levi, Roy Clary, Robert Fortune, Thomas Leigh Dickmann, Walter Williamson, Diane Hill, Jerry Hardin, Cherie Elledge, G. Leslie Muchmore, James Farmer, Lisa Galloway, Betsy Cornell, John Gilpin, Thomas Rowland, Henry Strozier, Marlene Caryl, Ben Tudor, Jayne Hardwick, Tracy Davis

PRODUCTIONS

"The Show-Off," "See How They Run," "Here Today," "The Incomparable Max," "The Winslow Boy," "The Hasty Heart," "U.S.A.," "There's a Girl in My Soup," "Money," "Merton of the Movies," "Arms and the Man"

Larry D. Webster Photos

"The Winslow Boy"
Above: "Here Today"

190

"The Incomparable Max"
Above: "There's a Girl in My Soup"
Top Left: "The Show-Off"

CENTER STAGE
Baltimore, Maryland
Peter W. Culman, Executive Director
Oct. 21, 1969 through May 24, 1970

Consulting Director, John Stix; General Manager, T. David Frank; Guest Directors, Peter W. Culman, Nathan George, Ben Piazza, Dennis Rosa, David Rounds, John Stix, Lee Theodore; Playwright in Residence, Paul Cherry; Guest Composers, Ryan Edwards, Lance Mulcahy; Guest Choreographer, Lee Theodore; Guest Musical Director, Oscar Kosarin; Designers, Jason Phillips, W. Scott Robinson, C. Mitch Rogers, Ritchie M. Spencer; Stage Managers, David Gregory, Christopher Parsons, William Radka; Technical Director, Dennis Shenk; Press, Flo Harbold.

PRODUCTIONS AND CASTS

"Slow Dance on the Killing Ground" with Clifton Davis, Roger De Koven, Madeline Miller. "The Knack" with Craig Carnelia, Michael Ebert, J. Frederick Jones, Maureen Silliman. "Long Day's Journey into Night" with Tom Brannum, Carlton Colyer, Vivian Nathan, William Prince, Margaret Sullivan. "The Tempest" with William Boesen, William Bolender, Kermit Brown, Frederick Coffin, Berkeley Cooley, Gregory Etchison, Barbara Frank, Wendy Girard, Bert Houle, Christopher Johnson, J. Frederick Jones, James Kleeman, David Leek, William Radka, Thurman Scott, Margaret Sullivan, Stephen Walker, Sophie Wibaux. World Premiere of musical "Park" with David Brooks, Joan Hackett, Ted LePlat, Julie Wilson. "The Indian Wants the Bronx" with Christopher Johnson, Ian Tucker, Glenn Walken, and "The Gnadiges Fraulein" with Gregory Etchison, Bert Houle, Christopher Johnson, Lucille Patton, Mary Louise Wilson. "Who's Got His Own" with Susan Batson, Harvey Denmark, Antonio Fargas, Minnie Gentry, Robert E. Russell, Sam Wilson. "The Glass Menagerie" with Frederick Coffin, Barbara Frank, Richard Greene, Vivienne Shub.

Touring Productions: "The Glass Menagerie," "Augustus Does His Bit," "The Zoo Story," "Ye Olde Generation Gappe," "Sir John Falstaff," "Nomoto the Samurai."

C. B. Nieberding Photos

Left: Mary Louise Wilson, Lucille Patton in "The Gnadiges Fraulein" Top: J. Frederick Jones (top center), Bert Houle (bottom center) in "The Tempest"

ton Colyer, Vivian Nathan, Tom Brannum, William Prince in "Long Day's Journey into Night"

Barbara Frank, Richard Greene, Vivienne Shub, Frederick Coffin in "The Glass Menagerie"

MUSIC CENTER OF LOS ANGELES
Center Theatre Group
Elliot Martin, Director

AHMANSON THEATRE

October 14 through November 22, 1969.
Center Theatre Group, Lester Osterman Productions, Bill Freedman, Charles Kasher present:

HADRIAN VII

(For cast, credits, and photos, see section on National Touring Companies)

AHMANSON THEATRE

December 2, 1969 through January 10, 1970.
Center Theatre Group and Herman Levin present:

THE GREAT WHITE HOPE

(For cast, credits, and photos, see section on National Touring Companies)

AHMANSON THEATRE

March 17 through April 25, 1970.
Center Theatre Group presents:

IDIOT'S DELIGHT

By Robert E. Sherwood; Director, Garson Kanin; Producer, Elliot Martin; Production Designed by Harry Horner; Costumes, Lewis Brown; Lighting, H. R. Poindexter; Choreographer and Associate Director, Wally Strauss; Production Supervisor, David Pardoll; Interpolated Music, John Uhler Lemmon III; Musical Arranger, John Guarnieri; Assistant Choreographer, Bill Richards; Sound Technician, Glenn Hayes.

CAST

Dumptsy	Leon Askin
Don Navadel	John Myhers
Paleta	John Guarnieri
Saxophonist	Georgie Auld
Drummer	Dick Berk
Violinist	Shirley Cornell
Pittaluga	Remo Pisani
Auguste	Reuben Singer
Captain Locicero	Anthony Caruso
Dr. Waldersee	Sam Jaffe
Mr. Cherry	Terence Scammell
Mrs. Cherry	Flora Plumb
Harry Van	Jack Lemmon
Shirley	Marti Rolph
Beulah	Trayce Johnson
Edna	Linda Gandell
Bebe	Lisa Pharren
Elaine	Corinne Carroll
Francine	Trish Mahoney
Flower Girl	Susan Ohman
Italian Officers	Dom Salinaro, Colin Higgins, Leo Morrell, Michael Sevareid
Quillery	Pierre Olaf
Major	Sam Scar
Anna	Jennifer Moore
Irene	Rosemary Harris
Weber	Sandor Szabo
Signora Rossi	Beppy De Vries
Signor Rossi	Peter Brocco

UNDERSTUDIES: Harry, Tommy Farrell; Irene, Marti Rolph; Navadel, Michael Sevareid; Quillery, Dumptsy, Reuben Singer; Auguste, Rossi, Dominic Salinaro; Locicero, Remo Pisani; Waldersee, Peter Brocco; Cherry, Colin Higgins; Mrs. Cherry, Jennifer Moore; Girls, Susan Ohman; Major, Weber, Leo Morrell

A Comedy in 3 acts and 5 scenes. The action takes place winter of 1936 in the Hotel Montegabriele in the Italian Alps.

Manager: Charles Mooney
Press: Dale Olson, David Bongard, Peter Frisch
Stage Manager: Dom Salinaro

Jack Lemmon, Rosemary Harris (also at top) Above: Jack Lemmon (C)

AHMANSON THEATRE

January 20 through February 28, 1970.
Center Theatre Group presents the NA-
TIONAL THEATRE COMPANY OF GREAT
BRITAIN (Laurence Olivier, Director) in:

THE BEAUX' STRATGEM

By George Farquhar; Director, William Gaskill;
Designer, Rene Allio; Music, John Cameron;
Choreography, Barry Moreland; Lighting, Andy
Philips; Stage Manager, John Rothenberg.

CAST

Thomas Aimwell	Ronald Pickup
Francis Archer	Robert Stephens
Squire Sullen	David Ryall
Sir Charles Freeman	Kenneth Mackintosh
Foirgard	Derek Jacobi
Gibbet	Paul Curran
Hounslow	Charles Kay
Bagshot	Patrick Carter
Boniface	Gerald James
Scrub	Bernard Gallagher
Lady Bountiful	Jeanne Watts
Mrs. Sullen	Maggie Smith
Dorinda	Sheila Reid
Gipsy	Louise Purnell
Cherry	Helen Fraser
Coachman	John Nightingale
Tapster	Richard Kay
Chamberlain	Bert Walker
Country woman	Mary Griffiths
Servant	Richard Kay

COACH PASSENGERS: Mary Griffiths, Norma
Streader, Judy Wilson, Patrick Carter, Michael
Edgar, Charles Kay

THREE SISTERS

By Anton Chekhov; Translation, Moura Bud-
berg; Director, Laurence Olivier; Settings, Josef
Svoboda; Costumes, Beatrice Dawson; Lighting,
Richard Pilbrow; Music and Sound Effects, Marc
Wilkinson; Special Orchestrations, Derek Hudson;
Piano, Chuck Mallett; Stage Manager, John Roth-
enberg.

CAST

Prosorov	Derek Jacobi
Olga Sergueevna (Olla)	Jeanne Watts
Maria Sergueevna (Masha)	Maggie Smith
Irina Sergueevna	Louise Purnell
Natalia Ivanovna	Sheila Reid
Kullighin	Kenneth Mackintosh
Anfissa	Daphne Heard
Feraport	Gerald James
Serving-maid	Judy Wilson
Maid	Mary Griffiths
Baron Tusenbach	Ronald Pickup
Chebutikin	Paul Curran
Solloni	Charles Kay
Vershinin	Robert Stephens
Fedotik	Richard Kay
Rode	David Ryall
Orderly	Bernard Gallagher
Officers	Robert Walker, Patrick Carter
Street Musician	Norma Streader

SOLDIERS: Patrick Carter, Michael Edgar,
Bernard Gallagher, John Nightingale, Robert
Walker

**Right Center: Maggie Smith, also at top with
Robert Stephens in "The Beaux' Stratagem"**

**Maggie Smith, Louise Purnell, Jeanne Watts
in "The Three Sisters"**

CENTER THEATRE GROUP
MARK TAPER FORUM
Los Angeles, California
Gordon Davidson, Artistic Director
June 1, 1969 through May 31, 1970

General Manager, David Lunney; Press, Richard Kitzrow, Farrar Cobb; Design Consultant, Peter Wexler; Staff Lighting Designer, Tharon Musser; Technical Supervisor, H. R. Poindexter; Production Managers, Robert Calhoun, John DeSantis; Stage Managers, Tom A. Larson, David Barber, Don Winton.

PRODUCTIONS AND CASTS
"Chemin de Fer" (American Premiere): Director, Stephen Porter; Designers, Peter Wexler, Lewis Brown, H. R. Poindexter; Music, Bernardo Segall; Cast: Al Alu, Jacques Aubuchon (succeeded by Rene Auberjonois), Eric Christmas, Peter Church, Jack Dodson, Ed Flanders, Mariette Hartley, Marvin Kaplan, Charles Kimbrough, Donald Moffat, Felton Perry, Pearl Shear, Joan Van Ark, Symma Winston.

"Uncle Vanya": Director, Harold Clurman; Designers, Peter Wexler, Richard Nelson; Cast: Richard Basehart, Eduard Franz, Marvin Kaplan, Ruth McDevitt, Lois Smith, Gale Sondergaard, Pamela Tiffin, Joseph Wiseman.

"Murderous Angels" (World Premiere) by Conor Cruis O'Brien; Director, Gordon Davidson; Designers, Peter Wexler, Lewis Brown, Gilbert V. Hemsley, Jr.; Sound, Pia Gilbert; Film Sequences, Sterling Johnson and Group One Productions; Cast: Gwen Arner, Paul Ballantyne, Georg Stanford Brown, Barbara Colby, Robert DoQui, David Dukes, Richard Easton, Bruce William Lucking, Robert Pastene, Joseph Ruskin, Tom Toner, George Voskovec, Ula Walker, Byron Webster, Ian Wolfe.

"Crystal & Fox" (American Premiere) by Brian Friel; Director, Hilton Edwards; Designers, Archie Sharp, Dorothy Jeakins, Gilbert V. Hemsley, Jr.; Cast: Peter Church, Kevin Coughlin, Robert Doyle, Dana Elcar, Jonathan Farwell, Salome Jens, Nancy Malone, Tom Toner, Jason Wingreen, Anthony Zerbe.

NEW THEATRE FOR NOW
Edward Parone, Director
June 1, 1969 through May 31, 1970

Associate Director, Robert Calhoun; Manager, Ellen Kaplan; Directors, Edward Parone, Jered Barclay, Robert Calhoun, Gordon Davidson; Designers, Ray Klausen, Marianna Elliott, Ken Fryer, Peter Wexler, Willa Kim, Tharon Musser.

CAST

Rene Auberjonois, Marge Champion, Jane Elliot, Philip Proctor, John Randolph, Peter Strauss, Bert Freed, Sally Kellerman, Ron Rifkin, Jan Sterling, Sian Barbara Allen, Roscoe Lee Browne, Al Checo, Odessa Cleveland, Richard Dreyfuss, Mary Frann, Gordon Hoban, Gail Kobe, Colgate Salsbury, Paul Winfield, Anthony Zerbe.

PRODUCTIONS

"The Dance Next Door," "Rosebloom," "Stars and Stripes," "The Girl and the Soldier," "Thoughts on the Instant of Greeting a Friend on the Street," "Punch and Judy in 'A Revenge Play,'" "Five Minutes," "Rats," "Camera Obscura," "Boats," "Photographs, "A3," "June/Moon," "Wandering," "Botticelli," "God Bless," "Tilt," "Line," and a special event: "Remembering Mr. Maugham" with Dennis King and Garson Kanin July 22 through July 27, 1969.

Right Center: Salome Jens, Nancy Malone, Robert Doyle, Anthony Zerbe, Tom Toner, Dana Elcar in American Premiere of "Crystal & Fox" Above: Mariette Hartley, Ed Flanders, Donald Moffat, Joan Van Ark in "Chemin de Fer" Top: Pamela Tiffin, Gale Sondergaard, Joseph Wiseman, Richard Basehart, Lois Smith, Eduard Franz, Daniel Ades, Ruth McDevitt, Marvin Kaplan in "Uncle Vanya"

Louis Gossett, George Voskovec in World Premiere of "Murderous Angels"

CHARLES PLAYHOUSE
Boston, Massachusetts
Frank Sugrue, Producing Director
Sept. 25, 1969 through May 31, 1970

General Manager, Peter Henderson; Press, Janet Sanders, Mary Jane Cotton; Stage Manager, David Shaver; Production Manager, Duncan Ross; Artistic Adviser, Louis Criss.

COMPANY

Victor Arnold, Tom Brannum, Dorrie Kavanaugh, Albert M. Ottenheimer, Wallace Rooney, Abe Vigoda, Robert Baines, Maxwell Glanville, Richard Kneeland, Adam Petroski, Nada Rwand, Aida Berlyn, Claude Horton, Sherman Lloyd, Frank Rohrback, Frank Savino, Joel Wolfe, Robert Brink, James Griffiths, Philip Gushee, Peter Hadreas, Percy Harkness, Sheila Hart, Nicholas Kepros, Ronald Roston, David Spielberg, Michael Stoddard, William Trotman, Antonie Becker, Kristina Callahan, Edward Finnegan, Dylan Green, John Horton, Nicholas Martin, Candace Tovar, Robert Benson, Christopher Carroll, Laurie Gould Dale Helward, Sherman Lloyd, Marrie Mumford, David Zirlin, Danny Davis, Joseph Maher, Warren Motley, Larry Swerdlove, Deborah Kipp, Roberta Maxwell, Leigh Woods, Elizabeth Eis, Paul Haggard, Jennifer Harmon, Stephen Keep, Christopher Kindy, John Watson, Morgan Freeman, Allen Hamilton, Michael Moriarty, Benjamin Slack, Carolyn Cardwell, Michael Heit, Lazaro Perez, Michael Hadge, Jack Kehoe, Andrew Winner, Elly Stone, Bill Copeland, Bob Jeffrey, Arlene Meadows, Stan Porter, Loro Farell, Judy Lander.

PRODUCTIONS

"The Iceman Cometh," "Narrow Road to the Deep North," "A Flea in Her Ear," "Antigone," "In the Jungle of Cities," "The Indian Wants the Bronx," "Rats," "Jacques Brel Is Alive and Well and Living in Paris."

Franklin Wing Photos

at: Victor Arnold, Aida Berlyn, Dorrie Kavanaugh "The Iceman Cometh" Above: Deborah Kipp, Roberta Maxwell in "Antigone" Top: Bob Jeffrey, Judy Lander, Arlene Meadows, Robert Guillaume in "Jacques Brel Is Alive…"

Kristina Callahan, Dale Helward, Antonie Becker, Dylan Green, David Zerlin, John Horton in "A Flea in Her Ear"

Andrew Winner, Jack Kehoe, Carolyn Cardwell in "Rats"

195

Associate Artistic Director, Gillian Walker; Managing Director, Paul Libin; Press, Judy Clericusio; Directors, Theodore Mann, Randall Brooks, William Francisco; Scenery, Marsha L. Eck, David Segal; Costumes, Leigh Rand, Michael Annals, Joseph G. Aulisi; Lighting, Jane Reisman, Paul Sullivan, Michael Destazio; Music Consultant, Edwin Sholz; Stage Managers, Kenneth M. Post, Jan Moerel, Deborah Foster, Randall Brooks, Guy Grasso; Technical Director, Richard Herr.

PRODUCTIONS AND CASTS

"Ah, Wilderness!" with Laurinda Barrett, Henry Calvert, Frank Coleman IV, Brenda Currin, William Dolive, Geraldine Fitzgerald, Larry Gates, Stefan Gierasch, Robert Legionaire, Peggy Pope, Camilla Ritchey, Hansford Rowe, Lucy Saroyan, Tony Schwab, Alex Wipf.

"Iphigenia in Aulis" with Jane White, Harris Yulin, Roderick Cook, Christopher Wines, Patricia Bower, Charles Herrick, Dan Mason, Jeremy Luban, Margaret Cathell, Maryce Carter, Carol Emshoff, Sarina Grant, Shirley Luban, Julie Prince, Marsha Sheiness, Linda Simon, Joanna Walton.

"Max Morath at the Turn of the Century" with Max Morath in a solo performance.

"The Fantasticks" with Stephen Douglass, Pamela Hall, Larry Small, William Larsen, Gwyllum Evans, Guy Grasso, George Curley, Richard Lederer, Glen Clugston, Karen Goldberg, Douglas Jones.

Peter Garfield Photos

Left: Christopher Wines, Jane White in "Iphigenia in Aulis" Top: Larry Gates, Laurinda Barrett, Stefan Gierasch, Tony Schwab, Geraldine Fitzgerald, Frank Coleman, Jr., Lucy Saroyan in "Ah, Wilderness!"

Max Morath

Pamela Hall, Stephen Douglass, Guy Grasso in "The Fantasticks"

CLEVELAND PLAYHOUSE
Cleveland, Ohio
William Greene, Executive Director
Sept. 19, 1969 through May 10, 1970

Associate Director, Rex Partington; Business Manager, Richard Allen; Executive Secretary, Eileen Willis; Production Coordinator, Larry Tarrant; Press, Ruth Fischer, Bonnie Jacobs; Directors, Jonathan Bolt, John Going, Richard Oberlin, Robert Snook, Larry Tarrant; Costumes, Joe Dale Lunday, Esther Eisenberg, Harriet Cone, Charlotte Hare; Technical Directors, Steve Waxler, Ben Letter; Lighting, Robert Allman; Sound, Bjorn Pernvik; Stage Manager, David Smith.

COMPANY

Robert Allman, Alexandra Barrett, Nolan D. Bell, Jonathan Bolt, John Buck, Jr., Margaret Christopher, David Frazier, Jana Gibson, John Going, Richard Halverson, Charlotte Hare, Allen Leatherman, Stuart Levin, Elizabeth Lowry, Vaughn McBride, Evie McElroy, Bob Moak, Richard Oberlin, Edith Owen, Dorothy Paxton, Marcie Ross, Robert Snook, Larry Tarrant, Robert Thorson, William Tomcho.

PRODUCTIONS

"The United States Vs. Julius and Ethel Rosenberg," "Royal Hunt of the Sun," "Joe Egg," "The Effect of Gamma Rays on Man-in-the-Moon Marigolds," "Harvey," "Black Comedy," "Bea, Frank, Richie and Joan," "The Country Wife," "Loot," "All the Way Home," "Red's My Color, What's Yours?," "Don Juan in Hell," "Taming of the Shrew," "Arsenic and Old Lace," "Whatever Happened to Hugging and Kissing?," "The Huff and the Puff."

Ben Bliss, Rebman Photos

Left: Vivienne Stotter, Stuart Levin in World Premiere of "The Huff and the Puff" Top: Charlotte Hare, Evie McElroy, Myriam Lipari in Premiere of "The Effect of Gamma Rays on Man-in-the-moon Marigolds"

Richard Halverson, Richard Oberlin, Cleo Holladay, Jack Devlin in World Premiere of "Red's My Color, What's Yours!"

David Berman, Mary Gallagher in World Premiere of "Whatever Happened to Hugging and Kissing?"

DALLAS THEATER CENTER
Dallas, Texas
Paul Baker, Managing Director
June 24, 1969 through May 31, 1970

Assistant Director, Mary Sue Jones; Administrative Director, John G. Goodlett; Administrative Assistant, Michael Dendy; Executive Coordinator, Deanna Dunagan; Costume Supervisor, Kathleen Latimer; Technical Director, Campbell Thomas; Production Coordinator, Jacque Thomas; Directors, Ken Latimer, Paul Baker, Mary Sue Jones, John Figlmiller, Kaki Dowling, Harry Buckwitz, Theodore Mann, Preston Jones, Campbell Thomas, Randolph Tallman, John Shepherd, Claudette Gardner, Edward Herrmann, Rosalie Robinson, Evangelos Voutsinas; Musical Director, Raymond Allen; Costumes and Sets, Jo Stalker, Charles, Jarrell, Judith Davis, Joan Meister, Gregory K. Caffy, Lydia Lee Weeks, Lynn Lester, A. J. Rogers, Nantawan Soonthorndhai, Harold Carle Sparks, Reginald Montgomery, Roberta Rude, Louise Mosley, Mary Sue Jones, Nancy Levinson, Deanna Dunagan, Kathleen Latimer, John Henson, Jean Progar, Campbell Thomas, Michael Wray; Lighting, Gene Clampitt, Ken Latimer, Randy Moore, Sally Netzel, Carleton Tanner, Robyn Baker Flatt, Margaret Yount, Steve Mackenroth, Fil Alvarado, Larry Wheeler, Robert Dickson, Allen Hibbard, A. J. Rogers.

COMPANY

Ella-Mae Brainard, Judith Davis, Don Davlin, Michael Dendy, Kaki Dowling, John Figlmiller, Robyn Baker Flatt, Claudette Gardner, James Nelson Harrell, Edward Herrmann, Mary Sue Jones, Preston Jones, Betty June Lary, Kathleen Latimer, Ken Latimer, Irene Lewis, John Logan, Ryland Merkey, Randy Moore, Louise Mosley, Sally Netzel, David Pursley, Mona Pursley, Synthia Rogers, Frank Schaefer, Barnett Shaw, Randolph Tallman, Campbell Thomas, Jacque Thomas, Lynn Trammell, Leonard T. Wagner, Ronald Wilcox.

PRODUCTIONS

KALITA HUMPHREYS THEATER: "A Gown for His Mistress," "You Can't Take It With You," "Cactus Flower," "Macbeth," "The Homecoming," "Project III: Is Law in Order?," "A Christmas Carol," "She Stoops to Conquer," "Marat/deSade," "Black Comedy," "Three to Get Ready," "The Top Loading Lover," "Little Murders".

DOWN CENTER STAGE: Black Reflections in a White Eye," "The Process Is the Product," "The Blacks," "Entertaining Mr. Sloane," "The Promise," "Halfway Up the Tree," "The Field," "Dear Liar," "Lovers," "The Nightwatchmen."

Andy Hanson Photos

Right: Randy Moore, Deanna Dunagan, Michael Dendy in "Marat/Sade" Above: Jane Burch, Mac Williams in "Lovers"

Tim Green, Kaki Dowling, Randy Moore in "The Homecoming"

Edward Herrmann, Preston Jones, Mary Sue Jones in "Little Murders"

DETROIT REPERTORY THEATRE
Detroit, Michigan
Bruce E. Millan, Producer
Dec. 4, 1969 through May 31, 1970

Directors, Bruce Millan, Barbara Busby; Scenic Artist, John Knox; Lighting, Dick Smith; Technical Director, Sean Andrus; Sound, David Reynolds; Costumes, Grace Spelvin, Karen Grossman; Stage Manager, Jesse Newton.

COMPANY

Barbara Busby, W. Paul Unger, Dolores Andrus, Jesse Newton, William Boswell, Jacqueline Thompson, Council Cargle, Janet Jackson.

PRODUCTIONS

"Naked," "Rose," Premier of "No Flowers in Cement," "The Blacks."

Right: William Boswell, Council Cargle in "Naked"

Dee Andrus, Janet Jackson, William Boswell, Council Cargle in "Rose"

GOODMAN THEATRE
Chicago, Illinois
John Reich, Producing Director
Oct. 20, 1969 through June 28, 1970

Associate Producing Director, Douglas Seale; Managing Director, Sheldon Kleinman; Press, Mel Kopp; Directors, Edward Payson Call, Douglas Seale, Joseph Slowik; Sets, Marc Cohen, James Maronek, Joseph Nieminski; Costumes, Alicia Finkel, Virgil Johnson, Al Tucci; Lighting, Jerrold Gorrell, G. E. Naselius; Stage Managers, Patricia Christian, George Boyd.

COMPANY

Ronald Bishop, Colostine Boatwright, Douglas Campbell, Ann Casson, Dewey Chapman, Leonardo Cimino, Will Cleary, Maurice Copeland, Clayton Corbin, Aviva Crane, Kathleen Doyle, Cordis Fejer, Fionnuala Flanagan, Brenda Forbes, Beatrice Fredman, Alice Gealy, Max Howard, Geraldine Kay, Stephen Keener, Michael Liscinsky, Fred Marlow, Douglas Mellor, Gerald Miller, Kent More, Vincent Park, Renee Rogoff, Rebecca Taylor, William Vinces, David Whitaker, Paxton Whitehead, Donald Woods, Lee Young.

PRODUCTIONS

"Soldiers," "You Can't Take It With You," "The Tempest," "The Basement," "Tea Party," "The Man in the Glass Booth," "Heartbreak House".

David Fishman, Susanne Seed Photos

Left Leonardo Cimino in "The Man in the Glass Booth" Above: David Whitaker, Cordis Fejer, Max Howard, Michael Liscinsky in "The Basement"

Maurice Copeland, Max Howard, Clayton Corbin in "The Tempest"

Donald Woods, Douglas Campbell in "Soldiers"

HARTFORD STAGE COMPANY
Hartford, Connecticut
Paul Weidner, Producing Director
Oct. 17, 1969 through June 21, 1970

Managing Director, William Stewart; Press, Ann Vermel, Ellen Jones; Production Manager, Harold Courchene; Costumer, Linda Fisher; Production Assistant, Edwin Siggelkow; Sets, Santo Loquasto; Lighting, Peter Hunt, Spencer Mosse, Joe Pacitti, John Wright Stevens; Stage Managers, Fred Hoskins, Carter Jahncke.

COMPANY

Eve Collyer, Jack Murdock, Victoria Zussin, Darthy Blair, David O. Petersen, Barbara Caruso, Tom Carson, Robert Britton, Jeremiah Sullivan, Al Corbin, Peter Stuart, John Dignan, Carter Jahncke, Glenn Lawrence, Charlotte Moore, Jane Orzech, Joanna Walton, Ted Graeber, Saylor Creswell, Katharine Houghton, Jack Murdock, Geddeth Smith, Robert Bright, Mel Winkler, Robert Kya-Hill, Earl Sydnor, Thomas Coley, Donald Gantry, Alan Gifford, Corinne Kason, Kenneth Cory, Jerry Rubino, Page Miller, Doug Kunz, Richard Schmeer, Frank Massey, Jan McElhaney, Marilynn Scott, Tania Hedrick, Paul Weidner.

PRODUCTIONS

"A Delicate Balance," "The Farce of Scapin," "Joe Egg," "Misalliance," World Premiere of "The Trial of A. Lincoln," "Anything Goes".

Siegfried Halus Photos

Left: Thomas Coley, Robert Kya-Hill in World Premiere of "The Trial of A. Lincoln" Above: Jeremiah Sullivan, Victoria Zussin, Tom Carson, Darthy Blair, Barbara Caruso in "The Farce of Scapin"

Charlotte Moore, Jeremiah Sullivan in "Joe Egg"

Darthy Blair, Katharine Houghton in "Misalliance"

THE JOHN FERNALD COMPANY OF THE MEADOW BROOK THEATRE
Rochester, Michigan
John Fernald, Artistic Director
Oct. 16, 1969 through May 31, 1970

Managing Director, Donald R. Britton; Press, Frank Bollinger; Directors, John Fernald, Malcolm Morrison, Ellen Pollock, Milo Sperber, Terence Kilburn; Scenery, Richard Davis, Bennet Averyt; Costumes, Ross B. Young; Lighting, Bennett Averyt, Pat Simmons; Stage Managers, Leon Leake, Bruce Blakemore, Roy Martin, Jan Heininger; Technical Director, Lyalls Phillips; Production Assistant, Phil Baker.

COMPANY

Barbara Bryne, Richard Curnock, Mikel Lambert, Elisabeth Orion, Toby Tompkins, Marshall Borden, Bonnie Hurren, Christopher Ross-Smith, Jeremy Rowe, Deborah Ardery, Raymond Clarke, Karin Fernald, Jenny Laird, Rhonda Rose, James Sutorius, K. C. Wilson, Pat Freni, Barry MacGregor, Colin Pinney, Jeffrey Winner, Leslie Yeo, William Needles, Dorothy Mallam, Andrea Stonorov, David Richmond, Bruce Lyman Blakemore, John Page Blakmore, Michael Tolaydo, Terence Kilburn, Harry Ellerbe, Vince Romano, Philip Mallet, Steven Leibman, Richmond Johnson, Kerry Welch, Glynis Bell, Diane Bugas, Linda Bowden, David Himes.

PRODUCTIONS

"The American Dream," "Black Comedy," "The Cocktail Party," "Pygmalion," "Hedda Gabler," "The Castle," "Summer and Smoke," "The Cherry Orchard," "Ah, Wilderness!"

Don Cutter Photos

Right: Karin Fernald, Marshall Borden, Elisabeth Orion, Raymond Clarke in "The Cocktail Party" Above: Richard Curnock, Toby Tompkins, Barbara Bryne, Jeremy Rowe, Christopher Ross-Smith, Bonnie Hurren in "Black Comedy"

Toby Tompkins, Barbara Bryne in "The American Dream" Above: James Sutorius, Jeremy Rowe, Mikel Lambert, Richard Curnock in "The Castle"

Mikel Lambert, William Needles in "Hedda Gabler"

LONG WHARF THEATRE
New Haven, Connecticut
Arvin Brown, Artistic Director
ct. 17, 1969 through May 23, 1970

Executive Director, M. Edgar Rosenblum; Associate Artistic Director, Maurice Breslow; Production Manager, Peter J. Hajduk; Press, Marjorie Shutkin, Margery Colloff; Directors, Harold Baldridge, Arvin Brown, Maurice Breslow, Barry Davis, Peter Hajduk, Mark Healy, George Spalding; Designers, Elizabeth Clinton, Marci Heiser, Ronald Wallace, John Conklin, Virginia Dancy, Robert Darling, Vaness James, Santo Loquasto, Thom J. Peterson, John Sherman, Alec Sutherland, David Taylor, Elmon Webb, Vernon Yates; Resident Composer-Musical Director, Gordon Emerson; Production Assistant, Joseph Gilinsky; Technical Directors, George Spalding, Peter Gordon, Paul Lalley; Stage Managers, William Garry, Jean Weigel, Craig Pierce.

COMPANY

Paul Blake, John Cazale, Tom Crawley, John Cromwell, Ray DeMattis, Mildred Dunnock, Joyce Ebert, Grayce L. Grant, William Hansen, George Hearn, Laurie Kennedy, Adelaide Klein, Richard Larson, Emily Lay, Vickie Mallory, Ruth Nelson, Peggy Pope, Chris Sarandon, Martha Schlamme, Benjamin H. Slack, William Swetland, Richard Venture, Jean Weigel, Kenneth Wickes, Dianne Wiest.

PRODUCTIONS

"Tartuffe," "Tango," "The Pirate," American Premiere of "Country People" by Maxim Gorky, "Black Comedy," "Joe Egg," "Spoon River Anthology," "A Thousand Clowns".

Maurice Breslow Photos

ght: Martha Schlamme, Tom Crawley in "Black medy" Top: Dianne Wiest, John Cazale in American Premiere of "Country People"

Heidi Mefford, William Cwikowski in "It's Called the Sugar Plum"

Joyce Ebert, Emily Lay in "Joe Egg"

203

McCARTER THEATRE
Princeton, N. J.
Arthur Lithgow, Executive Director
Oct. 17, 1969 through Apr. 25, 197(

Business Manager, Nancy Shannon; Press, Selika C. Conover, Alice McGrath, Amie Brockway; Production Consultant, Clyde Blakely; Technical Director, John C. Schenck, III; Sets, Hunter Nesbitt Spench; Lighting, F. Mitchell Dana; Costumes, Charles Blackburn, Martha Kelly, Ann Ward; Stage Managers, Peter B. Mumford, Nina Seeley, Anne Keefe; Directors, Robert Blackburn, Tom Brennan, Brendan Burke, Arthur Lithgow, John Lithgow.

COMPANY

Ray Aranha, Robert Blackburn, John Braden, Brendan Burke, Leila Cannon, Beth Dixon, James LaFerla, John Lithgow, Richard Mathews, Tom Oliver, Gordon Phillips, Donegan Smith, Holly Villaire, Kathryn Walker, Anne Hoffman, Richard Pilcher, Alice White.

PRODUCTIONS

"The Birthday Party," "Of Mice and Men," "The Firebugs," "The Way of the World," "Pygmalion," "Much Ado About Nothing," "Ah, Wilderness!," "Troilus and Cressida."

Jim McDonald Photos

Left: Tom Oliver, Arthur Lithgow, Robert Blackbu Beth Dixon in "Troilus and Cressida" Above: T Oliver, Donegan Smith, Christopher Reeve, Gene D Richard Pilcher, James LaFeria (foreground) in "T Firebugs"

Essie Miller, Sid Davis, Lily Miller in "Ah, Wilderness!"

John Lithgow, Richard Mathews in "Of Mice an Men" Above: Gordon Phillips, Ruby Holbrook "The Birthday Party"

MILWAUKEE REPERTORY COMPANY
Milwaukee, Wisconsin
Tunc Yalman, Artistic Director
Oct. 3, 1969 through May 31, 1970

Managing Director, Charles R. McCallum; Press, Donald Donne; Directors, Ronald L. Hufham, Eugene Lesser, John Olon-Scrymgeour, Anthony Perkins, Boris Tumarin, Tunc Yalman; Designer, William James Wall; Lighting, William Mintzer; Associate Director, Ronald L. Hufham; Assistant Set Designers, Jack Hilton Cunningham, Jay Depenbrock; Assistant Costume Designer, Janet C. Warren; Stage Managers, Merry Tigar, Julia Gillett, Margie Perkins.

COMPANY

Marc Alaimo, Rhoada B. Carrol, Al Corbin, Michael Fairman, John Glover, Anthony Heald, Tana Hicken, Stuart Kendall, Charles Kimbrough, Mary Jane Kimbrough, Diana Kirkwood, William Lafe, William McKereghan, David Metcalf, Maggie Olesen, Virginia Payne, Penelope Reed, Elizabeth Shepherd, Ronald Steelman, Jack Swanson, Michael Tucker, Ron Van Lieu, Eleanor Wilson, Ric Zank.

PRODUCTIONS

"A Midsummer Night's Dream," "The Burgomaster" (American Premiere), "The Kitchen," "Misalliance," "The Prince of Peasantmania" (World Premiere), "She Stoops to Conquer," "The Lesson," "The Chairs."

Jack Hamilton Photos

Left: Mary Jane Kimbrough, Michael Tucker, David Metcalf, William McKereghan, Eleanor Wilson in "Misalliance" Above: Penelope Reed, Ron Van Lieu, Michael Tucker in "The Chairs"

World Premiere of "The Prince of Peasantmania" Above: "A Midsummer Night's Dream"

Penelope Reed, Charles Kimbrough, Michael Fairman in American Premiere of "The Burgomaster"

PITTSBURGH PLAYHOUSE
Pittsburgh, Pennsylvania
S. Joseph Nassif, Executive Producer
Oct. 2, 1969 through May 31, 1970

Artistic Director, Ken Costigan; Associate Director, Tom Thomas; Production Managers, James Leslie, Susan Silversmith; Musical Director, James Reed Lawlor; Choreographer, Nicholas Petrov; Technical Director, Matthew Grant; Costumes, Mr. Vincente; Sound, Paul Kawecki; Sets, Ray Perry, Mary Ellen Kennedy, Matthew J. Grant; Lighting, Lee Waldron, Ralph Bloom III, Joe Dziedzic; Directors, Ken Costigan, Tom Thomas, Will Disney; Stage Managers, Paula Brindle, Sally Smith, David Jurlbert, James Martin, Sue Carroll, Rodney Loucks, Roy Backes, Jim Leslie, Lenora Nemetz.

COMPANY

Michele Shay, Wayne Claeren, Joe Franze, Linda Holeva, Genre Communale, Lenora Nemetz, Richard Cleary, Colette DiGiosio, Gloria Stein, Lincoln Maazel, Allan Pinsker, Peggy Greenberg, Virginia A. Heller, David Bird, James Reed Lawlor, Henry Sciullo, Johanna Lawrence, Harrison Shields, Steve Levycky, Dan Graham, Paul Greeno, Darby Cook, David Tompkins, A. C. MacDonald, Dick Picchiarini, Te D'Emilio, Milt Thompson, Tony Sgro, Dean Hyland, Peter Clay, Richard Rauh, Cheryl Houser, Ken Costigan, Kathy Medanic, Thomas Reichert, Rhoda Sikov, Barbara Bradshaw, Nan Mogg.

PRODUCTIONS

"Gypsy," "The Owl and the Pussycat," "Cindy," "Hay Fever," "The Streets of New York," "Joe Egg," "Irma La Douce," "Star Spangled Girl."

Guild, David van Deyeer Photos

Right: Ken Costigan, Kathy Medanic in "Joe Egg" Above: Diana Callahan, Will Disney in "Hay Fever"

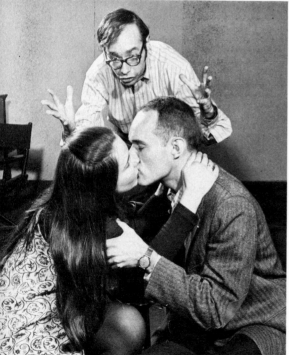

Cheryl Houser, Dick Rauh, Wayne Claeren in "Star Spangled Girl"

Michele Shay, Wayne Claeren in "The Owl and the Pussycat"

PLAYHOUSE IN THE PARK
Cincinnati, Ohio
Brooks Jones, Producer
Apr. 3 through Sept. 13, 1969

Managing Director, William Stewart; Associate Director, David Hooks; Press, William Casstevens; Business Manager, Jane Krause; Directors, Brooks Jones, Byron Ringland; Sets, Ed Wittstein, John Scheffler; Costumes, Caley Summers; Music, Conrad Susa; Lighting, Joe Pacitti; Stage Managers, Tom Warner, Allan Leicht.

COMPANY

Michael Beirne, Ronald Bishop, Leonardo Cimino, Jake Dengel, David Hooks, Hugh Hurd, Brooks Jones, Dick Latessa, John Marriott, Donald Marye, Patricia McAneny, Sandy McCallum, Leonard Norris, Joe Pacitti, Byron Ringland, Roy K. Stevens, William Stewart, Caley Summers, Conrad Susa, T. Klayer Warner, Mary Louise Wilson, Bernard Wurger, Ed Wittstein, Eve Collyer, Margaret Gathright.

PRODUCTIONS

"Volpone," "The Balcony," "3 Men on a Horse," "The Good Woman of Setzuan," "Lady Audley's Secret," "Six Characters in Search of an Author".

Right: Mary Louise Wilson, Ronald Bishop in "Volpone" Above: Dick Latessa, Donald Marye, Ronald Bishop, Eve Collyer in "The Balcony"

Dick Latessa, Margaret Gathright
in "The Balcony"

Dick Latessa, Jake Dengel
in "Volphone"

PURDUE PROFESSIONAL THEATRE
Lafayette, Indiana
Michael Flanagan, Director
Oct. 8, 1969 through May 2, 1970

Directors, Michael Flanagan, Wayne Lamb, Bernard Passeltiner, Joseph Stockdale, Word Baker; Choreographer, Wayne Lamb; Press, Dorothy Quinn, James R. Earle, Jr.; Lighting, and Technical Director, Randy Earle; Designers, Dusty Reeds, Robert T. Williams, Caley Summers, Ron Hall; Company Manager, Frank Schmitt; Stage Managers, James Bernardi, Fred Haskins, Lester Gruner.

COMPANY

Barry Bostwick, James Carruthers, Roni Eengal, Patricia Egglinger, Patrick Fox, Donald Gentry, Charles Haid, Don Linaham, Brian McMaster, Robert Moberly, Bernard Passeltiner, Earl Smith, Jill Tanner, Penelop Windust.

PRODUCTIONS

"A Midsummer Night's Dream," "Eh?" "Bury the Dead," "Dracula," "Guys and Dolls," "The Dumbwaiter," "Uncle Vanya," "King Lear," "Heartbreak House," "A Flea in Her Ear," "Celebration".

David Umberger Photos

Left: Candy Yelton, Patrick Fox in "A Midsummer Night's Dream" Above: Earl Smith Jill Tanner in "A Midsummer Night's Dream

**Bury The Dead" also above
with Lester Gruner (C)**

**Donald Gantry, Dan Von Bargen
in "Dracula"**

THE REPERTORY THEATRE
St. Louis, Missouri
Walter Perner, Jr., Managing Director
Oct. 16, 1969 through Mar. 14, 1970

Business Manager, Robert Olin; Directors, J. Robert Dietz, Nagle Jackson, Robert H. Livingston, Milton Lyon, William Woodman; Composer, Arthur Custer; Choreographer, Peter Hamilton; Sets, Clarke Dunham, Grady Larkins, Sandi Marks, Paul Staheli; Costumes, James Edmund Brady; Lighting, Peter E. Sargent; Press, Bruce Cleveland, Charles Sherwood; Stage Managers, George Nelson, John Economos; Technical Director, Jack Conant.

COMPANY

Chet Carlin, James Carruthers, Grace Chapman, Imogene Coca, John Devlin, J. Robert Dietz, James Donohue, King Donovan, Paddy Edwards, Gwyllum Evans, Pauline Flanagan, Elizabeth Franz, Tony Geary, Mike Genovese, Edward Grover, Kathleen Harper, Susan Harting, Earle Hyman, Andreas Katsulas, Bernard Levine, Michael Makman, Tanny McDonald, Marian Mercer, Carla Meyer, Page Miller, Terry O'Mara, Arthur Rosenberg, James Scott, April Shawhan, George Vafiadis, Paul Vincent, George Vogel, Paulette Waters, Arnold Wilkerson, G. Wood

PRODUCTIONS

American Premiere of "Ides of March," "You Can't Take It With You," "Once Upon a Mattress," "Othello," "Arms and the Man"

Robert J. Sokol Photos

Left: American Premiere of "The Ides of March"
Above: Grace Chapman, Chet Carlin, J. Robert Dietz in "Once Upon a Mattress"

Tanny McDonald, George Vafiadis in "Arms and the Man"

Earle Hyman, Marian Mercer in "Othello"
Above: Imogene Coca (R) in "You Can't Take It with You"

209

REPERTORY THEATRE NEW ORLEANS
New Orleans, La.
June Havoc, Artistic Director
Mar. 20 through Aug. 2, 1970

Designer, Ashton Smith; Costumes, Frank Bennett; Stage Manager, Phil King; Press, Ivan Rider

COMPANY

Brandy Barrett, Frank Bennett, Patrick Bolino, Ed Kearney, Elaine Kerr, June Havoc, DeHoun Lieteau, Gerald McRaney, Timothy Meyers, Lyla Hay Owen, Frank Root, Maureen Sadusk

GUEST ARTISTS: Myra Carter, Diane Deckard, Michael Ebert, Alice Evans, Julie Harris, Nanon-Kiam, Frances Koll, Richard Mulligan, Bill Nunnery, Ben Piazza, Shev Rodgers, Sandra Seacat, Ethel Smith, Art Wallace, Jessica Walter

PRODUCTIONS

"The Threepenny Opera," "Luv," "The Women," "A Streetcar Named Desire," "The Fantasticks"

John B. Barrois Photos

Right: June Havoc in "The Threepenny Opera"

Julie Harris, Myra Carter, Jessica Walter
in "The Women"

210

SCOTT THEATRE ACTORS
REPERTORY COMPANY
Fort Worth, Texas
Robert S. Telford, Managing Director
June 27 through Aug. 16, 1969

Directors, Gaylan Collier, Robert S. Telford, Arnold Kendall; Sets, Victor DiNapoli; Costumes, Judith Slattum; Lighting, Jack Ellis; Technical Director, Howard Parsons; Stage Managers, Steve Schoolar, Bill Newberry, Virginia Clyde, Olinda Sawyer, Barbara Ellis; Press, William Massad.

COMPANY

Joe Adams, Robert Anton, John Aydelotte, Joanna Bayless, Gaylan Collier, Michael S. Cook, James Covant, Victor DiNapoli, Mavourneen Dwyer, Jack Ellis, Dub Fisher, Sue Hamilton, Judy Harvey, Thomas Henvey, Arnold Kendall, Perry Langenstein, Sharon Langenstein, Travis Lockhart, Larry Martin, Garry Moore, Howard Parsons, Patricia Pearcy, Bill Roberts, Steve Schoolar, John Seeley, Judith Slattum, Ysidra Smith, Terry Tannen, Mary Lynn Tatarko, Robert S. Telford

PRODUCTIONS

"The Importance of Being Earnest," "The Lady's Not For Burning," "The Merry Wives of Windsor," "Volpone"

Right: "The Merry Wives of Windsor"

"The Importance of Being Earnest"
Above: "The Lady's Not For Burning"

"Volpone"
Above: "The Merry Wives of Windsor"   **211**

SEATTLE REPERTORY THEATRE
Seattle, Washington
Allen Fletcher, Artistic Director
Oct. 22, 1969 through Apr. 12, 1970

Executive Director, Donald Foster; General Manager, Peter Donnelly; Guest Directors, Pirie MacDonald, Byron Ringland; Sets and Costumes, Dahl Delu; Lighting, Steven A. Maze; Assistant Costume Designer, Linda Martin; Assistant Set Designer, Pater Maslan; Technical Director, Floyd Hart; Stage Managers, Mark S. Krause, Bethe Ward, Rodger Webster

COMPANY

Stanley Anderson, Earl Boen, Leslie Carlson, Clayton Corzatte, Jacqueline Coslow, Jeffery Craggs, Ted D'Arms, Kay Doubleday, Bernard Frawley, Patrick Gorman, Patricia Hamilton, Jana Hellmuth, Judith Long, Robert Loper, Wil Love, Marjorie Nelson, Daniel Putnam, Maureen Quinn, Rickey Ray, Archie Smith, Theodore Sorel, Roberta Williams, Beatrice Winde, David Beyer, Peter Brownell, Richard Gere, Dirk Niewoehner, Kim Syre, Pieternella Versloot

GUEST ARTISTS: Thomas Coley, Gordon Gould, Jeanne Hepple, Albert Ottenheimer, Josef Sommer, Carol Teitel, Douglass Watson, Joan White

PRODUCTIONS

"Volpone," "The Three Sisters," "Once in a Lifetime," "In the Matter of J. Robert Oppenheimer," "Little Foxes," "The Country Wife," "Joe Egg," "Summertree," World Premiere of "The Initiation"

Camera Craft Photos

Left: Douglass Watson, Kay Doubleday, Jeanne Hepple in "The Three Sisters" Above: Daniel Putnam, Patricia Gorman, Archie Smith, Bernard Frawley, Gordon Gould, D.H. Panchet, Thomas Coley, Frank Potter, Leslie Carlson, Stanley Anderson in "In the Matter of J. Robert Oppenheimer"

Theodore Sorel, Carol Teitel in World Premiere of "The Initiation"

Leslie Carlson, Patricia Hamilton, Theodore Sorel "Once in a Lifetime" Above: Clayton Corzatte Maureen Quinn in "Joe Egg"

STAGE/WEST AT STORROWTON
West Springfield, Massachusetts
Stephen E. Hays, Producing Director
Nov. 14, 1969 through May 2, 1970

COMPANY

Artistic Director, John Ulmer; Press, Wilma Barrows; Directors, John Ulmer, Peter Kipp; Sets, Richard Montfort Cary, William Hatch; Costumes, Tom Pazik, Sherry Watson; Lighting, Ronald Wallace, Steve Linn; Pianist, Stephen Hays; Stage Managers, Peter Kipp, Elaine T. Blank, Martha Fogg

COMPANY

Peter Blaxill, Jack Gianino, Max Gulack, Eric Tavaris, Lucy Martin, Michael Forella, Charles Hudson, Robert Patterson, Cathryn Roskam, Bill Capobianco, Wilma Barrows, Harry Watson, Thom Caron, Verne Cole, Vinnie Holman, Mara Lane, Dianne Wiest, Ronald Dawson, Arlene Nadel, Barbara Daytree, Jean Guild, Cash Baxter, Carol Couche, Hamp Watson

PRODUCTIONS

"The Taming of the Shrew," "The Fantasticks," "Waiting for Godot," "America Hurrah," "Uncle Vanya," "Luv," "The Flying Prince," "Keep Tightly Closed in a Cool Dry Place," "Muzeeka," "The Madness of Lady Bright"

Pecum, Akos Arnold Photos

Left: Peter Blaxill, Eric Tavaris in "The Fantasticks"
Below: Max Gulack, Lucy Martin, Cathryn Roskam, Charles Hudson, Robert Patterson in "The Taming of the Shrew"

Barbara Daytree, Ronald Dawson, Carol Couche in "Uncle Vanya"

Thom Caron, Eric Tavaris in "Waiting for Godot"

213

STUDIO ARENA THEATRE
Buffalo, New York
Neal Du Brock, Executive Producer
Sept. 16, 1969 through May 31, 1970

Director Emeritus, Jane Keeler; Executive Assistant, William Firestone; Press, Kate Selover, Blossom Cohan; Business Manager, William E. Lurie; Associate Director, Warren Enters; Directors, Neal Du Brock, Jose Quintero, Marvin Gordon, Warren Enters; Choreographers, Marvin Gordon, Lois Grandi; Sets, Ben Edwards, Larry Aumen, Stephen J. Hendrickson, Duane Anderson; Musical Director, Stuart Hamilton; Costumes, Jane Greenwood, Charles D. Tomlinson, Stephen J. Hendrickson, John Crespo, Duane Anderson, Fran Brassard; Lighting, Peter J. Gill, David Zierk; Technical Director, Jon Brittain

COMPANY

Stephen Chang, Danna Hansen, Mel Haynes, Charlotte Jones, Miller Lide, Betty Lutes, Gerald E. McGonagill, Betty Miller, Ronald Parady, Ted Pezzulo, Carla Pinza, Elsa Raven, Ralph Williams, Dean Dittmann, Irving Harmon, Gaye Edmond, Louise Armstrong, James O'Sullivan, Paul Glaser, Lloyd Hubbard, Gabor Morea, Brian Colbath, Sachi Nagasaki, Louisa Flaningam, Freda Vanterpool, Darcy Brown, Sean Feeley, Guy Grasso, Takeshi Hamagaki, Patricia Gage, Ron O'Neal, James Valentine, Patrick Horgan, Ronald Drake, Gene Lindsey, Ronnie Cunningham, Karen Lynn, Frank T. Wells, Joe Servello, Ira Rubin, Roy Monsell, Curtis Wheeler, Conrad J. Schuck, Jill Raisen, Norma Sandler, Gary Mueller, Pamela Raymond, Patrick McCullough, Alfred Hinckley, Elizabeth Hubbard, Lee McCain, Jean Hebborn, Michael Higgins, Patrick Horgan, Sherman Lloyd, Katherine Squire, Bonnie Bartlett, Kathryn Baumann, Charles Durning, Lee McCain, Shawn McGill, Frank Martinez III, Stuart Howard, Donna Monroe, Susan Stevens, Judith Gordon, Noreen Bartolomeo, Rita Dowling, Karen Dwyer, Lorraine Feather, Leone Gaylyn, Diane Lewis, Beatrice Mackin, Christopher Walken

PRODUCTIONS

"A Funny Thing Happened on the Way to the Forum," "Tiny Alice," "Don't Drink the Water," "The Only Game in Town," "Uncle Vanya," "Stop the World—I Want to Get Off," American Premiere of Jean Anouilh's "Episode in the Life of an Author" and "The Orchestra," World Premiere of "Lemon Sky"

Sherwin Greenberg, McGranahan & May Photos

Top Right: Stephen Chang, Charlotte Jones, Ralph Williams in American Premiere of "Episode in the Life of an Author" Below: Elizabeth Hubbard, Patrick Horgan, Lee McCain, Michael Higgins in "Uncle Vanya"

**Ron O'Neal, Patricia Gage
in "Tiny Alice"**

**Betty Miller, Elsa Raven, Danna Hansen, Betty Lut[e]
in American Premiere of "The Orchestra"**

THEATRE COMPANY OF BOSTON
Boston, Massachusetts
David Wheeler, Artistic Director
Sept. 17, 1969 through Apr. 19, 1970

Producer, Sara O'Connor; Associate Producer, Marsha Hanlon; Assistant to Producer, Peggy Forbes; Administrative Assistant, Barbara Necol; Designers, William Pitkin, John Jacobson, John Thornton, John Kavelin; Technical Directors, Geoffrey Richon, Lee Wheeler; Stage Managers, Boardman O'Connor, Ronald Schaeffer, William Guild, Arthur Merrow, Vincent Terrell, Eddie McKay, Gustave Johnson; Directors, Wayne Carson, David Wheeler, Gilbert Moses, James Spruill, Harold Scott.

COMPANY

Mary Alice, Phillip R. Allen, Sian Barbara Allen, Paul Benedict, Howland Bickerstaff, Donald R. Billett, Larry Bryggman, Marilyn Carrington, Faith Catlin, Roy Cato, Jr., Stockard Channing, Roberta Collinge, Darryl Croxton, Edward d'Amiata, Burr de Benning, Jake Dengel, Robert de Niro, Ronald Eddo, Jan Egleson, Mervyn Haines, Jr., Jack Honor, Barbara Houston, Hugh Hurd, Gustave Johnson, Christopher Josephs, Barbara Keel, Josephine Lane, Edward LeClair, Danny Lipman, Tracee Lyles, Sumner McClain, Arthur Merrow, George Neighbors, Novella Nelson, Katrina Nicke, Andrea Peterson, Christina Putnam, Roger Robinson, Harriet Rogers, Esther Rolle, Helane Rosenberg, Howard Rosenfield, Jan Ross, Catherine Sella, James Seymour, Mark Shapiro, James Sherwood, James Spruill, Robert Stocking, Bill Story, Dennis Tate, Will Teixeira, Naomi Thornton, Joan Tolentino, Ralph Waite, William Young

PRODUCTIONS

"Adaptation"—"Next," "The Basement," "Come and Go," "Captain Smight in His Glory," "In New England Winter," "El Hajj Malik," "The Blacks," "Murder in the Cathedral," "The Peacemaker"

Bradford F. Herzog Photos

Right: Marilyn Carrington, Dennis Tate in "The Blacks" Above: Burr DeBenning, Ralph Waite in World Premiere of "The Peacemaker"

Gustave Johnson, Barbara Keel in "El Hajj Malik"

Stockard Channing, Phillip R. Allen in "Adaptation"

THEATRE OF THE LIVING ARTS
Philadelphia, Pennsylvania
Jon Bos, Producing Director
Oct. 31, 1969 through Apr. 26, 1970

Artistic Director, Tom Bissinger; Business Manager, Steven Arnold; Press, George Keegan; Production Manager, Donald W. Earl; Sets, Eugene Lee; Lighting, Roger Morgan, Don Earl; Costumes, Nancy Christofferson, Franne Newman; Composers, Michael Bacon, Larry Gold, John Hall; Stage Managers, Lewis Rosen, Don Earl; Director, Tom Bissinger, Jerome Guardino; Projections, Shirley Kaplan, Bill Watkins; Movement Consultant, Rhoda Levine; Musicians, Don DeWilde, Terry Jones, Billi Mundi, Allen Rosenblum.

COMPANY

Alfonso Akeela, Lawrence Block, Gretel Cummings, Jeanne DeBaer, Bob DeFrank, Danny De Vito, Morgan Freeman, Betsy Henn, Judd Hirsch, Stacey Jones, Marion Killinger, Sally Kirkland, Phillip Morgan, Micheal Procaccino, Patti Perkins, Jerome Raphael, David Rounds, Amy Taubin

PRODUCTIONS

"The Recruiting Officer," "Harry, Noon and Night,' "Gargoyle Cartoons,""The Line of Least Existence."

Jack Hoffman Photos

Left: Marion Killinger, Alfonso Akeela, Larry Smith, Bob DeFrank in "Gargoyle Cartoons"

Amy Taubin, Judd Hirsch, Gretel Cummings in "The Line of Least Existence"

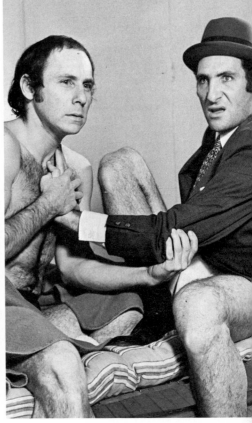

Lawrence Block, Judd Hirsch in "Harry, Noon and Night"

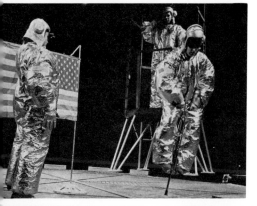

TRINITY SQUARE REPERTORY COMPANY
Providence, Rhode Island
Adrian Hall, Director
Sept. 30, 1969 through Apr. 11, 1970

Assistant to Director, Marion Simon; Resident Composer, Richard Cumming; Settings, Eugene Lee; Lighting, Roger Morgan; Costumes, John Lehmeyer; Technical Director, Steve Crowley; Press, Craig Scherfenberg; Stage Managers, Franklin Keysar, Rober Applegarth.

COMPANY

Robert Black Florence Bray, William Cain, Bree Cavazos, Robert J. Colonna, William Damkoehler, James Eichelberger, Ronald Frazier, James Gallery, Anthony George, Ed Hall, David C. Jones, Richard Kavanaugh, David Kennett, Marguerite H. Lenert, George Martin, Barbara Meek, Martin Molson, Pamela Payton-Wright, Dan Plucinski, Elizabeth Ann Sachs, Sylvia Soares, Donald Somers, Richard Steele

PRODUCTIONS

World Premieres of "House of Breath, Black/White," "Wilson in the Promise Land," and "Lovecraft's Follies," "The Skin of Our Teeth," "The Old Glory"

Images Photos

Left: Bob Black, David Kennett, Richard Steele Above: David C. Jones, Daniel Plucinski, Richard Kavanaugh, William Damkoehler, Ed Hall, Robert J. Colonna, George Martin in World Premiere of "Lovecraft's Follies"

ara Meek, Marguerite H. Lenert, David C. Jones, Sachs, David Kennett in "The Skin of Our Teeth"

Sylvia Soares, Marguerite H. Lenert in World Premiere of "House of Breath"

WASHINGTON THEATER CLUB
Washington, D.C.
Davey Marlin-Jones, Artistic/
Managing Director
May 29, 1969 through Aug. 9, 1970

Exexutive Director, Hazel H. Wentworth; Manager, Bryan E. Clark; Designers, James Parker, Susan Tuohy; Technical Director, William Butler; Sound, Fredric Lee; Stage Managers, Robert H. Leonard, Fredric Lee; Press, Leo Sullivan, Lillian Miller; Administrative Assistant, Charles Bryan; Directors, Davey Marlin-Jones, Darwin Knight, Robert Darnell; Choreographer, Darwin Knight; Designer, James Parker; Lighting, John Wilson, William Eggleston, Jim Albert Hobbes, T. C. Behrens, Joneal Joplin; Costumes, James Parker, Gail Singer, Carrie Curtis; Stage Manager, Robert H. Leonard

COMPANY

John Aman, Lois Balk, Jay Brower, Craig Carnelia, Harold C. Fleming, William Goldstein, George Haimsohn, Herbert Hartig, Marvin Himelfarb, Sue Lawless, Stephen Lesher, Davey Marlin-Jones, Bud McCreery, Eve Merriam, Peter O'Dell, Jim Rusk, Steve Schwartz, Robert Somerfeld, Leni Stern, Ralph Strait, Herb Sufrin, Don Tucker, Ira Wallach, Frank Lee Wilde, Susan Campbell, Diane Deckard, Jim Weston, Lynn Fitzpatrick, Mickey Hartnett, Michael Vita, Delores St. Amand, Bob Spencer, Verona Barnes, Danny Guerrero, Tray Christopher, Joneal Joplin, Richard Fancy, Maude Higgins, Camille Monte, Don Perkins, Marcia Wood, Cara Duff MacCormick, Leonard Yorr, Bryan Clark, Robert Darnell, Anny Lynn, Bob Spencer, Marcia Wood, Anne Chodoff, David Congdon, Ralph Cosham, Karen Cross, Robert Henninger, Dallas Teat, Eda Zahl, Jane Singer, Arlen Dean Snyder, Trinity Thompson, Ned Beatty, Howard Jerome

PRODUCTIONS

"The Decline and Fall of the Entire World as Seen Through the Eyes of Cole Porter," "Exit the King," "Before You Go," American Premiere of "Adventures in the Skin Trade" by Dylan Thomas, and World Premieres of "The Wolves" by Robert Koesis, "The Moths" by Raffi Arzoomanian, "Serenading Louie" by Lanford Wilson, and "Continental Divide" by Oliver Hailey

George DeVincent Photos

Right: Maude Higgins, Leonard Yorr in World Premiere of "The Moths" Above: Jane Singer, Arlen Dean Snyder, Robert Darnell, Anne Lynn in World Premiere of "Serenading Louie" Top: Marcia Wood, David Congdon, Karem Cross in American Premiere of "Adventures in the Skin Trade"

Arlen Dean Snyder, Bryan Clark in World Premiere of "Continental Divide"

Marcia Wood, Robert Darnell, Anne Lynn in World Premiere of "The Wolves"

218

Right: Henry Winkler, Elizabeth Parrish, Joan Pape in "Government Inspector" Above: Marc Flanagan, Jonathan Marks, Alvin Epstein in "The Government Inspector"

's Pryce-Jones, Louis Plante in "Transformations" ove: Alvin Epstein, John Cromwell in "Don Juan"

Carmen DeLavallade, David Ackroyd in "Crimes and Crimes"

219

PULITZER PRIZE PLAYS

1918-Why Marry?, 1919-No award, 1920-Beyond the Horizon, 1921-Miss Lulu Bett, 1922-Anna Christie 1923-Icebound, 1924-Hell-Bent Fer Heaven, 1925-They Knew What They Wanted, 1926-Craig's Wife, 1927-In Abraham's Bosom, 1928-Strange Interlude, 1929-Street Scene, 1930-The Green Pastures, 1931-Alison's House, 1932-Of Thee I Sing, 1933-Both Your Houses, 1934-Men in White, 1935-The Old Maid, 1936-Idiot's Delight, 1937-You Can't Take It With You, 1938-Our Town, 1939-Abe Lincoln in Illinois, 1940-The Time of Your Life, 1941-There Shall Be No Night, 1942-No award, 1943-The Skin of Our Teeth, 1944-No award, 1945-State of the Union, 1947-No award, 1948-A Streetcar Named Desire, 1949-Death of a Salesman, 1950-South Pacific, 1951-No award, 1952-The Shrike, 1953-Picnic, 1954-The Teahouse of the August Moon, 1955-Cat on a Hot Tin Roof, 1956-The Diary of Anne Frank, 1957-Long Day's Journey into Night, 1958-Look Homeward, Angel, 1959-J. B., 1960-Fiorello!, 1961-All the Way Home, 1962-How to Succeed in Business without Really Trying, 1963-No award, 1964-No award, 1965-The Subject Was Roses, 1966-No award, 1967-A Delicate Balance, 1968-No award, 1969-The Great White Hope, 1970-No Place to Be Somebody

NEW YORK DRAMA CRITICS CIRCLE AWARD PLAYS

1936-Winterset, 1937-High Tor, 1938-Of Mice and Men, Shadow and Substance, 1939-The White Steed, 1940-The Time of Your Life, 1941-Watch on the Rhine, The Corn Is Green, 1942-Blithe Spirit, 1943-The Patriots, 1944-Jacobowsky and the Colonel, 1945-The Glass Menagerie, 1946-Carousel, 1947-All My Sons, No Exit, Brigadoon, 1948-A Streetcar Named Desire, The Winslow Boy, 1949-Death of a Salesman, The Madwoman of Chaillot, South Pacific, 1950-The Member of the Wedding, The Cocktail Party, The Consul, 1951-Darkness at Noon, The Lady's Not for Burning, Guys and Dolls, 1952-I Am a Camera, Venus Observed, Pal Joey, 1953-Picnic, The Love of Four Colonels, Wonderful Town, 1954-Teahouse of the August Moon, Ondine, The Golden Apple, 1955-Cat on a Hot Tin Roof, Witness for the Prosecution, The Saint of Bleecker Street, 1956-The Diary of Anne Frank, Tiger at the Gates, My Fair Lady, 1957-Long Day's Journey into Night, The Waltz of the Toreadors, The Most Happy Fella, 1958-Look Homeward, Angel, Look Back in Anger, The Music Man, 1959-A Raisin in the Sun, The Visit, La Plume de Ma Tante, 1960-Toys in the Attic, Five Finger Exercise, Fiorello!, 1961-All the Way Home, A Taste of Honey, Carnival, 1962-Night of the Iguana, A Man for All Seasons, How to Succeed in Business without Really Trying, 1963-Who's Afraid of Virginia Woolf?, 1964-Luther, Hello, Dolly!, 1965-The Subject Was Roses, Fiddler on the Roof, 1966-The Persecution and Assassination of Marat as Performed by the Inmates of the Asylum of Charenton under the Direction of the Marquis de Sade, Man of La Mancha, 1967-The Homecoming, Cabaret, 1968-Rosencrantz and Guildenstern Are Dead, Your Own Thing, 1969-The Great White Hope, 1776, 1970-The Effect of Gamma Rays on Man-in-the-Moon Marigolds, Borstal Boy, Company

AMERICAN THEATRE WING
ANTOINETTE PERRY (TONY) AWARD PLAYS

1948-Mister Roberts, 1949-Death of a Salesman, Kiss Me, Kate, 1950-The Cocktail Party, South Pacific, 1951-The Rose Tattoo, Guys and Dolls, 1952-The Fourposter, The King and I, 1953-The Crucible, Wonderful Town, 1954-The Teahouse of the August Moon, Kismet, 1955-The Desperate Hours, The Pajama Game, 1956-The Diary of Anne Frank, Damn Yankees, 1957-Long Day's Journey into Night, My Fair Lady, 1958-Sunrise at Campobello, The Music Man, 1959-J. B., Redhead, 1960-The Miracle Worker, Fiorello tied with Sound of Music, 1961-Becket, Bye Bye Birdie, 1962-A Man for All Seasons, How to Succeed in Business without Really Trying, 1963-Who's Afraid of Virginia Woolf?, A Funny Thing Happened on the Way to the Forum, 1964-Luther, Hello, Dolly!, 1965-The Subject Was Roses, Fiddler on the Roof, 1966-The Persecution and Assassination of Marat as Performed by the Inmates of the Asylum of Charenton under the Direction of the Marquis de Sade, Man of La Mancha, 1967-The Homecoming, Cabaret, 1968-Rosencrantz and Guildenstern Are Dead, Hallelujah, Baby!, 1969-The Great White Hope, 1776, 1970-Child's Play, Applause

CHARLES GORDONE
1970 Pulitzer Prize Winner for "No Place to Be Somebody"

FORMER THEATRE WORLD AWARD WINNERS

1944-45: Betty Comden, Richard Davis, Richard Hart, Judy Holliday, Charles Lang, Bambi Linn, John Lund, Donald Murphy, Nancy Noland, Margaret Phillips, John Raitt

1945-46: Barbara Bel Geddes, Marlon Brando, Bill Callahan, Wendell Corey, Paul Douglas, Mary James, Burt Lancaster, Patrica Marshall, Beatrice Pearson.

1946-47: Keith Andes, Marion Bell, Peter Cookson, Ann Crowley, Ellen Hanley, John Jordan, George Keane, Dorothea MacFarland, James Mitchell, Patricia Neal, David Wayne

1947-48: Valerie Bettis, Edward Bryce, Whitfield Connor, Mark Dawson, June Lockhart, Estelle Loring, Peggy Maley, Ralph Meeker, Meg Mundy, Douglas Watson, James Whitmore, Patrice Wymore

1948-49: Tod Andrews, Doe Avedon, Jean Carson, Carol Channing, Richard Derr, Julie Harris, Mary McCarty, Allyn Ann McLerie, Cameron Mitchell, Gene Nelson, Byron Palmer, Bob Scheerer

1949-50: Nancy Andrews, Phil Arthur, Barbara Brady, Lydia Clarke, Priscilla Gillette, Don Hanmer, Marcia Henderson, Charlton Heston, Rick Jason, Grace Kelly, Charles Nolte, Roger Price

1950-51: Barbara Ashley, Isabel Bigley, Martin Brooks, Richard Burton, James Daly, Cloris Leachman, Russell Nype, Jack Palance, William Smithers, Maureen Stapleton, Marcia Van Dyke, Eli Wallach

1951-52: Tony Bavaar, Patricia Benoit, Peter Conlow, Virginia de Luce, Ronny Graham, Audrey Hepburn, Diana Herbert, Conrad Janis, Dick Kallman, Charles Proctor, Eric Sinclair, Kim Stanley, Marian Winters, Helen Wood

1952-53: Edie Adams, Rosemary Harris, Eileen Heckart, Peter Kelley, John Kerr, Richard Kiley, Gloria Marlowe, Penelope Munday, Paul Newman, Sheree North, Geraldine Page, John Stewart, Ray Stricklyn, Gwen Verdon

1953-54: Orson Bean, Harry Belafonte, James Dean, Joan Diener, Ben Gazzara, Carol Haney, Jonathan Lucas, Kay Medford, Scott Merrill, Elizabeth Montgomery, Leo Penn, Eva Marie Saint

1954-55: Julie Andrews, Jacqueline Brookes, Shirl Conway, Barbara Cook, David Daniels, Mary Fickett, Page Johnson, Loretta Leversee, Jack Lord, Dennis Patrick, Anthony Perkins, Christopher Plummer

1955-56: Diane Cilento, Dick Davalos, Anthony Franciosa, Andy Griffith, Laurence Harvey, David Hedison, Earle Hyman, Susan Johnson, John Michael King, Jayne Mansfield, Sarah Marshall, Gaby Rodgers, Susan Strasberg, Fritz Weaver

1956-57: Peggy Cass, Sydney Chaplin, Sylvia Daneel, Bradford Dillman, Peter Donat, George Grizzard, Carol Lynley, Peter Palmer, Jason Robards, Cliff Robertson, Pippa Scott, Inga Swenson

1957-58: Anne Bancroft, Warren Berlinger, Colleen Dewhurst, Richard Easton, Timmy Everett, Eddie Hodges, Joan Hovis, Carol Lawrence, Jacqueline McKeever, Wynne Miller, Robert Morse, George C. Scott

1958-59: Lou Antonio, Ina Balin, Richard Cross, Tammy Grimes, Larry Hagman, Dolores Hart, Roger Mollien, France Nuyen, Susan Oliver, Ben Piazza, Paul Roebling, William Shatner, Pat Suzuki, Rip Torn

1959-60: Warren Beatty, Eileen Brennan, Carol Burnett, Patty Duke, Jane Fonda, Anita Gillette, Elisa Loti, Donald Madden, George Maharis, John McMartin, Lauri Peters, Dick Van Dyke

1960-61: Joyce Bulifant, Dennis Cooney, Nancy Dussault, Robert Goulet, Joan Hackett, June Harding, Ron Husmann, James MacArthur, Bruce Yarnell

1961-62: Elizabeth Ashley, Keith Baxter, Peter Fonda, Don Galloway, Sean Garrison, Barbara Harris, James Earl Jones, Janet Margolin, Karen Morrow, Robert Redford, John Stride, Brenda Vaccaro

1962-63: Alan Arkin, Stuart Damon, Melinda Dillon, Robert Drivas, Bob Gentry, Dorothy Loudon, Brandon Maggart, Julienne Marie, Liza Minnelli, Estelle Parsons, Diana Sands, Swen Swenson

1963-64: Alan Alda, Gloria Bleezarde, Imelda De Martin, Claude Giraud, Ketty Lester, Barbara Loden, Lawrence Pressman, Gilbert Price, Philip Proctor, John Tracy, Jennifer West

1964-65: Carolyn Coates, Joyce Jillson, Linda Lavin, Luba Lisa, Michael O'Sullivan, Joanna Pettet, Beah Richards, Jaime Sanchez, Victor Spinetti, Nicholas Surovy, Robert Walker, Clarence Williams III

1965-66: Zoe Caldwell, David Carradine, John Cullum, John Davidson, Faye Dunaway, Gloria Foster, Robert Hooks, Jerry Lanning, Richard Mulligan, April Shawhan, Sandra Smith, Lesley Ann Warren

1966-67: Bonnie Bedelia, Richard Benjamin, Dustin Hoffman, Terry Kiser, Reva Rose, Robert Salvio, Sheila Smith, Connie Stevens, Pamela Tiffin, Leslie Uggams, Jon Voight, Christopher Walken

1967-68: Pamela Burrell, Sandy Duncan, Julie Gregg, Bernadette Peters, Alice Playten, Brenda Smiley, David Birney, Jordan Christopher, Jack Crowder, Stephen Joyce, Mike Rupert, Rusty Thacker

1968-69: Jane Alexander, David Cryer, Ed Evanko, Blythe Danner, Ken Howard, Lauren Jones, Ron Leibman, Marian Mercer, Jill O'Hara, Ron O'Neil, Al Pacino, Marlene Warfield

1969-1970 THEATRE WORLD AWARD WINNERS

Susan Browning of "Company"

Donny Burks of "Billy Noname"

Catherine Burns of "Dear Janet
Rosenberg, Dr. Mr. Kooning"

Len Cariou of "Henry V"
and "Applause"

223

Bonnie Franklin of "Applause"

David Holliday of "Coco"

**Katharine Houghton of
"A Scent of Flowers"**

David Rounds of "Child's Play"

Melba Moore of "Purlie"

Lewis J. Stadlen of "Minnie's Boys"

**Kristoffer Tabori of
"How Much, How Much?"**

**Fredricka Weber of "The Last
Sweet Days of Isaac"**

1970 THEATRE WORLD AWARD PARTY

Lauren Bacall, Donny Burks
Below: Bonnie Franklin, Lauren
Bacall, Len Cariou

Lauren Bacall, John Willis, Fredricka Weber Bel
Melba Moore, Lauren Bacall, Katharine Hough
Donny Burks

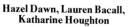

Hazel Dawn, Lauren Bacall,
Katharine Houghton

Lauren Bacall, David Rounds

Pepper Powell, Page Johnson, David Daniels, Mary
Ann Niles, Igors Gavon Below: Eileen Heckart, John
Willis, Maureen Stapleton, Frances Crampon

Blythe Danner, Susan Browning, Harold Stephens,
Sandy Duncan, Bruce Scott Below: (L) Bonnie Franklin,
(R) Bernadette Peters

Len Cariou, Catherine Burns

Boni Enten, Kristoffer Tabori, Alice Playten

Betty Bruce, Russell Nype

| Jack Aaron | Margot Albert | Hugh Alexander | Jane Alexander | Clinton J All |

BIOGRAPHIES

OF THIS SEASON'S CAST

AARON, JACK. Born May 1, 1933 in NYC. Attended Hunter Col., Actors Workshop. Has appeared Off-Bdwy in "Swim Low Little Goldfish," "Journey of the Fifth Horse," and "The Nest."

ABLE, WILL B. Born Nov. 21 in Providence, R.I. Has appeared on Bdwy in "Plain and Fancy," "Midgie Purvis," "All American, "Coco". Off-Bdwy in "Bella," "9 to 5 to 0," "Get Thee To Canterbury."

ABRAHAM, F. MURRAY. Born Oct. 24, 1939 in Pittsburgh. Attended U. Tex. Made Off-Bdwy bow in 1967 in "The Fantasticks," followed by "An Opening In The Trees," "The Fourteenth Dictator," "Young Abe Lincoln," ' 'Tonight in Living Color." Bdwy debut in "The Man In The Glass Booth" (1968).

ACKERMAN, LONI ZOE. Born Apr. 10, 1949 in NYC. Attended New School. Made Bdwy debut in 1968 in "George M!" appeared Off-Bdwy in "Dames at Sea."

ADAMS, MASON. Born Feb. 26, 1919 in NYC. Graduate U. Wisc. Neighborhood Playhouse. Has appeared in "Get Away, Old Man," "Public Relations," "Career Angel," Violet," "A Shadow of My Enemy," "Tall Story," "Inquest."

ADDY, WESLEY. Born Aug. 4, 1913 in Omaha, Neb. Attended UCLA. Made Bdwy debut in 1935 in "Panic," followed by "How Beautiful with Shoes," Howard's "Hamlet," Evans' "Richard II" and "Hamlet," "Henry IV," "Summer Night," "Romeo and Juliet," "Twelfth Night," "Antigone," Cornell's "Candida," "Another Part of the Forest," "Galileo," "Leading Lady," "The Traitor," "The Enchanted," "King Lear," "The Strong Are Lonely," "The First Gentleman," "A Month in the Country" (OB), "South Pacific" (CC), Holm's "Candida."

ADLER, LUTHER. Born in NYC, May 4, 1903. Attended Lewis Inst. Stage debut in 1908 in "Schmendrick." Other credits: "Night Over Taos," "Success Story," "Alien Corn," "Men In White," "Gold Eagle Guy," "Awake and Sing," "Paradise Lost," "Johnny Johnson," "Golden Boy," "Rocket To The Moon," "The Russian People," "Two On An Island," "Common Ground," "Beggars Are Coming To Town," "Dunnigan's Daughter," "A Flag Is Born," "Merchant of Venice," "A Month In The Country," "A Very Special Baby," "Passion of Josef D," "Three Sisters," "Fiddler On The Roof."

ADMIRE, JERE. Born Apr. 29 in Ft. Worth, Tex. Graduate TCU. Made Bdwy bow in 1959 in "Greenwillow," followed by "Tenderloin," "Sail Away," "No Strings," "Here's Love," "Do I Hear A Waltz?," "Royal Hunt of the Sun," "Cabaret," and OB in "On the Town," "Boys in the Band," "Steambath."

ALBERT, MARGOT. Born Oct. 3, 1943 in NYC. Attended Juilliard Made stage debut off Bdwy in 1969 in "Promenade."

ALDA, ROBERT. Born Feb. 26, 1914 in NYC. Attended NYU. Made Bdwy debut in 1950 in "Guys and Dolls," followed by "Harbor Lights," "What Makes Sammy Run?," "Your Daughter, My Son," "Front Page."

ALDREDGE, TOM. Born Feb. 28, 1928 in Dayton, O. Attended Dayton U., Goodman Theatre. Bdwy bow in 1959 in "The Nervous Set," followed by "UTBU," "Slapstick Tragedy," "Everything In The Garden," "Indians," "Engagement Baby," Off-Bdwy in "The Tempest," "Between Two Thieves," "Henry V," "The Premise," "Love's Labour's Lost," "Troilus and Cressida," "Butter and Egg Man," "Ergo," "Boys In The Band," "Twelfth Night."

ALEXANDER, HUGH. Born May 15, 1939 in Welland, Ont., Can. Attended U. Toronto, Central Sch. London. Made Bdwy bow in 1962 in "Beyond the Fringe," followed by Burton's "Hamlet," "Alfie," and OB in "The Fantasticks," "Unfair to Goliath."

ALEXANDER, JANE. Born Oct. 28, 1939 in Boston. Attended Sarah Lawrence College, U. Edinburgh. Was standby in "A Thousand Clowns" before Bdwy debut in "The Great White Hope" for which she received a THEATRE WORLD Award.

ALFASA, JOE. Born in NYC, Dec. 13, 1914. Attended Am. Theatre Wing, Columbia U. Made Bdwy debut in 1938 in "Pins and Needles." Other credits: "And The Wind Blows," "Capacity For Wings," "Out Of This World," "Look After Lulu," "Once Upon A Mattress," "The Wall," "Illya Darling," "Zorba," "The Penny Wars."

ALICE, MARY. Has appeared Off-Bdwy in "Strong Breed," "Trials of Brother Jero," "A Rat's Mass."

ALLEN, JONNY. Born Mar. 29, 1962 in Brooklyn. Made debut Off-Bdwy in 1969 in "Seven Days of Mourning."

ALLEN, MARC III. Born Mar. 3, 1943 in Los Angeles. Attended Mt. San Antonio Col. Made NY bow Off-Bdwy in 1969 in "Your Own Thing," followed by "Promenade," Bdwy debut in "Look to the Lilies."

ALLEN, NORMAN. Born Dec. 24, 1939 in London. Attended RADA. Made NY bow in 1963 in "Chips With Everything," followed by "Half A Sixpence," "Rockefeller and The Red Indians," "Get Thee To Canterbury" (OB), "Borstal Boy."

ALLAN, RAE. Born July 3, 1926 in Brooklyn. Attended Hunter College, AADA. Credits: "Where's Charley?," "Alive and Kicking," "Call Me Madam," "Pajama Game," "Damn Yankees," "Pictures In The Hallway" and "I Knock At The Door" (OB), "Oliver!," "Traveller Without Luggage," "On A Clear Day You Can See Forever," APA, "Henry IV" (CP) "Fiddler On The Roof."

ALLEN, SETH. Born July 13, 1941 in Brooklyn, Attended Musical Theatre Academy. Has appeared Off-Bdwy in "Viet Rock," "Futz," "Hair," "Candaules Commissioner."

ALLEN, WOODY. Born Dec. 1, 1935 in Brooklyn. Attended CCNY, NYU. Wrote both "Don't Drink The Water" and "Play It Again, Sam." Played lead in latter.

ALLINSON, MICHAEL. Born in London; attended Lausanne U, RADA. Made Bdwy bow in 1960 in "My Fair Lady," followed by "Importance of Being Earnest" (OB), "Hostile Witness," "Come Live with Me," "Coco."

ALLMON, CLINTON. Born June 13, 1941 in Monahans, Tex. Graduate Okla. State U. Has appeared Off-Bdwy in "The Bluebird," "Khaki Blue," made Bdwy bow in 1969 in "Indians."

ALLSBROOK, BILL. Born May 21, 1945 in Roanoke Rapids, NC. Graduate Temple U. Made Bdwy bow in 1968 in "Cabaret," followed by "Applause."

ALLYSON, JUNE. Born Oct. 7, 1923 in the Bronx. Made Bdwy debut in 1939 in "Very Warm for May," followed by "Best Foot Forward," "Panama Hattie," "Forty Carats."

ALMORAVIDS, TCHAKA. Born Sept. 7, 1939 in Pensacola, Fla. Attended Wash. Jr. Col., Harlem School of Arts. Made debut off Bdwy in 1969 in "Five on the Black Hand Side."

| rmen Alvarez | John Anania | Barbara Andres | Boris Aplon | Jeanne Arnold |

ALVAREZ, CARMEN. Born July 2 in Los Angeles. Bdwy debut in 1954 in "Pajama Game," followed by "Li'l Abner," "West Side Story," "Bye Bye Birdie," "Zorba," "Look to the Lillies," Off-Bdwy in "That Hat," and "Cole Porter Revisited.

AMES, CINDY. Born in Brooklyn. Attended Actors Lab. Made NY debut off Bdwy in 1970 in "Hedda Gabler."

ANANIA, JOHN. Born July 12, 1923 in Sicily. Attended Berghof Studio. Made Bdwy bow in 1947 in "Sweethearts," followed by "Christine," "What A Killing" (OB), "Little Me," "Fly Blackbird" (OB), "Cafe Crown," "Skyscraper," "Breakfast at Tiffany's," "Golden Rainbow," "The Penny Wars," "Applause."

ANDERSON, THOMAS. Brown in Pasadena, Cal. Made Bdwy debut in 1934 in "4 Saints in 3 Acts," followed by "Roll Sweet Chariot," "Cabin In The Sky," "Native Son," "Set My People Free," "How Long Till Summer," "A Hole In The Head," "The Great White Hope," Off-Bdwy: "Conquering Thursday," "The Peddler" and "The Dodo Bird."

ANDRE, FRANK. Born Dec. 30, 1942 in Philadelphia. Studied with Stella Adler. Made Bdwy bow in 1964 in "Ben Franklin In Paris," followed by "As I Lay Dying," "Brigadoon" (CC'67). "We Bombed In New Haven," Off-Bdwy: "Who's Who, Baby?," "Now," "Your Own Thing."

ANDRES, BARBARA. Born Feb. 11, 1939 in NYC. Graduate Catholic U. Made Bdwy debut in 1969 in ''Jimmy," followed by "The Boy Friend."

ANDREWS, NANCY. Born Dec. 16, 1924 in Minneapolis. Attended Pasadena Playhouse. Made Bdwy debut in 1948 in "Hilarities," followed by "Touch and Go" for which she received a THEATRE WORLD Award, "Gentlemen Prefer Blondes," "Hazel Flagg," "Plain and Fancy," "Pipe Dream," "Juno," "Christine," "Flower Drum Song," "Little Me," and Off-Bdwy in "Threepenny Opera," "Tiger Rag," "Maddame Aphrodite," "Say Nothing," "How Much, How Much?"

ANNEGAN, J. B. Born Apr. 18, 1944 in Clarksburg, WVa. Graduate Ohio State U. Made NY debut in 1970 in ELT's "Romeo and Jeannette."

ANTHONY, MICHAEL. Born June 7, 1943 in Sydney, Aust. Attended Waverley Col., AMDA. Made NY bow off Bdwy in 1967 in "Have I Got One For You," followed by "Gertrude Stein's First Reader."

APLON, BORIS. Born July 14 in Chicago. Attended U. Chicago, Goodman Theatre. Has appeared off Bdwy in "Makrapoulos Secret," "King of the Whole Damn World," at CC in "Carousel" and "Show Boat," on Bdwy in "Candide," "Anya," "Fiddler on the Roof."

ARNOLD, JEANNE. Born July 30 in Berkeley, Calif. Graduate U. Cal. Made NY debut off Bdwy in 1955 in "Threepenny Opera," followed by "Take Five," "Demi-Dozen," "Medium Rare," "Put It In Writing," on Bdwy in "The Happy Time," "Coco."

ARNOLD, VICTOR. Born July 1, 1936 in Herkimer, NY. Graduate, NYU. Off-Bdwy: "Shadow of Heroes," "Merchant of Venice," "3X3," "Lovey," "Fortune and Men's Eyes," "Time for Bed," "Take Me to Bed." Bdwy; "The Deputy," "Malcolm," "We Bombed In New Haven."

ATKINS, TOM. Born in Pittsburgh. Graduate Duquesne U., AADA. With LC Rep in "The Unknown Soldier and His Wife," "Cyrano," on Bdwy in "Keep It In The Family," "The Front Page" ('69). Off Bdwy in "Whistle in the Dark," "Nobody Hears a Broken Drum."

ATKINSON, DAVID. Born in Montreal, Oct. 20, 1921. Attended McGill U., Pasadena Playhouse. Credits: "Inside U.S.A.," "Girl In Pink Tights," "The Vamp," CC revivals of "Carousel," "Kiss Me, Kate," "Brigadoon," and "Annie Get Your Gun," "Man of LaMancha."

ATTLE, JOHN C. Born in Tacoma, Wash. Graduate U. Wash. Made Bdwy bow in 1964 in "Fiddler On The Roof," followed by "Jacques Brel Is Alive and Well and Living In Paris" (OB).

ATTLES, JOSEPH. Born Apr. 7, 1903 in Charleston, SC. Attended Harlem Musical Conservatory. Made Bdwy bow in "Blackbirds of 1928," followed by "John Henry," "Porgy and Bess," "Kwamina," "Tambourines To Glory." Off-Bdwy: "Jerico-Jim Crow," "Cabin In The Sky," "Prodigal Son," "Day of Absence," with LC Rep in "Cry of Players" and "King Lear," "The Reckoning," "Contributions."

AUBERJONOIS, RENE. Born June 1, 1940 in NYC. Graduate of Carnegie Inst. Has appeared with LC Rep in "A Cry of Players" and "King Lear," and on Bdwy in "Fire," "Coco."

AUMONT, JEAN-PIERRE. Born Jan. 5, 1913 in Paris. Attended French Ntl. School of Dramatic Art. Made US debut in 1942 in "Rose Burke," followed by "My Name Is Aquilon," "Heavenly Twins," "Second String," "Tovarich," "Camino Real" (LC).

AVALOS, LUIS. Born Sept. 2, 1946 in Havana. Graduate NYU. Made debut at CC in "Never Jam Today," followed by "Rules for the Running of Trains" (OB), and LC's "Camino Real" and "Beggar on Horseback."

AVERY, VAL. Born July 14, 1924 in Philadelphia. Attended Hedgerow Theatre School. Made Bdwy bow in 1962 in "Nowhere to Go But Up," followed by "Cafe Crown," "Front Page."

AWAD, JACQUELINE. Born Dec. 2, 1941 in Manila. PI. Graduate of Vassar, Juilliard. Has appeared with Am. Shakespeare Festival, in "The Drunkard" (OB), and with Natl. Theatre of Deaf.

AZZARA, CANDY. Born May 18, 1945 in Brooklyn. Attended Bklyn Col. Off-Bdwy credits: "On The First Day," "The Sexes," "Hills Like White Elephants," "Bedtime Story," "Fallen Angels." Made Bdwy debut in 1968 in "Lovers and Other Strnagers," followed by "Engagement Baby."

BABCOCK, BARBARA. Attended Lausanne U. Graduate Wellesley. Made NY debut in 1970 off Bdwy in "Nature of the Crime."

BACALL, LAUREN. Born Sept. 16, 1924 in NYC. Attended AADA. Made Bdwy debut in 1942 in "Johnny 2 x 4," followed by "Goodbye Charlie," "Cactus Flower," "Applause."

BACON, CATHERINE. Born Sept. 7, 1947 in Chelsea, Mass. Attended AADA. Made Bdwy debut in 1969 in "The Penny Wars."

BAFF, REGGIE. Born Mar. 31, 1949 in the Bronx. Attended Western Reserve, and Hunter Col. Made debut in 1969 off Bdwy in "The Brownstone Urge."

BAILEY, PEARL. Born Mar. 29, 1918 in Newport News, Va. Vaudeville and night club star before Bdwy debut in 1946 in "St. Louis Woman," Followed by "Arms and The Girl," "House of Flowers," "Hello, Dolly!"

BAIN, CONRAD. Born Feb. 4, 1923 in Lethbridge, Can. Attended AADA. Credits: "Sixth Finger In A Five Finger Glove," "Candide," "Hot Spot," "Advise and Consent," "The Cuban Thing." Off-Bdwy. "The Makropoulous Secret," "The Queen and The Rebels," "Hogan's Goat," "The Kitchen," "Scuba Duba." "Nobody Hears A Broken Drum," "Steambath."

BAKER, LENNY. Born Jan. 17, 1945 in Boston. Graduate of Boston U. Made NY bow Off-Bdwy in 1969 in "Frank Gagliano's City Scene," followed by "The Year Boston Won The Pennant" (LC); "The Time of Your Life" (LC), "Summertree."

BALABAN, ROBERT. Born Aug. 16, 1945 in Chicago. Attended Colgate, NYU. Made NY bow Off-Bdwy in 1967 in "You're A Good Man, Charlie Brown," followed by "Plaza Suite" (Bdwy 1968), "Up Eden," and "White House Murder Case" (OB).

| Raina Barrett | Louis Beachner | Donna Barry | Charles Beard | Kathryn Baun |

BALDAUFF, PATRICK. Born Feb. 18, 1938 in Butler, Pa. Appeared off Bdwy in "Barroom," "Like I'm Talking to You Now," "A Dream of Love." "Winter Journey," "Dream of a Blacklisted Actor," made Bdwy bow in 1967 in "The Natural Look," followed by "Criss-Crossing."

BARBOUR, THOMAS. Born July 25, 1921 in NYC. Graduate of Princeton and Harvard. Credits: Off-Bdwy "Twelfth Night," "Merchant of Venice," "The Admirable Bashville," "River Line," "The Lady's Not For Burning," "The Enchanted," "Antony and Cleopatra," "The Saintliness of Margery Kemp." "Dr. Willy Nilly," "Under The Sycamore Tree," "Epitaph For George Dillon." "Thracian Horse." "Old Glory," "Sjt. Musgrave's Dance." Bdwy: "Portrait of A Queen," "The Great White Hope."

BARCLAY, JERED. Born in Seattle, Wash. Attended U. Wash. Appeared off Bdwy in "Juana La Loca," "The Hero," "Next Time I'll Sing To You," "Zoo Story," "Sand Box," made Bdwy bow in 1967 in "Marat/deSade," followed by "A Patriot for Me."

BARNES, VERONA. Attended Winston-Salem State College. Appeared in stock before Bdwy debut in 1968 in "The Great White Hope."

BARRERA, JOSE. Born Sept. 29, 1929 in Spain. Made Bdwy debut with Vicente Escudero company of dancers. Has appeared with LC Rep in "Camino Real," "Operation Sidewinder," and "Beggar on Horseback."

BARRETT, RAINA. Born Jan. 5, 1941 in Detroit. Graduate Ithaca Col. Made debut in 1968 Off-Bdwy in "Recess," followed by "Oh, Calcutta."

BARRIE, BARBARA. Born May 23, 1931 in Chicago. Graduate of U. Tex. Made Bdwy debut in 1955 in "The Wooden Dish," followed by "Happily Never After," "Company." Off-Bdwy in "The Crucible," "The Beaux Stratagem." "Taming of The Shrew" and "All's Well That Ends Well" (CP), "Horseman, Pass by," "Twelfth Night" (CP).

BARRS, NORMAN. Born Nov. 6, 1917 in London. Made NY debut in 1948 with Dublin Gate Co. in "The Old Lady Says No!" and "Where Stars Walk," followed by "Now I Lay Me Down To Sleep," "The Little Glass Clock," "The Apple Cart," "The Little Moon of Alban," "Kwamina," "Poor Bitos," "The Zulu and the Zayda," "Hostile Witness," "Loot," "Little Boxes" (OB).

BARRY, DONNA. Born in NYC; attended Sorbonne. Appeared in stock and on tv before NY debut off Bdwy in "A Scent of Flowers."

BARTENIEFF, GEORGE. Born Jan. 24, 1933 in Berlin. Made Bdwy bow in 1947 in "The Whole World Over," followed by "Venus Is," "All's Well That Ends Well," "Walking To Waldheim" (OB), "Memorandum" (OB), "Quotations From Chairman Mao Tse-Tung," "Death of Bessie Smith," "Cop-Out," "The Increased Difficulty of Concentration" (LC), "Room Service."

BARTLETT, BONNIE. Born June 20, 1929 in Wisconsin Rapids, Wisc. Graduate Northwestern. Made Bdwy debut in 1957 in "Tunnel of Love," followed by "Natural Affection," off Bdwy in "Telemachus Clay," "Lemon Sky."

BASELEON, MICHAEL. Born in Tarkio, Mo. Attended Northwestern, Actors Studio. Has appeared in "Caligula," "Night Life," "Dear Me, The Sky Is Falling," "Venus Is," Off Bdwy in "Hamlet," "Henry IV," "Richard II," "Romeo and Juliet," "The Tempest," "Journey to the Day," "Harold and Sondra," "Peer Gynt" (CP).

BASS, EMORY. Born in Ga. Made Bdwy bow in 1952 in "Kiss Me, Kate," followed by "Teahouse of the August Moon," "Pal Joey" (CC), "Where's Charley?" (CC), "1776." Off-Bdwy: "Chic," "Bartleby," "Gay Divorce," "Boys From Syracuse," "By Jupiter."

BAUMANN, KATHRYN. Born Aug. 13, 1946 in NYC. Attended Neighborhood Playhouse. Made Bdwy debut in 1968 in "The Prime of Miss Jean Brodie," followed by "The Penny Wars," "Lemon Sky" (OB).

BAVAN, YOLANDE. Born June 1, 1942 in Ceylon. Attended U. Colombo. Made NY debut 1964 in "A Midsummer Night's Dream" (CP), followed by Off-Bdwy's "Jonah," "House of Flowers," "Salvation."

BAXLEY, BARBARA. Born Jan. 1, 1925 in Porterville, Cal. Attended Pacific Col., Neighborhood Playhouse. Made Bdwy debut in 1948 in "Private Lives," followed by "Out West of Eighth," "Peter Pan," "I Am A Camera," "Bus Stop," "Camino Real," "Frogs of Spring," "Oh, Men! Oh, Women!" "The Flowering Peach," "Period of Adjustment," "Brecht On Brecht" (OB), "She Loves Me," "Three Sisters," "Measure For Measure" (CP), "To Be Young, Gifted and Black" (OB), "Plaza Suite," "Oh, Pioneers" (OB).

BEACHNER, LOUIS. Born June 9, 1923 in Jersey City. Made Bdwy bow in 1942 in "Junior Miss," followed by "No Time for Sergeants," "Georgy," and Off Bdwy in "Time to Burn," "The Hostage."

BEAL, JOHN. Born Aug. 13, 1909 in Joplin, Mo. Graduate U. Pa. Many credits include "Wild Waves," "Another Language," "She Loves Me Not," "Russet Mantle," "Soliloquy," "Miss Swan Expects," "Liberty Jones," "Voice of The Turtle," "Lend An Ear," "Teahouse of The August Moon," "Calculated Risk," "Billy," "Our Town" (1970) Off-Bdwy in "Our Town," "Wilder's Triple Bill," "To Be Young, Gifted and Black."

BEAN, ORSON. Born July 22, 1928 in Burlington, Vt. Made Bdwy bow in 1953 in "Men of Distinction," followed by "John Murray Anderson's Almanac" for which he received a Theatre World Award, "Will Success Spoil Rock Hunter?," "Nature's Way," "Mister Roberts" (CC), "Subways Are For Sleeping," "Say, Darling" (CC), "Never Too Late," "Home Movies" (OB), "I Was Dancing," "Illya Darling," "A Round with Ring" (OB).

BEARD, CHARLES. Born July 24, 1945 in Lake Charles, La. Attended Butler U. Made NY bow in 1968 in "West Side Story" (LC), followed by "Carnival" (CC), "Gantry," "Dark of the Moon" (OB).

BEARD, JAMES. Born Feb. 27 in NYC., Has appeared Off-Bdwy in "The Scarecrow," "Henry V" (CP), "Him." "Smiling The Boy Fell Dead," "Taming of The Shrew" (CP), "My Fair Lady" (CC'68), on Bdwy in "The Egg," "Don't Drink The Water," "Hello, Dolly!"

BECHER, JOHN C. Born Jan. 13, 1915 in Milwaukee, Wisc. Graduate U. Wisc. Made Bdwy bow with Am. Rep. Theatre in 1946, followed by "Skipper Next To God," "Idiot's Delight" (CC). "Picnic," City Center revivals of "Brigadoon" (1957-'63), "No Time For Sergeants," "Ballad of The Sad Cafe," "Mame," "Harvey," (1970) Off-Bdwy in "American Dream," "Death of Bessie Smith," "Happy Days," "Dumbwaiter," "Child Buyer," "That Th ng At The Cherry Lane."

BECKER, EDWARD. Born in Astoria, NY. Attended Am. Theatre Wing. Made Bdwy bow in 1951 in "Paint Your Wagon," followed by "Silk Stockings," "Happy Hunting," "Body Beautiful," "Whoop-Up," "Bye Bye Birdie," "Family Affair," "Camelot," "Here's Love," "Illya Darling," "Brigadoon" (CC '67),"Mame," "Jimmy."

BECKER, RAY. Born May 18, 1934 in NYC. Attended HB Studio. Made Bdwy bow in "How To Succeed....," followed by "Curley McDimple" (OB), "George M!," "Applause."

BEDFORD, BRIAN. Born Feb. 16, 1935 in Morley, Eng. Attended RADA. Made NY bow in 1960 in "Five Finger Exercise," followed by "Lord Pengo," "The Private Ear," "The Knack" (OB). "The Astrakhan Coat," "The Unknown Soldier and His Wife," "Seven Descents of Myrtle," with APA in "Misanthrope," "Cocktail Party," and "Hamlet," "Private Lives."

BEDFORD, PATRICK. Born May 30, 1932 in Dublin. Appeared with Dublin Gate Theatre before Bdwy debut in 1966 in "Philadelphia, Here I Come," followed by "The Mundy Scheme."

BEERY, LEE. Born March 20 in Minneapolis. Made NY debut in 1965 off Bdwy in "Leonard Bernstein's Theatre Songs," followed by "Oklahoma!" (LC).

| Ted Beniades | Stellar Bennett | Ed Bernard | Dale Berg | Herschel Bernardi |

BENIADES, TED. Born Nov. 17 in NYC. Attended CCNY, Dramatic Workshop. Made Bdwy bow in 1950 in "Mr. Roberts," followed by "Wonderful Town," "Garden of Sweets," "The King and I" (CC), "Smiling the Boy Fell Dead" (OB), "Irregular Verb to Love," "Golden Boy," "Oklahoma!" (LC), "Pat O'Brien Movies" (OB).

BENJAMIN, FRED. Born Sept. 8, 1944 in Boston. Has appeared in "We're Civilized" (OB), "Hello, Dolly!," "Promises, Promises."

BENNETT, STELLAR. Born in Liverpool, Eng. Made NY debut in 1968 off Bdwy in "Your Own Thing," followed by Bdwy bow in 1970 revival of "Our Town."

BERDEEN, ROBERT. Born Aug. 6 in Arlington, Va. Attended Neighborhood Playhouse. Has appeared in "A Dream of Swallows" (OB), "The Passion of Josef D.," "Fiddler on the Roof," "Royal Hunt of the Sun," "Billy," "Me and Juliet" (ELT).

BERG, DALE. Born June 1, 1931 in NYC. Attended New School. Made Bdwy debut in 1969 in "Zelda." Off Bdwy credits: "Alan, Carlos, Theresa," "The Changing Grass," "Leonce and Lena," "Love Your Crooked Neighbor."

BERGHOF, HERBERT. Born Sept. 13, 1909 in Vienna. Made NY bow in 1942 in "Nathan The Wise," followed by "The Russian People," "Innocent Voyage," "Jacobowsky and The Colonel," "Temper The Wind," "The Whole World Over," "Miss Liberty," "Ghosts," "Hedda Gabbler," "The Deep Blue Sea," "The Andersonville Trial," "Krapp's Last Tape" (OB), "In The Matter of J. Robert Oppenheimer" (LC).

BERGMANN, ALAN. Born in Brooklyn; attended Syracuse U., Catholic U. Made Bdwy bow in 1961 in "Gideon," followed by "Here Come the Cowns," "Night Life," "Lorenzo," "Luther," Off-Bdwy in "Portrait of the Artist as a Young Man," "Barroom Monks," "Danton's Death" (LC), "Jumping Fool."

BERNARD, ED. Born July 4, 1939 in Philadelphia. Attended Temple U., Hedgerow Theatre, HB Studio. Made NY bow in 1969 off Bdwy in "To Be Young, Gifted and Black," followed by "Five on the Black Hand Side."

BERNARDI, HERSCHEL. Born in NYC in 1923. Began career at 3. Has appeared in "The World of Sholom Aleichem" (OB), "Fiddler On The Roof," "Bajour," "Zorba."

BETHENCOURT, FRANCIS. Born Sept. 5, 1924 in London. Attended Mayfield Col. Made NY bow in 1948 in 'Anne of the Thousand Days," followed by "The Happy Time," "Dial 'M' for Murder," "A Visit to a Small Planet," 'Ross," "The Right Honourable Gentleman," "Hamp" (OB), "Borstal Boy."

BIRNEY, DAVID. Born Apr. 23, 1939 in Washington, D.C. Graduate of Dartmouth, UCLA. Has appeared Off-Bdwy with NY Shakespeare Festival in "Comedy of Errors," "Titus Andronicus," and "King John" and in "MacBird," "Ceremony of Innocence," "Summertree" for which he received a THEATRE WORLD Award, "The Miser" (LC), "Crimes of Passion"(OB).

BLACKTON, JACK. Born Mar. 16, 1938 in Colorado Springs. Graduate of U. Colo. Has appeared Off-Bdwy in "The Fantasticks," "Put It In Writing," "Jacques Brel Is Alive..." Made Bdwy bow in 1966 in "Mame."

BLEEZARDE, GLORIA. Born Oct. 12, 1940 in Albany, NY. Attended Southern Seminary Jr. Col. Appeared Off-Bdwy in "Just for Fun" and "New York Coloring Book" before Bdwy debut in 1964 in "Never Live Over A Pretzel Factory" for which she received a THEATRE WORLD Award, followed by "New Faces of 1968," "Three Men on a Horse."

BLISS, IMOGENE. Born Feb. 24 in Cleveland, O. Attended Conn., Col., Cleveland Playhouse. Made Bdwy debut in 1967 in "Marat/Sade," followed by "Your Own Thing" (OB).

BLOCK, CHAD. Born May 1, 1938 in Twin Falls, Ida. Made Bdwy bow in 1954 in "The Vamp," followed by "Li'l Abner," "Destry Rides Again," "Take Me Along," "Do Re Mi," "Come On Strong," "Hello, Dolly!," "Walking Happy," "Hallelujah, Baby!," "Coco."

BOLIN, SHANNON. Born Jan. 1, 1917 in S. Dakota. Attended U. Md. Has appeared in "Helen Goes to Troy," "Golden Apple," "Regina," "Only in America," "Damn Yankees," "Student Gypsy," "Xmas in Las Vegas," "Promenade" (OB).

BOND, SUDIE. Born July 13, 1928 in Louisville, Ky. Attended Rollins Col. Off-Bdwy: "Summer and Smoke," "Tovarich,"y"American Dream," "Sandbox," "Endgame," "Theatre of The Absurd," "Home Movies," "Softly and Consider The Nearness," "The Memorandum," "The Local Stigmatic," On Bdwy in "Waltz of The Toreadors," "Auntie Mame." "The Egg," "Harold," "My Mother, My Father and Me," "The Impossible Years," "Keep It In The Family," "Quotations From Chrmn. Mao Tse-Tung," "American Dream," "Forty Carats."

BONELLE, DICK. Born Apr. 11, 1936 in Houston, Tex. Graduate U. Houston. Made NY debut off Bdwy in 1970 in "Lyle."

BONYNGE, LETA. Born May 11, 1917 in Los Angeles. Graduate of Wellesley. Made Bdwy debut in 1947 in "Strange Bedfellows," followed by "Ivy Green," "My Fair Lady"(CC), and at LC in "Inner Journey," "The Miser," "The Time of Your Life," and "Camino Real."

BOOTH, SHIRLEY. Born Aug. 30, 1907 in NYC. Made Bdwy debut in 1925 in "Hell's Bells," followed by "Bye Bye Baby," "Laff That Off," "War Song," Too Many Heroes," "Three Men on a Horse," "Excursion," "Philadelphia Story," "My Sister Eileen," "Tomorrow the World,' "Hollywood Pinafore,"'"Land's End,'"Goodbye, My Fancy," "Love Me Long," "Come Back, Little Sheba," "A Tree Grows in Brooklyn," "Time of the Cuckoo," "By the Beautiful Sea," "Miss Isobel,"'"Juno,'"Second String,"'Look to the Lilies."

BORDO, ED. Born Mar. 3, 1931 in Cleveland, O. Graduate of Allegheny Col. Appeared off Bdwy in "The Dragon" before Bdwy bow in 1964 in "The Last Analysis," followed by "Inquest."

BOSCO, PHILIP. Born Sept. 26, 1930 in Jersey City, NJ. Graduate of Catholic U. Has appeared in "Auntie Mame," "Rape of The Belt," "Ticket of Leave Man" (OB), "Donnybrook," "Man For All Seasons," with LCRep in "The Alchemist," "East Wind," "Galileo," "St. Joan," "Tiger At The Gates," "Cyrano," "King Lear," "A Great Career," "In The Matter of J. Robert Oppenheimer," "The Miser," "The Time of Your Life, ' "Camino Real," "Operation Sidewinder," "Amphitryon."

BOSTWICK, BARRY. Born Feb. 24, 1945 in San Mateo, Cal. Graduate of Cal-Western, NYU. Made Bdwy debut with APA in "War and Peace," "Pantagleize," "Misanthrope." "Cock-A-Doodle Dandy," "Hamlet," "Salvation" (OB); "Colette" (OB).

BOVA, JOSEPH. Born May 25 in Cleveland, O. Graduate of Northwestern. Made NY bow in 1959 in "On The Town" (OB), followed by "Once Upon A Mattress," "Rape of The Belt," "Irma La Douce," "Hot Spot," and NY Shakespeare Festival productions of "Taming of the Shrew," "Richard III," "Comedy of Errors," and "Invitation To A Beheading," "The Chinese."

BOVASSO, JULIE. Born Aug. 1, 1930 in Brooklyn. Attended CCNY. Appeared off Bdwy in "Naked," The Maids," "The Lesson," "The Typewriter," made Bdwy debut in 1957 in "Monique," followed by "Minor Miracle," "Gloria and Esperanza" which she wrote.

BOWAN, SIBYL Born Jan. 31 in NYC. Has appeared in "Visit To A Small Planet," "First Impressions," "Donnybrook," "Black Comedy," "Maggie Flynn," "Jimmy."

BOZYK, ROSE. Born in Poland on May 13, 1914. Star of many Yiddish productions before Bdwy debut in 1966 in "Let's Sing Yiddish," followed by "Sing, Israel, Sing," "Mirele Efros"(OB).

BRAGG, BERNARD. Born Sept. 27, 1928 in Brooklyn, Graduate of Gallaudet, and San Francisco State Colleges. Made Bdwy bow with National Theatre of The Deaf.

231

Roger Braun	Beverly Ann Bremers	James Brochu	Amy Burk	Herschell B

BRANNUM, TOM. Born June 17, 1941 in Shawnee, Pa. Made Bdwy bow in 1961 in "Once There Was A Russian," followed by "Take Her, She's Mine," "We Bombed In New Haven." "Room Service."

BRANON, JOHN. Born Oct. 7, 1939 in Chicago. Attended Chicago City Col. Appeared off Bdwy in "Scuba Duba" and "The Glorious Ruler," made Bdwy debut in 1968 in "The Guide."

BRASINGTON, ALAN. Born in Monticello, NY. Attended RADA. Made Bdwy debut in 1968 with APA in "Pantagleize," "The Misanthrope," "Cock-A-Doodle Dandy," and "Hamlet," "A Patriot for Me."

BRASWELL, CHARLES. Born Sept. 7 in McKinney, Tex. Attended Arlington State Col. Made Bdwy bow in 1960 in "A Thurber Carnival," followed by "Wildcat," "Sail Away," "Hot Spot," "Here's Love," "I Had A Ball," "Me and Thee," "Mame," "Company."

BRAUN, ROGER. Born Sept. 4, 1941 in Cleveland, O. Graduate Kent State U. Made Bdwy debut in 1968 in "George M!," followed by "Beggar on Horseback" (LC).

BREMERS, BEVERLY ANN. Born Mar. 10, 1950 in Chicago. Attended HB Studio. Made NY debut in 1969 in "Hair," followed by "The Me Nobody Knows" (OB).

BRESLIN, TOMMY. Born Mar. 24, 1946 in Norwich, Conn. Attended Iona Col. Appeared off Bdwy in "For Love or Money," "Freedom Is A Two-Edged Sword," "Who's Who, Baby?," "Beggar on Horseback" (LC).

BRINK, ROBERT. Born Nov. 9, 1944 in Milwaukee, Wisc. Yale graduate. Has appeared Off Bdwy in "Awakening of Spring," "Shout from the Rooftops," and with American Savoyards.

BROCHU, JAMES. Born Aug. 16, 1946 in NYC. Graduate St. Francis Col. Attended AADA. Made stage debut Off-Bdwy in 1968 in "Endecott and The Red Cross," followed by "Taming of the Shrew," "Unfair to Goliath."

BRODERICK, JAMES. Born Mar. 7, 1928 in Charlestown, NH. Attended UNH, Neighborhood Playhouse. Made Bdwy bow in 1953 in "Maggie," followed by "Johnny No Trump," and off Bdwy roles in "A Touch of the Poet," "Two by Saroyan," "The Firebugs," "Rooms," "The Time of Your Life" (LC).

BROOKES, JACQUELINE. Born July 24, 1930 in Montclair, NJ. Attended U. Iowa, RADA. Made Bdwy debut in 1955 in "Tiger at the Gates," followed by "Watercolor," and Off-Bdwy in "The Cretan Woman" for which she received a THEATRE WORLD Award, "The Clandestine Marriage," "Measure for Measure," "Duchess of Malfi," "Ivanov," "Six Characters in Search of an Author," "An Evening's Frost," "Come Slowly, Eden," "The Increased Difficulty of Concentration"(LC), "The Persians."

BROOKS, DAVID. Born Sept. 24, 1917 in Portland, Ore. Attended U. Wash, Curtis Inst. Made Bdwy bow in 1944 in "Bloomer Girl," followed by "Brigadoon," "Mr. President," "The Sunday Man," "Park."

BROOKS, GERALDINE. Born Oct. 29, 1925 in NYC. Attended Neighborhood Playhouse, AADA, Actors Studio. Made Bdwy debut in 1944 in "Follow the Girls," followed by "The Winter's Tale," "The Time of the Cuckoo," "Brighttower."

BROWN, ELIZABETH. Born in Mississippi. Made NY debut in "The Firebrand" (ELT), followed by "Dark of the Moon"(OB).

BROWN, GRAHAM. Born Oct. 24, 1924 in NYC. Graduate of Howard U. Off-Bdwy credits: "Widower's Houses," "The Emperor's Clothes," "Time of Storm," "Major Barbara," "A Land Beyond The River," "The Blacks," "The Firebugs," "God Is a (Guess What?)," "An Evening of One Acts" (NEC), "Man Better Man" (NEC), on Bdwy in "Weekend," and "The Man In The Glass Booth."

BROWN, R. G. Born April 24, 1933, in Flint, Mich. Attended LACC, U. Mich. Made Bdwy bow in "New Faces of 1962," followed by "A Great Career" (LC), "Spiro Who?"

BROWN, TALLY. Born Aug. 1, 1934 in NYC. Graduate NYU, Juilliard. Appeared Off-Bdwy in "The Jackass," on Bdwy in "Pajama Game," "Tenderloin," "Mame."

BROWNING, ROBERT. Born Apr. 30, 1942 in Syracuse, NY. Graduate Carnegie Tech, Purdue. Made Bdwy debut in 1970 in "Candida."

BROWNING, SUSAN. Born Feb. 25, 1941 in Baldwin, NY. Graduate Penn. State. Made Bdwy bow in 1963 in "Love and Kisses," followed by "Company" for which she received a THEATRE WORLD Award, and Off-Bdwy roles in "Jo," "Dime A Dozen," "Seventeen," "Boys from Syracuse," "Collision Course."

BRUNS, PHILIP. Born May 2, 1931 in Pipestone, Minn. Graduate Augustana College, and Yale. Made Bdwy bow in "The Deputy," appeared Off-Bdwy in "Mr. Simian," "The Cradle Will Rock," "He Who Gets Slapped," "Dr. Willy Nilly," "Come Play With Me," "Listen To The Mocking Bird," "The Bald Soprano," "Jack Or The Submission," "Endgame," "Servant of Two Masters," "Pantomania," "Square In The Eye," "The Butter and Egg Man," "Spitting Image," "Henry V."

BRYGGMAN, LARRY. Born Dec. 21, 1938 in Concord, Cal. Attended CCSF, Am. Theatre Wing. Made NY bow Off-Bdwy in "A Pair of Pairs," followed by "Live Like Pigs," "Stop, You're Killing Me!" "Mod Donna."

BUCKLEY, BETTY. Born July 3, 1947 in Big Spring, Tex. Graduate Tex. Christian U. Made Bdwy debut in 1969 in "1776."

BURGE, JAMES. Born Dec. 3, 1943 in Miami, Fla. Graduate U.Okla., Wayne State U. Made Bdwy bow in 1970 in "Grin and Bare It."

BURK, AMY. Born Apr. 16, 1944 in Bellingham, Wash. Graduate San Francisco State Col., UCLA. Made Bdwy debut in 1970 in "Borstal Boy."

BURKS, DONNY. Born in Martinsville, Va. Graduate St. John's U. Appeared Off-Bdwy in 1964 in "Dutchman," made Bdwy bow in 1968 in "Hair" followed by "Billy Noname"(OB) for which he received a THEATRE WORLD Award.

BURNS, CATHERINE. Born Sept. 25, 1945 in NYC. Attended AADA. Made Bdwy debut in 1968 in "The Prime of Miss Jean Brodie," followed by off Bdwy roles in "Dream of a Blacklisted Actor," LC's "The Disintegration of James Cherry" and "Operation Sidewinder," "Dear Janet Rosenberg, Dear Mr. Kooning" for which she received a THEATRE WORLD Award.

BURNS, DAVID. Born June 22, 1902 in NYC. Has appeared in "Polly Preferred," "Wonder Boy," "Face the Music," "The Man Who Came To Dinner," "Pal Joey," "My Dear Public," "Billion Dollar Baby," "Make Mine Manhattan," "Out of This World," "Two's Company," "Men of Distinction," "A Hole In The Head," "Music Man," "A Funny Thing Happened On The Way To The Forum," "Hello, Dolly!," "The Price," "Sheep on the Runway."

BURRUS, RON. Born Mar. 11, 1944 in Sioux City, Iowa. Attended Stella Adler Studio. Made NY bow off Bdwy in 1969 in "The Brownstone Urge."

BURSTEIN, MIKE. Born July 1, 1945 in The Bronx. Star in Israel before making Bdwy debut in 1968 in "The Megilla of Itzik Manger," "Inquest."

BURTON, HERSCHELL. Born in Georgia. Studied at Neighborhood Playhouse. Appeared off Bdwy in "Waiting for Lefty," "The Bond," "King Lear" and "Trumpets of the Lord," before making Bdwy bow in 1969 in "Buck White."

BURTON, WARREN. Born Oct. 23, 1944 in Chicago. Attended Wright Col. Made NY bow in "Hair," followed by "A Patriot for Me."

ina Callahan   Angus Cairns   Irene Cara   Nick Cantrell   Madlyn Cates

BUSH, NORMAN. Born Apr. 11, 1933 in Louisville, Ky. Attended AADA. Made NY bow off Bdwy in 1960 in "The Goose," followed by "The Connection," "Funny House of a Negro," "The Toilet," and NEC's "Daddy Goodness," "Kongi's Harvest," "Summer of the 17th Doll," "Song of the Lusitanian Bogey," "God Is A (Guess What?)," "Malcochon," "Man Better Man," "Day of Absence" and "Brotherhood."

BYRNE, GAYLEA. Born in Baltimore, Md. Graduate Peabody Conservatory. Made NY debut Off-Bdwy in 1961 in "All In Love," followed by "Music Man" (CC), "Man of LaMancha."

BYRNES, BURKE. Born Dec. 9, 1937 in Oceanside, NY Graduate American U., and Neighborhood Playhouse. Made Bdwy debut in 1968 in "The Great White Hope."

BYRNES, MAUREEN. Born May 14, 1944 in Chicago. Made Bdwy debut in 1965 in "La Grosse Valise," followed by "Oh, Calcutta!"(OB)

CAHILL, JAMES. Born May 31, 1940 in Brooklyn. Off-Bdwy in "The Hostage," "The Alchemist," "Johnny Johnson," made Bdwy bow in "Marat/DeSade" (1967), "Peer Gynt" (CP), LC's "An Evening for Merlin Finch," and "The Disintegration of James Cherry," "Crimes of Passion" (OB).

CAIRNS, ANGUS. Born Mar. 29, 1910 in Fitchburg, Mass. Made NY debut in 1941 in "Othello" (CC), followed by ART's "Henry VIII," "What Every Woman Knows," "Androcles and the Lion," "Yellow Jack," "Alice in Wonderland," and "Mock Turtle," "Brigadoon," "Kiss Me, Kate," "Paint Your Wagon," "Threepenny Opera" (OB), "The Engagement Baby."

CALDWELL, ZOE. Born Sept. 14, 1933 in Melbourne, Aust. Attended Methodist Ladies Coll. Made Bdwy debut in 1965 in "The Devils," followed by "Slapstick Tragedy" for which she received a THEATRE WORLD Award, "The Prime of Miss Jean Brodie," "Colette" (OB).

CALLAHAN, KRISTINA. Born in Atlanta, Ga. Attended Sarah Lawrence Col., London AMDA. Made NY debut off Bdwy in 1963 in "The Burning," followed by "The Blood of the Pig," "Fireworks."

CALVERT, HENRY. Born Jan. 8, 1920 in Chicago. Attended Dramatic Workshop, Theatre Wing. Appeared Off-Bdwy in "The Prodigal," "Hamlet," "Miss Julia," "The Country Girl," "There Is No End," "America Hurrah," "Spiro Who?"

CANTRELL, NICK. Born Oct. 7, 1943 in Hollywood, Cal. Studied at American Theatre, Stella Adler Studio. Made NY bow in 1967 off Bdwy in "Iphigenia in Aulis," followed by "Camino Real" (LC).

CARA, IRENE. Born Mar. 18, 1959 in NYC. Made Bdwy debut in 1968 in "Maggie Flynn," followed by "The Me Nobody Knows" (OB).

CAREY, FRANK. Born Oct. 12, 1934 in Tarrytown, NY. Attended AADA. Made debut off Bdwy in 1960 in "Nat Turner," followed by "The Brick and the Rose," "A Black Quartet."

CARIOU, LEONARD. Born Sept. 30, 1939 in Winnipeg, Can. Made Bdwy debut with Minn. Theatre Co. in "House of Atreus," followed by "Henry V," "Applause" for which he received a THEATRE WORLD Award.

CARLSON, LESLIE. Born Feb. 24, 1933 in Mitchell, SD. Graduate of U.S. Dak. Appeared with NY Shakespeare Festival in "Antony and Cleopatra," "As You Like It," and "Winter's Tale," and in "Your Own Thing" (OB).

CARNE, JUDY. Born Apr. 27, 1939 in Northampton, Eng. Attended Bush-Davis Theatrical School. Made Bdwy debut in 1970 in "The Boy Friend."

CARNELIA, CRAIG. Born Aug. 13, 1949 in Queens, NY. Attended Hofstra U. Made NY debut Off-Bdwy in "The Fantasticks" in 1969, followed by "Lend an Ear" (ELT).

CARNEY, KAY. Born in Rice Lake, Wisc. Graduate U. Wisc., Mt. Holyoke Col. Made NY debut in 1966 off Bdwy in "Viet Rock" followed by "Calling in Crazy."

CARPENTER, CARLETON. Born July 10, 1926 in Bennington, Vt. Attended Northwestern. Made Bdwy debut in 1944 in "Bright Boy," followed by "Career Angel," "Three to Make Ready," "Magic Touch," "John Murray Anderson's Almanac," "Hotel Paradiso," "A Box of Watercolors," "A Stage Affair" (OB), "Hello, Dolly!," "Boys in the Band" (OB), "Lyle"(OB).

CARPENTER, THELMA. Born Jan. 15, 1922 in Brooklyn. Appeared on Bdwy in "Memphis Bound," "Inside U.S.A.," "Shuffle Along" ('52). "Ankles Aweigh," "Hello, Dolly!"

CARR, KENNETH. Born May 3, 1943 in The Bronx. Made Bdwy debut in 1965 in "The Impossible Years," followed by off Bdwy roles in "Parents and Children," "Promenade," "Sambo."

CARROLL, HELENA. Born in Glasgow, Scot. Attended Weber-Douglas School of Drama, London. Came to US with Dublin Players. Founded, directed, acted with Irish Players off Bdwy. Made Bdwy debut in 1956 in "Separate Tables," followed by "Happy as Larry," "A Touch of the Poet," "Little Moon of Alban," "The Hostage," "Oliver!," "Pickwick," "Three Hand Reel" (OB), "Something Different," "Georgy," "Borstal Boy."

CASH, ROSALIND. Born Dec. 31, 1938 in Atlantic City, NJ. Attended CCNY. Made Bdwy debut in 1966 in "The Wayward Stork," followed by Off-Bdwy roles in "Junebug Graduates Tonight," "Fiorello" (CC). "To Bury A Cousin," with NEC in "Song of The Lusitanian Bogey," "Kongi's Harvest," "Ceremonies In Dark Old Men," "An Evening of One Acts," "Man Better Man," "The Harangues," "Day of Absence," "Brotherhood."

CASS, PEGGY. Born May 21, 1926 in Boston. Attended Wyndham. Appeared in "Touch and Go," "Live Wire," "Bernardine," "Phoenix '55" (OB), "Othello," "Henry V," "Auntie Mame" for which she received a THEATRE WORLD Award, "A Thurber Carnival," "Children From Their Games," "Don't Drink The Water," "The Front Page" ('69), "Plaza Suite."

CASSIDY, JACK. Born Mar. 5, 1927 in Richmond Hills, NY. Has appeared in "Something For The Boys," "Sadie Thompson," "Around The World," "Inside U.S.A.," "Small Wonder," "Music In My Heart," "Alive and Kicking," "Wish You Were Here," "Sandhog" (OB), "Shangri-La," "The Beggar's Opera" (CC), "She Loves Me," "Fade Out-Fade In," "It's Superman!," "Maggie Flynn," "The Mundy Scheme."

CASTELLANO, RICHARD. Born Sept. 4, 1933 in Jackson Heights, NY. Attended Columbia. Has appeared in "A View From The Bridge" (OB), "The Investigation," "That Summer—That Fall," "Mike Downstairs," "Lovers and Other Strangers," "Sheep on the Runway."

CATES, MADLYN. Born Mar. 8, 1925 in NYC. Attended Queens Col. Made debut in 1965 off Bdwy in "Sunset," followed by "The Kitchen," and Bdwy in "Marat/deSade" (1966), "A Patriot for Me."

CATLETT, MARY JO. Born Sept. 2, 1938 in Denver, Colo. Graduate of Loretto Hts. Coll. Has appeared in "Along Came A Spider" (OB), "New Girl In Town," "Fiorello," "Pajama Game," "Hello, Dolly!," "Canterbury Tales," "Promenade" (OB).

CAVANAUGH, MICHAEL. Born in NYC. Attended San Francisco State Col. Made NY bow in 1969 in "Oh, Calcutta."

Paul Charles   Louise Clay   Charles Cioffi   Jill Clayburgh   Edward Clin

CHACE, DOROTHY. Born in North Bergen, NJ. Attended San Diego and San Francisco State Colleges, Stanford, Yale. Has appeared with LC Rep in "The Caucasian Chalk Circle" and "Cyrano de Bergerac," and made Bdwy debut in 1969 in "Three Men on a Horse."

CHALLENGER, RUDY. Born Oct. 2, 1928 in NYC. Has appeared in "Tiger, Tiger Burning Bright," "Tambourines to Glory," "Golden Boy," "Do I Hear A Waltz?," "Shakespeare in Harlem," "Scuba Duba," "Mahagonny."

CHARLES, PAUL. Born July 29, 1947. Attended Quintano School. Has appeared in "Best Foot Forward" (OB), "Kelly," "Royal Hunt of the Sun," "A Joyful Noise," "La Strada."

CHARNEY, JORDAN. Born in NYC. Graduate Bklyn Col. Appeared off Bdwy in "Harry, Noon and Night," "A Place for Chance," "Hang Down Your Head and Die," "The Pinter Plays," "Telemachus Clay," "Zoo Story," "Viet Rock," "MacBird," "Red Cross," "The Glorious Ruler," and on Bdwy in "Slapstick Tragedy," "The Birthday Party."

CHEW, VIRGILIA. Born July 9, 1905 in Houston, Tex. Attended Bryn Mawr. Has appeared in "The Women," "Life With Father," "Anniversary Waltz," "Orpheus Descending," "Blue Denim," and Off-Bdwy in "Dumbbell People," "Days and Nights of Beebee Fenstermaker," "Suddenly Last Summer," "Winterset," and with LCRep in "Yerma," "A Cry of Players," "King Lear."

CHOBANIAN, HAIG. Born Oct. 26, 1937 in Racine, Wisc. Attended U. Wisc. Has appeared off Bdwy in "The Shoemaker and the Peddler," "Banquet for the Moon," "MacBird," "The Tenth Man" (CC'67), "Fireworks."

CHRISTIAN, ROBERT. Born Dec. 27, 1939 in Los Angeles. Attended UCLA. Has appeared Off-Bdwy in "The Happening," "Hornblend," "Fortune and Men's Eyes," "Boys in The Band," and on Bdwy in "We Bombed In New Haven," "Does A Tiger Wear A Necktie?"

CHRISTMAS, DAVID. Born May 2, 1942 in Pasadena, Cal. Attended Pasadena City College, HB Studio. Has appeared Off-Bdwy in "Butter and Egg Man," "Dames At Sea," made Bdwy bow in 1970 in "Grin and Bare It."

CIOFFI, CHARLES. Born Oct. 31, 1935 in NYC. Graduate of U. Minn. Has appeared Off-Bdwy with LCRep in "A Cry of Players," "King Lear," and "In The Matter of J. Robert Oppenheimer," "Whistle in the Dark."

CLARK, ALEXANDER. Born May 2, 1904 in NYC. Has appeared in "Merton of The Movies," "Excess Baggage," "Biography," "Too True To Be Good," "Victoria Regina," "Abe Lincoln In Illinois," "Margin For Error," "In Time To Come," "Sheppy," "Legend of Lovers," "The Captains and The Kings," "Calculated Risk," City Center revivals of "Brigadoon," "Carousel," and "Life With Father," "The Show-Off" (APA).

CLARK, DORT. Born Oct. 1, 1917 in Wellington, Kans. Attended Kan. State Teachers Col. Made NY bow off Bdwy in "The Years Between," followed by Bdwy roles in "Sweet Charity," "The First Million," "Lower North," "Snafu," "Happy Birthday," "South Pacific," "Wonderful Town," "Bells Are Ringing," "Let It Ride," "Take Me Along," "Fiorello" (CC), "Harvey."

CLARK, OLIVER. Born Jan. 4, 1939 in Buffalo, NY. Graduate Buffalo U. Made Bdwy bow in 1963 in "Arturo Ui," followed by "Ben Franklin In Paris," "Caucasian Chalk Circle" (LCRep), "Don't Drink The Water," off Bdwy in "Spiro Who?," "Two Times One," "Passing Through from Exotic Places."

CLARK, PHILLIP. Born Aug. 12, 1941 in San Diego, Calif. Attended US Cal. Made Bdwy bow in 1966 in "We Have Always Lived in the Castle", followed by "Boys in the Band" (OB).

CLARKE, DAVID. Born Aug. 30, 1908 in Chicago. Attended Butler U. Made Bdwy bow in 1930 in "Roadside," followed by "Let Freedom Ring," "Bury the Dead," "Washington Jitters," "200 Were Chosen," "Journey Man," "Abe Lincoln in Illinois," "See the Jaguar," "The Emperor's Clothes," "Madam, Will You Walk" (OB), "A View from the Bridge," "Ballad of the Sad Cafe," "Rose" (OB), "Inquest."

CLAY, LOUISE. Born Mar. 3, 1938 in Lafayette, La. Graduate La. State U., Manhattanville Col. Made Bdwy debut in 1966 in "Marat/deSade," followed by "Mike Downstairs," "Rondelay" (OB).

CLAYBURGH, JILL. Born Apr. 30, 1944 in NYC. Graduate Sarah Lawrence Col. Made Bdwy debut in 1970 in "The Sudden and Accidental Re-Education of Horse Johnson," appeared off Bdwy in "It's Called the Sugar Plum," "Calling in Crazy," "The Nest."

CLEIN, ED. Born Oct. 1944 in Atlanta, Ga. Graduate Emory U. Made NY bow in 1968 Off-Bdwy in "The Cannibals."

CLEMENT, DONALD. Born in Lakewood, NJ. Attended US Naval Academy. Made NY debut in 1970 Off Bdwy in "The Boys in the Band."

CLINTON, EDWARD. Born Sept. 23, 1948 in Evanston, Ill. Attended NYU. Made debut Off-Bdwy in 1970 in "The Pig Pen."

COATES, CAROLYN. Born Apr. 29, 1930 in Oklahoma City. Attended UCLA. Appeared Off-Bdwy in "The Innocents," "The Balcony," "Electra," "The Trojan Women" for which she received a THEATRE WORLD Award, "A Whitman Portrait," "Party On Greenwich Avenue," and "The Club Bedroom," with LCRep in "The Country Wife," "Condemned of Altona," "The Caucasian Chalk Circle," "The Disintegration of James Cherry"(LC), "A Scent of Flowers," and on Bdwy in "Death of Bessie Smith," "American Dream," "Fire!"

COBB, LEE J. Born Dec. 8, 1911 in NYC. Attended CCNY. Made Bdwy bow in 1935 in "Crime and Punishment," followed by "Waiting for Lefty," "Till The Day I Die," "Bitter Stream," "Johnny Johnson," "Golden Boy," "The Gentle People," "Thunder Rock," "Fifth Column," "Clash By Night," "Jason," "Winged Victory," "Death of A Salesman," "King Lear"(LC).

COCO, JAMES. Born Mar. 21, 1930 in NYC. Has appeared on Bdwy in "Hotel Paradiso," "Everybody Loves Opal," "A Passage To India," "Arturo Ui," "The Devils," "The Astrakhan Coat," "Here's Where I Belong," "The Last of the Red Hot Lovers," and Off-Bdwy in "Moon In The Yellow River," "That 5 A.M. Jazz," "Lovey," "Squat Betty and The Sponge Room," "Salome," "Fragments," "Witness," and "Next."

COE, JOHN. Born Oct. 19, 1925 in Hartford, Conn. Graduate of Tufts and Boston U. Has appeared Off-Bdwy in "The Marrying Maiden," "Thistle In My Bed," "John," "The Wicked Cooks," "June Bug Graduates Tonight," "Drums In The Night," "America Hurrah," "Father Uxbridge Wants To Marry," "Nobody Hears A Broken Drum," and on Bdwy in "The Passion of Josef D," "The Man In The Glass Booth," "La Strada."

COFFIELD, PETER. Born July 17, 1945 in Evanston, Ill. Graduate of Northwestern and U. Mich. Made NY debut with APA in "The Misanthrope," "Cock-A-Doodle Dandy" and "Hamlet."

COHEN, AL. Born Oct. 25, 1939 in NYC. Attended Queens Col. Appeared Off-Bdwy in "An Impudent Wolf." "Anything Goes," "Get Thee To Canterbury," with American Savoyards, and on Bdwy in "Illya Darling," "I'm Solomon," "Billy."

COHEN, MARGERY. Born June 24, 1947 in Chicago. Attended U. Wisc., U. Chicago, HB Studio. Made Bdwy debut in 1968 in "Fiddler on the Roof," followed by "Jacques Brel Is Alive and Well..."(OB).

Patricia Cope   **Peter Collins**   **Gretchen Corbett**   **Roderick Cook**   **Mariclare Costello**

COLEMAN, NANCY. Born Dec. 30, 1914 in Everett, Wash. Graduate of U. Wash. Has appeared in "Susan and God," "Liberty Jones," "The Sacred Flame," "The Male Animal" (1952), "The Desperate Hours," "Lemonade" (OB).

COLES, ZAIDA. Born Sept. 10, 1933 in Lynchburg, Va. Has appeared Off-Bdwy in "The Father," "Pins and Needles," and on Bdwy in "Weekend," "Zelda."

COLEY, THOMAS. Born July 29, 1918 in Bethayres, Pa. Attended Washington and Lee U. Made Bdwy debut in 1935 in "Taming of the Shrew," followed by "Swingin' the Dream," "Return Engagement," "Cue for Passion," "My Fair Ladies," "Mr. Peebles and Mr. Hooker," "Portrait in Black," "Harvey," "I Never Sang for My Father," "Our Town" ('69).

COLLINS, BLANCHE. Born May 12, 1918 in NYC. Attended LA State College, Actors Studio. Appeared in "Scarlet Sister Mary," "Strike Me Pink," "The Cradle Will Rock," "G.I. Hamlet" "On A Clear Day You Can See Forever," "My Fair Lady" (CC '68).

COLLINS, PETER. Born Aug. 7, 1923 in Kenosha, Wis. Graduate Marquette U. Made Bdwy bow in 1958 in "Night Circus," appeared off Bdwy in "Make Him Magnificent," "Spiro Who?"

COLTON, CHEVI. Born in NYC. Attended Hunter Col. Has appeared Off-Bdwy in "Time of Storm," "Insect Comedy" (CC). "The Adding Machine," "O Marry Me," "Penny Change," "The Mad Show," "Jacques Brel Is Alive...," and on Bdwy in "Cabaret."

COLSON, C. DAVID. Born Dec. 23, 1941 in Detroit. Graduate U. Mich. Made NY bow in 1970 in "The Last Sweet Days of Isaac" (OB), and Bdwy debut in "Purlie."

COLYER, AUSTIN. Born Oct. 29, 1935 in Brooklyn. Attended SMU. Has appeared in "Darwin's Theories," "Let It Ride," "Maggie Flynn," and City Center revivals of "Brigadoon," "Music Man," "How To Succeed In Business...," "Where's Charley?," "Elizabeth The Queen," "Carousel," "Finian's Rainbow," and "Wonderful Town," "Show Me Where The Good Times Are" (OB), "Jimmy."

CONDOS, DIMO. Born Feb. 29, 1932 in NYC. Has appeared Off-Bdwy in "The Celebration," "O'Flaherty," "The Cannibals," "Moths."

CONNELL, DAVID. Born Nov. 24, 1935 in Cleveland, O. Attended Kent State U. Made Bdwy debut in 1968 in "The Great White Hope."

CONNOLLY, GEORGE. Born Oct. 26, 1944 in Boston. Attended Boston U. Made Bdwy debut in 1968 in "The Happy Time," followed by "Up Eden" (OB), "Borstal Boy."

CONNOR, WHITFIELD. Born Dec. 3, 1916 in Ireland. Attended Wayne, and U. Mich. Has appeared in "Hamlet," Redgrave's "Macbeth" for which he received a THEATRE WORLD Award, "The Winner," "Lunatics and Lovers," "There Was A Little Girl," "Everything In The Garden," Off-Bdwy in "Six Characters In Search of An Author," "The Makropoulos Secret," "The Disenchanted" and "In The Matter of J. Robert Oppenheimer" (LC).

CONVY, BERT. Born July 23, 1935 in St. Louis. Graduate of UCLA. Made NY bow in "Billy Barnes Revue," followed by "Nowhere To Go But Up," "Morning Sun," "Love and Kisses," "Fiddler On The Roof," "The Impossible Years," "Cabaret," "Shoot Anything With Hair That Moves" (OB), "The Front Page" ('69).

CONWAY, DIANE. Born June 10, 1944 in NYC. Attended Teachers Col. Made Bdwy debut in 1967 in "Hello, Dolly!"

CONWAY, KEVIN BRYAN. Born May 29, 1942 in NYC. Made debut in 1968 off Bdwy in "Muzeeka," and on Bdwy in 1969 in "Indians."

COOK, PATRICK. Born Sept. 20, 1949 in Minneapolis. Attended Musical Theatre Workshop of US Cal. Made NY bow Off-Bdwy in "Treasure Island" in 1964, Bdwy debut in 1968 in "A Mother's Kisses," followed by "Dark of the Moon" (OB).

COOK, RODERICK. Born in 1932 in London. Attended Cambridge U. Made Bdwy debut in 1961 in "Kean," followed by "Roar Like A Dove," "The Girl Who Came to Supper," "Noel Coward's Sweet Potato," "A Scent of Flowers" (OB).

COONAN, SHEILA. Born June 28, 1922 in Montreal, Can. Attended McGill U. Has appeared in "Red Roses For Me," "A Taste of Honey," "The Hostage," "Hogan's Goat" (OB), "The Great White Hope."

COOPER, CHRISTINE. Born Aug 13, 1946 in El Paso, Tex. Graduate Kingsbord College, AADA. Made NY debut off Bdwy in 1970 in "Dark of the Moon."

COOPER, MARILYN. Born Dec. 14, 1936 in NYC. Attended NYU. Has appeared in "Mr. Wonderful," "West Side Story," "Brigadoon" (CC), "Gypsy," "I Can Get It For You Wholesale," "The Mad Show" (OB), "Hallelujah, Baby!" "Golden Rainbow," "Mame," "A Teaspoon Every 4 Hours."

COPE, PATRICIA. Born Sept. 3, 1943 in Meridian, Miss. Attended Lon Morris Col. Made Bdwy debut in 1965 in "Roar of the Greasepaint...," followed by "How to Succeed...," "Hooray! It's A Glorious Day (OB), "Wonderful Town" (CC)," "How Now Dow Jones," "Hello, Dolly!"

CORBETT, GRETCHEN. Born Aug. 13, 1947 in Portland, Ore. Attended Carnegie Tech. Appeared Off-Bdwy in "Arms and The Man," "The Bench," "Iphigenia In Aulis," and on Bdwy in "After The Rain," "Forty Carats."

CORBIN, BARRY. Born Oct. 16, 1940 in Lamesa, Tex. Attended Tex. Tech. Appeared with American Shakespeare Festival, and made Bdwy bow with company in "Henry V" in 1969.

COSTELLO, MARICLARE. Born in Peoria, Ill. Has appeared Off-Bdwy in "The Hostage" (1962), with LC Rep in "After The Fall" and "But For Whom Charlie," on Bdwy in "Lovers and Other Strangers," "A Patriot for Me," "Harvey."

COTSWORTH, STAATS. Born Feb. 17, 1908 in Oak Park, Ill. Attended Phila. College of Arts. Made NY debut with Civic Rep. Theatre in 1932. Among his many credits are "Romeo and Juliet," "Alice in Wonderland," "Rain from Heaven," "Murder at the Vanities," "Madame Capet," "Macbeth," "She Stoops to Conquer," "Richard III," "Advise and Consent," "Hamlet," "Right Honourable Gentleman," "Weekend," "A Patriot for Me," "Madwoman of Chaillot" (OB).

COTTRELL, RICHARD. Born Sept. 4, 1944 in Springfield, Ill. Graduate U. Ark. Made Bdwy debut with Minn. Theatre Co. in "House of Atreus" and "Arturo Ui."

COTTRELL, WILLIAM. Born June 6, 1918 in Medford, Ore. Graduate U. Ore. Made Bdwy bow in 1964 in "Traveler Without Luggage," followed by "Diamond Orchid," "Come Summer," and Off-Bdwy in "Six Characters In Search of An Author," "Taming of The Shrew," "Duchess of Malfi," "Ticket of Leave Man."

COUPE, DIANE. Born Nov. 19, 1939 in Widnes, Eng. Made Bdwy debut in 1962 in "Nowhere To Go But Up," followed by "Hot Spot," "Jenny," "Funny Girl," "La Grosse Valise," "Mame."

COURTNEY, ALEXANDER. Born Mar. 21, 1940 in NYC. Appeared in NY Shakespeare Festival in "Hamlet" and "Othello," with APA in "The Wild Duck," and "War and Peace," and in "Rosencrantz and Guildenstern Are Dead."

Don Crabtree　　**Kathleen Coyne**　　**Noel Craig**　　**Tandy Cronyn**　　**Darryl Croxton**

COVER, FRANKLIN. Born Nov. 20, 1928 in Cleveland, O. Graduate of Denison, Western Reserve U. Appeared Off- Bdwy in "Julius Caesar," "Henry IV," "She Stoops To Conquer," "The Plough and The Stars," "The Octoroon," "Hamlet," and "Macbeth," made Bdwy bow in 1962 in "Giants, Sons of Giants," followed by "Calculated Risk," "Abraham Cochrane," "Any Wednesday," "The Investigation," "Forty Carats."

COWLES, MATTHEW. Born Sept. 28, 1944 in NYC. Attended Neighborhood Playhouse. Made Bdwy bow in 1966 in "Malcolm," followed by Off-Bdwy roles in "King John" (CP), "The Indian Wants The Bronx," "Triple Play," "Stop, You're Killing Me!" "The Time of Your Life" (LC).

COYNE, KATHLEEN. Born July 29, 1945 in Seattle, Wash. Attended U. Wash. Made NY debut in 1969 off Bdwy in "Getting Married."

CRABTREE, DON. Born Aug. 21, 1928 in Borger, Tex. Attended Actors Studio. Made Bdwy bow in 1959 in "Destry Rides Again," followed by "Happiest Girl in the World," "Family Affair," "Unsinkable Molly Brown," "Sophie," "110 in the Shade," "Golden Boy," "Pousse Cafe," "Mahagonny" (OB).

CRAFT, THOMAS. Born Nov. 16, 1937 in London, Ky. Graduate Catholic U. Made NY bow in 1970 off Bdwy in "Dark of the Moon."

CRAIG, NOEL. Born Jan. 4 in St. Louis, Mo. Attended Northwestern, Goodman Theatre, Guildhall School London. Made Bdwy debut in 1967 in "Rosencrantz and Guildenstern Are Dead," followed by "A Patriot for Me."

CRAIG, PHYLLIS. Born Aug. 5, 1936 in London. Made NY debut Off-Bdwy in 1968 in "Scuba Duba," Bdwy bow in 1970 in "Borstal Boy."

CRANE, DEAN. Born Jan. 5, 1932 in Denver, Colo. Made Bdwy debut in 1953 in "John Murray Anderson's Almanac," followed by "Fanny," "Lute Song" (CC'59), "Carnival" (also 1968 CC revival).

CROFOOT, ALAN. Born June 2, 1929 in Toronto, Can. Graduate U. Toronto. Made Bdwy debut in 1964 in "Oliver!," followed by "Slapstick Tragedy," "Mahagonny" (OB).

CROFT, PADDY. Born in Worthing, Eng. Attended Avondale Col. Appeared Off-Bdwy in 1961 in "The Hostage," followed by "Billy Liar," "Live Like Pigs," "Hogan's Goat," and with APA, and on Bdwy in "The Killing of Sister George," "The Prime of Miss Jean Brodie."

CRONYN, HUME. Born in London, Ont., Can., July 18, 1911. Attended McGill U, AADA. Has appeared in "Hipper's Holiday," "High Tor," "Escape This Night," "Three Men On A Horse," "Boy Meets Girl," "Room Service," "Three Sisters," "Mr. Big," "Retreat to Pleasure," "The Fourposter," "The Honeys," "Man in the Dog Suit," "Triple Play," "Big Fish, Little Fish," "Hamlet," "The Physicists," "A Delicate Balance," "Hadrian VII."

CRONYN, TANDY. Born Nov. 26, 1945 in Los Angeles Attended Central School of Speech and Drama in London. Made Bdwy debut in 1969 in "Cabaret."

CROWDER, JACK. Born Nov. 15, 1939 in Miami, Fla. Attended U. Redlands. Appeared Off-Bdwy in "Fly Blackbird," and "The Fantasticks," on Bdwy in "Hello, Dolly!" (1967) for which he received a THEATRE WORLD Award.

CROWLEY, DICK. Born July 27, 1929 in Davenport, Iowa. Graduate Northwestern. Made Bdwy bow in 1951 in "Make A Wish," followed by "Ziegfeld Follies," "Bye, Bye, Birdie," "Hello, Dolly!"

CROWLEY, EDWARD. Born Sept. 5, 1926 in Lewiston, Me. Attended AADA. Appeared Off-Bdwy in "The Admirable Bashville," "An Evening With G.B.S.," "Once Around The Block," "I Want You." "Lion In Love," "Telemachus Clay," "Hair," "How To Steal An Election," and "An Evening for Merlin Finch" (LC), and on Bdwy in "Make A Million," "The Family Way."

CROXTON, DARRYL. Born Apr. 5, 1946 in Baltimore, Md. Attended AADA. Appeared off Bdwy in "Volpone" and "Murder in the Cathedral" before Bdwy debut in 1969 in "Indians."

CRYER, DAVID. Born Mar. 8, 1936 in Evanston, Ill. Attended DePauw U. Appeared Off-Bdwy in "The Fantasticks," "Streets of New York," and "Now Is The Time For All Good Men," and on Bdwy in "110 In The Shade." "Come Summer," for which he received a THEATRE WORLD Award, "1776."

CULLUM, JOHN. Born Mar. 2, 1930 in Knoxville, Tenn. Graduate U. Tenn. Made Bdwy bow in "Camelot," followed by "Infidel Caesar," "The Rehearsal," Burton's "Hamlet," "On A Clear Day You Can See Forever," for which he received a THEATRE WORLD Award, "Three Hand Reel" (OB), "Man of LaMancha," "1776."

CUMMINGS, CONSTANCE. Born May 15, 1910 in Seattle. Made Bdwy debut in 1928 in "Treasure Girl," followed by "The Little Show," "This Man's Town," "June Moon," "Accent On Youth," "Young Madame Conti," "Madame Bovary," "If I Were You," "One-Man Show," "The Rape of The Belt," "Hamlet," ('69).

CUNARD, LANCE. Born Mar. 20, 1910 in Collingswood, N.J. Attended Ursinus Col. Made NY bow in 1945 in "You Can't Take It With You," followed by "Legend of Lizzie," "The Visit," "The Trial," "Alcestis," "Spring's Awakening," "Volpone," "Richard III," "Henry V," "Rules of The Game," "As You Like It," "A Midsummer's Night Dream," "Taming of The Shrew," "Corruption In The Palace of Justice," "Colombe," "Sign of Winter," "Orphee," "Deadly Game," "Party On Greenwich Avenue," "The Great White Hope."

CUNNINGHAM, JOHN. Born June 22, 1932 in Auburn, NY. Graduate of Darmouth and Yale. Has appeared Off-Bdwy in "Love Me Little," "Pimpernel," "The Fantasticks," "Love and Let Love," on Bdwy in "Hot Spot," "Zorba," "Company."

CUNNINGHAM, SARAH. Born Sept. 8, 1918 in Greenville, SC. Attended Furman U, Actors Studio. Made Bdwy debut in 1948 in "The Respectful Prostitute," followed by "A Happy Journey," "Blood Wedding," "The Young and Fair," "Fair Game," "The Visit," "Toys in the Attic," "The Zulu and the Zayda," "My Sweet Charlie," Off-Bdwy in "Portrait of the Artist...," "Barroom Monks," "Christy," "Oh, Pioneers."

CUOZZO, ALBERTA. Born Oct. 5, in Newark, NJ. Graduate AADA. Made NY debut in 1969 Off-Bdwy in "The Man With The Flower In His Mouth."

CURNOCK, RICHARD. Born May 9, 1922 in London. Attended Italia Conti School. Made Bdwy bow in 1964 in "Oh, What a Lovely War," followed by "The Cherry Orchard" (1970).

CURTIS, KEENE. Born Feb. 15, 1925 in Salt Lake City. Graduate U. Utah. Made Bdwy bow in 1949 in "Shop At Sly Corner," joined APA in 1960 and has appeared with it in "School For Scandal," "The Tavern," "Anatole," "Scapin," "Right You Are," "The Importance of Being Earnest," "Twelfth Night," "King Lear," "The Seagull," "Lower Depths," "Man and Superman," "Judith," "War and Peace," "You Can't Take It With You," "Pantagleize," "The Cherry Orchard," "The Misanthrope," "The Cocktail Party," "Cock-A-Doodle Dandy," and "Hamlet," "A Patriot for Me," "Colette" (OB).

CUSACK, PHILIP. Born May 10, 1934 in Boston. Attended Emerson Col. Made Bdwy debut in 1966 in "Three Bags Full," followed by "The Boys in the Band" (OB).

| Jean David | Robert Darnell | Blanche Dee | Curt Dawson | Ruby Dee |

CYPHER, JON. Born Jan. 13, 1932 in Brooklyn. Graduate U. Vt. Made Bdwy bow in 1958 in "The Disenchanted," followed by "The Wives" (OB), "The Great Western Union" (OB), "Jennie," "Night of The Iguana," "Man of LaMancha," "Sherry!," "The Great White Hope," "1776," "Coco."

DABDOUB, JACK. Born Feb. 5 in New Orleans. Graduate of Tulane U. Has appeared Off-Bdwy in "What's Up," "Time For The Gentle People," "The Peddler" and "The Dodo Bird," on Bdwy in "Paint Your Wagon," "My Darlin' Aida," "Happy Hunting," "Hot Spot," "Camelot," "Baker Street," "Anya," "Annie Get Your Gun" (LC), "Her First Roman" "Man of LaMancha," "Coco."

DAILEY, DAN. Born 1918 in NYC. Has appeared on Bdwy in "Babes In Arms," "Stars In Your Eyes," "I Married An Angel," "Catch Me If You Can," "The Odd Couple," "Plaza Suite."

DALBEY, CYNTHIA. Born Nov. 1, 1944 in Spencer, Iowa. Graduate Northwestern U. Made Bdwy debut in 1969 in "Play It Again, Sam."

DAMON, CATHRYN. Born Sept. 11 in Seattle, Wash. Made Bdwy debut in 1954 in "By The Beautiful Sea," followed by "The Vamp," "Shinbone Alley," "A Family Affair," "Foxy," "The Boys From Syracuse" (OB), "Secret Life of Walter Mitty" (OB), "Flora, The Red Menace," "UTBU," "Come Summer," "Criss-Crossing," "Show Me Where the Good Times Are" (OB), "A Place for Polly."

DANA, BARBARA. Born Dec. 28, 1940 in NYC. Off Bdwy credits are "A Clearing In The Woods," "A Worm in the Horseradish," "Angels of Anadarko," "Second City." Made Bdwy debut in 1963 in "Enter Laughing," followed by "Who's Afraid of Virginia Woolf?," "Where's Daddy?," "Room Service."

DANA, LEORA. Born Apr. 1, 1923 in NYC. Attended Barnard Col., RADA. Made Bdwy debut in 1947 in "Madwoman of Chaillot," followed by "The Happy Time," "Point of No Return," "Sabrina Fair," "The Best Man," "Beekman Place," Natl. Rep. Theatre productions. Off-Bdwy in "In The Summer House," "Wilder's Triple Bill," "Collision Course," "The Bird of Dawning Singeth All Night Long," "The Increased Difficulty of Concentration" (LC).

DANIELE, GRACIELA. Born Dec. 8, 1939 in Buenos Aires. Made Bdwy debut in 1964 in "What Makes Sammy Run?" followed by "Here's Where I Belong," "Promises, Promises."

DANIELS, DAVID. Born Apr. 10, 1929 in Evanston, Ill. Attended Yale, Curtis Inst. Made Bdwy bow in "Plain and Fancy" for which he received a THEATRE WORLD Award, followed by Off-Bdwy roles in "Oh, Kay," "The Banker's Daughter," "The Boys In The Band."

DANIELS, WILLIAM. Born Mar. 31, 1927 in Brooklyn. Graduate of Northwestern U. Made Bdwy bow in 1943 in "Life With Father," followed by "Richard II," "Seagulls Over Sorrento," "Legend of Lizzie," "Cat On A Hot Tin Roof," "A Thousand Clowns," "The Zoo Story" (OB), "The Iceman Cometh" (OB), "Look Back In Anger" (OB), "Dear Me, The Sky Is Falling," "One Flew Over The Cuckoo's Nest," "On A Clear Day You Can See Forever," "Daphne In Cottage D," "1776."

DANNER, BLYTHE. Born in Philadelphia. Graduate of Bard Col. Made NY debut Off-Bdwy in 1966 in "The Infantry," followed by "Collision Course," "Summertree," "Up Eden," "Someone's Comin' Hungry," with LC Rep in "Cyrano," and "The Miser" for which she received a THEATRE WORLD Award, "Butterflies Are Free."

DARVELL, ROBERT. Born Sept. 26, 1929 in Los Angeles. Made Bdwy bow in 1962 in "Irma La Douce," followed by "Spoon River," "Luv," "You Know I Can't Hear You...," Off-Bdwy in "Threepenny Opera," "Young Abe Lincoln," "The Tempest," "On the Town," "In White America," "Who's Happy Now?"

DARROW, RICHARD. Born Aug. 20 in Ypsilanti, Mich. Graduate Northwestern. Made NY bow in 1968 off Bdwy in "Tartuffe" followed by "I Dreamt I Dwelt in Bloomingdale's."

DA SILVA, HOWARD. Born May 4, 1909 in Cleveland, O. Attended Carnegie Tech. Made debut with Civic Rep Co., followed by "Ten Million Ghosts," "Golden Boy," "The Cradle Will Rock," "Casey Jones," "Abe Lincoln In Illinois," "Summer Night," "Two On An Island," "Oklahoma!," "Shootin' Star," "Burning Bright," Off-Bdwy in "World of Sholom Aleichem," "The Adding Machine," "Diary of A Scoundrel," and "Volpone." "Compulsion," "Fiorello," "Romulus," "In The Counting House," "Dear Me, The Sky Is Falling," "Hamlet" (CP), "The Unknown Soldier and His Wife," "1776."

DAVID, CLIFFORD. Born June 30, 1932 in Toledo, O. Attended Toledo U., Actors Studio. Made Bdwy bow in 1960 in "Caligula," followed by "Wildcat," "The Aspern Papers," "Boys From Syracuse" (OB), "On A Clear Day You Can See Forever," "A Joyful Noise," "1776," "Camino Real" (LC).

DAVID, JEAN. Born May 4, 1931 in Denver, Colo. Graduate of Columbia. Made NY debut in 1963 Off-Bdwy in "Six Characters in Search of an Author," followed by "Miss Julie," "Hobbies," "Jack," "Oedipus," "Epitaph for George Dillon," "Now You See It," "Moondreamers," "Istanboul," "Triple Image," "Beclch," "Finnegan's Wake," "Dark of the Moon."

DAVID, JEFF. Born Sept. 16, 1940 in Philadelphia. Graduate Carnegie Tech. Has appeared Off-Bdwy in "Arms and the Man," "Phaedra," "Country Wife," "Caucasian Chalk Circle," "The Butter and Egg Man," "Francesca da Remini," "Hamlet," "Pequod," "Memory Bank."

DAVILA, DIANA. Born Nov. 5, 1947 in NYC. Made Bdwy debut in 1967 in "Song of The Grasshopper," followed by "The Prime of Miss Jean Brodie," "What the Butler Saw" (OB).

DAVIS, CLIFTON. Born Oct. 4 in Chicago. Attended Oakwood Col. Made NY debut off Bdwy in 1968 in "How to Steal an Election," followed by "Horseman, Pass By," "To Be Young, Gifted and Black," "No Place to Be Somebody," on Bdwy in "Hello, Dolly!," "Jimmy Shine," "Look to the Lilies," "The Engagement Baby."

DAWSON, CURT. Born Dec. 5, 1941 in Kansas. Graduate RADA. Made NY bow in 1968 Off-Bdwy in "Futz," followed by "Boys In The Band."

DEACON, RICHARD. Born May 14, 1922 in Philadelphia. Attended Ithaca College. Made Bdwy debut in 1969 in "Hello, Dolly!"

DeANDA, PETER. Born Mar. 10, 1940 in Pittsburgh. Attended Pittsburgh Playhouse, Actors Workshop. Made Bdwy bow in 1965 in "The Zulu and the Zayda," followed by "The Guide," and Off-Bdwy in "The Blacks," "Dutchman," "Sound of Silence," "The Kitchen," "Passing Through from Exotic Places," "House of Leather."

DEE, BLANCHE. Born Jan. 18, 1936 in Wheeling, W. Va. Graduate Bklyn Col. Appeared Off-Bdwy in "Rimers of Eldritch," "Tom Paine," made Bdwy debut in 1970 in "Grin and Bare It."

DEE, RUBY. Born Oct. 27 in Cleveland, O. Graduate Hunter Col. Made Bdwy debut in 1946 in "Jeb," followed by "Anna Lucasta," "The Smile of the World," "A Long Way Home," "The World of Sholom Aleichem" (OB), "A Raisin in the Sun," "Purlie Victorious," "Boesman and Lena" (OB).

237

Melinda Dillon　　**Michael Del Medico**　　**Gwyda DonHowe**　　**Paul Dooley**　　**Virginia Down**

DeKOVEN, ROGER. Born Oct. 22, 1907 in Chicago. Attended U. Chicago, Northwestern, Columbia. Made Bdwy bow in 1926 in "Juarez and Maximilian," followed by "Mystery Man," "Once in a Lifetime," "Counsellor-at-Law," "Murder in the Cathedral," "Eternal Road," "Brooklyn, USA," "The Assassins," "Joan of Lorraine," "Abie's Irish Rose," "The Lark," "Hidden River," "Compulsion," "Miracle Worker," "Fighting Cock," "Tovarich," "Arturo Ui," "Funny Girl," Off-Bdwy in "Deadly Game," "Steal the Old Man's Bundle," with LCRep in "St. Joan," "Tiger at the Gates," "Walking to Waldheim," "Cyrano."

DELBERT, ROBERT. Born Dec. 28, 1946 in Poinsitt, Ark. Graduate U. Mo. Made Bdwy debut in 1969 in "The Penny Wars."

DEL MEDICO, MICHAEL. Born Oct. 3, 1933 in Chicago. Attended DePaul U, American Theatre Wing. Made Bdwy bow in 1956 in "Inherit the Wind," followed by "The Disenchanted," and Off-Bdwy in "Cicero," "Rise, Marlowe," "Go Show Me A Dragon," "Witches' Sabbath," "Burn Me to Ashes," "Line," "I Dreamt I Dwelt in Bloomingdale's."

DeMAIO, PETER. Born in Hartford, Conn. Attended Juilliard, New School. Made NY debut Off-Bdwy in 1961 in "Threepenny Opera," followed by "Secret Life of Walter Mitty," "Dark of the Moon," Bdwy bow in 1969 in "Billy" and "Indians."

DEMAS, CAROLE. Born May 26, 1940 in Brooklyn. Attended U. Vt. and NYU. Appeared with NY Shakespeare Festival, and Off-Bdwy in "Morning Sun," "The Fantasticks," "How To Steal An Election," "Rondelay."

DEMPSEY, MARK. Born Jan. 29, 1936 in Hollywood, Calif. Graduate U Wash. Made NY debut in 1969 Off-Bdwy in "Oh, Calcutta."

DeSIMONE, B.J. Born Dec. 7, 1939 in Boston. Graduate of Tufts U. Made NY bow in 1964 in "West Side Story" (CC), followed by "Royal Hunt of The Sun," "The Unknown Soldier and His Wife," "Rosencrantz and Guildenstern Are Dead," "Hadrian VII," "Madwoman of Chaillot" (OB).

DESMOND, PATRICK. Born in Detroit. Graduate U. Detroit. Made NY bow in 1959 Off-Bdwy in "Our Town," followed by "Anything Goes," "All In Love," "The Lower Depths" (APA), Bdwy debut in 1969 in "The Front Page."

DEVLIN, JAY. Born May 8, 1929 in Ft. Dodge, Iowa. Has appeared Off-Bdwy in "The Mad Show," "Little Murders," "Unfair to Goliath," "Boys in the Band."

DEWHURST, COLLEEN. Born in Montreal, Can. Attended Downer Col., AADA. Made Bdwy debut in 1952 in "Desire under the Elms," followed by "Tamburlaine the Great," "Country Wife," "Caligula," "All the Way Home," "Great Day in the Morning," "Ballad of the Sad Cafe," "More Stately Mansions," Off-Bdwy in "Taming of the Shrew," "The Eagle Has Two Heads," "Camille," "Macbeth," "Children of Darkness" for which she received a THEATRE WORLD Award, "Antony and Cleopatra" (CP), "Hello and Goodbye."

DIENER, JOAN. Born Feb. 24, 1934 in Cleveland, O. Attended Sarah Lawrence Col. Made Bdwy debut in 1948 in "Small Wonder," followed by "Season in the Sun," "Kismet" for which she received a THEATRE WORLD Award, "Man of La Mancha," "Cry for Us All."

DILLER, PHYLLIS. Born July 17, 1917 in Lima, O. After films, tv, and night clubs, made Bdwy debut Dec. 26, 1969 in "Hello, Dolly!"

DILLON, MELINDA. Born Oct. 13, 1939 in Hope, Ark. Attended Goodman Theatre School. Made Bdwy debut in 1962 in "Who's Afraid of Virginia Woolf?" for which she received a THEATRE WORLD Award, followed by "You Know I Can't Hear You When The Water's Running," "A Way of Life," "A Round with Ring" (OB).

DONHOWE, GWYDA. Born Oct. 20, 1933 in Oak Park, Ill. Attended Drake U, Goodman Theatre, Made Bdwy debut in 1957 in "Separate Tables," followed by "Half a Sixpence," "The Flip Side," "Paris Is Out," with APA in "The Showoff," "War and Peace," "Right You Are...," "You Can't Take It with You," and Off-Bdwy in "Philosophy in the Boudoir," "Rondelay."

DORIN, PHOEBE. Born June 26, 1940 in NYC. Graduate Cooper Union. Made Bdwy debut in 1968 in "Happiness Is A Rolls Royce." Off-Bdwy credits: "2 by Saroyan," "Burn Me To Ashes," "To Be Young, Gifted and Black," "Awake and Sing."

DOOLEY, PAUL. Born Feb. 22, 1928 in Parkersburg, W.Va. Graduate W.Va.U. Has appeared on Bdwy in "The Odd Couple," and Off-Bdwy in "Threepenny Opera," "Toinette," "Fallout," "Dr. Willy Nilly," "Second City," "Adaptation," "White House Murder Case."

DOUGLAS, JOHANNA. Born July 23, 1917 in Minneapolis. Graduate U. Minn. Made Bdwy debut in 1965 in "Never Too Late," followed by "Mame."

DOUGLAS, LARRY. Born Feb. 17, 1914 in Philadelphia. Attended Bklyn Col. Made Bdwy bow in 1935 in "Jumbo," followed by "Frederika," "Three Waltzes," "Panama Hattie," "Star and Garter," "What's Up?," "The Duchess Misbehaves," "Hold It," "All For Love," "The King and I," "Her First Roman," "Jimmy."

DOWD, M'EL. Born Feb. 2 in Chicago. Attended Goodman Theatre. Appeared Off-Bdwy in "Macbeth," "A Midsummer Night's Dream," "Romeo and Juliet," and "Julius Caesar" before Bdwy debut in 1958 in "Methuselah," followed by "Royal Gambit" (OB), "A Case of Libel," "Sweet Bird of Youth," "Camelot," "The Emperor" (OB), "The Right Honourable Gentleman," "The Sound of Music" (CC), with LCRep in "The Unknown Soldier and His Wife" and "Tiger At The Gates," "Everything In The Garden," "Invitation To A Beheading" (OB), "Dear World," "Mercy Street" (OB).

DOWNING, DAVID. Born July 21, 1943 in NYC. Has appeared on Bdwy in "Green Pastures," "The Cool World," and Off-Bdwy with NEC in "Day of Absence," "Happy Ending," "Song of The Lusitanian Bogey," and "Ceremonies in Dark Old Men," "Man Better Man," "The Harangues," and "Brotherhood."

DOWNING, VIRGINIA. Born Mar. 7 in Washington, DC. Attended Bryn Mawr. Has appeared Off-Bdwy in "Juno and the Paycock," "Man with the Golden Arm," "Palm Tree in a Rose Garden," "Play with a Tiger," "The Wives," "The Idiot," "Medea," "Mrs. Warren's Profession," "Mercy Street," on Bdwy in "Father Malachy's Miracle," "Forward the Heart," "Cradle Will Rock," "Gift of Time," "We Have Always Lived in the Castle."

DRISCHELL, RALPH. Born Nov. 26, 1927 in Baldwin, NY. Attended Carnegie Tech. Has appeared Off-Bdwy in "Playboy of The Western World," "The Crucible," "The Balcony," "Time of Vengeance," "Barroom Monks," "Portrait of The Artist As A Young Man," "Abe Lincoln In Illinois," "The Caretaker," "A Slight Ache," "The Room," on Bdwy in "Rhinoceros," "All In Good Time," "Rosencrantz and Guildenstern Are Dead," with LCRep in "The Year Boston Won the Pennant," "The Time of Your Life," "Camino Real," "Operation Sidewinder," "Beggar on Horseback."

DRUMMOND, ALICE. Born May 21, 1929 in Pawtucket, R.I. Attended Pembroke Col. Appeared off Bdwy with Phoenix Co., and in "Royal Gambit," "Go Show Me a Dragon," "Sweet of You to Say So," "Gallows Humor," "American Dream," "Giants' Dance," made Bdwy debut in 1963 in "Ballad of the Sad Cafe," followed by "Malcolm," "The Chinese."

DUDA, ANDREA. Born June 1, 1945 in East Douglas, Mass. Attended Boston U, AADA. Made Bdwy debut in 1968 in "The Education of Hyman Kaplan," followed by "George M!," "Jimmy."

ace Engelhardt   Edloe   Michael Enserro   Marjory Edson   Ed Evanko

DUELL, WILLIAM. Born Aug. 30, 1923 in Corinth, NY. Attended Ill. Wesleyan, and Yale. Off-Bdwy credits: "Threepenny Opera," "Portrait of The Artist As A Young Man," "Barroom Monks," "A Midsummer Night's Dream," "Henry IV," "Taming of The Shrew," "The Memorandum," on Bdwy in "A Cook For Mr. General," "Ballad of The Sad Cafe," "Illya Darling," "1776."

DUFF-MacCORMICK, CARA. Born Dec. 12 in Woodstock, NB, Can. Attended AADA. Made NY debut in 1969 off Bdwy in "Love Your Crooked Neighbor."

DUKAS, JAMES. Born June 6, 1926 in Portsmouth, O. Graduate U. W.Va. Appeared off Bdwy in "Man with the Golden Arm," "Brothers Karamazov," "Threepenny Opera," "Incident at Vichy," "After the Fall," on Bdwy in "The Last Analysis," "Nobody Loves an Albatross," "Don't Drink the Water," "The Visit," "A Patriot for Me."

DULLEA, KEIR. Born May 30, 1936 in Cleveland, NJ. Attended Neighborhood Playhouse. Appeared off Bdwy in 1959 in "Season of Choice," made Bdwy bow in 1967 in "Dr. Cook's Garden," followed by "Butterflies Are Free."

DUNCAN, SANDY. Born Feb. 20, 1946 in Henderson, Tex. Attended Len Morris Col. Made NY debut in "The Music Man" (CC'65), followed by its revivals of "Carousel," "Finian's Rainbow," "Sound of Music," "Wonderful Town," and "Life With Father," Off-Bdwy in "Ceremony of Innocence" for which she received a THEATRE WORLD Award, "Your Own Thing," and made Bdwy debut in 1969 in "Canterbury Tales," followed by "Love is A Time of Day," "The Boy Friend."

DUNNOCK, MILDRED. Born Jan. 25 in Baltimore, Md. Graduate Goucher Col., Columbia. Made Bdwy debut in 1932 in "Life Begins," followed by "The Corn is Green," "Richard III," "Only the Heart," "Foolish Notion," "Lute Song," "Another Part of the Forest," "The Hallams," "Death of a Salesman," "Pride's Crossing," "The Wild Duck," "In the Summer House," "Cat on a Hot Tin Roof," "Child of Fortune," "The Milk Train Doesn't Stop Here Anymore," "Traveller without Luggage," off Bdwy in "The Trojan Women," "Phedre," "Willie Doesn't Live Here Anymore," "Colette."

DURNING, CHARLES. Born Feb. 28, 1933 in Highland Falls, NY. Attended Columbia. NYU. Bdwy credits: "Poor Bitos," "Drat! The Cat!," "Pousse Cafe," "The Happy Time," "Indians." Off-Bdwy in NY Shakespeare Festival productions, "Two By Saroyan," "The Child Buyer," "An Album of Gunther Grass," "Huui, Huui," "An Invitation To A Beheading," "Lemon Sky."

eda-YOUNG, BARBARA. Born Jan. 30, 1945 in Detroit, Mich. Made Bdwy debut in 1968 in "Lovers and Other Strangers," followed by "The Hawk" (OB), with LC Rep in "The Time of Your Life," "Camino Real," and "Operation Sidewinder,"

EDLOE. Born April 1943 in Baltimore, Md. Attended Neighborhood Playhouse. Made Bdwy debut in 1967 in "Hello, Dolly!," followed by "Salvation" (OB).

EDSON, MARJORY. Born Aug. 18, 1943 in Columbia, SC. Graduate Oberlin Cons. Made Bdwy debut in 1970 in "Minnie's Boys."

ELIAS, ELLEN. Born May 30, 1950 in Flint, Mich. Made Bdwy debut in 1969 in "Hello, Dolly!"

ELIZONDO, HECTOR. Born Dec. 22, 1936 in NYC. Attended CCNY. Has appeared Off-Bdwy in "Drums In The Night," "Steambath," and on Bdwy in "The Great White Hope."

ELLIN, DAVID. Born Jan. 10, 1925 in Montreal, Can. Attended AADA. Has appeared in "Swan Song," "West Side Story," "The Education of Hyman Kaplan," off Bdwy in "The Trees Die Standing," "Mirele Efros," "The End of All Things Natural."

ELLIOT, STEPHANIE. Born Dec. 7, 1931 in NYC. Attended New School. Has appeared Off-Bdwy in "Emperor's Clothes," "Glad Tidings," "Trouble In Mind," "Private Lives of The Master Race," "Summer of The 17th Doll," "To Be Young, Gifted and Black."

ELLIOTT, PATRICA. Born July 21, 1942 in Gunnison, Colo. Graduate U. Colo., London Academy. Made NY debut with LCRep in 1968 in "King Lear," and "A Cry of Players," followed by "Henry V," "The Persians" (OB).

EMMERSON, DOROTHY L. Born in Kyoto, Japan. Graduate Colorado Col. Made NY debut off Bdwy in 1967 in "The Mad Show," Bdwy bow in 1968 in "The Education of Hyman Kaplan," followed by "Jimmy Shine," "Norman, Is That You?"

ENGELHARDT, WALLACE. Born Apr. 30, 1923 in Oak Park, Ill. Graduate Cornell. Made NY bow in 1961 off Bdwy in "The Buskers," Bdwy debut in 1962 in "Never Too Late," followed by "The Great Indoors," "The Education of Hyman Kaplan," "Three Men on a Horse."

ENSERRO, MICHAEL. Born Oct. 5, 1918 in Soldier, Pa. Attended Allegheny Col., Pasadena Playhouse. Appeared in "Me and Molly," "The Passion of Josef D.," "Song of the Grasshopper," "Mike Downstairs," off Bdwy in "Penny Change," "The Fantasticks," "The Miracle," "The Kitchen," "Camino Real" (LC).

ENTEN, BONI. Born Feb. 20, 1947 in Baltimore. Attended Tex. Christian U. Made Bdwy debut in 1965 in "The Roar of The Greasepaint," off Bdwy "You're A Good Man, Charlie Brown," "Oh, Calcutta," "Salvation."

EPSTEIN, ALVIN. Born May 14, 1925 in NYC. Attended Queens Col., Decroux School of Mime, Habimah Theatre. Appeared with Marcel Marceau, and in "King Lear," "Waiting for Godot," "From A to Z," "No Strings," "The Passion of Josef D," "Postmark Zero," off Bdwy in "Purple Dust," "Pictures in a Hallway," "Clerambard," "Endgame," "Whores, Wars and Tin Pan Alley."

ESTERMAN, LAURA. Born Apr. 12, 1945 in NYC. Attended Radcliffe, London AMDA. Made NY debut in 1969 with LCRep in "The Time of Your Life," followed by "The Pig Pen" (OB).

EVANKO, ED. Born in Winnipeg, Can. Graduate U. Manitoba. Studied at Bristol Old Vic School. Made Bdwy debut in 1969 in "Canterbury Tales" for which he received a THEATRE WORLD Award.

EVANS, HARVEY. Born Jan. 7, 1941 in Cincinnati, O. Made Bdwy debut in 1957 in "New Girl in Town," Followed by "West Side Story," "Redhead," "Gypsy," "Anyone Can Whistle," "Hello, Dolly!," "George M!," "Our Town," "The Boy Friend."

EVERHART, REX. Born June 13, 1920 in Watseka, Ill. Graduate U. Mo., NYU. Made Bdwy bow in 1955 in "No Time For Sergeants," followed by "Tall Story," "Moonbirds," "Tenderloin," "A Matter of Position," "Rainy Day In Newark," "Skyscraper," "How Now, Dow Jones?," "1776."

FANT, LOU. Born Dec. 13, 1931 in Greenville, SC. Graduate Baylor U., Columbia. Made Bdwy debut with National Theatre of The Deaf in 1969.

FAY, BRENDAN. Born in NYC. Attended NY Maritime Acad. On Bdwy in "Legend of Lizzie," "First Love," "Borstal Boy." Off-Bdwy in "Heloise," "Threepenny Opera," "Donogoo," "King of The Whole Damned World," "Wretched The Lion-Hearted," "Time of The Key," "Thistle In My Bed," "Posterity For Sale," "Stephen D," with LCRep in "King Lear" and "A Cry of Players."

Jose Fernandez   Laura Figueroa   Ted Forlow   Frances Foster   Fred Forr

FAYE, JOEY. Born July 12, 1910 in NYC. Made Bdwy bow in 1938 in "Sing Out The News," followed by "Room Service," "Meet The People," "The Man Who Came To Dinner," "The Milky Way," "Boy Meets Girl," "Streets of Paris," "Allah Be Praised," "The Duchess Misbehaves," "Tidbits of 1948," "High Button Shoes," "Top Banana," "Tender Trap," "Man of LaMancha," "Lyle" (OB).

FEARL, CLIFFORD. Born in NYC. Graduate Columbia U. Made Bdwy debut in 1950 in "Flahooley," followed by "Three Wishes for Jamie," "Two's Company," "Kismet," "Happy Hunting," "Oh, Captain," "Redhead," "Let It Ride," "110 In The Shade," "Ben Franklin In Paris," "Mame," "La Plume de Ma Tante," "Dear World," "Jimmy."

FERNANDEZ, JOSE. Born Aug. 19, 1948 in Havana, Cuba. Attended HB Studio. Has appeared Off Bdwy in "Dark of the Moon," "The Me Nobody Knows."

FERRER, JOSE. Born Jan. 8, 1912 in Santurce, PR. Graduate Princeton. Has appeared in "A Slight Case of Murder," "Brother Rat," "In Clover," "Missouri Legend," "Mamba's Daughters," "Key Largo," "Charley's Aunt" (CC), "Vickie," "Let's Face It," "Othello," "Cyrano," "Silver Whistle," "20th Century," "Volpone," "The Shrike," "Angel Street" (CC), "Richard III," "Edwin Booth," "The Girl Who Came To Supper," "Man of La Mancha."

FIEDLER, JOHN. Born Feb. 3, 1925 in Plateville, Wisc. Attended Neighborhood Playhouse. Appeared off Bdwy in "The Seagull," "Sing Me No Lullaby," "The Terrible Swift Sword," on Bdwy in "One Eye Closed," "Howie," "Raisin' in the Sun," "Harold," "The Odd Couple," "Our Town."

FIELDING, ANNE. Born Jan. 30, 1943 in NYC. Has appeared in "Ivanov" (OB), with Am. Shake. Festival "Monserrat," NYS Festival's "Romeo and Juliet" and "Midsummer Night's Dream," "Hedda Gabler" (OB).

FIGUEROA, LAURA. Born Feb. 2, 1948 in San Turce, PR. Attended Pace Col. Appeared off Bdwy in "The Oxcart," "Theatre in the Street," and made Bdwy debut in 1969 in "Does A Tiger Wear A Necktie?"

FIORE, FRANK. Born Nov. 15, 1953 in Kew Gardens, NY. Attended Drama Workshop, Juilliard. Made Bdwy debut in 1970 in "Child's Play."

FITZGERALD, NEIL. Born Jan. 15, 1898 in Tipperary, Ire. Attended Trinity Col. Has appeared in "Leave Her To Heaven," "The Wookey," "Without Love," "Ten Little Indians," "Plan M," "You Touched Me," "The Play's The Thing," "Design For A Stained Glass Window," "The High Ground," "To Dorothy, A Son," "Mr. Pickwick," "Witness For The Prosecution," "Little Moon of Alban," "Hadrian VII," "The Mundy Scheme," and Off-Bdwy in "Portrait of The Artist As A Young Man," "Three Hand Reel," "Carricknabauna."

FLANAGAN, WALTER. Born Oct. 4, 1928 in Ponta, Tex. Graduate U. Houston. Appeared Off-Bdwy in "Bedtime Story," "Coffee and Windows," "The Opening of A Window," "The Moon Is Blue," "Laughwind," "The Dodo Bird," on Bdwy in "Once For The Asking," "The Front Page" ('69).

FLETCHER, JACK. Born Apr. 21, 1921 in Forest Hills, NY. Attended Yale. Has appeared Off-Bdwy in "Comic Strip," "The Way of The World," "Thieves' Carnival," "The Amorous Flea," "The American Hamburger League," "The Time of Your Life" (LC), "Lyle," at City Center in "Can-Can," "Cyrano," "Wonderful Town," on Bdwy in "Trial Honeymoon," "She Stoops To Conquer," "Romeo and Juliet," "Ben Franklin In Paris," "Drat! The Cat!."

FODOR, JOLEEN. Born Nov. 12, 1939 in Medina, O. Attended Denison U, U. Colo. Appeared off Bdwy in "Leave It to Jane," "Little Mary Sunshine," "Riverwind," "Babes in the Wood," "Great Scot!," made Bdwy debut in 1963 in "The Student Gypsy," followed by "A Funny Thing Happened on the Way to the Forum," "Grin and Bare It."

FONDA, HENRY. Born May 16, 1905 in Grand Island, Neb. Attended U. Minn. Made Bdwy debut in 1929 in "The Game of Love and Death," followed by "I Loved You Wednesday," "Forsaking All Others," "New Faces of 1934," "The Farmer Takes A Wife," "Mr. Roberts," "Point of No Return," "Caine Mutiny Court Martial," "Two for the Seesaw," "Silent Night, Lonely Night," "Critics Choice," "A Gift of Time," "Generation" "Our Town."

FORD, DAVID. Born Oct. 30, 1929 in LaJolla, Calif. Attended Ariz. State, U.S. Dak. Made NY bow Off-Bdwy in "Billy Budd," followed by "The Physicists," "Tea Party" (OB), "1776."

FORD, PAUL. Born Nov. 2, 1901 in Baltimore, Md. Attended Dartmouth. Made Bdwy bow in 1944 in "Decision," followed by "Lower North," "Kiss Them for Me," "Flamingo Road," "On Whitman Avenue," "Another Part of the Forest," "Command Decision," "Teahouse of the August Moon," "Whoop-Up," "Music Man," "Thurber Carnival," "Never Too Late," "3 Bags Full," "What Did We Do Wrong?," "3 Men on a Horse," "The Front Page."

FORLOW, TED. Born Apr. 29, 1931 in Independence, Mo. Attended Baker U. Made Bdwy debut in 1957 in "New Girl In Town," followed by "Juno," "Destry Rides Again," "Subways Are For Sleeping," "Can-Can," "Wonderful Town" (CC), "A Funny Thing Happened On The Way To The Forum," "Milk And Honey," "Carnival" (CC'68), "Man of La Mancha."

FORREST, FRED. Born Dec. 23, 1936 in Waxahachie, Tex. Graduate TCU. Made NY bow in 1966 off Bdwy in "Viet Rock," followed by "Tom Paine," "Futz," "Silhouettes."

FORREST, PAUL. Born July 2, 1923 in Philadelphia. Graduate U. Pa., Temple U. Made Bdwy debut in 1969 in "Jimmy."

FORSYTHE, HENDERSON. Born Sept. 11, 1917 in Macon, Mo. Attended U. Iowa. Appeared off Bdwy in "The Iceman Cometh," "The Collection," "The Room," "A Slight Ache," on Bdwy in "The Cellar and the Well," "Miss Lonelyhearts," "Who's Afraid of Virginia Woolf?," "Malcolm," "Right Honourable Gentleman," "Delicate Balance," "Birthday Party," "Harvey," "Engagement Baby."

FOSTER, FRANCES. Born June 11 in Yonkers, NY. Made Bdwy debut in 1955 in "The Wisteria Trees," followed by "Nobody Loves An Albatross," and "Raisin In The Sun," Off-Bdwy roles in "Take A Giant Step," "Edge of The City," "Tammy and The Doctor," "The Crucible," NEC's "Happy Ending," "Day of Absence," "An Evening of One Acts," "Man Better Man," "Brotherhood."

FOSTER, HERBERT. Born May 14, 1936 in Winnipeg, Can. Appeared with Natl. Rep. Theatre in 1967 in "The Imaginary Invalid," "A Touch of The Poet," and "Tonight At 8:30," followed by "Papers" (OB) "Henry V."

FOWKES, CONARD. Born Jan. 4, 1933 in Washington, D.C. Yale Graduate. Made Bdwy bow in 1958 in "Howie," followed by "The Wall," "Minor Miracle," off Bdwy in "Look Back in Anger," "That Thing at the Cherry Lane," "America Hurrah," "The Reckoning."

FRANCINE, ANNE. Born Aug. 8, 1917 in Philadelphia. Made bdwy debut in 1945 in "Marriage Is For Single People," followed by "By The Beautiful Sea," "The Great Sebastians," "Guitar" (OB), "Valmouth" (OB), "Tenderloin," "Asylum" (OB), "Mame."

FRANK, DOROTHY. Born July 8, 1942 in St. Louis, Mo. Made Bdwy debut in 1960 in "Tenderloin," followed by "Sail Away," "No Strings," "New Faces," "Once Upon a Mattress," "Boys from Syracuse" (OB), "Coco," "Beggar on Horseback" (LC).

| Nancy Franklin | Liam Gannon | Martha Galphin | David Garfield | Joy Garrett |

FRANKLIN, BONNIE. Born Jan. 6, 1944 in Santa Monica, Cal. Attended Smith Col., UCLA. Made NY debut off Bdwy in 1968 in "Your Own Thing," followed by "Dames at Sea," Bdwy bow in 1970 in "Applause" for which she received a THEATRE WORLD Award.

FRANKLIN, HUGH. Born Aug. 24, 1916 in Muskogee, Okla. Attended Northwestern. Made Bdwy bow in 1938 in "Gloriana," followed by "Harriet," "Alice in Wonderland," "Medea," "The Best Man," "Luther," "A Shot in the Dark," "Arturo Ui," "The Devils," "What Did We Do Wrong?," "How Much, How Much?" (OB)

FRANKLIN, NANCY. Born in NYC. Has appeared on Bdwy in "Happily Never After," "The White House," "Never Live Over A Pretzel Factory," off Bdwy in "Buffalo Skinner," "Power of Darkness," "Oh Dad, Poor Dad ...," "Theatre of Peretz," "Seven Days of Mourning."

FRANKS, LAURIE. Born Aug. 14, 1929 in Lucasville, Ore. Made Bdwy debut in 1956 in "Bells Are Ringing," followed by "Copper and Brass," "Pleasures and Palaces," "Leave It To Jane" (OB), "Something More," "Anya," "Mame."

FRANZ, EDUARD. Born Oct. 31, 1902 in Milwaukee. Has appeared in "Miss Swan Expects," "Farm of Three Echoes," "The Russian People," "Cafe Crown," "Outrageous Fortune," "The Cherry Orchard," "Embezzled Heaven," "The Stranger," "Home of The Brave," "The Big Two," "The Egghead," "Those That Play The Clowns," "In The Matter of J. Robert Oppenheimer" (LC).

FREEMAN, AL. JR. Born in 1934 in San Antonio, Tex. Attended CCLA. Has appeared on Bdwy in "The Long Dream," "Tiger Tiger Burning Bright," "The Living Premise," "Blues For Mr. Charlie," "The Dozens," "Look to the Lilies," Off-Bdwy in "The Slave," "Dutchman," "Trumpets of The Lord."

FREEMAN, ARNY. Born Aug. 28, 1908 in Chicago. Made Bdwy bow in 1949 in "Streetcar Named Desire," followed by "Dream Girl" (CC), "The Great Sebastians," "The Shrike" (CC), "Tall Story," "Hot Spot," "Gay Divorcee" (OB), "What Makes Sammy Run?," "Cactus Flower," "Minnie's Boys."

FREEMAN, MORGAN. Born June 1, 1937 in Memphis, Tenn. Attended LACC. Appeared Off-Bdwy in "Ostrich Feathers," "The Niggerlovers," "Exhibition," and made Bdwy bow in 1967 in "Hello, Dolly!"

FRENCH, ARTHUR. Born in NYC. Attended Bklyn Col. Appeared Off-Bdwy in "Raisin' Hell In The Son," "Ballad of Bimshire," "Day of Absence," "Happy Ending," "Jonah," with NEC in "Ceremonies In Dark Old Men," "An Evening of One Acts," "Man Better Man," "Brotherhood."

FRY, RAY. Born Feb. 22, 1923 in Hebron, Ind. Graduate SF State Col., Northwestern. Made Bdwy bow in 1944 in "Hickory Stick," followed by "Cyrano," "The Cradle Will Rock," with LCRep in "Danton's Death," "The Country Wife," "Caucasian Chalk Circle," "The Alchemist," "Galileo," "St. Joan," "Tiger At The Gates," "Cyrano," "A Cry of Players," "Bananas," "The Miser," "Operation Sidewinder," "Beggar on Horseback."

FULLER, PENNY. Born in Durham, NC, in 1940. Attended Northwestern. Has appeared in "Barefoot in the Park," "Cabaret," NY S. Festival's "Richard III," "As You Like It," and "Henry IV," "Applause."

GABEL, MARTIN. Born June 19, 1912 in Philadelphia. Attended Lehigh U, AADA. Has appeared in "Dead End," "Julius Caesar," "Danton's Death," "King Lear," "Reclining Figure," "Will Success Spoil Rock Hunter?," "The Rivalry," "Big Fish, Little Fish," "Children From Their Games," "Sheep on the Runway."

GABLE, JUNE. Born June 5, 1945 in NY. Graduate Carnegie Tech. Has appeared Off-Bdwy in "MacBird," "Jacques Brel Is Alive and Well and Living In Paris."

GALLAGHER, HELEN. Born in Brooklyn in 1926. Made Bdwy debut in 1947 in "Seven Lively Arts," followed by "Mr. Strauss Goes To Boston," "Billion Dollar Baby," "Brigadoon," "High Button Shoes," "Touch and Go," "Make A Wish," "Pal Joey," "Hazel Flagg," CC revivals of "Guys and Dolls." "Finian's Rainbow," and "Oklahoma," "Pajama Game," "Bus Stop," "Portofino," "Sweet Charity," "Mame," "Cry For Us All."

GALLISON, JOSEPH. Born Mar. 9, 1939 in Boston. Graduate Northwestern. Made Bdwy debut in 1967 in "Mame."

GALMAN, PETER W. Born Dec. 24, 1945 in Chicago. Attended Purdue, AADA. Made Bdwy debut in 1969 in "40 Carats," after "Welcome to Andromeda" (OB).

GALPHIN, MARTHA. Born in Louisville, Ky. Vassar graduate. Made Bdwy debut in 1969 in "The Penny Wars."

GAMBOA, MARCELO. Born Apr. 2, 1939 in Buenos Aires. Has appeared in "Flora The Red Menace," "La Grosse Valise," "Annie Get Your Gun," "Illya Darling," "Carnival" (CC'68), "Minnie's Boys," "The Boy Friend."

GAMPEL, MORISON. (formerly Chris) Born Feb. 19, 1921 in Montreal, Can. Made Bdwy bow in 1950 in "Flight Into Egypt," followed by "Capt. Brassbound's Conversion" (CC), "Richard II," "St. Joan," "Waltz of The Toreadors," "No Exit," "The Crucible," "Compulsion," "The Firstborn," "The Girl Who Came To Supper," "The Front Page."

GANIMIAN, CHARLES "CHICK." Born Jan. 18, 1926 in Troy, NY. Made stage debut off Bdwy in 1970 in "The Moths."

GANNON, LIAM. Born in Dublin, Ire. Studied at Abbey, and Dublin Gate Theatres. Made Bdwy bow in 1956 in "The Righteous Are Bold," followed by "Three Hand Reel" (OB), "The Mundy Scheme."

GARDENIA, VINCENT. Born Jan. 7 in Italy. Made NY bow Off-Bdwy in 1956 in "Man With The Golden Arm," followed by "Brothers Karamazov," "Power of Darkness," "Machinal," "Gallows Humor," "Endgame," "Little Murders," "Passing Through from Exotic Places," on Bdwy in "The Visit" (1957). "The Cold Wind and The Warm," "Roshomon," "Only In America," "The Wall," "Daughters of Silence," "Seidman and Son," "Dr. Fish."

GARFIELD, ALLEN. Born Nov. 22, 1939 in Newark, NJ. Attended Upsala Col., Actors Studio. Appeared off Bdwy in "Witness," "Dream of a Blacklisted Actor," made Bdwy bow in 1970 in "Inquest."

GARFIELD, DAVID. Born Feb. 6, 1941 in Brooklyn. Graduate Columbia, Cornell. Appeared off Bdwy in "Hang Down Your Head and Die" before Bdwy bow in 1967 in "Fiddler on the Roof."

GARFIELD, KURT. Born Jan. 10, 1931 in the Bronx. Attended Goodman Theatre. Made Bdwy debut in 1970 in "Sheep on the Runway."

GARLAND, GEOFF. Born June 10, 1932 in Warrington, Eng. Made NY bow Off-Bdwy in 1961 in "The Hostage," followed by Bdwy roles in "Hamlet," NRT's. "The Imaginary Invalid," "A Touch of The Poet," and "Tonight At 8:30," "The Front Page" ('69).

GARRETT, JOY. Born Mar. 2, 1945 in Ft. Worth, Tex. Graduate Tex. Wesleyan, AADA. Made NY bow off Bdwy in 1969 in "Gertrude Stein's First Reader," Followed by "The Drunkard."

GARY, DAVID. Born Dec. 9, 1946 in Zanesville, O. Graduate Miami U. Made Bdwy debut in 1970 in "Hello, Dolly!"

GASPER, EDD K. Born Oct. 2, 1937 in Pittsburgh. Attended Carnegie Tech. Appeared Off-Bdwy in "The Burning," and "Anna Kleiber" before Bdwy bow in 1968 in "The Great White Hope."

Carol Gelfand   **Wayne Geis**   **Ann Gibbs**   **Maxwell Glanville**   **Diana Lynn Gol**

GASSELL, SYLVIA. Born July 1, 1923 in NYC. Attended Hunter, New School. Made Bdwy debut in 1952 in "The Time of The Cuckoo," followed by "Sunday Breakfast," "Fair Game For Lovers," "Inquest," Off-Bdwy in "U.S.A.," "Romeo and Juliet," "Electra," "A Darker Flower," "Fragments," "Goa," "God Bless You, Harold Fineberg," "Philosophy In The Boudoir."

GAVON, IGORS. Born Nov. 14, 1937 in Latvia. Made Bdwy bow in 1961 in "Carnival," followed by "Hello, Dolly!" "Marat/DeSade," "Your Own Thing" (OB), "Billy," "Promenade" (OB), "Exchange" (OB).

GAYNES, EDMUND. Born May 14, 1947 in Brooklyn. Graduate CCNY. Made Bdwy bow in 1958 in "Body Beautiful," followed by "Greenwillow," "Bartleby" (OB), "Best Foot Forward" (OB), "The Fig Leaves Are Falling," "Promenade" (OB).

GEIS, WAYNE. Born Apr. 3, 1945 in Chicago. Made NY bow Off-Bdwy in "A View from the Bridge," followed by "Treasure Island," "Kicking the Castle Down," "Me and Juliet" (ELT)

GELFAND, CAROL. Born Aug. 16, 1937 in Chicago. Attended U. Ill., Columbia. Made NY debut off Bdwy in 1961 in "The Cage," Bdwy bow in 1970 in "Company."

GENTLES, AVRIL. Born Apr. 2, 1929 in Upper Montclair, NJ. Graduate U. NC. Made Bdwy debut in 1955 in "The Great Sebastians," followed by "Nude With Violin," "Present Laughter," "Dinny and The Witches" (OB), "My Mother, My Father and Me," "The Wives" (OB), "Jimmy Shine," "Grin and Bare It."

GERACI, FRANK. Born Sept. 8, 1939 in Brooklyn. Attended Yale, HB Studio. Made debut in 1961 off Bdwy in "Color of Darkness," followed by "Mr. Grossman," "Balm in Gilead," "The Fantasticks," "Tom Paine," "End of All Things Natural."

GERLACH, ROBERT. Born Sept. 1, in Dallas, Tex. Attended U. Tex. Made NY bow Off-Bdwy in 1964 in "The Alchemist," followed by "The White Devil" and Bdwy debut in 1968 in "Plaza Suite."

GERSTAD, JOHN. Born Sept. 3, 1925 in Boston. Attended Harvard. Made Bdwy bow in 1943 in "Othello," followed by "Dark of The Moon," "Joy To The World," "Not For Children," "The Male Animal (CC'52)," "Golden Fleecing," "Trial of Lee Harvey Oswald," "Come Summer," "Penny Wars," "Oklahoma!" (LC)

GIBBS, ANN. Born Sept. 26 in Oklahoma City. Attended U. Okla. Made NY debut off Bdwy in 1969 in "Your a Good Man, Charlie Brown."

GIERASCH, STEFAN. Born Feb. 5, 1926 in NYC. Appeared in "Kiss and Tell," "Snafu," "Billion Dollar Baby," "Montserrat," "Night-Music," "Hatful of Rain," "Compulsion," "Shadow of a Gunman," "War and Peace" (APA), "7 Days of Mourning" (OB).

GILBERT, LOU. Born Aug. 1, 1909 in Sycamore, Ill. Has appeared in "Common Ground," "Beggars Are Coming To Town," "Truckline Cafe," "The Whole World Over," "Volpone," "Hope's The Thing With Feathers," "Detective Story," "His and Hers," "The Great White Hope," Off-Bdwy in "A Month In The Country," "Big Man," "Dynamite Tonight."

GILFORD, JACK. Born July 25 in NYC. Made Bdwy bow in 1940 in "Meet the People," followed by "They Should Have Stood in Bed," "Count Me In," "The Live Wire," "Alive and Kicking," "Once Over Lightly," "Diary of Anne Frank," "Romanoff and Juliet," "The Tenth Man," "A Funny Thing Happened…," "Cabaret," "3 Men on a Horse."

GILLETTE, ANITA. Born Aug. 16, 1938 in Baltimore. Made NY debut Off-Bdwy in 1960 in "Russell Patterson's Sketchbook" for which she received a THEATRE WORLD Award, followed by "Carnival," "All American," "Mr. President," "Guys and Dolls" (CC'55), "Don't Drink the Water," "Cabaret," "Jimmy."

GIORDANO, FRANK. Born Oct. 29 in Chicago. Attended Northwestern. Made NY bow in 1969 off Bdwy in "Gertrude Stein's First Reader."

GIRARD, DONALD. Born June 17, 1953 in NYC. Made Bdwy debut Oct. 3, 1968 in "The Great White Hope."

GLANVILLE, MAXWELL. Born Feb. 11, 1918 in Antigua, BWI. Attended New School. Made Bdwy bow in 1946 in "Walk Hard," followed by "Anna Lucasta," "How Long Till Summer," "Freight," "Autumn Garden," "Take A Giant Step," "Cat On A Hot Tin Roof," "Simply Heavenly," "Interlock," "Cool World," "The Shrike," "Golden Boy," "We Bombed in New Haven," "Zelda," Off-Bdwy in over 250 shows including "The Blacks," "Nat Turner," "Rain," "Simple," "5 on the Blackhand Side."

GLASER, DAREL. Born Jan. 12, 1957 in Chicago. Made NY debut in 1966 in "Wozzeck" followed by "Tea Party" (OB), "Cry for Us All."

GLENN, FREDRIC. Born Oct. 26, 1939 in Houston, Tex. Attended U. Tex. Made Bdwy debut in 1969 in "Henry V."

GLENN-SMITH, MICHAEL. Born July 2, 1945 in Abilene, Tex. Attended N. Tex., State U. Made Bdwy debut in 1969 in "Celebration," followed by "The Fantastics."

GLOVER, DAVID. Born Sept. 24, 1927 in London. Made Bdwy debut in 1961 in "Ross," followed by "Private Lives."

GOBLE, DIANA. Born Aug. 23, 1946 in Richmond, Va. Attended Actors Studio. Made NY debut off Bdwy in 1967 in "The Drunkard," followed by "Up Eden," "We'd Rather Switch."

GOLDSMITH, MERWIN. Born Aug. 7, 1937 in Detroit, Mich. UCLA graduate. Studied at Old Vic. Made NY bow in 1967 off Bdwy in "Hamlet as a Happening," and Bdwy debut in 1970 in "Minnie's Boys."

GOODMAN, DODY. Born Oct. 28 in Columbus, O. Made Bdwy debut in 1947 in "High Button Shoes," followed by "Miss Liberty," "Call Me Madam," "Wonderful Town," "Fiorello" (CC), "A Rainy Day In Newark," "My Daughter, Your Son," "The Front Page," Off-Bdwy roles in "Shoestring Revue," "Shoestring '57," "Parade," "New Cole Porter Revue."

GORDONE, CHARLES. Born in 1925 in Cleveland, O. Has appeared off Bdwy in "The Blacks," and his own Pulitzer Prize-winning play "No Place to Be Somebody."

GORMAN, BOB. Born Dec. 30, 1928 in Peoria, Tenn. Graduate Ill. Wesleyan, Columbia. Made Bdwy bow in 1957 in "Li'l Abner," followed by "Music Man," "Subways Are for Sleeping," "Half a Sixpence," "Breakfast at Tiffany's," "Sweet Charity," "How Now, Dow Jones," "Gantry."

GOULD, HAROLD. Born Dec. 10, 1923 in Schenectady, NY. Graduate SUNY, Cornell. Made NY bow in 1969 at Lincoln Center in "The Increased Difficulty of Concentration," "Amphitryon."

GRAHAM, RICHARD. Born Jan. 1, 1915 in Detroit, Mich. Attended Princeton. Made Bdwy debut in 1933 in "Pursuit of Happiness," followed by "Romeo and Juliet," "St. Joan," "Saratoga," "Look to the Lilies."

GRANT, MICKI. Born June 30 in Chicago. Attended U. Ill., Geller School. Made Bdwy debut in 1963 in "Tambourines to Glory," followed by off Bdwy roles in "Fly Blackbird," "The Blacks," "Brecht on Brecht," "Jerico-Jim Crow," "The Cradle Will Rock," "Leonard Bernstein's Theatre Songs," "To Be Young, Gifted and Black."

GREENE, REUBEN. Born Nov. 24, 1938 in Philadelphia. Appeared with APA in "War and Peace," "You Can't Take It With You," and "Pantagleize," and Off-Bdwy in "Jericho-Jim Crow," "Happy Ending," "The Boys In The Band."

chael Greer   **Marian Hailey**   **Christopher Haden Guest**   **Margaret Hall**   **Peter Haig**

GREER, MICHAEL. Born Apr. 20, 1943 in Galesburg, Ill. Attended American Theatre Wing. Made NY debut in 1969 off Bdwy in "Fortune and Men's Eyes."

GREGORY, JAY. Born Sept. 16, 1939 in Albany, NY. Graduate Ithaca Col. Made Bdwy bow in 1966 in "A Time for Singing," followed by "Blood Red Roses."

GREGORY, WILL. Born Nov. 18, 1928 in Glasgow, Scot. Attended Western Reserve U., Cleveland Playhouse. Appeared Off-Bdwy in "Orpheus Descending," "Summer and Smoke," "A Streetcar Named Desire," "Eclipse Day," "Psalm For Fat Tuesdays," on Bdwy in "Cactus Flower," "A Warm Body," "The Front Page."

GREY, JOEL. Born Apr. 11, 1932 in Cleveland, O. Attended Cleveland, and Neighborhood Playhouses. Made NY bow Off-Bdwy in "The Littlest Revue," followed by "Borscht Capades," "Come Blow Your Horn," "Stop The World—I Want To Get Off," "Half A Sixpence," "Harry, Noon and Night" (OB), "Cabaret," "George M!"

GRIFFIS, WILLIAM. Born July 12, 1917 in Hollywood, Calif. Made Bdwy bow in 1953 in "A Pin to See the Peepshow," followed by "Look after Lulu," "Here's Love," "The Cradle Will Rock," "Never Too Late," "Philadelphia, Here I Come," "Jimmy," "Cry for Us All," Off-Bdwy in "The Corn Is Green," "Major Barbara," "Capacity for Wings," "No Trifling with Love," "Oklahoma!" (LC).

GRIMES, FRANK. Born in 1947 in Dublin, Ire. Attended Abbey Theatre School. Made Bdwy debut in 1970 in "Borstal Boy."

GRIMES, TAMMY. Born Jan. 30, 1934 in Lynn, Mass. Attended Stephens Col., Neighborhood Playhouse. Appeared off Bdwy in "The Littlest Revue," "Clerambard," made Bdwy debut in 1959 in "Look after Lulu" for which she received a THEATRE WORLD Award, followed by "The Unsinkable Molly Brown," "Rattle of a Simple Man," "High Spirits," "The Only Game in Town," "Private Lives."

GRIZZARD, GEORGE. Born Apr. 1, 1928 in Roanoke Rapids, NC. Graduate UNC. Made Bdwy bow in 1954 in "All Summer Long," followed by "The Desperate Hours," "The Happiest Millionaire" for which he received a THEATRE WORLD Award, "The Disenchanted," "Big Fish, Little Fish," with APA (1961-2), "Who's Afraid of Virginia Woolf?," "The Glass Menagerie" ('65), "You Know I Can't Hear You When the Water's Running," "Noel Coward's Sweet Potato," "The Gingham Dog," "Inquest."

GROSS, GENE. Born Feb. 17, 1920 in NYC. Made debut Off-Bdwy in 1957 in "Career," followed by "Handful of Fire," "J.B.," "The Passion of Josef D," "The Tenth Man" (CC'67), "Cannibals" (OB).

GROSSMAN, SUZANNE. Born in Switz. Graduate McGill U. Made Bdwy debut in 1966 in "The Lion In Winter," followed by "Cyrano" (LCRep), "The Show-Off" (APA), "Private Lives."

GROVER, STANLEY. Born Mar. 28, 1926 in Woodstock, Ill. Attended U Mo. Appeared in "Seventeen," "Wish You Were Here," "Time Remember'd," "Candide," "13 Daughters," "Mr. President," CC revivals of "South Pacific," "Finian's Rainbow," and "King and I," "Lyle" (OB).

GUEST, CHRISTOPHER HADEN. Born Feb. 5, 1948 in NYC. Attended Bard Col., NYU. Appeared off Bdwy in "Little Murders" before Bdwy bow in 1970 in "Room Service."

GUNN, MOSES. Born Oct. 2, 1929 in St. Louis. Graduate Tenn. AIU, U. Kan. Has appeared Off-Bdwy in "Measure For Measure," "Bohikee Creek," "Day of Absence," "Happy Ending," "Baal," "Hard Travelin'," "Lonesome Train," "In White America," "The Blacks," "Titus Andronicus" (CP), "A Hand Is On The Gate" (Bdwy), with NEC in "Song of The Lusitanian Bogey," "Summer of 17th Doll," "Kongi's Harvest," and "Daddy Goodness," "Cities In Bezique," "Perfect Party," "To Be Young, Gifted and Black."

HACKETT, JOAN. Born Mar. 1 in NYC. Attended Actors Studio. Made debut in 1959 off Bdwy in "A Clearing in the Woods," followed by Bdwy bow in 1959 in "Much Ado About Nothing," "Call Me by My Rightful Name" (OB) for which she received a THEATRE WORLD Award, "Peterpat," "Park."

HADGE, MICHAEL. Born June 6, 1932 in Greensboro, NC. Made Bdwy bow in 1958 in "The Cold Wind and the Warm," followed by "Lady of the Camellias," "The Impossible Years," "Local Stigmatic" (OB).

HAGEN, REIGH. Born Aug. 8, 1936 in Brooklyn. Made off Bdwy bow in 1959 in "Share My Lettuce," followed by "They Called Him Lincoln," "King Ubu," "4 By Night," "The Apollo of Bellac," "Gizmo," "If Adventure's Your Dish," "The Audition," "Moondreamers," "Gloria and Esperanza" (1970 Bdwy debut).

HAIG, PETER. Born June 24, 1939 in Philadelphia. Attended U. Chicago, AADA. Made NY bow in 1964 Off-Bdwy in "Othello," followed by Bdwy debut in 1967 in "Dr. Cook's Garden," "Mod Donna" (OB).

HAILEY, MARIAN. Born Feb. 1, 1941 in Portland, Ore. U. Wash graduate. Made Bdwy debut in 1965 in "Mating Dance," followed by "Any Wednesday," "Best Laid Plans," "Keep It In The Family," "Harvey," Off-Bdwy in "Under the Yum Yum Tree," and "Thornton Wilder's Triple Bill."

HAINES, A. LARRY. Born Aug. 3, 1917 in Mt. Vernon, NY. Attended CCNY. Made Bdwy bow in 1962 in "A Thousand Clowns," followed by "Generation," "Promises, Promises."

HAINES, MERVYN, JR. Born Aug. 20, 1933 in Newark, NJ. Attended AADA. Appeared with NY Shakespeare Festival in "All's Well That Ends Well," "Measure For Measure," and "Richard III," with LCRep in "King Lear," "A Cry of Players," "Henry V."

HALL, BRUCE. Born Dec. 7, 1919 in NYC. Attended Choate, Pasadena Playhouse. Has appeared on Bdwy in "Joan of Lorraine," "Traveling Lady," "Barefoot In Athens," "Seagulls Over Sorrento," "Song of Bernadette," "Southern Exposure," and Off-Bdwy in "To Be Young, Gifted and Black."

HALL, ED. Born Jan. 11, 1931 in Roxbury, Mass. Attended Harvard. Has appeared in "Climate of Eden," "No Time for Sergeants," "A Raisin in the Sun," "Wilson in the Promise Land," "The Zulu and the Zayda," Off-Bdwy in "Death of Bessie Smith," and "Trumpets of the Lord."

HALL, GEORGE. Born Nov. 19, 1916 in Toronto, Can. Attended Neighborhood Playhouse. Appeared in "Call Me Mister," "Lend an Ear," "Touch and Go," "Live Wire," "The Boy Friend," "There's A Girl in My Soup," Off-Bdwy in "The Balcony," "Ernest in Love," "A Round with Ring."

HALL, MARGARET. Born in Richmond, Va. Graduate Wm. & Mary Col. Made Bdwy debut in 1960 in "Becket," followed by "High Spirits," "Mame," Off-Bdwy in "The Boy Friend," "Fallout," "U.S.A.," "A Midsummer Night's Dream," "Little Mary Sunshine."

HALL, MARK. Born June 10, 1955 in Boston, Mass. Made NY debut Off-Bdwy in 1968 in "As You Like It," Bdwy bow in 1970 in "Child's Play."

HALLOW, JOHN. Born Nov. 28, 1942 in NYC. Attended Neighborhood Playhouse. Made Bdwy bow in 1954 in "Anastasia," followed by "Ross," "Visit To A Small Planet," "Foxy," "Oh, Dad, Poor Dad,...," "Ben Franklin In Paris," "3 Bags Full," "Don't Drink The Water," "Hadrian VII."

HAMER, JOSEPH. Born July 29, 1932 in Dayton, O. Graduate Miami U., UCLA. Has appeared Off-Bdwy in "Henry IV," "White Cargo," "Cicero," "A Month In The Country," "The White Rose and the Red," and made Bdwy bow in 1968 in "The Great White Hope."

Ronn Hansen   **Mary Hara**   **Gordon Heath**   **Tiffany Hendry**   **Bruce Heig**

HAMILTON, JEFFREY. Born Feb. 8, 1957 in Bridgeport, Conn. Made Bdwy debut in 1968 in "The Happy Time," followed by "The Penny Wars."

HAMILTON, MARGARET. Born Dec. 9, 1902 in Cleveland Playhouse. Made Bdwy debut in 1932 in "Another Language," followed by "Dark Tower," "The Farmer Takes A Wife," "Outrageous Fortune," "The Men We Marry," "Fancy Meeting You Again," "Annie Get Your Gun" (CC), "Goldilocks," "UTBU," "Show Boat" (LC), "Come Summer," "Oklahoma!" (LC), "Our Town."

HAMILTON, MURRAY. Born in Washington, DC. Made Bdwy debut in 1945 in "Strange Fruit," followed by "Mister Roberts," "The Chase," "Stockade" (OB), "Critic's Choice," "The Heroine," "Absence of A Cello," "Forty Carats."

HANLEY, ELLEN. Born May 15, 1926 in Lorain, O. Attended Juilliard. Made Bdwy debut in 1946 in "Annie Get Your Gun," followed by "Barefoot Boy with Cheek" for which she received a THEATRE WORLD Award, "High Button Shoes," "Two's Company," "First Impressions," "Fiorello!", "The Boys from Syracuse" (OB), "1776."

HANSEN, RONN. Born Oct. 18, 1939 in Madison, Wisc. Graduate U. Wisc. Made Bdwy bow in 1965 in "Slapstick Tragedy" followed by "Minnie's Boys."

HARA, MARY. Born in Nebraska; studied with Uta Hagen. Made Bdwy debut in 1968 in "Rosencrantz and Guildenstern Are Dead," appeared Off-Bdwy in "The Kitchen," "The Glorious Ruler."

HARRIS, BARBARA. Born in 1937 in Evanston, Ill. Made Bdwy debut in 1961 in "From the Second City," followed by roles off Bdwy in "Seacoast of Bohemia," "Alarums and Excursions," "Oh, Dad, Poor Dad..." for which she received a THEATRE WORLD Award, "Mother Courage and Her Children," "Dynamite Tonight," "On A Clear Day You Can See Forever," "The Apple Tree," "Mahagonny" (OB).

HARRIS, GEORGE, II. Born in Bronxville, NY. Attended Columbia U. Appeared Off-Bdwy in "Wide Open Cage" (1963), and "Gorilla Queen" ('67) before Bdwy bow in 1968 in "The Great White Hope."

HARRIS, JULIE. Born Dec. 2, 1925 in Grosse Point, Mich. Attended Yale. Made Bdwy debut in 1945 in "It's A Gift," followed by "Henry V," "Oedipus," "The Playboy of The Western World," "Alice In Wonderland," "Macbeth," "Sundown Beach" for which she received a THEATRE WORLD Award, "The Young and The Fair," "Magnolia Alley," "Montserrat," "The Member of The Wedding," "I Am A Camera," "Mlle. Colombe," "The Lark," "The Country Wife," "The Warm Peninsula," "Little Moon of Alban," "A Shot In The Dark," "Marathon '33," "Ready When You Are, C.B.," "Hamlet" (CP), "Skyscraper," "Forty Carats."

HAVESON, JIMMY. Born June 27, 1924 in Carthage, NC. Attended NC Col., NYU. Made NY debut in 1961 Off-Bdwy in "The Blacks," followed by "Melting Pot Park," "The Leader," "A Black Quartet."

HAWKINS, MICHAEL. Born in NYC. Attended Carnegie Tech. Has appeared off Bdwy in "MacBird," "Love and Let Love," "Getting Married."

HAYES, HELEN. Born Oct. 10, 1900 in Washington, DC. Graduate Sacred Heart Acad. Made Bdwy debut in 1909 in "Old Dutch," followed by "Summer Widowers," "Penrod," "Dear Brutus," "Clarence," "To The Ladies," "We Moderns," "Dancing Mothers," "Caesar and Cleopatra," "What Every Woman Knows," "Coquette," "Mary of Scotland," "Victoria Regina," "Twelfth Night," "Candle In The Wind," "Happy Birthday," "Wisteria Trees," "Mrs. McThing," "Glass Menagerie" (CC), "The Skin of Our Teeth," "Time Remember'd," "A Touch of The Poet," "A Program For Two Players," "The White House," and with APA in "School For Scandal," "Right You Are," "We Comrades Three," and "The Show-Off," "The Front Page," "Harvey."

HEATH, GORDON. Born Sept. 20, 1918 in NYC. Attended CCNY. Made Bdwy debut in 1945 in "Deep Are the Roots," appeared this season Off-Bdwy in "Oedipus" after many years in Europe.

HECHT, PAUL. Born Aug. 16, 1941 in London. Attended McGill U. Appeared with NY Shakespeare Festival, and Off-Bdwy in "Sjt. Musgrave's Dance," and "MacBird," on Bdwy in "Rosencrantz and Guildenstern Are Dead," "1776."

HECKART, EILEEN. Born Mar. 29, 1919 in Columbus, O. Graduate Ohio State U. Made NY debut Off-Bdwy in "Tinker's Dam," followed by "Our Town"(CC), "They Knew What They Wanted," "The Traitor," "Hilda Crane," "In Any Language," "Picnic" for which she received a THEATRE WORLD Award, "The Bad Seed," "A View From The Bridge," "The Dark At The Top of The Stairs," "Invitation To A March," "Pal Joey"(CC), "Everybody Loves Opal," "A Family Affair," "Too True To Be Good," "And Things That Go Bump In The Night," "Barefoot In The Park," "You Know I Can't Hear You When The Water's Running," "The Mother Lover," "Butterflies Are Free."

HEFFERNAN, JOHN. Born May 30, 1934 in NYC. Attended CCNY, Columbia, Boston U. Appeared Off-Bdwy in "The Judge," "Julius Caesar," "Great God Brown," "Lysistrata," "Peer Gynt," "Henry IV," "Taming of The Shrew," "She Stoops To Conquer," "The Plough and The Stars," "The Octoroon," "Hamlet," "Androcles and The Lion." "A Man's A Man," "Winter's Tale," "Arms and The Man," "St. Joan"(LCRep), "The Memorandum," "Invitation To A Beheading," on Bdwy in "Luther," "Tiny Alice," "Postmark Zero," "Woman Is My Idea," "Morning, Noon and Night," "Peer Gynt"(CP), "Purlie."

HEFLIN, MARTA. Born Mar. 29, 1945 in Washington, DC. Attended Northwestern, Carnegie Tech. Made NY debut in 1967 in "Life With Father"(CC), followed by "Salvation"(OB).

HEIGHLEY, BRUCE. Born May 7, 1939 in Liverpool, Eng. Attended St. Anselms Col. Made Bdwy debut in 1970 in "Borstal Boy."

HELMERS, JUNE. Born Oct. 21, 1941 in Middletown, O. Attended Carnegie Tech. Made Bdwy debut in 1967 in "Hello Dolly!" followed by "Oklahoma!"(LC).

HEMSLEY, SHERMAN. Born Feb. 1, 1938 in Philadelphia. Attended Phila. Academy of Dramatic Arts. Made NY bow in 1968 Off-Bdwy in "The People Vs. Ranchman," Bdwy in 1970 in "Purlie."

HENDERSON, MELANIE. Born Sept. 20, 1957 in NYC. Made debut in 1970 Off-Bdwy in "The Me Nobody Knows."

HENDRY, TIFFANY. Born Oct. 13, 1942 in Waterbury, Conn. Attended Boston U, Neighborhood Playhouse. Made NY debut in 1963 Off-Bdwy in "The Trojan Women," followed by "Getting Married," "Brotherhood"(NEC).

HENRITZE, BETTE. Born May 3 in Betsy Layne, Ky. Graduate U. Tenn. Off-Bdwy credits: "Lion In Love," "Abe Lincoln In Illinois," "Othello," "Baal," "Long Christmas Dinner," "Queens of France," "Rimers of Eldritch," "The Displaced Person," "The Acquisition," "Crimes of Passion," on Bdwy in "Jenny Kissed Me," "Pictures In The Hallway," "Giants, Sons of Giants," "Ballad of The Sad Cafe," "The White House," "Dr. Cook's Garden," "Here's Where I Belong."

HEPBURN, KATHARINE. Born Nov. 9, 1909 in Hartford, Conn. Attended Bryn Mawr. Made Bdwy debut in 1928 in "Night Hostess," followed by "A Month in the Country," "Art and Mrs. Bottle," "The Warrior's Husband," "The Lake," "Philadelphia Story," "Without Love," "As You Like It," "The Millionairess," "Coco."

HERMAN, MAXINE. Born Aug. 17, 1948 in NYC. Attended NYU. Made debut Off-Bdwy in 1970 in "The Nuns."

| ne Herman | Barton Heyman | Bonnie Hinson | Hal Holden | Anna Horsford |

HEWITT, ROBERT. Born Aug. 12, 1922 in Sydney, Aust. Member of Old Vic, London. Made Bdwy bow in 1963 in "Chips With Everything," followed by "The Zulu and The Zayda," "Hadrian VII."

HEYMAN, BARTON. Born Jan. 24, 1937 in Washington, DC. Attended UCLA. Appeared Off-Bdwy in 1967 in "A Midsummer Night's Dream," Bdwy debut in 1969 in "Indians."

HIGH, BOLEN. Born Nov. 27, 1945 in Houston, Tex. Graduate U Denver, Goodman Theatre. Made Bdwy debut in 1969 in "Henry V."

HILL, RALSTON. Born Apr. 24, 1927 in Cleveland, O. Graduate Oberlin Col. Appeared Off-Bdwy in "The Changeling," "Streets of New York," "Valmouth," "Carousel" (LC'65), on Bdwy in "1776."

HINGLE, PAT. Born July 19, 1923 in Denver. Graduate Tex. U. Made Bdwy bow in 1953 in "End As A Man," followed by "Festival," "Cat On A Hot Tin Roof," "Girls of Summer," "The Dark At The Top of The Stairs," "J.B.," "Deadly Game," "Strange Interlude"('63), "Blues For Mr. Charlie," "A Girl Could Get Lucky," "The Glass Menagerie" ('65), "Johnny No Trump," "The Price," "Child's Play."

HINNANT, BILL. Born Aug. 28, 1935 on Chincoteague Island, Va. Yale graduate. Appeared in "No Time for Sergeants," followed by "Here's Love," Off-Bdwy roles in "All Kinds of Giants," "Put It in Writing," "You're A Good Man, Charlie Brown," "American Hamburger League."

HINSON, BONNIE. Born Oct. 11, 1946 in Charlotte, NC. Graduate U Cin. Made NY debut in 1970 in "Me and Juliet" (ELT).

HODAPP, ANN. Born May 6, 1946 in Louisville, Ky. Attended Hunter, NYU. Made NY debut Off-Bdwy in 1968 in "You're A Good Man, Charlie Brown," followed by "A Round with Ring," "House of Leather."

HOFFMAN, JANE. Born July 24 in Seattle, Wash. Attended U Cal. Made Bdwy debut in 1940 in " 'Tis of Thee," followed by "Crazy With The Heat," "Something For The Boys," "One Touch of Venus," "Calico Wedding," "Mermaids Singing," "A Temporary Island," "Story For Strangers," "Two Blind Mice," "The Rose Tattoo," "The Crucible," "Witness For the Prosecution," "Third Best Sport," "Rhinoceros," "Mother Courage and Her Children," "Fair Game For Lovers," "A Murderer Among Us," and Off-Bdwy in "The American Dream," "The Sandbox," "Picnic On A Battlefield," "Theatre of The Absurd," "The Child Buyer," "A Corner of The Bed," and "Someone's Comin' Hungry," "The Increased Difficulty of Concentration"(LC), "American Hamburger League."

HOLGATE, RONALD. Born May 26, 1937 in Aberdeen, S.D. Attended Northwestern U., New Eng. Cons. Made NY bow in 1961 Off-Bdwy in "Hobo," followed by "A Funny Thing Happened On The Way To The Forum," "Milk and Honey," "Hooray, It's A Glorious Day"(OB), "1776."

HOLLAND, ANTHONY. Born Oct. 17, 1933 in Brooklyn. Graduate U Chicago. Off-Bdwy credits: "Venice Preserved," "Second City," "Victim of Duty," "The New Tenant," "Dynamite Tonight," "The Quare Fellow," "White House Murder Case," on Bdwy in "My Mother, My Father and Me," "We Bombed in New Haven."

HOLLANDER, JACK. Born Jan. 29, 1918 in Chicago. Graduate Goodman Theatre. Bdwy bow in 1959 in "The Miracle Worker," followed by "All The Way Home," "Gideon," "The Impossible Years," "Man In The Glass Booth," "Inquest," Off-Bdwy in "Girl of The Golden West," "The Dybbuk," "Journey To The Day," "Titus Andronicus"(CP), "Comedy of Errors"(CP), "Ergo."

HOLLIDAY, DAVID. Born Aug. 4, 1937 in Illinois. Attended Carthage Col. After appearing in London, made Bdwy bow in 1968 in "Man of La Mancha," followed by "Coco" for which he received a THEATRE WORLD Award.

HOLM, CELESTE. Born Apr. 29, 1919 in NYC. Bdwy debut in 1938 in "Gloriana," followed by "The Time of Your Life," "Another Sun," "The Return of The Vagabond," "Papa Is All," "Damask Cheek," "Oklahoma!," "She Stoops To Conquer," "Bloomer Girl," "Affairs of State," "Anna Christie"('51), "His and Hers," "Interlock," "Third Best Sport," "Invitation To A March," "A Month In The Country" (OB), "Mame," "Candida."

HOLM, JOHN CECIL. Born Nov. 4, 1904 in Philadelphia. Attended U Pa. Made Bdwy bow in 1929 in "The Front Page," followed by "Whirlpool," "Penal Law 2010," "The Up and Up," "Wonder Boy," "Bloodstream," "Dangerous Corner," "Mary of Scotland," "Midgie Purvis," "Gramercy Ghost," "Mr. President," "The Advocate," "A Mighty Man Is He," "Philadelphia, Here I Come!," "Forty Carats."

HOOKS, ROBERT. Born Apr. 18, 1937 in Washington, DC. Attended Temple U. Made Bdwy bow in 1959 in "A Raisin in the Sun," followed by "A Taste of Honey," "Tiger, Tiger, Burning Bright," "Arturo Ui," "The Milk Train Doesn't Stop Here Anymore," "Where's Daddy?" for which he received a THEATRE WORLD Award, "Hallelujah, Baby!," Off-Bdwy in "Henry V," "Ballad of Bimshire," "The Blacks," "Dutchman," "Happy Ending," "Day of Absence," with NEC (that he co-founded) in "Kongi's Harvest," "The Harangues."

HOREN, BOB. Born Oct. 12, 1925 in Aberdeen, SD. Graduate U Minn., U Mo. Off-Bdwy credits: "Hogan's Goat," on Bdwy in "An Enemy of The People," "A Minor Miracle," "The Great White Hope."

HORSFORD, ANNA MARIA. Born Mar. 6, 1947 in NYC. Attended Inter-American U. Made NY debut Off-Bdwy in 1969 in "The Black Quartet," followed by "The Perfect Party."

HOUGHTON, KATHARINE. Born Mar. 10, 1945 in Hartford, Conn. Graduate Sarah Lawrence Co. Made Bdwy debut in 1965 in "A Very Rich Woman," followed by "The Front Page"('69), "A Scent of Flowers" Off-Bdwy for which she received a THEATRE WORLD Award.

HOWARD, KEN. Born Mar. 28, 1944 in El Centro, Calif. Graduate Amherst and Yale. Made Bdwy debut in 1968 in "Promises, Promises," followed by "1776" for which he received a THEATRE WORLD Award, "Child's Play."

HOWELL, MARGARET. Born Sept. 9, 1947 in Raleigh, NC. Graduate UNC. Made NY debut in 1970 Off-Bdwy in "Dark of the Moon."

HOWLAND, BETH. Born May 28, 1941 in Boston. Made NY debut Off-Bdwy in 1960 in "Once Upon A Mattress," followed by Bdwy roles in "Bye, Bye, Birdie," "High Spirits," "Drat! The Cat!," "Darling of the Day," "Company."

HUGHES, BARNARD. Born July 16, 1915 in Bedford Hills, N.Y. Attended Manhattan Col. Off-Bdwy credits: "Rosmersholm," "A Doll's House," "Hogan's Goat," on Bdwy in "The Ivy Green," "Dinosaur Wharf," "Teahouse of The August Moon"(CC'56), "A Majority of One," "Advise and Consent," "The Advocate," "Hamlet"('64), "I Was Dancing," "Generation," "How Now, Dow Jones?," "Wrong Way Light Bulb," "Sheep On The Runway."

HUGHES, TRESA. Born Sept. 17, 1929 in Washington, DC. Attended Wayne U. Has appeared Off-Bdwy in "Electra," "The Crucible," "Hogan's Goat," "Party On Greenwich Avenue," "Fragments," "Passing Through from Exotic Places," "Beggar On Horseback"(LC). On Bdwy in "The Miracle Worker," "The Devil's Advocate," "Dear Me, The Sky Is Falling," "The Last Analysis," "Spofford," "The Man In The Glass Booth."

HULL, TOM. Born Mar. 10, in Durham, NC. Attended UNC. Made NY debut in 1969 Off-Bdwy in "A Round With Riug," followed by "I Dreamt I Dwelt in Bloomingdale's."

L. Errol Jaye   **Salome Jens**   **Clay Johns**   **Karen Johnson**   **Page Johns**

HUMPHREY, CAVADA. Born June 17 in Atlantic City, NJ. Graduate Smith Col. Made NY debut Off-Bdwy in 1943 in "A Man's House," followed by Bdwy bow in '44 in "The House in Paris," "Song of Bernadette," "As the Girls Go," "The Devil's Disciple"(CC), "Time Remember'd," CC productions of "Richard II," "Taming of the Shrew," "Love's Labour's Lost," "Richard III," "Othello," and "Henry IV," "You Can't Take It With You" (APA), "Candida," Off-Bdwy in "Moon in Capricorn," "Girl of the Golden West," "Dear Liar," "Life Is A Dream."

HUNTER, KIM. Born Nov. 12, 1922 in Detroit, Mich. Member Actors Studio. Made Bdwy debut in 1947 in "A Streetcar Named Desire," followed by "Darkness at Noon," "The Chase," "The Children's Hour," "The Tender Trap," "Come Slowly, Eden"(OB), "Write Me A Murder," "Weekend," "The Penny Wars."

HUSTON, MARTIN. Born Feb. 8, 1941 in Lexington, Ky. Attended Columbia. Made Bdwy bow in 1959 in "Only in America," followed by "Take Her, She's Mine," "Come Blow Your Horn," "A Race of Hairy Men," "Harold," "Sondra" (OB), "Norman, Is That You?"

IRVING, GEORGE S. Born Nov. 1, 1922 in Springfield, Mass. Attended Leland Powers Sch. Made Bdwy bow in 1943 in "Oklahoma!," followed by "Call Me Mister," "Along Fifth Avenue," "Two's Company," "Me and Juliet," "Can-Can," "Shinbone Alley," "Bells Are Ringing," "The Good Soup," "Tovarich," "A Murderer Among Us," "Alfie," "Sanya," "Galileo"(LC), "The Happy Time," "Up Eden" (OB), "Promenade"(OB).

JACKSON, ANNE. Born Sept. 3, 1926 in Allegheny, Pa. Attended Neighborhood Playhouse, Actors Studio. Made Bdwy debut in 1945 in "Signature," followed by "Yellow Jack," "John Gabriel Borkman," "The Last Dance," "Summer and Smoke," "Magnolia Alley," "Love Me Long," "Lady from the Sea," "Never Say Never," "Oh, Men! Oh, Women!," "Rhinoceros," "Luv," "The Exercise," "Inquest," Off-Bdwy in "Brecht on Brecht," "The Tiger" and "The Typists."

JACOBI, LOU. Born Dec. 28, 1913 in Toronto, Can. Made Bdwy bow in 1955 in "The Diary of Anne Frank," followed by "The Tenth Man," "Come Blow Your Horn," "Fade Out-Fade In," "Don't Drink The Water," "A Way of Life," "Norman, Is That You?"

JACOBY, SCOTT. Born Nov. 26, 1955 in Chicago. Made NY debut Off-Bdwy in "Dandelion Wine," Bdwy bow in 1968 in "Golden Rainbow," followed by "The Time of Your Life"(LC), "Summertree"(OB), "Cry For Us All."

JAMES, ERIC. Born Jan. 14, 1943 in Westmont, Ill. Attended Loyola U. Made NY debut in 1969 Off-Bdwy in "The Boys In The Band."

JANIS, CONRAD. Born Feb. 11, 1928 in NYC. Appeared on Bdwy in "Junior Miss," "Dark of the Moon," "The Next Half Hour," "The Brass Ring" for which he received a THEATRE WORLD Award, "Time Out For Ginger," "The Terrible Swift Sword," "Visit To A Small Planet," "Make A Million," "Sunday In New York," "Marathon '33," "The Front Page ('69)."

JANNEY, LEON. Born Apr. 1, 1917 in Ogden, Utah. Made Bdwy bow in 1934 in "Every Thursday," followed by "Simpleton of the Unexpected Isle," "Parade," "Mulatto," "Foreigners," "Ghost for Sale," "Flowering Peach," "Madam, Will You Walk?," "Measure for Measure," "Country Wife," "Damn Yankees," "The Gazebo," "Summer of the 17th Doll," "Nobody Loves an Albatross," "The Last Analysis," "3 Men on A Horse."

JARRETT, JERRY. Born Sept. 9, 1918 in Brooklyn. Attended New Theatre School. Appeared Off-Bdwy in "Waiting For Lefty," "Nat Turner," "Me Candido," "That 5 A.M. Jazz," made Bdwy bow in 1948 in "At War With The Army," followed by "Gentlemen Prefer Blondes," "Stalag 17," "Fiorello," "Fiddler On The Roof."

JASPER, ZINA. Born Jan. 29, 1939 in the Bronx. Attended CCNY. Made Bdwy debut in 1967 in "Something Different," followed by "Saturday's Children" (OB), "Moondreamers" (OB), "Paris Is Out."

JAY, WILLIAM. Born May 15, 1935 in Baxter Springs, Kan. Attended Omaha U. Made NY bow Off-Bdwy in 1963 in "Utopia," followed by "The Blacks," "Loop The Loop," "Happy Ending," "Day of Absence," "Hamlet" (CP), "Othello" (CP), NEC's "Song of The Lusitanian Bogey," "Ceremonies In Dark Old Men," "Man Better Man," "The Harangues," and "Brotherhood."

JAYE, L. ERROL. Born Feb. 7, 1928 in Jacksonville, Fla. Graduate Fisk U., AMDA. Made NY bow in 1966 off Bdwy in "Happy Ending" and "Day of Absence, followed by NYSF's "Troilus and Cressida" and "Henry V," "Who's Got His Own," "The Electronic Nigger and Others," "A Black Quartet," "5 on the Blackhand Side," made Bdwy debut in 1968 in "The Great White Hope."

JEANNETTE, GERTRUDE. Born, Nov. 28, 1918 in Little Rock, Ark. Attended New School. Has appeared in "Lost In The Stars," "The Long Dream," "The Amen Corner," "Nobody Loves An Albatross," and Off-Bdwy in "This Way Forward," "Deep Are The Roots," "417," "Moon On A Rainbow Shawl," "To Be Young, Gifted and Black."

JENS, SALOME. Born May 8, 1935 in Milwaukee, Wisc. Attended Northwestern, U. Wisc. Made Bdwy debut in 1956 in "Sixth Finger In A Five-Finger Glove," followed by "The Disenchanted," "A Far Country," "Night Life," "I'm Solomon," "A Patriot for Me," Off-Bdwy in "The Bald Soprano," "Jack," "Deidre of The Sorrows," "U.S.A.," "The Balcony," "Desire Under The Elms," "Posterity For Sale," LCRep's "After The Fall," "But For Whom Charlie," and "Tartuffe," "A Moon For The Misbegotten."

JOBIN, PETER. Born Feb. 1, 1944 in Montreal, Can. Attended Williams U. Made Bdwy debut in 1969 in "Hadrian VII."

JOHANN, JOHN. Born Dec. 23, 1942 in Madison, Wisc. Attended Los Angeles State Col. Made NY bow in 1966 Off-Bdwy in "Autumn's Here," followed by "My Fair Lady" (CC'68), "Come Summer," "Me and Juliet" (ELT).

JOHNS, CLAY. Born June 6, 1934 in Lima, O. Has appeared off Bdwy in "Tiger at the Gates," "The Disenchanted," "Under the Gaslight," "The Queen and the Rebels," "The Drunkard."

JOHNSON, BOBBY. Born Oct. 26, 1946 in San Francisco. Studied dancing before making Bdwy debut in 1968 in "Hello, Dolly!"

JOHNSON, KAREN. Born July 18, 1939 in Kane, Pa. Graduate Holyoke Col. Made NY debut in 1965 off Bdwy in "The 4th Pig," followed by "Plain and Fancy" (ELT), "You're a Good Man, Charlie Brown."

JOHNSON, PAGE. Born Aug. 25, 1930 in Welch, W.Va. Graduate Ithaca Col. Made Bdwy bow in 1951 in DeHavilland's "Romeo and Juliet," followed by "Electra," "Oedipus," "Camino Real," "In April Once" for which he received a THEATRE WORLD Award, "Red Roses For Me," "The Lovers," Off-Bdwy in "Military Taps," "The Enchanted," "Guitar," "4 In 1," "Journey of The Fifth Horse," "Yucca Trail," and "Ruby's Revenge," with APA in "School For Scandal," "The Tavern," and "The Seagull," "The Odd Couple," "The Boys In The Band."

JONES, DEAN. Born Jan. 25, 1930 in Decatur, Ala. Attended Ashburn Col., UCLA. Made Bdwy debut in 1960 in "There Was a Little Girl," followed by "Under the Yum-Yum Tree," "Company."

JONES, JAMES EARL. Born Jan. 17, 1931 in Arkabutla, Miss. Graduate Mich. U. Off-Bdwy credits: "The Pretender," "The Blacks," "Clandestine On The Morning Line," "The Apple," "A Midsummer Night's Dream," "Moon On A Rainbow Shawl" for which he received a THEATRE WORLD Award, "PS 193," "The Last Minstrel," "The Love Nest," "Bloodknot," "Othello," "Baal," "Danton's Death" (LCRep), on Bdwy in "The Egghead," "Sunrise At Campobello," "The Cool World," "A Hand Is On The Gate," "The Great White Hope."

Marilyn Joseph **Jimmy Justice** **Patti Karr** **James Karen** **Corinne Kason**

JONES, TOM LEE. Born Sept. 15, 1946 in San Saba, Tex. Harvard graduate. Made Bdwy debut in 1969 in "A Patriot for Me."

JONES, NEIL. Born May 6, 1942 in Boston. Attended Boston Cons. Has appeared in "The Music Man," "Hello, Dolly!," "Promises, Promises."

JORDAN, RICHARD. Born July 19, 1938 in NYC. Attended Harvard. Made Bdwy bow in 1961 in "Take Her, She's Mine," followed by "Bicycle Ride to Nevada," APA's "War and Peace" and "Judith," "Generation," "All's Well That Ends Well" (NYSF), "A Patriot for Me."

JOSEPH, MARILYN. Born Feb. 17, 1948 in London. Attended Neighborhood Playhouse. Made Bdwy debut in 1968 in "Cabaret," followed by "A Patriot for Me."

JOYCE, STEPHEN. Born Mar. 7, 1933 in NYC. Attended Fordham. Made Bdwy bow in 1966 in "Those That Play the Clowns," followed by "The Exercise," and off Bdwy roles in "Three Hand Reel," LCRep's "Galileo" and "St. Joan," "Stephen D" for which he received a THEATRE WORLD Award, "Fireworks."

JULIA, RAUL. Born Mar. 9, 1940 in San Juan, PR. Graduate UPR. Has appeared Off-Bdwy in "Macbeth" "Titus Andronicus" (CP), "Theatre In The Streets," "Life Is A Dream," "Blood Wedding," "The Ox Cart," "No Exit," "The Memorandum," "Frank Gagliano's City Scene," "Your Own Thing," "The Persians," and made Bdwy bow in 1968 in "The Cuban Thing," followed by "Indians."

JUSTICE, JIMMY. Born Dec. 31, 1941 in Erie, Pa. Juilliard graduate. Made Bdwy debut in 1969 in "Helly, Dolly!" followed by "Mahagonny" (OB).

KAHL, HOWARD. Born Sept. 17, 1930 in New Albany, Ind. Graduate Ind. U. Made Bdwy bow in 1962 in "Camelot," followed by "Hot Spot," "Fade Out — Fade In," "Pleasures and Palaces," "Anya," "On A Clear Day You Can See Forever," "Cabaret," "Applause."

KAHN, MADELINE. Born Sept. 29, 1942 in Boston. Graduate Hostra U. Made Bdwy debut in "New Faces of 1968," followed by "Promenade" (OB).

KAMINSKA, IDA. Born Sept. 4, 1899 in Odessa, Rus. Made Bdwy debut in 1967 in "Mirele Efros," followed by "Mother Courage," "The Trees Die Standing" (OB).

KAMLOT, ROBERT. Born Nov. 28, 1926 in Vienna. Attended Syracuse U., Hunter Col. Has been company or general manager for many productions, and appeared in "The Plough and The Stars," "Jimmy Shine."

KAPEN, BEN. Born July 2, 1928 in NYC. Graduate NYU. Has appeared Off-Bdwy in "No Trifling With Love," "Good News," and on Bdwy in "The Happy Time," "The Man In The Glass Booth," "The Penny Wars."

KAPLAN, JEANNE. Born in Brooklyn. Has appeard Off-Bdwy in "A View From The Bridge," "The Ox Cart," "The Electronic Nigger," and made Bdwy debut in 1968 in "The Cuban Thing."

KARATY, TOMMY. Born Mar. 25, 1940 in Paterson, NJ. Graduate Notre Dame, Catholic U. Made Bdwy bow in 1960 in "West Side Story," followed by "Cindy" (OB), "Pousse Cafe," "Mame."

KAREN, JAMES. Born Nov. 28, 1923 in Wilkes-Barre, Pa. Attended Neighborhood Playhouse. Made Bdwy bow in 1948 in "Streetcar Named Desire," followed by "An Enemy of the People," "Time of Storm" (OB), "Third Best Sport," "A Cook for Mr. General," "Who's Afraid of Virginia Woolf?," "Tiny Alice," "Cactus Flower," "Birthday Party," "Everything in the Garden." "Only Game in Town," "Engagement Baby."

KARIN, RITA. Born Oct. 24, 1919 in Warsaw, Poland. Made Bdwy debut in 1960 in "The Wall," followed by "A Call On Kuprin," "The Penny Wars, Off-Bdwy roles in "The Pocket Watch," "Scuba Duba."

KARR, PATTI. Born July 10 in St. Paul, Minn. Attended Tex. Christian U. Bdwy credits: "Maggie," "Carnival In Flanders," "Pipe Dream," "Bells Are Ringing," "New Girl In Town," "Body Beautiful," "Bye Bye Birdie," "New Faces of 1962," "Come On Strong," "Look to the Lilies," "Off-Bdwy in "A Month of Sundays," "Up Eden."

KASON, CORINNE. Born Mar. 10 in San Francisco. Attended San Jose State Col. Made NY debut Off-Bdwy in 1968 in "Futz" followed by "By Jupiter," "Unfair to Goliath," Bdwy bow in 1969 in "Fiddler on the Roof."

KAYE, ANNE. Born Sept. 6, 1942 in New Haven, Conn. Attended Emerson Col., AMDA. Has appeared Off-Bdwy in "Now Is The Time For All Good Men," "Have I Got One For You," "The Fantasticks," "Mahagonny."

KEACH, STACY. Born June 2, 1941 in Savannah, Ga. Graduate U. Cal, Yale, London Acad. Has appeared Off-Bdwy in "MacBird," "The Niggerlovers," "Henry IV" (CP), with LCRep in "The Country Wife," "King Lear," "Peer Gynt" (CP), Bdwy debut in "Indians" (1969).

KEEFE, ADAM. Born Jan. 8, 1931 in the Bronx. Appeared in clubs and tv before Off-Bdwy bow in 1970 in "Nature of the Crime."

KELTON, GENE. Born Oct. 21, 1938 in Flag Staff, Ariz. Has appeared in "Once Upon a Mattress," "Destry Rides Again," "Subways Are for Sleeping," "Here's Love," "Fade Out — Fade In," "Skyscraper," "Mame," "Dear World," "Applause."

KENDALL, RICHARD. Born Jan. 6, 1945 in Ottawa, Can. Made Bdwy debut with National Theatre of The Deaf.

KERCHEVAL, KEN. Born July 15, 1935 in Indiana. Attended Pacific U., Neighborhood Playhouse. Off-Bdwy credits: "Dead End," "Young Abe Lincoln," "Black Monday," "A Man's A Man," "23 Pat O'Brien Movies," "Father Uxbridge Wants To Marry," "Horseman, Pass By," "Who's Happy Now?," on Bdwy in "Something About A Soldier," "Fiddler On The Roof," "Happily Never After," "The Apple Tree," "Cabaret."

KERR, PHILIP. Born Apr. 9, 1940 in NYC. Attended Harvard, London AMDA. Made Bdwy bow in 1969 with ACT in "Tiny Alice," "A Flea in Her Ear," "The Three Sisters."

KERT, LARRY. Born Dec. 5, 1934 in Los Angeles. Attend LACC. Made NY bow in "John Murray Anderson's Almanac," followed by "Ziegfeld Follies," "Mr. Wonderful," "Walk Tall," "Look, Ma, I'm Dancin'," "Tickets, Please," "West Side Story," "A Family Affair," "Breakfast At Tiffany's," "Cabaret," "La Strada," "Company."

KEYES, DANIEL. Born Mar. 6, 1914 in Concord, Mass. Attended Harvard. Made Bdwy bow in 1954 in "The Remarkable Mr. Pennypacker," followed by "Bus Stop," "Only In America," "Christine," "First Love," "Take Her, She's Mine," "Baker Street," "Dinner At 8," "I Never Sang For My Father," "Wrong Way Light Bulb," "A Place For Polly," Off-Bdwy in "Our Town," "Epitaph For George Dillon," "Plays For Bleecker St.," "Hooray, It's A Glorious Day!," "Six Characters In Search of An Author," "Sjt. Musgrave's Dance," "Arms and The Man."

KEZER, GLENN. Born Apr. 2, 1923 In Okemah, Okla. Graduate U. Okla. Has appeared in "My Fair Lady," "Camelot," "Fade Out — Fade In," "Half A Sixpence," "Little Murders," "The Trial of Lee Harvey Oswald," "The Other Man," Off-Bdwy in "Walk In Darkness," "Brigadoon" (CC'64), "Oh, Say Can You See L.A.," "Firebugs," "The David Show," "Promenade."

KIDWELL, GENE. Born Oct. 14, 1946 in Lafayette, Ind. Attended Ind. U. Made NY debut in 1968 in "You're A Good Man, Charlie Brown."

KILLMER, NANCY. Born Dec. 16, 1936 in Homewood, Ill. Graduate Northwestern. Made Bdwy debut in 1969 in "Coco."

Carolyn Kirsch

Yaphet Kotto

Virginia Kiser

Bob Larkin

Jenny Laird

KIMBROUGH, CHARLES. Born May 23, 1936 in St. Paul, Minn. Graduate Ind. U., Yale. Appeared Off-Bdwy in "All In Love," "Struts and Frets," made Bdwy bow in 1969 in "Cop-Out," followed by "Company."

KING, DENNIS. Born Nov. 2, 1897 in Coventry, Eng. Made Bdwy debut in 1921 in "Claire de Lune," followed by "Romeo and Juliet," "Antony and Cleopatra," "Vagabond King," "Three Musketeers," "I Married an Angel," "A Doll's House," "Three Sisters," "Dunnigan's Daughter," "He Who Gets Slapped," "Medea," "Edward, My Son," "Devil's Disciple," "Billy Budd," "Music In The Air," "The Strong Are Lonely," "Lunatics and Lovers," "A Day by the Sea," "Affair of Honor," "Shangri-La," "Hidden River," "The Greatest Man Alive," "Love and Libel," "Photo Finish," "Minor Miracle," "Loves of Cass McGuire," "Portrait of a Queen," "A Patriot for Me."

KING, WOODIE, JR. Born July 27, 1937 in Detroit. Attended Wayne State U. Appeared Off-Bdwy in "Benito Cereno," "Displaced Person," "Day of Absence," "Who's Got His Own," "Study In Color," "Lost In The Stars," "The Perfect Party," on Bdwy in "The Great White Hope."

KIRKHAM, SAM. Born Apr. 28, 1923 in Gainesville, Tex. Attended U. Chicago, SMU. Made Bdwy bow in 1946 in "Cyrano de Bergerac," followed by "South Pacific," "Alive and Kicking," "That's the Ticket," "Stalag 17," "Marat/deSale," "Don't Drink the Water," "Oklahoma!" (LC).

KIRSCH, CAROLYN. Born May 24, 1942 in Shreveport, La. Attended Ballet Russe School. Made Bdwy debut in 1963 in "How to Succeed...," followed by "Folies Bergere," "La Grosse Valise," "Skyscraper," "Breakfast at Tiffany's," "Sweet Charity," "Hallelujah, Baby!," "Dear World," "Promises, Promises," "Coco."

KISER, TERRY. Born Aug. 1, 1939 in Omaha, Neb. Graduate U. Kan. Made NY bow in 1966 Off-Bdwy in "Night of The Dunce," followed by "Fortune and Men's Eyes" for which he received a THEATRE WORLD Award, "Horseman, Pass By," "Frank Gagliano's City Scene," "The Ofay Watcher," made Bdwy debut in 1970 in "Paris Is Out."

KLIBAN, KEN. Born July 26, 1942 in Norwalk, Conn. Attended Oberlin, U. Miami. Has appeared with APA in "Judith," "Man and Superman," and "War and Peace," in "Elizabeth the Queen" (CC), "And Puppy Dog Tails" (OB).

KLUNIS, TOM. Has appeared on Bdwy in "Gideon," "The Devils," "Henry V," Off-Bdwy in "The Immoralist," "Hamlet," "Arms and the Man," "Potting Shed," "Measure for Measure," "Romeo and Juliet," "The Balcony," "Our Town," "Man Who Never Died," "God Is My Ram," "Rise, Marlowe," "Iphigenia in Aulis."

KOBART, RUTH. Born Apr. 24, 1924 in Des Moines, Iowa. Graduate Chi. Cons., Hunter Col. Made Bdwy debut in 1955 in "Pipe Dream," followed by "Maria Golovin," "How to Succeed...," "A Funny Thing Happened...," "Oklahoma," (CC), with NYC opera, ACT's "A Flea in Her Ear" and "Three Sisters."

KOTTO, YAPHET. Born Nov. 15, 1937 in NYC. Made Bdwy bow in 1965 in "The Zulu and the Zayda" after other Bdwy roles in "Bloodknot," "In White America," "Black Monday," "Great Western Union," "Cyrano de Bergerac." Succeeded James Earl Jones in "The Great White Hope."

KRAMER, JOHN. Born July 9, 1938 in NYC. Attended Bucknell U. Made bow in 1966 Off-Bdwy in "The Kitchen," followed by "Viet Rock," "America Hurrah," on Bdwy in "Of Love Remembered," "Hadrian VII," "A Patriot for Me."

KRAMER, LLOYD. Born Nov. 25, 1947 in Lynn, Mass. Graduate Trinity Col. Made Bdwy debut in 1970 in "Child's Play."

KROSS, RONALD. Born Feb. 24, 1936 in Nanticoke, Pa. Graduate Wilkes Col., Penn. State. Made Bdwy debut in 1969 in "1776."

KUBIAK, THOMAS J. Born Dec. 29, 1936 in Lackawanna, NY. Attended Actors Studio. Made debut in 1969 off Bdwy in "End of All Things Natural."

KUHNER, JOHN. Born Dec. 27, 1942 in Cleveland, O. Graduate Denison U. Made NY debut in 1968 Off-Bdwy in "Your Own Thing," followed by "House of Leather."

KUPPERMAN, ALVIN. Born Oct. 14, 1945 in Brooklyn. Graduate Emerson Col. Appeared Off-Bdwy in "If We Grow Up," before Bdwy debut in 1970 in "Minnie's Boys."

KURTZ, SWOOSIE. Born Sept. 6, 1944 in Omaha, Nebr. Attended USCal. London Academy. Made NY debut Off-Bdwy in 1968 in "The Firebugs," followed by "The Effect of Gamma Rays on Man-in-the-Moon Marigolds."

KUSSACK, ELAINE. Born Dec. 30 in Brooklyn. Graduate Hunter Col., Columbia. Made Bdwy debut in 1969 in "Fiddler on the Roof."

LACY, JERRY. Born Mar. 27, 1936 in Sioux City, Iowa. Attended LACC. Appeared Off-Bdwy in "Desire Under The Elms" ('63) before Bdwy bow in "Play It Again, Sam."

LACY, TOM. Born Aug. 30, 1933 in NYC. Has appeared Off-Bdwy in "The Fourth Pig," "The Fantasticks," "Shoemaker's Holiday," "Love and Let Love," "The Millionairess," "Crimes of Passion."

LADD, MARGARET. Born Nov. 8, 1942 in Providence, RI. Graduate Bard Col. Off-Bdwy roles in "The Knack" and "Free, Free, Free" before Bdwy debut in 1966 in "The Great Indoors," followed by "The Experiment" (OB), "Sheep on the Runway."

LAGIOIA, JOHN P. Born Nov. 24, 1937 in Philadelphia. Graduate Temple U. Appeared Off-Bdwy in "Keyhole," "Lovers in the Metro," "The Cherry Orchard," "Titus Andronicus" (NYSF), made Bdwy bow in 1969 in "Henry V."

LAIRD, JENNY. Born Feb. 13, 1917 in Manchester, Eng. Graduate U. College, London. Made Bdwy debut in 1970 in "The Cherry Orchard" with John Fernald's Co.

LaMOTTA, JOHNNY. Born Jan. 8, 1939 in Brooklyn. Has appeared in "Dead Survivors" (OB), "Illya Darling," "I'm Solomon," "Zorba."

LAMPERT, ZOHRA. Born May 13, 1936 in NYC. Attended Chicago U. Off-Bdwy credits: "Venus Observed," "Diary of A Scoundrel," with LCRep in "After The Fall" and "Marco Millions," on Bdwy in "Major Barbara," "Maybe Tuesday," "Look, We've Come Through," "First Love," "Mother Courage," "Nathan Weinstein, Mystic Conn.," "Lovers and Other Strangers."

LANCASTER, LUCIE. Born Oct. 15, 1907 in Chicago. Made Bdwy debut in 1947 in "Heads or Tails," followed by "Mr. Pickwick," "Girl Who Came to Supper," "Bajour," "How Now, Dow Jones," "Little Boxes" (OB).

LANCHESTER, ROBERT. Born Aug. 2, 1941 in Boston. Graduate MIT, UC Berkeley. Made Bdwy debut in 1969 with ACT in "A Flea in Her Ear" and "Three Sisters."

LAND, ROBERT E. Born Aug. 9, 1948 in Winnipeg, Can. Made NY debut in 1970 Off-Bdwy in ELT's "Me and Juliet."

LANGELLA, FRANK. Graduate of Syracuse U. Has appeared Off-Bdwy in "The Immoralist," "Good Day," "The Old Glory," "The White Devil," "A Cry of Players" (LCRep).

LANSBURY, ANGELA. Born Oct. 16, 1925 in London. Made Bdwy debut in 1957 in "Hotel Paradiso," followed by "A Taste of Honey," "Anyone Can Whistle," "Mame," "Dear World."

LARKIN, BOB. Born Mar. 9, 1929 in Cleveland, O. Graduate NYU. Appeared Off-Bdwy in "Squaring the Circle," "Way of the World," "The Shy and the Lonely," "The Day the Lid Blew Off," "The Pocket Watch," Bdwy debut in 1969 in "The Front Page," followed by "Great White Hope."

| Jerry Laws | Laryssa Lauret | Peter Lazer | Barbara Lester | Henry LeClair |

LARSEN, WILLIAM. Born Nov. 20, 1927 in Lake Charles, La. Attended U. Tex. Appeared Off-Bdwy in "The Crucible," "The Fantasticks," "Legend of Lovers," "Twelfth Night," "Troilus and Cressida," with APA in "The Tavern," "Lower Depths," and "School For Scandal," on Bdwy in "Ballad of The Sad Cafe," "Half A Sixpence," "Funny Girl," "Halfway Up The Tree," "There's A Girl In My Soup," "Dear World."

LATHAM, CYNTHIA. Born Apr. 21, 1897 in London. Made Bdwy debut in 1914 in "The Eldest Son," followed by, among others, "The Living Room," "Ring Round the Moon," "The Heiress," "Country Wife," "Matchmaker," "Write Me A Murder," "Photo Finish," "Redhead," "Georgy."

LAUDICINA, DINO. Born Dec. 22, 1939 in Brooklyn. Made Bdwy bow in 1960 in "Christine," followed by "King of the Dark Chamber" (OB), "Rosencrantz and Guildenstern Are Dead," "Indians."

LAUGHLIN, SHARON. Graduate U. Wash. Made Bdwy debut in 1964 in "One by One," appeared Off-Bdwy in "Henry IV" (NYSF), "Huui, Huui," "Mod Donna."

LAURENCE, PAULA. Born Jan. 25 in Brooklyn. Made Bdwy debut in 1936 in "Horse Eats Hat," followed by "Dr. Faustus," "Junior Miss," "Something for the Boys," "One Touch of Venus," "Cyrano de Bergerac," "The Liar," "Season in the Sun," "Tovarich," "The Time of Your Life," "Beggar's Opera," "Hotel Paradiso," "Night of the Iguana," "Have I Got A Girl for You," "Ivanov," "7 Days of Mourning" (OB).

LAURET, LARYSSA. Born Aug. 9, 1939 in Poland. Graduate Hunter, Columbia. Made Bdwy debut in 1961 in "Julia, Jake and Uncle Joe," followed by "Night of the Iguana," "Paris Is Out," Off-Bdwy in "One-Eyed Man Is King," "Don Juan," "Minna von Barhelm," "Noble Woman," "The Chair," "Ashes of April," "Royal Gambit."

LAVIN, LINDA. Born Oct. 15, 1939 in Portland, Me. Graduate William & Mary Col. Made Bdwy bow in 1962 in "A Family Affair," followed by "The Riot Act," "Wet Paint" (OB) for which she received a THEATRE WORLD Award, "The Game Is Up," "Hotel Passionato," "The Mad Show" (OB), "It's Superman!," "On A Clear Day You Can See Forever," "Something Different," "Little Murders" (OB), "Cop-Out," "Last of the Red Hot Lovers."

LAWLESS, SUE. Born Sept. 26 in Freeport, Ill. Graduate DePaul U. Made NY debut in 1961 Off-Bdwy in "The Sudden End of Anne Cinquefoil," followed by "Shoemaker's Holiday," "In The Nick of Time," "Don't Shoot, Mable, It's Your Husband," "Now."

LAWS, JERRY. Born Mar. 25, 1912 in New Haven, Conn. Has appeared in "Blackbirds of 1939," "Porgy and Bess," "St. Louis Woman," "Finian's Rainbow," "Along Came A Spider" (OB), "The Great White Hope."

LAWSON, ROGER. Born Oct. 11, 1942 in Tarrytown, NY. Attended Fredonia Col. Made Bdwy debut in 1967 in "Hello, Dolly!," Off-Bdwy in "Pins and Needles," "Billy Noname."

LAZER, PETER. Born Apr. 12, 1946 in NYC. Attended NYU. Made Bdwy debut in 1957 in "Hide and Seek," followed by "Miss Isobel," "Watercolor," "Criss-Crossing."

LeCLAIR, HENRY. Born July 27 in Cranston, RI. Has appeared in "Flora, The Red Menace," "A Time For Singing," "Wonderful Town" (CC'67), "1776."

LEE, VALERIE. Born in NYC. Made Bdwy debut in 1959 in "Sound of Music" followed by "Here's Love," "The Glorious Ruler" (OB).

LEEDS, PHIL. Born in NYC. Made Bdwy bow in 1942 in "Of V We Sing," followed by "Make A Wish," "Let Freedom Ring," "Can-Can," "Romanoff and Juliet," "Girls Against the Boys," "Christine," "Banker's Daughter" (OB), "Nowhere to Go But Up," "Sophie," "Nobody Loves an Albatross," "Dinner at 8," "Little Murders," "Inquest."

LEIBMAN, RON. Born Oct. 11, 1937 in NYC. Attended Ohio Wesleyan, Actors Studio. Appeared Off-Bdwy in "The Academy," "John Brown's Body," "Scapin," "Legend of Lovers," "Dead End," "The Poker Session," "The Premise," "Transfers," "Room Service," made Bdwy bow in 1963 in "Dear Me, The Sky Is Falling," followed by "Bicycle Ride To Nevada," "The Deputy," "We Bombed in New Haven" for which he received a THEATRE WORLD Award, "Cop-out."

LeMASSENA, WILLIAM. Born May 23, 1916 in Glen Ridge, NJ. Attended NYU. Made Bdwy bow in 1940 in "Taming Of The Shrew," followed by "There shall Be No Night," "The Pirate," "Hamlet," "Call Me Mister," "Inside U.S.A.," "I Know, My Love," "Dream Girl," "Nina," "Ondine," "Fallen Angels," "Redhead," "The Conquering Hero," "The Beauty Part," "The Coop" (OB), "Brigadoon" (CC), "Life With Father" (CC), "Come Summer," "Grin and Bare It."

LENS, PATRICIA. Born May 3, 1947 in Philadelphia. Attended Northwestern U. Made Bdwy debut in 1969 in "Celebration," followed by "Man of LaMancha."

LENZ, RICK. Born Nov. 21, 1939 in Springfield, Ill. Graduate U. Mich. Made Bdwy bow in 1965 in "Mating Dance," followed by "The Infantry" (OB), "Cactus Flower," "Calling in Crazy" (OB).

LEONARDOS, URYLEE. Born May 14 in Charleston, SC. Attended Manhattan School of Music, Chicago Conserv. Has appeared in "Carmen Jones," "Shangri-La," "Bells Are Ringing," "Wildcat," "Sophie," "Milk and Honey," "110 In The Shade," "Bajour," "Illya Darling," "Dear World," "Billy Noname" (OB).

LeROY, KEN. Born Aug. 17, 1927 in Detroit. Attended Neighborhood Playhouse. Appeared in "The American Way," "Morning Star," "Anne of England," "Oklahoma!," "Carousel," "Brigadoon," "Call Me Madam," "Pajama Game," "West Side Story," "Fiddler On The Roof."

LESTER, BARBARA. Born Dec. 27, 1928 in London. Graduate Columbia U. Made Bdwy debut in 1956 in "Protective Custody," followed by "Legend of Lizzie," "Luther," "Inadmissable Evidence," "Johnny No-Trump," "Grin and Bare It," Off-Bdwy in "Electra," "Queen after Death," "Summer of the 17th Doll," "Richard II" and "Much Ado About Nothing" (NYSF), "One Way Pendulum."

LeSTRANGE, PHILIP. Born May 9, 1942 in the Bronx. Graduate Catholic U., Fordham. Made NY debut in 1970 Off-Bdwy in "Getting Married."

LEVENE, SAM. Born Aug. 28, 1905 in NYC. Graduate AADA. Made Bdwy bow in 1927 in "Wall Street," followed by "3 Men on a Horse," "Dinner at 8," "Room Service," "Margin for Error," "Sound of Hunting," "Light Up the Sky," "Guys and Dolls," "Hot Corner," "Fair Game," "Make A Million," "Heartbreak House," "Good Soup," "Devil's Advocate," "Let It Ride," "Seidman & Son," "Cafe Crown," "Last Analysis," "Nathan Weinstein, Mystic, Conn.," "The Impossible Years," "3 Men on a Horse" ('69), "Paris Is Out."

LEVIN, MICHAEL. Born Dec. 8, 1932 in Minneapolis. Graduate U. Minn. Made Bdwy debut in 1965 in "Royal Hunt of the Sun," followed by "End of All Things Natural" (OB), LC's "Camino Real" and "Operation Sidewinder."

LEWIS, GILBERT. Born Apr. 6, 1941 in Philadelphia. Attended Morgan State Col. Appeared off Bdwy in "Who's Got His Own," "Transfers," made Bdwy bow in 1969 in "The Great White Hope."

LEWIS, MARCIA. Born Aug. 18, 1938 in Melrose, Mass. Attended U. Cincinnati. Has appeared Off-Bdwy in "The Impudent Wolf," "Who's Who, Baby?," "The Time of Your Life" (LC), Bdwy debut in "Hello, Dolly."

LEYDEN, LEO. Born Jan. 28, 1929 in Dublin, Ire. Attended Abbey Theatre School. Made Bdwy debut in 1960 in "Love and Libel," followed by "Darling of the Day," "The Mundy Scheme."

Jillian Lindig   **Clifford Lipson**   **Dorothy Lyman**   **Luis Lopez-Cepero**   **Janice Ly**

LICHTERMAN, MARVIN. Born May 12, 1938 in Brooklyn. Graduate Bklyn. Col., Yale. Appeared Off-Bdwy in "Anthology of Love," "Saturday Night," "Adaptation," on Bdwy in "Happiness Is Just A Little Thing Called A Rolls Royce," "Lovers and Other Strangers," "Dr. Fish."

LIGON, TOM. Born Sept. 10, 1945 in New Orleans. Yale graduate. Made NY debut Off-Bdwy in 1968 in "Your Own Thing," followed by Bdwy roles in "Angela," "Love Is A Time of Day."

LINDER, CEC. Born Mar. 10, 1921 in Radziechow, Poland. Attended Acad. of Radio Arts, Toronto. Made NY debut in 1969 with LCRep in "In The Matter of J. Robert Oppenheimer."

LINDIG, JILLIAN. Born Mar. 19, 1944 in Johnson City, Tex. Graduate U. Tex. Made NY debut Off-Bdwy in 1969 in "The Brownstone Urge."

LINDSAY, KEVIN-JOHN. Born Sept. 7, 1957 in NYC. Made debut in 1970 Off-Bdwy in "The Me Nobody Knows."

LINDSAY, PHILIP. Born July 31, 1924 in Cairo, Ill. Attended U. Chicago, Goodman Th. School. Has appeared Off-Bdwy in "Clandestine On The Morning Line," "Orpheus Descending," "3 By Wilder," "Mamba's Daughter," "The Blacks," on Bdwy in "Member of The Wedding," "The Great White Hope."

LINN, MARGARET. Born Aug. 21, 1934 in Richmond, Ind. Attended Northwestern U., Denver U. Off-Bdwy credits: "Pale Horse, Pale Rider," "The Room," "Billy Liar," "Huui, Huui," "The Disintegration of James Cherry" (LC), on Bdwy in "How's The World Treating You?," "Halfway Up The Tree."

LiPARI, MARJORIE. Born June 1, 1945 in Brooklyn. Made Bdwy debut in 1968 in "Hair."

LIPSON, CLIFFORD. Born Feb. 10, 1947 in Providence, RI. Attended Neighborhood Playhouse, AMDA. Off-Bdwy credits: "Great Scot!," "Hooray, It's A Glorious Day," "The Indian Wants the Bronx," "Salvation," made Bdwy bow in 1970 in "Hair."

LIPSON, PAUL. Born Dec. 23, 1913 in Brooklyn. Attended Ohio State, American Theatre Wing. Made Bdwy bow in 1942 in "Lily of the Valley," followed by "Heads or Tails," "Dectective Story," "Remains to Be Seen," "Carnival in Flanders," "I've Got Sixpence," "The Vamp," "Bells Are Ringing," "Fiorello" (CC), "Sound of Music," "Fiddler on the Roof."

LIPTON, MICHAEL. Born Apr. 27, 1925 in NYC. Attended Queens Col. Appeared in "Caesar and Cleopatra," "The Moon Is Blue," "Sing Me No Lullaby," "Wake Up, Darling," "The Tenth Man," "Separate Tables," "Inquest," Off-Bdwy in "The Lover," "Trigon," "Long Christmas Dinner," "Hamp," "The Boys In The Band."

LISA, LUBA. Born in Brooklyn. Attended Am. Th. Wing. Made Bdwy debut in 1961 in "Carnival," followed by "I Can Get It for You Wholesale," "West Side Story" (CC), "I Had a Ball" for which she received a THEATRE WORLD Award, "Your Own Thing" (OB).

LITTLE, CLEAVON. Born June 1, 1939 in Chickasha, Okla. Attended San Diego State U, AADA. Made NY bow Off-Bdwy in 1967 in "MacBird," followed by "Hamlet" (NYSF), "Someone's Coming Hungry," "The Ofay Watcher," "Scuba Duba," Bdwy debut in 1968 in "Jimmy Shine" followed by "Purlie."

LoBIANCO, TONY. Born Oct. 19, 1936 in NYC. Appeared in "Threepenny Opera," "Answered The Flute," "Camino Real," "Oh, Dad, Poor Dad...," "Journey To The Day," "Zoo Story," "Nature of the Crime," with LCRep in "Incident At Vichy," "Tartuffe," on Bdwy in "The Office," "Royal Hunt of The Sun," "Rose Tattoo," "90 Day Mistress," "The Goodbye People."

LOGGIA, ROBERT. Born Jan. 3, 1930 in Staten Island, NY. Attended U.Mo., Actors Studio. Has appeared Off-Bdwy in "The Man With The Golden Arm," "The Three Sisters," "World War 2 1/2", "Passing Through from Exotic Places."

LOMBARD, MICHAEL. Born Aug. 8, 1934 in Brooklyn. Graduate Bklyn Col. Appeared off Bdwy in "King Lear," "Merchant of Venice," "Cages," "Pinter Plays," "La Turista," "Elizabeth the Queen" (CC), "Room Service," on Bdwy in "Poor Bitos."

LONG, TAMARA. Born Nov. 7, 1941 in Oklahoma City. Graduate Okla. U. Made NY debut in 1968 Off-Bdwy in "Dames At Sea."

LONGO, PEGGY. Born Oct. 1, 1943 in Brooklyn. Graduate Ithaca Col. Appeared with NYC Opera before Bdwy debut in 1967 in "Fiddler on the Roof."

LOPEZ-CEPERO, LUIS. Born Dec. 5 in Fairfield, Conn. Attended Emerson, Tufts, Harvard. Made Bdwy debut in 1969 in "Dear World," followed by "A Patriot for Me."

LOWRY, JUDITH. Born July 1890 in Morristown, NJ. Made Bdwy debut in 1915 in "Romeo and Juliet," followed by many productions. Currently in "The Effect of Gamma Rays on Man-in-the-Moon Marigolds."

LORRING, JOAN. Born Apr. 17, 1931 in Hong Kong. Made Bdwy debut in 1950 in "Come Back, Little Sheba," followed by "Autumn Garden," "Dead Pigeon," "A Clearing in the Woods," "Awake and Sing" (OB).

LUCKINBILL, LAURENCE. Born Nov. 21, 1938 in Ft. Smith, Ark. Graduate U.Ark., Catholic U. Made Bdwy bow in "A Man For All Seasons," followed by "Beekman Place," Off-Bdwy roles in "Oedipus Rex," "There Is A Play Tonight," "The Fantasticks," "Tartuffe," "The Boys In The Band," "Horseman, Pass By," "Memory Bank," "What the Butler Saw."

LUDWIG, SALEM. Born July 31, 1915 in Brooklyn. Attended Bklyn Col. Off-Bdwy roles in "The Brothers Karamazov," "The Victim," "The Troublemaker," "Man of Destiny," "Night of The Dunce," "A Corner of The Bed," "Awake and Sing," on Bdwy in "Miracle In The Mountains," "Camino Real," "An Enemy of The People," "All You Need Is One Good Break," "Inherit The Wind," "The Disenchanted," "Rhinoceros," "The Three Sisters," "The Zulu and The Zayda."

LYDIARD, BOB. Born Apr. 28, 1944 in Glen Ridge, NJ. Attended Atlantic U., Wayne State U. Made NY bow in 1968 Off-Bdwy in "You're A Good Man, Charlie Brown," followed by "A Round with Ring."

LYMAN, DOROTHY. Born Apr. 18, 1947 in Minneapolis. Attended Sarah Lawrence Col. Made NY debut Off-Bdwy in "America Hurrah," followed by "Pequod." "The American Hamburger League."

LYNDE, JANICE. Born Mar. 28, 1947 in Houston, Tex. Attended U. Ind. Made NY debut in 1969 Off-Bdwy in "3 One-Act Plays by Richard Lenz," followed by "Sambo."

LYNDECK, EDMUND. Born Oct. 4, 1925 in Baton Rouge, La. Graduate Montclair State Col., Fordham U. Made Bdwy debut in 1969 in "1776."

MacCAULEY, MARK. Born Dec. 11, 1948 in NYC. Attended Ind. U. Made bow Off-Bdwy in 1969 in "Crimes of Passion."

MacGREGOR, BARRY. Born Sept. 10, 1936 in Strathpeyfr, Scot. Attended Foster Drama Col., London. Made Bdwy debut in 1964 with Royal Shakespeare Co., followed by "Don't Shoot, Mable, It's Your Husband" (OB), with ACT in "A Flea in Her Ear."

MacKAY, JOHN. Has appeared on Bdwy in "Under the Yum-Yum Tree," "A Gift of Time," "A Man for All Seasons," "The Lovers," "Borstal Boy."

h Mackey   **Helen Martin**   **Donald Mark**   **Avis McCarther**   **Alec McCowen**

MACKENZIE, WILL. Born July 24, 1938 in Providence, RI. Graduate Brown U. Off-Bdwy credits include "Wonderful Town," "Put It In Writing," "Morning Sun," "Brigadoon," (CC), on Bdwy in "Half A Sixpence," "Hello, Dolly!," "Sheep on the Runway."

MACKEY, KEITH. Born Nov. 6, 1918 in Columbus, O. Graduate OSU. Made Bdwy debut in 1970 in Celeste Holm's "Candida."

MacLEAN, PETER. Born Jan. 2, 1936 in Dorchester, Mass. Graduate Emerson Col. Made Bdwy bow in 1969 in "Fire!," followed by "Indians," "Child's Play."

MACY, WILLIAM. Born May 18, 1922 in Revere, Mass. Graduate NYU. Made Bdwy bow in 1959 in "Once More With Feeling," followed by Off-Bdwy roles in "Threepenny Opera," "Machinal," "The Balcony," "America Hurrah," "Cannibals," "The Guns of Carrar," "Oh, Calcutta," "Awake and Sing."

MAGGART, BRANDON. Born Dec. 12, 1933 in Carthage, Tenn. Graduate U. Tenn. Appeared Off-Bdwy in "Sing, Muse!," "Like Other People," "Put It In Writing" for which he received a THEATRE WORLD Award, made Bdwy debut in 1965 in "Kelly," followed by "New Faces of 1968," "Applause."

MAHER, JOSEPH. Born Dec. 29, 1933 in Westport, Ire. Made Bdwy bow in 1964 in "Chinese Prime Minister," followed by "The Prime of Miss Jean Brodie," "Henry V," Off-Bdwy in "The Hostage," "Live Like Pigs," "The Importance of Being Earnest," "Eh?," "The Local Stigmatic."

MAISELL, JOE. Born Oct. 27, 1939 in Brooklyn. Appeared Off-Bdwy in "Cindy," "Jacques Brel Is Alive…," made Bdwy debut in 1969 in "Dear World."

MANDAN, ROBERT. Born Feb. 2, 1932 in Clever, Mo. Attended Pomona Col. Has appeared in "Debut," "Speaking of Murder," "No Exit" (OB), "Maggie Flynn," "But Seriously," "Applause."

MANSON, ALAN. Born in NYC. Made Bdwy bow in 1940 in "Journey to Jerusalem," followed by "This Is The Army," "Call Me Mister," "Southern Exposure," "Angels Kiss Me," "The Ponder Heart," "Maybe Tuesday," "Tenth Man," "Gideon," "Nobody Loves an Albatross," "Funny Girl," "A Place for Polly," Off-Bdwy in "Dr. Jekyll and Mr. Hyde," "A Midsummer Night's Dream," "Oh Say Can You See L.A.?," "The Other Man."

MARCH, KENDALL. Born in Boston. Graduate Sarah Lawrence Col. Has appeared Off-Bdwy in "The Ballad of John Ogilvie," "The Autograph Hound," made Bdwy debut in 1969 in "The Front Page."

MARCHAND, NANCY. Born June 19, 1928 in Buffalo, NY. Graduate Carnegie Tech. Made NY debut in "The Taming of The Shrew" (CC), followed by "Merchant of Venice," "Much Ado About Nothing," "The Balcony" (OB), with APA in repertory, "Three Bags Full," "After The Rain," LCRep's "The Alchemist," "Yerma," and "Cyrano," "Forty Carats."

MARIANO, PATTI. Born June 12, 1945 in Philadelphia. Made Bdwy debut in 1957 in "The Music Man," followed by "Bye Bye Birdie," "Sail Away," "I Had A Ball," "Country Girl" (OB), "George M!," "Me and Juliet" (ELT).

MARK, DONALD. Born Oct. 14, 1944 in NYC. Attended CCNY. Has appeared in CC's "Most Happy Fella," and "My Fair Lady," "Show Boat" (LC), "Me and Juliet" (ELT).

MARKLIN, PETER. Born Dec. 22, 1939 in Buffalo, NY. Graduate Northwestern U. Has appeared in "The Brig" (OB), "Fiddler on the Roof."

MARR, RICHARD. Born May 12, 1928 in Baltimore, Md. Graduate U. Pa. Bdwy credits "Baker Street," "How To Succeed…" (cc'66), "Here's Where I Belong," "Coco," Off-Bdwy in "Sappho," "Pilgrim's Progress," "Pimpernel," "Witness."

MARSHALL, SID. Born July 15, 1941 in Mt. Pleasant, NY. Attended Dramatic Workshop. Appeared Off-Bdwy in "Bachelor Toys," "Sambo."

MARTIN, HELEN. Born in St. Louis. Attended Paul Mann Workshop. Made Bdwy debut in 1941 in "Native Son," followed by "Take a Giant Step," "The Long Dream," "Deep Are the Roots," "Amen Corner," "Period of Adjustment," "Purlie Victorious," "My Mother, My Father and Me," "Purlie," Off-Bdwy in "Major Barbara," "Juno and the Paycock," "A Land Beyond the River," "Ballad of Jazz Street," "The Blacks," "Stevedore," "The Cat and the Canary."

MARUNAS, P. RAYMOND. Born Mar. 5, 1939 in Lithuania. Graduate U. Conn. Made NY debut in 1966 Off Bdwy in "The Kitchen," followed by "Deer Park," "The Visit" (ELT), "The Glorious Ruler."

MASCOLO, JOSEPH. Born Mar. 13, 1935 in Hartford, Conn. Has appeared in "Night Life," "A View from the Bridge," NY Shakespeare Festival, "Dinner at 8," "To Clothe the Naked" (OB), LCRep's "The Time of Your Life" and "Camino Real."

MASSI, BERNICE. Born Aug. 23 in Camden, NJ. Made Bdwy debut in 1952 in "South Pacific," followed by "Wish You Were," "By The Beautiful Sea," "Can-Can," "The Vamp," "Two For The Seesaw," "Beg, Borrow or Steal," "No Strings," "What Makes Sammy Run?," "Man of La Mancha."

MASTERSON, PETER. Born June 1, 1936 in Houston, Tex. Graduate Rice U. Made NY debut in 1961 in "Call Me By My Rightful Name" (OB), followed by "Marathon '33," "Blues For Mr. Charlie," "The Trial of Lee Harvey Oswald," "The Great White Hope."

MATHEWS, GEORGE. Born Oct. 10, 1911 in NYC. Made Bdwy bow in 1937 in "Professional," followed by "Life of Reilly," "Cuckoos On The Hearth," "Eve of St. Mark," "Kiss Them For Me," "Antigone," "Temper The Wind," "Silver Whistle," "Streetcar Named Desire," "Barefoot In Athens," "Desperate Hours," "Holiday For Lovers," "Shadow of A Gunman," "Triple Play," "Luther," "Catch Me If You Can," "A Time For Singing," "A Joyful Noise," "The Great White Hope."

MATTHAEI, KONRAD. Born in Detroit. Graduate Yale, U. Mich. Made NY bow in 1961 Off-Bdwy in "She Stoops To Conquer," followed by other OB roles in "Thracian Horses," "Trelawney of The Wells," "King of The Dark Chamber," "Don Carlos," "A Man's A Man," "Riverwind," "The Boys In The Band," on Bdwy in "13 Daughters," "Luther," "The Milk Train Doesn't Stop Here Anymore" ('66), "A Place for Polly."

MATTHEWS, ART. Born in NYC. Made debut Off-Bdwy with American Savoyards, followed by "Leave It To Jane" (OB), "Mame."

McCARTHER, AVIS. Born May 6, 1947 in NC. Attended New School. Appeared Off-Bdwy in "A Roof Over Your Head," "The Pig Pen," made Bdwy debut in 1969 in "The Penny Wars."

McCLANAHAN, RUE. Born Feb. 21 in Healdton, Okla. Has appeared Off-Bdwy in "The Secret Life of Walter Mitty," "The Big Man," "MacBird," "Tonight in Living Color," "Who's Happy Now?," "Dark of the Moon," and on Bdwy in "The Best Laid Plans," "Jimmy Shine."

McCONNELL, TY. Born Jan. 13, 1940 in Coldwater, Mich. Graduate U. Mich. Made NY bow in 1962 Off-Bdwy in "The Fantasticks," followed by "Promenade," on Bdwy in "The Lion In Winter," "Dear World."

McCOWEN, ALEC. Born May 26 in Tunbridge Wells, Eng. Attended RADA. Made NY debut in 1952 in "Antony and Cleopatra" and "Caesar and Cleopatra," followed by "King Lear" and "Comedy of Errors" at LC in 1964, "After The Rain," "Hadrian VII."

251

Stephen McHattie   **DeAnn Mears**   **Robert McLane**   **Lynn Milgrim**   **John Mer**

McGIVER, JOHN. Born Nov. 5, 1913 in NYC. Attended Fordham, Columbia, Catholic U. Made Bdwy bow in 1956 in "Little Glass Clock," followed by "Cloud 7," "Drink To Me Only," "God and Kate Murphy," "A Thurber Carnival," "A Cook For Mr. General," "Happiness Is Just A Little Thing Called A Rolls Royce," "A Way of Life," "The Front Page" ('69).

McGRATH, PAUL. Born Apr. 11, 1904 in Chicago. Attended Carnegie Tech. Made Bdwy bow in 1920 in "The First Year," followed by "Ned McCobb's Daughter," "John Ferguson," "Green Bay Tree," "Ode to Liberty," "Susan and God," "Lady in the Dark," "Tomorrow the World," "Common Ground," "Command Decision," "The Big Knife," "Small Hours," "Love and Let Love," "Touchstone," "A Girl Can Tell," "A Case of Libel," "The Child Buyer"(OB), "Brightower."

McGUIRE, BIFF. Born Oct. 25, 1926 in New Haven, Conn. Attended Mass. State Col. Has appeared in "Make Mine Manhattan," "South Pacific," "Dance Me A Song," "The Time of Your Life"(CC&LC), "A View from the Bridge," "Greatest Man Alive," "The Egghead," "Triple Play," "Happy Town," "Beg, Borrow or Steal," "Finian's Rainbow" (CC), "Beggar on Horseback"(LC).

McGUIRE, MITCHELL. Born Dec. 26, 1936 in Chicago. Attended Goodman Th. School, Santa Monica City Col. Appeared Off-Bdwy in "The Rapists," "Go, Go, Go, God Is Dead," "Waiting For Lefty," "The Bond," "The Guns of Carrar," "Cannibals," "Oh, Calcutta."

McHATTIE, STEPHEN (formerly Stephen Smith). Born Feb. 3 in Antigonish, Nova Scotia. Graduate Acadia U. AADA. Appeared with NY Shakespeare Festival in "Henry IV," on Bdwy in "The American Dream"('68), "The Persians" (OB).

McINTIRE, JANET. Born July 14, 1945 in Manchester, NH. Attended RADA. Made Bdwy debut in 1970 with John Fernald Co. in "The Cherry Orchard."

McKAY, TONY. Born on Cat Island, Bahamas. Made NY debut in 1962 Off-Bdwy in "Moon on a Rainbow Shawl," followed by "The Brighter Shading," "Man Better Man."

McKECHNIE, DONNA. Born in Nov. 1944 in Detroit. Made Bdwy debut in "How To Succeed...," followed by "Promises, Promises," "Company."

McKENZIE, RICHARD. Born June 2, 1930 in Chattanooga, Tenn. Attended U Mo., U Tenn., RADA. Made Bdwy debut in 1969 in "Indians," appeared Off-Bdwy in "Whistle in the Dark," "Nobody Hears a Broken Drum."

McLANE, ROBERT. Born Aug. 4, 1944 in Macon, Ga. Attended AMDA. Appeared Off-Bdwy in "Antigone," "Madonna in the Orchard," made Bdwy debut in 1969 in "Indians."

McNAMARA, DERMOT. Born Aug. 24, 1925 in Dublin, Ire. Made Bdwy bow in 1959 in "A Touch of the Poet," followed by "Philadelphia, Here I Come," Off-Bdwy in "The Wise Have Not Spoken," "3 by Synge," "Playboy of the Western World," "Shadow and Substance," "Happy as Larry," "Sharon's Grave," "A Whistle in the Dark."

McMILLAN, KENNETH. Born July 2, 1934 in Brooklyn. Attended HB Studio. Off-Bdwy in "Red Eye of Love," "King of the Whole Damn World," "Little Mary Sunshine," "Babes in the Wood," made Bdwy bow in 1970 in "Borstal Boy."

McNEIL, CLAUDIA. Born Aug. 13, 1917 in Baltimore. Made Bdwy debut in 1952 in "The Crucible," followed by "Simply Heavenly," "A Raisin In The Sun," "Tiger Tiger Burning Bright," "Something Different," "Her First Roman," "Wrong Way Light Bulb," "Contributions"(OB).

McQUEEN, BUTTERFLY. Born Jan. 8, 1911 in Tampa, Fla. Attended CCLA, UCLA. Made Bdwy debut in 1937 in "Brother Rat," followed by "What A Life," "Swingin' the Dream," "3 Men On A Horse," "Front Page," Off-Bdwy in "School for Wives," "Athenian Touch," "Curley McDimple."

McVEY, PATRICK. Born Mar. 17, 1913 in Ft. Wayne, Ind. Graduate Ind. Law School, Pasadena Playhouse. Has appeared in "State of The Union," "Detective Story," "Hold It," "Bus Stop," "Catch Me If You Can," "On Vacation"(OB), "The Transgressor Rides Again"(OB), LC Rep's "Camino Real" and "The Time of Your Life."

MEADE, JULIA. Born Dec. 17, 1928 in Boston. Attended Yale Drama School. Made Bdwy debut in 1954 in "The Tender Trap," followed by "Double In Hearts," "Roman Candle," "Mary, Mary," "The Front Page"('69).

MEARS, DeANN. Born in Ft. Fairfield, Me. Attended Westbrook Col. Made NY debut in 1961 Off-Bdwy in "The Decameron," followed by "Ernest in Love," "A Sound of Silence," Bdwy bow in 1963 in "Too True to Be Good," and with ACT in "Tiny Alice."

MENKEN, FAYE. Born Feb. 19, 1947 in NYC. Graduate NYU. Made Bdwy debut in 1969 in "Fiddler On The Roof."

MERANDE, DORO. Born in Columbia, Kan. Made Bdwy debut in 1935 in "Loose Moments," followed by "One Good Year," "Fulton of Oak Falls," "Red Harvest," "Angel Island," "Our Town," "Love's Old Sweet Song," "Beverly Hills," "The More The Merrier," "Junior Miss," "Hope For A Harvest," "Three's A Family," "Naked Genius," "Pick-Up Girl," "Violet," "Hope For The Best," "Apple of His Eye," "Silver Whistle," "Rat Race," "4 Twelves Are 48," "Lo and Behold," "Diary of A Scoundrel"(OB), "The Front Page"('69).

MERCER, MARIAN. Born Nov. 26, 1935 in Akron, O. Graduate U. Mich. Made Bdwy debut in 1960 in "Greenwillow," followed by "Fiorello!" "Promises, Promises" for which she received a THEATRE WORLD Award, "A Place For Polly," Off-Bdwy in "Little Mary Sunshine," "Hotel Passionato," "Your Own Thing."

MERENSKY, JOHN. Born Nov. 4, 1943 in NYC. Attended Neighborhood Playhouse, HB Studio. Has appeared with APA in "Judith," "Man and Superman," and "War and Peace," Off-Bdwy in "Something for Kitty Genovese," "The Nun," "Two Gentlemen from Verona," "As You Like It," "Are You Prepared To Be A US Marine?," "The Disintegration of James Cherry"(LC).

MERMAN, ETHEL. Born Jan. 16, 1912 in Astoria, NY. Appeared in vaudeville before Bdwy debut in 1930 in "Girl Crazy," followed by "George White's Scandals," "Take A Chance," "Anything Goes," "Red, Hot and Blue," "Stars In Your Eyes," "Panama Hattie," "Something For The Boys," "Annie Get Your Gun," "Call Me Madam," "Happy Hunting," "Gypsy," "Hello, Dolly!"

MICHAELS, LAURA. Born Nov. 17, 1953 in NYC. Attended HB Studio. Made Bdwy debut in 1962 in "Sound of Music," followed by "Roar Of The Greasepaint...," "A Time For Singing," NYSF, ASF, "The Me Nobody Knows" (OB).

MICHAELS, TIMMY. Born Mar. 6, 1963 in NYC. Made debut Off-Bdwy in 1969 in "7 Days of Mourning."

MICHELL, KEITH. Born Dec. 1, 1926 in Adelaide, Aust. Attended Aust. School of Arts. Made Bdwy debut in 1960 in "Irma La Douce," followed by "The Rehearsal," "Man of La Mancha."

MIDDLETON, RAY. Born Feb. 8, 1907 in Chicago. Graduate U. Ill., Juilliard. Made Bdwy bow in 1933 in "Roberta," followed by "Knickerbocker Holiday," "George White's Scandals," "Annie Get Your Gun," "Love Life," "South Pacific," "Too True To Be Good," "Man of LaMancha."

MILGRIM, LYNN. Born Mar. 17, 1944 in Philadelphia. Graduate Swarthmore, Harvard. Made NY debut in 1969 Off-Bdwy in "Frank Gagliana's City Scene," followed by "Crimes of Passion."

MILLER, ANN. Born Apr. 12, 1919 in Chireno, Tex. Made film debut in 1937, and Bdwy debut in 1940 in "George White's Scandals." Appeared this season in "Mame."

| ut Miller | Madeline Miller | Michael Misita | Pamela Myers | Angelo Nazzo |

MILLER, DROUT. Born Sept. 18, 1942 in Trenton, NJ. Attended Lafayette Col. Made Bdwy debut in 1970 in "Boral Boy."

MILLER, MADELINE. Born Apr. 4, 1945 in NYC. Attended AMDA. Made Bdwy debut in 1964 in "Bajour" followed by "Slow Dance On The Killing Ground"(OB).

MILLER, MARY BETH. Born Dec. 18, 1942 in Louisville, Ky. Attended Gallaudet Col. Made Bdwy debut with National Theatre of the Deaf.

MILLI, ROBERT. Born Mar. 15, 1933 in Brooklyn. Graduate U Md., Catholic U. Appeared in "Write Me A Murder," "Ross," "The Rehearsal," "Hamlet," "The Front Page" '69).

MILLS, STEVE. Born Oct. 9, 1895 in Boston. Appeared n burlesque and vaudeville, on Bdwy in "3 Little Girls," A Wonderful Night," "Pleasure Bound," "A Lady Says Yes," "This Was Burlesque."

MINTUN, JOHN. Born Jan. 16, 1941 in Decatur, Ill. Princeton graduate. Made debut in 1969 Off-Bdwy in "Get Thee o Canterbury," followed by "Boys in the Band."

MISITA, MICHAEL. Born Jan. 10, 1947 aboard HMS Queen Mary at sea. Graduate Boston Cons. Made Bdwy debut in 1968 in "Fig Leaves Are Falling," followed by Mame," "Applause."

MITCHELL, GARRY. Born Mar. 22, 1938 in Medicine Hat, Can. Graduate U Alberta. Made NY debut in 1968 Off-Bdwy in "Moon For The Misbegotten," followed by Bdwy bow in "We Bombed In New Haven," "Nobody Hears A Broken Drum."

MITCHELL, KEN. Born Nov. 6, 1944 in Wichita, Kan. Graduate U Utah. Made Bdwy debut in 1969 in "Mame," followed by "The Boy Friend."

MOBERLY, ROBERT. Born Apr. 15, 1939 in Excelsior Springs, Mo. Graduate U Kan. Made NY bow in 1967 Off-Bdwy in "Arms And The Man" followed by "The Millionairess," "A Place For Polly."

MOONEY, WILLIAM. Born in Bernie, Mo. Attended U Colo. Made Bdwy bow in "A Man For All Seasons," followed by "Half Horse, Half Alligator"(OB), "A Place For Polly."

MOOR, BILL. Born July 13, 1931 in Toledo, O. Attended Northwestern, Denison U. Made Bdwy bow in 1964 in "Blues For Mr. Charlie," followed by Off-Bdwy roles in "Dandy Dick," "Love Nest," "Days and Nights of Beebee Fenstermaker," "The Collection," "The Owl Answers," "Long Christmas Dinner," "Fortune and Men's Eyes," with LCRep in "King Lear," and "A Cry Of Players," "Boys In The Band."

MOORE, CHARLES. Born May 22 in Cleveland, O. Appeared on Bdwy in "Jamaica," "Kwamina," "The Zulu and The Zayda," Off-Bdwy in "Ballad For Bimshire," "House Of Flowers," "Billy Noname."

MOORE, EDWARD J. Born June 2, 1935 in Chicago. Graduate Goodman Theatre. Made Bdwy debut in 1967 in "After the Rain," followed by "The White House Murder Case" (OB).

MOORE, JONATHAN. Born Mar. 24, 1923 in New Orleans. Attended Piscator's Workshop. Made NY bow in 1961 Off-Bdwy in "After The Angels," followed by "Dylan," "1776."

MOORE, MELBA. Born in 1945 in NYC. Graduate Montclair State Col. Made Bdwy debut in 1968 in "Hair," followed by "Purlie" for which she received a THEATRE WORLD Award.

MORRIS, GARRETT. Born Feb. 1, 1944 in New Orleans. Graduate Dillard U. Appeared Off-Bdwy in "Bible Salesman," "Slave Ship," "Transfers," "Operation Sidewinder" (LC), on Bdwy in "Porgy and Bess," "Hallelujah, Baby!," "I'm Solomon," "The Great White Hope."

MORSE, RICHARD. Born May 31, 1927 in Brookline, Mass. Attended Principia Col., Neighborhood Playhouse. Made NY bow in Off-Bdwy in "Teach Me How To Cry," followed by "Thor With Angels," "The Makropoulis Secret," "All Kinds of Giants," and on Bdwy in "Mother Courage," "Fiddler On The Roof."

MORTON, BROOKS. Born Oct. 3, 1932 in Ky. Attended Northwestern. Made NY bow in 1962 Off-Bdwy in "Riverwind," followed by "Beyond The Fringe," "Marathon '33," "The Three Sisters," "Ivanov," "The Prime of Miss Jean Brodie," "Her First Roman," at CC in "West Side Story" and "Say, Darling!," "The Penny Wars."

MULLIKIN, BILL. Born Apr. 1, 1927 in Baltimore, Md. Graduate Loyola. Made Bdwy bow in "New Faces of 1952," followed by "The Boy Friend"(OB), "Hello, Dolly!"

MURCH, ROBERT G. Born Apr. 17, 1935 in Jefferson Barracks, Mo. Graduate Wash. U. Made Bdwy bow in 1966 in "Hostile Witness," followed by "The Harangues"(NEC).

MURRAY, BRIAN. Born Oct. 9, 1939 in Johannesburg, S.A. Made NY debut in 1964 Off-Bdwy in "The Knack," followed by "King Lear"(LC), and on Bdwy in "All In Good Time," "Rosencrantz and Guildenstern Are Dead."

MURRAY, PEG. Born in Denver, Colo. Attended Western Reserve U. Appeared Off-Bdwy in "Children Of Darkness," "A Midsummer Night's Dream," and "Oh, Dad, Poor Dad ...," on Bdwy in "The Great Sebastians," "Gypsy," "Blood, Sweat and Stanley Poole," "She Loves Me," "Anyone Can Whistle," "The Subject Was Roses," "Something More," "Cabaret," "Fiddler On The Roof."

MYERS, MICHAELE. Born July 2 in Brems, Ind. Attended Goodman Theatre, Cleveland Playhouse. Made Bdwy debut in 1958 in "Sunrise At Campobello," followed by "Who's Afraid of Virginia Woolf?," "Hogan's Goat" (OB), "You Know I Can't Hear You When The Water's Running," "Angela."

MYERS, PAMELA. Born July 15, 1947 in Hamilton, O. Graduate Cincinnati Cons. of Music. Appeared at "Upstairs At The Downstairs" before making Bdwy debut in 1970 in "Company."

MYLES, LYNDA. Attended Mich. State Col, Columbia. Appeared Off-Bdwy in "Two Gentlemen of Verona," "The Trojan Women," "Rocking Chair," "No Exit," and "Iphigenia In Aulis," on Bdwy in "Plaza Suite."

NATWICK, MILDRED. Born June 19, 1908 in Baltimore, Md. Made Bdwy debut in 1932 in "Carrie Nation," followed by "The Wind And The Rain," "The Distaff Side," "End Of Summer," "Love From A Stranger," "Candida," "Star Wagon," "Missouri Legend," "Blithe Spirit," "Playboy Of The Western World," "Grass Harp," "Coriolanus," "Waltz Of The Toreadors," "Day The Money Stopped," "The Firstborn," "Critic's Choice," "Barefoot In The Park," "Our Town," "Landscapes" (LC).

NAZZO, ANGELO. Born Aug. 1, 1939 in Bombay, India. Made NY debut in 1968 in "The People Vs. Ranchman."

NELSON, BARRY. Born in 1925 in Oakland, Cal. Graduate U Cal. Made Bdwy bow in 1943 in "Winged Victory," followed by "Light Up The Sky," "The Moon Is Blue," "Wake Up Darling," "The Rat Race," "Mary, Mary," "Nobody Loves An Albatross," "Cactus Flower," "Everything in The Garden," "The Only Game In Town," "Fig Leaves Are Falling," "Engagement Baby."

NELSON, RUTH. Born Aug. 2, 1905 in Saginaw, Mich. Attended Sacred Heart Conv., Am. Lab. Theatre. Made Bdwy debut in 1931 with Group Theatre in "House of Connolly," and appeared with Group until 1941, followed by "Grass Harp," "Colette" (OB).

Mary Ann Niles **Richard Novello** **Jenny O'Hara** **Michael O'Sullivan** **Bibi Oste**

NESOR, AL. Born Mar. 31, 1920 in NYC. Made Bdwy debut in 1953 in "Guys and Dolls," followed by "Li'l Abner," "Do Re Mi," "One Flew Over The Cuckoo's Nest," "I Had A Ball," "3 Men On A Horse," Off-Bdwy in "How Much, How Much?"

NEVINS, CLAUDETTE. Born in Wilkes-Barre, Pa. Graduate NYU. Appeared Off-Bdwy in "The Emperor," "In White America," with LCRep in "Danton's Death," on Bdwy in "The Wall," "Wait Until Dark," "Plaza Suite."

NICHOLLS, RICHARD. Born Oct. 21, 1900 in Plymouth, Eng. Made Bdwy debut in 1926 in "The Half-Naked Truth," followed by 19 productions including "John," "L'Aiglon," "The Jealous Moon," "The Jade God," "The Lark," "Jane Eyre," "A Distant Bell," "Abraham Cochrane," "Hadrian VII."

NICHOLS, NOREEN. Born Oct. 17, 1945 in NYC. Attended AMDA. Made debut in 1970 Off-Bdwy in "Lyle."

NILES, MARY ANN. Born May 2, 1933 in NYC. Attended Miss Finchley's, and Ballet Acad. Made Bdwy debut in 1945 in "Girl From Nantucket," followed by "Dance Me A Song," "Call Me Mister," "Make Mine Manhattan," "La Plume de Ma Tante," "Carnival," "Flora The Red Menace," "Sweet Charity," "George M!," Off-Bdwy in "The Boys From Syracuse," "Little Brown Road," "Big Spender," "Your Sister Rose," "Wonderful Town" (CC'67), "Carnival" (CC'68).

NOBLE, JAMES. Born Mar. 5, 1922 in Dallas, Tex. Attended SMU. Made Bdwy bow in 1949 in "The Velvet Glove," followed by "Come of Age," "A Far Country," "Strange Interlude," Off-Bdwy in "Wilder's Triple Bill," "Night of The Dunce," "Rimers of Eldritch," "The Acquisition," "A Scent of Flowers."

NOVAK, NORMA. Born Dec. 14, 1937 in Brooklyn. Graduate Hunter Col. Has appeared Off-Bdwy in "The Decapitated Taxi," "Hedda Gabler."

NOVELLO, RICHARD. Born in Rome, Italy. Appeared Off-Bdwy in 1962 in "Romeo and Juliet," Made Bdwy bow in 1969 in "Indians."

NYPE, RUSSELL. Born Apr. 26, 1924 in Zion, Ill. Attended Lake Forest Col. Made Bdwy bow in 1949 in "Regina," followed by "Call Me Madam" for which he received a THEATRE WORLD Award, "Tender Trap," "Tunnel Of Love," "Wake Up, Darling," "Carousel" (CC), "Goldilocks," "Brigadoon" (CC), "Brouhaha" (OB), "The Owl And The Pussycat," "Girl in the Freudian Slip," "Private Lives" (OB), "Hello, Dolly!"

OAKLAND, SIMON. Born Aug. 28, 1920 in Brooklyn. Attended Columbia. Has appeared in "Skipper Next To God," "Light Up The Sky," "Caesar and Cleopatra," "Harvey," "The Shrike," "The Sands of Negev," "The Great Sebastians," "Angela."

O'BRIEN, DAVID. Born Oct. 1, 1935 in Chicago. Graduate Stanford, London Acad. Appeared on Bdwy in "A Passage To India," "Arturo Ui," "A Time For Singing," Off-Bdwy in "Under Milk Wood," "A Month In The Country," "Henry IV" (CP), "The Boys In The Band."

O'BRIEN, SYLVIA. Born May 4, 1924 in Dublin, Ire. Made NY debut in 1961 Off-Bdwy in "O Marry Me," followed by "Red Roses For Me," "Every Other Evil," "3 By O'Casey," "Essence of Women," on Bdwy in "The Passion of Josef D," "The Right Honourable Gentleman," "The Loves of Cass McGuire," "Hadrian VII."

O'CONNOR, KEVIN. Born May 7, 1938 in Honolulu. Attended Hawaii U, U Cal, Neighborhood Playhouse. Has appeared Off-Bdwy in "Up To Thursday," "Six From La Mama," "Rimers of Eldritch," "Tom Paine," "Boy On The Straight-Back Chair," "Dear Janet Rosenberg....," made Bdwy bow in 1970 in "Gloria and Esperanza."

O'HARA, JENNY. Born Feb. 24 in Sonora, Cal. Attended Carnegie Tech. Made Bdwy debut in 1964 in "Dylan," followed by "Fig Leaves Are Falling," "Criss-Crossing," Off-Bdwy in "Hang Down Your Head and Die," "Play With A Tiger," "Arms And The Man," "Sambo."

O'HARA, JILL. Born Aug. 23, 1947 in Warren, Pa. Attended Edinburgh State Teachers Col. Appeared Off-Bdwy in "Hang Down Your Head and Die," and "Hair," before Bdwy debut in 1968 in "George M!" followed by "Promises, Promises," for which she received a THEATRE WORLD Award.

OMENS, ESTELLE. Born Oct. 11, 1928 in Chicago. Graduate U Iowa. Appeared Off-Bdwy in "Summer and Smoke," "Grass Harp," "Legend of Lovers," "Plays of Bleecker Street," "Pullman Car Hiawatha," "Brownstone Urge," made Bdwy debut in 1969 in "The Watering Place."

O'NEAL, FREDERICK. Born Aug. 27, 1905 in Brooksville, Miss. Attended Am. Th. Wing. Co-founded Am. Negro Theatre in 1940 and appeared in its productions. Made Bdwy bow in 1944 in "Anna Lucasta," followed by "Take A Giant Step," "The Winner," "House Of Flowers." Off-Bdwy in "Man With The Golden Arm," "Ballad of Bimshire," "Madwoman of Chaillot." Is president of Equity.

O'NEAL, RON. Born Sept. 1, 1937 in Utica, N.Y. Attended Ohio State U. Made NY debut in 1968 Off-Bdwy in "Americana Pastoral," followed by "No Place To Be Somebody" for which he received a THEATRE WORLD Award.

O'NEILL, DICK. Born Aug. 29, 1928 in The Bronx. Attended Utica Col. Made Bdwy bow in 1961 in "The Unsinkable Molly Brown," followed by "Skyscraper," "Have I Got One For You" (OB), "Promises, Promises."

ORBACH, JERRY. Born Oct. 20, 1935 in NYC. Attended U. Ill., Northwestern. Made Bdwy bow in 1961 in "Carnival," followed by "Guys and Dolls" (CC), LC revivals of "Carousel" and "Annie Get Your Gun," "The Natural Look," "Promises, Promises," appeared Off-Bdwy in "Threepenny Opera," "The Fantasticks," "The Cradle Will Rock," "Scuba Duba."

ORFALY, ALEXANDER. Born Oct. 10, 1935 in Brooklyn. Appeared in "South Pacific" (LC), "How Now, Dow Jones," Off-Bdwy in "The End Of All Things Natural," "Mahagonny."

OSTERWALD, BIBI. Born Feb. 3, 1920 in New Brunswick, NJ. Attended Catholic U. Made Bdwy debut in 1945 in "Sing Out, Sweet Land," followed by "3 to Make Ready," "Sally," "Gentlemen Prefer Blondes," "Golden Apple," "The Vamp," "Look Homeward, Angel," "New Girl in Town," "A Family Affair," "Hello, Dolly!"

OSTRIN, ART. Born Aug. 30, 1935 in NYC. Appeared in CC revivals of "The Time of Your Life," "Carnival," "Finian's Rainbow," and "South Pacific," "Promenade," "Beggar on Horseback" (LC), on Bdwy in "Irma La Douce," "Slapstick Tragedy."

O'SULLIVAN, MAIRIN D. Born Jan. 1 in Ireland. Member of Abbey Theatre before Bdwy debut in 1966 in "Philadelphia, Here I Come," followed by "Borstal Boy."

O'SULLIVAN, MAUREEN. Born May 17, 1911 in Roscommon, Ire. Made Bdwy debut in 1962 in "Never Too Late," followed by "The Subject Was Roses," "Keep It in the Family," "Front Page."

O'SULLIVAN, MICHAEL. Born Mar. 4, 1934 in Phoenix, Ariz. Attended Denver U., Goodman Theatre. Appeared Off-Bdwy in "6 Characters in Search of an Author," "In White America," with LCRep in "Tartuffe" (for which he received a THEATRE WORLD Award) and "The Alchemist," made Bdwy bow in 1964 in "The White House," followed by "It's a Bird, It's a Plane, It's Superman!," "Love and Let Love," "The Bench" (OB), with ACT in "A Flea in Her Ear" and "Three Sisters."

| Liz Otto | Jimmy Pelham | Lara Parker | Seymour Penzner | Erika Petersen |

OTTO, LIZ. Born in Coral Gables, Fla. Graduate U. Fla. Made NY debut in 1963 Off-Bdwy in "The Plot against the Chase Manhattan Bank," followed by "I Dreamt I Dwelt in Bloomingdale's."

PACINO, AL. Born Apr. 25, 1940 in NYC. Member of Actors Studio. Appeared Off-Bdwy in "Why Is A A Crooked Letter," "The Peace Creeps," "The Indian Wants The Bronx," "Local Stigmatic," "Camino Real" (LC), and made Bdwy bow in 1969 in "Does A Tiger Wear A Necktie?" for which he received a THEATRE WORLD Award.

PAGE, GERALDINE. Born Nov. 22, 1924 in Kirksville, Mo. Attended Goodman Theatre. Appeared Off-Bdwy in "7 Mirrors" and "Summer and Smoke" before Bdwy debut in 1953 in "Midsummer" (for which she received a THEATRE WORLD Award), followed by "The Immoralist," "The Rainmaker," "The Innkeepers," "Separate Tables," "Sweet Bird of Youth," "Strange Interlude," "Three Sisters," "P.S. I Love You," "The Great Indoors," "White Lies," "Black Comedy," "The Little Foxes," "Angela."

PALMER, ANTHONY. Born July 19, 1934 in Eagle Pass, Tex. Appeared with NYSF in "Antony and Cleopatra," "Macbeth," and "Winter's Tale," made Bdwy bow in 1964 in "The Passion of Josef D," followed by "Traveller without Luggage," Off-Bdwy in "A Whistle in the Dark," "Nobody Hears a Broken Drum."

PALMIERI, JOSEPH. Born Aug. 1, 1939 in Brooklyn. Attended Catholic U. Appeared with Ntl. Rep. Theatre (1965-6), NYSF(1965-6), LC's "Cyrano," Off-Bdwy in "Butter and Egg Man," "Boys in the Band."

PARISH, MICHAEL J. Born July 31 in NYC. Attended Frankel Theatre Workshop. Appeared with LCRep in 1967 in "Yerma" and "Galileo," made Bdwy bow in 1969 in "Henry V."

PARKER, LARA. Born Oct. 27, 1942 in Knoxville, Tenn. Graduate Southwestern U., U. Iowa. Made Bdwy debut in 1968 in "Woman Is My Idea," followed by "Lulu (OB)."

PARSONS, ESTELLE. Born Nov. 20, 1927 in Lynn, Mass. Attended Boston U., Conn. Col., Actors Studio. Appeared Off-Bdwy in "Threepenny Opera," "Automobile Graveyard," "Mrs. Dally Has A Lover" for which she received a THEATRE WORLD Award, "In The Summer House," "Monopoly," "Peer Gynt" (CP), "Mahagonny," with LC Rep in "East Wind" and "Galileo," on Bdwy in "Happy Hunting," "Whoop-Up!," "Beg, Borrow or Steal," "Ready When You Are, C.B.," "Malcolm," "The Seven Descents of Myrtle," "A Way of Life."

PASLE-GREEN, JEANNE. Born Oct. 24 in Mass. Attended Boston U. Made Bdwy debut in 1970 in "Grin and Bare It."

PASSANTINO, ANTHONY. Born July 9, 1945 in Brooklyn. Attended Hofstra U. Appeared in NYSF's "Hamlet" and "Othello" in 1964, made Bdwy bow in 1969 in "Henry V."

PATERSON, WILLIAM. Born July 7, 1919 in Buffalo, NY. Graduate Western Reserve in ACTS's "The Three Sisters" in 1969.

PATTERSON, JAMES. Born June 29, 1932 in Derry, Pa. Off-Bdwy credits: "Brothers Karamazov," "Epitaph For George Dillon," "Zoo Story," "The Collection," "Benito Cereno," "Silence" (LC), made Bdwy bow in 1964 in "Conversation At Midnight," followed by "Inadmissible Evidence," "The Birthday Party," "Wrong Way Light Bulb," "Amphitryon" (LC).

PATTON, LUCILLE. Born in NYC; attended Neighborhood Playhouse, Actors Studio. Made Bdwy debut in 1946 in "The Winter's Tale," followed by "Topaze," "Arms and The Man," "Joy To The World," "All You Need Is One Good Break," "The Fifth Season," "Heavenly Twins," "Rhinoceros," "Marathon '33," "The Last Analysis," "Dinner at 8" ('66), "La Strada," Off-Bdwy in "Ulysses In Nighttown," "The Failures," "Three Sisters," "Yes, Yes, No, No," "Tango."

PAUL, STEVEN. Born May 16, 1959 in NYC. Attended AADA. Made debut Off-Bdwy in 1970 in "Lyle," followed by "Lemon Sky."

PAYTON-WRIGHT, PAMELA. Born Nov. 1, 1941 in Pittsburgh. Graduate Birmingham Southern Col., RADA. Made Bdwy debut in 1967 with APA in "The Show-Off," "Exit The King," and "The Cherry Orchard," "Jimmy Shine," Off-Bdwy in "The Effect of Gamma Rays on Man-in-the-Moon Marigolds."

PEARL, IRWIN. Born Oct. 14, 1945 in Brooklyn. Graduate Hofstra U. Appeared Off-Bdwy in "Big Hotel," "Ergo," "Invitation To A Beheading," "Babes In Arm" (ELT), made Bdwy bow in 1970 in "Minnie's Boys."

PEARLMAN, STEPHEN. Born Feb. 26, 1935 in NYC. Dartmouth graduate. Made Bdwy bow in 1964 in "Barefoot in the Park," followed by "La Strada," Off-Bdwy roles in "Threepenny Opera," "Time of the Key," "Pimpernel," "In White America," "Viet Rock," "Chocolates."

PEARSON, SCOTT. Born Dec. 13, 1941 in Milwaukee. Attended Valparaiso U., U. Wisc. Made Bdwy debut in 1966 in "A Joyful Noise," followed by "Promises, Promises."

PEARSON, SUSAN G. Born Jan. 3, 1941 in Minneapolis. Attended U. Minn. Made NY debut in 1969 Off-Bdwy in "No Place to Be Somebody."

PELHAM, JIMMY. Born in Goldsboro, NC. Graduate NYU. Made Bdwy debut in 1968 in "The Great White Hope."

PENDLETON, AUSTIN. Born Mar. 27, 1940 in Warren, O. Attended Yale. Appeared with LCRep (1962-3), in "Oh, Dad, Poor Dad...," "Fiddler on the Roof," "Hail Scrawdyke," "The Little Foxes," "Last Sweet Days of Isaac" (OB).

PENDLETON, WYMAN. Born Apr. 18, 1916 in Providence, RI. Graduate Brown U. Off-Bdwy credits: "Gallows Humor," "American Dream," "Zoo Story," "Corruption In The Palace of Justice," "The Giant's Dance," "The Child Buyer," "Happy Days," "The Butter and Egg Man," on Bdwy in "Tiny Alice," "Malcolm," "Quotations From Chairman Mao Tse-Tung," "Happy Days," "Henry V."

PENNOCK, CHRISTOPHER. Born June 7, 1944 in Jackson Hole, Wyo. Attended Hobart Col., AADA. Made NY bow in 1966 in "The Rose Tattoo" (CC), and Bdwy debut in 1969 in "A Patriot for Me."

PENTECOST, GEORGE. Born July 15, 1939 in Detroit. Graduated Wayne State, U. Mich. With APA in "Scapin," "Lower Depths," "The Tavern," "School For Scandal," "Right You Are," "War and Peace," "The Wild Duck," "The Show-Off," "Pantagleize," and "The Cherry Orchard," "The Boys in the Band."

PENZNER, SEYMOUR. Born July 29, 1915 in Yonkers, NY. Attended CCNY. Appeared Off-Bdwy in "Crystal Heart," "Guitar," on Bdwy in "Oklahoma!," "Finian's Rainbow," "Call Me Madam," "Paint Your Wagon," "Can-Can," "Kean," "Baker Street," "Man of La Mancha."

PERKINS, DON. Born Oct. 23, 1928 in Boston. Graduate Emerson Col. Appeared Off-Bdwy in "Drums under the Window," made Bdwy bow in 1970 in "Borstal Boy."

PETERS, BERNADETTE. Born Feb. 28, 1948 in Jamaica, NY. Appeared Off-Bdwy in "Penny Friend," "Curley McDimple," "Most Happy Fella" (CC), and "Dames At Sea," made Bdwy debut in 1967 in "The Girl In The Freudian Slip," followed by "Johnny No Trump," "George M!" for which she received a THEATRE WORLD Award, "La Strada."

PETERSEN, ERIKA. Born Mar. 24, 1949 in NYC. Attended NYU. Appeared Off-Bdwy in "One Is A Lonely Number" ('63), "I Dreamt I Dwelt in Bloomingdale's."

PETERSON, KURT. Born Feb. 12, 1948 in Stevens Point, Wisc. Attended AMDA. Appeared in "An Ordinary Miracle" (OB), "West Side Story" (LC'68), made Bdwy debut in 1969 in "Dear World," followed by "Dames at Sea" (OB).

Don Plumley

Eleanor Phelps

Teno Pollick

Mary Bracken Phillips

Ed Preble

PHALEN, ROBERT. Born May 10, 1937 in San Francisco. Attended CCSF., U. Cal. Appeared with LCRep in "Danton's Death," "The Country Wife," "Caucasian Chalk Circle," "The Alchemist," "Yerma," "Galileo," "St. Joan," "Tiger At The Gates," "Cyrano," "King Lear," "A Cry of Players," "In The Matter of J. Robert Oppenheimer," "Operation Sidewinder," and "Beggar on Horseback."

PHELPS, ELEANOR. Born in Baltimore, graduate of Vassar. Made Bdwy debut in 1928 with George Arliss in "The Merchant of Venice," many subsequent credits include "Richard II," "Criminal Code," "Trick for Trick," "Seen but Not Heard," "Flight to the West," "Queen Bee," "We the People," "6 Characters in Search of an Author," "Naughty-Naught," "The Disenchanted," "Picnic," "My Fair Lady," "Garden District," "Color of Darkness" (OB), "40 Carats."

PHILLIPS, DIANE. Born Sept. 25, 1945 in NYC. Attended AADA. Made Bdwy debut in 1966 in "Joyful Noise," followed by "Coco."

PHILLIPS, MARY BRACKEN. Born Aug. 15, 1946 in Kansas City, Mo. Attended Kansas U. Made NY debut in 1969 Off-Bdwy in "Perfect Party," followed by Bdwy bow in "1776."

PHILLIPS, RANDY. Born Jan. 22, 1926 in NYC. Attended Juilliard. Appeared Off-Bdwy in "HMS Pinafore," on Bdwy in "How to Succeed...," "Hello Dolly!," "Skyscraper," "Mame."

PICON, MOLLY. Born Feb. 28, 1898 in NYC. International Yiddish theatre star, has appeared on Bdwy in "Morning Star," "For Heaven's Sake, Mother," "Milk and Honey," "How to Be A Jewish Mother," "Front Page," "Paris Is Out."

PLAYTEN, ALICE. Born Aug. 28, 1947 in NYC. Attended NYU, Bklyn Col. Made stage debut in 1959 in Met's "Wozzeck," Bdwy bow in 1960 in "Gypsy," followed by "Oliver!," "Hello, Dolly!," "Henry, Sweet Henry" for which she recevied a THEATRE WORLD Award, "George M!," Off-Bdwy in "Promenade," "The Last Sweet Days of Isaac."

PLUMLEY, DON. Born Feb. 11, 1934 in Los Angeles. Graduate Pepperdine Col. Made NY bow Off-Bdwy in 1961 in "The Cage," followed by NYSF's "Midsummer Night's Dream," "Richard II," and "Much Ado About Nothing," "Saving Grace," "A Whistle in the Dark," "Operation Sidewinder" (LC).

POINTER, PRISCILLA. Born in NYC. Has appeared with LCRep from 1965, and in "Summertree," "An Evening For Merlin Finch," "Inner Journey," "The Disintegration of James Cherry," "The Time of Your Life," "Camino Real," "Amphitryon."

POLITO, PHILIP. Born Feb. 17, 1944 in Hackensack, NJ. Graduate Ill. Wesleyan U., Yale. Made Bdwy debut in 1969 in "1776."

POLLICK, TENO. Born July 14, 1935 in NYC. Attended LA-CC. Made Bdwy debut in 1954 in "Peter Pan," followed by "Much Ado About Nothing," "Steambath" (OB).

POLLOCK, NANCY R. Born Feb. 10, 1905 in Brooklyn. Attended U. Cuba, Columbia, NYU. Made Bdwy debut in 1950 in "Diamond Lil," followed by "One Bright Day," "In The Summer House," "Middle of The Night," "Period of Adjustment," "Come Blow Your Horn," "In The Counting House," "Have I Got A Girl For You," "Ceremony of Innocence" (OB), "A Day In The Death of Joe Egg," "Wrong Way Light Bulb."

PONAZECKI, JOE. Born Jan. 7, 1934 in Rochester, NY. Attended Rochester U, Columbia. Made Bdwy bow in 1959 in "Much Ado About Nothing," followed by "Send Me No Flowers," "A Call On Kuprin," "Take Her, She's Mine," "The Dragon," "Fiddler On The Roof," "Xmas In Las Vegas," "3 Bags Full," "Love In E-Flat," "90 Day Mistress," "Muzeeka" (OB), "Witness" (OB), "Harvey."

POOLE, ROY. Born Mar. 31, 1924 in San Bernardino, Cal. Graduate Stanford. Credits: "Now I Lay Me Down To Sleep," "St. Joan" ('56), "The Bad Seed," "I Knock At The Door," "Long Day's Journey Into Night," "Face of A Hero," "Moby Dick," "Poor Bitos," "1776."

POPE, PEGGY. Born May 15, 1929 in Montclair, NJ. Attended Smith Col. Appeared in "The Doctor's Dilemma" (1955), "Volpone," "The Rose Tattoo," "Muzeeka" (OB), "The Front Page."

PORTER, DON. Born Sept. 24 in Miami, Okla. Attended Oregon Tech. Has appeared in "Calculated Risk," "Any Wednesday," "The Front Page" ('69).

PORTER, STAN. Born July 1, 1928 in Brooklyn. Made Bdwy debut in 1967 in "Hello, Solly!," and Off-Bdwy in 1968 in "Jacques Brel Is Alive and Well..."

POSTON, TOM. Born Oct. 17, 1921 in Columbus, O. Attended Bethany Col., AADA. Made Bdwy bow in 1947 in "Cyrano," followed by "The Insect Comedy" (CC), "King Lear" ('50), "Stockade," "Grand Prize," "Will Success Spoil Rock Hunter?," "Goodbye Again," "Romanoff and Juliet," "Drink To Me Only," "Golden Fleecing," "Come Play With Me" (OB), "The Conquering Hero," "Come Blow Your Horn," "Mary, Mary," "But Seriously," "40 Carats."

POTTER, DON. Born Aug. 15, 1932 in Philadelphia. Made NY bow in 1961 Off-Bdwy in "What A Killing," followed by "Sunset," "You're A Good Man, Charlie Brown."

PREBLE, ED. Born Nov. 9, 1919 in Chicago. Made Bdwy bow in 1957 in "Inherit the Wind," followed by "The Family Way," Off-Bdwy's "Press Cuttings," "Failures," "Krapp's Last Tape," "Marcus in the High Grass," "A Figleaf in Her Bonnet," "Calling in Crazy."

PRICE, GILBERT. Born Sept. 10, 1942 in NYC. Attended Am. Th. Wing. Made Bdwy bow in 1965 in "The Roar of the Greasepaint...," appeared Off-Bdwy in "Kicks & Co.," "Fly Blackbird," "Jerico-Jim Crow" for which he received a THEATRE WORLD Award, "Promenade," "Slow Dance on the Killing Ground."

PRICE, PAUL B. Born Oct. 7, 1933 in Carteret, NJ. Attended Pasadena Playhouse. Made NY bow in 1960 in "Dead End" (OB), followed by "A Cook for Mr. General," "Banquet for the Moon," "O Say Can You See," "Dumbwaiter," "Live Like Pigs," "Medea," "4H Club."

PRIEST, DAN. Born Feb. 29, 1924 in Altus, Okla. Attended W. Tex. State Teachers Col. Appeared Off-Bdwy in "The Crucible," "Deep Are The Roots," "A View From The Bridge," on Bdwy in "The Investigation," "The Trial of Lee Harvey Oswald," "The Great White Hope."

PRIEUR, DON. Born Jan. 1, 1942 in Detroit, Mich. Attended Wayne State U. Made Bdwy debut in 1970 in "Look to the Lilies."

PRIMROSE, ALEK. Born Aug. 20, 1934 in San Joaquin, Cal. Attended Col. of The Pacific, Goodman Theatre. Off-Bdwy credits: "In Good King Charles' Golden Days," "The Golem," "Leave It To Jane," "The Balcony," "Rules of The Game," "A Man's A Man," "In White America," "The Kitchen," "Room Service," with LCRep in "Incident at Vichy" and "Tartuffe," on Bdwy in "A Cook For Mr. General" with Minn. Theatre Co. in "House of Atreus," and "Arturo Ui."

PRIMUS, BARRY. Born Feb. 16, 1938 in NYC. Attended CCNY. Made Bdwy bow in 1960 in "The Nervous Set," followed by "Oh, Dad, Poor Dad...," LCRep productions, "Henry IV" (CP), "Huui, Huui" (OB), "The Criminals" (OB).

| Prud'homme | Richard Quarry | Teri Ralston | Lee Roy Reams | Elsa Raven |

PRINCE, WILLIAM. Born Jan. 26, 1913 in Nicholas, NY. Attended Cornell. Appeared in "Richard II," "Hamlet," "Ah, Wilderness," "Guest in the House," "Across the Board on Tomorrow Morning," "Eve of St. Mark," "John Loves Mary," "Forward the Heart," "As You Like It," "I Am A Camera," "Affair of Honor," "Third Best Sport," "Highest Tree," "Venus at Large," "Strange Interlude," "Ballad of the Sad Cafe," "Stephen D" (OB), "The Little Foxes," "Mercy Street" (OB).

PRUD'HOMME, JUNE. Born June 8 in San Francisco. Attended SF Jr. Col., AADA. Made NY debut in 1953 in "Richard II" (CC), followed by "Halfway Up The Tree," "Henry V," Off-Bdwy in "Blood Wedding," "Church Street," "Bruno and Sidney," "Sugar and Spice," "Scarecrow Richard," "The Potting Shed" (ELT).

PRYOR, NICHOLAS. Born Jan. 28, 1935 in Baltimore, Md. Attended Yale. Appeared in "Small War on Murray Hill," "The Egghead," "Love Me Little," "Who's Afraid of Virginia Woolf?," Off-Bdwy in "Borak," "A Party for Divorce," "Boys in the Band."

PUGH, TED. Born Apr. 24, 1937 in Anadarko, Okla. Graduate U. Okla. Has appeared Off-Bdwy in "In The Nick of Time," "Have I Got One For You," "Don't Shoot, Mable, It's Your Husband," "Now," "Lend an Ear" (ELT).

PUMA, MARIE. Born in Brooklyn; CUNY graduate. Made debut in 1969 in ELT's "Romeo and Jeanette."

QUARRY, RICHARD. Born Aug. 9, 1944 in Akron, O. Graduate U. Akron, NYU. Made Bdwy bow in 1970 in "Georgy."

RABY, ROGER ALLAN. Born Sept. 2, 1939 in Houston, Tex. Graduate U. Tex. Made NY bow in 1961 Off-Bdwy in "Bella" and on Bdwy in 1964 in "Fade Out-Fade In," followed by "Sherry!," "Mame."

RACHINS, ALAN. Born Oct. 3, 1942 in Brookline, Mass. Attended U. Pa. Made Bdwy debut in 1967 in "After The Rain," followed by "Hadrian VII," "Oh, Calcutta" (OB).

RACIOPPI, JAMES. Born Feb. 11, 1946 in Newark, NJ. Attended HB Studio. Made NY debut Off-Bdwy in 1969 in "Silhouettes."

RAE, CHARLOTTE. Born Apr. 22, 1926 in Milwaukee. Graduate Northwestern. Off-Bdwy credits: "Threepenny Opera," "The Littlest Revue," "The Beggar's Opera," "The New Tenant," "Victims of Duty," "Henry IV" (CP), on Bdwy in "Three Wishes For Jamie," "Golden Apple," "Li'l Abner," "The Beauty Part," "Pickwick," "Morning, Noon and Night," "The Chinese."

RALL, TOMMY. Born Dec. 27, 1929 in Kansas City, Mo. Soloist with Ballet Theatre before Bdwy debut in 1948 in "Look Ma, I'm Dancin'," followed by "Small Wonder," "Miss Liberty," "Call Me Madam," "Juno," "Milk and Honey," "Cry For Us All."

RALSTON, TERI. Born Feb. 16, 1943 in Holyoke, Colo. Graduate SF State Col. Made NY debut in 1969 Off-Bdwy in "Jacques Brel Is Alive...," Bdwy bow in 1970 in "Company."

RAMSAY, REMAK. Born Feb. 2, 1937 in Baltimore, Md. Princeton graduate. Appeared Off-Bdwy in 1964 in "Hang Down Your Head and Die," Bdwy bow in 1965 in "Half a Sixpence," followed by "Sheep on the Runway."

RANDOLPH, JOHN. Born June 1, 1915 in the Bronx. Attended CCNY, Actors Studio. Made Bdwy bow in 1937 in "Revolt of the Beavers," followed by "The Emperor's New Clothes," "Capt. Jinks," "No More Peace," "Coriolanus," "Medicine Show," "Hold on to Your Hats," "Native Son," "Command Decision," "Come Back, Little Sheba," "Golden State," "Peer Gynt," "Paint Your Wagon," "Seagulls over Sorrento," "Grey-Eyed People," "Room Service," "All Summer Long," "House of Flowers," "The Visit," "Mother Courage and Her Children," "Sound of Music," "Case of Libel," "Conversation at Midnight," "An Evening's Frost" (OB), "My Sweet Charlie," "The Peddler and the Dodo Bird" (OB), "Our Town."

RATCLIFFE, SAMUEL D. Born Mar. 30, 1945 in Eagle Lake, Fla. Graduate Birmingham Southern Col. Made NY debut in 1969 Off-Bdwy in "The Fantasticks," followed by Bdwy bow in "Fiddler on the Roof" same year.

RAVEN, ELSA. Born Sept. 21, 1929 in Charleston, SC. Attended Charleston Col. Made Bdwy debut in 1959 in "Legend of Lizzie," followed by "Taming of the Shrew" (NYSF), "In a Bar in a Tokyo Hotel" (OB).

RAWLINS, LESTER. Born Sept. 24, 1924 in Farrell, Pa. Attended Carnegie Tech. Appeared in "Othello," "King Lear," "The Lovers," "A Man For All Seasons," Off-Bdwy in "Endgame," "Quare Fellow," "Camino Real," "Hedda Gabler," "Old Glory," "The Child Buyer," "Winterset," "In The Bar of A Tokyo Hotel," "The Reckoning."

RAY, JAMES. Born July 4, 1932 in Calgra, Okla. Attended Okla. A&M. Made Bdwy debut in 1957 in "Compulsion," followed by "J.B.," "The Wall," "Dylan," "The Glass Menagerie" ('65), and Off-Bdwy in "The Creditors," "The Collection," "Love's Labour's Lost" (CP), "Henry IV" (CP), "The Basement," with Am. Sh. Festival from 1961, LC Rep's "Disintegration of James Cherry," and "Amphitryon."

REAMS, LEE ROY. Born Aug. 23, 1942 in Covington, Ky. Graduate U. Cinn. Cons. Made Bdwy debut in 1966 in "Sweet Charity," followed by "Oklahoma!" (LC), "Applause."

REILEY, ORRIN. Born Aug. 12, 1946 in Santa Monica, Cal. Graduate UCLA. Made Bdwy debut in 1969 in "Dear World," followed by "Man of La Mancha," "Applause."

REINHARDT, STEPHEN. Born Nov. 30, 1947 in Philadelphia. Attended Juilliard. Made NY bow in 1968 in "West Side Story" (LC), followed by Bdwy roles in "The Happy Time," "Noel Coward's Sweet Potato," "Minnie's Boy."

REISER, ROBERT. Born Dec. 3, 1946 in Chicago. Graduate Goodman Theatre. Made Bdwy debut in 1970 in "Watercolor-Criss-Crossing."

REY, ANTONIA. Born Oct. 12, 1927 in Havana, Cuba. Graduate Havana U. Made NY debut in 1964 in "Bajour," followed by "Yerma" (OB), "Mike Downstairs," "Fiesta In Madrid" (CC), "Engagement Baby," "Camino Real" (LC).

REYNOLDS, EUGENE. Born May 11, 1944 in Panama City, Fla. Attended National Black Theatre. Made NY bow Off-Bdwy in 1969 in "5 on the Black Hand Side."

RICH, RON. Born Oct. 29, 1938 in Pittsburgh, Pa. Made NY debut in 1968 in "Big Time Buck White" Off and On Bdwy.

RICHARDS, JEAN. Born in NYC. Attended Yale. Made debut Off-Bdwy in 1969 in "Man With the Flower in His Mouth," followed by "Madwoman of Chaillot."

RICHARDS, PAUL. Born Aug. 31, 1934 in Bedford, Ind. Graduate Ind. U. Made Bdwy debut in 1960 in "Once Upon A Mattress," followed by "Camelot," "Superman," "A Joyful Noise," "1776."

RILEY, ED. Born Apr. 1, 1933 in Kulpmont, Pa. Attended Georgetown U. Appeared Off-Bdwy in "Little Mary Sunshine" (1959), and made Bdwy bow in 1969 in "The Front Page."

RITCHEY, CAMILLA. Born July 30, 1945 in Ft. Worth, Tex. Graduate Trinity U. Made NY debut in 1969 Off-Bdwy in "7 Days of Mourning."

ROBBINS, REX. Born in Pierre, S.Dak. Yale graduate. Bdwy debut in 1964 in "One Flew over the Cuckoo's Nest," Off-Bdwy in "Servant of Two Masters," "Alchemist," "Arms and the Man," "Boys in the Band."

ROBERTS, ANTHONY. Born Oct. 22, 1939 in NYC. Graduate Northwestern. Made Bdwy bow in 1962 in "Something About A Soldier," followed by "Take Her, She's Mine," "The Last Analysis," "The Cradle Will Rock" (OB), "Never Too Late," "Barefoot In The Park," "Don't Drink The Water," "How Now, Dow Jones," "Play It Again, Sam."

Enid Rodgers   **Arthur Roberts**   **Suzanne Rogers**   **Irwin Rosen**   **Rosalind Ross**

ROBERTS, ARTHUR. Born Aug. 10, 1938 in NYC. Harvard graduate. Made NY bow in 1964 in NYSF's "Hamlet" and "Othello," followed by "Galileo" (LC), "Boys in the Band," Bdwy debut in 1970 in "Borstal Boy."

ROBERTS, DORIS. Born in St. Louis, Mo. Attended Neighborhood Playhouse, Actors Studio. Off Bdwy credits: "Death of Bessie Smith," "American Dream," "Color of Darkness," "Don't Call Me By My Rightful Name," "Christy," "Boy in the Straightback Chair," "A Matter of Position," "Natural Affection," made Bdwy debut in 1956 in "The Desk Set," followed by "Have I Got A Girl for You," "The Time of Your Life" (CC), "Malcolm," "Marathon '33," "Under the Weather," "The Office," "The Natural Look," "Last of the Red Hot Lovers."

ROBERTS, MARILYN. Born Oct. 30, 1939 in San Francisco. Graduate SF State Col. Made NY debut in 1963 Off-Bdwy in "Telemachus Clay," followed by "The Maids," "The Class," "Gabriella," "Tom Paine," "Futz," "Candaules, Commissioner."

ROBERTSON, WILLIAM. Born Oct. 9, 1908 in Portsmouth, Va. Graduate Pomona Col. Made Bdwy debut in 1936 in "Tapestry in Grey," followed by "Cup of Trambling," "Liliom," "Our Town" (1969) Off-Bdwy in "Uncle Harry," "Shining Hour," "The Cenci," "Aspern Papers," "Madame Is Served," "Tragedian in spite of Himself," "The Kibosh," "Sun-Up."

ROBINSON, ANDY. Born Feb. 14, 1942 in NYC. Graduate New School, London AMDA. Made debut in 1967 Off-Bdwy in "MacBird," followed by "The Cannibals," "Futz," "The Young Master Dante," "Operation Sidewinder" (LC).

ROBINSON, LESLIE. Born Jan. 5, 1940 in Selma, Ala. Attended U. Ala. Made NY debut in 1970 Off-Bdwy in "The Madwoman of Chaillot."

RODD, MARCIA. Born July 8 in Lyons, Kan. Attended Northwestern, Yale. Appeared Off-Bdwy in "Oh Say Can You See," "Cambridge Circus," "Mad Show," "Madame Mousse," "Love and Let Love," "Your Own Thing," made Bdwy debut in 1964 in "Oh What A Lovely War," followed by "Love in E-Flat," "Last of the Red Hot Lovers."

RODGER-REID, PAUL. Born Jan. 26, 1938 in Philadelphia. Attended Temple U., AFDA. Made NY bow in 1969 Off-Bdwy in "A Black Quartet."

RODGERS, ENID. Born Apr. 29, 1924 in London. Attended Royal Col., Webber-Douglas School of Drama. Made NY debut in 1969 Off-Bdwy in "Sourball," followed by "Getting Married" (ELT).

RODGERS, LOU. Born Oct. 15, 1935 in London. Graduate New England Cons. Made Bdwy bow in 1967 in "Illya, Darling," followed by "Mahagonny" (OB).

ROE, PATRICIA. Born Sept. 18, 1932 in NYC. Attended US Cal., Carnegie, Actors Studio. Made Bdwy debut in 1951 in "Romeo and Juliet," followed by "Cat On A Hot Tin Roof," "Compulsion," "By The Beautiful Sea," "Night Circus," "A Distant Bell," "Look After Lulu," "Night of The Iguana," "The Collection" (OB), with LCRep in "After The Fall," and "But For Whom Charlie," "The Homecoming," "Bananas" (LC), "Transfers" (OB).

ROGERS, GIL. Born Feb. 4, 1934 in Lexington, Ky. Attended Harvard. Has appeared Off-Bdwy in "The Ivory Branch," "The Vanity of Nothing," "Warrior's Husband," "Hell Bent For Heaven," "Gods of Lightning," "Pictures In The Hallway," "Rose," "Memory Bank," and made Bdwy bow in 1968 in "The Great White Hope."

ROGERS, SUZANNE. Born July 9, 1947 in Richmond, Va. Attended Stella Adler School. Made Bdwy debut in 1967 in "Hallelujah, Baby!," followed by "Her First Roman," "Cabaret," "Coco."

ROLIN, JUDI. Born Nov. 6, 1946 in Chicago. Made Bdwy debut in "40 Carats."

ROLLE, ESTHER. Born Nov. 8 in Pompano Beach, Fla. Attended Hunter Col. Made Bdwy debut in 1964 in "Blues For Mr. Charlie," followed by "Purlie Victorious," "The Amen Corner," and Off-Bdwy in "The Blacks," "Happy Ending," "Day of Absence," in NEC's "Evening of One Acts," "Man Better Man," and "Brotherhood."

RONAN, ROBERT. Born Feb. 17, 1938 in Richmond Hills, NY. Attended Hofstra U. Has appeared Off-Bdwy in "Dr. Faustus," "Colombe," in Central Park in "Love's Labour's Lost," "All's Well That Ends Well," "Comedy of Errors," and "Henry IV," "The Memorandum," "Invitation To A Beheading," "Twelfth Night" (CP).

ROONEY, WILLIAM. Born Feb. 28, 1945 in Jamaica, NY. Attended HB Studio. Made Bdwy debut in 1969 in "The Mundy Scheme."

ROSE, GEORGE. Born Feb. 19, 1920 in Bicester, Eng. Made NY bow with Old Vic in 1946 in "Henry IV," followed by "Much Ado About Nothing," "A Man For All Seasons," "Hamlet" ('64), "Royal Hunt of The Sun," "Walking Happy," "Loot," "My Fair Lady" (CC'68), "Canterbury Tales," "Coco."

ROSEN, IRWIN. Born May 17, 1936 in Brooklyn. Attended Bklyn. Col. Has appeared Off-Bdwy in "Winterset," "The Advocate," "Awake and Sing."

ROSQUI, TOM. Born June 12, 1928 in Oakland, Calf. Graduate Col. of Pacific. With LCRep in "Danton's Death," "Condemned of Altoona," "Country Wife," "Caucasian Chalk Circle," "Alchemist," "Yerma," and "East Wind," Off-Bdwy in "Collision Course," NEC's "Day of Absence" and "Brotherhood," "What the Butler Saw."

ROSS, HELEN. Born Jan. 16, 1914 in NYC. Appeared in vaudeville, with Federal Theatre, made Bdwy debut in 1967 in "Marat/deSade," followed by "Our Town."

ROSS, LARRY. Born Oct. 18, 1945 in Brooklyn. Attended AADA. Made Bdwy debut in 1963 in "How to Succeed in Business....," followed by "Fiddler on the Roof."

ROSS, ROSALIND. Born Nov. 26, 1934 in London. Attended Bedford Col., RADA. Made Bdwy debut in 1965 in "All in Good Time," followed by "Rockefeller and the Red Indians," "Little Boxes" (OB).

ROUNDS, DAVID. Born Oct. 9, 1938 in Bronxville, NY. Attended Denison U. Appeared Off-Bdwy in "You Never Can Tell," "Money," made Bdwy debut in 1965 in "Foxy" followed by "Child's Play" for which he received a THEATRE WORLD Award.

ROUNSEVILLE, ROBERT. Born Mar. 25, 1919 in Attleboro, Mass. Attended Tufts U. Made Bdwy bow in 1937 in "Babes In Arms," followed by "Two Bouquest," "Knickerbocker Holiday," "Higher and Higher," "Up In Central Park," "Show Boat" ('54), "The Merry Widow," "Candide," "Brigadoon" (CC), "Man of La Mancha."

ROWLES, POLLY. Born Jan. 10 in Philadelphia. Graduate Carnegie Tech. Made Bdwy debut in 1938 in "Julius Caesar," followed by "Richard III," "Anne of The Thousand Days," "Golden State," "The Small Hours," "Gertie," "Time Out For Ginger," "Wooden Dish," "Goodbye Again," "Auntie Mame," "Look After Lulu," "A Mighty Man Is He," "No Strings," "The Killing of Sister George," "Forty Carats."

ROY, RENEE. Born Jan. 2, 1935 in Buffalo, NY. Attended Hartford, Col. Made Bdwy debut in 1954 in "Ankles A-weigh," followed by "Nature's Way," "By Jupiter" (ELT), "Zelda."

RUDD, PAUL. Born May 15, 1940 in Boston. Attended RADA. Appeared with NY Shakespeare Festival in "Henry IV," with LCRep in "King Lear," "A Cry of Players," "An Evening For Merlin Finch," and "In The Matter of J. Robert Oppenheimer."

RULE, CHARLES. Born Aug. 4, 1928 in Springfield, Mo. Made Bdwy bow in 1951 in "Courtin' Time," followed by "Happy Hunting," "Oh, Captain!," "The Conquering Hero," "Donnybrook," "Bye Bye Birdie," "Fiddler On The Roof," "Henry, Sweet Henry," "Maggie Flynn," "1776," "Cry For Us All."

| John P. Ryan | Charlene Ryan | Nicholas Saunders | Donna Sanders | Roger Omar Serbagi |

RUSKIN, SHIMEN. Born Feb. 25, 1907 in Vilno, Poland. Made Bdwy debut in 1937 in "Having Wonderful Time," has appeared Off-Bdwy in "Saturday Night," "Little Murders," "7 Days of Mourning."

RUSSOM, LEON. Born Dec. 6, 1941 in Little Rock, Ark. Attended Southwestern U. Has appeared Off-Bdwy in "Futz," "Cyrano" (LCRep), "The Boys In The Band," "Oh, Calcutta."

RYAN, CHARLENE. Born in NYC. Made Bdwy debut in 1964 in "Never Live Over A Pretzel Factory," followed by "Sweet Charity," "Fig Leaves Are Falling," "Coco."

RYAN, JOHN P. Born July 30, 1938 in NYC. Graduate CCNY. Appeared Off-Bdwy in "Big Man," "Nobody Hears A Broken Drum," made Bdwy bow in 1967 in "Daphne in Cottage D."

RYAN, ROBERT. Born Nov. 11, 1913 in Chicago. Attended Dartmouth. Made Bdwy bow in 1941 in "Clash By Night," followed by "Coriolanus" ('53 OB), "Mr. President," "The Front Page" ('69).

RYLAND, JACK. Born July 2, 1935 in Lancaster, Pa. Attended AFDA. Appeared Off-Bdwy in "Palm Tree in a Rose Garden," "Lysistrata," "The White Rose and the Red," "The Old Glory," "Cyrano de Bergerac" (LC), with NYSF, on Bdwy in "The World of Suzie Wong," "A Very Rich Woman," "Henry V."

SABIN, DAVID. Born Apr. 24, 1937 in Washington, DC. Graduate Catholic U. Made NY bow in 1965 in "The Fantasticks" (OB), followed by "The Yearling," "Slapstick Tragedy," "Now Is The Time For All Good Men" (OB), "Jimmy Shine," "Gantry."

ST. JOHN, MARCO. Born May 7, 1939 in New Orleans. Graduate Fordham U. Off-Bdwy credits: "Angels of Anadarko," "Man of Destiny," on Bdwy in "Poor Bitos," "And Things That Go Bump In The Night," with APA in "We Comrades Three," and "War and Peace," "The Unknown Soldier and His Wife," "Weekend," "Forty Carats."

SALT, JENNIFER. Born Sept. 4, 1944 in Los Angeles. Attended Sarah Lawrence Col. Made Bdwy debut in 1970 in "Watercolor."

SALVIO, ROBERT. Born Feb. 14, 1942 in NYC. Graduate UCLA. Appeared Off-Bdwy in "The Awakening of Spring," "Night of The Dunce," and "Hamp" for which he received a THEATRE WORLD Award, "Awake and Sing," on Bdwy in "Cabaret," "Billy."

SANDERS, DONNA. Born Mar. 3 in Greenville, Tex. Attended Juilliard. Made Bdwy debut in 1954 in "Me and Juliet," followed by "Saint of Bleecker St.," "The Vamp," "Bells Are Ringing," "Do Re Mi," "Come on Strong," "110 in the Shade," "La Grosse Valise," Off-Bdwy in "The Drunkard."

SANDS, DOROTHY. Born Mar. 5, 1900 in Cambridge, Mass. Attended Radcliffe Col. Has appeared in "Grand Street Follies," "The Seagull," "The Stairs," "All The Comforts of Home," "Papa Is All," "Tomorrow The World," "A Joy Forever," "Bell, Book and Candle," "Misalliance," "Quadrille," "First Gentleman," "Moonbirds," "Once For The Asking," "Come Summer," Off-Bdwy in "Mary Stuart," "Whisper To Me," and "The Club Bedroom," "Paris Is Out."

SANFORD, JANE. Born Mar. 15, 1943 in NYC. Graduate Carengie Tech. Appeared Off-Bdwy in "The Moondreamers," made Bdwy debut in 1970 in "Gloria and Esperanza."

SANTELL, MARIE. Born July 8 in Brooklyn. Made Bdwy debut in "Music Man," followed by "A Funny Thing Happened on the Way...," "Flora, the Red Menance," Off-Bdwy in "Hi, Paisano!," "Boys from Syracuse," "Peace," "Promenade," "The Drunkard."

SANTORO, DEAN. Born Jan. 30, 1938 in Johnstown, Pa. Graduate Penn. State. Made NY debut with APA in "War and Peace" and "Man and Superman," followed by "Philosophy In The Boudoir" (OB), "Hadrian VII," "Borstal Boy."

SAPPINGTON, MARGO. Born July 30, 1947 in Baytown, Tex. Made NY debut in 1965 with Joffrey Ballet, Bdwy debut in "Sweet Charity," followed by "Oh, Calcutta" (OB).

SAROYAN, LUCY. Born Jan. 17, in San Francisco. Attended Northwestern, Neighborhood Playhouse. Made NY debut in 1970 Off-Bdwy in "I Dreamt I Dwelt in Bloomingdale's," followed by "Room Service."

SAUNDERS, MARILYN. Born Apr. 28, 1948 in Brooklyn. Attended Bklyn Col. Appeared Off-Bdwy in "Dames at Sea" before Bdwy debut in 1970 in "Company."

SAUNDERS, NICHOLAS. Born June 2, 1914 in Kiev, Russia. Made Bdwy debut in 1942 in "Lady in the Dark," followed by "A New Life," "Highland Fling," "Happily Ever After," "Magnificent Yankee," "Anastasia," "Take Her, She's Mine," "A Call on Kuprin," "Passion of Josef D," Off-Bdwy in "An Enemy of the People," "End of All Things Natural."

SAVINO, FRANK. Born May 7, 1936 in Chicago. Graduate Goodman Theatre. Made Bdwy debut in 1961 in "Daughter of Silence," Off-Bdwy in "Medea," "Serjeant Musgrave's Dance," "The Firebugs," "Room Service."

SCHACHT, SAM. Born Apr. 19, 1936 in The Bronx. Graduate CCNY. Has appeared Off-Bdwy in "Fortune and Men's Eyes," "The Cannibals," "I Met a Man," "The Increased Difficulty of Concentration" (LC).

SCHELL, MAXIMILIAN. Born Dec. 8, 1930 in Vienna. Graduate U. Zurich. Made Bdwy debut in 1958 in "Interlock," followed by "A Patriot for Me" (1969).

SCHNABEL, STEFAN. Born Feb. 2, 1912 in Berlin, Ger. Attended U. Bonn, Old Vic. Made NY bow in 1937 in "Julius Caesar," followed by "Shoemaker's Holiday," "Glamour Preferred," "Land of Fame," "The Cherry Orchard," "Around The World," "Now I Lay Me Down To Sleep," "Idiot's Delight" (CC), "The Love of Four Colonels," "Plain and Fancy," "Small War On Murray Hill," "A Very Rich Woman," "Tango" (OB), "In The Matter of J. Robert Oppenheimer" (LC), "A Patriot for Me."

SCOGIN, ROBERT. Born Nov. 15, 1937 in Moulton, Ala. Graduate Florence State U. Appeared Off-Bdwy in "Children of the Ladybug," made Bdwy debut in 1969 in "Henry V."

SCOTT, STEPHEN. Born Feb. 8, 1928 in London. Attended Central School of Speech. Made Bdwy debut in 1967 in "There's a Girl in My Soup," followed by "Borstal Boy."

SELDES, MARIAN. Born Aug. 23, 1928 in NYC. Attended Neighborhood Playhouse. Made Bdwy debut in 1947 in "Medea," followed by "Crime and Punishment," "That Lady," "Tower Beyond Tragedy," "Ondine," "High Ground," "Come of Age," "Chalk Garden," "The Milk Train Doesn't Stop Here Anymore," "The Wall," "A Gift of Time," "A Delicate Balance," "Before You Go," Off-Bdwy in "Diff'rent," "Ginger Man," "Mercy St."

SELL, JANIE. Born Oct. 1 in Detroit, Mich. Appeared Off-Bdwy in "Upstairs at the Downstaris," "Dames at Sea," made Bdwy debut in 1968 in "George M!"

SELLERS, ARTHUR D. Born Aug. 16, 1945 in Terre Haute, Ind. Graduate NYU. Made NY bow in 1969 with LCRep in "The Time of Your Life," "Camino Real," "Operation Sidewinder," and "Beggar on Horseback."

SELMAN, LINDA. Born Sept. 14, in NYC. Graduate U. CNY. Made Bdwy debut in 1968 in "You Know I Can't Hear You...," followed by "The Criminals" (OB).

SERBAGI, ROGER OMAR. Born July 26, 1937 in Waltham, Mass. Attended American Theatre Wing. Appeared Off-Bdwy in "A Certain Young Man" in 1967, made Bdwy bow in 1969 in "Henry V," followed by "Awake and Sing" (OB).

SEROFF, MUNI. Born Jan. 8, 1905 in Russia. Attended U Odessa. Made NY debut in 1960 in "The Wall," followed by "The Tenth Man"(CC), "Soldiers," Off-Bdwy in "Between Two Thieves," "Shadow of Heroes," "Corruption In The Palace Of Justice," "The Day The Whores Came Out To Play Tennis," "The Kitchen," "Javelin," "End Of All Things Natural."

259

Patrick Shea   **Harriet Slaughter**   **Don Simms**   **Susan Slavin**   **Arlen Dean Sn**

SHAKAR, MARTIN. Born in Detroit, Jan. 1, 1940. Attended Wayne State U. Has appeared Off-Bdwy in "Lorenzaccio," "Macbeth," "The Infantry," "Americana Pastoral," "No Place To Be Somebody," The World of Mrs. Solomon," Bdwy bow in 1969 in "Our Town."

SHANNON, MARK. Born Dec. 13, 1948 in Indianapolis, Ind. Attended U Cin. Made NY debut Off-Bdwy in 1969 in "Fortune and Men's Eyes."

SHATTUCK, ROBERT. Born Apr. 26, 1940 in Vermont. Graduate Hiram Col. Made NY bow Off-Bdwy in 1967 in "Ceremony of Innocence," on Bdwy in 1969 in "Hadrian VII."

SHAW, ROBERT. Born Aug. 9, 1927 in Westhoughton, Eng. Attended RADA. Made Bdwy debut in 1961 in "The Caretaker," followed by "The Physicists," "Gantry."

SHAWHAN, APRIL. Born Apr. 10, 1940 in Chicago. Attended AADA. Made NY debut in 1964 in "Jo," Bdwy bow in 1965 in "A Race of Hairy Men," followed by '3 Bags Full," for which she received a THEATRE WORLD Award, "Dinner At 8"('69), "Hamlet"(OB), "Cop-Out," "Oklahoma!" (LC), "Mod Donna"(OB).

SHAWN, MICHAEL. Born July 3, 1944 in Springfield, Ill. Made Bdwy debut in 1968 in "Golden Rainbow" followed by "Promises, Promises."

SHEA, PATRICK. Born Oct. 7, 1946 in NYC. Graduate AADA. Appeared in 1969 with NYSF in "Peer Gynt" and "Twelfth Night," made Bdwy bow in 1970 in "Child's Play."

SHEEN, MARTIN. Born Aug. 3, 1940 in Dayton, O. Appeared Off-Bdwy in "The Connection," "Many Loves," "Jungle Of Cities," "Wicked Cooks," "Hamlet," "Romeo and Juliet (CP)," "Hello and Goodbye," made Bdwy debut in 1964 in "Never Live Over A Pretzel Factory," followed by "The Subject Was Roses."

SHELLEY, CAROLE. Born Aug. 16, 1939 in London. Made Bdwy debut in 1965 in "The Odd Couple," followed by "The Astrakhan Coat," "Loot," "Noel Coward's Sweet Potato," "Little Murders"(OB).

SHELLY, NORMAN. Born May 3, 1921 in Denver, Colo. Attended New School. Made Bdwy bow in 1950 in "Peter Pan," followed by "Daughter of Silence," "Promises, Promises."

SHENAR, PAUL. Born Feb. 12, 1936 in Milwaukee, Wisc. Graduate U Wisc. Appeared Off-Bdwy in "6 Characters In Search Of An Author," made Bdwy debut in 1969 with ACT in "Tiny Alice," and "Three Sisters."

SHEPHERD, ELIZABETH. Born Aug. 12, 1936 in London. Graduate U Bristol. Made NY debut in 1970 Off-Bdwy in "The Jumping Fool."

SHERWELL, YVONNE. Born May 27, 1934 in Waterbury, Conn. Attended Columbia. Made NY debut in 1970 Off-Bdwy in "Contributions."

SHERWOOD, WILLIAM. Born in Ann Arbor, Mich. Made NY debut Off-Bdwy in 1970 in "Getting Married."

SHIMONO, SAB. Born in Sacramento, Cal. Graduate U Cal. Made NY bow in 1965 in "South Pacific"(CC), followed by "Mame."

SHULL, RICHARD B. Born Feb. 24, 1929 in Elmhurst, Ill. Graduate Iowa State U. Made Bdwy debut in 1954 in "Black-Eyed Susan," followed by "Wake Up, Darling," "Red Roses For Me," "I Knock At The Door," "Pictures In The Hallway," "Have I Got A Girl For You," "Minnie's Boys," Off-Bdwy roles in "Purple Dust," "Journey To The Day," "American Hamburger League."

SICARI, JOSEPH R. Born Apr. 29, 1939 in Boston. Graduate Catholic U. Has appeared Off-Bdwy in "The Parasite," "Comedy of Errors"(CP), "Love and Let Love," "Henry IV"(CP), "Dames At Sea."

SILBER, DON. Born Dec. 11, 1936 in Utica, NY. Attended Colgate, Syracuse. U. Made Bdwy bow in 1965 in "Royal Hunt of the Sun," Off-Bdwy in "Hamp," "The Glorious Ruler."

SILLMAN, LEONARD. Born May 9, 1908 in Detroit, Mich. Made Bdwy debut in 1927 in "Loud Speaker," followed by "Merry-Go-Round Revue," "Polly," "Lady Be Good," "Greenwich Village Follies," "New Faces of 1968" (11th in the series he has produced), "Madwoman of Chaillot" (OB).

SILVIA, LESLIE. Born Dec. 11, 1958 in NYC. Made Bdwy debut in 1967 in "Fiddler On The Roof."

SIMMONDS, STANLEY. Born July 13, in Brooklyn. Attended Roosevelt Col. Bdwy bow in 1927 in "My Maryland," followed by "Castles In The Air," "Simple Simon," "If The Shoe Fits," "Brigadoon" (CC), "Call Me Madam," "Silk Stockings," "Li'l Abner," "Fiorello," "Let It Ride," "I Can Get It For You Wholesale," "How To Succeed...," "Pickwick," "Kelly," "Half A Sixpence," "How Now, Dow Jones," "Maggie Flynn," "Jimmy."

SIMMS, DON. Born in NYC. Appeared on Bdwy in "The Impossible Years," "3 Men On A Horse," Off-Bdwy in "Kiss Mama."

SIMMS, HILDA. Born in Minneapolis, Minn. Graduate Hampton Inst., AADA. Made Bdwy debut in "Anna Lucasta," followed by "Cool World," "Tambourines To Glory," "Madwoman Of Chaillot"(OB).

SINGLETON, SAM. Born Feb. 11, 1940 in Charleston, SC. Attended Dramatic Workshop. Appeared Off-Bdwy in "Aria Da Capo," "The Dumb Waiter," "Beautiful Dreamer," "Great Goodness Of Life."

SLAUGHTER, HARRIET. Born Apr. 2, 1937 in Ft. Worth, Tex. Graduate U Tex. Made Bdwy debut in 1960 in "The Hostage," followed by "Fiddler On The Roof."

SLAVIN, SUSAN. Born Nov. 21 in Chicago. Attended HB Studio. Made NY debut in 1968 Off-Bdwy in "The Mad Show," followed by "Dark Of The Moon."

SMALL, NEVA. Born Nov. 17, 1952 in NYC. Made Bdwy debut in 1964 in "Something More," followed by "The Impossible Years," "Henry, Sweet Henry," Off-Bdwy in "Ballad For A Firing Squad," "Tell Me Where The Good Times Are," "How Much, How Much?"

SMITH, DELOS, V., Jr. Born June 2, 1906 in Hutchinson, Kan. Attended Harvard, Actors Studio. Appeared Off-Bdwy in "The Making Of Moo," "When We Dead Awaken," "Tiger Rag," "In The First Place," "Do You Know The Milky Way?" "Winter Journey," on Bdwy in "The Fun Couple," "Three Sisters," "Front Page," "Our Town."

SMITH, SHEILA. Born Apr. 3, 1933 in Conneaut, O. Attended Kent State U., Cleveland Playhouse. Made Bdwy debut in 1963 in "Hot Spot," followed by roles Off-Bdwy in "Taboo Revue," "Anything Goes," and "Sweet Miani," "Fiorello"(CC'62). "Mame" for which she received a THEATRE WORLD Award.

SNYDER, ARLEN DEAN. Born Mar. 3, 1933 in Rice, Kan. Graduate U Tulsa, U Iowa. Made Bdwy bow in 1965 in "The Family Way," followed by Off-Bdwy in "Benito Cereno," "Hogan's Goat," "Miss Pete," "Open 24 Hours."

SOBOLOFF, ARNOLD. Born Nov. 11, 1930 in NYC. Attended Cooper Union. Off-Bdwy credits: "Threepenny Opera," "Career," "Brothers Karamazov," "Vincent," "Bananas," "Papp," on Bdwy in "Mandingo," "The Egg," "The Beauty Part," "One Flew Over The Cuckoo's Nest," "Anyone Can Whistle," "Bravo Giovanni," "Sweet Charity," "Mike Downstairs," "Camino Real"(LC).

SPIEGEL, BARBARA. Born Mar. 12 in NYC. Made debut in 1969 with LC Rep in "Camino Real," "Operation Sidewinder," and "Beggar On Horseback."

SPIVAK, ALICE. Born Aug. 11, 1935 in Brooklyn. Attended HB Studio. Made debut Off-Bdwy in 1954 in "Early Primrose," followed by "Of Mice and Men," "Secret Concubine," "Port Royal," "Time For Bed-Take Me To Bed."

STADLEN, LEWIS J. Born Mar. 7, 1947 in Brooklyn. Attended Neighborhood Playhouse, Stella Adler Studio. After touring in "Fiddler On The Roof," made Bdwy debut in 1970 in "Minnie's Boys" for which he received a THEATRE WORLD Award.

| rence Stanley | Tony Stevens | Sally Stark | Ted Story | Vikki Summers |

STANG, ARNOLD. Born Sept. 28 in Chelsea, Mass. Made Bdwy debut in 1941 in "All In Favor," followed by "Sailor Beware," "Same Time Next Week," "Wallflower," "Wedding Breakfast," "A Funny Thing Happened On The Way To The Forum," "The Front Page."

STANLEY, FLORENCE. Born July 1 in Chicago. Graduate Northwestern. Appeared Off-Bdwy in "Machinal," "Electra," before Bdwy debut in 1965 in "Glass Menagerie," followed by "Fiddler On The Roof."

STAPLETON, MAUREEN. Born June 21, 1925 in Troy, NY. Attended HB Studio. Made Bdwy debut in 1946 in "Playboy of The Western World," followed by "Antony and Cleopatra," "Detective Story," "The Bird Cage," "The Rose Tattoo" for which she received a THEATRE WORLD Award, "The Emperor's Clothes," "The Crucible," "Richard III," "The Seagull," "27 Wagons Full Of Cotton," "Orpheus Descending," "The Cold Wind And The Warm," "Toys In The Attic," "The Glass Menagerie"('65), "Plaza Suite," "Norman, Is That You?"

STARK, SALLY. Born May 28, 1938 in Riverhead, NY. Attended St. Elizabeth Col. Made NY debut in 1967 Off-Bdwy in "Babes In Arms," followed by "Your Own Thing," "Dames At Sea."

STARKAND, MARTIN. Born in Brooklyn. Attended Bklyn Col. Made debut in 1959 Off-Bdwy in "The Young Provincials," followed by "Machnial," "Tender Trap," "Brownstone Urge."

STATTEL, ROBERT. Born Nov. 20, 1937 in Floral Park, NY. Graduate Manhattan Col. Has appeared Off-Bdwy in "Heloise," "When I Was A Child," "Man and Superman," "The Storm," "Don Carlos," "Taming of The Shrew," "Titus Andronicus"(CP), "Henry IV"(CP), "Iphigenia In Aulis," "Ergo," with LC Rep in "Danton's Death," "The Country Wife," "Caucasian Chalk Circle," "King Lear," "Peer Gynt" (CP), "A Patriot For Me," "The Persians"(OB).

STEIN, MICHAEL. Born Aug. 17, 1933 in NYC. Graduate Boston U. Appeared Off-Bdwy in "Witches' Sabbath," "The Brig," made Bdwy bow in 1968 in "Hadrian VII."

STERLING, JAN. Born Apr. 3, 1923 in NYC. Attended Fay Compton's School, London. Made Bdwy debut in 1938 in "Bachelor Born," followed by "When We Are Married," "Grey Farm," "This Rock," "The Rugged Path," "Dunnigan's Daughter," "This Too Shall Pass," "Present Laughter," "Two Blind Mice," "Small War On Murray Hill," "Perfect Setup," "Friday Night"(OB), "Front Page."

STEVENS, FRAN. Born Mar. 8 in Washington, DC. Attended Notre Dame, Cleveland Playhouse. Appeared in "Pousse Cafe," "Most Happy Fella," "A Funny Thing Happened On The Way To The Forum," "How Now, Dow Jones," "Her First Roman," "Frank Gagliano's City Scene" (OB), "Cry For Us All."

STEVENS, TONY. Born May 2, 1948 in St. Louis, Mo. Made NY debut in 1967 City Center revival of "Wonderful Town," followed by "The Fig Leaves Are Falling," "Billy," "Jimmy," "The Boy Friend."

STEWART, FRED. Born Dec. 7, 1906 in Atlanta, Ga. Graduate Oglethorpe U. Made Bdwy bow in 1931 in "Ladies Of Creation," followed by "Experience Unnecessary," "200 Were Chosen," "Excursion," "Robin Landing," "Washington Jitters," "The Devil and Daniel Webster," "Night Music," "Retreat to Pleasure," "Land's End," "The Whole World Over," "Brigadoon," "The Crucible," "Cat On A Hot Tin Roof," "The Girls in 509," "Romulus," "Strange Interlude," "Galileo"(LC), "More Stately Mansions," Off-Bdwy in "Memory Bank," "Room Service."

STEWART, JEAN-PIERRE. Born May 4, 1946. Graduate CCNY, Neighborhood Playhouse. Appeared in "Henry IV"(CP'68), and with LC Rep in "King Lear," "A Cry Of Players," "In The Matter of J. Robert Oppenheimer," "The Miser."

STEWART, RAY. Born Apr. 21, 1932 in San Benito, Tex. Graduate U Tex., Neighborhood Playhouse. Appeared Off-Bdwy in "Black Monday," "Conerico Was Here To Stay," "Second City," "Play," "The Experiment," "The Fantasticks," with LC Rep in "King Lear," "A Cry of Players," and "Inner Journey," made Bdwy debut in 1970 in "Grin And Bare It."

STICKNEY, DOROTHY. Born June 21, 1900 in Dickinson, SD. Attended Northwestern. Made Bdwy debut in 1926 in "The Squall," followed by "Chicago," "March Hares," "Beaux Stratagem," "Front Page," "Philip Goes Forth," "Another Language," "On Borrowed Time," "Life With Father," "Life With Mother," "The Small Hours," "To Be Continued," "Kind Sir," "The Honeys," "Riot Act," "A Lovely Light" (solo show), "The Mundy Scheme."

STOCKWELL, JEREMY. Born in Houston, Tex. Graduate U Tex. Made NY debut in 1969 Off-Bdwy in "Fortune And Men's Eyes."

STORY, TED. Born May 13, 1942 in Batavia, NY. Columbia graduate. Made Bdwy debut in 1964 in "Thurber Carnival"(ELT), "South Pacific"(LC), "Booth Is Back in Town"(LC), "Me and Juliet"(ELT).

STRASSBERG, MORRIS. Born Apr. 18,1897 in Lemberg. Trained with Yiddish Art Theatre. Made Bdwy debut in 1921 in "The Dybbuk," followed by "Merchant Of Venice," "We Americans," "Spring Song," "Awake And Sing," "Welcome Stranger," "Kosher Kitty Kelly," "A Hole in The Head," "The Tenth Man," "The World Of Mrs. Solomon"(OB), "Awake And Sing"(OB).

STRAUS, SYLVIE. Born June 28, 1923 in NYC. Attended Hunter Col. Appeared Off-Bdwy in "Babel, Babel, Little Tower," "Orpheus Descending," "Camino Real," "Middle Of The Night," "Walking to Waldheim"(LC), Bdwy debut in 1970 in "Inquest."

STRIMPELL, STEPHEN. Born Jan. 17, 1937 in NYC. Graduate Columbia. Made Bdwy bow in 1964 in "The Sunday Man," appeared Off-Bdwy in "School For Scandal," "Henry IV," "Dumbbell People In A Barbell World," "To Be Young, Gifted and Black," "The Disintegration of James Cherry"(LC).

STRITCH, ELAINE. Born Feb. 2, 1925 in Detroit, Mich. Attended Dramatic Workshop. Made Bdwy debut in 1946 in "Loco," followed by "Made In Heaven," "Angel In The Wings," "Call Me Madam," "Pal Joey," "On Your Toes," "Bus Stop," "The Sin Of Pat Muldoon," "Goldilocks," "Sail Away," "Who's Afraid of Virginia Woolf?," "Wonderful Town"(CC), "Private Lives"(OB), "Company."

STUART, LAURA. Born May 26, 1938 in Philadelphia. Attended Catholic U. Appeared Off-Bdwy in "Electra," "The Trojan Women," "The Women At The Tomb," and made Bdwy debut in 1968 in "Fiddler On The Roof."

STUCKMANN, EUGENE. Born Nov. 16, 1917 in NYC. Made Bdwy bow in 1943 in "Richard III," followed by "Counsellor-At-Law," "Othello," "The Tempest," "Foxhole In The Parlor," "Henry VIII," "Androcles And The Lion," "Yellow Jack," "Skipper Next To God," "A Patriot For Me."

SULLIVAN, JEREMIAH. Born Sept. 22, 1937 in NYC. Graduate Harvard. Appeared in "Compulsion"(1957), "Ardele"(OB), "The Astrakhan Coat," "Philadelphia, Here I Come!," "The Lion In Winter," "Hamlet," "A Scent Of Flowers"(OB).

SULLIVAN, JOSEPH. Born Nov. 29, 1918 in NYC. Attended Fordham, Am. Theatre Wing. Appeared in "Sundown Beach," "Command Decision," "The Live Wire," "Country Girl," "Oh, Men! Oh, Women!," "The Rainmaker," "Best Man," "Fiddler On The Roof."

SUMMERS, VIKKI. Born In Denmark, Tenn. Attended LACC, Ntl. Black Theatre. Made NY debut in 1969 Off-Bdwy in "A Black Quartet."

SUTORIUS, JAMES L. Born Dec. 14, 1944 in Euclid, O. Graduate Ill. Wesleyan U., AMDA. Made Bdwy debut in 1970 with John Fernald's Co. in "The Cherry Orchard."

John Swearingen   **Barbara Tarbuck**   **Tony Thomas**   **Rebecca Thompson**   **Evan Thomp**

SWANSON, LARRY. Born Nov. 10, 1930 in Roosevelt, Okla. Graduate Okla. U. Off-Bdwy credits: "Dr. Faustus Lights The Lights," "A Thistle In My Bed," "A Darker Flower," "Vincent," "MacBird," "The Unknown Soldier And His Wife"(LC Rep), "The Sound Of Music"(CC'61), on Bdwy in "Those That Play The Clowns," "The Great White Hope."

SWEET, DOLPH. Born July 18, 1920 in NYC. Graduate Columbia. Appeared Off-Bdwy in "The Dragon," "Too Much Johnson," "Sjt. Musgrave's Dance," "Ceremony Of Innocence," on Bdwy in "Rhinoceros," "Romulus," "The Advocate," "Sign In Sidney Brustein's Window," "The Great Indoors," "The Natural Look," "Billy," "The Penny Wars."

SWEARINGEN, JOHN. Born July 23, 1935 in Knob Noster, Mo. Graduate Central Mo. State, Guildhall Drama School in London. Made Bdwy debut in 1963 in "A Man For All Seasons," followed by "Me And Juliet"(ELT).

SYMONDS, ROBERT. Born Dec. 1, 1926 in Bristow, Okla. Attended Tex. U, U Mo. Made NY bow with LC Rep in "Danton's Death," followed by roles in their "Country Wife," "The Alchemist," "Galileo," "St. Joan," "Tiger At The Gates," "Cyrano," "A Cry of Players," "Inner Journey," "The Miser," "The Time Of Your Life," "Camino Real," "The Disintegration Of James Cherry," "Silence," "Landscape," "Amphitryon."

SYMS, SYLVIA. Born Dec. 3, 1920 in NYC. Attended NYU. Made Bdwy debut in 1949 in "Diamond Lil," followed by CC's "Dream Girl" and "South Pacific," "Whoop-Up," "Camino Real"(LC).

TABORI, KRISTOFFER. Born Aug. 4, 1952 in Calif. Made Bdwy debut in 1969 in "The Penny Wars," followed by "Henry V," appeared Off-Bdwy in "Emil And The Detectives," "Guns Of Carrar," "A Cry Of Players"(LC), "Dream Of A Blacklisted Actor," "How Much, How Much?" for which he received a THEATRE WORLD Award.

TALCOTT, MICHAEL. Born Jan. 9, 1939 in NYC. Graduate Pasadena Playhouse, NYU. Made bow Off-Bdwy in 1966 in "Winterset," followed by "As You Like It," "7 Days Of Mourning."

TANDY, JESSICA. Born June 7, 1909 in London. Attended Greet Acad. Made Bdwy debut in 1930 in "The Matriarch," followed by "The Last Enemy," "Time And The Conways," "The White Steed," "Geneva," "Jupiter Laughs," "Anne Of England," "Yesterday's Magic," "A Streetcar Named Desire," "Hilda Crane," "The Fourposter," "The Honeys," "A Day By The Sea," "The Man In The Dog Suit," "Triple Play," "5 Finger Exercise," "The Physicists," "A Delicate Balance," "Camino Real"(LC).

TANNER, TONY. Born July 27, 1932 in Hillingdon, Eng. Attended Webber-Douglas Drama School. Made Bdwy debut in 1966 in "Half A Sixpence," followed by "Little Boxes"(OB).

TARBUCK, BARBARA. Born Jan. 15, 1942 in Detroit, Mich. Graduate U Mich., LAMDA. Made NY debut in 1970 in LC's "Landscape."

TARLOW, FLORENCE. Born Jan. 19, 1929 in Philadelphia. Graduate Hunter Col. Off-Bdwy credits: "Beautiful Day," "Istanbul," "Gorilla Queen," "America Hurrah," "Red Cross," "Promenade," made Bdwy debut in 1968 in "The Man In The Glass Booth."

TARPEY, TOM. Born June 3, 1943 in NYC. Attended Carnegie-Mellon U, LAMDA. Made NY bow in 1969 Off-Bdwy in "The Glorious Ruler," followed by "Crimes Of Passion."

TARTEL, MICHAEL. Born Mar. 21, 1936 in Newark, NJ. Attended Manhattan Col. Appeared Off-Bdwy in "The Fantasticks," made Bdwy debut in 1969 in "Billy."

TASK, MAGGIE. Born July 4 in Marion, O. Attended Wright Jr. Col. Made Bdwy debut in 1960 in "Greenwillow," followed by "Family Affair," "Tovarich," CC's "Most Happy Fella," and "Carousel," "Funny Girl," "Kelly," "Anya," "A Time For Singing," "Darling Of The Day," "Education of Hyman Kaplan."

TATE, DENNIS. Born Aug. 31, 1938 in Iowa City, Iowa. Attended Iowa U. Appeared Off-Bdwy in "Black Monday," "The Blacks," "The Hostage," "Bohikee Creek," "The Happy Bar," "Trials of Brother Jero," "The Strong Breed," "Goa," "The Electronic Nigger," "Black Quartet."

TAUPIER, GERALD. Born Apr. 11, 1941 in Pawtucket, RI. Attended Brown U. Made NY debut Off-Bdwy in "Their Golden Coffins" (1964), followed by "Footprint in the Sand," "7 Anachronisms," "Rhode Island," "Boys in the Band."

TAYLOR, CLARICE. Born Sept. 20, in Buckingham County, Va. Attended New Theater School. Made NY bow in 1943 Off-Bdwy in "Striver's Row," followed by other roles OB in "Major Barbara," "Family Portrait," "Trouble In Mind," "The Egg And I," "A Medal For Willie," "Nat Turner," "Simple Speaks His Mind," "Gold Through The Trees," "The Owl Answers," with NEC in "Song of The Lusitanian Bogey," "Summer Of The 17th Doll," "Kongi's Harvest," "Daddy Goodness," "God Is A (Guess What?)," "An Evening Of One Acts," "5 On The Black Hand Side," "Man Better Man," "Day Of Absence," and "Brotherhood."

TAYLOR, HOLLAND. Born Jan. 14, 1943 in Philadelphia. Graduate Bennington Col. Made Bdwy debut in 1965 in "The Devils," followed by Off-Bdwy roles in "The Poker Session," "The David Show," "Tonight In Living Color," "Colette."

TEITEL, CAROL. Born Aug. 1, 1929 in NYC. Attended Am. Theatre Wing. Appeared on Bdwy in "The Country Wife," "The Entertainer," "Hamlet," "Marat/de Sade," Off-Bdwy in "The Way of the World," "The Plough And The Stars," "The Anatomist," "Country Scandal," "Under Milkwood," "The Bench," "7 Days Of Mourning."

THOMA, CARL. Born Aug. 29, 1947 in Manila, PI. Attended SUNY at Buffalo. Made NY debut in 1970 Off-Bdwy in "The Me Nobody Knows."

THOMAS, TONY. Born in Atlanta, Ga. Attended Temple U. Appeared Off-Bdwy in "Cities in Bezique," "The Pig Pen," made Bdwy bow in 1969 in "Henry V."

THOMPSON, EVAN. Born Sept. 3, 1931 in NYC. Graduate U Cal. Made Bdwy bow in 1969 in "Jimmy" followed by "Mahagonny"(OB).

THOMPSON, REBECCA. Born Apr. 14, 1942 in Dover, NH. Graduate Penn State U. Made NY debut in 1961 Off-Bdwy in "Love's Old Sweet Song," followed by "St. Joan," "Red Roses For Me," "Shakespeare's Hamlet Revisited," "The White Rose And The Red," "Hedda Gabler."

THOMPSON, RONNIE. Born Jan. 31, 1941 in Louisville, Ky. Made NY debut in "No Place To Be Somebody" on and Off-Bdwy.

THOMPSON, SADA. Born Sept. 27, 1929, in Des Moines, Iowa. Graduate Carnegie Tech. Made NY debut Off-Bdwy in 1953 in "Under Milk Wood," followed by "The Clandestine Marriage," "Murder In The Cathedral," "The White Devil," "The Carefree Tree," "The Misanthrope," "USA," "River Line," "Ivanov," "The Last Minstrel," "An Evening For Merlin Finch," "The Effect Of Gamma Rays On The Man-In-The-Moon Marigolds," on Bdwy in "Festival," "Juno," "Johnny No Trump," "The American Dream," "Happy Days."

THORNE, RAYMOND. Born Nov. 27, 1934 in Lackawanna, NY. Graduate U Conn. Made NY bow in 1966 Off-Bdwy in "Man With A Load Of Mischief," followed by "Rose," "Dames At Sea."

THURSTON, TED. Born Jan. 9, 1920 in St. Paul, Minn. Attended Drake U, Wash. U. Has appeared in "Bonanza Bound," "Flahooley," "Paint Your Wagon," "Girl In Pink Tights," "Kismet," "Buttrio Square," "Seventh Heaven," "Most Happy Fella," "Li'l Abner," "13 Daughters," "Happiest Girl In Town," "Let It Ride," "Sophie," "Luther," "Cafe Crown," "Bible Salesman"(OB), "I Had A Ball," "Wonderful Town"(CC'67), "Celebration," "Gantry."

| Lou Tiano | Marie Toussaint | Matthew Tobin | Lisa Tracy | Frank Torren |

TIANO, LOU. Born Feb. 5, 1935 in NYC. Attended NYU. Made Bdwy debut in 1969 in "The Penny Wars."

TILLINGER, JOHN. Born June 28, 1938 in Tabriz, Iran. Attended U Rome. Made Bdwy debut in 1966 in "How's The World Treating You?," followed by "Halfway Up The Tree," Off-Bdwy in "Tea Party," "Pequod," "A Scent Of Flowers," "Crimes Of Passion."

TILSTON, JENNIFER. Born Mar. 29, 1947 in Tilston, Eng. Attended Tulane, AADA. Made Bdwy debut in 1967 in "Black Comedy," followed by "Little Boxes"(OB).

TIPPIT, WAYNE. Born Dec. 19, 1932 in Lubbock, Tex. Graduate U Iowa. Made Bdwy bow in 1959 in "Tall Story," followed by "Only In America," "Gantry," Off-Bdwy roles in "Dr. Faustus," "Under The Sycamore Tree," "Misalliance," "The Alchemist," "MacBird," "Trainor, Dean. Liepolt & Co.," "The Young Master Dante," "The Boys In The Band."

TOBIN, MATTHEW. Born Aug. 10, 1933 in Indianapolis, Ind. Carnegie Tech graduate. Made NY debut Off-Bdwy in 1959 in "The Hasty Heart," followed by "Boys from Syracuse," "Mad Show," "Boys in the Band," "Empire Builders," "Lyle," Bdwy bow in 1960 in "Redhead."

TOLL, DAVID. Born June 14, 1943 in Philadelphia. Graduate Temple U. Made NY bow Off-Bdwy in 1968 in "But It Is Nothing," followed by "The Alchemist," "Me And Juliet" (ELT).

TORMEY, JOHN. Born Aug. 4, 1937 in Willimantic, Conn. Graduate Boston U. Made Bdwy bow in 1960 in "Beg, Borrow Or Steal," followed by "Bajour," "Marat/deSade," "Mike Downstairs," "Our Town."

TORN, RIP. Born Feb. 6, 1931 in Temple, Tex. Graduate U Tex. Made Bdwy bow in 1956 in "Cat On A Hot Tin Roof," followed by "Chapparal"(OB) for which he received a THEATRE WORLD Award, "Sweet Bird Of Youth," "Daughter Of Silence," "Strange Interlude"('63), "Blues For Mr. Charlie," "The Country Girl," (CC'66), "The Kitchen"(OB), "Deer Park"(OB), "The Cuban Thing," "Dream Of A Blacklisted Actor"(OB).

TORREN, FRANK. Born Jan. 5, 1939 in Tampa, Fla. Attended U Tampa, AADA. Made NY bow in 1964 Off-Bdwy in "Jo," followed by "No Corner In Heaven," "Treasure Island," "Open Season For Butterflies," "Brownstone Urge."

TOUSSAINT, MARI. Born in Brooklyn. Has appeared with NEC in "Song of The Lusitanian Bogey," "God Is A (Guess What?)," "An Evening of One Acts," "Man Better Man."

TOWBIN, BERYL. Born June 14, 1938 in NYC. Made Bdwy debut in 1951 in "The King And I," followed by "Hazel Flagg," "Girl In Pink Tights," "Ziegfeld Follies," "Plain And Fancy," "A to Z," "Bells Are Ringing," "Family Affair," "Hallelujah, Baby," "Education Of Hyman Kaplan," "Beggar On Horseback"(LC).

TOWERS, CONSTANCE. Born May 20, 1933 in Whitefish, Mont. Attended Juilliard, AADA. Made Bdwy debut in 1965 in "Anya," followed by "Show Boat"(LC), CC's "Carousel," "Sound Of Music," and "King And I," "Engagement Baby."

TOWNES, HARRY. Born Sept. 18, 1918 in Huntsville, Ala. Attended U Ala., Columbia. Has appeared in "Tobacco Road," "Strip For Action," "Mr. Sycamore," "Finian's Rainbow," "Twelfth Night," "Gramercy Ghost," "In The Matter of J. Robert Oppenheimer"(LC Rep).

TOZERE, FREDERIC. Born July 19, 1901 in Brookline, Mass. Made Bdwy debut in 1924 in "Sweet Little Devil," followed by "Stepping Stones," "Journey's End," "Key Largo," "Watch On The Rhine," "Outrageous Fortune," "In Bed We Cry," "Signature," "Rich Full Life," "King Of Friday's Men," "Tower Beyond Tragedy," "First Lady," "Caligula," "St. Joan"(OB), "Happy Town," "Daughter Of Silence," "Hidden Stranger," "Mr. Simian"(OB), "Little Boxes"(OB).

TRACT, JO. Born Dec. 25, 1939 in Urbana, O. Made Bdwy debut in 1964 in "Fade Out-Fade In," followed by "Catch Me If You Can," "Mame."

TRACY, LISA. Born July 20, 1945 in Lexington, Va. Graduate Oberlin Col. Made NY debut in 1970 Off-Bdwy in "Dark Of The Moon."

TROOBNICK, GENE. Born Aug. 23, 1926 in Boston. Attended Ithaca Col., Columbia. Made Bdwy bow in 1960 in "Second City," followed by "The Odd Couple," "Dynamite Tonight"(OB), "Before You Go," "The Time Of Your Life" (LC).

TRIBUSH, NANCY. Born Dec. 18, 1940 in NYC. Graduate Bklyn. Col. Made Bdwy debut in 1961 in "Bye, Bye, Birdie," followed by "Happily Never After," Off-Bdwy in "Riverwind," "Hang Down Your Head And Die," "Oh, Calcutta."

TROY, HECTOR. Born May 25, 1941 in NYC. Appeared Off-Bdwy in "Waiting For Lefty," "The Miser," "Winterset," "Summertree," Bdwy debut in 1969 in "Does A Tiger Wear A Necktie?"

TRUEMAN, PAULA. Born Apr. 25, 1907 in NYC. Graduate Hunter Col., Neighborhood Playhouse. Made Bdwy debut in 1922 in "Thunderbird," followed by "Grand St. Follies," "Sweet And Low," "Grand Hotel," "You Can't Take It With You," "George Washington Slept Here," "Kiss And Tell," "Violet," "For Love Or Money," "Gentlemen Prefer Blondes," "Solid Gold Cadillac," "Mrs. McThing," "Wake Up Darling," "Family Affair," "Wonderful Town," "Sherry," "The Chinese," Off-Bdwy in "Sunday Man," "Wilder's Triple Bill," "Postcards."

TUCCI, MARIA. Born June 19, 1941 in Florence, Italy. Attended Actors Studio. Appeared Off-Bdwy in "Corruption In The Palace of Justice," "Five Evenings," "The Trojan Women," "The White Devil," "Horseman, Pass By," with NY Shakespeare Festival, "Yerma"(LC Rep), "Shepherd Of Avenue B," on Bdwy in "The Milk Train Doesn't Stop Here Anymore," "The Rose Tattoo"('66), "The Little Foxes" ('67), "The Cuban Thing," "The Great White Hope."

TUPOU, MANU. Born in 1939 in Fiji Islands. Attended San Francisco State Col., U London. Made Bdwy bow in 1969 in "Indians."

TURNER, DOUGLAS. Born May 5, 1930 in Burnside, La. Attended U. Mich. Made Bdwy bow in 1959 in "A Raisin In The Sun," followed by "One Flew Over The Cuckoo's Nest," Off-Bdwy in "The Iceman Cometh," "The Blacks," "Pullman Car Hiawatha," "Bloodknot," "Happy Ending," "Day Of Absence," and with NEC (was co-founder) in "Kongi's Harvest," "Ceremonies In Dark Old Men," "The Harangues," and "The Reckoning."

TYRRELL, SUSAN. Born in San Francisco. Made Bdwy debut in 1952 in "Time Out For Ginger," has appeared Off-Bdwy in "The Knack," "Futz," LC's "A Cry Of Players," "The Time Of Your Life," and "Camino Real."

URICH, TOM. Born Mar. 26 in Toronto, O. Attended Cin. Cons. Appeared Off-Bdwy in "The Streets Of New York," "The Fantasticks," "Shoemaker's Holiday," made Bdwy bow in 1970 in "Applause."

VAHANIAN, MARC. Born Apr. 17, 1956 in Detroit, Mich. Attended AADA. Made NY debut in 1969 in "The Time Of Your Life"(LC).

VALE, MICHAEL. Born June 28, 1922 in Brooklyn. Attended New School. Made Bdwy bow in 1961 in "The Egg," followed by "Cafe Crown," "The Last Analysis," "The Impossible Years," "The Autograph Hound"(OB), "The Moths" (OB).

VALENTI, MICHAEL. Born Nov. 21, 1943 in NYC. Attended Juilliard. Made Bdwy bow in "How To Succeed...," and appeared Off-Bdwy in "Leave It To Jane," and "Your Own Thing."

VANDIS, TITOS. Born Nov. 7, 1917 in Athens, Greece. Attended Ntl. Theatre Drama School. Made Bdwy bow in 1965 in "On A Clear Day You Can See Forever," followed by "Illya, Darling," "The Guide," "Look to the Lilies," "Man of La Mancha."

van GRIETHUYSEN, TED. Born Nov. 7, 1934 in Ponca City, Okla. Graduate U. Tex., RADA. Made Bdwy bow in 1962 in "Romulus," followed by "The Moon Besieged," "Inadmissible Evidence," Off-Bdwy in "The Failures," "Lute Song" (CC), "O Marry Me!," "Red Roses For Me," "The Basement," "Hedda Gabler."

VANNUYS, ED. Born Dec. 28, 1930 in Lebanon, Ind. Attended Ind. U. Made NY bow Off-Bdwy in 1969 in "No Place To Be Somebody."

VAN ORE, HARRY. Born July 3, 1944 in Philadelphia. Graduate St. Joseph's Col. Made NY debut in 1970 Off-Bdwy in "Lulu."

VAN PATTEN, DICK. Born Dec. 9, 1928 in NYC. Made Bdwy bow in 1935 in "Tapestry In Gray," followed by "Eternal Road," "Home Sweet Home," "The American Way," "The Woman Brown," "The Lady Who Came To Stay," "Run, Sheep, Run," "The Land Is Bright," "Kiss and Tell," "Decision," "The Skin of Our Teeth," "Too Hot For Maneuvers," "The Wind Is Ninety," "O Mistress Mine," "Mr. Roberts," "The Male Animal," "Have I Got A Girl For You," "I Was Dancing," "A Very Rich Woman," "Lovers and Other Strangers," "But Seriously," "Adaptations" (OB).

VAN SCOTT, GLORY. Attended Goddard Col. Appeared in CC revivals of "Carmen Jones," "Porgy and Bess," and "Show Boat," Off-Bdwy in "Fly Blackbird," "Prodigal Son," "Who's Who, Baby?," "Billy NoName," on Bdwy in "House of Flowers," "Kwamina," American Ballet Theatre, "The Great White Hope."

VASNICK, ANDREW. Born Dec. 31, 1926 in Philadelphia. Graduate Gallaudet, U. Pa. Made Bdwy debut in 1969 with Natl. Theatre of The Deaf.

VAUGHAN, DAVID. Born May 17, 1924 in London. Attended Wadham Col. Made Bdwy debut in 1957 in "The Country Wife," followed by "Epitaph For George Dillon," "Minnie's Boys," Off-Bdwy in "The Boy Friend," "The Fantasticks," "The Way of The World," "The Wedding," "Madrigal of War," "The Promenade," "In Circles," "Peace."

VENTANTONIO, JOHN. Born Aug. 13, 1943 in Orange, NJ. Attended AADA. Made Bdwy debut in 1969 in "Our Town."

VESTOFF, VIRGINIA. Born Dec. 9, 1940 in NYC. Off-Bdwy credits: "The Boy Friend," "Crystal Heart," "Fall Out," "New Cole Porter Revue," "Man With A Load of Mischief," "Love and Let Love," on Bdwy in "From A To Z" (1960), "Irma La Douce," "Baker Street," "1776."

VIGODA, ABE. Born Feb. 24, 1921 in NYC. Off-Bdwy credits: "Dance of Death," "Feast of Panthers," "Witches' Sabbath," "The Cherry Orchard," "Mrs. Warren's Profession," "A Darker Flower," "The Cat and The Canary," with NY Shakespeare Festival, and on Bdwy in "Marat/DeSade," "The Man In The Glass Booth," "Inquest."

VON SCHERLER, SASHA. Born Dec. 12 in NYC. Made Bdwy debut in 1959 in "Look after Lulu," followed by "Rape of the Belt," "The Good Soup," "Great God Brown," "First Love," "Alfie," Off-Bdwy in "The Admirable Bashville," "The Comedian," "Conversation Piece," "Good King Charles' Golden Days," "Under Milkwood," "Plays for Bleecker Street," "Ludlow Fair," "Harold," "Twelfth Night" (CP), "Sondra," "Cyrano" (LC), "Crimes of Passion."

VOSKOVEC, GEORGE. Born June 19, 1905 in Sazava, Czech. Graduate Dijon U. Made NY bow in 1945 in "The Tempest," followed by "The Love of 4 Colonels," "His and Hers," "The Seagull," "Festival," "Uncle Vanya" (OB), "A Call On Kuprin," "The Tenth Man," "Big Fish, Little Fish," "Do You Know The Milky Way?," "Hamlet," "Brecht On Brecht" (OB), with LCRep in "The Alchemist," "East Wind," and "Galileo," "Oh, Say Can You See L.A." (OB), "Cabaret," "The Penny Wars," "Room Service" (OB).

WALKEN, CHRISTOPHER. Born Mar. 31, 1943 in Astoria, NY. Attended Hofstra U. Made Bdwy debut in 1958 in "J.B.," followed by "Best Foot Forward" (OB), "High Spirits," "Baker Street," "The Lion In Winter," "Measure For Measure" (CP), "The Rose Tattoo" ('66) for which he received a THEATRE WORLD Award, "The Unknown Soldier and His Wife," "Iphigenia In Aulis" (OB), "Rosencrantz and Guildenstern Are Dead," "Lemon Sky" (OB).

WALKER, DIANA. Born June 28, 1942 in NYC. Appeared Off-Bdwy in "The Fourth Pig," "The Cat and The Canary" before Bdwy debut in 1966 in "Mame."

WALKER, ELIZABETH. Born Feb. 19, 1947 in NYC. Made debut Off-Bdwy in 1969 in "Summertree."

WALKER, SYDNEY. Born May 4, 1921 in Philadelphia. Attended Conservatoire Nationale, Paris. Made Bdwy bow in 1960 in "Becket," Off-Bdwy in "Volpone," "Julius Caesar,""King Lear," "The Collection," "A Scent of Flowers," with APA in "You Can't Take It With You," "War and Peace," "Right You Are," "School For Scandal," "We Comrades Three," "The Wild Duck," "Pantagleize," "The Cherry Orchard," "The Misanthrope," "The Cocktail Party," and "Cock-A-Doodle Dandy," "Blood Red Roses."

WALLACE, MARCIA. Born Nov. 1, 1942 in Creston, Iowa. Attended HB Studio. Made NY debut in 1968 Off-Bdwy in "The Fourth Wall," followed by "Calling in Crazy," "Dark of the Moon."

WALSH, SEAN J. Born Oct. 9, 1938 in Rocky River, O. Graduate John Carroll U. Has appeared in CC revival of "Carousel," and "Guys and Dolls," and made Bdwy bow in 1968 in "The Great White Hope."

WANDREY, DONNA. Born May 11, 1947 in Chicago. Attended Northern Ill. U., HB Studio. Made NY debut in 1969 Off-Bdwy in "The Brownstone Urge."

WARD, JANET. Born Feb. 19 in NYC. Attended Actors Studio. Made Bdwy debut in 1945 in "Dream Girl," followed by "Anne of the Thousand Days," "Detective Story," "King of Friday's Men," "Middle of the Night," "Miss Lonelyhearts," "Chapparal" (OB), "J.B.," "Cheri," "The Egg," "The Typists" and "The Tiger" (OB), "The Impossible Years," "Of Love Remembered," Off-Bdwy in "Summertree," "Dream of a Blacklisted Actor," and "Cruising Speed 600 MPH."

WARFIELD, MARLENE. Born June 19, 1941 in Queens, NY. Attended Actors Studio. Has appeared Off-Bdwy in "The Blacks," "All's Well That Ends Well" (CP), "Volpone" (CP), "Taming of The Shrew," "Who's Got His Own," "Elektra," "2 By Cromwell," and made Bdwy debut in 1968 in "The Great White Hope" for which she received a THEATRE WORLD Award.

WARIK, JOSEF. Born in McKeesport, Pa. Attended Carnegie Mellon U. Made NY bow in 1969 Off-Bdwy in "Crimes of Passion."

WARREN, JOSEPH. Born June 5, 1916 in Boston. Graduate Denver U. Made Bdwy bow in 1951 in "Barefoot in Athens," followed by "One Bright Day," "Love of Four Colonels," "Hidden River," "The Advocate," "Brecht on Brecht" (OB), "Philadelphia, Here I Come," "Jonah" (OB), "Borstal Boy."

WATERMAN, WILLARD. Born Aug. 29, 1914 in Madison, Wisc. Attended U. Wisc. Made Bdwy debut in 1966 in "Mame."

WATERSTON, SAM. Born Nov. 15, 1940 in Cambridge, Mass. Graduate Yale. Made Bdwy bow in 1963 in "Oh, Dad, Poor Dad...," followed by "First One Asleep Whistle," "Halfway Up The Tree," "Indians," and Off-Bdwy in "As You Like It," "Thistle In My Bed," "The Knack," "Fitz," "Biscuit," "La Turista," "Posterity For Sale," "Ergo," "Muzeeka," "Red Cross," "Henry IV" (CP), "Spitting Image," "I Met A Man," "Brass Butterfly."

WATERSTREET, EDMUND. Born May 5, 1943 in Algoma, Wisc. Graduate Gallaudet Col. Made Bdwy debut in 1969 with the Natl. Theatre of The Deaf.

WATSON, SUSAN. Born Dec. 17, 1938 in Tulsa, Okla. Attended Juilliard. Off-Bdwy credits: "The Fantasticks," "Lend An Ear," "Follies of 1910," "Carousel" (LC), CC revivals of "Oklahoma!," "Where's Charley?," on Bdwy in "Bye Bye Birdie," "Carnival," "Ben Franklin In Paris," "A Joyful Noise," "Celebration," "Beggar on Horseback" (LC).

WEAVER, FRITZ. Born Jan. 19, 1926 in Pittsburgh. Graduate U. Chic. Off-Bdwy credits: "The Way of The World," "The White Devil," "The Doctor's Dilemma," "Family Reunion," "The Power and The Glory," "Great God Brown," "Peer Gynt," "Henry IV," "My Fair Lady" (CC'68), on Bdwy in "Chalk Garden" for which he received a THEATRE WORLD Award, "Protective Custody," "Miss Lonelyhearts," "All American," "Lorenzo," "The White House," "Baker Street," "Child's Play."

WEBB, ALYCE ELIZABETH. Born June 1, 1934 in NYC. Graduate NYU. Made Bdwy debut in 1946 in "Street Scene," followed by "Lost in the Stars," "Finian's Rainbow," "Porgy and Bess," "Show Boat," "Guys and Dolls," "Kiss Me, Kate," "Wonderful Town," "Hello, Dolly!," Off-Bdwy in "Simply Heavenly," "Ballad of Bimshire," "Trumpets of the Lord."

WEBER, FREDRICKA. Born Dec. 22, 1940 in Beardstown, Ill. Attended Northwestern. Made Bdwy debut in 1965 in "Those That Play the Clowns," followed by "Upstairs at the Downstairs" Revues, Off-Bdwy in 1970 in "The Last Sweet Days of Isaac" for which she received a THEATRE WORLD Award.

| John Ventantonio | Marcia Wallace | Robert E. Weil | Alyce Elizabeth Webb | Charles White |

WEEDE, ROBERT. Born Feb. 22, 1903 in Baltimore, Md. Appeared in opera before Bdwy debut in 1956 in "The Most Happy Fella," followed by "Milk and Honey," "Cry for Us All."

WEIL, ROBERT E. Born Nov. 18, 1914 in NYC. Attended NYU. Made Bdwy bow in "New Faces of 1942," followed by "Burlesque," "Becket," "Once Upon A Mattress," "Blood, Sweat and Stanley Poole," "Night Life," "Arturo Ui," "Love Your Crooked Neighborhood" (OB), "Beggar on Horseback" (LC).

WELBES, GEORGE M. Born Sept. 14, 1934 in Sioux Falls, SD. Graduate USD. Made NY bow in 1968 Off-Bdwy in "Oh Say Can You See L.A.," followed by "The Other Man," "Oh, Calcutta."

WELDON, ANN. Born Feb. 28, 1938 in Haldanville, Okla. Attended Am. Cons. Theatre. Made Bdwy debut in 1969 with ACT's "A Flea in Her Ear."

WELDON, CHARLES. Born June 1, 1940 in Wetumka. Okla. Made Bdwy debut in 1969 in "Big Time Buck White."

WELLS, MARY K. Born in Omaha, Neb. Attended BH Studio. Made Bdwy debut in 1958 in "Interlock," followed by "Any Wednesday," "Everything in the Garden," "3 Men on a Horse."

WEST, BERNIE. Born May 30, 1918 in NYC. Graduate CCNY. Made Bdwy bow in "New Faces of 1943," followed by "Early to Bed," "Bells Are Ringing," "Do Re Mi," "All American," "The Beauty Part," "Children from Their Games," "Poor Bitos," "The Wayward Stork," "Oh, Kay" (OB), "A Teaspoon Every 4 Hours," "The Front Page."

WESTCOTT, LYNDA. Born June 17, 1942 in Muskegon, Mich. Attended City Col. Appeared Off-Bdwy in "Deep Are The Roots," "Finian's Rainbow," "International Wrestling Match," "No Place To Be Somebody."

WHITE, CHARLES. Born Aug. 29, 1920 in Perth Amboy, NJ. Graduate Rutgers U., Neighborhood Playhouse. Has appeared in "Career," "Cloud 7," "Gypsy," "Philadelphia, Here I Come," "Inherit The Wind," "Comes A Day," "The Front Page" ('69).

WHITE, JESSE. Born Jan. 3, 1918 in Buffalo, NY. Made Bdwy bow in 1943 in "Sons and Soldiers," followed by "My Dear Public," "Mrs. Kimball Presents," "Helen Goes To Troy," "Harvey," "The Cradle Will Rock," "Red Gloves," "Born Yesterday," "Kelly," "Kiss Me, Kate" (CC'65), "The Front Page," "Harvey."

WHITEHEAD, PAXTON. Born in Kent, Eng. Attended Webber-Douglas Drama School. Made Bdwy debut in 1962 in "The Affair," followed by "Beyond the Fringe," "Candida," Off-Bdwy in "Gallows Humour," "One Way Pendulum," "A Doll's House," "Rondelay."

WHITESIDE, ANN. Born in Philadelphia. Attended Chestnut Hill Col. Made Bdwy debut in 1955 in "A Roomful of Roses," followed by "Wake Up, Darling," "Jumping Fool" (OB).

WHITMORE, JAMES. Born Oct. 1, 1922 in White Plains, NY. Attended Yale. Made Bdwy debut in 1947 in "Command Decision," followed by "A Case of Libel," "Inquest."

WHYTE, DONN. Born Feb. 23, 1941 in Chicago. Attended Northwestern. Made NY debut in 1969 Off-Bdwy in "The Brownstone Urge."

WILKINSON, KATE. Born Oct. 25 in San Francisco. Attended San Jose State Col. Made Bdwy debut in 1967 in "Little Murders," followed by "Johnny No-Trump," "Watercolor," "Postcards," Off-Bdwy in "La Madre," "Ernest in Love," "Story of Mary Surratt" (ELT), "Bring Me a Warm Body," "Child Buyer," "Rimers of Eldritch."

WILLARD, FRED. Born Sept. 18 in Cleveland, O. Graduate Va. Military Inst. Made NY debut Off-Bdwy in 1969 in "Little Murders" followed by "Arf."

WILLIAMS, BILLY DEE. Born Apr. 6, 1938 in NYC. Attended Natl. Acad. of Fine Arts. Has appeared in "Firebrand of Florence," "Cool World," "A Taste of Honey," "Hallelujah, Baby!," Off-Bdwy in "Blue Boy in Black," "Firebugs," "Ceremonies in Dark Old Men," "Slow Dance on the Killing Ground."

WILLIS, HORTON. Born Apr. 13, 1946 in Magnolia, Ark. Graduate Baylor U., AMDA. Made NY debut Off-Bdwy in 1968 in "Your Own Thing," followed by "And Puppy Dog Tails."

WILLISON, WALTER. Born June 24, 1947 in Monterey Park, Calif. Made Bdwy debut in 1970 in "Norman, Is That You?"

WILSON, CARRIE. Born Sept. 15, 1944 in Philadelphia. Graduate Barnard Col., Neighborhood Playhouse. Made NY debut in 1969 Off-Bdwy in "Promenade."

WILSON, ELIZABETH. Born Apr. 4, 1925 in Grand Rapids, Mich. Attended Neighborhood Playhouse. Has appeared in "Picnic," "The Desk Set," "The Tunnel of Love," "Big Fish, Little Fish," Off-Bdwy in "Plaza 9," "Eh?," "Little Murders," "Sheep on the Runway."

WILSON, LISLE. Born Sept. 2, 1943 in Brooklyn. Attended AADA. Appeared with NY Shakespeare Festival in "Coriolanus," "Troilus and Cressida," and "Volpone," Off-Bdwy in "The Niggerlovers," "Hamlet," "Americana Pastoral," "5 on the Black Hand Side," on Bdwy in "Blues For Mr. Charlie," "The Death of Bessie Smith."

WILSON, LOIS. Born June 28, 1900 in Pittsburgh. Made Bdwy debut in 1937 in "Farewell Summer," followed by "Chicken Every Sunday," "The Mermaids Singing," "Madwoman of Chaillot" (OB).

WILSON, MARY LOUISE. Born Nov. 12, 1936 in New Haven, Conn. Graduate Northwestern. Has appeared Off-Bdwy in "Our Town," "Upstairs At The Downstairs," "Threepenny Opera," "A Great Career," on Bdwy in "Hot Spot," "Flora, The Red Menace," "Criss-Crossing."

WINSTON, HATTIE. Born Mar. 3, 1945 in Greenville, Miss. Attended Howard U. Appeared Off-Bdwy in "Prodigal Son," "Day of Absence," "Pins and Needles," "Weary Blues," "Man Better Man" (NEC), "Billy Noname," "Sambo," "The Me Nobody Knows."

WINSTON, HELENE. Born in Winnipeg, Can. Made Bdwy debut in 1963 in "Milk and Honey," followed by "The Time of Your Life" (LC).

WINTER, EDWARD. Born June 3, 1937 in Roseburg, Ore. Attended U. Ore. Appeared with LCRep. in "The Country Wife," "Condemned of Altona," and "The Caucasian Chalk Circle," on Bdwy in "Cabaret," "The Birthday Party," "Promises, Promises."

WINTERS, ROLAND. Born Nov. 22, 1904 in Boston. Attended Boston School of Fine Arts. Made Bdwy debut in 1924 in "The Firebrand," followed by "Who Was that Lady I Saw You With?," "A Cook for Mr. General," "Take Her, She's Mine," "Calculated Risk," "Minnie's Boys."

WINTERS, SHELLEY. Born Aug. 18, 1922 in East St. Louis, Ill. Attended Drama Workshop, Actors Studio. Made Bdwy debut in 1941 in "The Night Before Christmas," followed by "Meet the People," "Rosalinda," "Oklahoma!," "A Hatful of Rain," "Girls of Summer," "Night of the Iguana," "Cages" (OB), "Under the Weather," "Minnie's Boys."

WISEMAN, JOSEPH. Born May 15, 1919 in Montreal, Can. Attended CCNY. Has appeared in "Abe Lincoln In Illinois," "Journey To Jerusalem," "Candle In The Wind," "Three Sisters," "Storm Operation," "Joan of Lorraine," "Antony and Cleopatra," "Detective Story," "That Lady," "King Lear" ('50). "Golden Boy," "The Lark," "Duchess of Malfi" (OB), with LCRep in "Marco Millions," "Incident At Vichy," "In The Matter of J. Robert Oppenheimer."

| Joel Wolfe | Bryan Young | Pam Zarit | Louis Zorich | Darrell Zwerling |

WITHERS, IVA. Born July 7, 1917 in Rivers, Can. Made Bdwy debut in 1945 in "Carousel," followed by "Oklahoma!," "As The Girls Go," "Make A Wish," "Guys and Dolls," "Redhead," "The Unsinkable Molly Brown," "Rattle of A Simple Man," "High Spirits," "I Do! I Do!," "The Happy Time," "40 Carats."

WOLFE, JOEL. Born Sept. 19, 1936 in NYC. CCNY graduate. Made debut Off-Bdwy in "Ergo," followed by "Room Service."

WOLFSON, MARTIN. Born Apr. 4, 1904 in NYC. Attended CCNY. Appeared in "Black Pit," "Counsellor-at-Law," "Co-Respondent Unknown," "Gentle People," "Ladies and Gentlemen," "Brooklyn USA," "Counterattack," "Cup of Trembling," "South Pacific," "Threepenny Opera," "Guys and Dolls" (CC), "A Month in the Country" (OB), "Goldilocks," "The Great White Hope."

WOMBLE, ANDRE. Born Feb. 11, 1940 in Brooklyn. Attended NYU. Has appeared in "Miss Julie" (OB), "Slow Dance On The Killing Ground," "The Zulu and The Zayda," "The Little Foxes" ('67), "To Be Young, Gifted and Black" (OB).

WOOD, EUGENE R. Born Oct. 27, 1903 in Bowling Green, Mo. Graduate Colo. State, and Cornell. Has appeared Off-Bdwy in "Borak," "The Crucible," "The Anvil," "Night of The Auk," "This Here Nice Place," "Kiss Me, Kate" (CC), on Bdwy in "Porgy and Bess," "Pajama Game," "Look Homeward, Angel," "Subways Are For Sleeping," "West Side Story," "The Devils," "The Great White Hope."

WOOD, G. Born Dec. 31, 1919 in Forrest City, Ark. Graduate Carnegie Tech, NYU. Made Bdwy bow in 1953 in "Cyrano de Bergerac," followed by "Richard III," "Shangri-La," "The Crucible," "The Seagull," NRT's "The Imaginary Invalid," "A Touch of the Poet" and "Tonight at 8:30," "Henry V," Off-Bdwy in "La Ronde," "Cradle Song," "The Lesson," "Thor with Angels," "A Box of Watercolors," "Tobias and the Angels," "The Potting Shed."

WOOD, NORMA JEAN. Born Sept. 27, 1942 in Flagstaff, Ariz. Graduate U. Minn. Made NY debut in 1970 Off-Bdwy in "The House of Leather."

WOOD, PEGGY. Born Feb. 9, 1894 in Brooklyn. Made Bdwy debut in 1910 in "Naughty Marietta," followed by "Lady of the Slipper," "Love O' Mike," "Maytime," "Candida," "Trelawney of the Wells," "Merchant of Venice," "Bitter Sweet," "Old Acquaintance," "Blithe Spirit," "The Happiest Years," "Getting Married," "Charley's Aunt," "Girls in 509," Off-Bdwy in "Transposed Heads," "Opening Night," "Pictures in a Hallway," "A Madrigal for Shakespeare," "Madwoman of Chaillot."

WOODS, ALLIE. Born Sept. 28, 1940 in Houston, Tex. Graduate Tex. Southern. Has appeared Off-Bdwy in "The Blunderers," and with NEC in "Song of The Lusitanian Bogey," "Kongi's Harvest," "Daddy Goodness," "God Is A (Guess What?)," "Man Better Man," "Brotherhood" and "Day of Absence."

WOODS, JAMES. Born Apr. 18, 1947 in Vernal, Utah. Graduate Mass. Inst. Tech. Made Bdwy debut in 1970 in "Borstal Boy."

WOODS, RICHARD. Born May 9, 1930 in Buffalo, NY. Graduate Ithaca Col. Appeared in "Beg, Borrow or Steal," "Capt. Brassbound's Conversion," "Sail Away," Off-Bdwy in "The Crucible," "Summer and Smoke," "American Gothic," "Four-In-One," "My Heart's In The Highlands," "Eastward In Eden," "The Long Gallery," "The Year Boston Won The Pennant" (LC), "In The Matter of J. Robert Oppenheimer" (LCRep), with APA from 1962 in "You Can't Take It With You," "War and Peace," "School For Scandal," "Right You Are," "The Wild Duck," "Pantagleize," "Exit The King," "The Cherry Orchard," "Cock-A-Doodle Dandy," and "Hamlet," "Coco."

WRIGHT, BOB. Born in 1911 in Columbia, Mo. Attended U. Mo. Made Bdwy bow in 1948 in "Make Mine Manhattan," "Kiss Me, Kate," "Hit The Trail," "South Pacific" (CC'57), "Tall Story," "The Merry Widow" (LC), "The Sound of Music" (CC'67), "Man of La Mancha."

WRIGHT, CATHERINE. Born Mar. 19, 1948 in San Francisco. Attended SF State Col. Made Bdwy debut in 1969 in "Henry V," and Off-Bdwy in "Crimes of Passion."

WRIGHT, TERESA. Born Oct. 27, 1918 in NYC. Made Bdwy debut in 1938 in "Our Town," followed by "Life with Father," "The Dark at the Top of the Stairs," "Mary, Mary," "I Never Sang for My Father," "Who's Happy Now?" (OB).

YARNELL, BRUCE. Born Dec. 28, 1935 in Los Angeles. Attended CCLA. Has appeared in "Camelot," "The Happiest Girl in the World" for which he received a THEATRE WORLD Award, "Carousel" (CC), "Annie Get Your Gun" (LC), "Oklahoma!" (LC).

YOUNG, ASTON S. Born June 6, 1930 in NYC. Made Off-Bdwy bow in 1965 in "The Old Glory," followed by "The Outside Man," "Arms and the Man," "Benito Cerino," "Trials of Brother Jero," "The Strong Breed," "Man Better Man."

YOUNG, BRYAN. Born Dec. 27, 1945 in Shrewsbury, Pa. Attended Ind. U., AADA. Made Bdwy debut in 1969 in "A Patriot for Me," followed by "Madwoman of Chaillot" (OB).

YOUNG, RONALD. Born June 11, 1941 in Tulsa, Okla. Graduate Tulsa U. Made Bdwy debut in "Hello, Dolly!," followed by "Mame," "George M!," "The Boy Friend."

YURKA, BLANCHE. Born June 18, 1887 in St. Paul, Minn. Attended Inst. of Musical Art. Made Bdwy debut in 1907 in "The Warrens of Virginia," followed by "Hamlet," "The Wild Duck," "Goat Song," "Hedda Gabler," "Lady from the Sea," "Lysistrata," "Troilus and Cressida," "Carrie Nation," "Romeo and Juliet," "Gloriana," "The Wind Is Ninety," "Temper the Wind," "Jane Eyre," "Dinner at 8," Off-Bdwy in "The Carefree Tree," "Diary of a Soundrel," "Madwoman of Chaillot" (OB).

ZANG, EDWARD. Born Aug. 19, 1934 in NYC. Graduate Boston U. Has appeared Off-Bdwy in "The Good Soldier Schweik," "St. Joan" (LCRep), "The Boys In The Band."

ZARIT, PAM. Born Mar. 7, 1944 in Chicago. Attended Denver U., Northwestern. Made Bdwy debut in 1969 in "Promises, Promises."

ZIMMERMANN, ED. Born Mar. 30, 1935 in NYC. Graduate Columbia. Appeared Off-Bdwy in "20 Poems of E. E. Cummings," "Hamlet," "Tea Party" and "The Basement," on Bdwy in "Luther," "The Right Honourable Gentleman," "Venus Is," "A Day in the Death of Joe Egg," "A Patriot for Me."

ZORICH, LOUIS. Born Feb. 12, 1924 in Chicago. Attended Roosevelt U., Goodman Theatre. Off-Bdwy credits: "Six Characters In Search of An Author," "Crimes and Crimes," "Henry V," "Thracian Horses," "All Women Are One," "The Good Soldier Schweik," "Shadow of Heros," "To Clothe The Naked," with LCRep Co., on Bdwy in "Becket," "Moby Dick," "The Odd Couple," "Hadrian VII."

ZWERLING, DARRELL. Born in Pittsburgh. Attended Northern Ill. Col., HB Studio. Made NY bow in 1963 Off-Bdwy in "Along Came A Spider," followed by "Room Service."

OBITUARIES

ARMSTRONG, WILL STEVEN, 39, stage designer, died Aug. 12, 1969 while on vacation in New Mexico. He received a "Tony" Award in 1962 for "Carnival." Other Bdwy credits include "Caligula," "Tchin Tchin," "Something Different," "The Three Sisters," "The Lion In Winter," and "Forty Carats." He also designed for the American Shakespeare Festival, National Repertory Theatre, NYC Opera, and Phoenix Theatre. His widow and daughter survive.

ARNELL, NYDIA, 74, musical comedy star, died May 15, 1970 in a Southampton, NY hospital after a short illness. George M. Cohan picked her from a church choir for the lead in "Little Nelly Kelly." She also starred in "My Maryland," among others. She retired in 1930 when she married Harry A. Bruno.

BACCALONI, SALVATORE, 69, Metropolitan Opera's basso buffo for 22 years, died Dec. 31, 1969 in a NYC hospital following deterioration of a number of organs. He also appeared in several films. His widow survives.

BARRAT, ROBERT, 78, stage, film, and tv character actor, died of a heart ailment in a Hollywood hospital on Jan. 7, 1970. His career spanned more than 50 years. His Broadway successes included "Marco Millions" and "Lilly Turner." His widow survives.

BEGLEY, ED, 69, versatile character actor of stage, screen, vaudeville, radio, and tv, collapsed and died at a Hollywood party on Apr. 28, 1970 of a heart attack. Made Bdwy bow in 1943 in "Land of Fame," followed by "Pretty Little Parlor," "Get Away, Old Man," "All My Sons," "All Summer Long," "Inherit The Wind," "A Shadow Of My Enemy" "Look Homeward, Angel," "Semi-Detached," "Advise and Consent," "Zelda," and "Our Town" this season. Surviving are his third wife, 2 sons and 2 daughters.

BOLTON, WHITNEY, 69, Broadway columnist and drama critic for The Morning Telegraph, died of cancer on Nov. 4, 1969 in a NYC hospital. He was one of the founders of the Drama Critics Circle. He is survived by his second wife, actress Nancy Coleman, 2 daughters and a son.

BOZYK, MAX, 71, Yiddish actor, collapsed and died of a heart attack on Apr. 5, 1970 backstage after a performance at Town Hall. Appeared in many Yiddish stage and film productions before making Bdwy bow in 1966 in "Let's Sing Yiddish," followed by "Sing, Israel, Sing." His widow and partner Rose, and a daughter survive.

BROWN, LILLIAN, 83, actress, singer, and male impersonator, died in NYC of cancer on June 8, 1969. Her career began at 11 in a minstrel show. She was later billed as Elbrown or "The Kate Smith of Harlem," and appeared on Bdwy in "Queen at Home," "Baby Pompadour," "Kiss Me, Kate" revival, "Regina," and in revues "Hi-De-Ho," "Sing Out The Blues," and "Dixie Singers." Twice married and widowed, she left no survivors.

BURKE, BILLIE, 84, renowned Bdwy beauty and film comedienne for 50 years, died in her Beverly Hills home on May 14, 1970. At an early age, went to England with her parents and became a star at 17. Made NY debut in 1907 starring with John Drew in "My Wife" and became the toast of Bdwy. Subsequently, between films, she appeared in "Love Watches," "Mrs. Dot," "The Mind-the-Paint Girl," "The Amazons," "Rose Briar," "The Marquise," "Family Affairs," "This Rock," "Mrs. January and Mr. X," "Accidentally Yours," "Life With Mother," and "Listen To The Mocking Bird." Retired in 1960. She was the widow of Florenz Ziegfeld and their only daughter survives.

CHANEY, STEWART, 59, prolific stage and film designer, died Nov. 9, 1969 in his Easthampton, NY home. Among his many credits are "Life With Father," "Voice of the Turtle," "The Late George Apley," "The Moon Is Blue," "Arsenic and Old Lace," "Late Love," and "A Severed Head." Surviving are 2 brothers and 2 sisters.

CIANNELI, EDUARDO, 80, a stage and film character actor for 45 years, died of cancer Oct. 8, 1969 in Rome, after completing a film. Italian-born, he made his Bdwy bow in 1925 in "Rose Marie," followed by "Winterset," "The Front Page," "Yellow Jack," "Reunion in Vienna," "Foolscap," "St. Joan," and his last "The Devils Advocate" in 1961. Two sons survive.

COLLYER, BUD, 61, stage and radio actor, and popular television host, died Sept. 8, 1969 of a circulatory ailment in a Greenwich, Conn., hospital. He had bit parts in several Bdwy plays before turning to radio acting in 1935. He was MC for two of tv's longest-running shows, "Beat The Clock" and "To Tell the Truth."

Ed Begley

Billie Burke

Vicki Cummings

CUMMINGS, VICKI, 50, actress, died in her NYC apartment on Nov. 30, 1969 after a long illness. Her Bdwy debut was in 1931 in "Here Goes The Bride." Her many credits in musicals and straight plays include "Furnished Rooms," "The Time, The Place, The Girl," "The Man Who Came To Dinner," "Skylark," "The Voice Of The Turtle," "For Love Or Money," "Oh, Mr. Meadowbrook," "A Phoenix Too Frequent," "Buy Me Blue Ribbons," "Mid-Summer," "Lunatics and Lovers," and her last in 1966 in "The Butter and Egg Man." Her husband, actor William Gibberson, survives.

D'ARCY, ROY, 75, stage and screen actor, died Nov. 15, 1969 in Redlands, Calif. He was a leading tenor in Shubert revues, Earl Carroll's Vanities, and the musical "Oh, Boy!" He also appeared at the Palace, and in numerous films.

DAVIS, HALLIE FLANAGAN, 78, educator, writer, director of the Federal Theatre Project, and a leader in experimental theatre Off-Broadway and in colleges, died of Parkinsonism in Tappan, NJ. In 1968 she received the first annual National Theatre Conference citation for "distinguished service" in the American theatre. Twice widowed, 2 step-daughters and a step-son survive.

DIXON, HARLAND, 83, vaudeville and Broadway comic dancer, and film coach, died June 27, 1969 in Jackson Heights, NY. He appeared in "Stop, Look, and Listen," "Honeymoon Express," "Oh, Kay," "Top Speed," "Tip-Top," "Dancing Around," "Manhattan Mary," "Kid Boots," "Good Morning, Dearie," "Rainbow," "Ziegfeld Follies," and "A Tree Grows in Brooklyn." His widow survives.

DOLLY, ROSIE, 77, of the dancing vaudeville and musical comedy sister act, died of a heart attack in a NY hospital on Feb. 1, 1970. She and her twin Jenny were international favorites from 1911 to 1927. After a year in vaudeville, they made their Bdwy debut in 1910 in "The Echo," followed by "Ziegfeld Follies," "A Winsome Widow," "The Merry Countess," "Her Bridal Night," "Oh Look," and "The Greenwich Village Follies." They retired in 1927. Jennie died in 1941. Dolly's third husband, Irving Netcher, died in 1953. There are no surviving relatives.

DOWLING, CONSTANCE, 49, former stage and screen actress, died Oct. 28, 1969 in Los Angeles of a cardiac arrest. She appeared on Bdwy in "Panama Hattie," "Hold On To Your Hats," "The Strings, My Lord, Are False," "Strawberries, in January." Her film career began in 1943. Surviving are her film producer husband, Ivan Tors, 4 sons, and her actress sister Doris Dowling.

DRUCKER, FRANCES, 69, Off-Broadway producer, died of a heart attack in the Meadowbrook, L.I., Hospital. With the late Stella Holt, she had produced many plays at the Greenwich Mews Theatre. Two nieces survive.

EASTMAN, CARL, 62, former radio actor, and for 15 years an actors agent, died in his NYC home in his sleep on Jan. 16, 1970. A daughter survives.

EASTMAN, JOAN, 32, actress, died in a NYC hospital on Aug. 24, 1969 after a short illness. She had appeared in "Stop the World, I Want To Get Off," "Oliver!," and "Cactus Flower." Her parents survive.

EDWARDS, JAMES, 48, stage, film, and tv actor, died Jan. 4, 1970 of a heart attack in a San Diego hospital. His Bdwy appearances were in "Almost Faithful," "Lady Passing Fair," and "Deep Are the Roots." He made his film debut in 1949. His widow and daughter survive.

FLETCHER, LAWRENCE, 70, stage and screen actor, died Feb. 11, 1970 in a Bridgeport, Conn., hospital. Began his career with the Stewart Walker Company and among his Bdwy credits that began in 1927 are "The Poor Nut," "Marriage on Approval," "Another Language," "Sailor, Beware," "Boy Meets Girl," "Antony and Cleopatra," "Julius Caesar," "No Time For Comedy," "Spring Again," "The Rugged Path," "Made in Heaven," "Allegro," "The Silver Whistle," and "Mr. Johnson." He appeared in several early talkies. A sister survives.

FORD, EDWARD H., 82, better known as Senator Ford the vaudeville and radio comedian, died of lung cancer on Jan. 27, 1970 in Greenport, NY. He appeared at the Palace and on Bdwy and originated the long-running panel show "Can You Top This?" He also wrote a weekly column "Senator Ford says." Surviving is his widow.

FOSTER, DONALD, 80, character actor of stage, films, and tv, died in his Hollywood home on Dec. 22, 1969 after a long illness. His Bdwy credits include "Daddy Long Legs," "Thank U," "Alias the Deacon," "In Love With Love," "Tomorrow's A Holiday," "The Curtain Rises," "Carrie Nation," "Girl Crazy," "My Sister Eileen," "Career Angel," "No Way Out," "State Of The Union," "Dr. Social," "20th Century," "Of Thee I Sing," "Men of Distinction," "The Ponder Heart," and "Witness For The Prosecution." Surviving are his widow, a son and daughter.

FREDERICKS, CHARLES, 51, stage, radio, tv, and film actor, died May 14, 1970 in Los Angeles of a heart attack. Appeared in clubs before Bdwy debut in 1946 in "Show Boat," followed by "Music In My Heart," and "My Romance." His widow, 3 sons, and a daughter survive.

FREEDLEY, VINTON, 77, producer, died from a heart condition in a NY hospital on June 5, 1969. Made Bdwy debut as an actor in 1917 and appeared in minor parts until 1923 when he became a producer. His impressive list of productions include "The New Poor," "Lady, Be Good," "Tip Toes," "Oh, Kay!," "Funny Face," "Girl Crazy," "Anything Goes," "Leave It To Me," "Red, Hot and Blue," "Let's Face It," "Dancing In The Streets," and his last "Great To Be Alive." He served 20 terms as president of Actors Fund of America. A son and daughter survive.

GARLAND, JUDY, 47, vaudeville, stage, and screen star, was found dead June 22, 1969 in her London home from an accidental over-dose of sleeping pills. Her career began at 30 months in vaudeville, and her last NY appearance was at the Palace in 1967. She appeared in over 35 films. Surviving are her fifth husband of 3 months, Mickey Deans, and 3 children, Lorna and Joseph Luft, and singer-actress Liza Minelli.

GORCEY, LEO, 52, retired stage and film actor, died June 2, 1969 in his Oakland, Calif., home after a long illness. He was one of the original Dead End Kids in the 1935 Bdwy hit, when he was signed for films. His fifth wife, a son and daughter survive.

GREENE, WILLIAM, 43, actor, and executive director of the Cleveland Playhouse, died of a heart attack in his Cleveland Heights, Ohio, home on Mar. 12, 1970. Before assuming duties at the Playhouse, he appeared in London and on Bdwy. His parents survive.

HARRIS, RENEE, 93, Bdwy's first female producer and a survivor of the Titanic, died in a NYC hospital on Sept. 2, 1969. She was a former owner of the Hudson Theatre, and gave the first Bdwy roles to Barbara Stanwyck and Judith Anderson. She was married four times.

HEALY, DAN, 80, song and dance man of the 1920's, died Aug. 31, 1969 in his home in Jackson Heights, NY. He was known as "Night Mayor of Broadway" and "Broadway's Boy" from the musical in which he appeared in 1929. He also appeared in the "Ziegfeld Follies," "Midnight Frolic," "Betsy," "Yip, Yip, Yaphank," and "This Is The Army." Later he operated several night clubs. He was the widower of singer Helen Kane. A sister survives.

HECHT, TED, 61, stage and film actor, died June 24, 1969 in Hollywood. A daughter survives.

HUNT, MARTITA, 69, Argentina-born, English-educated stage and film actress, died in her London home on June 13, 1969 of bronchial asthma. She won a "Tony" Award in 1948 for her Bdwy debut in "The Madwoman of Chaillot." She had been acclaimed in London since 1921. She is probably best known for her performance in the film "Great Expectations." No survivors were listed.

INGRAM, REX, 73, stage, film an tv actor for 50 years, died of a heart attack on Sept. 19, 1969 in Hollywood. Made his Bdwy debut in 1929 in "Lulu Belle," followed by "Theodora the Queen," "Stevedore," "Marching Song," "Haiti," "Sing Out The News," "Cabin In The Sky," "St. Louis Woman," and an all-Negro version of "Waiting For Godot." He is probably best remembered for his role of De Lawd in the film version of "Green Pastures." His second wife, and a daughter survive.

JOHNSON, HALL, 82, composer, arranger, and founder of Hall Johnson choir, died of burns received in a fire in his Harlem apartment on Apr. 30, 1970. In addition to concerts, his choir appeared in "Green Pastures," and "Run Little Chillun" which he wrote. He also worked on several films.

KORNZWEIG, BEN, 59, veteran theatrical press agent, died Oct. 10, 1969 of a heart attack in NYC. During his 35 year career he had represented over 250 productions, and the Phoenix and APA. His widow and daughter survive.

LA FOLLETTE, FOLA, 87, retired actress and suffrage leader, died Feb. 17, 1970 of pneumonia in Arlington, Va. Among her stage credits are "The Scarecrow" and "Tradition." She was the widow of playwright George Middleton. A sister survives.

Judy Garland   **Martita Hunt**   **Gypsy Rose Lee**   **Jules Munshin**   **Conrad Nagel**

LANGLEY, STUART, 60, singer-actor, died Apr. 2, 1970 in NYC. He had appeared in "Best Foot Forward," "Something For the Boys," "Winged Victory," and "The Red Mill" among others. Surviving is his widow.

LA ROCQUE, ROD, 70, stage and former famous film star, died Oct. 15, 1969 in his Beverly Hills home after a brief illness. Began career on stage at 8, and appeared on Bdwy in several William Brady productions, "Cherries Are Ripe" with his wife Vilma Banky, and in "Domino" in 1932. His widow survives.

LAWTON, FRANK, 64, British stage and film actor, died June 10, 1969 in his London home after a brief illness. Among his Bdwy credits are "The Wind And The Rain," and "French Without Tears." He was the husband of musical comedy star Evelyn Laye who survives.

LEE, GYPSY ROSE, 56, strip tease artist, actress, and author, died Apr. 26, 1970 of cancer in UCLA Medical Center. Began career at 4 in an act with her sister June Havoc. She became the world's most acclaimed stripper, a profession to which she added sophistication and art. Her NY debut was in 1931 and she became a sensation in "Ziegfeld Follies of 1937." She also appeared in "Hotcha," "George White's Scandals," "Melody," "I Must Love Someone," "The Streets of New York," "DuBarry Was A Lady," "Star and Garter," and her last appearance was Off-Broadway in 1961 in "A Curious Evening with Gypsy Rose Lee." She made several films, was a popular tv personality, and wrote 3 books, one of which became the musical hit "Gypsy." Three times married and divorced, she leaves a son by her second husband actor Alexander Kirkland.

LIEBLING, WILLIAM, 75, retired theatrical agent, died in a NYC hospital on Dec. 29, 1969. For 25 years he represented top stars of Bdwy and Hollywood. His widow and partner, Audrey Wood, survives.

LIGHT, NORMAN, 70, general manager of the Shubert theatres, died Mar. 1, 1970 after a long illness. He helped his cousins build their national theatre chain, and managed many of their productions. He was a founding member of the Association of Theatrical Press Agents and Managers. Surviving is his widow.

LOESSER, FRANK, 59, composer-lyricist for stage and films, died in a NYC hospital of lung cancer on July 28, 1969. His shows and songs are among some of Bdwy's greatest: "Guys and Dolls," the Pulitzer Prize-winning "How To Succeed in Business Without Really Trying," "Where's Charley?," and "The Most Happy Fella." His second wife, actress-singer Jo Sullivan, 3 daughters and a son survive.

LONG, W. BETHELL, JR., 53, former stage and tv actor, died Nov. 2, 1969 in his Redding, Conn., home after a long illness. Among his credits are "She Stoops To Conquer," "The Reluctant Debutante," "A Streetcar Named Desire," "Dial M For Murder," "Burlesque," and "Gigi." He retired in 1956. Surviving are his mother and sister.

MALCOLM, JOHN, 63, actor, died in his NYC home after a long illness on Oct. 21, 1969. He had appeared in "Scarlet Sister Mary," "Love Duel," "Kingdom of God," "Payment Deferred," "Come Of Age," "Love Goes To Press," "The Living Room," "Witness For The Prosecution," "The Hasty Heart," "A Majority Of One," "The Affair," "Jane Eyre," and his last in 1966 "A Time for Singing." His widow actress Edith Fisk survives.

MALONE, RAY, 44, actor dancer, died Apr. 18, 1970 in a NYC hospital after a short illness. He had appeared in several Bdwy productions.

MARCH, HAL, 49, stage and radio actor, and tv host, died Jan. 19, 1970 at UCLA Medical Center of pneumonia following the removal of a cancerous lung. On Bdwy he appeared in "Two For The Seesaw," and "Come Blow Your Horn." He was MC for the popular tv show "The $64,000 Question." Surviving are his actress-model wife, Candy Toxton, 3 sons and 2 daughters.

MARSH, HOWARD, retired musical comedy star, died Aug. 7, 1969 in a Long Branch, NJ, hospital. Made his NY bow in 1917 in "The Grass Widow," followed by "Blossom Time" "Cherry Blossoms," "The Student Prince," "Show Boat," "The Well of Romance," and Gilbert and Sullivan operettas. He retired from the stage and became a banker in NJ.

MASON, RICHARD, 24, actor, was found dead Apr. 30, 1970 in his NYC apartment from an acute reaction to heroin. He had appeared with the Negro Ensemble Co. in such plays as "Daddy Goodness," and "Kongi's Harvest," and in "Dope."

MASTERS, RUTH, 75, stage and tv actress, died Sept. 22, 1969 in Stamford, Conn. Her career began at 19 in "Romeo and Juliet," and she was active until six months before her death. Among her many Bdwy credits are "Lady Christilinda" and "Middle Of The Night." She was a regular on the tv series "Car 54." Her husband, John Saxelby survives

MORELLI, CARLO, 72, former Metropolitan Opera baritone, died of a heart attack on May 12, 1970 in Mexico City where he had lived for 20 years. Chilean-born, he was at the Met from 1935 to 1940. His widow and daughter survive.

MORRIS, MARY, 74, former Bdwy star, died Jan. 16, 1970 in a NYC hospital after a long illness. Made NY debut in 1916 in "The Clod," subsequently appearing in "Fashion," "Desire Under The Elms," "Cross Roads," "The House Of Connelly," "Double Door," and "Within The Gates." She became a member of Carnegie Tech's faculty, and also at the American Shakespeare Festival Academy. Her two marriages ended in divorce.

MOSCONI, LOUIS, 74, top vaudeville and Bdwy dancer, died Aug. 1, 1969 in Hollywood where he operated a dancing school. Appeared with his brothers as vaudeville headliners, and in "The World Of Pleasure," "Ziegfeld Follies," "Hitchy-Koo," and others. Surviving is his son, Lou, Jr., also a song-and-dance man.

MUNSHIN, JULES, 54, stage and film comedian, died Feb. 19, 1970 in his NYC home of a heart attack. He was rehearsing Off-Bdwy in "Duet For Solo Voice." Began career in vaudeville, became singer with George Olsen's band, and appeared on Bdwy in "The Army Play-By-Play," "Call Me Mister," "Bless You All," "Mrs. McThing," "The Good Soup," "Show Girl," "The Gay Life," "Oliver!," "Oklahoma!" (CC), "Barefoot in the Park," "The Front Page." His widow and 2 sons survive.

MURRAY, KATHLEEN, 41, stage and tv actress, died Aug. 24, 1969 in her NYC home of cancer. Began her career at 6 and had appeared in "Leave It To Jane," "Maybe Tuesday," "A Swim In The Sea," "Purple Dust," "Summer and Smoke," "The Enchanted," "Legend Of Lovers," and "An Ordinary Man," most of them Off-Broadway. She was Kitty Foyle in the tv series of that name. Surviving are her theatre producer-manager husband, Joseph Beruh, and 2 sons.

NAGEL, CONRAD, 72, star of stage and films, was found dead in his NYC home on Feb. 24, 1970. His Bdwy career began in 1918 in "Forever After," followed by "The First Apple," "The Moon Is Down," "The Skin Of Our Teeth," "Susan And God," "Tomorrow The World," "A Goose For The Gander," "State Of The Union," "For Love Or Money," "Goodbye, My Fancy," "Music In The Air," "Be Your Age," "Four Winds," "The Captains And The Kings," and toured in many others. He made over 200 films. His 3 marriages ended in divorce. A son and daughter survive.

PECHNER, GERHARD, 66, Metropolitan Opera bass, died Oct. 22, 1969 in a NYC hospital after a long illness. Berlin-born, he made his US debut in 1940, and sang over 30 roles at the Met from 1941 to 1966. His wife died in 1966, and he had no immediate survivors.

Eric Portman

Inger Stevens

Nydia Westman

Raymond Walburn

Ruth White

PORTMAN, ERIC, 66, English-born stage and film actor, died in his Cornwall home on Dec. 7, 1969. He had appeared on Bdwy in "Madame Bovary," "I Have Been Here Before," "Separate Tables," "Jane Eyre," "A Touch Of The Poet," and his last in 1963 "A Passage To India." He retired a few months before his death because of heart trouble.

POWERS, LEONA, 73, stage, radio, and tv actress, died in NYC on Jan.7, 1970. Began career at 5, and made her NY debut in 1903 in "The Charity Nurse." For a while she had her own company in New Orleans. Among her many Bdwy credits are "Mary Of Scotland," "End Of Summer," "The Moon Is Down," "Dear Ruth," "The Big Knife," "Wallflower," "My Mother, My Father and Me," "Bicycle Ride To Nevada," and "Once For The Asking." She appeared in "The Aldrich Family" on radio. Her husband, retired actor Howard Miller, survives.

ROBB, LOTUS, former Bdwy leading lady, died Sept. 28, 1969 in a Washington, D.C., hospital. Her last appearance in NY was in 1945 with Walter Hampden in "And Be My Love," prior to that she had appeared in "The Green Goddess," "Why Marry?," "Fair and Warmer," "Rollo's Wild Oat," "The Constant Nymph," "Kempy," and "The Rivals." Her third husband, curator Marvin C. Ross, and a daughter survive.

ROBBINS, RICHARD, 50, stage, film, and tv actor died Oct. 23, 1969 in a NYC hospital of a heart attack. On Bdwy he appeared in "Born Yesterday," "The Egghead," "Sunrise At Campobello," among others. Surviving are his mother and sister.

ROMER, TOMI, 45, stage and tv actress, died July 21, 1969 in NYC after a brief illness. She had appeared in "Holiday for Lovers," "Speaking Of Murder," among others, and with the American Shakespeare Festival.

ST. CLAIR, LYDIA, stage, film, and tv actress, died Jan. 1, 1970 in New Milford, Conn. A leading actress in Frankfurt, Germany, she came to U.S. in 1940. Among her credits are "Flight To The West," "Trio," "Time Of The Cuckoo." Her husband survives.

SCHWEID, MARK, 78, star of Yiddish theatre, died Dec. 2, 1969 in the Bronx from Parkinson's disease. He had played over 300 roles in classical and modern plays in English, Yiddish, and German, translated or adapted 40 plays, and directed 20. He appeared with the Theatre Guild in "Volpone" and "Marco Millions." He was a past president of the Hebrew Actors Union. His widow, a son and daughter survive.

SHRINER, HERB, 51, radio, stage, and tv humorist, was killed with his wife Apr. 24, 1970 in a car wreck in Delray Beach, Fla. His only Bdwy performance was in 1948 in "Inside U.S.A." He was a popular radio and tv host. A daughter and 2 sons survive.

SINCLAIR, ROBERT B., 64, retired Broadway, film, and tv director, was stabbed to death Jan. 2, 1970 in his Montecito, Calif., home when he surprised a burglar. His Bdwy credits include "The Philadelphia Story," "Pride and Prejudice," "The Postman Always Rings Twice," "Babes in Arms," and "Dodsworth." Surviving are his British actress wife, Heather Angel, a son and stepdaughter.

STEVENS, INGER, 35, Swedish-born stage, film, and tv actress was found dead Apr. 30, 1970 in her Hollywood home from acute barbiturate intoxication. Came to U.S. at 13 and appeared in stock before making Bdwy bow in 1957 in "Debut" which took her to Hollywood for films. She returned to Bdwy for "Mary, Mary," "Roman Candle," and began a 3 year run on tv as "The Farmer's Daughter." Surviving are her parents.

SULLIVAN, BRIAN, 49, operatic tenor, was found dead June 17, 1969 in Lake Geneva, Switz. where he had gone to sing Siegfried in "Gotterdammerung." He appeared with the Metropolitan Opera from 1948 to 1964, and on Bdwy in "Show Boat," and "Street Scene." He is survived by his widow, a son and 2 daughters.

SWARTHOUT, GLADYS, 64, former Metropolitan Opera mezzo-soprano, died July 8, 1969 in her villa outside Florence, Italy. Her beauty and voice made her one of our most popular opera, film, radio, and concert singers. She was best known for her portrayal of Carmen, and was at the Met from 1929 until she retired in 1945. Twice widowed, a sister survives.

THORBORG, KERSTIN, 73, Wagnerian opera star, died Apr. 12, 1970 in Falun, Sweden. Appeared at the Met from 1936 to 1947, and appeared in concert until 1950 when she retired to her native Sweden.

WALBURN, RAYMOND, 81, stage and film actor, died July 26, 1969 in a NYC hospital. His career began on stage at 16, and his last role was in "A Very Rich Woman" in 1965 Other Bdwy roles were in "Manhattan," "The Awful Truth," "The Show-Off," "If I Were Rich," "Sinner," "Take My Advice," "The Great Necker," "Zeppelin," "Freddy," "Three Little Girls," "Bridal Wise," "Man Bites Dog," "The Pursuit Of Happiness," "Park Avenue," and "A Funny Thing Happened On The Way To The Forum." His second wife survives.

WALDRON, JACK, 76, actor and shepherd of The Lambs Club, died Nov. 21, 1969 in his NYC home of a heart attack. Began his career in 1916 as half of a comedy and dancing act, appearing in vaudeville and night clubs. Appeared on Bdwy in "Gingham Girl," "Keep Kool," "Flossie," "Great Temptations," "The Pajama Game," "Say Darling," and a revival of "Pal Joey." His widow survives.

WESTMAN, NYDIA, 68, stage, film, and tv actress, died May 23, 1970 in Burbank, Calif. Began career in vaudeville with family act. Made Bdwy debut at 16 in "Pigs." Among her many credits are "Jonesy," "Ada Beats The Drum," "Lysistrata," "Merchant Of Yonkers," "Life with Father," "Strange Bedfellows," "Madwoman Of Chaillot," "Mr. Pickwick," "The Emperor's Clothes," "The Sleeping Prince," "Endgame," "Rape Of The Belt," and "Midgie Purvis." A daughter survives.

WHITE, JOSH, 61, folk singer, died Sept. 5, 1969 in a Manhasset, NY, hospital while undergoing heart surgery. He usually performed in clubs and concerts but appeared on Bdwy in "John Henry," "Blue Holiday," "The Lower Depths," "A Long Way From Home," and "How Long Till Summer." Surviving are his widow, a son and 4 daughters.

WHITE, RUTH, 55, stage screen, and tv actress, died Dec. 3, 1969 of cancer in a Perth Amboy, NJ, hospital. She appeared in many stock productions before making her Bdwy debut in 1949 in "The Ivy Green," followed by "The Ponder Heart," "The Happiest Millionaire," "Rashomon," "The Warm Peninsula," "Whisper To Me," "Big Fish, Little Fish," "Happy Days," "Lord Pengo," "Absence Of A Cello," "Malcolm," "Little Murders," and her last in 1967 "The Birthday Party." A sister and 2 brothers survive.

WIDDECOMBE, WALLACE, 100, oldest member of Actors Equity, died July 12, 1969 in Somers, NY. English-born, he came to NY in 1901 and remained active for 60 years. Some of his credits include "The Queen's Husband," "The Green Hat," "Jane Eyre," "Victoria Regina," "The Red Planet," "The Bat," "Sheppey," "The Play's The Thing," and his last "Cyrano de Bergerac" with Jose Ferrer in 1953. His widow, actress Jane Houston, survives.

WILLIAMS, HUGH, 65, stage and film actor and playwright died Dec. 7, 1969 in his native London. He appeared on Bdwy in "Flowers Of The Forest," "Once Is Enough," "Journey's End," "The Cocktail Party." With his actress wife Margaret Vyner, he collaborated on several successful plays, including "Past Imperfect" and "The Irregular Verb To Love." His widow survives, as do a daughter and 2 sons.

WILSON, WAYNE, 71, veteran actor, died Jan. 4, 1970 in San Antonio, Tex. Made his Bdwy debut in 1917, and his most recent roles were in "The Amazing Mr. Pennypacker," and "The World Of Suzie Wong." He also performed on radio, tv, and in films. His widow and 2 daughters survive.

INDEX